Essential Grammar in Use

Deutsche Ausgabe

Nachschlage- und Übungsgrammatik für Englischlernende mit Grundkenntnissen

Dritte Auflage
mit Schlüssel und E-book

Raymond Murphy

mit Almut Köster

Shaftesbury Road, Cambridge CB2 8EA, United Kingdom

One Liberty Plaza, 20th Floor, New York, NY 10006, USA

477 Williamstown Road, Port Melbourne, VIC 3207, Australia

314–321, 3rd Floor, Plot 3, Splendor Forum, Jasola District Centre, New Delhi – 110025, India

103 Penang Road, #05–06/07, Visioncrest Commercial, Singapore 238467

Cambridge University Press & Assessment is a department of the University of Cambridge.

We share the University's mission to contribute to society through the pursuit of education, learning and research at the highest international levels of excellence.

www.cambridge.org
Information on this title: www.cambridge.org/9781316505304

Third Edition © Cambridge University Press & Assessment 2016

This publication is in copyright. Subject to statutory exception and to the provisions of relevant collective licensing agreements, no reproduction of any part may take place without the written permission of Cambridge University Press & Assessment.

First published 2002
Third edition 2016

20 19 18 17 16 15 14

Printed in Poland by Opolgraf

A catalogue record for this publication is available from the British Library

Library of Congress Cataloguing data applied for.

ISBN 978-1-316-50530-4

Cambridge University Press & Assessment has no responsibility for the persistence or accuracy of URLs for external or third-party internet websites referred to in this publication and does not guarantee that any content on such websites is, or will remain, accurate or appropriate. Information regarding prices, travel timetables, and other factual information given in this work is correct at the time of first printing but Cambridge University Press & Assessment does not guarantee the accuracy of such information thereafter.

Inhalt

Danke vii
An die Lernenden viii
An die Unterrichtenden x

Gegenwart
1 **am/is/are**
2 **am/is/are** (*Frageform*)
3 **I'm hungry / I'm scared** *usw.*
4 **I am doing** (present continuous)
5 **are you doing?** (present continuous: *Fragen*)
6 **I do/work/like** *usw.* (present simple: *bejahte Form*)
7 **I don't ...** (present simple: *Verneinung*)
8 **Do you ... ?** (present simple: *Frageform*)
9 **I am doing** (present continuous) *und* **I do** (present simple)
10 **I have ...** *und* **I've got ...**

Vergangenheit
11 **was/were**
12 **worked/got/went** *usw.* (past simple)
13 **I didn't ...   Did you ... ?** (past simple: *Verneinung und Frageform*)
14 **I was doing** (past continuous)
15 **I was doing** (past continuous) *und* **I did** (past simple)

Present perfect
16 **I have done** (present perfect 1)
17 **I've just ...   I've already ...   I haven't ... yet** (present perfect 2)
18 **Have you ever ... ?** (present perfect 3)
19 **How long have you ... ?** (present perfect 4)
20 **for   since   ago**
21 **I have done** (present perfect) *und* **I did** (past)

Passiv
22 **is done   was done** (*Passiv 1*)
23 **is being done   has been done** (*Passiv 2*)

Verbformen
24 **be/have/do** (Gegenwarts- und Vergangenheitsformen)
25 Regelmäßige und unregelmäßige Verben

Zukunft
26 **What are you doing tomorrow?**
27 **I'm going to ...**
28 **will/shall** 1
29 **will/shall** 2

Modale Hilfsverben, Imperativ usw.
30 **might**
31 **can** *und* **could**
32 **must   mustn't   don't need to**
33 **should**
34 **I have to ...**
35 **Would you like ... ?   I'd like ...**
36 **Do this!   Don't do that!   Let's do this!** (*der Imperativ*)
37 **I used to ...**

There und **it**
38 **there is   there are**
39 **there was/were   there has/have been   there will be**
40 **It ...**

Hilfsverben
41 **I am, I don't** *usw.*
42 **Have you?   Are you?   Don't you?** *usw.*
43 **too/either   so am I / neither do I** *usw.*
44 **isn't**, **haven't**, **don't** *usw.* (*Verneinung*)

Fragen
45 **is it ... ?   have you ... ?   do they ... ?** *usw.* (*Fragen 1*)
46 **Who saw you?   Who did you see?** (*Fragen 2*)
47 **Who is she talking to?   What is it like?** (*Fragen 3*)
48 **What ... ?   Which ... ?   How ... ?** (*Fragen 4*)
49 **How long does it take ... ?**
50 **Do you know where ... ?   I don't know what ...** *usw.*

Die indirekte Rede
51 **She said that ...   He told me that ...**

-ing und **to ...**
52 **work/working   go/going   do/doing**
53 **to ...** (**I want to do**) *und* **-ing** (**I enjoy doing**)
54 **I want you to ...   I told you to ...**
55 **I went to the shop to ...**

Go, **get**, **do**, **make** und **have**
56 **go to ...   go on ...   go for ...   go -ing**
57 **get**
58 **do** *und* **make**
59 **have**

Pronomen und Possessivbegleiter
60 **I/me   he/him   they/them** *usw.*
61 **my/his/their** *usw.*
62 **Whose** is this?   It's **mine/yours/hers** *usw.*
63 **I/me/my/mine**
64 **myself/yourself/themselves** *usw.*
65 **-'s** (**Kate's** camera / **my brother's** car *usw.*)

Artikel: **a** *und* **the**
66 **a/an ...**
67 **train(s)   bus(es)** (*Singular und Plural*)
68 **a bottle / some water** (*zählbar / nicht zählbar 1*)
69 **a cake / some cake / some cakes** (*zählbar / nicht zählbar 2*)
70 **the ...**
71 **go to work   go home   go to the cinema**
72 I like **music**   I hate **exams**
73 **the ...** (*geographische Bezeichnungen*)

Bestimmungswörter und Pronomen
74 **this/that/these/those**
75 **one/ones**
76 **some** *und* **any**
77 **not** + **any   no   none**
78 **not** + **anybody/anyone/anything   nobody/no-one/nothing**
79 **somebody/anything/nowhere** *usw.*
80 **every** *und* **all**
81 **all   most   some   any   no/none**
82 **both   either   neither**
83 **a lot   much   many**
84 **(a) little   (a) few**

Adjektive und Adverbien
85 **old/nice/interesting** *usw.* (*Adjektive*)
86 **quickly/badly/suddenly** *usw.* (*Adverbien*)
87 **old/older   expensive / more expensive**
88 **older than ...   more expensive than ...**
89 **not as ... as**
90 **the oldest   the most expensive**
91 **enough**
92 **too**

Satzbau
93 He **speaks English** very well. (*Satzbau 1*)
94 **always/usually/often** *usw.* (*Satzbau 2*)
95 **still   yet   already**
96 **Give me that book!   Give it to me!**

Konjunktionen und Relativsätze
97 **and   but   or   so   because**
98 **When ...**
99 **If we go ...   If you see ...** *usw.*
100 **If I had ...   If we went ...** *usw.*
101 a person **who ...**   a thing **that/which ...** (*Relativsätze 1*)
102 the people **we met**   the hotel **you stayed at** (*Relativsätze 2*)

Präpositionen
103 **at 8 o'clock   on Monday   in April**
104 **from ... to   until   since   for**
105 **before   after   during   while**
106 **in   at   on** (*räumliche Präpositionen 1*)
107 **in   at   on** (*räumliche Präpositionen 2*)
108 **to   in   at** (*räumliche Präpositionen 3*)
109 **under, behind, opposite** *usw.*
110 **up, over, through** *usw.*
111 **on   at   by   with   about**
112 **good at ... , interested in ...** *usw.*   **of/at/for** *usw.* (*Präpositionen*) + **-ing**
113 **listen to ... , look at ...** *usw.* (*Verb + Präposition*)

Phrasal verbs
114 **go in, fall off, run away** *usw.* (*phrasal verbs 1*)
115 **put on** your shoes   **put** your shoes **on** (*phrasal verbs 2*)

WENN SIE UNSICHER SIND, WELCHE UNITS RELEVANT FÜR SIE SIND, VERWENDEN SIE DIE LERNHILFE AUF SEITE 271.

Anhang
Anhang 1 Aktiv und Passiv   243
Anhang 2 Liste der unregelmäßigen Verben   244
Anhang 3 Unregelmäßige Verben nach Gruppen   245
Anhang 4 Kurzformen (**he's** / **I'd** / **don't** usw.)   246
Anhang 5 Rechtschreibung   248
Anhang 6 Phrasal verbs (**take off** / **give up** usw.)   250
Anhang 7 Phrasal verbs + Objekt (**put out** a fire / **give up** your job usw.)   251

Zusätzliche Übungen   252

Lernhilfe   271

Schlüssel zu den Übungen   282
Schlüssel zu den zusätzlichen Übungen   312
Schlüssel zur Lernhilfe   314

Index   315

WENN SIE UNSICHER SIND, WELCHE UNITS RELEVANT FÜR SIE SIND, VERWENDEN SIE DIE LERNHILFE AUF SEITE 271.

Danke

Die Autoren möchten sich bei Rebecca Hill, Petra Bryce, Emer Corrigan, Ruth Atkinson, Lynn Townsend, Jane Coates, Liz Driscoll, Alison Sharpe, Jeanne McCarten und Martina von Harten bedanken, die auf unterschiedliche Weise zu dieser deutschen Ausgabe von *Essential Grammar in Use* beigetragen haben.

Design
Kamae Design

Illustrationen
Adz, Paul Boston, Christopher Flint, John Goodwin, Katie Mac, Martina - KJA artists, Lucy Truman

Digitale Entwicklung
Datamatics Ltd.

An die Lernenden (für das Selbststudium)

Essential Grammar in Use, Deutsche Ausgabe ist eine Grammatik der englischen Sprache für Lernende mit geringen Grundkenntnissen. Das Buch besteht aus 115 Lektionen oder 'Units', wobei jede Unit einen bestimmten Aspekt der englischen Grammatik behandelt. Sie finden eine Liste der Units im Inhaltsverzeichnis am Anfang des Buches.

Arbeiten Sie das Buch nicht von Anfang bis Ende durch, sondern wählen Sie den Lernstoff je nach Ihren Bedürfnissen aus. Sollten Sie zum Beispiel Schwierigkeiten mit der Zeitform *present perfect* haben (*I have been*, *he has done*? usw.), lesen Sie die Units 16–21.

Um die relevanten Unit(s) zu finden, verwenden Sie die *Inhaltsangabe* oder den *Index* (am Ende des Buches).

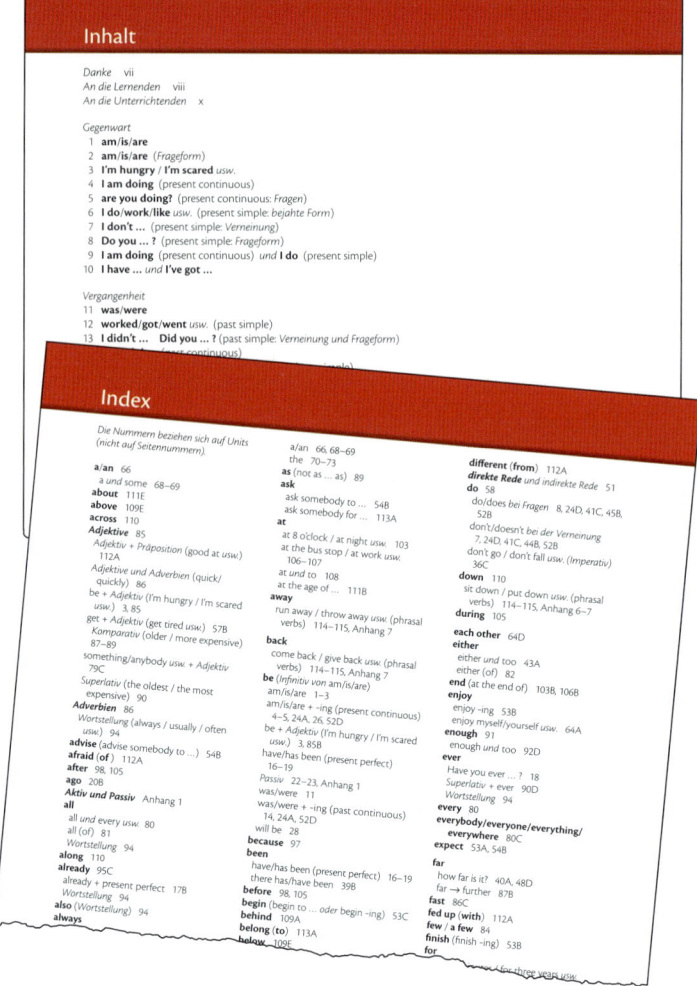

Wenn Sie unsicher sind, welche Units relevant für Sie sind, verwenden Sie die *Lernhilfe* am Ende des Buches.

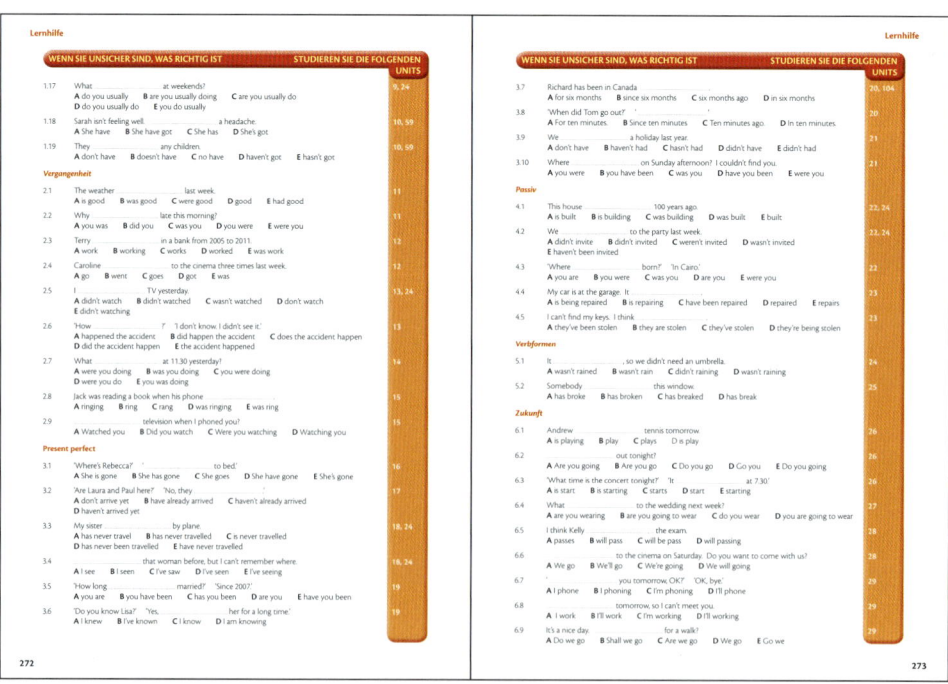

Lernhilfe (Seiten 271–281)

Jede Unit besteht aus zwei Seiten. Die Erklärungen und Beispiele befinden sich auf der linken Seite, während die Übungen auf der rechten Seite stehen.

Lesen und studieren Sie die Grammatikerklärungen und Beispiele auf der linken Seite und machen Sie die Übungen auf der rechten Seite.

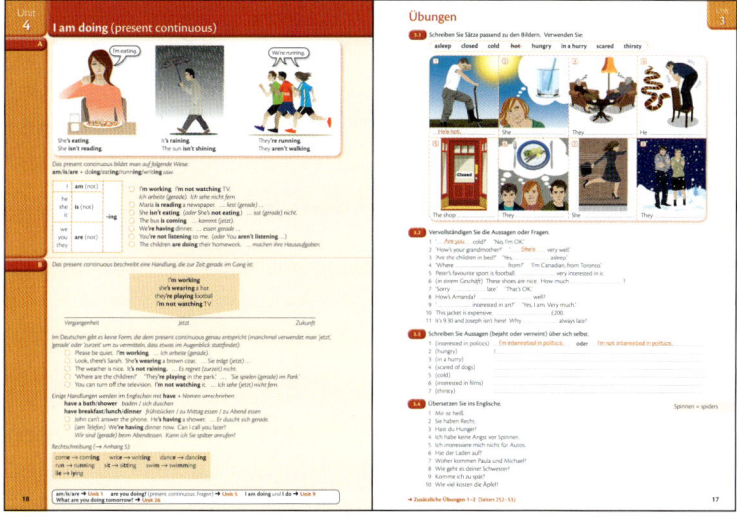

Erklärungen **Übungen**

Überprüfen Sie Ihre Antworten anhand des Schlüssels zu den Übungen. Diesen finden Sie auf den Seiten 282–312.

Wenn notwendig, studieren Sie abermals die Informationen auf der linken Seite.

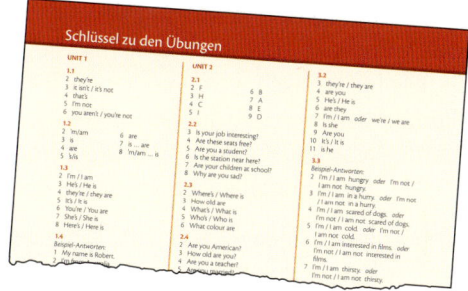

Weitere Hilfe bietet der siebenteilige *Anhang* am Ende des Buches (auf Seiten 243–251). Hier finden Sie Informationen über Passiv- und Aktivformen, unregelmäßige Verben, Kurzformen, Rechtschreibung und *phrasal verbs*.

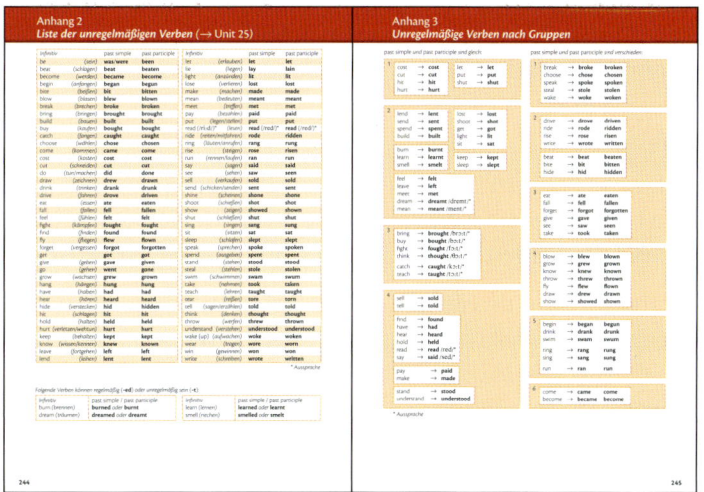

Zusätzliche Übungen zu verschiedenen Grammatikthemen finden Sie am Ende des Buches (auf Seiten 252–270) mit einer Liste der Übungen auf Seite 252.

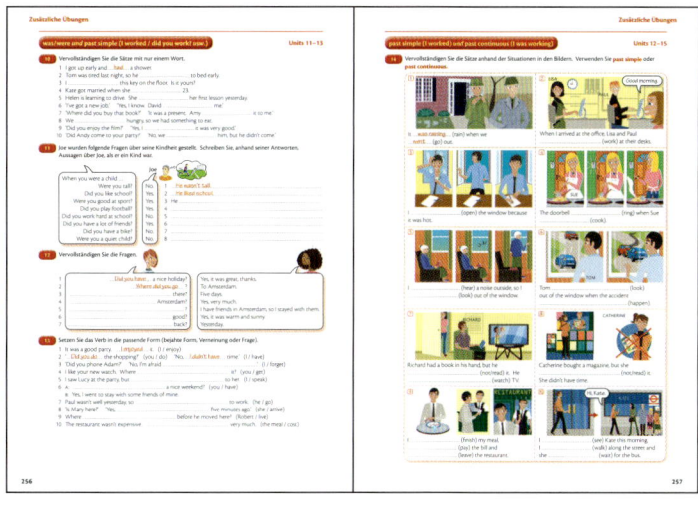

An die Unterrichtenden

Dies sind die wichtigsten Merkmale von *Essential Grammar in Use, Deutsche Ausgabe*:
- Dieses Buch ist eine Grammatik und eignet sich nicht als allgemeines Lehrwerk.
- Das Buch richtet sich an Lernende mit geringen Grundkenntnissen (*elementary level*). Es befasst sich **nicht** mit Aspekten der Grammatik, die nicht in der Regel in der Elementarstufe behandelt werden.
- Es ist ein Nachschlagewerk mit Übungen.
- Grammatikerklärungen sind auf Deutsch, wobei wichtige Unterschiede zwischen der englischen und der deutschen Grammatik hervorgehoben werden.
- Das Buch wendet sich an Lernende und ist zum Selbststudium gedacht.

Aufbau des Buches

Das Buch besteht aus 115 Units, die je einen bestimmten Aspekt der englischen Grammatik behandeln. Der Lernstoff ist nach grammatischen Themen organisiert, zum Beispiel nach Zeitform, Fragestellung oder Artikel. Die Reihenfolge der Units richtet sich *nicht* nach dem Schwierigkeitsgrad. Sie sollten deshalb nicht der Reihe nach durchgearbeitet, sondern je nach den Bedürfnissen der Lernenden ausgewählt und verwendet werden. Die Units sind im *Inhaltsverzeichnis* aufgelistet, und ein umfassender *Index* befindet sich am Ende des Buches.

Jede Unit hat den gleichen Aufbau mit zwei gegenüberliegenden Seiten. Der Grammatikpunkt wird auf der linken Seite vorgestellt und erläutert – eventuell mit Hinweisen auf Unterschiede zwischen der englischen und deutschen Grammatik. Die Erklärungen werden mit zum Teil übersetzten Beispielen veranschaulicht. Übungen zu diesem Grammatikpunkt befinden sich auf der rechten Seite. Der *Anhang* besteht aus sieben Teilen (*Anhang* 1–7, Seiten 243–251) und befasst sich mit Aktiv- und Passivformen, unregelmäßigen Verben, Kurzformen, Rechtschreibung und *phrasal verbs*. Es wird empfohlen, Lernende auf den *Anhang* aufmerksam zu machen.

Am Ende des Buches befindet sich eine Anzahl *zusätzlicher Übungen* (Seiten 252–270), die Grammatikthemen – vor allem in Bezug auf Verbformen – aus verschiedenen Units zusammenbringen. Eine vollständige Liste der 35 zusätzlichen Übungen finden Sie auf Seite 252.

Außerdem verfügt das Buch über eine *Lernhilfe* (Seiten 271–280), die Lernenden bei der Auswahl der zu studierenden Units hilft. Ein *Schlüssel zu den Übungen* befindet sich am Ende des Buches (Seiten 281–309), damit Lernende ihre Antworten eigenständig überprüfen können.

Lernstufe

Das Buch richtet sich an Lernende mit geringen Vorkenntnissen, eignet sich jedoch nicht für 'Nullanfänger'. Es eignet sich auch für Lernende der Mittelstufe, deren Grammatik schwächer ist als ihre übrigen Englischkenntnisse. Es kann auch verwendet werden, um bestimmte grundlegende Aspekte der Grammatik aufzufrischen.

Das Vokabular, das in den Beispielen und Übungen verwendet wird, beschränkt sich in der Regel auf Wörter, die bei dieser Lernstufe generell bekannt sind. Trotzdem werden viele Beispiele teilweise oder vollständig übersetzt, vor allem wenn sie schwierigere Wörter enthalten. Bei den Übersetzungsübungen werden schwierigere Wörter auf Englisch angegeben.

Arbeiten mit dem Buch

Das Buch kann von Lernenden im Selbststudium (siehe *An die Lernenden*) oder als zusätzliches Kursmaterial im Unterricht verwendet werden. In beiden Fällen eignet es sich als Grammatik für die oben genannte Lernstufe.

Als Zusatzmaterial kann das Buch entweder für die unmittelbare Festigung der gelernten Grammatik oder für das spätere Üben verwendet werden. Je nach Bedarf kann die ganze Klasse oder können einzelne Kursteilnehmer/innen oder Schüler/innen, die zusätzliche Hilfe oder Übung brauchen, mit dem Buch arbeiten.

Obwohl es möglich ist, die linke Seite einer Unit (mit Erklärungen und Beispielen) im Unterricht zu verwenden, sollte darauf hingewiesen werden, dass diese Seiten speziell für das Selbststudium und zum Nachschlagen geschrieben wurden. Darum ist es in der Regel besser, wenn Sie – als Kursleiter/in oder Lehrer/in – die Grammatik mit Ihren eigenen Methoden vorstellen und die Übungen als Hausaufgaben machen lassen. Die linke Seite kann dann später von den Kursteilnehmer/innen oder Schüler/innen als Wiederholung eigenständig studiert werden.

Wird das Buch nur zur Übung und Wiederholung verwendet, können bestimmte Units von der Klasse – oder von einzelnen Kursteilnehmer/innen (Schüler/innen) – zu Hause im Selbststudium oder als zusätzliche Hausaufgaben gemacht werden.

Deutsche Grammatikbegriffe (überwiegend lateinischen Ursprungs – zum Beispiel Substantiv, Verb) werden verwendet. Ist kein entsprechender deutscher Begriff vorhanden – wenn es sich zum Beispiel um einen 'typisch englischen' Grammatikpunkt handelt – wird der englische Begriff verwendet, zum Beispiel: *present perfect, phrasal verbs*.

Am Ende jeder Unit gibt es eine zusätzliche Übersetzungsübung. Diese besteht aus deutschen Sätzen oder Mini-Dialogen, die Lernende ins Englische übersetzen sollen. Die englischen Zielsätze wiederholen den Grammatikpunkt der jeweiligen Unit. Gelegentlich werden Vokabeln in Englisch angegeben, besonders um Fehler zu vermeiden, die nicht vom Grammatikpunkt der Unit behandelt werden. In der Übung 12.6.5 zum Beispiel wird 'in die Stadt' als *to town* (und nicht *in the town*) übersetzt.

Unit 1   am/is/are

A

- My name **is** Lisa.
- I'**m** 22.
- My favourite colour **is** blue.
- I'**m** American. I'**m** from Chicago.
- My favourite sports **are** football and swimming.
- I'**m** a student.
- My father **is** a doctor and my mother **is** a journalist.
- I'**m not** interested in politics.

LISA

B

bejahte Form

I	am	(I'**m**)
he		(he'**s**)
she	**is**	(she'**s**)
it		(it'**s**)
we		(we'**re**)
you	**are**	(you'**re**)
they		(they'**re**)

Kurzform

Verneinung

I	**am not**	(I'**m not**)		
he		(he'**s not**	*oder*	he **isn't**)
she	**is not**	(she'**s not**	*oder*	she **isn't**)
it		(it'**s not**	*oder*	it **isn't**)
we		(we'**re not**	*oder*	we **aren't**)
you	**are not**	(you'**re not**	*oder*	you **aren't**)
they		(they'**re not**	*oder*	they **aren't**)

Kurzformen

You're very busy today.

- I'**m** 32 years old. My sister **is** 29.
  Ich bin 32 Jahre alt. Meine Schwester ist 29.
- Steve **is** ill. He'**s** in bed. Steve ist krank. Er ist im Bett.
- My car **is** very old. Mein Auto ist sehr alt.
- You'**re** very busy today. Sie sind heute sehr beschäftigt.
- Ann and I **are** good friends. … sind gut befreundet.
- Your keys **are** on the table. Deine Schlüssel sind auf dem Tisch.

- I'**m not** very fit. Ich bin nicht sehr fit.
- James **isn't** a teacher. He'**s** a student.
  James ist kein Lehrer. Er ist Student.
- Those people **aren't** English. They'**re** Australian.
  Die Leute dort sind keine Engländer. Sie sind …
- It'**s** sunny today, but it **isn't** warm.
  Es ist heute sonnig, aber es ist nicht warm.

Beachten Sie, dass man **a/an** für Berufe und Tätigkeiten verwendet:
- I'm **a** student. Ich bin Student.
- My brother is **an** electrician. Mein Bruder ist Elektriker.

C

that'**s** = that **is**   there'**s** = there **is**   here'**s** = here **is**

- Thank you. That'**s** very kind of you.
  Das ist sehr nett von Ihnen.
- Look! There'**s** Chris. Guck mal! Dort ist Chris.
- A: Here'**s** your key. Hier ist Ihr Schlüssel.
  B: Thank you.

Here's your key.

Thank you.

Beachten Sie, dass **am/is/are** in manchen Fällen nicht mit 'sein' ins Deutsche übersetzt werden (→ Unit 3).

---

am/is/are (*Fragen*) → **Unit 2**   I'm hungry / I'm scared *usw.* → **Unit 3**   there is/are → **Unit 38**   It → **Unit 40**
a/an → **Unit 66**   Kurzformen → **Anhang 4**

Übungen

1.1 Schreiben Sie die Kurzformen (**she's** / **we aren't** usw.).

1 she is   she's
2 they are
3 it is not
4 that is
5 I am not
6 you are not

1.2 Vervollständigen Sie die Sätze mit **am**, **is** oder **are**.

1 The weather is nice today.
2 I .... not rich.
3 This bag .... heavy.
4 These bags .... heavy.
5 Look! There .... Helen.
6 My brother and I .... good tennis players.
7 Emily .... at home. Her children .... at school.
8 I .... a taxi driver. My sister .... a nurse.

1.3 Vervollständigen Sie die Sätze.

1 Steve is ill.   He's in bed.
2 I'm not English. .... American.
3 Mr Thomas is a very old man. .... 98.
4 These chairs aren't beautiful, but .... comfortable.
5 The weather is nice today. .... warm and sunny.
6 You are a good swimmer. .... very fit.
7 Catherine isn't at home. .... at work.
8 '........ your coat.' 'Oh, thank you very much.'

1.4 Sehen Sie sich Lisas Aussagen an (→ Unit 1A). Schreiben Sie jetzt Sätze über sich selbst.

1 (name?) My
2 (from?) I
3 (age?) I
4 (job?) I
5 (favourite colour or colours?) My
6 (interested in … ?) I

1.5 Schreiben Sie Sätze passend zu den Bildern. Verwenden Sie:

angry   ~~happy~~   sad   strong   tall   tired

1 She's happy.
2 He
3 They
4
5
6

1.6 Schreiben Sie wahre Aussagen. Verwenden Sie: **is/isn't** oder **are/aren't**.

1 (it / hot today)   It isn't hot today. oder It's hot today.
2 (it / windy today)   It
3 (my hands / cold)   My
4 (Brazil / a very big country)
5 (diamonds / cheap)
6 (Toronto / in the US)

Schreiben Sie wahre Aussagen. Verwenden Sie **I'm/I'm not**.

7 (tired)   I'm tired. oder I'm not tired.
8 (fit)   I
9 (a good swimmer)

1.7 Übersetzen Sie ins Englische.

1 Claire ist Französin. Sie ist aus Paris.
2 Mike ist sehr stark.
3 Deine Freunde sind nett.
4 Ich bin heute sehr beschäftigt.
5 Wir sind nicht verheiratet.
6 Die Kinder sind heute müde.
7 Ich bin Lehrer.
8 Tom ist nicht zu Hause.
9 Die Straße ist sehr laut.
10 Das Wetter ist heute nicht schön, aber es ist nicht kalt.

stark = strong
nett = nice
laut = noisy
schön = nice

Unit 1

Unit 2: am/is/are (Frageform)

A

bejahte Form

I	am	I'm
he		he's
she	is	she's
it		it's
we		we're
you	are	you're
they		they're

Frageform

am	I?
	he?
is	she?
	it?
	we?
are	you?
	they?

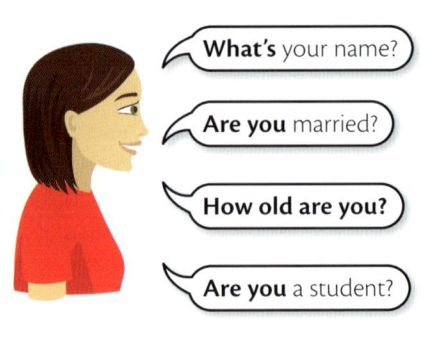
- What's your name?
- Are you married?
- How old are you?
- Are you a student?

- David.
- No, I'm not.
- 25.
- Yes, I am.

- ☐ A: **Are you** English? *Sind Sie Engländer?*
  B: No, **I'm** Scottish. *Nein, ich bin Schotte.*
- ☐ A: **Is your mother** at home? *Ist deine Mutter zu Hause?*
  B: No, **she's** out. *Nein, sie ist weg.*
- ☐ A: **Are your parents** at home? *Sind deine Eltern zu Hause?*
  B: No, **they're** out. *Nein, sie sind weg.*
- ☐ A: **Is it** late? *Ist es spät?*
  B: No, **it's** only 9 o'clock. *Nein, es ist erst 9 Uhr.*
- ☐ Your shoes are nice. **Are they** new? *Deine Schuhe sind schön. Sind sie neu?*

B

Where ... ? / What ... ? / Who ... ? / How ... ? / Why ... ?

- ☐ **Where is** your mother? Is she at home? *Wo ist deine Mutter? ...*
- ☐ **Where are** your parents? Are they at home? *Wo sind deine Eltern? ...*
- ☐ '**What colour is** your car?' 'It's red.' *'Welche Farbe hat Ihr Auto?' ...*
- ☐ '**How old is** Joe?' 'He's 24.' *'Wie alt ist Joe?' ...*
- ☐ '**How tall are** you?' 'One metre 70.' *'Wie groß sind Sie?' ...*
- ☐ This hotel isn't very good. **Why is** it so expensive? *... Warum ist es so teuer?*

what**'s** = what **is**   who**'s** = who **is**   how**'s** = how **is**   where**'s** = where **is**

- ☐ **What's** the time? *Wie viel Uhr ist es?*
- ☐ **Where's** Lucy? *Wo ist Lucy?*
- ☐ **Who's** that man? *Wer ist dieser Mann?*

C

Kurzantworten

Yes,	I	am.
	he	
	she	is.
	it	
	we	
	you	are.
	they	

No,	I'm	
	he's	
	she's	
	it's	not.
	we're	
	you're	
	they're	

oder

No,	he	
	she	isn't.
	it	
	we	
	you	aren't.
	they	

- That's my seat.
- No, it isn't.

Häufig verwendet man im Englischen Kurzantworten dieser Art:

- ☐ A: **Are you** tired? *Bist du müde?*
  B: **Yes, I am.** *Ja.*
- ☐ A: **Are you** English? *Sind Sie Engländer?*
  B: **No, I'm not.** I'm Scottish. *Nein, (bin ich nicht). Ich bin Schotte.*
- ☐ A: **Is your friend** English?
  B: **Yes, he is.**
- ☐ A: **Are these** your keys?
  B: **Yes, they are.**
- ☐ A: **That's** my seat.
  B: **No, it isn't.**

am/is/are ➜ Unit 1   I'm hungry / I'm scared *usw.* ➜ Unit 3   Fragen 1 ➜ Unit 45   what/which/how ➜ Unit 48

Übungen

2.1 Ordnen Sie den Fragen die passende Antwort zu.

1	Where's the camera?	A	No, I'm not.	1	G
2	Is your car blue?	B	Black.	2	
3	Is Kate here?	C	Yes, you are.	3	
4	Am I a good student?	D	My sister.	4	
5	Where's Amy?	E	Tuesday.	5	
6	What colour is your bag?	F	No, it's black.	6	
7	Are you tired?	G	In your bag.	7	
8	What day is it?	H	No, she's out.	8	
9	Who's that woman?	I	At work.	9	

2.2 Bilden Sie Fragen mit den angegebenen Wörtern. Setzen Sie die Wörter in die richtige Reihenfolge und verwenden Sie **is** oder **are**.

1 (is / at home / your mother)   *Is your mother at home* ?
2 (your parents / are / at home)   *Are your parents at home* ?
3 (interesting / is / your job)   ?
4 (these seats / are / free)   ?
5 (a student / you / are)   ?
6 (is / near here / the station)   ?
7 (at school / are / your children)   ?
8 (why / you / are / sad)   ?

2.3 Vervollständigen Sie die Fragen. Verwenden Sie: **What … / Who … / Where … / How …** .

1 *What's* the time? — Half past eleven.
2 .... the bus stop? — At the end of the street.
3 .... your children? — Five, six and ten.
4 .... your favourite sport? — Skiing.
5 .... the man in this photo? — That's my father.
6 .... your new shoes? — Black.

2.4 Schreiben Sie passende Fragen zu den Antworten auf der rechten Seite.

PAUL

1 (name?) *What's your name?* — Paul.
2 (American?) — No, I'm Australian.
3 (how old?) — I'm 30.
4 (a teacher?) — No, I'm a lawyer.
5 (married?) — Yes, I am.
6 (wife a lawyer?) — No, she's a designer.
7 (from?) — She's Italian.
8 (her name?) — Anna.
9 (how old?) — She's 27.

2.5 Schreiben Sie Kurzantworten (**Yes, I am.** / **No, he isn't.** usw.).

1 Are you married?   *No, I'm not.*
2 Are you at home?
3 Is it Monday today?
4 Are the children tired?
5 Is it dark now?
6 Are you a teacher?

2.6 Übersetzen Sie ins Englische.

1 Sind Sie Deutscher/Deutsche?
2 Wo sind wir?
3 Ist dein Mantel neu?
4 Wer ist das?
5 Sind die Kinder zu Hause?
6 Bist du müde?
7 Sind deine Eltern bei der Arbeit?
8 Was ist das?
9 Wie alt sind deine Katzen?
10 'Ist deine Mutter Lehrerin?'   'Nein, sie ist Ärztin.'

Unit 2

Unit 3

I'm hungry / I'm scared *usw.*

A

Bei einigen Redewendungen mit **am**/**is**/**are** verwendet man im Deutschen 'haben':

I'm hungry/thirsty = *ich habe Hunger/Durst (ich bin hungrig/durstig)*
- **Are** you **hungry**? *Haben Sie Hunger?*
- **I'm** not **hungry**. *Ich habe keinen Hunger.*
- The children **are thirsty**. *Die Kinder haben Durst. (Die Kinder sind durstig.)*

I'm right/wrong = *ich habe Recht/Unrecht*
- Who's **right**? You or me? *Wer hat Recht? …*
- We're **right**. They're **wrong**. *Wir haben Recht. Sie haben Unrecht.*

I'm scared = *ich habe Angst*
- Why **is** John **scared** of dogs? *Warum hat John Angst vor Hunden?*
- **I'm** not **scared** of dogs. *Ich habe keine Angst vor Hunden.*

I'm scared of dogs.
Woof !!!!

I'm in a hurry = *ich habe es eilig*
- **Are** you **in a hurry**? *Haben Sie es eilig?*

Außerdem:
- The shops **are open/closed**. *Die Läden haben auf/zu.*

B

Beachten Sie auch Unterschiede im Gebrauch zwischen dem Englischen und dem Deutschen bei den folgenden Redewendungen:

I'm hot/cold = *mir ist heiß/kalt*
- **I'm hot**. Can I open the window?
  Mir ist heiß. Darf ich das Fenster öffnen?
- '**Are** you **cold**?' 'No, I'm OK.'
  'Ist dir kalt?' …

I'm hot. Can I open the window?

I'm well = *mir geht es gut*
- **How are** you? **Are** you **well**? *Wie geht es Ihnen? Geht es Ihnen gut?*
- Mary **isn't well**. She's at home in bed. *Mary geht es nicht gut. …*

I'm interested in = *ich interessiere mich für …*
- **I'm interested** in politics. *Ich interessiere mich für Politik.*
- Jenny **isn't** very **interested** in music.
  Jenny interessiert sich nicht sehr für Musik.

I'm interested in politics.

I'm late = *ich komme zu spät / ich habe mich verspätet / ich bin spät dran*
- Sorry **I'm late**. *Es tut mir leid, dass ich zu spät komme.*
- Hurry up! We're **late**. *Mach schnell! Wir sind spät dran.*

he's/she's/they're asleep = *er/sie schläft, sie schlafen*
- Joe is in bed. He's **asleep**. *… Er schläft.*
- **Are** the children **asleep**? *Schlafen die Kinder?*

Where are you from? = *Woher kommen Sie?*
- **I'm from Berlin**. **Where are** you **from**? *Ich komme aus Berlin. Woher kommen Sie?*

Man kann auch sagen: Where **do** you **come from**? (→ Unit 8)

How much is/are … ? = *Wie viel kostet … ?*
- **How much is** this shirt? *Wie viel kostet dieses Hemd?*
- These oranges **are** forty pence each. *Diese Orangen kosten … pro Stück.*

am/is/are ➜ Units 1–2

Übungen

Unit 3

3.1 Schreiben Sie Sätze passend zu den Bildern. Verwenden Sie:

asleep   closed   cold   ~~hot~~   hungry   in a hurry   scared   thirsty

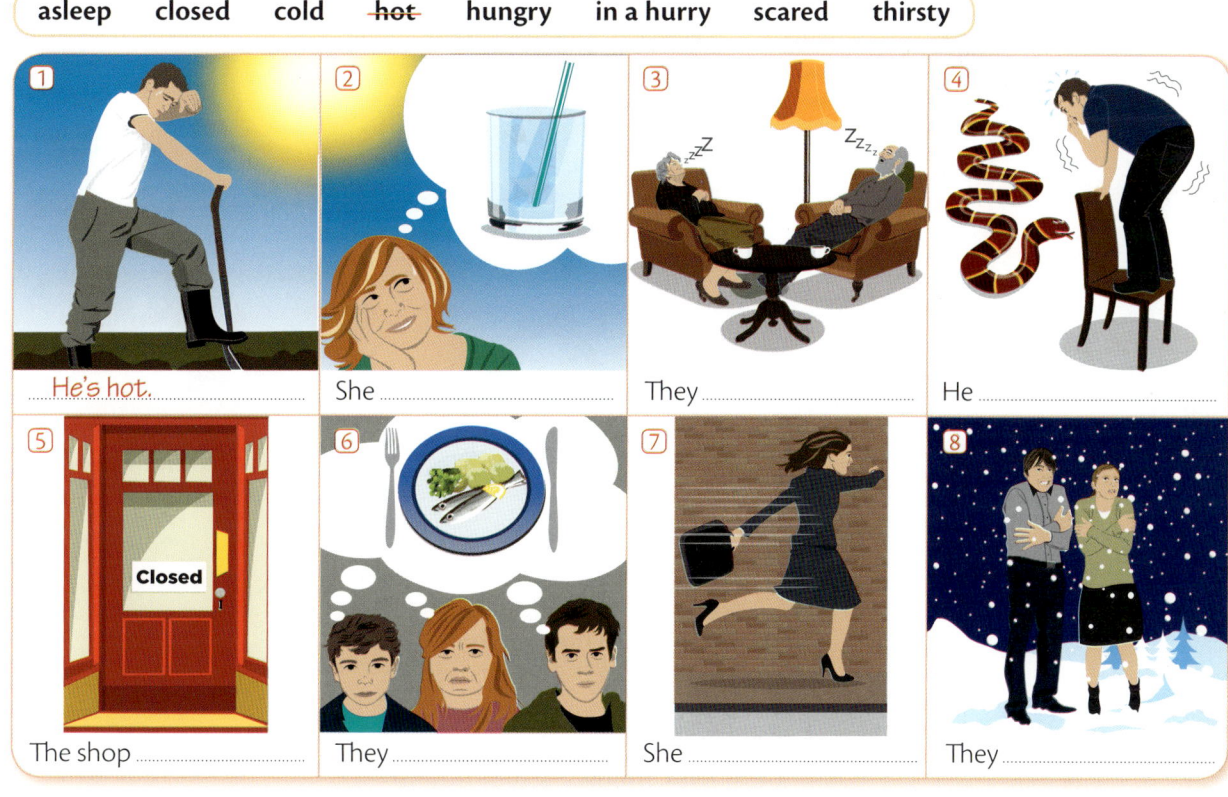

1. He's hot.
2. She ....
3. They ....
4. He ....
5. The shop ....
6. They ....
7. She ....
8. They ....

3.2 Vervollständigen Sie die Aussagen oder Fragen.

1. '_Are you_ cold?'   'No, I'm OK.'
2. 'How's your grandmother?'   '_She's_ very well.'
3. 'Are the children in bed?'   'Yes, ... asleep.'
4. 'Where .... from?'   'I'm Canadian, from Toronto.'
5. Peter's favourite sport is football. .... very interested in it.
6. (*in einem Geschäft*) These shoes are nice. How much .... ?
7. 'Sorry .... late.'   'That's OK.'
8. How's Amanda? .... well?
9. '.................. interested in art?'   'Yes, I am. Very much.'
10. This jacket is expensive. .... £200.
11. It's 9.30 and Joseph isn't here! Why .... always late?

3.3 Schreiben Sie Aussagen (bejaht oder verneint) über sich selbst.

1. (interested in politics)   I'm interested in politics.   oder   I'm not interested in politics.
2. (hungry)   I ....
3. (in a hurry) ....
4. (scared of dogs) ....
5. (cold) ....
6. (interested in films) ....
7. (thirsty) ....

3.4 Übersetzen Sie ins Englische.

Spinnen = spiders

1. Mir ist heiß.
2. Sie haben Recht.
3. Hast du Hunger?
4. Ich habe keine Angst vor Spinnen.
5. Ich interessiere mich nicht für Autos.
6. Hat der Laden auf?
7. Woher kommen Paula und Michael?
8. Wie geht es deiner Schwester?
9. Komme ich zu spät?
10. Wie viel kosten die Äpfel?

➔ Zusätzliche Übungen 1–2 (Seiten 252–53)

Unit 4: I am doing (present continuous)

A

She's eating.
She isn't reading.

It's raining.
The sun isn't shining.

They're running.
They aren't walking.

Das present continuous bildet man auf folgende Weise:
am/**is**/**are** + do**ing**/eat**ing**/runn**ing**/writ**ing** usw.

I	**am** (not)	
he she it	**is** (not)	-ing
we you they	**are** (not)	

- **I'm working**. **I'm not watching** TV.
  Ich arbeite (gerade). Ich sehe nicht fern.
- Maria **is reading** a newspaper. *… liest (gerade) …*
- She **isn't eating**. (oder She's **not eating**.) *… isst (gerade) nicht.*
- The bus **is coming**. *… kommt (jetzt).*
- We**'re having** dinner. *… essen gerade …*
- You**'re not listening** to me. (oder You **aren't listening** …)
- The children **are doing** their homework. *… machen ihre Hausaufgaben.*

B

Das present continuous *beschreibt eine Handlung, die zur Zeit gerade im Gang ist:*

> I'm working
> she's wearing a hat
> they're playing football
> I'm not watching TV

Vergangenheit   *Jetzt*   *Zukunft*

Im Deutschen gibt es keine Form, die dem present continuous genau entspricht (manchmal verwendet man 'jetzt', 'gerade' oder 'zurzeit' um zu vermitteln, dass etwas im Augenblick stattfindet):
- Please be quiet. **I'm working**. *… Ich arbeite (gerade).*
- Look, there's Sarah. She**'s wearing** a brown coat. *… Sie trägt (jetzt) …*
- The weather is nice. It**'s not raining.** *… Es regnet (zurzeit) nicht.*
- 'Where are the children?' 'They**'re playing** in the park.' *… 'Sie spielen (gerade) im Park.'*
- You can turn off the television. **I'm not watching** it. *… Ich sehe (jetzt) nicht fern.*

Einige Handlungen werden im Englischen mit **have** + Nomen umschrieben:
have a bath/**shower** *baden / sich duschen*
have breakfast/**lunch**/**dinner** *frühstücken / zu Mittag essen / zu Abend essen*
- John can't answer the phone. He**'s having** a shower. *… Er duscht sich gerade.*
- (am Telefon) We**'re having** dinner now. Can I call you later?
  Wir sind (gerade) beim Abendessen. Kann ich Sie später anrufen?

Rechtschreibung (→ Anhang 5):

| com**e** → com**ing**   writ**e** → writ**ing**   danc**e** → danc**ing** |
| run → ru**nn**ing   si**t** → si**tt**ing   swi**m** → swi**mm**ing |
| **lie** → **ly**ing |

am/is/are → **Unit 1** are you doing? (present continuous: *Fragen*) → **Unit 5** I am doing *und* I do → **Unit 9**
What are you doing tomorrow? → **Unit 26**

Übungen

Unit 4

4.1 Was machen die Leute gerade? Verwenden Sie die folgenden Verben, um die Sätze zu vervollständigen:

| ~~eat~~ have lie play sit wait |

1 _She's eating_ an apple.
2 He .... for a bus.
3 They .... football.
4 .... on the floor.
5 .... breakfast.
6 .... on the table.

4.2 Vervollständigen Sie die Sätze mit der passenden Form folgender Verben:

| build cook go have stand stay swim ~~work~~ |

1 Please be quiet. I _'m working_ .
2 'Where's John?' 'He's in the kitchen. He ....'
3 'You .... on my foot.' 'Oh, I'm sorry.'
4 Look! Somebody .... in the river.
5 We're here on holiday. We .... at the Central Hotel.
6 'Where's Sue?' 'She .... a shower.'
7 They .... a new hotel in the city centre at the moment.
8 I .... now. Goodbye.

4.3 Schreiben Sie Sätze über Jane. Verwenden Sie **She's -ing** oder **She isn't -ing**.

Jane

1 (have dinner)   _Jane isn't having dinner._
2 (watch TV)   _She's watching TV._
3 (sit on the floor)   She ....
4 (read a book) ....
5 (play the piano) ....
6 (laugh) ....
7 (wear a hat) ....
8 (drink coffee) ....

4.4 Was machen Sie gerade, oder was passiert jetzt gerade? Schreiben Sie wahre Aussagen.

1 (I / wash / my hair)   _I'm not washing my hair._
2 (it / snow)   _It's snowing._   oder   _It isn't snowing._
3 (I / sit / on a chair) ....
4 (I / eat) ....
5 (it / rain) ....
6 (I / learn / English) ....
7 (I / listen / to music) ....
8 (the sun / shine) ....
9 (I / wear / shoes) ....
10 (I / read / a newspaper) ....

4.5 Übersetzen Sie ins Englische.

Guck mal an =
Look at

1 Ich habe jetzt keine Zeit. Ich schreibe (gerade) eine E-mail.
2 Guck mal Matt an! Er tanzt mit Steph.
3 Ich esse gerade zu Mittag. Hast du Hunger?
4 Sie arbeitet (jetzt) nicht; sie sieht fern.
5 'Wo sind Tom und Sue?' 'Sie spielen Tennis.'
6 Die Sonne scheint und wir liegen am Strand.
7 Die Kinder spielen (jetzt) nicht; sie schlafen.
8 Jamie trägt heute einen neuen Schlips.
9 Amy kann nicht ans Telefon gehen. Sie badet gerade.

Unit 5: are you doing? (present continuous: *Fragen*)

A

bejahte Form

I	am	
he / she / it	is	doing working going staying *usw.*
we / you / they	are	

Frageform

am	I	
is	he / she / it	doing? working? going? staying? *usw.*
are	we / you / they	

What are you doing?

- A: **Are** you **feeling** OK?   *Fühlst du dich wohl?*
  B: Yes, I'm fine, thanks.
- A: **Is** it **raining**?   *Regnet es?*
  B: Yes, take an umbrella.
- Why **are** you **wearing** a coat? It's not cold.
  Warum trägst du einen Mantel? …
- A: What**'s** Paul **doing**?   *Was macht Paul (gerade)?*
  B: He**'s studying** for his exams.   *Er lernt für seine Prüfungen.*
- A: What **are** the children **doing**?   *Was machen die Kinder (gerade)?*
  B: They**'re watching** TV.   *Sie sehen fern.*
- Look, there's Emily! Where**'s** she **going**? … *Wohin geht sie?*
- Who **are** you **waiting** for? **Are** you **waiting** for Sue?
  Auf wen wartest du? Wartest du auf Sue?

B

Beachten Sie die Wortfolge bei der Fragestellung: das Subjekt kommt zwischen **is**/**are** und **-ing**:

is/**are** + *Subjekt* + **-ing**

	Is	he	**working** today?
	Is	Ben	**working** today? (*nicht* Is working Ben today?)
Where	are	they	**going**?
Where	are	those people	**going**? (*nicht* Where are going those people?)

C Kurzantworten

Yes,	I	am.
	he / she / it	is.
	we / you / they	are.

No,	I'm	
	he's / she's / it's	not.
	we're / you're / they're	

oder

No,	he / she / it	isn't.
	we / you / they	aren't.

- A: **Are** you **going** now?   *Gehen Sie jetzt?*
  B: **Yes, I am.**   *Ja, (ich gehe).*
- '**Is** Ben **working** today?'   '**Yes, he is.**'
- '**Is** it **raining**?'   '**No, it isn't.**'
- A: **Are** your friends **staying** at a hotel?   *Wohnen deine Freunde im Hotel?*
  B: **No, they aren't.** They're staying with me.   *Nein, sie wohnen bei mir.*

I am doing (present continuous) → Unit 4   What are you doing tomorrow? → Unit 26   Fragen → Units 45–48

Übungen

Unit 5

5.1 Schreiben Sie für jedes Bild passende Fragen zu den Antworten.

5.2 Vervollständigen Sie die Sprechblasen mit einer Frage. Verwenden Sie die folgenden Verben:

cry   eat   go   laugh   look at   ~~read~~

5.3 Bilden Sie Fragen mit den angegebenen Wörtern. Setzen Sie die Wörter in die richtige Reihenfolge.

1 (is / working / Ben / today) Is Ben working today ?
2 (what / the children / are / doing) What are the children doing ?
3 (you / are / listening / to me) ?
4 (where / your friends / are / going) ?
5 (are / watching / your parents / TV) ?
6 (what / Jessica / is / cooking) ?
7 (why / you / are / looking / at me) ?
8 (is / coming / the bus) ?

5.4 Schreiben Sie Kurzantworten (**Yes, I am.** / **No, he isn't.** usw.).

1 Are you watching TV? No, I'm not.
2 Are you wearing a watch?
3 Are you eating something?
4 Is it raining?
5 Are you sitting on the floor?
6 Are you feeling well?

5.5 Übersetzen Sie ins Englische.

1 Trägt John heute einen Schlips?
2 'Schneit es?' 'Nein, es regnet.'
3 'Was machen Sie?' 'Ich überlege gerade.'
4 Da ist Emily. Wo geht sie hin?
5 Warum lachen sie? Das ist nicht witzig.
6 Wo ist James? Arbeitet er heute?
7 A: Was liest du?
   B: Ein sehr interessantes Buch.
8 A: Sehen die Kinder fern?
   B: Nein, sie spielen im Garten.

überlegen = think
Dort ist = There's
witzig = funny

→ **Zusätzliche Übungen 3** (Seite 253)

Unit 6

I do/work/like usw. (present simple: *bejahte Form*)

A

They have a lot of books.
They **read** a lot. *Sie lesen viel.*

He's eating an ice cream.
He **likes** ice cream. *Er mag Eis.*

They **read** / he **likes** / I **work** usw. sind in der Form des present simple:

I/we/you/they	read	like	work	live	watch	do	have
he/she/it	reads	likes	works	lives	watches	does	has

Beachten Sie, dass man bei **he/she/it** ein **s** am Verb benötigt:
he work**s** / **she** live**s** / **it** rain**s** *usw.*
- **I work** in a shop. **My brother works** in a bank. (*nicht* My brother work)
  Ich arbeite … Mein Bruder arbeitet …
- **Lucy lives** in London. **Her parents live** in Scotland.
  Lucy lebt in London. Ihre Eltern leben …
- **It rains** a lot in winter. *Es regnet viel …*

I **have** → he/she/it **has**:
- **Joe has** a shower every day. *Joe duscht sich jeden Tag.*

Rechtschreibung (→ Anhang 5):
nach **-s** / **-sh** / **-ch** schreibt man **-es**: pas**s** → pas**ses**   fini**sh** → fini**shes**   wat**ch** → wat**ches**
-y → **-ies**: stud**y** → stud**ies**   tr**y** → tr**ies**
außerdem: do → do**es**   go → go**es**

B

Man verwendet das present simple *um auszudrücken, dass etwas allgemein gültig ist, zum Beispiel für regelmäßige oder wiederholte Handlungen:*
- I **like** big cities. *Ich mag …*
- Your English is good. You **speak** very well. *… Sie sprechen sehr gut.*
- Tom **works** very hard. He **starts** at 7.30 and **finishes** at 8 o'clock in the evening.
  Tom arbeitet sehr fleißig. Er fängt um … an und ist um … fertig.
- The earth **goes** round the sun. *Die Erde dreht sich um die Sonne.*
- We **do** a lot of different things in our free time.
  Wir machen in unserer Freizeit viele verschiedene Sachen.
- It **costs** a lot of money to build a hospital. *Es kostet sehr viel Geld …*

Beachten Sie, dass man **I like** (= ich mag) / **he likes** (= er mag) usw. auch mit 'mir gefällt/gefallen' / 'ihm gefällt/gefallen' übersetzen kann:
- I **like** big cities. *Ich mag … oder Mir gefallen …*

C

Beachten Sie die Stellung von **always/never/often/usually/sometimes** beim present simple:
- Sue **always gets** to work early. (*nicht* Sue gets always) *Sue kommt immer …*
- I **never eat** breakfast. (*nicht* I eat never) *Ich frühstücke nie.*
- We **often go** away at weekends. *Wir fahren oft am Wochenende weg.*
- Mark **usually plays** football on Sundays. *… spielt meistens …*
- I **sometimes walk** to work, but not very often. *Ich gehe manchmal zu Fuß …*

I don't … (Verneinung) → **Unit 7**   **Do you** … ? (Fragen) → **Unit 8**   **I am doing** und **I do** → **Unit 9**
always/usually/often *usw.* (Satzbau) → **Unit 94**

Übungen

Unit 6

6.1 Schreiben Sie die passende Form für die folgenden Verben (–s oder –es).

1. (read) she *reads*
2. (think) he ....
3. (fly) it ....
4. (dance) he ....
5. (have) she ....
6. (finish) it ....

6.2 Vervollständigen Sie die Sätze über die Personen in den Bildern. Verwenden Sie die folgenden Verben:

eat   go   live   ~~play~~   play   sleep

1. *He plays* the piano.
2. They .... in a very big house.
3. .... a lot of fruit.
4. .... tennis.
5. .... to the cinema a lot.
6. .... seven hours a night.

6.3 Vervollständigen Sie die Sätze mit den folgenden Verben:

boil   close   cost   cost   like   like   meet   open   ~~speak~~   teach   wash

1. Maria *speaks* four languages.
2. The shops in the city centre usually .... at 9 o'clock in the morning.
3. The City Museum .... at 5 o'clock in the evening.
4. Tina is a teacher. She .... mathematics to young children.
5. My job is very interesting. I .... a lot of people.
6. Peter's car is always dirty. He never .... it.
7. Food is expensive. It .... a lot of money.
8. Shoes are expensive. They .... a lot of money.
9. Water .... at 100 degrees Celsius.
10. Laura and I are good friends. I .... her and she .... me.

6.4 Bilden Sie Sätze mit den angegebenen Wörtern. Setzen Sie die Verben in die korrekte Form (**arrive** oder **arrives** usw.).

1. (always / early / Sue / arrive) *Sue always arrives early.*
2. (to the cinema / never / I / go) I ....
3. (work / Martina / hard / always) ....
4. (like / chocolate / children / usually) ....
5. (Jackie / parties / enjoy / always) ....
6. (often / people's names / I / forget) ....
7. (TV / Sam / watch / never) ....
8. (usually / dinner / we / have / at 7.30) ....
9. (Kate / always / nice clothes / wear) ....

6.5 Schreiben Sie Aussagen über sich selbst. Verwenden Sie **always**/**never**/**often**/**usually**/**sometimes**.

1. (watch TV in the evening) *I usually watch TV in the evening.*
2. (read in bed) I ....
3. (get up before 7 o'clock) ....
4. (go to work/school by bus) ....
5. (drink coffee in the morning) ....

6.6 Übersetzen Sie ins Englische.

aufgehen = rise

1. Ich mag Schokolade.
2. Wir leben in Frankfurt.
3. Die Bank schließt um 3.30.
4. Die Sonne geht im Sommer früh auf.
5. Sam sieht abends immer fern.
6. Rachel und Mark gehen oft ins Kino.
7. Er macht nie seine Hausaufgaben.
8. Ich fahre meistens mit dem Zug, aber manchmal fahre ich mit dem Auto.

Unit 7

I don't ... (present simple: *Verneinung*)

A

Die Verneinung im present simple bildet man mit **don't**/**doesn't** + Verb:

She **doesn't drink** coffee.
Sie trinkt keinen Kaffee.

He **doesn't like** his job.
Ihm gefällt seine Arbeit nicht.

bejahte Form		Verneinung		
I, we, you, they	work, like, do, have	I, we, you, they	**don't** (do not)	work, like, do, have
he, she, it	works, likes, does, has	he, she, it	**doesn't** (does not)	

- I **drink** coffee, but I **don't drink** tea. *Ich trinke Kaffee, aber ich trinke keinen Tee.*
- Sue **drinks** tea, but she **doesn't drink** coffee. *Sue trinkt ... , aber sie trinkt keinen ...*
- You **don't work** very hard. *Du arbeitest nicht sehr fleißig.*
- We **don't watch** TV very often. *Wir sehen nicht sehr oft fern.*
- The weather is usually nice. It **doesn't rain** very often. *... Es regnet nicht sehr oft.*
- Sam and Chris **don't know** many people. *Sam und Chris kennen nicht ...*

B

Beachten Sie die Form der Verneinung:

| I/we/you/they | **don't** ... |
| he/she/it | **doesn't** ... |

- **I don't** like football.
- **He doesn't** like football.

- **I don't** like Fred and **Fred doesn't** like me. (*nicht* Fred don't like)
- **My car doesn't** use much petrol. (*nicht* My car don't use)
- Sometimes he is late, but **it doesn't** happen very often. *... es passiert nicht sehr oft.*

C

Nach **don't**/**doesn't** verwendet man den Infinitiv des Verbs (don't **like** / doesn't **speak** / doesn't **do** usw.):

- I **don't like** washing the car. I **don't do** it very often.
  Ich wasche nicht gerne das Auto. Ich mache es nicht sehr oft.
- Sarah **speaks** Spanish, but she **doesn't speak** Italian. (*nicht* doesn't speaks)
  Sarah spricht Spanisch, aber sie spricht kein ...
- David **doesn't do** his job very well. (*nicht* David doesn't his job)
  David macht seine Arbeit nicht sehr gut.
- Paula **doesn't** usually **have** breakfast. (*nicht* doesn't ... has) *Paula frühstückt meistens nicht.*

Vorsicht, wenn das Hauptverb **do** (= *machen*) ist:

- I **don't do** it very often. *Ich mache es nicht sehr oft.*
- David **doesn't do** his job very well. *David macht seine Arbeit nicht sehr gut.*

In diesen Beispielen zeigen **don't** und **doesn't** die Verneinung an, während **do** die Bedeutung 'machen' hat.

I do/work/like usw. (present simple: *bejahte Form*) → Unit 6   **Do you ... ?** (present simple: *Frageform*) → Unit 8

Übungen

7.1 Schreiben Sie die Verneinung.

1. I play the piano very well. — *I don't play the piano very well.*
2. Anna plays the piano very well. — Anna ....
3. They know my phone number. — They ....
4. We work very hard.
5. He has a bath every day.
6. You do the same thing every day.

7.2 Schreiben Sie Sätze mit **like** anhand der Informationen in der Tabelle.

Do you like ...?	BEN AND SOPHIE	KATE	YOU
1 classical music?	yes	no	?
2 boxing?	no	yes	
3 horror movies?	yes	no	

1. *Ben and Sophie like classical music.*
   Kate ....
   I .... classical music.
2. Ben and Sophie ....
   Kate ....
   I ....
3. ....

7.3 Schreiben Sie über sich selbst. Verwenden Sie:

I never ... oder **I often ...** oder **I don't ... very often**.

1. (watch TV) *I don't watch TV very often.* oder *I never watch TV.* oder *I often watch TV.*
2. (go to the theatre)
3. (ride a bike)
4. (eat in restaurants)
5. (travel by train)

7.4 Vervollständigen Sie die Sätze mit der Verneinung folgender Verben (**don't**/**doesn't** + Verb):

cost   go   know   ~~rain~~   see   use   wear

1. The weather here is usually nice. It *doesn't rain* much.
2. Paul has a car, but he .... it very often.
3. Paul and his friends like films, but they .... to the cinema very often.
4. Amanda is married, but she .... a ring.
5. I .... much about politics. I'm not interested in it.
6. The Regent Hotel isn't expensive. It .... much to stay there.
7. Ed lives very near us, but we .... him very often.

7.5 Setzen Sie das Verb in die passende Form: Bejahung oder Verneinung.

1. Margaret *speaks* four languages – English, French, German and Spanish. (speak)
2. I *don't like* my job. It's very boring. (like)
3. 'Where's Steve?' 'I'm sorry. I ....' (know)
4. Sue is a very quiet person. She .... very much. (talk)
5. Andy .... a lot of tea. It's his favourite drink. (drink)
6. It's not true! I .... it! (believe)
7. That's a very beautiful picture. I .... it very much. (like)
8. Mark is a vegetarian. He .... meat. (eat)

7.6 Übersetzen Sie ins Englische.

1. Ich kenne deinen Bruder nicht.
2. Sonntags steht Ben nicht früh auf.
3. Mir gefällt das Kleid nicht sehr gut.
4. Wir gehen nicht sehr oft aus.
5. Jenny mag Äpfel, aber sie mag keine Bananen.
6. Steve und Amy machen am Wochenende nicht sehr viel.
7. Lisa spielt kein Tennis, aber sie spielt Squash.

Unit 8

Do you … ? (present simple: *Frageform*)

A Man bildet Fragen im present simple mit **do**/**does**:

bejahte Form		Frageform		
I / we / you / they	work / like / do / have	do	I / we / you / they	work? / like? / do? / have?
he / she / it	works / likes / does / has	does	he / she / it	

Do you play the guitar?

- Do you **like** Greek food? *Mögen Sie griechisches Essen?*
- **Does** Chris **play** tennis? *Spielt Chris Tennis?*
- Where **do** your parents **live**? *Wo wohnen deine Eltern?*
- How much **does** it **cost**? *Wie viel kostet es?*

B Beachten Sie die Wortstellung bei Fragen:

do/**does** + *Subjekt* + *Infinitiv*

	Do	you	**play**	the guitar?
	Do	your friends	**live**	near here?
	Does	Chris	**work**	on Sundays?
	Does	it	**rain**	a lot here?
Where	**do**	your parents	**live?**	
How often	**do**	you	**wash**	your hair?
What	**does**	this word	**mean?**	
How much	**does**	it	**cost**	to fly to Rome?

Beachten Sie auch die Stellung von **always** und **usually**:

	Does	Chris	**always**	**work**	on Sundays?
What	**do**	you	**usually**	**do**	at weekends?

Vorsicht, wenn das Hauptverb **do** (= machen) ist! In diesem Beispiel zeigt das erste **do** an, dass eine Frage gestellt wird, während das zweite **do** die Bedeutung 'machen' hat:
- **Do** you **do** much at weekends? *Machen (unternehmen) Sie viel am Wochenende?*

What do you **do**? = *Was machen Sie (beruflich)? (Welchen Beruf üben Sie aus?)*:
- '**What do** you **do**?' 'I work in a bank.' '*Was machen Sie?*' …
- '**What does** Sarah **do**?' 'She's a student.' '*Was macht Sarah?*' …

C Vorsicht beim Gebrauch von **do** und **does**! Man sagt:

| **do** I/we/you/they … |
| **does** he/she/it … |

- **Do they** like music? *Mögen Sie Musik?*
- **Does he** like music? *Mag er Musik?*

D Kurzantworten

Yes,	I/we/you/they **do**.		No,	I/we/you/they **don't**.
	he/she/it **does**.			he/she/it **doesn't**.

- '**Do you** play the guitar?' '**No, I don't**.' '*Spielen Sie … ?*' '*Nein, (ich spiele nicht).*'
- '**Do your parents** speak English?' '**Yes, they do**.'
- '**Does James** work hard?' '**Yes, he does**.'
- '**Does your sister** live in London?' '**No, she doesn't**.'

I do/**work**/**like** usw. (present simple: *bejahte Form*) → **Unit 6**   **I don't** … (present simple: *Verneinung*) → **Unit 7**
Fragen → **Units 45–48**

Übungen

Unit 8

8.1 Bilden Sie Fragen mit **Do ... ?** und **Does ... ?**

1. I like chocolate. How about you? — Do you like chocolate ?
2. I play tennis. How about you? — .... you .... ?
3. You live near here. How about Lucy? — .... Lucy .... ?
4. Tom plays tennis. How about his friends? — .... ?
5. You speak English. How about your brother? — .... ?
6. I do yoga every morning. How about you? — .... ?
7. Sue goes away a lot. How about Paul? — .... ?
8. I want to be famous. How about you? — .... ?
9. You work hard. How about Anna? — .... ?

8.2 Bilden Sie Fragen mit den Wörtern in Klammern. Verwenden Sie **do/does** und setzen Sie die Wörter in die richtige Reihenfolge.

1. (where / live / your parents) — Where do your parents live ?
2. (you / early / always / get up) — Do you always get up early ?
3. (how often / TV / you / watch) — .... ?
4. (you / want / what / for dinner) — .... ?
5. (like / you / football) — .... ?
6. (your brother / like / football) — .... ?
7. (what / you / do / in your free time) — .... ?
8. (your sister / work / where) — .... ?
9. (breakfast / always / you / have) — .... ?
10. (what / mean / this word) — .... ?
11. (in winter / snow / it / here) — .... ?
12. (go / usually / to bed / what time / you) — .... ?
13. (how much / to phone New York / it / cost) — .... ?
14. (you / for breakfast / have / usually / what) — .... ?

8.3 Vervollständigen Sie die Fragen, indem Sie die folgenden Verben verwenden:

~~do~~ do enjoy go like start teach work

1. What do you do ? — I work in a bookshop.
2. .... it? — It's OK.
3. What time .... in the morning? — At 9 o'clock.
4. .... on Saturdays? — Sometimes.
5. How .... to work? — Usually by bus.
6. And your husband. What .... ? — He's a teacher.
7. What .... ? — Science.
8. .... his job? — Yes, he loves it.

8.4 Schreiben Sie Kurzantworten (**Yes, he does.** / **No, I don't.** usw.).

1. Do you watch TV a lot? — No, I don't. oder Yes, I do.
2. Do you live in a big city? — ....
3. Do you often ride a bike? — ....
4. Does it rain a lot where you live? — ....
5. Do you play the piano? — ....

8.5 Übersetzen Sie ins Englische.

mieten = rent

1. Gefällt dir mein Kleid?
2. Arbeitet er sehr viel?
3. Mögen Sie Fisch?
4. Wo wohnt Tom?
5. Spielt sie Gitarre?
6. Wie oft geht ihr abends aus?
7. Fahren sie oft nach London?
8. Was macht deine Mutter beruflich?
9. Was machen Sie gewöhnlich nach der Arbeit?
10. Wie viel kostet es, ein Auto zu mieten?

→ Zusätzliche Übungen 4–7 (Seiten 253–54)

Unit 9

I am doing (present continuous) und I do (present simple)

A

Jack is watching television.
He is *not* playing the guitar.

But Jack has a guitar.
He often plays it and he plays very well.

Jack **plays** the guitar,
but he **is not playing** the guitar now.
Jack spielt Gitarre, aber jetzt gerade spielt er nicht.

Is he playing the guitar?   **No, he isn't.**   (present continuous)
Does he play the guitar?   **Yes, he does.**   (present simple)

B

*Das present continuous (**I am doing**) verwendet man für Handlungen, die im Moment des Sprechens gerade im Gang sind:*

I'm doing
(im Augenblick, gerade)

Vergangenheit — *Jetzt* — *Zukunft*

- Please be quiet. **I'm** work**ing**. (*nicht* I work)
  … *Ich arbeite (gerade).*
- Tom **is** hav**ing** a shower at the moment. (*nicht* Tom has)
  Tom duscht jetzt gerade.
- Take an umbrella with you. It**'s** rain**ing**. … *Es regnet (jetzt).*
- You can turn off the television. **I'm** not watch**ing** it. … *Ich sehe (jetzt) nicht fern.*
- Why are you under the table? What **are** you do**ing**? … *Was machst du (gerade)?*

C

*Das present simple (**I do**) verwendet man für allgemein gültige Aussagen und wiederholte, regelmäßige Handlungen:*

I do
(allgemein, immer, manchmal)

Vergangenheit — *Jetzt* — *Zukunft*

- I **work** every day from 9 o'clock to 5.30. *Ich arbeite jeden Tag …*
- Tom **has** a shower every morning. *Tom duscht sich jeden Morgen.*
- It **rains** a lot in winter. *Im Winter regnet es viel.*
- I **don't watch** TV very often. *Ich sehe nicht oft fern.*
- What **do** you usually **do** at weekends? *Was machen Sie gewöhnlich … ?*

Das present continuous und present simple werden beide mit der Gegenwartsform ins Deutsche übersetzt:
- 'Where is Karin?' 'She**'s** work**ing**.' '*Wo ist Karin?' 'Sie arbeitet (im Moment).*'
- Karin is a doctor. She **works** in a hospital. *Karin ist Ärztin. Sie arbeitet in … (allgemein).*

D

*Folgende Verben werden nicht im present continuous (**I am -ing**) verwendet:*

like	want	know	understand	remember
prefer	**need**	**mean**	**believe**	**forget**

*Mit diesen Verben verwendet man nur das present simple (**I want** / **do you like?** usw.):*
- I'm tired. **I want** to go home. (*nicht* I'm wanting) *Ich will …*
- '**Do** you **know** that girl?' 'Yes, but **I don't remember** her name.'
  '*Kennen Sie … ?' 'Ja, aber ich kann mich nicht an ihren Namen erinnern.*'
- **I don't understand**. What **do** you **mean**? *Ich verstehe nicht. Was meinen Sie?*

---

present continuous → **Units 4–5**   present simple → **Units 6–8**   Gegenwartsformen mit Zukunftsbedeutung → **Unit 26**

Übungen

9.1 Beantworten Sie die Fragen zu den Personen auf den Bildern.

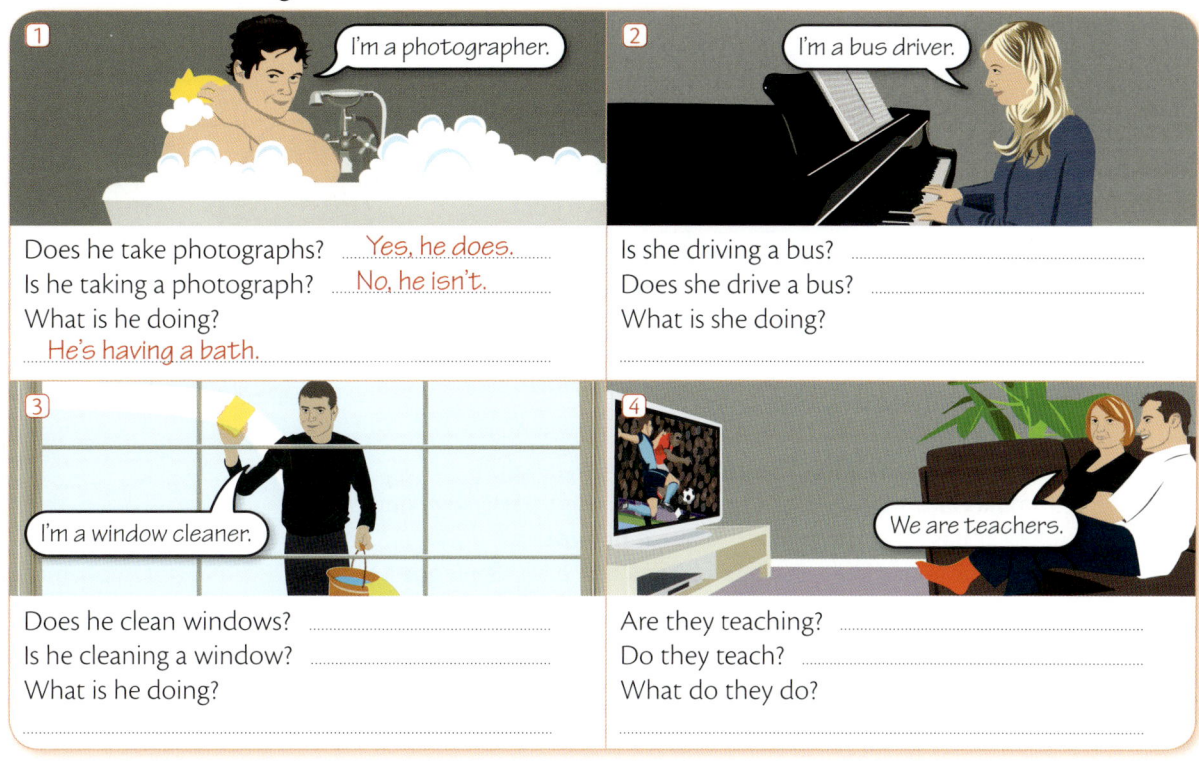

1. Does he take photographs? Yes, he does.
   Is he taking a photograph? No, he isn't.
   What is he doing? He's having a bath.

2. Is she driving a bus? ____
   Does she drive a bus? ____
   What is she doing? ____

3. Does he clean windows? ____
   Is he cleaning a window? ____
   What is he doing? ____

4. Are they teaching? ____
   Do they teach? ____
   What do they do? ____

9.2 Vervollständigen Sie die Sätze mit **am**/**is**/**are** oder **do**/**don't**/**does**/**doesn't**.

1. Excuse me, ...do... you speak English?
2. 'Where's Kate?' 'I .... know.'
3. What's funny? Why .... you laughing?
4. 'What .... your sister do?' 'She's a dentist.'
5. It .... raining. I .... want to go out in the rain.
6. 'Where .... you come from?' 'Canada.'
7. How much .... it cost to stay at this hotel? Is it expensive?
8. Steve is a good tennis player, but he .... play very often.

9.3 Vervollständigen Sie die Sätze mit den Wörtern in Klammern und verwenden Sie entweder present continuous (**I am doing**) oder present simple (**I do**).

1. Excuse me, ...do you speak... (you/speak) English?
2. 'Where's Tom?' '...He's having... (he/have) a shower.'
3. ...I don't watch... (I/not/watch) TV very often.
4. Listen! Somebody .... (sing).
5. Sarah is tired. .... (she/want) to go home now.
6. How often .... (you/use) your car? Every day?
7. 'Excuse me, but .... (you/sit) in my seat.' 'Oh, I'm sorry.'
8. I'm sorry, ... (I/not/understand). Can you speak more slowly?
9. It's late. .... (I/go) home now. .... (you/come) with me?
10. What time .... (your father / finish) work every day?
11. You can turn off the radio. .... (I/not/listen) to it.
12. 'Where's Paul?' 'In the kitchen. .... (he/cook) something.'
13. Mark .... (not/usually/drive) to work.
    He .... (usually/walk).
14. Sue .... (not/like) coffee. .... (she/prefer) tea.

9.4 Übersetzen Sie ins Englische.

unmöglich = impossible
lernen = study

1. A: Was machst du?
   B: Ich mache meine Hausaufgaben.
2. Mein kleiner Sohn schläft viel, aber jetzt weint er gerade.
3. Verstehst du, was ich meine?
4. Die Kinder wollen nicht ins Bett gehen.
5. Das ist unmöglich! Das glaube ich nicht!
6. Gehst du oft ins Kino?
7. A: Arbeitest du?
   B: Nein, ich mache ein Spiel.
8. 'Wo sind die Kinder?' 'Sie spielen im Garten.'
9. Jane lernt sehr viel, aber jetzt spielt sie gerade mit der Katze.

Unit 10: I have ... und I've got ...

A

Man kann **I have** oder **I have got** sagen. Die Bedeutung bleibt gleich.

I / we / you / they	**have**	oder	I / we / you / they	**have got**	(I**'ve got**) (we**'ve got**) (you**'ve got**) (they**'ve got**)
he / she / it	**has**	oder	he / she / it	**has got**	(he**'s got**) (she**'s got**) (it**'s got**)

Kurzformen

I've got a headache.

- **I have** blue eyes. oder I**'ve got** blue eyes. *Ich habe ...*
- Tom **has** two sisters. oder Tom **has got** two sisters. *Tom hat ...*
- Our car **has** four doors. oder Our car **has got** four doors. *... hat vier Türen.*
- Sarah isn't feeling well. She **has** a headache. oder She**'s got** a headache. *... Sie hat Kopfschmerzen.*
- They like animals. They **have** a horse, three dogs and six cats. oder They**'ve got** a horse ... *... Sie haben ...*

B

I **don't have** / I **haven't got** usw. (Verneinung)

Man sagt:

I/you we/they	**don't**	**have**	oder	I/you we/they	**haven't**	**got**
he/she it	**doesn't**			he/she it	**hasn't**	

- I **don't have** a car. oder I **haven't got** a car. *Ich habe kein Auto.*
- They **don't have** any children. oder They **haven't got** any children. *Sie haben keine Kinder.*
- It's a nice house, but it **doesn't have** a garden. oder ... it **hasn't got** a garden. *..., aber es hat keinen Garten.*
- Amy **doesn't have** a job at the moment. oder Amy **hasn't got** a job ... *Amy hat gerade keine Arbeit.*

C

do you **have**? / **have** you **got**? usw. (Frageform)

Man sagt:

do	I/you we/they	**have**		**have**	I/you we/they	**got**
does	he/she it			**has**	he/she it	

- 'Do you **have** a camera?' 'No, I **don't**.' oder
  Have you **got** a camera?' 'No, I **haven't**.' *'Hast du / Haben Sie ...?' 'Nein.'*
- '**Does** Helen **have** a car?' 'Yes, she **does**.' oder
  '**Has** Helen **got** a car?' 'Yes, she **has**.' *'Hat Helen ...?' 'Ja.'*
- What kind of car **does** she **have**? oder ... **has** she **got**? *Was für ein Auto hat sie?*
- How many children **do** they **have**? oder ... **have** they **got**? *Wie viele Kinder haben sie?*

D

Beachten Sie, dass **is** und **has** beide in der Kurzform zu **'s** zusammengezogen werden:
- It**'s** (It **is**) a small house, but it**'s got** (it **has** got) a big garden. *..., aber es hat einen großen Garten.*
- She**'s** (She **is**) tired and she**'s got** (she **has** got) a headache. *... und sie hat Kopfschmerzen.*

Die Kurzform **'s** für **has** wird jedoch nur in Verbindung mit **got** verwendet:
- She **has** a headache. oder She**'s got** a headache. (nicht She's a headache)

---

had / didn't have (Vergangenheit) → Units 12–13   have breakfast / have a shower usw. → Units 4, 59
some/any → Unit 76

Übungen

Unit 10

10.1 Schreiben Sie die Sätze mit **got**. Die Bedeutung bleibt gleich.
1. They have two children. — *They've got two children.*
2. She doesn't have a key. — *She hasn't got a key.*
3. He has a new job. — He ....
4. Do you have an umbrella? ....
5. We have a lot of work to do. ....
6. I don't have your phone number. ....
7. Does your father have a car? ....
8. How much money do we have? ....

10.2 Schreiben Sie die Sätze mit **do/does/don't/doesn't**. Die Bedeutung bleibt gleich.
1. Have you got any money? — *Do you have any money?*
2. I haven't got many clothes. — I ....
3. Has Tom got a brother? ....
4. How many children have they got? ....
5. Have you got any questions? ....
6. Sam hasn't got a job. ....

10.3 Lesen Sie die Fragen und Antworten. Schreiben Sie anschließend Sätze über Mark.

1. Have you got a car? — No. — *He hasn't got a car.*
2. Have you got a bike? — Yes. — He ....
3. Have you got a dog? — No. — ....
4. Have you got a mobile phone? — Yes. — ....
5. Have you got a watch? — No. — ....
6. Have you got any brothers or sisters? — Yes, two brothers and a sister. — ....

Und Sie? Schreiben Sie Sätze mit **I've got** oder **I haven't got**.

7. (a dog) ....
8. (a bike) ....
9. (brothers/sisters) ....

10.4 Vervollständigen Sie Sätze. Verwenden Sie **have**, **has**, **don't have** oder **doesn't have**.
1. Sarah *doesn't have* a car. She goes everywhere by bike.
2. They like animals. They *have* three dogs and two cats.
3. Charles isn't happy. He .... a lot of problems.
4. They are always busy. They .... much free time.
5. 'What's wrong?' 'I .... something in my eye.'
6. 'Where's my pen?' 'I don't know. I .... it.'
7. Amy wants to go to the concert, but she .... a ticket.

10.5 Vervollständigen Sie die Sätze. Verwenden Sie **have/has got** oder **haven't/hasn't got**.

six legs   a key   ~~a headache~~   a lot of friends   a job   much time

1. I'm not feeling very well. I *'ve got a headache.*
2. Everybody likes Tom. He ....
3. She can't open the door. She ....
4. Quick! We ....
5. An insect ....
6. I'm unemployed. I ....

10.6 Übersetzen Sie ins Englische.
Laptop = laptop

1. Tom hat einen neuen Laptop.
2. Wir haben keinen Fernseher.
3. Wie viel Zeit haben wir?
4. Hat Emily ein Fahrrad?
5. A: Haben Sie Kinder?
   B: Ja, wir haben ein Mädchen und einen Jungen.
6. Kate hat drei Brüder, aber sie hat keine Schwestern.
7. Es ist ein großes Haus, aber es hat eine kleine Küche.

→ Zusätzliche Übungen 5–7 (Seite 254)

Unit 11
was/were

A

last night | now

Now Robert **is** at work.

At midnight last night he **wasn't** at work.
Um Mitternacht ... war er nicht ...

He **was** in bed. Er war im Bett.
He **was** tired. Er war müde.

am/is (*Gegenwart*) → **was** (*Vergangenheit*):
- I **am** tired. *Ich bin müde.*
- Where **is** Kate? *Wo ist Kate?*
- The weather **is** good today.

- I **was** tired **last night**. *Ich war gestern Abend müde.*
- Where **was** Kate **yesterday**? *Wo war Kate gestern?*
- The weather **was** good **last week**.

are (*Gegenwart*) → **were** (*Vergangenheit*):
- You **are** late today. *Sie sind heute spät.*
- They **aren't** here. *Sie sind nicht hier.*

- You **were** late **yesterday**. *Sie waren gestern spät.*
- They **weren't** here **last Sunday**. *Sie waren ... nicht hier.*

B

bejahte Form	Verneinung	Frageform
I / he / she / it **was**	I / he / she / it **was not** (**wasn't**)	**was** I? / he? / she? / it?
we / you / they **were**	we / you / they **were not** (**weren't**)	**were** we? / you? / they?

- Last year Rachel **was** 22, so she is 23 now. *Letztes Jahr war Rachel 22, also ist sie jetzt 23.*
- When I **was** a child, I **was** scared of dogs. *Als ich ein Kind war, hatte ich Angst vor ...*
- We **were** hungry, but we **weren't** tired. *Wir hatten Hunger, aber wir waren nicht müde.*
- The hotel **was** comfortable, but it **wasn't** expensive. *Das Hotel war gemütlich, aber es war nicht teuer.*

- **Was** the weather nice when you **were** on holiday? *War das Wetter angenehm, als Sie im Urlaub waren?*
- Your shoes are nice. **Were** they expensive? *Deine Schuhe sind schön. Waren sie teuer?*
- Why **were** you late this morning? *Warum bist du heute Früh zu spät gekommen?*

Beachten Sie, dass man bei einigen Redewendungen mit **was/were** im Deutschen 'haben' verwendet (→ Unit 3):
- I **was** scared. *Ich hatte Angst.*
- We **were** hungry/thirsty. *Wir hatten Hunger/Durst. (Wir waren hungrig/durstig.)*

Beachten Sie außerdem:
was/were asleep = *schlief/schliefst/schliefen*
- The children were in bed. They **were asleep**. *... Sie schliefen.*

I **was late** = *ich habe mich verspätet / ich bin zu spät gekommen*
- I **was late** for the meeting. *Ich bin zu spät zur Konferenz gekommen.*

C

Kurzantworten

Yes,	I/he/she/it **was**.	No,	I/he/she/it **wasn't**.
	we/you/they **were**.		we/you/they **weren't**.

- '**Were you** late?' 'No, I wasn't.'
- '**Was Tom** at work yesterday?' 'Yes, he was.'
- '**Were Sue and Steve** at the party?' 'No, they weren't.'

am/is/are → Units 1–3   I was doing → Unit 14

Übungen

Unit 11

11.1 Wo waren die Personen um 3 Uhr gestern Nachmittag? Schreiben Sie passende Sätze.

JOE   JACK   KATE   SUE   MR AND MRS HALL   BEN

1 *Joe was in bed.*
2 Jack and Kate ....
3 Sue ....
4 ....
5 ....
6 And you? I ....

11.2 Vervollständigen Sie die Sätze mit am/is/are (Gegenwart) oder was/were (Vergangenheit).

1 Last year she .....*was*..... 22, so she .....*is*..... 23 now.
2 Today the weather .... nice, but yesterday it .... very cold.
3 I .... hungry. Can I have something to eat?
4 I feel fine this morning, but I .... very tired last night.
5 Where .... you at 11 o'clock last Friday morning?
6 Don't buy those shoes. They .... very expensive.
7 I like your new jacket. .... it expensive?
8 This time last year I .... in Paris.
9 'Where .... Sam and Joe?' 'I don't know. They .... here a few minutes ago.'

11.3 Vervollständigen Sie die Sätze mit was/were oder wasn't/weren't.

1 We weren't happy with the hotel. Our room .....*was*..... very small and it .....*wasn't*..... clean.
2 Mark .... at work last week because he .... ill. He's better now.
3 Yesterday .... a public holiday, so the banks .... closed. They're open today.
4 '................ Kate and Ben at the party?' 'Kate .... there, but Ben ....'
5 Where are my keys? They .... on the table, but they're not there now.
6 You .... at home last night. Where .... you?

11.4 Bilden Sie Fragen. Setzen Sie die Wörter in Klammern in die richtige Reihenfolge und verwenden Sie was/were.

1 (late / you / this morning / why?)
   Why were you late this morning? → The traffic was bad.
2 (difficult / your exam?)
   .... → No, it was easy.
3 (last week / where / Sue and Chris?)
   .... → They were on holiday.
4 (your new camera / how much?)
   .... → A hundred pounds.
5 (angry / you / yesterday / why?)
   .... → Because you were late.
6 (nice / the weather / last week?)
   .... → Yes, it was beautiful.

11.5 Übersetzen Sie ins Englische.

1 Gestern Abend war ich auf einem Fest, und heute bin ich sehr müde!
2 Ben war letzte Woche im Krankenhaus, aber jetzt ist er wieder bei der Arbeit.
3 War Jenny gestern in der Schule?
4 'Wo wart ihr letztes Wochenende?' 'Wir waren in den Bergen.'
5 Warum warst du heute Früh müde?
6 'Wo sind meine braunen Schuhe?' 'Ich weiß nicht. Gestern waren sie unter dem Tisch.'
7 Als Beth klein war, hatte sie Angst vor dem Dunkeln.

bei = at
das Dunkel = the dark

Unit 12

worked/got/went usw. (past simple)

A

They **watch** TV every evening. (present simple)
Sie sehen ... fern.

They **watched** TV yesterday evening. (past simple)
Sie haben gestern Abend ferngesehen.

watched ist im past simple:

| I/we/you/they | watched |
| he/she/it | |

B

Das past simple *von regelmäßigen Verben bildet man mit der Endung* **-ed**, *zum Beispiel:*

| work → **worked** | start → **started** | stay → **stayed** |
| clean → **cleaned** | dance → **danced** | need → **needed** |

- I clean my teeth every morning. This morning I **cleaned** my teeth.
  Ich putze jeden Morgen meine Zähne. Heute Früh habe ich meine Zähne geputzt.
- Terry **worked** in a bank from 2005 to 2011. *Terry hat von ... bis ... in einer Bank gearbeitet.*
- Yesterday it **rained** all morning. It **stopped** at lunchtime.
  Gestern hat es den ganzen Morgen geregnet. Es hat um die Mittagszeit aufgehört.
- We **enjoyed** the party last night. We **danced** a lot and **talked** to a lot of people. The party **finished** at midnight. *... hat uns gefallen ... haben ... getanzt und haben ... geredet. ... hat ... geendet.*

Rechtschreibung (→ Anhang 5):

| tr**y** → tr**ied** | sto**p** → sto**pped** | stud**y** → stud**ied** | pla**n** → pla**nned** | cop**y** → cop**ied** |

C

Manche Verben sind unregelmäßig und bilden die Vergangenheit nicht mit **-ed**. Hier ist die past simple Form einiger wichtiger unregelmäßiger Verben (→ Anhang 2–3):

begin *(anfangen)* → **began**	get (→ Unit 57) → **got**	say *(sagen)* → **said**
break *(brechen)* **broke**	give *(geben)* **gave**	see *(sehen)* **saw**
bring *(bringen)* **brought**	go *(gehen)* **went**	sell *(verkaufen)* **sold**
build *(bauen)* **built**	have *(haben)* **had**	sit *(sitzen)* **sat**
buy *(kaufen)* **bought**	hear *(hören)* **heard**	sleep *(schlafen)* **slept**
catch *(fangen)* **caught**	know *(wissen/kennen)* **knew**	speak *(sprechen)* **spoke**
come *(kommen)* **came**	leave *(fortgehen)* **left**	stand *(stehen)* **stood**
do *(machen/tun)* **did**	lose *(verlieren)* **lost**	take *(nehmen)* **took**
drink *(trinken)* **drank**	make *(machen)* **made**	tell *(sagen)* **told**
eat *(essen)* **ate**	meet *(treffen)* **met**	think *(denken)* **thought**
fall *(fallen)* **fell**	pay *(bezahlen)* **paid**	win *(gewinnen)* **won**
find *(finden)* **found**	put *(legen/stellen)* **put**	write *(schreiben)* **wrote**
fly *(fliegen)* **flew**	read *(lesen)* **read** /red/*	
forget *(vergessen)* **forgot**	ring *(läuten/anrufen)* **rang**	* Aussprache

- I usually get up early, but this morning I **got** up at 9 o'clock.
  Meistens stehe ich früh auf, aber heute Morgen bin ich um 9 Uhr aufgestanden.
- We **did** a lot of work yesterday. *Wir haben gestern viel Arbeit geleistet.*
- Caroline **went** to the cinema three times last week. *Caroline ist ... dreimal ins Kino gegangen.*

Das past simple entspricht im Deutschen meistens dem Perfekt:

- It **rained** yesterday. *Es hat gestern geregnet.*
- He **came** in. *Er ist hereingekommen.*

In manchen Fällen wird das past simple aber auch mit dem Präteritum (ich war, er hatte usw.) übersetzt:

- Jane **was** tired yesterday and she **had** a headache. *Jane war gestern müde und sie hatte Kopfschmerzen.*

---

was/were → Unit 11   I didn't / Did you ... ? *(Verneinung und Frageform)* → Unit 13   ago → Unit 20

Übungen

Unit 12

12.1 Vervollständigen Sie die Sätze mit der past simple Form eines der folgenden Verben:

~~clean~~   die   enjoy   finish   happen   open   rain   start   stay   want

1 I __cleaned__ my teeth three times yesterday.
2 It was hot in the room, so I _____ the window.
3 The film was very long. It _____ at 7.15 and _____ at 10 o'clock.
4 When I was a child, I _____ to be a doctor.
5 The accident _____ last Sunday afternoon.
6 The weather is nice today, but yesterday it _____ all day.
7 We _____ our holiday last year. We _____ at a very nice place.
8 Anna's grandfather _____ when he was 90 years old.

12.2 Schreiben Sie die past simple Form der folgenden Verben:

1 get __got__
2 see _____
3 play _____
4 pay _____
5 visit _____
6 buy _____
7 go _____
8 think _____
9 copy _____
10 know _____
11 put _____
12 speak _____

12.3 Lesen Sie über Lisas Reise nach Madrid und setzen Sie die Verben in die passende Form.

Last Tuesday Lisa (1) __flew__ from London to Madrid. She (2) _____ up at 6 o'clock in the morning and (3) _____ a cup of coffee. At 6.30 she (4) _____ home and (5) _____ to the airport. When she (6) _____ there, she (7) _____ the car, (8) _____ to the airport building, and (9) _____ in. Then she (10) _____ breakfast at a cafe and (11) _____ for her flight. The plane (12) _____ on time and (13) _____ in Madrid two hours later. Finally she (14) _____ a taxi from the airport to her hotel in the centre of Madrid.

fly, get
have
leave, drive
get, park, walk
check, have
wait, depart
arrive, take

12.4 Lesen Sie die Sätze, und schreiben Sie entsprechende Sätze über die Vergangenheit (**yesterday** / **last week** usw.).

1 James always goes to work by car. Yesterday __he went to work by car.__
2 Rachel often loses her keys. She _____ last week.
3 Kate meets her friends every evening. She _____ yesterday evening.
4 I buy a newspaper every day. Yesterday I _____
5 We often go to the cinema at weekends. Last Sunday we _____
6 I eat an orange every day. Yesterday I _____
7 Tom always has a shower in the morning. This morning he _____
8 Our friends often come to see us. They _____ last Friday.

12.5 Schreiben Sie, was Sie gestern gemacht haben.

1 __I went to the theatre.__
2 _____
3 _____
4 _____
5 _____
6 _____

12.6 Übersetzen Sie ins Englische.

1 Lisa hat auf dem Fest mit Tom getanzt.
2 Als ich ein Kind war, hatte ich einen Hund.
3 Meine Schwester hat von 2010 bis 2012 in Frankreich gearbeitet.
4 Meistens fahre ich am Wochenende weg, aber letztes Wochenende bin ich zu Hause geblieben.
5 Gestern sind Kate und ich in die Stadt gegangen, und ich habe ein Kleid gekauft.
6 Meine Eltern sind gestern Abend spät nach Hause gekommen.

wegfahren = go away
in die Stadt = to town
nach Hause kommen = come home

→ Zusätzliche Übungen 10 (Seite 256)

Unit 13

I didn't ...   Did you ... ?
(past simple: *Verneinung und Frageform*)

A

Man verwendet **did**, um Verneinungen und Fragen im past simple zu bilden:

Infinitiv	bejahte Form		Verneinung			Frageform		
play	I	**played**	I		play		I	play?
start	we	**started**	we		start		we	start?
watch	you	**watched**	you	**did not**	watch	**did**	you	watch?
have	they	**had**	they	**(didn't)**	have		they	have?
see	he	**saw**	he		see		he	see?
do	she	**did**	she		do		she	do?
go	it	**went**	it		go		it	go?

B

do/does present simple *wird im* past simple **did**:

- I **don't** watch TV very often. → I **didn't** watch TV **yesterday**.
  Ich sehe nicht sehr oft fern.   *Ich habe gestern nicht ferngesehen.*

- **Does** she often go away? → **Did** she go away **last week**?
  Fährt sie oft weg?   *Ist sie letzte Woche weggefahren?*

C

did/**didn't** *verwendet man mit dem Infinitiv* (**watch**/**play**/**go** *usw.*):

I **watched**	*aber*	I **didn't watch**	(*nicht* I didn't watched)
they **went**		**did** they **go**?	(*nicht* did they went?)
he **had**		he **didn't have**	
you **did**		**did** you **do**?	

- I **played** tennis yesterday, but I **didn't win**.
  Ich habe ... gespielt, aber ich habe nicht gewonnen.
- '**Did** you **do** the shopping?'   'No, I **didn't have** time.'
  'Hast du ... gemacht?'   'Nein, ich hatte keine Zeit.'
- We **went** to the cinema, but we **didn't enjoy** the film.
  Wir sind ins Kino gegangen, aber der Film hat uns nicht gefallen.

Vorsicht bei folgenden Beispielen:
- **Did** you **do** the shopping?   *Hast du die Besorgungen gemacht?*
- Sam **didn't do** his homework.   *Sam hat ... nicht gemacht.*

Did *und* **didn't** *zeigen die Fragestellung oder die Verneinung an, während* **do** *die Bedeutung 'machen' hat.*

D

Beachten Sie die Wortstellung bei Fragen:

did + *Subjekt* + *Infinitiv*

	Did	your sister	**call**	you?
What	**did**	you	**do**	last night?
How	**did**	the accident	**happen**?	
Where	**did**	your parents	**go**	for their holiday?

E

Kurzantworten

| Yes, | I/we/you/they he/she/it | **did**. | | No, | I/we/you/they he/she/it | **didn't**. |

- '**Did you** see Joe yesterday?'   '**No, I didn't.**'
- '**Did it** rain on Sunday?'   '**Yes, it did.**'
- '**Did Helen** come to the party?'   '**No, she didn't.**'
- '**Did your parents** have a good holiday?'   '**Yes, they did.**'

worked/got/went *usw.* (past simple) → **Unit 12**

Übungen

Unit 13

13.1 Vervollständigen Sie die Sätze mit der Verneinung des Verbs.
1. I saw Barbara, but I **didn't see** Jane.
2. They worked on Monday, but they _____ on Tuesday.
3. We went to the post office, but we _____ to the bank.
4. She had a pen, but she _____ any paper.
5. Jack did French at school, but he _____ German.

13.2 Bilden Sie Fragen mit **Did ... ?**
1. I watched TV last night. How about you? **Did you watch TV last night** ?
2. I enjoyed the party. How about you? _____ ?
3. I had a good holiday. How about you? _____ ?
4. I finished work early. How about you? _____ ?
5. I slept well last night. How about you? _____ ?

13.3 Schreiben Sie, was Sie gestern gemacht oder nicht gemacht haben.
1. (watch TV) **I watched TV.** oder **I didn't watch TV.**
2. (get up before 7 o'clock) I _____
3. (have a shower) _____
4. (buy a magazine) _____
5. (eat meat) _____
6. (go to bed before 10.30) _____

13.4 Welche Fragen stellt B in den folgenden Dialogen? Vervollständigen Sie die Fragen mit:

arrive   cost   go   go to bed late   happen   have a nice time   ~~stay~~   win

1 A: We went to New York last month. B: Where **did you stay** ? A: With some friends.	5 A: We came home by taxi. B: How much _____ ? A: Ten pounds.
2 A: I was late for the meeting. B: What time _____ ? A: Half past nine.	6 A: I'm tired this morning. B: _____ ? A: No, but I didn't sleep very well.
3 A: I played tennis this afternoon. B: _____ ? A: No, I lost.	7 A: We went to the beach yesterday. B: _____ ? A: Yes, it was great.
4 A: I had a nice holiday. B: Good. Where _____ ? A: To the mountains.	8 A: The window is broken. B: How _____ ? A: I don't know.

13.5 Setzen Sie die Wörter in Klammern in die passende Form: bejahte Form, Verneinung oder Frage.
1. We went to the cinema, but the film wasn't very good. We **didn't enjoy** it. (enjoy)
2. Tom _____ some new clothes yesterday – two shirts, a jacket and a pullover. (buy)
3. '_____ yesterday?' 'No, it was a nice day.' (rain)
4. We were tired, so we _____ long at the party. (stay)
5. It was very warm in the room, so I _____ a window. (open)
6. 'Did you phone Chris this morning?' 'No, I _____ time.' (have)
7. 'I cut my hand this morning.' 'How _____ that?' (do)
8. 'Why weren't you at the meeting yesterday?' 'I _____ about it.' (know)

13.6 Übersetzen Sie ins Englische.
1. Hast du David letzte Woche gesehen?
2. Lisa hat mich gestern nicht angerufen.
3. Wie haben Sie Ihren Arm gebrochen?
4. Wir haben gestern in einem Restaurant gegessen, aber das Essen hat uns nicht geschmeckt.
5. Was haben die Kinder gestern gemacht?
6. Ich habe heute Früh nicht gefrühstückt.
7. A: Seid ihr gestern Abend auf das Fest gegangen?
   B: Nein, wir sind zu Hause geblieben.
8. Ich habe in meinem Urlaub nicht sehr viel gemacht.

➔ Zusätzliche Übungen 10–13 (Seite 256)

Unit 14

I was doing (past continuous)

A

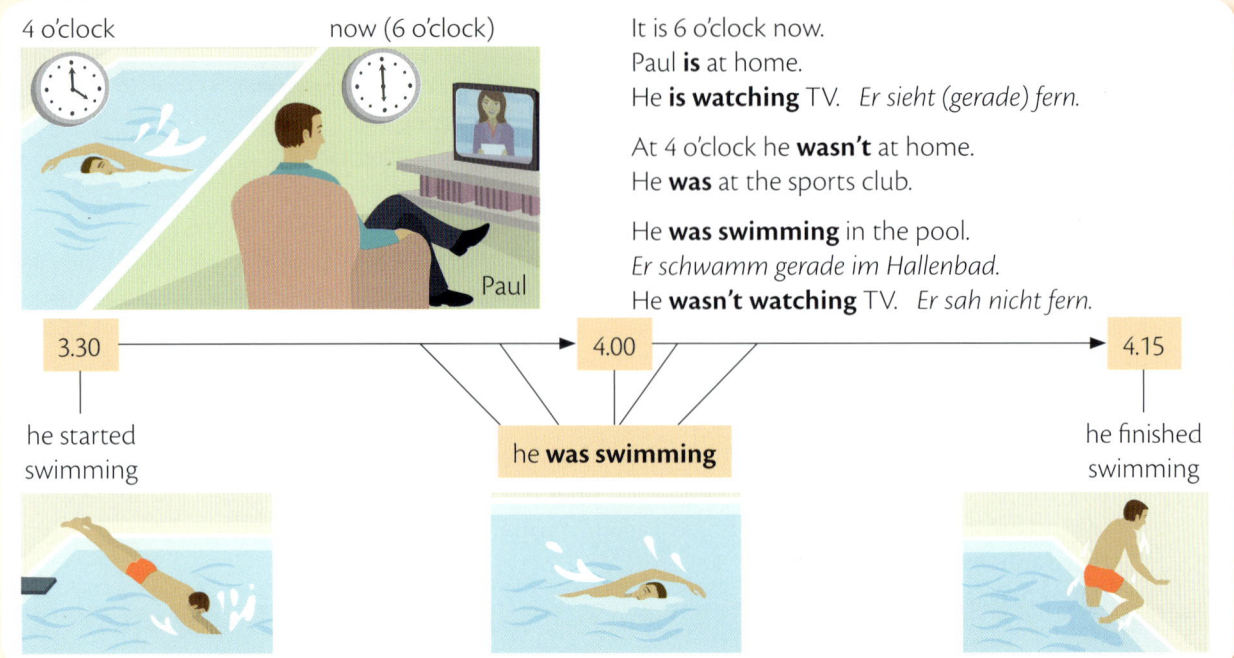

4 o'clock   now (6 o'clock)

It is 6 o'clock now.
Paul **is** at home.
He **is watching** TV.   *Er sieht (gerade) fern.*

At 4 o'clock he **wasn't** at home.
He **was** at the sports club.

He **was swimming** in the pool.
Er schwamm gerade im Hallenbad.
He **wasn't watching** TV.   *Er sah nicht fern.*

3.30 — he started swimming
4.00 — he **was swimming**
4.15 — he finished swimming

B

Das *past continuous* bildet man mit **was/were** + **-ing**.
Es beschreibt eine Handlung, die zu einem Zeitpunkt in der Vergangenheit gerade im Gang war:

bejahte Form		Verneinung		Frageform		
I / he / she / it	**was**	I / he / she / it	**was not** (**wasn't**)	**was**	I / he / she / it	doing? watching? playing? swimming? living?
we / you / they	**were**	we / you / they	**were not** (**weren't**)	**were**	we / you / they	
			doing watching playing swimming living *usw.*		doing watching playing swimming living *usw.*	

○ What **were** you **doing** at 11.30 yesterday? **Were** you **working**?
    Was hast du um … gerade gemacht? Hast du gearbeitet?
○ 'What did he say?' 'I don't know. I **wasn't listening**.' '… Ich hörte gerade nicht zu.'
○ In 2009 we **were living** in Canada. … *lebten wir in Kanada.*
○ Today she's wearing a skirt, but yesterday she **was wearing** trousers. … *gestern trug sie eine Hose.*
○ I woke up early yesterday. It was a beautiful morning. The sun **was shining** and the birds **were singing**.
    … *Die Sonne schien und die Vögel sangen.*

Rechtschreibung (liv**e** → liv**ing** / ru**n** → ru**nning** / l**ie** → l**ying** usw.) → Anhang 5

C

Das *past continuous* (**was playing** / **were doing** usw.) entspricht im Deutschen dem Präteritum ('spielte', 'machten' usw.) oder dem Perfekt ('habe gespielt' / 'haben gemacht' usw.):
○ It **was raining**, so we didn't go out. *Es regnete/hat geregnet, also sind wir nicht rausgegangen.*

Manchmal verwendet man im Deutschen 'gerade' um zu vermitteln, dass eine Handlung im Gang war:
○ What **were** you **doing** yesterday afternoon at 5 o'clock?
    Was haben Sie gestern Nachmittag um … gerade gemacht? / Was machten Sie gerade … ?

D

Vergleichen Sie:

present continuous **am/is/are** + **-ing**	past continuous **was/were** + **-ing**
○ I**'m working** (now).	○ I **was working** at 10.30 last night.
○ It **isn't raining** (now).	○ It **wasn't raining** when we went out.
○ What **are** you **doing** (now)?	○ What **were** you **doing** at 3 o'clock?

was/were → Unit 11   I was doing (past continuous) *und* I did (past simple) → Unit 15

Übungen

Unit 14

14.1
Die Bilder zeigen, wo die verschiedenen Personen gestern Nachmittag um drei Uhr waren und was sie gemacht haben. Schreiben Sie zwei Sätze für jedes Bild.

RACHEL	JACK KATE	TOM	TRACEY	MR AND MRS HALL
at home	at the cinema	in his car	at the station	in the park
watch TV	watch a film	drive	wait for a train	walk

1 *Rachel was at home. She was watching TV.*
2 Jack and Kate .... They ....
3 Tom ....
4 ....
5 ....
6 And you? I ....

14.2
Sarah hat gestern viel gemacht. Vervollständigen Sie die Sätze über Sarahs gestrigen Tagesablauf anhand der Informationen in den Bildern.

1 At 8.45 *she was washing her car.*
2 At 10.45 she ....
3 At 8 o'clock ....
4 At 12.10 ....
5 At 7.15 ....
6 At 9.30 ....

14.3
Vervollständigen Sie die Fragen mit **was/were -ing**. Verwenden Sie bei Bedarf **what/where/why**.

1 (you/live) *Where were you living* in 2012? — In London.
2 (you/do) .... at 2 o'clock? — I was asleep.
3 (it/rain) .... when you got up? — No, it was sunny.
4 (Sue/drive) .... so fast? — Because she was late.
5 (Tom/wear) .... a suit yesterday? — No, a T-shirt and jeans.

14.4
Im Bild sehen Sie Joe. Gestern Nachmittag sind Sie Joe auf der Straße begegnet. Schreiben Sie, was er gerade machte oder nicht machte und was er trug oder nicht trug.

Hi. I'm going shopping.

1 (wear / a jacket) *He wasn't wearing a jacket.*
2 (carry / a bag) ....
3 (go / to the dentist) ....
4 (eat / an ice cream) ....
5 (carry / an umbrella) ....
6 (go / home) ....
7 (wear / a hat) ....
8 (ride / a bike) ....

14.5
Übersetzen Sie ins Englische.

1 Um 7.30 duschte ich mich (gerade).
2 Heute Früh schneite es nicht.
3 Jenny trug einen warmen Mantel, aber keinen Hut.
4 Wir spielten gestern Abend um 10 Uhr (gerade) Karten.
5 Das Wetter war komisch heute Früh. Es regnete, aber die Sonne schien auch.
6 Joe trägt heute einen Schlips, aber gestern trug er keinen.
7 Warum weinte das Baby um 2 Uhr in der Frühe?

Unit 15

I was doing (past continuous) *und* I did (past simple)

A

Jack was reading a book.   His phone rang.   He stopped reading.   He answered his phone.
Jack las (gerade) …   *Sein Handy hat geklingelt.*   *Er hat aufgehört zu lesen.*   *Er ist ans Handy gegangen.*

What **happened**? His phone **rang**. (past simple)
What **was** Jack **doing** when his phone rang? ⎫
    He **was reading** a book. ⎭ (past continuous)

What **did** he **do** when his phone rang? ⎫
    He **stopped** reading and **answered** his phone. ⎭ (past simple)

Jack began reading *before* his phone rang.   *Jack hat angefangen zu lesen bevor sein Handy geklingelt hat.*
So *when* his phone rang, he **was reading**.   *Also als sein Handy geklingelt hat, las er (gerade).*

```
he started                           his phone      he stopped        he answered
reading                              rang           reading           his phone
    |─────────────────────────────────|──────────────|                 |
              he was reading
```

Wenn das past continuous eine unterbrochene Handlung beschreibt – wie im Beispiel oben – wird es auch manchmal mit 'dabei sein …' oder 'beim (am) -en' übersetzt:
- Jack **was reading** when his phone rang.   *Jack war dabei zu lesen, als …*
- Sue hurt herself while she **was playing** tennis.   *Sue hat sich beim Tennisspielen verletzt.*

B

Das past simple (**we played**) *beschreibt eine abgeschlossene Handlung in der Vergangenheit.*

- A: What **did** you **do** yesterday morning?
  Was haben Sie gestern Früh gemacht?
  B: We **played** tennis. (from 10 to 11.30)
  Wir haben Tennis gespielt (von … bis …).

```
Anfang                        Ende
10 o'clock                   11.30
    |─────────────────────────|
         we played
    (abgeschlossene Handlung)
```

- Jack **read** a book yesterday.
  Jack hat gestern ein Buch gelesen.
- **Did** you **watch** the game on TV last night?
  Hast du das Spiel gestern Abend … gesehen?
- It **didn't rain** while we were on holiday.
  Es hat nicht geregnet, während wir ….

Das past continuous (**we were playing**) *beschreibt eine Handlung, die zu einem Zeitpunkt in der Vergangenheit gerade im Gang war.*

- A: What **were** you **doing** at 10.30?
  Was haben Sie um 10.30 (gerade) gemacht?
  B: We **were playing tennis**.
  Wir spielten Tennis / haben (gerade) Tennis gespielt.

```
Anfang
10 o'clock
    |─────────↑─↑─↑─↑─↑──────────
         we were playing
         (Handlung im Gang)
```

- Jack **was reading** a book when his phone rang. *Jack las (gerade) ein Buch, als …*
- **Were** you **watching** TV when I phoned you?
  Hast du (gerade) ferngesehen, als ich …
- It **wasn't raining** when I got up.
  Es regnete nicht, als ich aufgestanden bin.

- I **started** work at 9 o'clock and **finished** at 4.30. At 2.30 I **was working**.
  Ich habe um … angefangen und um … aufgehört. Um 2.30 war ich am Arbeiten.
- Kelly **fell** asleep while she **was reading**. *Kelly ist beim Lesen eingeschlafen.*

I did (past simple) → Units 12–13   I was doing (past continuous) → Unit 14   while → Unit 105

Übungen

15.1 In den Kästchen sehen Sie drei Bildgeschichten. Setzen Sie die passende Form (past continuous oder past simple) der Wörter in Klammern in den Lückentext ein.

1  Lucy *broke* (break) her arm last week. It .... (happen) when she .... (paint) her room. She .... (fall) off the ladder.

2  The train .... (arrive) at the station and Paula .... (get) off. Two friends of hers, Jon and Rachel, ... (wait) to meet her.

3 Yesterday Sue .... (walk) along the road when she .... (meet) James. He .... (go) to the station to catch a train and he .... (carry) a bag. They .... (stop) to talk for a few minutes.

15.2 Verwenden Sie die passende Form der Wörter in Klammern: past continuous oder past simple.

1 A: What was the weather like when you *got* (get) up this morning?
   B: It *was raining* (rain).
2 A: Was Jane busy when you went to see her?
   B: Yes, she .... (study).
3 A: .... (Paul/call) you this morning?
   B: Yes, he .... (call) while I .... (have) breakfast.
4 A: Was Tracey at work today?
   B: No, she .... (not/go) to work. She was ill.
5 A: How fast .... (you/drive) when the police .... (stop) you?
   B: I'm not sure, but I .... (not/drive) very fast.
6 A: .... (your team / win) the football match yesterday?
   B: The weather was very bad, so we .... (not/play).
7 A: How .... (you/break) the window?
   B: We .... (play) football. I .... (kick) the ball and it .... (hit) the window.
8 A: .... (you/see) Jessica last night?
   B: Yes, she .... (wear) a very nice jacket.
9 A: What .... (you/do) at 2 o'clock this morning?
   B: I was asleep.
10 A: I .... (lose) my key last night.
   B: How .... (you/get) into your room?
   A: I .... (climb) in through a window.

15.3 Übersetzen Sie ins Englische.

1 Wann ist Ihr Flugzeug angekommen?
2 Ich war dabei mich zu duschen, als mein Telefon geklingelt hat.
3 Was machte Joe (gerade), als du ihn gesehen hast?
4 'Wie haben Sie sich das Bein gebrochen?' 'Ich bin beim Skifahren hingefallen.'
5 Ich habe Tom und Anna gestern in der Stadt gesehen. Sie waren (gerade) beim Einkaufen.
6 Hast du Jenny auf dem Fest am Samstagabend gesehen? Sie hatte ein sehr schönes Kleid an.
7 'Was machten die Kinder als du nach Hause gekommen bist?' 'Sie spielten gerade.'
8 Wir waren dabei ins Bett zu gehen, als wir ein eigenartiges Geräusch gehört haben.

das Bein brechen
= break your leg
ein eigenartiges Geräusch
= a strange noise

→ Zusätzliche Übungen 14–15 (Seiten 257–58)

Unit 16

I have done (present perfect 1)

A

His shoes are dirty.

He is cleaning his shoes.

I've cleaned my shoes.
He **has cleaned** his shoes.
Er hat seine Schuhe geputzt.

They are at home.

They are going out.

They **have gone** out.
Sie sind weggegangen.

B

Das present perfect *bildet man mit* **have** + (past participle) (**has cleaned** / **have gone** *usw.*):

I / we / you / they	**have** (**'ve**) / **have not** (**haven't**)	cleaned / finished / started / lost
he / she / it	**has** (**'s**) / **has not** (**hasn't**)	done / been / gone

↑ past participle

regelmäßige Verben

have	I / we / you / they	cleaned? / finished? / started? / lost?
has	he / she / it	done? / been? / gone?

unregelmäßige Verben

regelmäßige Verben: Das past participle *endet in* **-ed** *(wie beim* past simple*)*:

> clean → I have clean**ed**   finish → we have finish**ed**   start → she has start**ed**

unregelmäßige Verben: Das past participle *wird nicht mit* **-ed** *gebildet.*
Manchmal haben past simple *und* past participle *die gleiche Form:*

gleich: buy → I **bought** / I have **bought**   have → he **had** / he has **had**

Manchmal haben past simple *und* past participle *unterschiedliche Formen:*

anders: break → I **broke** / I have **broken**   see → you **saw** / you have **seen**
fall → it **fell** / it has **fallen**   go → they **went** / they have **gone**

C

Man verwendet das present perfect *für Handlungen in der Vergangenheit, die ein Ergebnis in der Gegenwart haben:*
- I**'ve lost** my passport.   *Ich habe meinen Pass verloren. (Ich kann ihn jetzt nicht finden.)*
- 'Where's Rebecca?'   'She**'s gone** to bed.'
  … 'Sie ist ins Bett gegangen.' (Sie ist jetzt im Bett.)
- We**'ve bought** a new car.   *Wir haben ein neues Auto gekauft. (Wir haben das Auto jetzt.)*
- It's Rachel's birthday tomorrow and I **haven't bought** her a present.
  … , und ich habe ihr (noch) kein Geschenk gekauft.
- 'Bob is away on holiday.'   'Oh, where **has** he **gone**?'   … 'Ach so? Wo ist er hingefahren?'
- Can I take this newspaper?   **Have** you **finished** with it?   … *Sind Sie damit fertig?*

D

Das present perfect *wird generell mit dem Perfekt ins Deutsche übersetzt:*
- Tom **has done** his homework.   *Tom hat seine Hausaufgaben gemacht.*
- They **have gone** home.   *Sie sind nach Hause gegangen.*

Beachten Sie jedoch, dass auch andere englische Zeitformen mit dem Perfekt ins Deutsche übersetzt werden können
(→ Units 12, 14, 21).

---

present perfect → Units 17–20   present perfect *und* past simple → Unit 21   unregelmäßige Verben → Unit 25, Anhang 2–3

Übungen

16.1 Beschreiben Sie, was in den Situationen unten passiert ist. Wählen Sie aus der folgenden Liste, und setzen Sie das Verb in die richtige Form.

go to bed   ~~clean his shoes~~   stop raining
close the door   fall down   have a shower

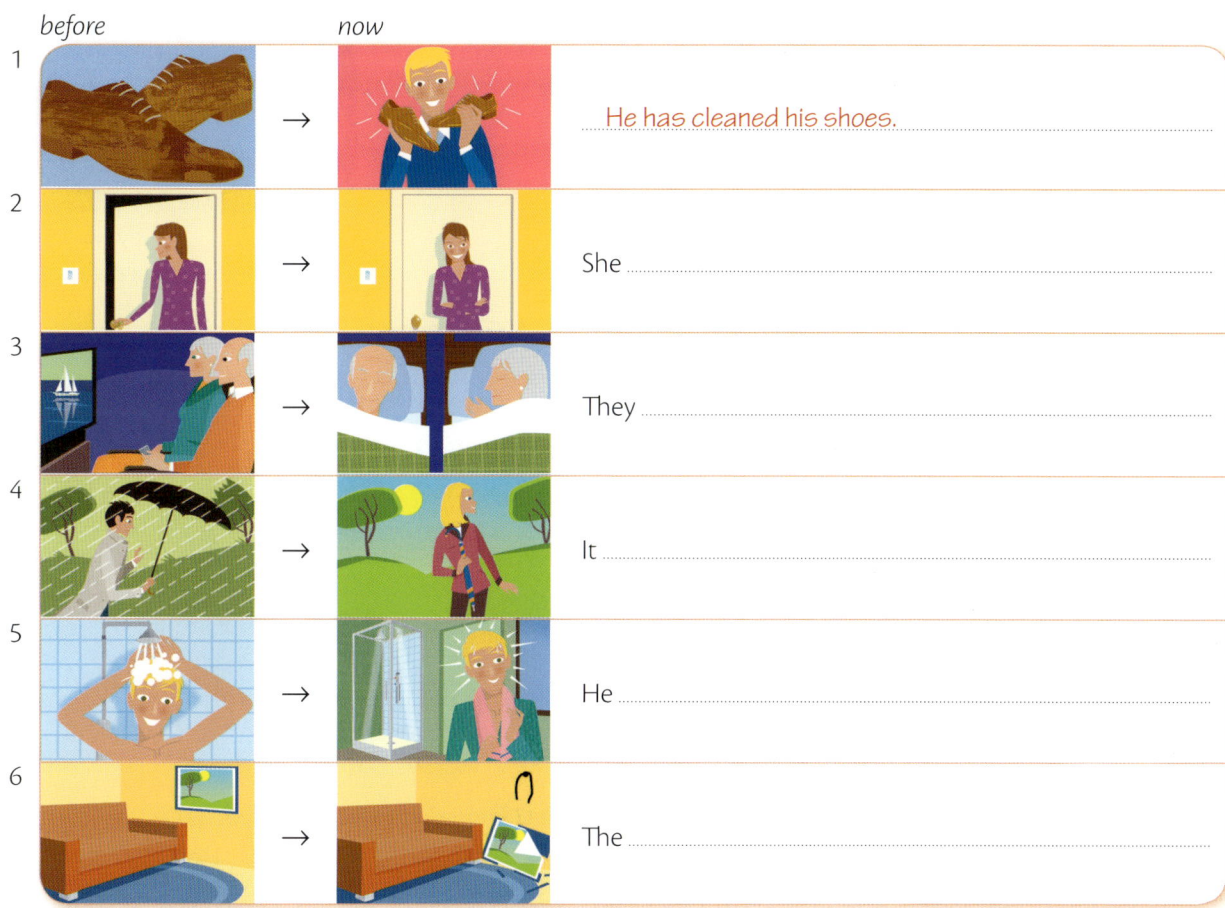

1 He has cleaned his shoes.
2 She
3 They
4 It
5 He
6 The

16.2 Vervollständigen Sie die Sätze mit einem Verb aus der Liste.

break   buy   decide   finish   forget   go   go
invite   ~~lose~~   see   not/see   take   tell   not/tell

1 I **'ve lost** my keys. I don't know where they are.
2 I .... some new shoes. Do you want to see them?
3 'Where is Helen?'   'She's not here. She .... out.'
4 I'm looking for Paula. .... you .... her?
5 Look! Somebody .... that window.
6 'Does Lisa know that you're going away?'   'Yes, I .... her.'
7 I can't find my umbrella. Somebody .... it.
8 'Where are my glasses?'   'I don't know. I .... them.'
9 I'm looking for Sarah. Where .... she .... ?
10 I know that woman, but I .... her name.
11 Sue is having a party tonight. She .... a lot of people.
12 What are you going to do? .... you .... ?
13 A: Does Ben know about the meeting tomorrow?
     B: I don't think so. I .... him.
14 I .... with this magazine. Do you want it?

16.3 Übersetzen Sie ins Englische.

1 Laura hat ein neues Handy gekauft.
2 Ich habe meine Handtasche verloren!
3 Hast du deine Zähne geputzt?
4 Du hast deine Milch nicht getrunken.
5 'Wo ist Rachel?'   'Sie ist zur Arbeit gegangen.'
6 Es tut mir leid. Ich habe das Glas zerbrochen.
7 Ist der Zug angekommen?
8 Das Auto ist schmutzig. Wir haben es nicht gewaschen.
9 A: Wo sind die Kinder?
    B: Sie sind ins Bett gegangen.

Handy = (mobile) phone

Unit 17

I've just ... I've already ... I haven't ... yet (present perfect 2)

A I've just ... (Ich habe gerade ...)

In Verbindung mit dem present perfect bedeutet **just** 'gerade' (= vor kurzer Zeit):

- A: Are Laura and Paul here?
  B: Yes, they**'ve just arrived**.
  ... sie sind gerade angekommen.

- A: Are you hungry?
  B: No, I**'ve just eaten**.
  ... ich habe gerade gegessen.

- A: Is Tom here?
  B: No, I'm afraid he**'s just gone**.
  ... leider ist er gerade gegangen.

They **have just arrived**.
Sie sind gerade angekommen.

B I've already ... (Ich habe schon ...)

Already in einem Aussagesatz bedeutet 'schon' (= früher als erwartet):

- A: What time are Laura and Paul coming?
  B: They**'ve already arrived**.
  Sie sind schon angekommen.

- It's only 9 o'clock and Anna **has already gone** to bed.
  Es ist erst ... Anna ist schon ins Bett gegangen.

- A: Jon, this is Emma.
  B: Yes, I know. We**'ve already met**.
  ... Wir haben uns schon kennen gelernt.

C I haven't ... yet (Ich habe noch nicht ...) / Have you ... yet? (Hast du / Haben Sie schon ... ?)

Yet verwendet man bei der Verneinung und bei Fragen. Meistens steht **yet** am Ende des Satzes.
Not (n't) ... **yet** entspricht im Deutschen 'noch nicht':

- A: Are Laura and Paul here?
  B: No, they **haven't arrived yet**.
  ... sie sind noch nicht angekommen.

- A: Does James know that you're going away?
  B: No, I **haven't told** him **yet**.
  ... ich habe es ihm noch nicht gesagt.

- Silvia has bought a new dress, but she **hasn't worn** it **yet**.
  ... sie hat es noch nicht getragen.

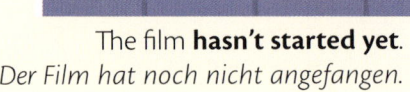

The film **hasn't started yet**.
Der Film hat noch nicht angefangen.

D Have you ... yet?

Bei Fragen entspricht **yet** im Deutschen 'schon':

- A: **Have** Laura and Paul **arrived yet**?
  Sind ... schon angekommen?
  B: No, not **yet**. We're still waiting for them.
  Nein, noch nicht. Wir warten immer noch auf sie.

- A: **Has** Nicola **started** her new job **yet**?
  Hat Nicola schon bei ihrer neuen Arbeit angefangen?
  B: No, she starts next week.

- A: This is my new dress.
  B: Oh, it's nice. **Have** you **worn** it **yet**?
  ... Hast du es schon getragen?

NB: Beachten Sie, dass **already** in bejahten Aussagesätzen und **yet** in Fragen beide mit 'schon' ins Deutsche übersetzt werden.

present perfect → **Units 16, 18–21**   Wortstellung → **Unit 94**   still, yet und already → **Unit 95**

Übungen

17.1 Schreiben Sie einen Satz mit **just** für jedes Bild.

1 They've just arrived.
2 He ....
3 They ....
4 The race ....

17.2 Beantworten Sie die Fragen, indem Sie **already** + present perfect verwenden.

1 What time is Paul arriving? — He's already arrived.
2 Do your friends want to see the film? — No, they .... it.
3 Don't forget to phone Tom. — I ....
4 When is Mark going away? — He ....
5 Do you want to read the newspaper? — I ....
6 When does Sarah start her new job? — She ....

17.3 Bilden Sie für jede Situation einen Satz mit **just** (They've just ... / She's just ... usw.) oder einen verneinten Satz mit **yet** (They haven't ... yet / She hasn't ... yet usw.).

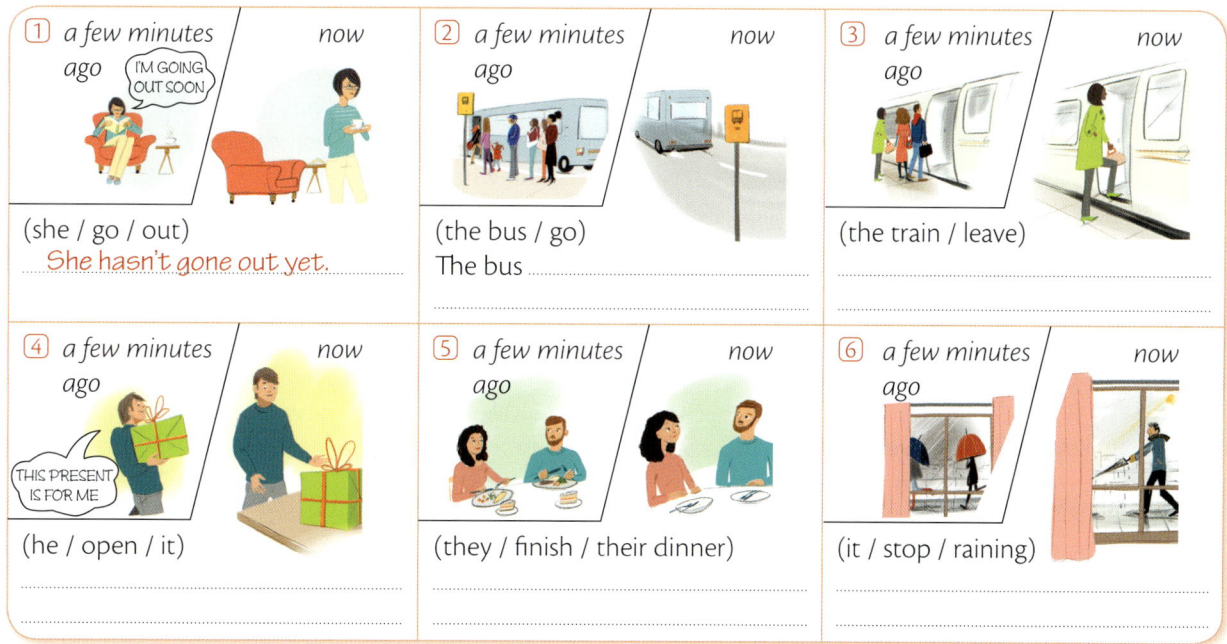

1 (she / go / out) She hasn't gone out yet.
2 (the bus / go) The bus ....
3 (the train / leave) ....
4 (he / open / it) ....
5 (they / finish / their dinner) ....
6 (it / stop / raining) ....

17.4 Bilden Sie Fragen mit **yet**.

1 Eine Freundin hat eine neue Arbeitsstelle. Vielleicht hat sie dort schon angefangen. Sie fragen Ihre Freundin:
   Have you started your new job yet?
2 Ein Freund hat neue Nachbarn. Vielleicht hat er sie inzwischen kennengelernt. Sie fragen Ihre Freundin:
   .... you ....
3 Eine Freundin muss ihre Stromrechnung bezahlen. Vielleicht hat sie schon bezahlt. Sie fragen Ihre Freundin:
   ....
4 Tom versucht sein Auto zu verkaufen. Vielleicht hat er es inzwischen verkauft. Sie fragen einen Bekannten über Tom:
   ....

17.5 Übersetzen Sie ins Englische.

1 A: Möchten Sie eine Tasse Kaffee?
  B: Nein danke. Ich habe gerade Kaffee getrunken.
2 A: Vergiss nicht, das Fenster zu schließen.
  B: Ich habe es schon gemacht.
3 Das Flugzeug ist noch nicht angekommen.
4 Es ist ein wunderschöner Tag. Wart ihr schon draußen?
5 Hast du dein Zimmer schon sauber gemacht?
6 'Wo ist der Bus?' 'Er ist schon weggefahren.'

Unit 18

Have you ever … ? (present perfect 3)

A

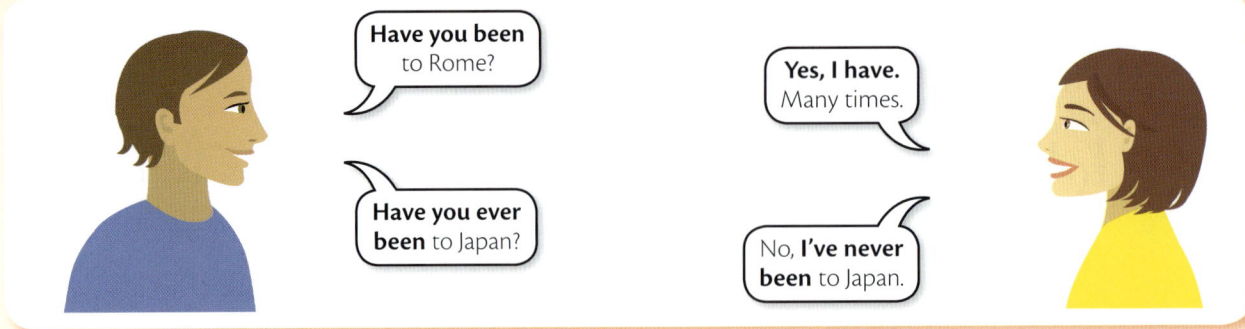

Das present perfect (**have been** / **have had** / **have played** usw.) wird verwendet, wenn man über einen nicht abgeschlossenen Zeitraum spricht, der von der Vergangenheit bis zum heutigen Zeitpunkt reicht – dieser Zeitraum könnte zum Beispiel das Leben einer Person sein:

Have you ever been to Japan?
Waren Sie schon mal in Japan?

——— Zeitraum von der Vergangenheit bis zum heutigen Zeitpunkt ———

Vergangenheit — *Gegenwart*

- A: **Have** you **been** to France? *Waren Sie schon mal in Frankreich?*
  B: No, I **haven't**. *Nein.*
- I**'ve been** to Canada, but I **haven't been** to the United States.
  Ich war schon mal in Kanada, aber noch nie in den Vereinigten Staaten.
- Mary is an interesting person. She **has had** many different jobs and **has lived** in many places.
  … Sie hat viele unterschiedliche Arbeitsstellen gehabt und in vielen Ländern gelebt.
- I**'ve seen** that woman before, but I can't remember where.
  Ich habe diese Frau schon mal gesehen, …
- How many times **has** Brazil **won** the World Cup?
  Wie oft hat Brasilien die Fußball-Weltmeisterschaft gewonnen?
- A: **Have** you **read** this book? *Haben Sie dieses Buch gelesen?*
  B: Yes, I**'ve read** it twice. *Ja, ich habe es zweimal gelesen.*

B

Mit dem present perfect *wird oft* **ever** (= schon mal / jemals) *bei Fragen und* **never** (= noch nie) *verwendet:*
- A: **Has** Ann **ever been** to Australia? *Ist Ann jemals in Australien gewesen?*
  B: Yes, once. (**once** = one time)
- A: **Have** you **ever played** golf? *Haben Sie schon mal Golf gespielt?*
  B: Yes, I play a lot.
- My sister **has never travelled** by plane. *Meine Schwester ist noch nie geflogen.*
- I**'ve never ridden** a horse. *Ich bin noch nie auf einem Pferd geritten.*
- A: Who is that man?
  B: I don't know. I**'ve never seen** him before. *… Ich habe ihn noch nie gesehen.*

Beachten Sie, dass man nach **been** die Präposition **to** verwendet:
- Ben has never **been to** Spain. *Ben ist noch nie in Spanien gewesen.*
- Have you ever **been to** Japan?

C

Das present perfect entspricht im Deutschen meistens dem Perfekt:
- I**'ve read** this book twice. *Ich habe dieses Buch zweimal gelesen.*

In manchen Fällen wird das present perfect aber auch mit dem Präteritum ins Deutsche übersetzt, zum Beispiel:
- I**'ve** never **been** to Canada. *Ich war noch nie in Kanada.*

Beachten Sie jedoch, dass auch andere englische Zeitformen mit dem Perfekt ins Deutsche übersetzt werden können (→ Units 12, 14, 21).

present perfect → **Units 16–17, 19**   present perfect *und* past simple → **Unit 21**

Übungen

Unit 18

18.1 Stellen Sie Fragen an Helen. Beginnen Sie mit **Have you ever ... ?**

Helen

1. (be / London?)
2. (play / golf?)
3. (be / Australia?)
4. (lose / your passport?)
5. (fly / in a helicopter?)
6. (win / a race?)
7. (be / New York?)
8. (drive / a bus?)
9. (break / your leg?)

Have you ever been to London?
Have you ever played golf?
Have ....

No, never.
Yes, many times.
Yes, once.
No, never.
Yes, a few times.
No, never.
Yes, twice.
No, never.
Yes, once.

18.2 Schreiben Sie Sätze über Helen anhand ihrer Antworten in 18.1.

1. (be / New York)   She's been to New York twice.
2. (be / Australia)   She ....
3. (win / a race) ....
4. (fly / in a helicopter) ....

Schreiben Sie jetzt über sich selbst. Wie oft haben Sie folgende Sachen schon gemacht?

5. (be / New York)   I ....
6. (play / tennis) ....
7. (drive / a lorry) ....
8. (be / late for work or school) ....

18.3 Setzen Sie das Verb ins present perfect.

1. **I've seen** (I/see) that woman before, but I can't remember where.
2. 'Do you know Amy's brother?'   'No, ... (I/never/meet) him.'
3. George has hundreds of books, and .... (he/read) all of them.
4. .... (you/ever/write) a poem?
5. .... (I/not/be) to China, but .... (my brother/be) there twice.
6. My parents like to travel a lot. .... (they/visit) many places.

18.4 Mary ist 65 Jahre alt. Sie hat ein interessantes Leben gehabt. Was hat sie alles gemacht? Schreiben Sie Sätze über ihre Erfahrungen.

Mary

~~have~~	be
do	write
travel	meet

all over the world	a lot of interesting things
~~many different jobs~~	a lot of interesting people
ten books	married three times

1. She has had many different jobs.
2. She ....
3. ....
4. ....
5. ....
6. ....

18.5 Übersetzen Sie ins Englische.

1. Ich habe diesen Film dreimal gesehen.
2. 'Waren Sie schon mal in Irland?'   'Ja, schon oft.'
3. A: Hast du schon mal mexikanisch gegessen?
   B: Nein, noch nie.
4. Mein Bruder war noch nie in den USA.
5. Wir haben ihn noch nie besucht.
6. 'Wie oft hat er sie gesehen?'   'Nur einmal.'
7. War er schon jemals verheiratet?
8. Sarah und Michael waren (schon) dreimal in Las Vegas.

➜ Zusätzliche Übungen 16, 18 (Seiten 258–59, 260)

Unit 19

How long have you … ? (present perfect 4)

A

Helen is on holiday in Ireland. She is there now.
She arrived in Ireland on Monday.
Sie ist am Montag … angekommen.
Today is Thursday.

How long **has she been** in Ireland?
Wie lange ist sie schon in Irland?

She **has been** in Ireland { **since Monday.** / **for three days**.

Sie ist { seit Montag / drei Tagen } in Irland.

How long have you been in Ireland?
Since Monday.

Vergleichen Sie **is** *und* **has been**:

She **is** in Ireland **now**.   **is** = present

She **has been** in Ireland { since Monday. / for three days.   **has been** = present perfect

Monday — now / Thursday

Um auszudrücken, wie lange ein Zustand oder eine Handlung schon andauert, verwendet man im Englischen das present perfect und nicht wie im Deutschen die Gegenwartsform.

B

Vergleichen Sie den Gebrauch von present simple *und* present perfect simple *(im Deutschen verwendet man in beiden Fällen die Gegenwartsform):*

present simple	present perfect simple (**have been** / **have lived** / **have known** *usw*.)
Dan and Kate **are** married. *… sind verheiratet.*	They **have been** married **for five years**. *Sie sind seit fünf Jahren verheiratet.* (nicht They are married for five years.)
Are you married? *Sind Sie verheiratet?*	How long have you **been** married? *Wie lange sind Sie schon verheiratet?* (nicht How long are you married?)
Do you **know** Lisa? *Kennst du Lisa?*	How long have you **known** her? *Wie lange kennst du sie schon?* (nicht How long do you know her?)
I **know** Lisa. *Ich kenne Lisa.*	I've **known** her **for a long time**. *Ich kenne sie schon lange.* (nicht I know her for a long time.)
Vicky **lives** in London. *Vicky lebt in London.*	How long has she **lived** in London? *Wie lange lebt sie schon in London?* She **has lived** there **all her life**. *Sie lebt schon ihr ganzes Leben dort.*
I **have** a car. *Ich habe ein Auto.*	How long have you **had** your car? *Wie lange hast du schon dein Auto?* I've **had** it **since April**. *Ich habe es seit April.*

present continuous	present perfect continuous (**have been** + **-ing**)
I'm **learning** French. *Ich lerne zurzeit Französisch.*	How long have you **been learning** French? (nicht How long are you learning French?) *Wie lange lernen Sie schon Französisch?* I've **been learning** French **for two years**. *Ich lerne seit zwei Jahren Französisch.*
David **is watching** TV. *David sieht gerade fern.*	How long has he **been watching** TV? He's **been** (= He **has been**) **watching** TV **since 5 o'clock**. *Er sieht schon seit 5 Uhr fern.*
It's **raining**. *Es regnet gerade.*	It's **been** (= It **has been**) **raining all day**. *Es regnet schon den ganzen Tag.*

for und **since** → Units 20, 104

Übungen

19.1 Vervollständigen Sie die Sätze.

1 Helen is in Ireland. She ....has been.... in Ireland since Monday.
2 I know Lisa. I ....have known.... her for a long time.
3 Sarah and Andy are married. They .... married since 2005.
4 Ben is ill. He .... ill for the last few days.
5 We live in Scott Road. We .... there for a long time.
6 Catherine works in a bank. She .... there for five years.
7 Alan has a headache. He .... a headache since he got up this morning.
8 I'm learning English. I .... English for six months.

19.2 Bilden Sie Fragen mit **How long ... ?**

1 Helen is on holiday.   How long has she been on holiday ?
2 Steve and Nadia are in Brazil.   How long .... ?
3 I know Amy.   How long .... you ?
4 Emily is learning Italian.   ?
5 My brother lives in Canada.   ?
6 I'm a teacher.   ?
7 It is raining.   ?

19.3 Schreiben Sie passende Sätze zu den Situationen in den Bildern. Verwenden Sie für jeden Satz eine der folgenden Satzendungen.

for ten minutes   all day   all her life   ~~for ten years~~   since he was 20   since Sunday

1 They have been married for ten years.
2 She ....
3 They ....
4 The sun ....
5 She ....
6 He ....

19.4 Wählen Sie die richtige Form: present oder present perfect.

1 Mark ~~lives~~ / has lived in Canada since April. (has lived ist richtig)
2 Jane and I are friends. I know / I've known her very well.
3 Jane and I are friends. I know / I've known her for a long time.
4 A: Sorry I'm late. How long are you waiting / have you been waiting?
  B: Not long. Only five minutes.
5 Luke works / has worked in a hotel now. He likes his job a lot.
6 Ruth is reading a newspaper. She is reading / She has been reading it for two hours.
7 'How long do you live / have you lived in this house?' 'About ten years.'
8 'Is that a new coat?' 'No, I have / I've had this coat for a long time.'
9 Tom is / has been in Spain at the moment. He is / He has been there for the last three days.

19.5 Übersetzen Sie ins Englische.

1 A: Anna ist jetzt in England.
  B: Wie lange ist sie schon da?
2 A: Mein Bruder lebt in Hamburg.
  B: Wie lange lebt er schon da?
3 A: Wie lange kennst du schon John?
  B: Ich kenne ihn seit 10 Jahren.
4 Jenny hat seit Mai ein neues Auto.
5 A: Wo ist Helen?
  B: Ich weiß nicht. Wir warten bereits seit 20 Minuten auf sie.
6 Wie lange lernen Sie schon Englisch?
7 Es regnet schon seit einer Woche.

seit = for (Sätze 3, 5)
seit = since (Satz 4)
warten auf = wait for

Unit 20: for since ago

A for und since

Man verwendet **for** und **since** um zu sagen, wie lange oder seit wann etwas andauert.
Sowohl **for** als auch **since** werden mit 'seit' ins Deutsche übersetzt.

Beachten Sie den Unterschied zwischen dem Englischen und dem Deutschen.
Englisch: present perfect + **for** oder **since**:   Deutsch: Gegenwart + 'seit':

○ Helen **has been** in Ireland { **for three days**. / **since Monday**. }   Helen ist { seit drei Tagen / seit Montag } in Irland.

*Man verwendet **for** mit einem Zeitraum (**three days** / **two years** usw.):*

Vergangenheit   Jetzt

for	
three days	ten minutes
an hour	two hours
a week	four weeks
a month	six months
five years	a long time

*Man verwendet **since** mit dem Beginn des Zeitraums (**Monday** / **9 o'clock** usw.):*

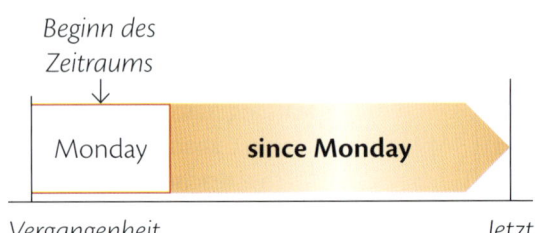

Vergangenheit   Jetzt

since	
Monday	Wednesday
9 o'clock	12.30
24 July	Christmas
January	I was ten years old
1985	we arrived

○ Richard has been in Canada **for six months**.
  (*nicht* since six months)
  Richard ist seit sechs Monaten in Kanada.
○ We've been waiting **for two hours**.
  (*nicht* since two hours)
  Wir warten bereits seit zwei Stunden.
○ I've lived in London **for a long time**.
  Ich lebe schon lange in London.

○ Richard has been in Canada **since January**.
  Richard ist seit Januar in …
○ We've been waiting **since 9 o'clock**.
  (= from 9 o'clock to now)
  Wir warten bereits seit 9 Uhr.
○ I've lived in London **since I was ten years old**.
  Ich lebe in London seitdem ich zehn Jahre alt war.

B ago

ago entspricht im Deutschen 'vor' und wird in Verbindung mit dem past (**started**/**did**/**was** usw.) verwendet:
○ Susan started her new job **three weeks ago**. Susan hat vor drei Wochen … angefangen.
○ 'When did Tom go out?' '**Ten minutes ago**.' … 'Vor zehn Minuten.'
○ I had dinner **an hour ago**. Ich habe vor einer Stunde zu Abend gegessen.
○ Life was very different **a hundred years ago**. Das Leben war vor hundert Jahren sehr anders.

Vergleichen Sie **ago** und **for**:
○ **When did** Helen **arrive** in Ireland?
  She **arrived** in Ireland **three days ago**.
  Sie ist vor drei Tagen … angekommen.

○ **How long has** she **been** in Ireland?
  She **has been** in Ireland **for three days**.
  Sie ist seit drei Tagen …

present perfect + for/since → Unit 19   from … to/until/since/for → Unit 104   for und during → Unit 105

Übungen

20.1 Vervollständigen Sie die Sätze mit **for** oder **since**.
1. Helen has been in Ireland ..*since*.. Monday.
2. Helen has been in Ireland ..*for*.. three days.
3. My aunt has lived in Australia .... 15 years.
4. Tina is in her office. She has been there .... 7 o'clock.
5. India has been an independent country .... 1947.
6. The bus is late. We've been waiting .... 20 minutes.
7. Nobody lives in those houses. They have been empty .... many years.
8. Michael has been ill .... a long time. He has been in hospital .... October.

20.2 Beantworten Sie die Fragen mit **ago**.
1. When was your last meal? — *Three hours ago.*
2. When was the last time you were ill?
3. When did you last go to the cinema?
4. When was the last time you were in a car?
5. When was the last time you went on holiday?

20.3 Vervollständigen Sie die Sätze. Verwenden Sie die Wörter in Klammern mit **for** oder **ago**.
1. Helen arrived in Ireland ..*three days ago.*.. (three days)
2. Helen has been in Ireland ..*for three days.*.. (three days)
3. Lynn and Mark have been married .... (20 years)
4. Lynn and Mark got married .... (20 years)
5. Dan arrived .... (an hour)
6. I bought these shoes .... (a few days)
7. Silvia has been learning English .... (six months)
8. Have you known Lisa .... ? (a long time)

20.4 Schreiben Sie passende Sätze mit **for** oder **since** zu den unten geschilderten Situationen.
1. (Helen is in Ireland – she arrived there three days ago)
   Helen has been in Ireland for three days.
2. (Jack is here – he arrived on Tuesday)
   Jack has
3. (It's raining – it started an hour ago)
   It's been
4. (I know Sue – I first met her in 2008)
   I've
5. (Claire and Matt are married – they got married six months ago)
   Claire and Matt have
6. (Laura is studying medicine at university – she started three years ago)
   Laura has
7. (David plays the piano – he started when he was seven years old)
   David has

20.5 Schreiben Sie Sätze über sich selbst. Beginnen Sie mit:

| I've lived … | I've been … | I've been learning … | I've known … | I've had … |

1. *I've lived in this town for three years.*
2.
3.
4.
5.

20.6 Übersetzen Sie ins Englische.
1. Ich bin seit 5 Uhr zu Hause.
2. John ist seit zwei Wochen in Australien.
3. Wir sind vor drei Jahren nach Deutschland gekommen.
4. James und Ali sind vor fünf Minuten weggegangen.
5. Hannah ist seit Donnerstag krank.
6. A: Wie lange leben Sie schon in Boston?
   B: Seit 2010.
7. Ich kenne Ben seit drei Monaten.
8. A: Wann ist der Zug angekommen?
   B: Vor einer Stunde.

→ **Zusätzliche Übungen 16–18** (Seiten 258–60)

Unit 21

I have done (present perfect) und I did (past)

A

Wenn man sich auf einen abgeschlossenen Zeitraum (**yesterday** / **last week** usw.) bezieht, verwendet man das past (**arrived**/**saw**/**was** usw.).

past + abgeschlossener Zeitraum

| We **arrived** | yesterday. last week. at 3 o'clock. in 2002. six months ago. |

yesterday / last week / six months ago — abgeschlossener Zeitraum

Vergangenheit — Jetzt

Man verwendet nicht das present perfect (**have arrived** / **have done** / **have been** usw.), wenn man sich auf einen abgeschlossenen Zeitraum bezieht:

- I **saw** Paula **yesterday**. (nicht I have seen Paula) *Ich habe Paula gestern gesehen.*
- Where **were** you **on Sunday afternoon**? (nicht Where have you been) *Wo warst du / bist du gewesen … ?*
- We **didn't have** a holiday **last year**. (nicht We haven't had) *Wir haben letztes Jahr keinen Urlaub gemacht.*
- A: What **did** you **do last night**? *Was hast du gestern Abend gemacht?*
  B: I **stayed** at home. *Ich bin zu Hause geblieben.*
- William Shakespeare **lived from 1564 to 1616**. He **was** a writer. He **wrote** many plays and poems. *… hat von … bis … gelebt. Er war ein Schriftsteller. Er hat viele Theaterstücke und Gedichte geschrieben.*

Man verwendet das past mit den Fragen **When … ?** (Wann … ?) oder **What time … ?** (Um wie viel Uhr … ?):

- **When did** you **buy** your computer? (nicht When have you bought)
- **What time did** Andy **go** out? (nicht What time has Andy gone out?)

B

Vergleichen Sie present perfect und past. Meistens entsprechen beide Formen dem deutschen Perfekt:

present perfect	past
I **have lost** my key. (= Ich kann ihn jetzt nicht finden.)	I **lost** my key **last week**.
Ben **has gone** home. (= Er ist jetzt nicht hier.)	Ben **went** home **ten minutes ago**.
Have you **seen** Kate? (= Wo ist sie jetzt?)	**Did** you **see** Kate **on Saturday**?
My friend is a writer. He **has written** many books.	Shakespeare **wrote** many plays and poems.
Sam **hasn't phoned** me yet. *… hat mich noch nicht angerufen.*	Sam **didn't phone** me yesterday. *… hat mich gestern nicht angerufen.*
Zeitraum bis jetzt	abgeschlossener Zeitraum
Vergangenheit — Jetzt	Vergangenheit — Jetzt

Beachten Sie außerdem, dass in manchen Fällen present perfect und past im Deutschen dem Präteritum entsprechen:

- **Have** you **ever been** to Spain? *Waren Sie schon einmal in Spanien?*
- **Did** you **go** to Spain **last year**? *Waren Sie letztes Jahr in Spanien?*

Das present perfect + **for** oder **since** entspricht im Deutschen der Gegenwartsform:

- We**'ve lived** in Singapore for six years. *Wir leben seit sechs Jahren in …* (= Wir leben jetzt dort.)
- We **lived** in Glasgow for six years, but now we live in Singapore. *Wir haben sechs Jahre in Glasgow gelebt, aber jetzt leben wir in …*
- He**'s been** in France **since** Friday. *Er ist seit Freitag in Frankreich.*
- Before that, he **was** in Spain. *Vorher war er in Spanien.*

past simple → Units 12–13   present perfect → Units 16–19

Übungen

Unit 21

21.1 Vervollständigen Sie die Antworten auf die Fragen.

1. Have you seen Kate? — Yes, **I saw her** five minutes ago.
2. Have you started your new job? — Yes, I .... last week.
3. Have your friends arrived? — Yes, they .... at 5 o'clock.
4. Has Sarah gone away? — Yes, ... on Friday.
5. Have you worn your new suit? — Yes, ... yesterday.

21.2 Entscheiden Sie, ob die unterstrichenen Verben in der korrekten Form stehen. Schreiben Sie OK (richtig) oder korrigieren Sie die Fehler.

1. <u>I've lost</u> my key. I can't find it. — **OK**
2. <u>Have you seen</u> Kate yesterday? — **Did you see**
3. <u>I've finished</u> my work at 2 o'clock. — ....
4. I'm ready now. <u>I've finished</u> my work. — ....
5. What time <u>have you finished</u> your work? — ....
6. Sue isn't here. <u>She's gone</u> out. — ....
7. Steve's grandmother <u>has died</u> two years ago. — ....
8. Where <u>have you been</u> last night? — ....

21.3 Setzen Sie die Wörter in den Klammern in die korrekte Form: present perfect oder past.

1. My friend is a writer. He **has written** (write) many books.
2. We **didn't have** (not/have) a holiday last year.
3. I .... (play) tennis yesterday afternoon.
4. What time .... (you/go) to bed last night?
5. .... (you/ever/meet) a famous person?
6. The weather .... (not/be) very good yesterday.
7. Kathy travels a lot. She .... (visit) many countries.
8. I .... (switch) off the light before going out this morning.
9. I live in New York now, but I .... (live) in Mexico for many years.
10. 'What's Canada like? Is it beautiful?' 'I don't know. I .... (not/be) there.'

21.4 Setzen Sie die Wörter in den Klammern in die korrekte Form: present perfect oder past.

1. A: **Have you ever been** (you/ever/be) to Florida?
   B: Yes, we **went** (go) there on holiday two years ago.
   A: .... (you/have) a good time?
   B: Yes, it .... (be) great.

2. A: Where's Alan? .... (you/see) him?
   B: Yes, he .... (go) out a few minutes ago.
   A: And Rachel?
   B: I don't know. I .... (not/see) her.

3. Rose works in a factory. She .... (work) there for six months.
   Before that she .... (be) a waitress in a restaurant.
   She .... (work) there for two years, but she .... (not/enjoy) it very much.

4. A: Do you know Mark's sister?
   B: I .... (see) her a few times, but I .... (never/speak) to her. .... (you/ever/speak) to her?
   A: Yes. I .... (meet) her at a party last week. She's very nice.

21.5 Übersetzen Sie ins Englische.

1. Jane ist gestern Abend angekommen.
2. 'Wo ist John?' 'Er ist zum Supermarkt gegangen.'
3. Wir leben seit sechs Monaten in New York.
4. Ich habe von 2010 bis 2012 in London studiert.
5. War dein Sohn schon mal in den USA?
6. Was hast du letztes Wochenende gemacht?
7. A: Wann hast du gefrühstückt?
   B: Vor drei Stunden.
8. Haben Sie schon mal Hummer gegessen?
9. Wir haben gerade das Haus sauber gemacht.
10. A: Das ist ein schönes Kleid.
    B: Ich habe es gestern gekauft.

→ Zusätzliche Übungen 19–23, 29–31 (Seiten 260–62, 265–67)

Unit 22: is done   was done (Passiv 1)

A

The office **is cleaned** every day.
Das Büro wird jeden Tag sauber gemacht.

The office **was cleaned** yesterday.
Das Büro wurde gestern sauber gemacht.

Vergleichen Sie das Aktiv und das Passiv:

Somebody **cleans** the office every day.   (Aktiv)

The office **is cleaned** every day.   (Passiv)

Somebody **cleaned** the office yesterday.   (Aktiv)

The office **was cleaned** yesterday.   (Passiv)

B

Das Passiv bildet man mit:

			past participle	
present simple	**am/is/are**	(not) +	cleaned done	
past simple	**was/were**		invented built	
			injured taken	*usw.*

Das *past participle* von regelmäßigen Verben ist **-ed** (clean**ed**/damag**ed** usw.).
Sie finden eine Liste der unregelmäßigen Partizipien (**done/built/taken** usw.) in Anhang 2–3.

Im Deutschen bildet man das Passiv mit 'werden' + past participle:
- Butter **is made** from milk.   *Butter wird aus Milch gemacht.*
- Oranges **are imported** into Britain.   *... werden ... importiert.*
- How often **are** these rooms **cleaned**?   *... werden diese Räume gereinigt?*
- I **am** never **invited** to parties.   *Ich werde nie ... eingeladen.*

- This house **was built** 100 years ago.   *... wurde vor 100 Jahren gebaut.*
- These houses **were built** 100 years ago.   *... wurden ... gebaut.*
- When **was** the telephone **invented**?   *Wann wurde ... erfunden?*
- We **weren't invited** to the party last week.   *... wurden nicht ... eingeladen.*
- A: **Was** anybody **injured** in the accident?   *Wurde irgendjemand bei dem Unfall verletzt?*
  B: Yes, two people **were taken** to hosptial.   *... wurden ins Krankenhaus gebracht.*

Bei einigen allgemeinen Aussagen verwendet man im Englischen das Passiv und im Deutschen 'man':
- The passive **is used** mainly in writing.
  Das Passiv verwendet man vor allem in der Schriftsprache.

C

was/were born entspricht im Deutschen 'bin/bist usw. geboren':
- I **was born** in Berlin in 1993.   (*nicht* I am born)   *Ich bin 1993 in Berlin geboren.*
- 'Where **were** you **born**?'   'In Cairo.'   *'Wo sind Sie geboren?'   'In Kairo.'*

D

Passiv + **by** ... (= von)
- The telephone was invented **by Alexander Bell** in 1876.   (*nicht* from Alexander Bell)
  Das Telefon wurde 1876 von ... erfunden.
- I was bitten **by a dog** a few days ago.
  ... wurde ... von einem Hund gebissen.
- Do you like these paintings?   They were painted **by a friend of mine**.
  ... Sie wurden von einem meiner Freunde gemalt.

---

is being done / has been done → Unit 23   unregelmäßige Verben → Unit 25, Anhang 2–3   by → Unit 111
Aktiv und Passiv → Anhang 1

Übungen

Unit 22

22.1
Bilden Sie Sätze mit den Wörtern in Klammern. Einige Sätze sind Fragen.
Sätze 1–7 sind in der Gegenwartsform.

1. (the office / clean / every day) — The office is cleaned every day.
2. (these rooms / clean / every day?) — Are these rooms cleaned every day?
3. (glass / make / from sand) — Glass ....
4. (the windows / clean / every two weeks)
5. (this room / not / use / very much)
6. (we / allow / to park here?)
7. (how / this word / pronounce?)

Sätze 8–15 sind in der Vergangenheitsform.

8. (the office / clean / yesterday) — The office was cleaned yesterday.
9. (the house / paint / last month) — The house ....
10. (my phone / steal / a few days ago)
11. (three people / injure / in the accident)
12. (when / this bridge / build?)
13. (I / not / wake up / by the noise)
14. (how / these windows / break?)
15. (you / invite / to Jon's party last week?)

22.2
Korrigieren Sie die Fehler in den Sätzen.

1. This <u>house built</u> 100 years ago. — This house was built
2. Football plays in most countries of the world.
3. Why did the letter send to the wrong address?
4. A film studio is a place where films make.
5. Where are you born?
6. How many languages are speaking in Switzerland?
7. Somebody broke into our house, but nothing stolen.
8. When was invented the bicycle?

22.3
Vervollständigen Sie die Sätze. Verwenden Sie das Passiv (Gegenwart oder Vergangenheit) folgender Verben:

~~clean~~   damage   find   give   invite   make   make   show   steal   ~~take~~

1. The room **is cleaned** every day.
2. I saw an accident yesterday. Two people **were taken** to hospital.
3. Paper .... from wood.
4. There was a fire at the hotel last week. Two of the rooms ....
5. 'Where did you get this picture?' 'It .... to me by a friend of mine.'
6. Many American programmes .... on British TV.
7. 'Did James and Sue go to the wedding?' 'No. They ...., but they didn't go.'
8. 'How old is this film?' 'It .... in 1985.'
9. My car .... last week, but the next day it .... by the police.

22.4
Wo sind diese Leute geboren?

1. (Ian / Edinburgh) — Ian was born in Edinburgh.
2. (Sarah / Manchester) — Sarah ....
3. (her parents / Ireland) — Her ....
4. (you / ???) — I ....
5. (your mother / ???)

22.5
Übersetzen Sie ins Englische.

1. Die Straßen werden jeden Tag gereinigt.
2. Das Haus wurde gestern im Sturm beschädigt.
3. Wann wurde diese Kirche gebaut?
4. Zwei Computer wurden gestern aus dem Büro gestohlen.
5. Wann sind deine Eltern geboren?
6. Welche Sprachen spricht man in Südamerika?
7. Zwei Männer wurden gestern von der Polizei festgenommen.

beschädigen = damage
festnehmen = arrest

Unit 23

is being done   has been done (Passiv 2)

A   is/are being ... (Passiv des present continuous)

Somebody **is painting** the door .   (Aktiv)
The door **is being painted**.   (Passiv)

Jemand streicht die Tür.
Die Tür wird gestrichen.

- My car is at the garage. It **is being repaired**.   Mein Auto ist in der Werkstatt. Es wird (gerade) repariert.
- Some new houses **are being built** opposite the park.
  Zurzeit werden einige neue Häuser gegenüber vom Park gebaut.

Wie bei der Aktivform, gibt es beim Passiv im Deutschen keine Form, die dem present continuous genau entspricht. (Manchmal verwendet man 'jetzt', 'gerade' oder 'zurzeit' um zu vermitteln, dass etwas im Augenblick stattfindet.)

Vergleichen sie das present continuous und present simple der Passivform:
- The office **is being cleaned** at the moment.   (present continuous: Handlung im Gang)
  The office **is cleaned** every day.   (present simple: regelmäßig wiederholte Handlung)
- Football matches **are** often **played** at the weekend, but no matches **are being played** next weekend.
  Fußball wird oft am Wochenende gespielt, aber dieses Wochenende wird nicht gespielt.

Für den Gebrauch des present continuous im Vergleich zum present simple siehe Units 9 und 26.

B   has/have been ... (Passiv des present perfect)

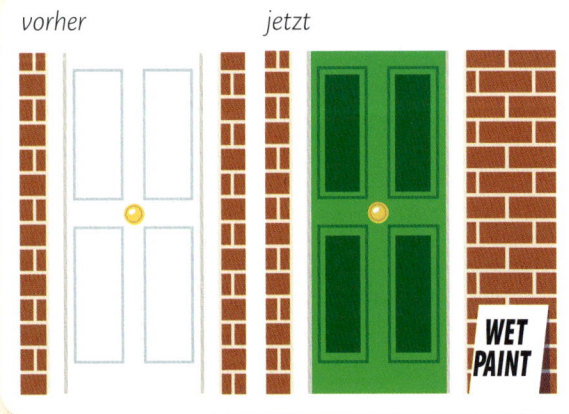

Somebody **has painted** the door .   (Aktiv)
The door **has been painted**.   (Passiv)

Jemand hat die Tür gestrichen.
Die Tür ist gestrichen worden.

- My key **has been stolen**.   Mein Schlüssel ist gestohlen worden.
- My keys **have been stolen**.   ... sind gestohlen worden.
- I'm not going to the party. I **haven't been invited**.   ... Ich wurde nicht eingeladen.
- **Has** this shirt **been washed**?   Wurde dieses Hemd gewaschen?

Vergleichen Sie das present perfect und past simple der Passivform:
- The room isn't dirty any more. It **has been cleaned**.   (present perfect: nicht abgeschlossener Zeitraum)
  The room w**as cleaned** yesterday.   (past simple: abgeschlossener Zeitraum)
- I can't find my keys. I think they**'ve been stolen**.   (present perfect)
  My keys **were stolen** last week.   (past simple)

Für den Gebrauch des present perfect im Vergleich zum past simple siehe Unit 21.

is done / was done → Unit 22   Aktiv und Passiv → Anhang 1

Übungen

Unit 23

23.1 Was passiert gerade in den Bildern? Verwenden Sie die Passivform.

1 The car ..... is being repaired.
2 A bridge .....
3 The windows .....
4 The grass .....

23.2 Beschreiben Sie, was in den Bildern gerade passiert oder was gerade passiert ist. Verwenden Sie die Passivform des present continuous (**is**/**are being ...**) oder present perfect (**has**/**have been ...**).

1 (the office / clean) The office is being cleaned.
2 (the shirts / iron) The shirts have been ironed.
3 (the window / break) The window .....
4 (the roof / repair) The roof .....
5 (the car / damage) .....
6 (the houses / knock / down) .....
7 (the trees / cut / down) .....
8 (they / invite / to a party) .....

23.3 Vervollständigen Sie die Sätze mit den Wörtern in Klammern. Beziehen Sie sich auf Unit 22.
1 I can't use my office at the moment. It ..... is being painted ..... (paint).
2 We didn't go to the party. We ..... weren't invited ..... (not/invite).
3 The washing machine was broken, but it's OK now. It ..... (repair).
4 The washing machine ..... (repair) yesterday afternoon.
5 A factory is a place where things ..... (make).
6 How old are these houses? When ..... (they/build)?
7 A: ..... (the photocopier / use) at the moment?
   B: No, you can go ahead and use it.
8 I've never seen these flowers before. What ..... (they/call)?
9 My sunglasses ..... (steal) at the beach yesterday.
10 The bridge is closed at the moment. It ..... (damage) last week
    and it ..... (not/repair) yet.

23.4 Übersetzen Sie ins Englische.

glauben = think
untersuchen = examine

1 'Wo ist dein Fahrrad?' 'Es wird gerade repariert.'
2 Das Abendessen wird jeden Abend um 7 Uhr serviert.
3 Ich kann mein Geld nicht finden. Ich glaube, es ist gestohlen worden.
4 Gestern wurde ein Bild aus dem Museum gestohlen.
5 Sieh mal die Häuser an! Sie sind im Sturm beschädigt worden.
6 Letzte Woche wurde das Büro nicht gereinigt.
7 David wird (gerade) vom Arzt untersucht.

➜ Zusätzliche Übungen 24–27 (Seiten 263–64)

Unit 24

be/have/do
(Gegenwarts- und Vergangenheitsformen)

A
be (= **am**/**is**/**are**/**was**/**were**) + **-ing** (**cleaning**/**working** usw.) beim *present continuous* und *past continuous*

am/**is**/**are** + -ing
(*present continuous*)
→ Units 4–5 und 26

- Please be quiet. I**'m working**. Ich arbeite (gerade).
- It **isn't raining** at the moment. Es regnet (gerade) nicht.
- What **are** you **doing** this evening? Was machst du heute Abend?

was/**were** + -ing
(*past continuous*)
→ Unit 14

- I **was working** when she arrived.
  Ich arbeitete gerade (war gerade beim Arbeiten), als sie angekommen ist.
- It **wasn't raining**, so we didn't need an umbrella.
  Es regnete nicht, also brauchten wir keinen Schirm.
- What **were** you **doing** at 3 o'clock?
  Was hast du um 3 Uhr (gerade) gemacht?

B
be + past participle (**cleaned**/**made**/**eaten** usw.) beim Passiv

am/**is**/**are** + past participle
(*Passiv des* present simple)
→ Unit 22

- I**'m** never **invited** to parties.
  Ich werde nie … eingeladen.
- Butter **is made** from milk.
  … wird aus Milch gemacht.
- These offices **aren't cleaned** every day.
  … werden nicht jeden Tag gereinigt.

was/**were** + past participle
(*Passiv des* past simple)
→ Unit 22

- The office **was cleaned** yesterday.
  … wurde gestern gereinigt.
- These houses **were built** 100 years ago.
  … wurden vor 100 Jahren gebaut.
- How **was** the window **broken**?
  Wie wurde das Fenster eingeschlagen?
- Where **were** you **born**? Wo sind Sie geboren?

C
have/**has** + past participle (**cleaned**/**lost**/**eaten**/**been** usw.) beim *present perfect*

have/**has** + past participle
(*present perfect*)
→ Units 16–19

- I**'ve cleaned** my room. Ich habe mein Zimmer geputzt.
- Tom **has lost** his passport. … hat seinen Pass verloren.
- Kate **hasn't been** to Canada. … war noch nie in Kanada.
- Where **have** Paul and Emma **gone**? Wo sind … hingegangen?

D
do/**does**/**did** + Infinitiv (**clean**/**like**/**eat**/**go** usw.) bei der Verneinung und Frageform des *present simple* und *past simple*

do/**does** + Infinitiv
(*present simple* Verneinung
und Frageform)
→ Units 7–8

- I like coffee, but I **don't like** tea.
  … aber ich mag keinen Tee.
- Chris **doesn't go** out very often.
  … geht nicht sehr oft aus.
- What **do** you usually **do** at weekends?
  Was machen Sie gewöhnlich … ?
- **Does** Sam **live** alone? Lebt Sam allein?

did + infinitiv
(*past simple* Verneinung
und Frageform)
→ Unit 13

- I **didn't watch** TV yesterday.
  Ich habe gestern nicht ferngesehen.
- It **didn't rain** last week. Es hat … nicht geregnet.
- What time **did** Paul and Emma **go** out?
  Um wie viel Uhr sind … ausgegangen?

unregelmäßige Verben ➜ Unit 25, Anhang 2–3

Übungen

Unit 24

24.1 Schreiben Sie **is**/**are** oder **do**/**does**.

1. *Do* you work in the evenings?
2. Where *are* they going?
3. Why .... you looking at me?
4. .... Ben live near you?
5. .... you like cooking?
6. .... the sun shining?
7. What time .... the shops close?
8. .... Maria working today?
9. What .... this word mean?
10. .... you feeling all right?

24.2 Vervollständigen Sie die Sätze mit den folgenden Verneinungen: **am not**/**isn't**/**aren't** oder **don't**/**doesn't**.

1. Tom *doesn't* work at weekends.
2. I'm very tired. I .... want to go out this evening.
3. I'm very tired. I .... going out this evening.
4. Gary .... working this week. He's on holiday.
5. My parents are usually at home. They .... go out very often.
6. Nicola has travelled a lot, but she .... speak any foreign languages.
7. You can turn off the television. I .... watching it.
8. Lisa has invited us to her party next week, but we .... going.

24.3 Vervollständigen Sie die Sätze mit **was**/**were**/**did**/**have**/**has**.

1. Where *were* your shoes made?
2. .... you go out last night?
3. What .... you doing at 10.30?
4. Where .... your mother born?
5. .... Laura gone home?
6. What time .... she go?
7. When .... these houses built?
8. .... Steve arrived yet?
9. Why .... you go home early?
10. How long .... they been married?

24.4 Vervollständigen Sie die Sätze mit **is**/**are**/**was**/**were**/**have**/**has**.

1. Joe *has* lost his passport.
2. This bridge .... built ten years ago.
3. .... you finished your work yet?
4. This town is always clean. The streets .... cleaned every day.
5. Where .... you born?
6. I .... just made some coffee. Would you like some?
7. Glass .... made from sand.
8. This is a very old photograph. It .... taken a long time ago.
9. David .... bought a new car.

24.5 Vervollständigen Sie die Sätze mit der passenden Form der Verben aus der Liste.

| damage | ~~rain~~ | enjoy | ~~go~~ | pronounce | eat |
| listen | use | open | go | understand | |

1. I'm going to take an umbrella with me. It's *raining*.
2. Why are you so tired? Did you *go* to bed late last night?
3. Where are the chocolates? Have you .... them all?
4. How is your new job? Are you .... it?
5. My car was badly .... in the accident, but I was OK.
6. Kate has got a car, but she doesn't .... it very often.
7. Lisa isn't at home. She has .... away for a few days.
8. I don't .... the problem. Can you explain it again?
9. Mark is in his room. He's .... to music.
10. I don't know how to say this word. How is it ....?
11. How do you .... this window? Can you show me?

24.6 Übersetzen Sie ins Englische.

1. Guck mal! Es schneit.
2. Wir sind gestern Nachmittag nicht rausgegangen, weil es geregnet hat.
3. Yoghurt wird aus Milch gemacht.
4. Mein Büro wurde gestern nicht geputzt.
5. 'Was machen die Kinder?' 'Sie spielen.'
6. Ich gehe nicht sehr oft ins Theater.
7. Mögen Sie japanisches Essen?
8. Was hast du letztes Wochenende gemacht?
9. Amy und Steven haben ein neues Haus gekauft.
10. Jenny ist gestern nicht zur Arbeit gegangen.
11. Ben hat seine Hausaufgaben fertig gemacht und jetzt sieht er fern.
12. Unser Haus wurde 1950 gebaut.

Unit 25: Regelmäßige und unregelmäßige Verben

A Regelmäßige Verben

Das *past simple* und das *past participle* von regelmäßigen Verben haben: die Endung **-ed**:
clean → clean**ed**   live → liv**ed**   paint → paint**ed**   study → stud**ied**

past simple (→ Unit 12):
- I **cleaned** my room yesterday.
  Ich habe mein Zimmer gestern geputzt.
- Chris **studied** engineering at university.
  Chris hat ... Maschinenbau studiert.

Das *past participle* verwendet man bei der Bildung des *present perfect* und des Passivs:

have/has + past participle (present perfect → Units 16–19):
- I **have cleaned** my room.
  Ich habe ... geputzt.
- Tina **has lived** in London for ten years.
  Tina lebt seit zehn Jahren in London.

be (**is/are/were/has been** usw.) + past participle (Passiv → Units 22–23):
- These rooms **are cleaned** every day.
  ... werden jeden Tag gereinigt.
- My car **has been repaired**.
  Mein Auto ist repariert worden.

B Unregelmäßige Verben

Das *past simple* und das *past participle* von unregelmäßigen Verben haben nicht die Endung **-ed**:

	make	break	cut
past simple	made	broke	cut
past participle	made	broken	cut

In manchen Fällen haben das *past simple* und das *past participle* die gleiche Form, zum Beispiel:

	make	find	buy	cut
past simple / past participle	made	found	bought	cut

- I **made** a cake yesterday. (past simple)
  Gestern habe ich einen Kuchen gebacken.
- I **have made** some coffee. (past participle *beim* present perfect)
  Ich habe Kaffee gekocht.
- Butter **is made** from milk. (past participle *beim* Passiv *des* present simple)
  Butter wird aus Milch gemacht.

In manchen Fällen haben das *past simple* und das *past participle* eine unterschiedliche Form, zum Beispiel:

	break	know	begin	go
past simple	broke	knew	began	went
past participle	broken	known	begun	gone

- Somebody **broke** this window last night. (past simple)
  Jemand hat gestern Nacht dieses Fenster eingeschlagen.
- Somebody **has broken** this window. (past participle *beim* present perfect)
  ... hat ... eingeschlagen.
- This window **was broken** last night. (past participle *beim* Passiv *des* past simple)
  Dieses Fenster wurde ... eingeschlagen.

Liste der unregelmäßigen Verben → **Anhang 2–3**   Rechtschreibung der regelmäßigen Verben → **Anhang 5**

Übungen

Unit 25

25.1 Schreiben Sie das past simple / past participle folgender Verben (in dieser Übung sind beide Formen identisch).

1. make — made
2. cut — cut
3. get
4. bring
5. pay
6. enjoy
7. buy
8. sit
9. leave
10. happen
11. hear
12. put
13. catch
14. watch
15. understand

25.2 Schreiben Sie das past simple und das past participle folgender Verben.

1. break — broke — broken
2. begin
3. eat
4. drink
5. drive
6. speak
7. write
8. come
9. know
10. take
11. go
12. give
13. throw
14. forget
15. run

25.3 Setzen Sie die passende Form des Verbs ein.

1. I ..washed.. my hands because they were dirty. (wash)
2. Somebody has ..broken.. this window. (break)
3. I feel good. I .... very well last night. (sleep)
4. We .... a really good film yesterday. (see)
5. It .... a lot while we were on holiday. (rain)
6. I've .... my bag. Have you .... it? (lose / see)
7. Rosa's bike was .... last week. (steal)
8. I .... to bed early because I was tired. (go)
9. Have you .... your work yet? (finish)
10. The shopping centre was .... about 20 years ago. (build)
11. Anna .... to drive when she was 18. (learn)
12. I've never .... a horse. (ride)
13. Jessica is a good friend of mine. I've .... her for a long time. (know)
14. Yesterday I .... and .... my leg. (fall / hurt)
15. My brother .... in the London Marathon last year. Have you ever in a marathon? (run / run)

25.4 Vervollständigen Sie die Sätze mit den folgenden Verben und setzen Sie diese in die passende Form.

> cost   drive   fly   ~~make~~   meet   sell   speak   swim   tell   think   wake up   win

1. I have ..made.. some coffee. Would you like some?
2. Have you .... John about your new job?
3. We played basketball on Sunday. We didn't play very well, but we .... the game.
4. I know Gary, but I've never .... his wife.
5. We were .... by loud music in the middle of the night.
6. Stephanie jumped into the river and .... to the other side.
7. 'Did you like the film?' 'Yes, I .... it was very good.'
8. Many different languages are .... in the Philippines.
9. Our holiday .... a lot of money because we stayed in an expensive hotel.
10. Have you ever .... a very fast car?
11. All the tickets for the concert were .... very quickly.
12. A bird .... in through the open window while we were having our dinner.

25.5 Übersetzen Sie ins Englische.

einen Kuchen backen = make a cake
Treppen = stairs

1. Ich habe Englisch an der Universität studiert.
2. Ich habe einen Kuchen gebacken. Möchten Sie ein Stück?
3. Emma ist gestern ins Theater gegangen.
4. 'Wo ist Joe?' 'Er ist rausgegangen.'
5. Die Treppen werden jeden Donnerstag geputzt.
6. *Romeo and Juliet* wurde von William Shakespeare geschrieben.
7. Lisa ist müde. Sie ist heute 500 Kilometer gefahren.
8. Wo ist unser Auto? Es ist gestohlen worden!
9. Ich habe auf dem Fest viel gegessen und getrunken.

Unit 26

What are you doing tomorrow?

A

They **are playing** tennis (**now**).
Sie spielen (jetzt) Tennis.

today is Sunday

"I'm playing tennis tomorrow."

He **is playing** tennis **tomorrow**.
Er spielt morgen Tennis.

Man verwendet **am**/**is**/**are** + **-ing** (present continuous) *für eine Handlung, die zurzeit im Gang ist:*
- A: Where are Tina and Helen?
  B: They**'re playing** tennis in the park.   Sie spielen im Park Tennis.
- Please be quiet. **I'm working**.   Sei bitte still! Ich arbeite.

Man verwendet **am**/**is**/**are** + **-ing** *auch für die Zukunft ('morgen' / 'nächste Woche' usw.):*
- Andrew **is playing** tennis tomorrow.   Andrew spielt morgen Tennis.
- I**'m** not **working** next week.   Ich arbeite nächste Woche nicht.

B

I am doing something tomorrow (= *Ich mache morgen etwas*) *bedeutet, dass ich einen Plan oder eine Vereinbarung habe etwas zu tun:*

"I'm going to a concert tomorrow."

- Sophie **is going** to the dentist on Friday.
  Sophie geht am Freitag zum Zahnarzt. (= sie hat einen Termin)
- We**'re having** a party next weekend.
  Wir machen nächstes Wochenende ein Fest.
- **Are** you **meeting** your friends tonight?
  Triffst du dich heute Abend mit deinen Freunden?
- What **are** you **doing** tomorrow evening?
  Was machst du morgen Abend?
- I**'m** not **going** out tonight. I**'m staying** at home.
  Ich gehe heute Abend nicht aus. Ich bleibe zu Hause.

Man kann für Zukunftspläne auch '**I'm going to** do something' sagen (→ Unit 27).

C

Man verwendet das present continuous (**I'm staying** / **are you coming**? usw.) für Pläne und Vereinbarungen:
- I**'m staying** at home this evening. (*nicht* I stay)
- **Are** you **going** out tonight? (*nicht* Do you go)
- Lisa **isn't coming** to the party next week. (*nicht* Lisa doesn't come)

Das present simple (**start** / **arrives** usw.) verwendet man jedoch für Stundenpläne, Fahrpläne, Programme, usw.:
- The train **arrives** at 7.30.   Der Zug kommt um 7.30 an.
- What time **does** the film **finish**? Um wie viel Uhr ist der Film zu Ende?

Vergleichen Sie den Gebrauch des present continuous und present simple für Zukunftshandlungen:

present continuous:	present simple:
bezieht sich meistens auf Menschen	Fahrpläne, Programme usw.

Im Deutschen verwendet man in beiden Fällen die Gegenwartsform.

I**'m going** to a concert tomorrow.	The concert **starts** at 7.30.
Morgen gehe ich in ein Konzert.	Das Konzert beginnt um …
What time **are** you **leaving**?	What time **does** your train **leave**?
Um wie viel Uhr fahren Sie los?	Um wie viel Uhr fährt Ihr Zug ab?

present continuous → Units 4–5   present simple → Units 6–8   I'm going to … → Unit 27

Übungen

Unit 26

26.1 Schreiben Sie, was die Personen in den Bildern nächsten Freitag machen.

1	2	3	4	5
ANDREW	RICHARD	RACHEL	KAREN	SUE AND TOM

1 *Andrew is playing tennis on Friday.*
2 Richard .... to the cinema.
3 Rachel ....
4 .... lunch with Will.
5 ....

26.2 Bilden Sie Fragen über die Zukunft mit den Wörtern in Klammern.

1 (you / go / out / tonight?) *Are you going out tonight?*
2 (you / work / next week?)
3 (what / you / do / tomorrow evening?)
4 (what time / your friends / come?)
5 (when / Lisa / go / on holiday?)

26.3 Schreiben Sie über Ihre Pläne in den nächsten Tagen.

1 *I'm staying at home tonight.*
2 *I'm going to the theatre on Monday.*
3
4
5
6

26.4 Setzen Sie die Verben in die passende Zeitform: present continuous (**he is leaving** usw.) oder present simple (**the train leaves** usw.).

1 '*Are you going* (you/go) out tonight?' 'No, I'm too tired.'
2 *We're going* (we/go) to a concert tonight. *It starts* (it/start) at 7.30.
3 Do you know about Sarah? .... (she/get) married next month!
4 A: My parents .... (go) on holiday next week.
   B: Oh, that's nice. Where .... (they/go)?
5 Silvia is doing an English course at the moment. The course .... (finish) on Friday.
6 There's a party tomorrow night, but .... (I/not/go).
7 .... (I/go) out with some friends tonight. Why don't you come too?
   .... (we/meet) at the Royal Hotel at 8 o'clock.
8 A: How .... (you/get) home after the party tomorrow? By taxi?
   B: No, I can go by bus. The last bus .... (leave) at midnight.
9 A: .... (you/come) with us to the cinema tonight?
   B: Yes, what time .... (the film / begin)?
10 A: What .... (you/do) tomorrow afternoon?
   B: .... (I/work).

26.5 Übersetzen Sie ins Englische.

1 Ich fahre am Wochenende in die Berge.
2 Tom geht morgen nicht zur Arbeit.
3 Gehst du heute Abend auf das Fest?
4 Sarah und Michael fahren nächsten Sommer nach Irland.
5 Um wie viel Uhr kommst du heute Abend nach Hause?
6 Das Fußballspiel beginnt heute um 4 Uhr.
7 'Was macht ihr am Freitagabend?' 'Wir gehen ins Kino.'
8 Um wie viel Uhr kommt Ihr Flugzeug morgen an?

Unit 27
I'm going to ...

A I'm going to do something

morning   this evening

She **is going to watch** TV this evening.   Sie sieht heute Abend fern / Sie hat vor ... fernzusehen.

Man verwendet **am**/**is**/**are going to** ... für die Zukunft:

I	**am**		do ...	**am**	I		buy ... ?
he/she/it	**is**	(not) **going to**	drink ...	**is**	he/she/it	**going to**	eat ... ?
we/you/they	**are**		watch ...	**are**	we/you/they		wear ... ?

B

I am going to do something bedeutet so viel wie 'Ich werde etwas tun' oder 'Ich habe vor etwas zu tun'.
Man verwendet diese Form, wenn man entschieden hat, oder die Absicht hat, etwas zu tun:

I decided to do it ⟶   **I'm going to do it**

Vergangenheit   Jetzt   Zukunft

- I**'m going to buy** some books tomorrow.   Ich werde morgen einige Bücher kaufen.
- Sarah **is going to sell** her car.   Sarah hat vor, ihr Auto zu verkaufen.
- I**'m not going to have** breakfast this morning. I'm not hungry.   Ich frühstücke heute Früh nicht. ...
- What **are** you **going to wear** to the wedding next week?   Was wirst du ... tragen?
- 'Your hands are dirty.'   'Yes, I know. I**'m going to wash** them.'   ... 'Ich werde sie waschen.'
- **Are** you **going to invite** Mark to your party?   Hast du vor Mark ... einzuladen?

Man verwendet auch das present continuous (**I am doing**) für die Zukunft; meistens für Vereinbarungen (→ Unit 26):
- I **am playing** tennis with Julia tomorrow.   Ich spiele morgen ... Tennis.

C Something is going to happen

Man verwendet auch **am**/**is**/**are going to** ... , wenn es offensichtlich ist, dass etwas geschehen wird.
- Look at the sky! It**'s going to rain**.
  Sieh mal den Himmel an! Es wird regnen. / Es regnet bald.
- Oh dear! It's 9 o'clock and I'm not ready.
  I**'m going to be** late.   ... Ich werde zu spät kommen.

It's going to rain.

D

Wie die Beispiele oben zeigen, gibt es mehrere Möglichkeiten, wie man **am**/**is**/**are going to** ... ins Deutsche übersetzen kann:

- I **am going to do** something.   Ich werde etwas tun.
                                   Ich habe vor etwas zu tun.
                                   Ich tue (in der Zukunft) etwas.

- I **am going to meet** Tom tonight.   Ich werde mich heute Abend mit Tom treffen.
                                   Ich habe vor ... , mich mit Tom zu treffen.
                                   Ich treffe mich heute Abend mit Tom.

- It**'s going to rain**.   Es wird regnen.
                      Es regnet bald.

die Gegenwartsform für die Zukunft → **Unit 26**   will → **Units 28–29**

Übungen

Unit 27

27.1 Was haben die Personen auf den Bildern vor? Schreiben Sie in die Sprechblasen, was sie sagen.

27.2 Vervollständigen Sie die Sätze mit **going to** + einem der folgenden Verben:

| do | eat | give | lie down | stay | walk | ~~wash~~ | watch | ~~wear~~ |

1. My hands are dirty. _I'm going to wash_ them.
2. What _are you going to wear_ to the party tonight?
3. It's a nice day. I don't want to take the bus. I ....
4. Steve is going to London next week. He .... with some friends.
5. I'm hungry. I .... this sandwich.
6. It's Sarah's birthday next week. We .... her a present.
7. Sue says she's feeling very tired. She .... for an hour.
8. Your favourite programme is on TV tonight. .... you .... it?
9. What .... Rachel .... when she leaves school?

27.3 Schreiben Sie, was demnächst in den Bildern passieren wird.

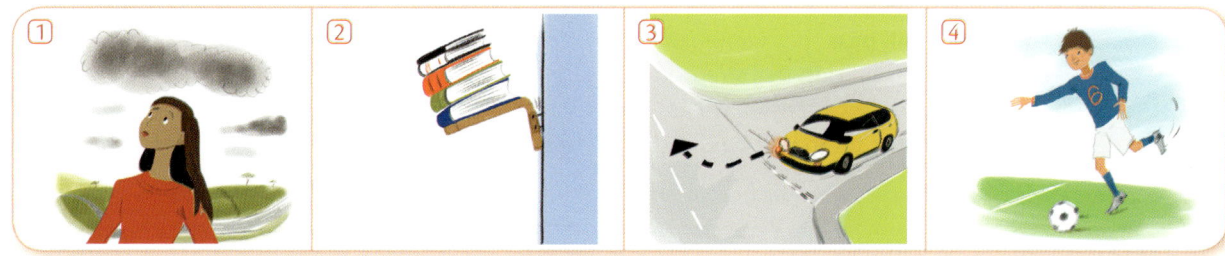

1. _It's going to rain._
2. The shelf ....
3. The car ....
4. He ....

27.4 Was haben Sie heute oder morgen vor? Schreiben Sie drei Sätze.

1. I'm ....
2. ....
3. ....

27.5 Übersetzen Sie ins Englische. Verwenden Sie **going to …** .

1. Ich bin müde. Ich werde heute Abend zu Hause bleiben.
2. Paul hat vor, ein neues Smartphone zu kaufen.
3. Was machen die Kinder in den Schulferien?
4. Helen und Ben haben vor zu heiraten.
5. Besucht deine Mutter uns am Sonntag?
6. Wann hat Sarah vor Urlaub zu machen?
7. Es ist kalt. Ich glaube, es wird schneien.
8. Mach schnell! Wir werden zu spät kommen.

heiraten = get married
Urlaub machen = have a holiday
Mach schnell! = Hurry up

Unit 28: will/shall 1

A

SARAH

Sarah goes to work every day. She is always there from 8.30 until 4.30.

It is 11 o'clock now. Sarah **is** at work.
… Sarah ist bei der Arbeit.

At 11 o'clock yesterday, she **was** at work.
… gestern war sie bei der Arbeit.

At 11 o'clock tomorrow, she **will be** at work.
… morgen wird sie bei der Arbeit sein.

will + Infinitiv (**will be** / **will win** / **will come** usw.):

I/we/you/they he/she/it	**will** (**'ll**) **will not** (**won't**)	**be win eat come** usw.

will	I/we/you/they he/she/it	**be? win? eat? come?** usw.

Kurzformen:
'll = **will**: I**'ll** (I will) / you**'ll** / she**'ll** usw.
won't = **will not**: I **won't** (= I will not) / you **won't** / she **won't** usw.

B

Man verwendet **will** für die Zukunft (tomorrow / next week usw.):
- Sue travels a lot. Today she is in Madrid. Tomorrow she**'ll be** in Rome. Next week she**'ll be** in Tokyo.
  … Morgen ist sie in Rom. Nächste Woche wird sie in Tokio sein.
- You can call me this evening. I**'ll be** at home. … Ich werde zu Hause sein.
- Leave the old bread in the garden. The birds **will eat** it. … Die Vögel werden es essen.
- We**'ll** probably **go** out this evening. Wir gehen heute Abend wahrscheinlich aus.
- **Will** you **be** at home this evening? Bist du heute Abend zu Hause?

- I **won't be** here tomorrow. (= I will not be here)
  Ich werde morgen nicht hier sein.
- Don't drink coffee before you go to bed. You **won't sleep**.
  … Sie werden nicht schlafen.

Oft sagt man **I think** … **will** … :
- **I think** Kelly **will pass** the exam. Ich glaube, Kelly wird die Prüfung bestehen.
- **I don't think** it **will rain** this afternoon. (nicht I think it will not rain)
  Ich glaube nicht, dass es regnen wird …
- **Do you think** the exam **will be** difficult? Glaubst du, die Prüfung wird schwierig sein?

Beachten Sie, dass **will** oft – jedoch nicht immer – im Deutschen 'werden' entspricht (→ Units 26–27).

C

Man verwendet nicht **will**, wenn man etwas geplant hat, oder entschieden hat, etwas zu tun (→ Units 26–27):
- We**'re going** to the cinema on Saturday. Do you want to come with us? (nicht We will go)
- I**'m** not **working** tomorrow. (nicht I won't work)
- **Are** you **going to do** the exam? (nicht Will you do)

D shall

Man kann auch **I shall** und **we shall** (anstatt I will und we will) sagen:
- **I shall be** late tomorrow.   oder   **I will** (**I'll**) **be** late tomorrow.
- I think **we shall win**.   oder   I think **we will** (**we'll**) **win**.

Man verwendet **shall** jedoch nicht mit **you/they/he/she/it**:
- **Tom will** be late. (nicht Tom shall be)

Übungen

28.1 Helen ist auf Reisen in Europa. Vervollständigen Sie die Sätze mit **she was**, **she's** oder **she'll be**.

1. Yesterday _she was_ in Paris.
2. Tomorrow .... in Amsterdam.
3. Last week .... in Barcelona.
4. Next week .... in London.
5. At the moment .... in Brussels.
6. Three days ago .... in Munich.
7. At the end of her trip .... very tired.

Helen

28.2 Wo werden Sie sein? Schreiben Sie Sätze über sich selbst. Verwenden Sie:

I'll be ... oder **I'll probably be ...** oder **I don't know where I'll be.**

1. (at 10 o'clock tomorrow) _I'll probably be on the beach._
2. (one hour from now) ....
3. (at midnight tonight) ....
4. (at 3 o'clock tomorrow afternoon) ....
5. (two years from now) ....

28.3 Vervollständigen Sie die Sätze mit **will** ('ll) oder **won't**.

1. Don't drink coffee before you go to bed. You _won't_ sleep.
2. 'Are you ready yet?' 'Not yet. I .... be ready in five minutes.'
3. I'm going away for a few days. I'm leaving tonight, so I .... be at home tomorrow.
4. It .... rain, so you don't need to take an umbrella.
5. A: I don't feel very well this evening.
   B: Well, go to bed early and you .... feel better in the morning.
6. It's Ben's birthday next Monday. He .... be 25.
7. I'm sorry I was late this morning. It .... happen again.

28.4 Beginnen Sie die Sätze mit **I think ...** oder **I don't think ...** .

1. (Kelly will pass the exam) _I think Kelly will pass the exam._
2. (Kelly won't pass the exam) _I don't think Kelly will pass the exam._
3. (we'll win the game) I ....
4. (I won't be here tomorrow) ....
5. (Sue will like her present) ....
6. (they won't get married) ....
7. (you won't enjoy the film) ....

28.5 Welcher Satz ist richtig? (Studieren Sie zuerst Unit 26!)

1. ~~We'll go~~ / We're going to the theatre tonight. We've got tickets. (We're going ist richtig)
2. 'What will you do / are you doing tomorrow evening?' 'Nothing. I'm free.'
3. They'll go / They're going away tomorrow morning. Their train is at 8.40.
4. I'm sure your aunt will lend / is lending us some money. She's very rich.
5. 'Why are you putting on your coat?' 'I'll go / I'm going out.'
6. Do you think Clare will phone / is phoning us tonight?
7. Steve can't meet us on Saturday. He'll work / He's working.
8. Will you / Shall you be at home tomorrow evening?
9. A: What are your plans for the weekend?
   B: Some friends will come / are coming to stay with us.

28.6 Übersetzen Sie ins Englische.

1. Der amerikanische Präsident wird morgen in Irland sein.
2. Sie können mich morgen anrufen. Ich werde den ganzen Tag im Büro sein.
3. Wir werden in einer Stunde zu Hause sein.
4. Ich glaube, Tom wird Kelly heiraten.
5. Ich bin morgen nicht bei der Arbeit.
6. Glaubst du, dass es morgen regnen wird?
7. Es wird nicht sehr schwierig sein.
8. Ich glaube nicht, dass Jenny auf das Fest kommt.

Unit 29 will/shall 2

A

Man kann **I'll** … (**I will**) verwenden, wenn man anbietet etwas zu tun, oder wenn man entscheidet etwas zu tun. In diesem Fall entspricht **will** meistens der Gegenwartsform im Deutschen:
- 'My bag is very heavy.'   '**I'll carry** it for you.'   … 'Ich trage sie für dich.'
- '**I'll phone** you tomorrow, OK?'   'OK, bye.'   'Ich ruf' dich morgen an, OK?' …

Oft sagt man **I think I'll** … / **I don't think I'll** … wenn man entscheidet etwas zu tun (im Deutschen verwendet man 'werden' oder die Gegenwartsform):
- I'm tired. **I think I'll go** to bed early tonight.
  … Ich glaube, ich werde heute Abend früh ins Bett gehen. / … ich gehe … früh ins Bett.
- It's a nice day. **I think I'll sit** outside.   … Ich glaube, ich sitze draussen.
- It's raining. **I don't think I'll go** out.   … Ich glaube nicht, dass ich rausgehen werde.

In Aussagen dieser Art verwendet man nicht das present simple (**I go** / **I phone** usw.):
- I**'ll phone** you tomorrow, OK?   (nicht I phone you)
- I think I**'ll go** to bed early.   (nicht I go to bed)

B

I'll verwendet man nicht, wenn man schon entschieden hat, oder die Absicht hat, etwas zu tun (→ Units 26–27):
- I**'m working** tomorrow.   (nicht I'll work)
- I don't want my car any more. I**'m going to sell** it.   (nicht I'll sell)
- What **are** you **doing** at the weekend?   (nicht What will you do)

C Shall I … ? Shall we … ?

Shall I / Shall we … ? verwendet man, um jemanden um Rat zu bitten oder um einen Vorschlag zu machen:
- It's very warm in this room. **Shall I open** the window?   … Soll ich das Fenster öffnen?
- '**Shall I phone** you this evening?'   'Yes, please.'   'Soll ich dich heute Abend anrufen?' …
- I'm going to a party tonight. What **shall I wear**?   … Was soll ich anziehen?
- It's a nice day. **Shall we go** for a walk?
  … Sollen/Wollen wir spazieren gehen? / Gehen wir spazieren?
- Where **shall we go** for our holidays this year?   Wohin fahren wir dieses Jahr in Urlaub?
- 'Let's go out this evening.'   'OK, what time **shall we meet**?'
  '… um wie viel Uhr sollen/wollen wir uns treffen?'

What are you doing tomorrow? → Unit 26   I'm going to … → Unit 27   will/shall 1 → Unit 28   Let's → Units 36, 54

Übungen

Unit 29

29.1 Vervollständigen Sie die Sätze mit I'll (I will) + einem der folgenden Verben:

~~carry~~   do   eat   show   sit   stay

1 My bag is very heavy.   I'll carry .... it for you.
2 I don't want this banana.   Well, I'm hungry. .... it.
3 Do you want a chair?   No, it's OK. .... on the floor.
4 Did you phone Jenny?   Oh no, I forgot. .... it now.
5 Are you coming with me?   No, I don't think so. .... here.
6 How do you use this camera?   Give it to me and .... you.

29.2 Vervollständigen Sie die Sätze mit I think I'll ... oder I don't think I'll ... + einem der folgenden Verben:

buy   buy   ~~go~~   have   play

1 It's cold today. I don't think I'll go .... out.
2 I'm hungry. I .... something to eat.
3 I feel very tired. .... tennis.
4 I like this hat. .... it.
5 This camera is too expensive. .... it.

29.3 Welcher Satz ist richtig?

1 ~~I phone~~ / I'll phone you tomorrow, OK?   (I'll phone ist richtig)
2 I haven't done the shopping yet. I do / I'll do it later.
3 I like sport. I watch / I'll watch a lot of sport on TV.
4 I need some exercise. I think I go / I'll go for a walk.
5 Carl is going to buy / will buy a new car. He told me last week.
6 'This book belongs to Tina.' 'OK. I give / I'll give / I'm going to give it to her.'
7 A: Are you doing / Will you do anything this evening?
   B: Yes, I'm going / I'll go out with some friends.
8 I can't go out with you tomorrow night. I work / I'm working / I'll work.

29.4 Schreiben Sie Fragen mit Shall I ... ? Verwenden Sie für jede Frage Wörter aus den Kästchen.

make   turn off   some sandwiches   the TV
~~open~~   turn on   the light   ~~the window~~

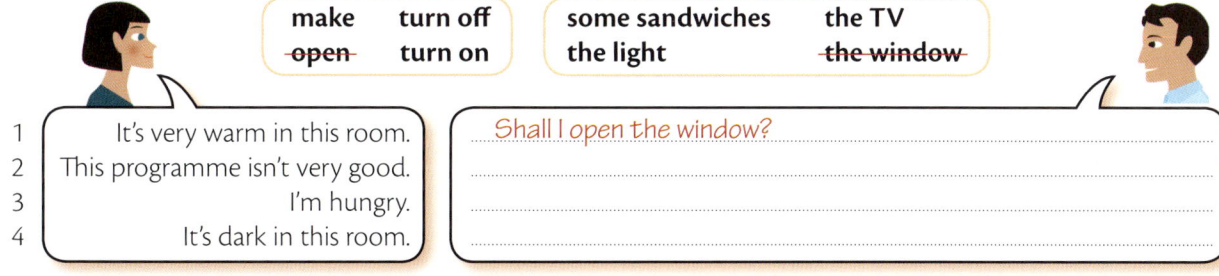

1 It's very warm in this room.   Shall I open the window?
2 This programme isn't very good.   ....
3 I'm hungry.   ....
4 It's dark in this room.   ....

29.5 Schreiben Sie Fragen mit Shall we ... ? Verwenden Sie für jede Frage Wörter aus den Kästchen.

what   where   buy   invite
~~what time~~   who   go   ~~meet~~

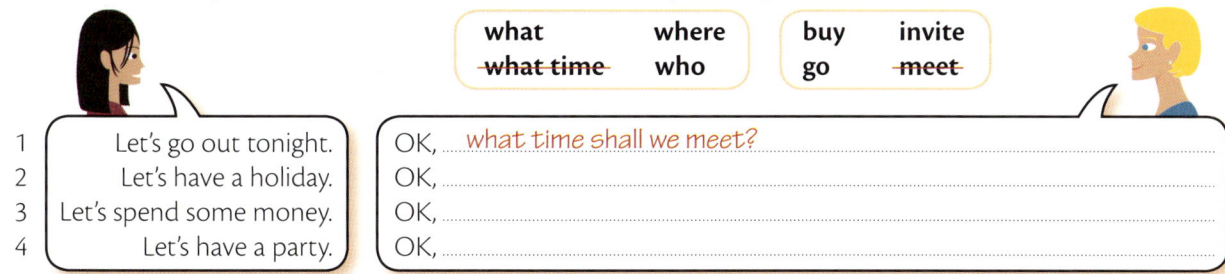

1 Let's go out tonight.   OK, what time shall we meet?
2 Let's have a holiday.   OK, ...
3 Let's spend some money.   OK, ...
4 Let's have a party.   OK, ...

29.6 Übersetzen Sie ins Englische.

1 'Es ist kalt.' 'Ich mach' das Fenster zu.'
2 Es ist heute sehr heiß. Ich glaube, ich gehe schwimmen.
3 A: Meine Hausaufgaben sind sehr schwierig.
   B: Ich helf' dir.
4 Wo sollen wir uns morgen treffen?
5 Ich fühle mich nicht wohl. Ich glaube nicht, dass ich heute Abend ausgehen werde.
6 Das Wetter ist schön. Wollen wir in die Berge fahren?
7 A: Soll ich die Tür aufmachen?
   B: Nein, ich mach's.

→ Zusätzliche Übungen 28–31 (Seiten 264–67)

Unit 30 might

A

He **might go** to New York.
Er fährt vielleicht nach New York.

It **might rain**.
Es könnte regnen.

might + *Infinitiv* (**might go** / **might be** / **might rain** usw.):

I/we/you/they he/she/it	**might** (not)	be go play come *usw.*

B

Man verwendet **might** um zu sagen, dass etwas möglich, aber nicht sicher, ist.
Might kann mit 'vielleicht …' oder 'könnte / es könnte (sein, dass …)' übersetzt werden:

- I **might go** to the cinema this evening, but I'm not sure.
  Ich gehe heute Abend vielleicht … / Es könnte sein, dass ich heute Abend …
- A: When is Rebecca going to phone you? *Wann wird Rebecca dich anrufen?*
  B: I don't know. She **might phone** this afternoon.
       … Es könnte sein, dass sie heute Nachmittag anruft.
- Take an umbrella with you. It **might rain**. *… Es könnte regnen.*
- Buy a lottery ticket. You **might be** lucky. *… Du könntest Glück haben.*
- A: Are you going out tonight?
  B: **I might**. *Vielleicht (werde ich ausgehen).*

Vergleichen Sie:

sicher
- I**'m playing** tennis tomorrow.
  Ich spiele morgen …
- Rebecca **is going to phone** later.
  … wird … anrufen.

möglich
- I **might play** tennis tomorrow.
  Ich spiele vielleicht …
- Rebecca **might phone** later.
  … wird vielleicht später anrufen.

C

Die Verneinung von **might** ist **might not**:
- I **might not go** to work tomorrow.
  Ich werde morgen vielleicht nicht zur Arbeit gehen.
- Sue **might not come** to the party.
  Sue kommt vielleicht nicht …

D may

Man kann auch **may** anstelle von **might** verwenden, um zu sagen, dass etwas möglich ist:
- I **may go** to the cinema this evening. *Ich gehe vielleicht …*
- Sue **may not come** to the party. *Sue kommt vielleicht nicht …*

May I … ? (= *Darf ich … ?*) wird auch verwendet, wenn man um Erlaubnis bittet:
- **May I** ask a question?
  Darf ich eine Frage stellen?
- '**May I** sit here?' 'Yes, of course.'
  'Darf ich mich hier hinsitzen?' 'Ja, natürlich.'

NB: **Can I … ?** (*Kann ich … ?*) ist eine weniger formelle Art, um Erlaubnis zu bitten (→ Unit 31).

will → Units 28–29   can → Unit 31

Übungen

Unit 30

30.1 Formulieren Sie folgende Sätze um – verwenden Sie **might**.

1. (it's possible that I'll go to the cinema) — I might go to the cinema.
2. (it's possible that I'll see you tomorrow) — I ....
3. (it's possible that Sarah will forget to phone) ....
4. (it's possible that it will snow today) ....
5. (it's possible that I'll be late tonight) ....

Schreiben Sie nun Sätze mit **might not**.

6. (it's possible that Mark will not be here next week) ....
7. (it's possible that I won't have time to go out) ....

30.2 Sie werden über Ihre Pläne befragt. Sie haben einige Ideen, sind aber noch nicht sicher. Wählen Sie Wörter aus der Liste und schreiben Sie Sätze mit **I might**.

fish   go away   ~~Italy~~   Monday   a new car   taxi

1. Where are you going for your holidays? — I'm not sure. I might go to Italy.
2. What are you doing at the weekend? — I don't know. I ....
3. When will you see Kate again? — I'm not sure. ....
4. What are you going to have for dinner? — I don't know. ....
5. How are you going to get home tonight? — I'm not sure. ....
6. I hear you won some money. What are you going to do with it? — I haven't decided yet. ....

30.3 Sie befragen Ben über seine Pläne. Manchmal hat er feste Pläne, aber meistens ist er noch nicht sicher.

1. Are you playing tennis tomorrow? — Yes, in the afternoon.
2. Are you going out tomorrow evening? — Possibly.
3. Are you going to get up early? — Perhaps.
4. Are you working tomorrow? — No, I'm not.
5. Will you be at home tomorrow morning? — Maybe.
6. Are you going to watch TV? — I might.
7. Are you going out in the afternoon? — Yes, I am.
8. Are you going shopping? — Perhaps.

Ben

Schreiben Sie nun Sätze über Ben. Verwenden Sie bei Bedarf **might**.

1. He's playing tennis tomorrow afternoon.
2. He might go out tomorrow evening.
3. He ....
4. ....
5. ....
6. ....
7. ....
8. ....

30.4 Schreiben Sie drei Dinge, die Sie vielleicht morgen machen werden. Verwenden Sie **might**.

1. ....
2. ....
3. ....

30.5 Übersetzen Sie ins Englische. Verwenden Sie, wenn möglich, **might**.

1. Vielleicht gehe ich heute Abend ins Theater.
2. Es könnte morgen schneien.
3. 'Spielen die Jungen morgen Fußball?' 'Vielleicht.'
4. Es könnte sein, dass Tina uns morgen besucht.
5. James fühlt sich nicht wohl. Er wird heute Abend vielleicht nicht ausgehen.
6. 'Was macht ihr heute Nachmittag?' 'Wir werden vielleicht im Garten arbeiten.'
7. Ich bin heute Nachmittag vielleicht nicht zu Hause, aber ich werde heute Abend da sein.
8. Darf ich hereinkommen?

Unit 31: can und could

A

"I can play the piano."

He **can play** the piano.
Er kann Klavier spielen.

"Could you open the door, please?"

Könnten Sie bitte die Tür öffnen?

can + Infinitiv (**can do** / **can play** / **can come** usw.):

I/we/you/they he/she/it	**can** **can't** (**cannot**)	do play see come usw.

can	I/we/you/they he/she/it	do? play? see? come? usw.

B

I can do something = Ich kann etwas tun:
- I **can play** the piano. My brother **can play** the piano too.
  Ich kann Klavier spielen. Mein Bruder kann auch Klavier spielen.
- Sarah **can speak** Italian, but she **can't speak** Spanish.
  Sarah kann Italienisch sprechen, aber sie kann nicht …
- '**Can** you **swim**?' 'Yes, but I'm not a very good swimmer.' 'Kannst du schwimmen?' …
- A: **Can** you **change** twenty pounds? Können Sie zwanzig Pfund wechseln?
  B: I'm sorry, I **can't**. Leider (kann ich) nicht.
- I'm having a party next week, but Paul and Rachel **can't come**. … können nicht kommen.

C

Für die Vergangenheit verwendet man **could/couldn't**:
- When I was young, I **could run** very fast. … konnte ich sehr schnell laufen.
- Before Maria came to Britain, she **couldn't understand** much English. Now she **can understand** everything.
  … konnte sie nicht viel Englisch verstehen. Jetzt kann sie alles verstehen.
- I was tired last night, but I **couldn't sleep**. … aber ich konnte nicht schlafen.
- I had a party last week, but Paul and Rachel **couldn't come**. … konnten nicht kommen.

D

Can … ? und **Could** … ? für Bitten

Man verwendet **Can you** … ? oder **Could you** … ?, wenn man jemanden bittet etwas zu tun:
- **Can you** open the door, please? oder **Could you** open the door, please?
  Können/Könnten Sie bitte die Tür öffnen?
- **Can you** wait a moment, please? oder **Could you** wait … ?
  Kannst/Könntest du bitte einen Moment warten?

Man verwendet **Can I have** … ? oder **Can I get** … ?, wenn man um etwas bittet:
- **Can I have** a glass of water, please? oder **Can I get** … ?
  Kann/Könnte ich bitte … haben?

Man verwendet **Can I** … ? oder **Could I** … ?, wenn man um Erlaubnis bittet:
- **Can I** sit here?
  Kann ich hier sitzen?
- Tom, **could I** borrow your umbrella?
  Tom, kann/darf ich mir deinen Regenschirm ausleihen?

May I … ? ➔ Unit 30

Übungen

31.1
Fragen Sie Steve, ob er alle diese Sachen machen kann.

chess

10 kilometres

You / Steve
1. Can you swim?
2. ....
3. ....
4. ....
5. ....
6. ....

Können Sie diese Sachen machen? Schreiben Sie Aussagen über sich selbst und verwenden Sie **I can** oder **I can't**.

7. I ....
8. ....
9. ....
10. ....
11. ....
12. ....

31.2
Vervollständigen Sie die Sätze mit **can** oder **can't** und einem der folgenden Verben:

~~come~~   find   hear   see   speak

1. I'm sorry, but we ...can't come... to your party next Saturday.
2. I like this hotel room. You .... the mountains from the window.
3. You are speaking very quietly. I .... you.
4. Have you seen my bag? I .... it.
5. Catherine got the job because she .... five languages.

31.3
Vervollständigen Sie die Sätze mit **can't** oder **couldn't** und einem der folgenden Verben:

decide   eat   find   go   go   ~~sleep~~

1. I was tired, but I ...couldn't sleep... .
2. I wasn't hungry yesterday. I .... my dinner.
3. Kate doesn't know what to do. She ....
4. I wanted to speak to Mark yesterday, but I .... him.
5. James .... to the concert next Saturday. He has to work.
6. Paula .... to the meeting last week. She was ill.

31.4
Was würden Sie in den folgenden Situationen sagen? Verwenden Sie **can** oder **could**.

1. (open/door) — Could you open the door, please?
2. (pass/salt)
3. (have/postcards)
4. (turn off /radio)
5. (borrow/newspaper)
6. (use/pen)

31.5
Übersetzen Sie ins Englische.

1. Alice kann vier Sprachen sprechen.
2. James kann nicht Tennis spielen.
3. Können Sie um 3 Uhr kommen?
4. Michael und Anna können Tango tanzen.
5. Ich kann meinen Schlüssel nicht finden.
6. Kannst du mir bitte helfen?
7. Als Laura jung war, konnte sie zehn Kilometer laufen.
8. Darf ich Ihr Telefon benutzen?
9. Wir konnten am Wochenende nicht ausgehen. Wir hatten keine Zeit.

Unit 32

must   mustn't   don't need to

A

It's a fantastic film. You must see it.

must + *Infinitiv* (**must do** / **must work** *usw.*):

I/we/you/they he/she/it	must	do go see eat *usw.*

B

I must (do something) = *ich muss etwas tun*:
- I'm very hungry. I **must eat** something. … *Ich muss etwas essen.*
- It's a fantastic film. You **must see** it. … *Du musst ihn sehen!*
- The windows are very dirty. We **must clean** them. … *Wir müssen sie putzen.*

Für die Vergangenheit (yesterday / last week *usw.*) *verwendet man* **had to** … (*nicht* must):
- I was very hungry. I **had to eat** something. (*nicht* I must eat)
  … *Ich musste etwas essen.*
- We **had to walk** home last night. There were no buses. (*nicht* We must walk)
  Wir mussten gestern zu Fuß nach Hause gehen. …

Zum Unterschied zwischen **must** *und* **have to** *siehe Unit 34D.*

C

mustn't (= must not)

mustn't (do something) *entspricht im Deutschen 'nicht dürfen' oder 'nicht sollen'*:
- I **must go**. I **mustn't be** late.
  Ich muss weg. Ich darf nicht zu spät kommen.
- I **mustn't forget** to phone Chris.
  Ich darf nicht vergessen, Chris anzurufen.
- Be happy! You **mustn't be** sad.
  Sei froh! Du darfst/sollst nicht unglücklich sein.
- You **mustn't touch** the pictures.
  Du darfst/sollst die Bilder nicht anfassen!

You mustn't touch the pictures.

D

don't need to

I **don't need** (to do something) *entspricht im Deutschen 'nicht müssen'*:
- I **don't need to go** yet. I can stay a little longer.
  Ich muss noch nicht gehen. …
- You **don't need to shout**. I can hear you OK.
  Du muss nicht schreien. Ich kann dich gut hören.

Man kann auch sagen **don't have to** … :
- I **don't have to go** yet. I can stay a little longer.

Vergleichen Sie **don't need to** *und* **mustn't**:
- You **don't need to** go. You can stay here if you want.
  Du musst nicht gehen. …
- You **mustn't** go. You must stay here.
  Du darfst nicht gehen. …

I have to … → Unit 34

Übungen

Unit 32

32.1 Vervollständigen Sie die Sätze mit **must** und einem der folgenden Verben:

be   ~~eat~~   go   learn   meet   wash   win

1. I'm very hungry. I ...**must eat**... something.
2. Marilyn is a very interesting person. You .... her.
3. My hands are dirty. I .... them.
4. You .... to drive. It will be very useful.
5. I .... shopping. I need to buy some food.
6. The game tomorrow is very important for us. We ....
7. You can't always have things immediately. You .... patient.

32.2 Schreiben Sie **I must** oder **I had to**.

1. ...**I had to**... walk home last night. There were no buses.
2. It's late. .... go now.
3. I don't usually work on Saturdays, but last Saturday .... work.
4. .... get up early tomorrow. I have a lot to do.
5. I came here by train. The train was full and .... stand all the way.
6. I was nearly late for my appointment this morning. .... run to get there on time.
7. I forgot to phone David yesterday. .... phone him later today.

32.3 Vervollständigen Sie die Sätze mit **mustn't** oder **don't need to** und einem der folgenden Verben:

forget   ~~go~~   lose   phone   rush   wait

1. I ...**don't need to go**... home yet. I can stay a little longer.
2. We have a lot of time. We ....
3. Keep these papers in a safe place. You .... them.
4. I'm not ready yet, but you .... for me. You can go now and I'll come later.
5. We .... to turn off the lights before we leave.
6. I must contact David, but I .... him – I can send him an email.

32.4 Finden Sie Sätze im rechten Kästchen mit der gleichen Bedeutung wie die Sätze im linken Kästchen.

1 We can leave the meeting early.	A We must stay until the end.	1 E
2 We must leave the meeting early.	B We couldn't stay until the end.	2 ....
3 We mustn't leave the meeting early.	C We can't stay until the end.	3 ....
4 We had to leave the meeting early.	D We can stay until the end.	4 ....
5 We don't need to leave the meeting early.	E We don't need to stay until the end.	5 ....

32.5 Vervollständigen Sie die Sätze mit **must**, **had to**, **mustn't** oder **don't need to**.

1. You ...**don't need to**... go. You can stay here if you want.
2. It's a fantastic film. You ...**must**... see it.
3. The restaurant won't be busy tonight. We .... reserve a table.
4. I was very busy last week. I .... work every evening.
5. I want to know what happened. You .... tell me.
6. I don't want Sue to know what happened. You .... tell her.
7. I .... go now or I'll be late for my appointment.
8. 'Why were you so late?' 'I .... wait half an hour for a bus.'
9. We .... decide now. We can decide later.
10. It's Lisa's birthday next week. I .... forget to buy her a present.

32.6 Übersetzen Sie ins Englische.

Verspätung haben = be delayed

1. Ich muss dieses Wochenende das Haus putzen.
2. Simon musste heute Früh aufstehen.
3. Du darfst das nicht tun!
4. Du musst vorsichtig sein!
5. Du musst nicht mitkommen, wenn du müde bist.
6. Wir dürfen nicht vergessen Milch zu kaufen.
7. Ich kann es alleine machen. Sie müssen mir nicht helfen.
8. Unser Flugzeug hatte Verspätung. Wir mussten vier Stunden am Flughafen warten.

75

Unit 33: should

A

You shouldn't watch TV so much.

should + *Infinitiv*
(**should do** / **should watch** *usw.*):

I/we/you/they he/she/it	should shouldn't	do stop go watch *usw.*

B

You **should** do something = *Du solltest etwas tun*:
- Tom doesn't study enough. He **should study** harder.
  Tom lernt nicht genug. Er sollte mehr lernen.
- It's a good film. You **should go** and see it. ... *Du solltest ihn sehen.*
- When you play tennis, you **should** always **watch** the ball.
  Wenn Sie Tennis spielen, sollten Sie immer den Ball beobachten.

C

Die Verneinung von **should** ist **shouldn't** (= should not):
- Tom **shouldn't go** to bed so late. *Tom sollte nicht so spät ins Bett gehen.*
- You watch TV all the time. You **shouldn't watch** TV so much.
  Du siehst immer fern. Du solltest nicht so viel fernsehen.

D

Man verwendet oft **think** mit **should** um eine Meinung auszudrücken.

I think ... **should** ... (*Ich meine/glaube/finde, du solltest / er sollte usw.*):
- **I think** Lisa **should buy** some new clothes.
  Ich meine, Lisa sollte neue Kleider kaufen.
- It's late. **I think** I **should go** home now.
  ... *Ich glaube, ich sollte jetzt nach Hause gehen.*
- A: Shall I buy this coat?
  B: Yes, **I think** you **should**.
  Ja, ich finde, du solltest (ihn kaufen).

Do you think I should buy this hat?

I don't think ... **should** ... (*Ich meine/glaube/finde, du solltest / er sollte usw. nicht*):
- **I don't think** you **should work** so hard.
  Ich finde, Sie sollten nicht so viel arbeiten.
- **I don't think** we **should go** yet. It's too early.
  Ich glaube, wir sollten noch nicht gehen ...
  (*wörtlich: 'Ich glaube nicht, dass wir schon gehen sollten.'*)

Do you think ... **should** ... ?:
- **Do you think** I **should buy** this hat?
  Meinst du, ich sollte diesen Hut kaufen?
- What time **do you think** we **should go** home?
  Um wie viel Uhr glaubst du, dass wir nach Hause gehen sollten?

E

Anstatt **should** kann man auch **ought to** sagen:
- It's a good film. You **ought to go** and see it. ... *Du solltest ...*
- I think Lisa **ought to buy** some new clothes. *Ich finde, Lisa sollte ...*

shall → Units 28–29   must → Unit 32

Übungen

Unit 33

33.1 Vervollständigen Sie die Sätze mit **you should** und einem der folgenden Verben:

> eat   go   take   visit   ~~watch~~   wear

1. When you play tennis, *you should watch* the ball.
2. It's late and you're very tired. _____ to bed.
3. _____ plenty of fruit and vegetables.
4. If you have time, _____ the Science Museum. It's very interesting.
5. When you're driving, _____ a seat belt.
6. It's too far to walk from here to the station. _____ a taxi.

33.2 Schreiben Sie, was die Leute in den Bildern nicht tun sollten. Verwenden Sie **He/She shouldn't ... so ...** .

1. You watch TV too much.
2. You eat too much.
3. You work too hard.
4. You drive too fast.

1. *She shouldn't watch TV so much.*
2. He _____
3. _____ hard.
4. _____

33.3 Schreiben Sie Sätze über folgende Situationen. Verwenden Sie:
I think ... should ... oder **I don't think ... should ...**

1. We have to get up early tomorrow. (go home now) *I think we should go home now.*
2. That coat is too big for you. (buy it) *I don't think you should buy it.*
3. You don't need your car. (sell it) _____
4. Karen needs a rest. (have a holiday) _____
5. Sarah and Dan are too young. (get married) _____
6. You're not well this morning. (go to work) _____
7. James isn't well today. (go to the doctor) _____
8. The hotel is too expensive for us. (stay there) _____

33.4 Schreiben Sie Ihre eigene Meinung. Verwenden Sie **should**.

1. I think *everybody should learn another language.*
2. I think everybody _____
3. I think _____
4. I don't think _____
5. I think I should _____

33.5 Übersetzen Sie ins Englische.

1. Du solltest öfter schwimmen gehen.   öfter = more often
2. Kinder sollten mehr Bücher lesen.
3. Sie sollten nicht immer so spät kommen.
4. Meinst du, ich sollte dieses Kleid tragen?
5. Tom sollte nicht so oft ausgehen. Er ist immer müde.
6. Ich finde, wir sollten Jenny ein Buch zum Geburtstag kaufen.
7. Meinen Sie, dass ich zur Polizei gehen sollte?
8. Ich glaube, dass wir nicht so lange bleiben sollten.
9. Ich finde, dass du nicht so viel Fleisch essen solltest. Du solltest mehr Salat essen.

Unit 34: I have to ...

A

This is my medicine. I have to take it three times a day.

I have to do something = *ich muss etwas tun; ich bin verpflichtet es zu tun*

I/we/you/they	**have**	to do
		to work
he/she/it	**has**	to go
		to wear *usw.*

- I'll be late for work tomorrow. I **have to go** to the dentist. ... *Ich muss zum Zahnarzt.*
- Jane starts work at 7 o'clock, so she **has to get** up at 6. ... *also muss sie um 6 aufstehen.*
- You **have to pass** a test before you can get a driving licence. *Sie müssen eine Prüfung bestehen ...*

B

Die Vergangenheit von **have/has to** *ist* **had to** (= *musste/mussten*):
- I was late for work yesterday. I **had to go** to the dentist. ... *Ich musste zum Zahnarzt gehen.*
- We **had to walk** home last night. There were no buses.
  Wir mussten gestern Abend zu Fuß nach Hause gehen. ...

C

Die Frageform und die Verneinung bildet man mit **do/does** (*Gegenwart*) *und* **did** (*Vergangenheit*):

Gegenwart

do	I/we/you/they	have to ... ?
does	he/she/it	

I/we/you/they	**don't**	have to ...
he/she/it	**doesn't**	

Vergangenheit

did	I/we/you/they he/she/it	have to ... ?

I/we/you/they he/she/it	**didn't have to** ...

- What time **do** you **have to go** to the dentist tomorrow?
  Um wie viel Uhr müssen Sie morgen ... gehen?
- **Does** Jane **have to work** on Sundays? *Muss Jane sonntags arbeiten?*
- Why **did** they **have to leave** the party early?
  Warum mussten sie das Fest früh verlassen?

I **don't have to** (do something) = *Ich muss nicht etwas tun; ich bin nicht verpflichtet, es zu tun*:
- I'm not working tomorrow, so I **don't have to get** up early.
  ... *also muss ich nicht früh aufstehen.*
- Ian **doesn't have to work** very hard. He's got an easy job.
  Ian muss nicht sehr hart arbeiten. ...
- We **didn't have to wait** very long for the bus – it came in a few minutes.
  Wir mussten nicht sehr lange ... warten ...

D

must *und* **have to**

Wenn man die eigene Meinung ausdrückt, kann man **must** *oder* **have to** *verwenden*:
- It's a fantastic film. You **must** see it. *oder* You **have to** see it. ... *Du musst ihn sehen!*

Wenn man nicht die eigene Meinung ausdrückt, verwendet man **have to** (*nicht* **must**). **Have to** *drückt aus, dass die Verpflichtung oder Notwendigkeit als von außen kommend (nicht selbst bestimmt) empfunden wird*:
- Jane won't be at work this afternoon. She **has to** go to the doctor. ... *Sie muss zum Arzt.*
  (*Dies ist nicht meine Meinung, sondern eine Tatsache, die ich berichte.*)
- Jane isn't well. She doesn't want to go to the doctor, but I told her she **must** go.
  (*Dies ist meine Meinung.*)

must / mustn't / don't need to → Unit 32

Übungen

Unit 34

34.1 Vervollständigen Sie die Sätze. Verwenden Sie **have to** oder **has to** und eines der folgenden Verben:

| do | hit | read | speak | travel | ~~wear~~ |

1. My eyes are not very good. I ....*have to wear*.......... glasses.
2. At the end of the course all the students .... a test.
3. Sarah is studying literature. She .... a lot of books.
4. Albert doesn't understand much English. You .... very slowly to him.
5. Kate is often away from home. She .... a lot in her job.
6. In tennis you .... the ball over the net.

34.2 Vervollständigen Sie die Sätze. Verwenden Sie **have to** oder **had to** und eines der folgenden Verben:

| answer | buy | change | go | ~~walk~~ |

1. We ....*had to walk*.......... home last night. There were no buses.
2. It's late. I .... now. I'll see you tomorrow.
3. I went to the supermarket after work yesterday. I .... some food.
4. This train doesn't go all the way to London. You .... at Bristol.
5. We did an exam yesterday. We .... six questions out of ten.

34.3 Vervollständigen Sie die Fragen. Beachten Sie, dass manche in der Gegenwart und andere in der Vergangenheit sind.

1. I have to get up early tomorrow. — What time ....*do you have to get up*.......... ?
2. George had to wait a long time. — How long .... ?
3. Lisa has to go somewhere. — Where .... ?
4. We had to pay a lot of money. — How much .... ?
5. I have to do some work. — What exactly .... ?

34.4 Schreiben Sie Sätze mit **don't/doesn't/didn't have to ...** .

1. Why are you going out? You ....*don't have to go out.*..........
2. Why is Sue waiting? She ....
3. Why did you get up early? You ....
4. Why is Paul working so hard? He ....
5. Why do you want to leave now? We ....

34.5 Welcher Satz ist richtig? In manchen Fällen sind **must** und **have to** beide möglich. Manchmal ist nur eins von beiden möglich.

1. It's a fantastic film. You <u>must see / have to</u> see it. (*beide sind richtig*)
2. Jessica won't be at work this afternoon. She ~~must go~~ / has to go to the doctor. (<u>has to go</u> *ist richtig*)
3. You can't park your car here for nothing. You <u>must pay / have to pay</u>.
4. I didn't have any money with me last night, so I <u>must borrow / had to borrow</u> some.
5. I eat too much chocolate. I really <u>must stop / have to stop</u>.
6. Paul is in a hurry. He <u>must meet / has to meet</u> somebody in five minutes.
7. What's wrong? You <u>must tell / have to tell</u> me. I want to help you.

34.6 Schreiben Sie Sätze über einiges, was Sie (oder Ihre Familie und Freunde) machen müssen oder machen mussten.

1. (every day)   *I have to travel ten miles every day.*
2. (every day)   ....
3. (yesterday)   ....
4. (tomorrow)   ....

34.7 Übersetzen Sie ins Englische.   *lernen = study*

1. Ich muss jeden Morgen um 8 Uhr im Büro sein.
2. Ben muss heute Abend für seine Prüfung lernen.
3. Ich muss die Fenster putzen. Sie sind schmutzig.
4. Für diesen Kurs müssen Sie keine Prüfung machen.
5. Wir mussten ein Taxi nach Hause nehmen, weil es keine Busse gab.
6. Musst du morgen arbeiten?
7. Muss Rachel eine Brille tragen, wenn sie liest?
8. Die Kinder mussten gestern nicht früh ins Bett gehen.
9. Es ist sehr wichtig. Du musst zuhören!

Unit 35

Would you like … ?   I'd like …

A

Would you like … ? = *Möchten Sie … ?*

Man verwendet **Would you like … ?** *um etwas anzubieten:*
- A: **Would you like** some coffee?
  Möchten Sie Kaffee?
  B: No, thank you. *Nein danke.*
- A: **Would you like** a chocolate?
  Möchten Sie eine Praline?
  B: Yes, please. *Ja, gerne.*
- A: What **would you like**, tea or coffee?
  Was möchten Sie – Tee oder Kaffee?
  B: Tea, please. *Tee bitte.*

Man verwendet **Would you like to … ?** *auch um jemanden einzuladen:*
- **Would you like to go** for a walk? *Möchtest du spazierengehen?*
- A: **Would you like to eat** with us on Sunday? *Möchten Sie am Sonntag mit uns essen gehen?*
  B: Yes, **I'd love to**. *Ja, sehr gerne.*
- What **would you like to do** this evening? *Was möchtest du heute Abend machen?*

B

Man verwendet **I'd like …** (*Ich möchte … / Ich hätte gerne …*), um Bitten auszudrücken.

I'd like = **I would** like (*I'd like ist höflicher als* I want.):
- I'm thirsty. **I'd like** a drink. *Ich hätte gerne etwas zu trinken.*
- (in einem Fremdenverkehrsamt) **I'd like** some information about hotels, please.
  Ich hätte gerne einige Informationen …
- I'm feeling tired. **I'd like to stay** at home this evening. *… Ich möchte heute Abend zuhause bleiben.*

C

Would you like … ? *und* **Do you like … ?**

Would you like … ? / I'd like …	**Do you like … ? / I like …**
Möchten Sie (Möchtest du) … ? / Ich möchte …	*Mögen Sie (Magst du) … ? / Ich mag … / Mir gefällt … / Ich mache gerne … Gefällt Ihnen (Gefällt dir) … ? Machen Sie (Machst du) gerne … ?*

Would you like some tea? *Möchten Sie etwas Tee?*
- A: **Would you like** to go to the cinema tonight?
  Möchtest du heute Abend ins Kino gehen?
  B: Yes, I'd love to. *Ja, gerne.*
- **I'd like** an orange, please.
  Ich möchte eine Orange, bitte.
- What **would you like** to do next weekend?
  Was möchtest du nächstes Wochenende machen?

Do you like tea? *Mögen Sie Tee?*
- A: **Do you like** going to the cinema?
  Gehst du gerne ins Kino?
  B: Yes, I go to the cinema a lot.
  Ja, ich gehe oft ins Kino.
- **I like** oranges.
  Ich mag Orangen.
- What **do you like** to do at weekends?
  Was machst du gerne am Wochenende?

like to do *und* like -ing → Unit 53   I would do *something* if … → Unit 100

Übungen

35.1 Was sagen die Personen auf in den Bildern? Verwenden Sie **Would you like ... ?**

1. Would you like a chocolate?
2.
3.
4.
5.
6.

35.2 Was würden Sie Sue in folgenden Situationen fragen? Verwenden Sie **Would you like to ... ?**

1. You want to go to the cinema tonight. Perhaps Sue will go with you. (go)
   You say: _Would you like to go to the cinema tonight?_
2. You want to play tennis tomorrow. Perhaps Sue will play too. (play)
   You say: ____
3. You have an extra ticket for a concert next week. Perhaps Sue will come. (come)
   You say: ____
4. It's raining and Sue is going out. She doesn't have an umbrella, but you have one. (borrow)
   You say: ____

35.3 Welcher Satz ist richtig?

1. '~~Do you like~~ / Would you like a chocolate?' 'Yes, please.' (Would you like ist richtig)
2. 'Do you like / Would you like bananas?' 'Yes, I love them.'
3. 'Do you like / Would you like an ice cream?' 'No, thank you.'
4. 'What do you like / would you like to drink?' 'A glass of water, please.'
5. 'Do you like / Would you like to go out for a walk?' 'Not now. Perhaps later.'
6. I like / I'd like tomatoes, but I don't eat them very often.
7. What time do you like / would you like to have dinner this evening?
8. 'Do you like / Would you like something to eat?' 'No, thanks. I'm not hungry.'
9. 'Do you like / Would you like your new job?' 'Yes, I'm enjoying it.'
10. I'm tired. I like / I'd like to go to sleep now.
11. 'I like / I'd like a sandwich, please.' 'Sure. What kind of sandwich?'
12. 'What kind of music do you like / would you like?' 'All kinds.'

35.4 Übersetzen Sie ins Englische.

Ski fahren = go skiing

1. 'Möchten Sie ein Glas Saft?' 'Ja, gerne.'
2. Ich möchte eine Tasse Kaffee und ein Stück Kuchen, bitte.
3. Möchtest du einen Apfel oder eine Orange?
4. A: Möchtest du mit uns Ski fahren?
   B: Ja, sehr gerne.
5. Fährst du gerne in die Berge?
6. Ich hätte gerne drei Äpfel und vier Bananen.
7. A: Gehen Sie gerne ins Theater?
   B: Ja, aber ich gehe nicht sehr oft.
8. Ich trinke gerne Tee, aber jetzt möchte ich ein Glas Wasser.

Unit 36

Do this! Don't do that! Let's do this! *(der Imperativ)*

A

Man verwendet **come/look/go/wait/be** usw. wie im Deutschen, um jemanden aufzufordern etwas zu tun:
- '**Come** here and **look** at this!' 'What is it?' *'Komm her und sieh dir das an!'* ...
- I don't want to talk to you. **Go** away! ... *Geh weg!*
- I'm not ready yet. Please **wait** for me. ... *Bitte warte(t) auf mich.*
- Please **be** quiet. I'm working. *Sei(d) bitte still.*

Es gibt nur eine Form für Singular und Plural:
- Are you ready? **Follow** me. *Bist du bereit? Folge mir!*
- Are you both ready? **Follow** me. *Seid Ihr (Sind Sie) beide bereit? Folgt (Folgen Sie) mir!*

B

Man verwendet auch den Imperativ, um gute Wünsche auszudrücken:
- Bye! **Have** a good holiday! *Schönen Urlaub!*
- **Have** a nice time! **Have** fun! ... *Viel Spaß!*
- **Have** a good flight! *Guten Flug!*

Es ist auch möglich den Imperativ zu verwenden, um jemandem etwas anzubieten:
- '**Have** a chocolate.' 'Oh, thanks.'
  'Wie wär's mit einer Praline?' 'Oh, danke.'

C

Die Verneinung des Imperativs bildet man mit **don't** ... :
- Be careful! **Don't fall**. *Sei vorsichtig! Fall nicht hinunter!*
- Please **don't go**. Stay here with me. *Bitte geh nicht. Bleib hier bei mir!*
- Be here on time. **Don't be** late. *Sei bitte rechtzeitig hier. Komm nicht zu spät!*

D

Um andere aufzufordern, etwas gemeinsam mit einem zu tun, verwendet man **Let's** ... . **Let's** = Let us.
- It's a nice day. **Let's go** out.
  ... *Gehen wir raus!*
- Come on! **Let's dance**.
  Komm! Tanzen wir!
- Are you ready? **Let's go**.
  Bist du bereit? Gehen wir!
- **Let's have** fish for dinner tonight.
  Wollen wir heute Abend Fisch essen?
- A: Shall we go out tonight?
  B: No, I'm tired. **Let's stay** at home.
  ... *Bleiben wir zuhause.*

Die Verneinung ist **Let's not** ... :
- It's cold. **Let's not** go out. Let's stay at home.
  Es ist kalt. Gehen wir nicht raus. Bleiben wir zuhause.
- **Let's not** have fish for dinner tonight. Let's have chicken.
  Essen wir lieber keinen Fisch heute Abend. Wie wär's mit Hähnchen?

shall we ... ? → Unit 29

Übungen

Unit 36

36.1 Was sagen die Personen auf den Bildern? Vervollständigen Sie die Sprechblasen mit der Imperativform (**buy**/**come** usw.) folgender Verben. In manchen Fällen müssen Sie die Verneinung verwenden (**don't buy** / **don't come** usw.).

be   buy   ~~come~~   ~~drink~~   drop   forget   have   sit   sleep   smile

1. Come in!
2. Don't drink the water!
3. It's too expensive. .... it.
4. OK, are you ready? .... !
5. .... on the cat!
6. Bye! .... a nice time!
7. .... to phone me. Don't worry. I won't.
8. I'm going to bed now. OK. .... well.
9. .... careful with that vase. .... it!

36.2 Vervollständigen Sie die Sätze. Verwenden Sie **let's** und:

~~go for a swim~~   go to a restaurant   take a taxi   wait a little   watch TV

1 Would you like to play tennis?   No, let's go for a swim.
2 Do you want to walk home?   No, ...
3 Shall I put a CD on?   No, ...
4 Shall we eat at home?   No, ...
5 Would you like to go now?   No, ...

36.3 Beantworten Sie die Fragen mit **No, don't …** oder **No, let's not …** .

1 Shall I wait for you?   No, don't wait for me.
2 Shall we go home now?   No, let's not go home yet.
3 Shall we go out?
4 Do you want me to close the window?
5 Shall I phone you tonight?
6 Do you think we should wait for Andy?
7 Do you want me to turn on the light?
8 Shall we go by bus?

36.4 Übersetzen Sie ins Englische.

1 Die Türe ist abgeschlossen. Mach sie bitte auf!
2 Das Baby schläft. Seid bitte ruhig!
3 Das ist ein Geheimnis. Erzähl es nicht unsern Freunden!
4 Gehen wir in die Stadt!
5 Auf Wiedersehen. Gute Reise!
6 Ich bin müde. Spielen wir heute nicht Tennis!
7 A: Wie wär's mit noch einem Stück Kuchen?
   B: Nein danke.
8 A: Was machen wir Samstag Abend?
   B: Gehen wir ins Kino!

abgeschlossen = locked
Geheimnis = secret
Reise = trip

Unit 37 I used to …

A

DAVE vor einigen Jahren — I work in a factory.
DAVE heute — I work in a supermarket. I used to work in a factory.

Dave **used to work** in a factory. Now he **works** in a supermarket.
Dave hat einmal in einer Fabrik gearbeitet. Jetzt arbeitet er in einem Supermarkt.

he **used to** work	he works
Vergangenheit	Jetzt

B

Man sagt **I used to work** … / **she used to have** … / **they used to be** … usw.:

| I/you/we/they he/she/it | used to | be work have play usw. |

Used to drückt Zustände oder Gewohnheiten in der Vergangenheit aus, die nicht mehr bestehen.
Used to kann im Deutschen mit der Vergangenheit + 'einmal' oder 'früher' wiedergegeben werden.

- When I was a child, I **used to like** chocolate.
  Als Kind mochte ich gerne Schokolade.
- I **used to read** a lot of books, but I don't read much these days.
  Ich habe früher viel gelesen, aber heutzutage …
- Lisa has got short hair now, but it **used to be** very long.
  Lisa hat jetzt … aber früher war es sehr lang.
- They **used to live** in the same street as us, so we **used to see** them a lot. We don't see them much these days.
  Sie haben früher in derselben Straße gewohnt wie wir. …
- Helen **used to have** a piano, but she sold it a few years ago.
  Helen hatte einmal ein Klavier, aber …

I used to have very long hair.

Die Verneinung ist **I didn't use to** … :
- When I was a child, I **didn't use to like** tomatoes.
  Als Kind mochte ich keine …

Die Frageform ist **did you use to** … **?**:
- Where **did** you **use to live** before you came here?
  Wo haben Sie gelebt bevor Sie …

C

Used to wird nur für die Vergangenheit verwendet. Es gibt keine Gegenwartsform wie 'I use to …':
- I **used to play** tennis. These days I **play** golf. (nicht I use to play golf)
  Ich habe früher … gespielt. Heutzutage spiele ich …
- We usually **get** up early. (nicht We use to get up early)
  Meistens stehen wir früh auf.

Übungen

37.1 Schreiben Sie Sätze mit **used to ...** passend zu den Situationen in den Bildern.

1. She used to have long hair.
2. He .... football.
3. .... a taxi driver.
4. .... in the country.
5. ....
6. This building ....

37.2 Karen arbeitet sehr viel und hat wenig Freizeit. Vor einigen Jahren war das anders.

Schreiben Sie über Karen und verwenden Sie **used to ...** .

1. She used to swim every day.
2. She ....
3. ....
4. ....
5. ....
6. ....

37.3 Vervollständigen Sie die Sätze mit **used to** oder mit dem present simple (**I play** / **he lives** usw.).

1. I _used to play_ tennis. I stopped playing a few years ago.
2. 'Do you do any sport?' 'Yes, I _play_ basketball.'
3. 'Do you have a car?' 'No, I .... one, but I sold it.'
4. George .... a waiter. Now he's the manager of a hotel.
5. 'Do you go to work by car?' 'Sometimes, but most days I .... by train.'
6. When I was a child, I never .... meat, but I eat it now.
7. Mary loves watching TV. She .... TV every evening.
8. We .... near the airport, but we moved to the city centre a few years ago.
9. Normally I start work at 7 o'clock, so I .... up very early.
10. What games .... you .... when you were a child?

37.4 Übersetzen Sie ins Englische. Verwenden Sie, wenn möglich, **used to ...** .

Gemüse = vegetables

1. Als Kind habe ich Fußball gespielt.
2. Kate hat früher in einer Bank gearbeitet.
3. John und Linda haben einmal in Paris gelebt.
4. Als Kind mochte ich kein Gemüse.
5. Tom hat früher keine Brille getragen.
6. Wir sind früher viel ins Kino gegangen.
7. Wir gehen Samstagabends meistens aus.
8. Hattest du früher mal lange Haare?

Unit 38: there is   there are

A

There's a man on the roof.
Da ist ein Mann auf dem Dach.

There's a train at 10.30.
Es gibt einen Zug um 10.30.

SUNDAY
MONDAY
TUESDAY
WEDNESDAY
THURSDAY
FRIDAY
SATURDAY
} 7

There are seven days in a week.
Es gibt sieben Tage in der Woche.

There is / **There are** entspricht im Deutschen 'es gibt/ist/sind' ('Es steht/stehen') oder 'da gibt/ist/sind' ('Da steht/stehen'):

Singular

there is …	(**there's**)
is there … ?	
there is not …	(**there isn't**)
	oder **there's not**)

- **There's** a big tree in the garden. *Da steht ein großer Baum …*
- A: Do you have any money?
  B: Yes, **there's** some in my bag.
    Ja, ich habe welches in meiner Tasche. (Es ist welches …)
- A: Excuse me, **is there** a hotel near here?
    … gibt es hier in der Nähe ein Hotel?
  B: Yes, **there is**. / No, **there isn't**.
    Ja (es gibt eins). / Nein (es gibt keins).
- We can't go skiing. **There isn't** any snow.
    … Es gibt keinen Schnee.

Plural

there are …	
are there … ?	
there are not …	(**there aren't**)

- **There are** some big trees in the garden. *Da stehen …*
- **There are** a lot of accidents on this road.
    Es gibt viele Unfälle auf dieser Straße.
- A: **Are there** any restaurants near here?
    Gibt es einige Restaurants hier in der Nähe?
  B: Yes, **there are**. / No, **there aren't**.
    Ja (es gibt einige). / Nein (es gibt keine).
- This restaurant is very quiet. **There aren't** many people here.
    … Es sind nicht viele Leute hier.

B

Vergleichen Sie **there is** und **it is**:

there is

There's a book on the table.
(*nicht* It's a book on the table.)
Es/Da ist ein Buch auf dem Tisch.

it is

I like this book . **It's** interesting.
(**It** = this book)
Dieses Buch gefällt mir. Es ist interessant.

Vergleichen Sie:

- 'What's **that noise**?' '**It**'s a train.' (**It** = that noise)
  'Was ist das für ein Geräusch?' 'Das ist ein Zug.'
  There's a train at 10.30. **It**'s a fast train. (**It** = the 10.30 train)
  Es gibt einen Zug um 10.30. Es ist ein schneller Zug.

- **There's** a lot of salt in this soup. *Es ist viel Salz in dieser Suppe.*
  I don't like **this soup**. **It**'s too salty. (**It** = this soup)
  Mir schmeckt diese Suppe nicht. Sie ist zu salzig.

there was / were / has been *usw.* → Unit 39   it *und* there → Unit 40   some *und* any → Unit 76

Übungen

Unit 38

38.1
Kentham ist eine Kleinstadt. Schreiben Sie Aussagen über Kentham mit **There is**/**are** oder **There isn't**/**aren't** anhand der Informationen in der Tabelle.

1	a castle?	No
2	any restaurants?	Yes (a lot)
3	a hospital?	Yes
4	a swimming pool?	No
5	any cinemas?	Yes (two)
6	a university?	No
7	any big hotels?	No

1 *There isn't a castle.*
2 *There are a lot of restaurants.*
3 ....
4 ....
5 ....
6 ....
7 ....

38.2
Schreiben Sie Aussagen über Ihre Stadt (oder über eine Stadt, die Sie kennen). Verwenden Sie: **There is**/**are** oder **There isn't**/**aren't**.

1 *There are a few restaurants.*
2 *There's a big park.*
3 ....
4 ....
5 ....
6 ....

38.3
Vervollständigen Sie die Sätze mit **there is** / **there isn't** / **is there** oder **there are** / **there aren't** / **are there**.

1 Kentham isn't an old town. *There aren't* any old buildings.
2 Look! .... a picture of your brother in the newspaper!
3 'Excuse me, ... a bank near here?' 'Yes, at the end of the street.'
4 .... five people in my family: my parents, my two sisters and me.
5 'How many students .... in the class?' 'Twenty.'
6 The road is usually very quiet. .... much traffic.
7 '.................... a bus from the city centre to the airport?' 'Yes, every 20 minutes.'
8 '.................... any problems?' 'No, everything is OK.'
9 .... nowhere to sit down. .... any chairs.

38.4
Schreiben Sie Sätze mit **There are …**. Verwenden Sie Begriffe aus den drei Kästchen.

~~seven~~	twenty-six		letters	~~days~~		September	the solar system
eight	thirty		players	days		the USA	~~a week~~
fifteen	fifty		planets	states		a rugby team	the English alphabet

1 *There are seven days in a week.*
2 ....
3 ....
4 ....
5 ....
6 ....

38.5
Vervollständigen Sie die Sätze mit **there's** / **is there** oder **it's** / **is it**.

1 '*There's* a train at 10.30.' '*Is it* a fast train?'
2 I'm not going to buy this shirt. .... too expensive.
3 'What's wrong?' '.................... something in my eye.'
4 .... a red car outside your house. .... yours?
5 '.................... anything good on TV tonight?' 'Yes, ... a programme I want to see at 8.15.'
6 'What's that building?' '.................... a school.'
7 '.................... a restaurant in this hotel?' 'No, I'm afraid not.'

38.6
Übersetzen Sie ins Englische. Verwenden Sie wenn möglich **there**.

Dorf = village
vor = in front of

1 Es gibt eine alte Kirche im Dorf.
2 Es gibt keinen Flughafen in unserer Stadt.
3 Es sind viele Blumen in unserem Garten.
4 'Das ist unser Haus.' 'Es ist sehr schön.'
5 Gibt es ein gutes Restaurant hier in der Nähe?
6 Eine Katze ist auf dem Sofa.
7 Es ist Sonntag. Es sind heute viele Leute im Park.
8 Da ist eine Tasche auf dem Tisch. Ist das Ihre?
9 Es steht ein alter Baum vor dem Haus. Er ist sehr groß.

Unit 39: there was/were   there has/have been   there will be

A

there was / there were = 'es gab' oder 'es war/waren' ('es stand/standen')

There is a train every hour.
Es gibt jede Stunde einen Zug.

The time now is 11.15.
There was a train at 11 o'clock.
Es gab einen Zug um 11 Uhr.

Vergleichen Sie:

there is/are (Gegenwart)

- **There is** nothing on TV tonight.
  Es gibt nichts (sehenswertes) …
- **There are** a lot of people here today.
  Es sind heute viele Leute hier.
- Is everything OK? **Are there** any problems?
  … Gibt es Probleme?
- I'm hungry, but **there isn't** anything to eat.
  … aber es gibt nichts zu essen.
- **There's** a small house next to the church.
  Da steht ein kleines Haus …

there was/were (Vergangenheit)

- **There was** nothing on TV last night.
  Es gab nichts (sehenswertes) …
- **There were** a lot of people here yesterday.
  Es waren gestern …
- Was everything OK yesterday? **Were there** any problems? … *Gab es Probleme?*
- I was hungry when I got home, but **there wasn't** anything to eat.
  … aber es gab nichts zu essen.
- **There was** a small house next to the church 30 years ago.
  Vor dreißig Jahren stand ein kleines Haus …

B

there has been / there have been (present perfect) = 'es hat gegeben' oder 'es gab'

There's been an accident.

- Look! **There's been** an accident.
  (**there's been** = there **has** been)
  Es hat einen Unfall gegeben. / Es ist ein Unfall passiert.
- This road is very dangerous. **There have been** many accidents.   *… Es hat (schon) viele Unfälle gegeben.*

Vergleichen Sie mit **there was** (Vergangenheit):

- **There was** an accident **last night**.
  (*nicht* There has been an accident last night.)
  Es ist gestern ein Unfall passiert.

Siehe Unit 21 zum Vergleich von *past simple* und *present perfect*.

C

there will be = 'es wird/werden sein', 'es wird geben' oder 'es gibt'

There will be rain tomorrow afternoon.

- Do you think **there will be** a lot of people at the party on Saturday?
  Glaubst du, es werden viele Leute auf dem Fest … sein?
- The manager of the company is leaving, so **there will be** a new manager soon.
  … also wird es bald einen neuen Leiter geben.
- I'm going away tomorrow. I'll do my packing today because **there won't be** time tomorrow.
  (**there won't be** = there **will not** be)
  Ich werde heute packen, weil ich morgen keine Zeit haben werde (… weil morgen dafür keine Zeit ist).

---

was/were ➔ **Unit 11**   has/have been ➔ **Units 16–19**   will ➔ **Unit 28**   there is/are ➔ **Unit 38**
there *und* it ➔ **Unit 40**   some *und* any ➔ **Unit 76**

Übungen

Unit 39

39.1 In den Bildern sehen Sie dasselbe Zimmer heute und letzte Woche. Jetzt ist das Zimmer leer, aber was war letzte Woche noch darin? Schreiben Sie Aussagen mit **There was ...** oder **There were ...** und den Wörtern in der Liste.

an armchair   a carpet   some flowers   a sofa
some books   ~~a clock~~   three pictures   a small table

last week

now

1 *There was a clock* .... on the wall near the window.
2 .... on the floor.
3 .... on the wall near the door.
4 .... in the middle of the room.
5 .... on the table.
6 .... on the shelves.
7 .... in the corner near the door.
8 .... opposite the armchair.

39.2 Vervollständigen Sie die Sätze mit **there was** / **there wasn't** / **was there** oder **there were** / **there weren't** / **were there**.

1 I was hungry, but *there wasn't* anything to eat.
2 Was everything OK yesterday? *Were there* any problems?
3 I opened the envelope, but it was empty. .... nothing in it.
4 'We stayed at a very nice hotel.' 'Really? .... a swimming pool?'
5 'Did you buy any bananas?' 'No, ... any in the shop.'
6 The wallet was empty. .... any money in it.
7 '............................. many people at the meeting?' 'No, very few.'
8 We didn't visit the museum. .... enough time.
9 I'm sorry I'm late. .... a lot of traffic.
10 Twenty years ago .... many tourists here. Now there are a lot.

39.3 Vervollständigen Sie die Sätze mit **there** + **is** / **are** / **was** / **were** / **has been** / **have been** / **will be**.

1 *There was* a good film on TV last night.
2 .... 24 hours in a day.
3 .... a party at the club last Friday, but I didn't go.
4 'Where can I get something to eat?' '............................. a cafe at the end of the street.'
5 'Why are the police outside the bank?' '............................. a robbery.'
6 When we arrived at the theatre, ... a long queue outside.
7 When you arrive tomorrow, ... somebody at the station to meet you.
8 Ten years ago .... 500 children at the school. Now .... more than a thousand.
9 Last week I went back to the town where I was born. It's very different now. .... a lot of changes.
10 I think everything will be OK. I don't think .... any problems.

39.4 Übersetzen Sie ins Englische. Verwenden Sie **there**.

1 Letzte Woche gab es hier ein großes Konzert.
2 Das Wetter war gestern schön. Es waren viele Kinder im Park.
3 Es wird diesen Winter viel Schnee geben.
4 Waren viele Leute auf der Party gestern Abend?
5 Vor 50 Jahren standen hier keine Häuser.
6 Glauben Sie, es wird heute Nachmittag viel Verkehr in der Stadt sein?
7 A: Warum ist das Flugzeug verspätet?
   B: Es hat ein technisches Problem gegeben.
8 Morgen wird es kein Fußballspiel geben.

verspätet = delayed
Verkehr = traffic

Unit 40

It ...

A

Man verwendet **it** für die Uhrzeit, Tag und Datum, Entfernungen und für das Wetter.
It entspricht hier meistens 'es' im Deutschen:

Uhrzeit

- What time is **it**? Wie viel Uhr ist es?
- **It**'s half past ten. Es ist halb elf.
- **It**'s late. Es ist spät.
- **It**'s time to go home. Es ist Zeit nach Hause zu gehen.

Tag/Datum

- What day is **it**? Welcher Tag ist heute? / Welcher Tag ist es?
- **It**'s Thursday. Es ist Donnerstag.
- **It**'s 16 March. Es ist der 16. März.
- **It** was my birthday yesterday. Gestern war mein Geburtstag.

Entfernungen

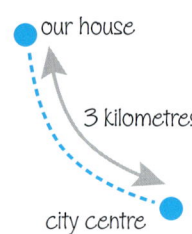

- **It**'s three kilometres from our house to the city centre.
  Es sind drei Kilometer von ... bis ...
- How far is **it** from New York to Los Angeles? Wie weit ist es ... ?

Man verwendet **far** (= weit) in Fragen (**is it far**?) und Verneinungen (**it isn't far**):
- Where's the station? **Is it far**? ... Ist es weit?
- We can walk home. **It isn't far**. ... Es ist nicht weit.

In bejahten Sätzen verwendet man **a long way** (**it's a long way**):
- **It's a long way** from here to the station. Es ist weit von hier bis zum Bahnhof.

Wetter

- **It**'s raining.   **It** isn't raining.   Is **it** snowing?
  Es regnet.   Es regnet nicht.   Schneit es?
- **It** rains a lot here.   **It** didn't rain yesterday.   Does **it** snow very often?
  Es regnet hier viel.   Es hat gestern nicht geregnet.   Schneit es sehr oft?
- **It**'s warm/hot/cold/fine/cloudy/windy/sunny/foggy/dark usw.
  Es ist warm/heiß/kalt/schön/bewölkt/windig/sonnig/neblig/dunkel usw.
- **It**'s a nice day today. Heute ist ein schöner Tag.

Vergleichen Sie **it** und **there**:
- **It rains** a lot in winter. Es regnet viel im Winter.
  There is **a lot of rain** in winter. Im Winter gibt es viel Regen.
- **It** was very **windy**. Es war sehr windig.
  There was **a strong wind** yesterday. Gestern gab es einen starken Wind.

B

It's nice to ... usw. = Es ist schön ... zu ...

It's	easy / difficult / impossible / dangerous / safe / expensive / interesting / nice / wonderful / terrible usw.	to ...

- **It**'s nice **to see you again**. Es ist schön dich wieder zu sehen.
- **It**'s impossible **to understand her**. Es ist unmöglich sie zu verstehen.
- **It** wasn't easy **to find your house**. Es war nicht einfach euer Haus zu finden.

there is → Unit 38

Übungen

40.1
Schreiben Sie über das Wetter in den Bildern. Verwenden Sie **It's ...** .

1. It's raining.
2. ....
3. ....
4. ....
5. ....
6. ....

40.2
Vervollständigen Sie die Sätze mit **it is** (**it's**) oder **is it**.

1. What time ___is it___ ?
2. We have to go now. _____ very late.
3. _____ true that Ben can fly a helicopter?
4. 'What day _____ today? Tuesday?' 'No, _____ Wednesday.'
5. _____ ten kilometres from the airport to the city centre.
6. _____ OK to call you at your office?
7. 'Do you want to walk to the hotel?' 'I don't know. How far _____ ?'
8. _____ Lisa's birthday today. She's 27.
9. I don't believe it! _____ impossible.

40.3
Bilden Sie Fragen mit **How far ... ?**

1. (here / the station) — How far is it from here to the station?
2. (the hotel / the beach) — How ....
3. (New York / Washington) ....
4. (your house / the airport) ....

40.4
Schreiben Sie **it** oder **there**.

1. The weather isn't so nice today. ___It___ 's cloudy.
2. ___There___ was a strong wind yesterday.
3. _____ 's hot in this room. Open a window.
4. _____ was a nice day yesterday. _____ was warm and sunny.
5. _____ was a storm last night. Did you hear it?
6. I was afraid because _____ was very dark.
7. _____ 's often cold here, but _____ isn't much rain.
8. _____ 's a long way from here to the nearest shop.

40.5
Vervollständigen Sie die Sätze, indem Sie Begriffe aus beiden Kästchen verbinden.

it's | easy   dangerous | to | work here   get up early
     | difficult nice | | visit different places go out alone
     | impossible interesting| | see you again   make friends

1. If you go to bed late, ___it's difficult to get up early___ in the morning.
2. Hello, Jane. .... How are you?
3. .... There is too much noise.
4. Everybody is very nice at work. ....
5. I like travelling. ....
6. Some cities are not safe. .... at night.

40.6
Übersetzen Sie ins Englische.

Stadtzentrum = city centre
Nebel = fog

1. Es ist heute sehr heiß.
2. Es ist 7.30. Es ist Zeit in die Schule zu gehen.
3. Es schneit nicht sehr oft hier.
4. Es sind fünf Kilometer zum Stadtzentrum.
5. Es gab heute Früh am Flughafen ein wenig Nebel.
6. Wie weit ist es von London nach Paris?
7. Es ist leicht Englisch zu lernen.
8. Es ist teuer jeden Tag in einem Restaurant zu essen.

Unit 41

I am, I don't usw.

A

She isn't tired, but **he is**.
(**he is** = he is tired)

He likes tea, but **she doesn't**.
(**she doesn't** = she doesn't like tea)

*Die Beispiele zeigen, wie man bestimmte Verben (hier **is** und **does**) alleine benutzen kann, um schon verwendete Wörter nicht wiederholen zu müssen.*

*Folgende Verben kann man auf diese Weise (wie **is** und **does** oben) benutzen:*

| am/is/are |
| was/were |
| have/has |
| do/does/did |
| can |
| will |
| might |
| must |

- I haven't got a car, but my sister **has**. (= my sister has got a car)
  Ich habe kein Auto, aber meine Schwester schon.
- A: Please help me. *Hilf mir bitte.*
  B: I'm sorry. I **can't**. (= I can't help you) *Leider kann ich nicht.*
- A: Are you tired? *Bist du müde?*
  B: I **was**, but I'**m not** now. *Vorher war ich (müde), aber jetzt nicht.*
- A: Do you think Laura will come and see us? *Meinst du, Laura wird uns besuchen?*
  B: She **might**. *(Sie wird uns) vielleicht (besuchen).*
- A: Are you going now? *Gehen Sie jetzt?*
  B: Yes, I'm afraid I **must**. *Ja, leider muss ich.*

Man kann die Kurzformen ('m*/*'s*/*'ve* usw.) der Verben im Kästchen nicht auf diese Weise benutzen.*
*Man muss **am**/**is**/**have** usw. verwenden:*

- She isn't tired, but he **is**. (*nicht* but he's)

*Man kann jedoch verneinte Kurzformen verwenden: **isn't** / **haven't** / **won't** usw. :*

- My sister has got a car, but I **haven't**. *Meine Schwester hat ein Auto, aber ich nicht.*
- A: Are you and Jane working tomorrow? *Arbeitet ihr morgen – Jane und du?*
  B: I am, but Jane **isn't**. *Ich schon, aber Jane nicht.*

B

I am / **I'm not** usw. werden auch für Kurzantworten nach **Yes** oder **No** verwendet:

- 'Are you tired?' 'Yes, I **am**. / No, I'**m not**.' *'Bist du müde?' 'Ja (bin ich). / Nein (bin ich nicht).'*
- A: Will Alan be here tomorrow? *Wird Alan morgen hier sein?*
  B: Yes, he **will**. / No, he **won't**. *Ja (er wird morgen hier sein). / Nein (er wird morgen nicht hier sein).*
- A: Is there a bus to the airport? *Gibt es einen Bus zum Flughafen?*
  B: Yes, there **is**. / No, there **isn't**. *Ja, es gibt einen. / Nein, es gibt keinen.*

C

*Beim present simple verwendet man **do**/**does** auf die gleiche Weise (→ Units 7–8):*

- I don't like hot weather, but Sue **does**. (= Sue likes hot weather)
  Ich mag kein heißes Wetter, aber Sue schon.
- Sue works hard, but I **don't**. (= I don't work hard) *… aber ich nicht.*
- 'Do you enjoy your work?' 'Yes, I **do**.' *'Gefällt Ihnen Ihre Arbeit?' 'Ja (sie gefällt mir).'*

*Beim past simple verwendet man **did** auf diese Art: (→ Unit 13):*

- A: Did you and Chris enjoy the film? *Hat dir und Chris der Film gefallen?*
  B: I **did**, but Chris **didn't**. *Mir schon, aber Chris nicht.*
- 'I enjoyed the film.' 'I **did** too.' *'Mir hat der Film gefallen.' 'Mir auch.'*
- 'Did it rain yesterday?' 'No, it **didn't**.' *'Hat es gestern geregnet?' 'Nein (hat es nicht).'*

have you? / don't you? usw. → Unit 42   so am I / neither do I usw. → Unit 43

Übungen

Unit 41

41.1 Vervollständigen Sie die Sätze mit jeweils nur einem Verb (**is**/**have**/**can** usw.).

1. Kate wasn't hungry, but we _were_ .
2. I'm not married, but my brother _____ .
3. Ben can't help you, but I _____ .
4. I haven't seen the film, but Tom _____ .
5. Karen won't be here, but Chris _____ .
6. You weren't late, but I _____ .

41.2 Vervollständigen Sie die Sätze mit einer Verneinungsform (**isn't**/**haven't**/**can't** usw.).

1. My sister can play the piano, but I _can't_ .
2. Sam is working today, but I _____ .
3. I was working, but my friends _____ .
4. Mark has been to China, but I _____ .
5. I'm ready to go, but Tom _____ .
6. I've got a key, but Sarah _____ .

41.3 Vervollständigen Sie die Sätze mit **do**/**does**/**did** oder **don't**/**doesn't**/**didn't**.

1. I don't like hot weather, but Sue _does_ .
2. Sue likes hot weather, but I _don't_ .
3. My mother wears glasses, but my father _____ .
4. You don't know Paul very well, but I _____ .
5. I didn't enjoy the party, but my friends _____ .
6. I don't watch TV much, but Peter _____ .
7. Kate lives in London, but her parents _____ .
8. You had breakfast this morning, but I _____ .

41.4 Schreiben Sie Sätze über sich selbst und über andere Leute nach dem Beispiel.

1. I didn't _go out last night, but my friends did._
2. I like _____ , but _____
3. I don't _____ , but _____
4. I'm _____
5. I haven't _____

41.5 Vervollständigen Sie die Sätze mit einem Verb in der bejahten oder der verneinten Form.

1. 'Are you tired?' 'I _was_ earlier, but I'm not now.'
2. Steve is happy today, but he _____ yesterday.
3. The bank isn't open yet, but the shops _____ .
4. I haven't got a telescope, but I know somebody who _____ .
5. I would like to help you, but I'm afraid I _____ .
6. I don't usually go to work by car, but I _____ yesterday.
7. A: Have you ever been to the United States?
   B: No, but Sandra _____ . She went there on holiday last year.
8. 'Do you and Chris watch TV a lot?' 'I _____ , but Chris doesn't.'
9. I've been invited to Sam's wedding, but Kate _____ .
10. 'Do you think Sarah will pass her driving test?' 'Yes, I'm sure she _____ .'
11. 'Are you going out tonight?' 'I _____ . I don't know for sure.'

41.6 Beantworten Sie die Fragen über sich selbst mit Kurzantworten (**Yes, I have.** / **No, I'm not.** usw.):

1. Are you American? _No, I'm not._
2. Have you got a car? _____
3. Do you feel OK? _____
4. Is it snowing? _____
5. Are you hungry? _____
6. Do you like classical music? _____
7. Will you be in Paris tomorrow? _____
8. Have you ever broken your arm? _____
9. Did you buy anything yesterday? _____
10. Were you asleep at 3 a.m.? _____

41.7 Übersetzen Sie ins Englische.

1. Ich bin nicht groß, aber meine Schwester schon.
2. Sam kann tanzen, aber Sarah nicht.
3. Das Wetter war gestern nicht schön, aber heute schon.
4. Mein Bruder hat Kinder, aber ich nicht.
5. 'Wart ihr gestern auf dem Fest?' 'Ich nicht, aber Emma schon.'
6. Ich spiele Tennis, aber mein Mann nicht.
7. Wir mögen keine Hunde, aber unsere Kinder schon.
8. 'Habt ihr gestern das Fußballspiel gesehen?' 'Ich schon, aber Jenny nicht.'
9. 'Werdet ihr morgen zu Hause sein?' 'Ich nicht, aber Thomas schon.'

Unit 42

Have you?   Are you?   Don't you? usw.

A

- I've bought a new car. — Oh, have you?
- I'm writing a book. — Are you really? What about?
- I don't like George. — Don't you? Why not?

Man kann **have you?** / **is it?** / **can't he?** usw. verwenden, um Interesse zu zeigen oder Überraschung auszudrücken. (Im Deutschen verwendet man 'wirklich?' / 'ach so?' / 'nein?' usw.) Dabei wiederholt man das erste Verb des Gesprächspartners (A: I**'ve** bought … B: **Have** you?).

Wirklich? / Ach so?
- 'You're late.' 'Oh, **am I?** I'm sorry.' 'Du kommst zu spät.' 'Wirklich? Das tut mir leid.'
- A: **I was** ill last week. Ich war letzte Woche krank.
  B: **Were you?** I didn't know that. Ach so? Das wusste ich nicht.
- '**It's** raining again.' '**Is it?** It was sunny five minutes ago.'
- '**There's** a problem with the car.' '**Is there?** What's wrong with it?'

Wirklich? / Ach so? / Nein? / Nicht?
- A: **Bill can't** drive. Bill kann nicht Auto fahren.
  B: **Can't he?** I didn't know that. Nein? Das wusste ich nicht.
- '**I'm not** hungry.' '**Aren't you?** I am.' 'Ich habe keinen Hunger.' 'Wirklich? Ich schon.'
- '**Sue isn't** at work today.' '**Isn't she?** Is she ill?'

Beim present simple verwendet man **do/does** und beim past simple **did**:
- '**I speak** four languages.' '**Do you?** Which ones?' 'Ich spreche vier Sprachen.' 'Wirklich? Welche?'
- '**Ben doesn't** eat meat.' '**Doesn't he?** Does he eat fish?'
- '**Nicola got** married last week.' '**Did she?** Really?' …'Ach so? Wirklich?'

B Question tags

Das sind kurze Fragen (**have you?** / **is it?** / **can't she?** usw.), die man an eine Aussage anhängen kann. Sie entsprechen im Deutschen 'nicht wahr?' / 'nicht?' / 'oder?'.

Beim bejahten Satz wird der question tag verneint.
Beim verneinten Satz wird der question tag bejaht.

It's a beautiful day, isn't it? — Yes, it's perfect.

bejahte Form → Verneinung

It's a beautiful day,	**isn't it?**		Yes, it's perfect.
Kate lives in London,	**doesn't she?**		Yes, that's right.
You closed the window,	**didn't you?**	… nicht wahr?	Yes, I think so.
Those shoes are nice,	**aren't they?**		Yes, very nice.
Tom will be here soon,	**won't he?**		Yes, probably.

Verneinung → bejahte Form

That isn't your car,	**is it?**		No, it's my mother's.
You haven't met my mother,	**have you?**	… oder?	No, I haven't.
Helen doesn't go out much,	**does she?**		No, she doesn't.
You won't be late,	**will you?**		No, I'm never late.

I am / I don't usw. → Unit 41

Übungen

42.1 Antworten Sie mit Do you? / Doesn't she? / Did they? usw.

1 I speak four languages. — Do you? Which ones?
2 I work in a bank. — ....? I work in a bank too.
3 I didn't go to work yesterday. — ....? Were you ill?
4 Jane doesn't like me. — ....? Why not?
5 You look tired. — ....? I feel fine.
6 Kate phoned me last night. — ....? What did she say?

42.2 Antworten Sie mit Have you? / Haven't you? / Did she? / Didn't she? usw.

1 I've bought a new car. — Have you? What make is it?
2 Tim doesn't eat meat. — Doesn't he? Does he eat fish?
3 I've lost my key. — ....? When did you last have it?
4 Sue can't drive. — ....? She should learn.
5 I was born in Italy. — ....? I didn't know that.
6 I didn't sleep well last night. — ....? Was the bed uncomfortable?
7 There's a film on TV tonight. — ....? Are you going to watch it?
8 I'm not happy. — ....? Why not?
9 I saw Paula last week. — ....? How is she?
10 Maria works in a factory. — ....? What kind of factory?
11 I won't be here next week. — ....? Where will you be?
12 The clock isn't working. — ....? It was working yesterday.

42.3 Vervollständigen Sie die Sätze mit einem question tag (isn't it? / haven't you? usw.).

1 It's a beautiful day, isn't it? — Yes, it's perfect.
2 These flowers are nice, ...? — Yes, what are they?
3 Jane was at the party, ...? — Yes, but I didn't speak to her.
4 You've been to Paris, ...? — Yes, many times.
5 You speak German, ...? — Yes, but not very well.
6 Martin looks tired, ...? — Yes, he works very hard.
7 You'll help me, ...? — Yes, of course I will.

42.4 Vervollständigen Sie die Sätze mit einem bejahten question tag (is it? / do you? usw.) oder einem verneinten question tag (isn't it? / don't you? usw.).

1 You haven't got a car, have you? — No, I can't drive.
2 You aren't tired, ...? — No, I feel fine.
3 Lisa is a very nice person, ...? — Yes, everybody likes her.
4 You can play the piano, ...? — Yes, but I'm not very good.
5 You don't know Mike's sister, ...? — No, I've never met her.
6 Sarah went to university, ...? — Yes, she studied psychology.
7 The film wasn't very good, ...? — No, it was terrible.
8 Anna lives near you, ...? — That's right. In the same street.
9 You won't tell anybody what I said, ...? — No, of course not.

42.5 Übersetzen Sie ins Englische. Verwenden Sie have you? / is it? / doesn't he? usw.

kennen lernen = meet

1 'Es ist spät.' 'Wirklich? Wie viel Uhr ist es?'
2 A: Ich bin müde.
   B: Wirklich? Willst du nach Hause gehen?
3 Tim ist nicht verheiratet, oder?
4 A: Ich habe keinen Fernseher.
   B: Wirklich? Warum nicht?
5 Du kannst Auto fahren, oder?
6 A: Ben war gestern nicht bei der Arbeit.
   B: Ach so? War er krank?
7 A: Tom spielt Fußball.
   B: Ach so? Wie oft spielt er?
8 Sie kommen aus London, nicht wahr?
9 A: Ich habe Mia gestern gesehen.
   B: Wirklich? Wo?
10 Du warst gestern nicht zu Hause, oder?
11 Kate hat dich gestern nicht angerufen, oder?
12 Sie haben meine Frau kennen gelernt, nicht wahr?

Unit 43

too/either   so am I / neither do I usw.

A too und either

Too (*auch*) und **either** (*auch nicht*) setzt man ans Ende eines Satzes.

Man verwendet **too** nach einem bejahten Verb:
- A: I'm happy.
  B: **I'm** happy **too**.
  Ich freue mich auch. / Ich bin auch froh.

- A: I enjoyed the film.
  B: I **enjoyed** it **too**. *Er hat mir auch gefallen.*

- Jane is a doctor. Her husband **is** a doctor **too**.
  ... Ihr Mann ist auch Arzt.

Man verwendet **either** nach einem verneinten Verb:
- A: I'm not happy.
  B: **I'm not** happy **either**.
  Ich freue mich auch nicht. / Ich bin auch nicht froh.

- A: I can't cook.
  B: I **can't either**. *Ich kann auch nicht kochen.*

- Ben doesn't watch TV. He **doesn't** read newspapers **either**.
  ... Er liest auch keine Zeitung.

B so am I / neither do I usw. (*ich auch / ich auch nicht usw.*):

so	am/is/are ... was/were ... do/does ... did ... have/has ... can ... will ... would ...
neither	

so am I = I am too
so have I = I have too (*usw.*):
- A: **I'm** working. *Ich arbeite (gerade).*
  B: **So am I**. *Ich auch.*
- A: **I was** late for work today.
  B: **So was Sam**. *Sam auch.*
- A: **I work** in a bank.
  B: **So do I**.
- A: **We went** to the cinema last night.
  Wir sind gestern ins Kino gegangen.
  B: Did you? **So did we**.
  Wirklich? Wir auch.
- A: **I'd** like to go to Australia.
  Ich würde gerne nach Australien reisen.
  B: **So would I**. *Ich auch.*

neither am I = I'm not either
neither can I = I can't either (*usw.*):
- A: **I haven't** got a key.
  Ich habe keinen Schlüssel.
  B: **Neither have I**. *Ich auch nicht.*
- A: **Kate can't** cook.
  B: **Neither can Tom**. *Tom auch nicht.*
- A: **I won't** (= will not) be here tomorrow.
  Ich werde morgen nicht hier sein.
  B: **Neither will I**. *Ich auch nicht.*
- A: **I never go** to the cinema.
  Ich gehe nie ...
  B: **Neither do I**. *Ich auch nicht.*

Man kann auch **Nor** ... anstatt **Neither** ... sagen:
- A: I'm not married.
  B: **Nor am I**. oder **Neither am I**.

Beachten Sie die Wortstellung:
- So **am I**. (*nicht* So I am)
- Neither **have I**. (*nicht* Neither I have)

I am / I don't *usw.* ➔ Unit 41

Übungen

43.1 Vervollständigen Sie die Sätze mit **too** oder **either**.

1. I'm happy. — I'm happy _too_.
2. I'm not hungry. — I'm not hungry _____.
3. I'm going out. — I'm going out _____.
4. It rained on Saturday. — It rained on Sunday _____.
5. Rachel can't drive a car. — She can't ride a bike _____.
6. I don't like shopping. — I don't like shopping _____.
7. Emma's mother is a teacher. — Her father is a teacher _____.

43.2 Reagieren Sie auf die Aussagen mit **So ... I** (**So am I** / **So do I** / **So can I** usw.).

1. I went to bed late last night. — _So did I._
2. I'm thirsty.
3. I've just eaten.
4. I need a holiday.
5. I'll be late tomorrow.
6. I was very tired this morning.

Reagieren Sie auf die Aussagen mit **Neither ... I**.

7. I can't go to the party.
8. I didn't phone Alex last night.
9. I haven't got any money.
10. I'm not going out tomorrow.
11. I don't know what to do.

43.3 Sie sprechen mit Maria. Schreiben Sie wahre Aussagen über sich selbst. Verwenden Sie, wenn möglich, **So ... I** oder **Neither ... I**. Folgen Sie den Beispielen:

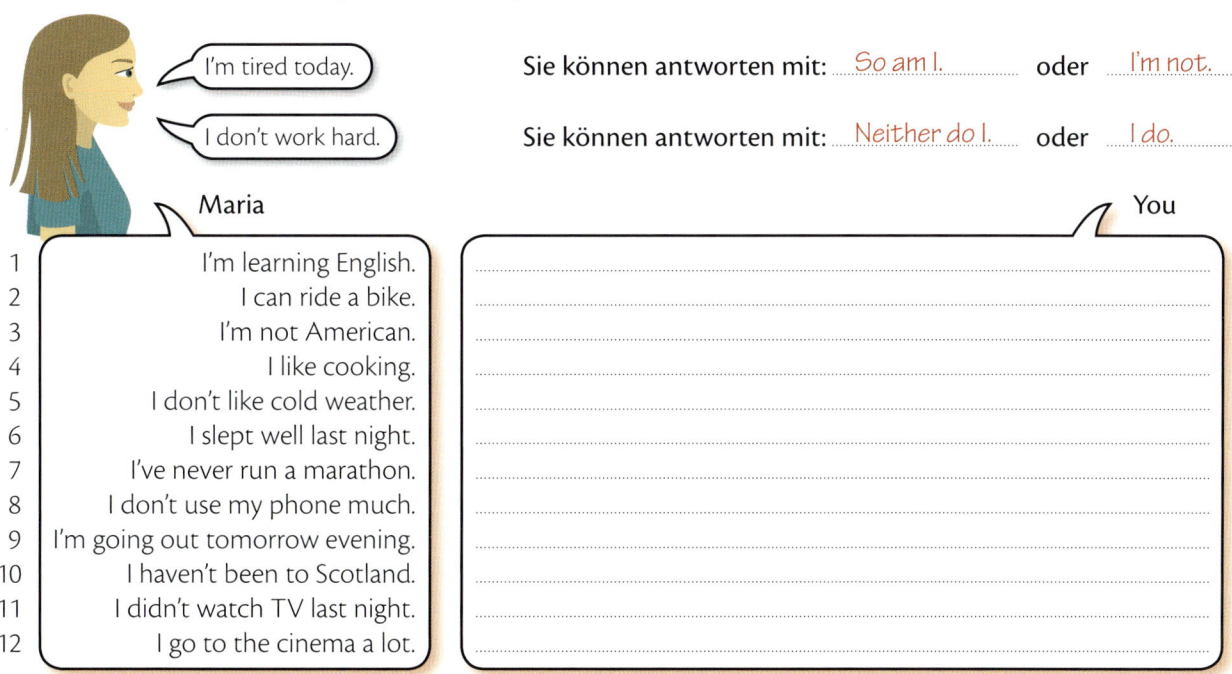

Maria: I'm tired today. — Sie können antworten mit: _So am I._ oder _I'm not._
Maria: I don't work hard. — Sie können antworten mit: _Neither do I._ oder _I do._

1. I'm learning English.
2. I can ride a bike.
3. I'm not American.
4. I like cooking.
5. I don't like cold weather.
6. I slept well last night.
7. I've never run a marathon.
8. I don't use my phone much.
9. I'm going out tomorrow evening.
10. I haven't been to Scotland.
11. I didn't watch TV last night.
12. I go to the cinema a lot.

43.4 Übersetzen Sie ins Englische.

1. A: Ich komme aus Deutschland.
   B: Ich komme auch aus Deutschland.
2. 'Ich bin müde.' 'Ich auch.'
3. Rebecca ist Lehrerin. Jenny ist auch Lehrerin.
4. A: Ich kann nicht Tennis spielen.
   B: Ich auch nicht.
5. John geht früh ins Bett. Er steht auch früh auf.
6. 'Wir haben einen Hund.' 'Wir auch.'
7. Tony ist nicht verheiratet. Anna ist auch nicht verheiratet.
8. A: Wir sind letztes Wochenende in die Berge gefahren.
   B: Wir auch.
9. Ben geht nicht sehr oft aus. Nicola auch nicht.

Unit 44: isn't, haven't, don't usw. (Verneinung)

A

not (**n't**) verwendet man für die Verneinung:

bejahte Form → verneinte Form

am	**am not** (**'m not**)	I**'m not** tired.
is	**is not** (**isn't** *oder* **'s not**)	It **isn't** (*oder* It**'s not**) raining.
are	**are not** (**aren't** *oder* **'re not**)	They **aren't** (*oder* They**'re not**) here.
was	**was not** (**wasn't**)	Julian **wasn't** hungry.
were	**were not** (**weren't**)	The shops **weren't** open.
have	**have not** (**haven't**)	I **haven't** finished my work.
has	**has not** (**hasn't**)	Sue **hasn't** got a car.
will	**will not** (**won't**)	We **won't** be here tomorrow.
can	**cannot** (**can't**)	George **can't** drive.
could	**could not** (**couldn't**)	I **couldn't** sleep last night.
must	**must not** (**mustn't**)	I **mustn't** forget to phone Jane. *
should	**should not** (**shouldn't**)	You **shouldn't** work so hard.
would	**would not** (**wouldn't**)	I **wouldn't** like to be an actor.

*Beachten Sie: **must** = 'müssen' aber **mustn't** = 'nicht dürfen' (Ich darf nicht vergessen Jane anzurufen.)

B

don't/doesn't/didn't

present simple negative	I/we/you/they	**do not** (**don't**)	**work/live/go** *usw.*
	he/she/it	**does not** (**doesn't**)	
past simple negative	I/they/he/she *usw.*	**did not** (**didn't**)	

bejahte Form → verneinte Form

I **want** to go out.	→	I **don't want** to go out.
They **work** hard.	→	They **don't work** hard.
Lisa **plays** the guitar.	→	Lisa **doesn't play** the guitar.
My father **likes** his job.	→	My father **doesn't like** his job.
I **got** up early this morning.	→	I **didn't get** up early this morning.
They **worked** hard yesterday.	→	They **didn't work** hard yesterday.
We **played** tennis.	→	We **didn't play** tennis.
Emily **had** dinner with us.	→	Emily **didn't have** dinner with us.

Don't … (beim Imperativ)
Die Verneinung des Imperativs bildet man mit **don't** + Infinitiv (**don't go/don't be** *usw.*):

Look!	→	**Don't look!**
Wait for me.	→	**Don't wait** for me.

Vorsicht bei den folgenden Beispielen:

Do something!	→	**Don't do** anything!
Sue **does** a lot at weekends.	→	Sue **doesn't do** much at weekends.
I **did** what you said.	→	I **didn't do** what you said.

In diesen Beispielen zeigt **don't/doesn't/didn't** die Verneinung an, während **do** die Bedeutung 'tun'/'machen' hat.

---

present simple (Verneinung) ➜ Unit 7 past simple (Verneinung) ➜ Unit 13
don't look / don't wait *usw.* ➜ Unit 36   Why **isn't/don't** … ? ➜ Unit 45

Übungen

44.1 Bilden Sie die Verneinung folgender Sätze.
1. He's gone away.   He hasn't gone away.
2. They're married.
3. I've had dinner.
4. It's cold today.
5. We'll be late.
6. You should go.

44.2 Bilden Sie die Verneinung folgender Sätze. Verwenden Sie **don't**/**doesn't**/**didn't**.
1. She saw me.   She didn't see me.
2. I like cheese.
3. They understood.
4. He lives here.
5. Go away!
6. I did the shopping.

44.3 Bilden Sie die Verneinung folgender Sätze.
1. She can swim.   She can't swim.
2. They've arrived.
3. I went to the bank.
4. He speaks German.
5. We were angry.
6. He'll be pleased.
7. Call me tonight.
8. It rained yesterday.
9. I could hear them.
10. I believe you.

44.4 Vervollständigen Sie die Sätze mit einem verneinten Verb (**isn't**/**haven't**/**don't** usw.).
1. They aren't rich. They _haven't_ got much money.
2. 'Would you like something to eat?' 'No, thank you. I .... hungry.'
3. I .... find my glasses. Have you seen them?
4. Steve .... go to the cinema much. He prefers to watch DVDs at home.
5. We can walk to the station from here. It .... very far.
6. 'Where's Jane?' 'I .... know. I .... seen her today.'
7. Be careful! .... fall!
8. We went to a restaurant last night. I .... like the food very much.
9. I've been to Japan many times, but I .... been to Korea.
10. Julia .... be here tomorrow. She's going away.
11. 'Who broke that window?' 'Not me. I .... do it.'
12. We didn't see what happened. We .... looking at the time.
13. Lisa bought a new coat a few days ago, but she .... worn it yet.
14. You .... drive so fast. It's dangerous.

44.5 Sie haben Gary folgende Fragen gestellt und er hat Ihnen mit 'Yes' oder 'No' geantwortet. Schreiben Sie nun die Ergebnisse Ihres Interviews: Schreiben Sie einen bejahten oder verneinten Satz über Gary für jede seiner Antworten.

You — Gary

Are you married?	No.	1	He isn't married.
Do you live in London?	Yes.	2	He lives in London.
Were you born in London?	No.	3	
Do you like London?	No.	4	
Would you like to live in the country?	Yes.	5	
Can you drive?	Yes.	6	
Have you got a car?	No.	7	
Do you read newspapers?	No.	8	
Are you interested in politics?	No.	9	
Do you watch TV most evenings?	Yes.	10	
Did you watch TV last night?	No.	11	
Did you go out last night?	Yes.	12	

44.6 Übersetzen Sie ins Englische.
1. Ich bin nicht traurig.
2. David war gestern nicht zu Hause.
3. Wir können morgen nicht kommen.
4. Ich kenne deine Schwester nicht.
5. Wir sind gestern Abend nicht ausgegangen.
6. Geh nicht zu spät ins Bett!
7. Es wird morgen nicht regnen.
8. Kommt nicht zu spät. Wir haben nicht viel Zeit.
9. Ich konnte meinen Schlüssel heute früh nicht finden.
10. Du solltest nicht darüber sprechen.
11. Tu das nicht! Das ist nicht nett.

Unit 44

Unit 45: is it … ? have you … ? do they … ? usw. (Fragen 1)

A

Aussage **you** **are** → **You are** eating.

Frage **are** **you** → **Are you** eating?   What **are you** eating?

In Fragen kommt das erste Verb (**is**/**are**/**have** usw.) vor dem Subjekt:

Aussage Subjekt + Verb		Frage Verb + Subjekt	
I	**am** late.	→ **Am**	**I** late?
That seat	**is** free.	→ **Is**	**that seat** free?
She	**was** angry.	→ Why **was**	**she** angry?
David	**has** gone.	→ Where **has**	**David** gone?
You	**have** got a car.	→ **Have**	**you** got a car?
They	**will** be here soon.	→ When **will**	**they** be here?
Paula	**can** swim.	→ **Can**	**Paula** swim?

B

Fragen mit **do** … ? / **does** … ? / **did** … ?

Fragen im present simple und past simple bildet man mit **do** (**do**/**does**/**did**):

present simple questions	**do** I/we/you/they **does** he/she/it	**work**/**live**/**go** usw. … ?
past simple questions	**did** I/they/he/she usw.	

Aussage   Frage

They **work** hard.	→	**Do** they **work** hard?
You **watch** television.	→	How often **do** you **watch** television?
Chris **works** hard.	→	**Does** Chris **work** hard?
She **gets up** early.	→	What time **does** she **get** up?
They **worked** hard.	→	**Did** they **work** hard?
You **had** dinner.	→	What **did** you **have** for dinner?
She **got** up early.	→	What time **did** she **get** up?

Do wird auch als gewöhnliches Verb verwendet, und bedeutet 'tun' oder 'machen':
- I can **do** it. Ich kann das tun.
- She **does** the same thing every day. Sie macht jeden Tag das Gleiche.

In folgenden Beispielen zeigt das erste **do** an, dass eine Frage gestellt wird. Das zweite **do** ist ein gewöhnliches Verb mit der Bedeutung 'tun'/'machen':
- What **do** you usually **do** at weekends? Was tun Sie gewöhnlich am Wochenende?
- A: What **does** your brother **do**? Was macht Ihr Bruder beruflich?
  B: He works in a bank. Er arbeitet in einer Bank.
- A: I broke my finger last week.
  B: How **did** you **do** that? Wie hast du das gemacht?

C

Why isn't … ? / **Why don't** … ? usw. (verneinte Fragen mit **Why**):

- Where's John? **Why isn't he** here?
  … Warum ist er nicht hier?
- **Why can't Paula** come to the meeting tomorrow?
  Warum kann Paula nicht … ?
- Why **didn't you** phone me last night?
  Warum hast du mich gestern Abend nicht angerufen?

---

present simple (Frageform) → Unit 8   past simple (Frageform) → Unit 13   Fragen 2–3 → Units 46–47
what/which/how → Units 48–49

Übungen

45.1 Bilden Sie vollständige Fragen anhand der Wörter in den Klammern.

1. I can swim. (and you?) — Can you swim?
2. I work hard. (and Jack?) — Does Jack work hard?
3. I was late this morning. (and you?)
4. I've got a key. (and Kate?)
5. I'll be here tomorrow. (and you?)
6. I'm going out this evening. (and Paul?)
7. I like my job. (and you?)
8. I live near here. (and Nicola?)
9. I enjoyed the film. (and you?)
10. I had a good holiday. (and you?)

45.2 Sie sprechen mit jemandem über das Autofahren. Stellen Sie vollständige Fragen.

You:
1. (have / a car?) — Have you got a car? — Yes, I have.
2. (use / a lot?) .... it — Yes, nearly every day.
3. (use / yesterday?) — Yes, to go to work.
4. (enjoy driving?) — Not very much.
5. (a good driver?) — I think I am.
6. (ever / have / an accident?) — No, never.

45.3 Bilden Sie Fragen, indem Sie die Wörter in die richtige Reihenfolge bringen.

1. (has / gone / where / David?) — Where has David gone?
2. (working / Rachel / is / today?) — Is Rachel working today?
3. (the children / what / are / doing?) What
4. (made / is / how / cheese?)
5. (to the party / coming / is / your sister?)
6. (you / the truth / tell / don't / why?)
7. (your guests / have / yet / arrived?)
8. (leave / what time / your train / does?)
9. (to work / Emily / why / go / didn't?)
10. (your car / in the accident / was / damaged?)

45.4 Sie wollen mehr über die Aussagen unten links wissen. Vervollständigen Sie die Fragen.

1. I want to go out. — Where do you want to go?
2. Kate and Paul aren't going to the party. — Why aren't they going?
3. I'm reading. — What
4. Sue went to bed early. — What time
5. My parents are going on holiday. — When
6. I saw Tom a few days ago. — Where
7. I can't come to the party. — Why
8. Tina has gone away. — Where
9. I need some money. — How much
10. Angela doesn't like me. — Why
11. It rains sometimes. — How often
12. I did the shopping. — When

45.5 Übersetzen Sie ins Englische.

1. Sind die Kinder müde?
2. Kann Jenny Französisch sprechen?
3. War der Film interessant?
4. Wirst du heute Abend zu Hause sein?
5. Mögen Sie chinesisches Essen?
6. Hast du David heute gesehen?
7. Wo arbeitet deine Mutter?
8. Hat Rachel dich gestern angerufen?
9. Was habt ihr letztes Wochenende gemacht?
10. Warum magst du Emma nicht?

Unit 46: Who saw you? Who did you see?
(Fragen 2)

A

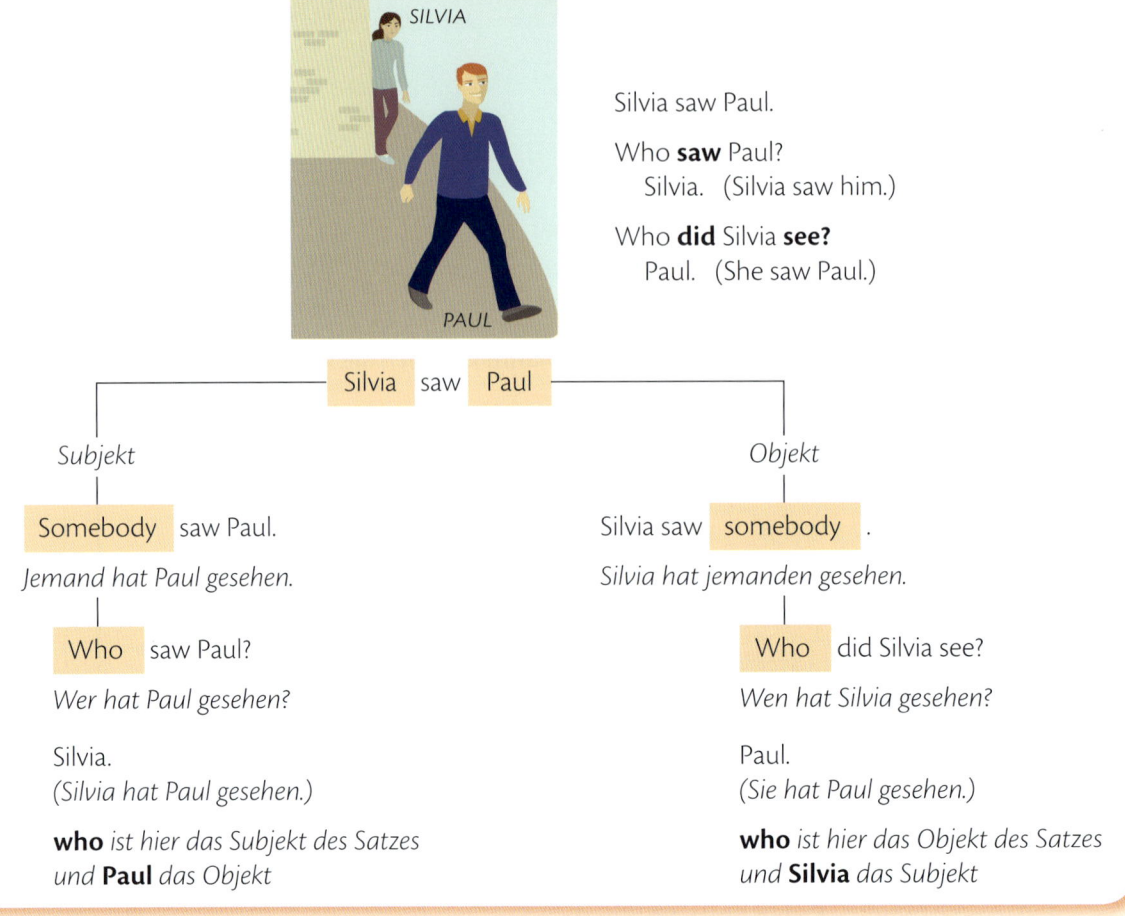

Silvia saw Paul.

Who **saw** Paul?
   Silvia. (Silvia saw him.)

Who **did** Silvia **see**?
   Paul. (She saw Paul.)

Silvia saw Paul

Subjekt

Somebody saw Paul.
Jemand hat Paul gesehen.

Who saw Paul?
Wer hat Paul gesehen?

Silvia.
(Silvia hat Paul gesehen.)

who ist hier das Subjekt des Satzes und **Paul** das Objekt

Objekt

Silvia saw **somebody**.
Silvia hat jemanden gesehen.

Who did Silvia see?
Wen hat Silvia gesehen?

Paul.
(Sie hat Paul gesehen.)

who ist hier das Objekt des Satzes und **Silvia** das Subjekt

B

Man bildet Fragen auf unterschiedliche Weise je nachdem, ob **who**/**what** Subjekt oder Objekt des Satzes ist.

Fragen in denen **who**/**what** das Subjekt ist, werden wie Aussagesätze gebildet:
- **Who lives** in this house? (*nicht* Who does live?)
  Wer wohnt in diesem Haus?
- **What happened**? (*nicht* What did happen?)
  Was ist passiert?
- **What's happening**? (What's = What **is**)
  Was passiert gerade?
- **Who's got** my key? (Who's = Who **has**)
  Wer hat meinen Schlüssel?

Fragen in denen **who**/**what** Objekt des Satzes ist, bildet man nach den normalen Regeln der Fragestellung:
- Who did **you** meet yesterday? Wen hast du gestern getroffen?
- What did **Paul** say? Was hat Paul gesagt?
- Who are **you** phoning? Mit wem telefonieren Sie?
- What was **Silvia** wearing? Was hatte Silvia an?

Vergleichen Sie die unterschiedliche Fragestellung in den folgenden Beispielen:
- George likes oranges. → **Who likes** oranges? – George.
  What does George like? – Oranges.
- Jane won a new car. → **Who won** a new car? – Jane.
  What did Jane win? – A new car.

C

Beachten Sie, dass **who** ('wer/wen/wem') und **where** ('wo') leicht verwechselt werden wegen der verwirrenden Ähnlichkeit mit 'wo' und 'wer':
- **Who** is your sister? Wer ist deine Schwester?
- **Where** is your sister? Wo ist deine Schwester?

Fragen → Units 45, 47 what/which/how → Unit 48

Übungen

Unit 46

46.1 Stellen Sie Fragen mit **who** oder **what**. In diesen Fragen ist **who**/**what** Subjekt.

1. Somebody broke the window.
2. Something fell off the shelf.
3. Somebody wants to see you.
4. Somebody took my umbrella.
5. Something made me ill.
6. Somebody is coming.

Who broke the window?
What ....
.... me?

46.2 Stellen Sie Fragen mit **who** oder **what** (als Subjekt oder Objekt).

1. I bought something.
2. Somebody lives in this house.
3. I phoned somebody.
4. Something happened last night.
5. Somebody knows the answer.
6. Somebody did the washing-up.
7. Jane did something.
8. Something woke me up.
9. Somebody saw the accident.
10. I saw somebody.
11. Somebody has got my pen.
12. This word means something.

What did you buy?
Who lives in this house?

46.3 Sie wollen die fehlenden Informationen (XXXXX) erfragen. Stellen Sie Fragen mit **who** oder **what**.

1. I lost **XXXXX** yesterday, but fortunately **XXXXX** found it and gave it back to me.

   What did you lose?
   Who found it?

2. **XXXXX** phoned me last night. She wanted **XXXXX**.

   Who ....
   What ....

3. I needed some advice, so I asked **XXXXX**. He said **XXXXX**.

4. I hear that **XXXXX** got married last week. **XXXXX** told me.

5. I met **XXXXX** on my way home this evening. She told me **XXXXX**.

6. Steve and I played tennis yesterday. **XXXXX** won. After the game we **XXXXX**.

7. It was my birthday last week and I had some presents. **XXXXX** gave me a book and Catherine gave me **XXXXX**.

46.4 Übersetzen Sie ins Englische.

riechen = smell

1. Wer hat mein Englischbuch?
2. Wer kann die Frage beantworten?
3. Wo sind die Kinder?
4. Das riecht gut. Was kochst du?
5. Wer sind diese Leute?
6. Was ist runtergefallen?
7. Wer hat das Spiel am Samstag gewonnen?
8. Wo hast du Thomas heute Morgen gesehen?
9. Was hast du gestern zum Abendessen gegessen?
10. Ich kann Musik hören. Wer spielt (gerade) Klavier?

Unit 47

Who is she talking to?   What is it like?
(Fragen 3)

A

Jessica is talking to somebody.

Who is she talking **to**?

In Fragen mit **Who** … **?** / **What** … **?** / **Where** … **?** / **Which** … **?** stellt man Präpositionen (**to**/**from**/**with** usw.) meistens an das Satzende:

- '**Where** are you **from**?'   'I'm from Thailand.'   'Woher kommen Sie?' …
- 'Jack was afraid.'   '**What** was he afraid **of**?' …   'Wovor hatte er Angst?'
- '**Who** do these books belong **to**?'   'They're mine.'   'Wem gehören diese Bücher?' …
- 'Tom's father is in hospital.'   '**Which hospital** is he **in**?' …   'In welchem Krankenhaus ist er?'
- A: Kate is going on holiday.
  B: **Who with**? / **Who** is she going **with**?   Mit wem? / Mit wem geht sie?
- A: Can we talk?
  B: Sure.   **What** do you want to talk **about**? …   Worüber möchten Sie sprechen?

B

What's it like? / **What are they like?** usw.

What's your new house **like**?

It's very big.

What**'s** it like? = What **is** it like?

What's it like? = tell me something about it – is it good or bad, big or small, old or new (usw.)?

What's it like? / **What are … like?** = Wie ist/sind … ?
Like bedeutet hier 'wie' und nicht 'mögen'/'gefallen'.

- A: There's a new restaurant in our street.
  B: **What's** it **like**? Is it good?   Wie ist es? Ist es gut?
  A: I don't know. I haven't eaten there yet. … Ich habe noch nicht dort gegessen.
- A: **What's** your new teacher **like**?   Wie ist eure neue Lehrerin?
  B: She's very good. We learn a lot.
- A: I met Nicola's parents yesterday.   Ich habe Nicolas Eltern gestern kennen gelernt.
  B: Did you? **What** are they **like**?   Ach so? Wie sind sie so? (Wie fandst du sie?)
  A: They're very nice.
- A: Did you have a good holiday? **What** was the weather **like**? … Wie war das Wetter?
  B: It was lovely. It was sunny every day.

C

Vergleichen Sie folgende Fragen:
- A: **What** is Julia **like**?   Wie ist Julia? (= Was für eine Person ist sie?)
  B: She's very nice.
- A: **How** is Julia?   Wie geht es Julia?
  B: She's very well.
- A: **What does** Julia **look like**?   Wie sieht Julia aus?
  B: She's tall and she's got long blonde hair.

Fragen 1–2 → **Units 45–46**   what/which/how → **Unit 48**   Präpositionen → **Units 103–113**

Übungen

Unit 47

47.1
Sie wollen die fehlenden Informationen (XXXXX) erfragen. Stellen Sie Fragen mit **who** oder **what**.

1. The letter is from **XXXXX**. — Who is the letter from?
2. I'm looking for a **XXXXX**. — What .... you
3. I went to the cinema with **XXXXX**. —
4. The film was about **XXXXX**. —
5. I gave the money to **XXXXX**. —
6. The book was written by **XXXXX**. —

47.2
Schreiben Sie Fragen zu den Bildern mit den angegebenen Verben und einer Präposition.

go   listen   look   ~~talk~~   talk   wait

1. Who is she talking to?
2. What .... they
3. Which restaurant ....
4. What ....
5. What ....
6. Which bus ....

47.3
Sie wollen mehr über die Aussagen unten links wissen. Stellen Sie Fragen mit **Which ... ?**

1. Tom's father is in hospital. — Which hospital is he in?
2. We stayed at a hotel. — .... you ....
3. Jack plays for a football team.
4. I went to school in this town.

47.4
Sie wollen sich über ein anderes Land informieren. Fragen Sie jemanden, der das Land kennt. Verwenden Sie **What is/are ... like?**

1. (the roads)   What are the roads like?
2. (the food)
3. (the people)
4. (the weather)

47.5
Stellen Sie Fragen mit **What was/were ... like?** Folgen Sie jeweils den Anweisungen.

1. Your friend has just come back from holiday. Ask about the weather.
   What was the weather like?
2. Your friend has just come back from the cinema. Ask about the film.
3. Your friend has just finished an English course. Ask about the lessons.
4. Your friend has just come back from holiday. Ask about the hotel.

47.6
Übersetzen Sie ins Englische.

Strand = beach

1. 'Woher kommt Jim?' 'Aus Australien.'
2. Worüber denkst du nach?
3. Wie sind die Strände in Thailand?
4. In welchem Haus wohnt Becky?
5. Worauf wartet ihr?
6. Wie war das Essen in Spanien?
7. A: Kate war gestern auf einer Party.
   B: Mit wem ist sie hingegangen?
8. 'Wie geht es deinem Vater?' 'Es geht ihm besser, danke.'
9. Wie ist Joe? Ist er freundlich?

105

Unit 48: What ... ? Which ... ? How ... ?
(Fragen 4)

A

What ... ? = *Was ... ?*
- **What's** your favourite colour? *Was ist deine Lieblingsfarbe?*
- **What** do you want to do tonight? *Was willst du heute Abend machen?*

Wird **what** jedoch in Verbindung mit einem Nomen verwendet (**What colour ... ?** / **What kind ... ?** usw.), wird es häufig mit 'Welche(r)' übersetzt:
- **What colour** are your eyes? *Welche Farbe ... ?*
- **What size** is this shirt? *Welche Größe ... ?*
- **What make** is your TV? *Welche Marke ... ?*
- **What day** is it today? *Welcher Tag ist heute?*

Beachten Sie auch folgende Fragen mit **what**:
- **What time** is it? *Wie viel Uhr ist es? / Wie spät ist es?*
- **What kind** of job do you want? (*oder* **What type** / **What sort** of job ... ?) *Was für eine Arbeit ... ?*

B

Which + *Nomen* = *Welche(r)/Welchen usw.* :
- **Which train** did you catch – the 9.50 or the 10.30? *Welchen Zug haben Sie genommen ... ?*
- **Which doctor** did you see – Doctor Ellis, Doctor Gray or Doctor Hill? *Welchen Arzt ... ?*

Which *ohne Nomen* = *Was/Welche(r) usw.* :
- **Which** is bigger – Canada or Australia? *Was (Welches Land) ist größer ... ?*

Für Menschen verwendet man **who** (= *wer/wen usw.*), wenn das Fragewort nicht in Verbindung mit einem Nomen verwendet wird:
- **Who** is taller – Joe or Gary? (*nicht* Which is taller?) *Wer ist größer ... ?*

C

What *oder* **which**?

Man verwendet **which**, wenn es sich um eine begrenzte Anzahl von Möglichkeiten oder Alternativen handelt:
- We can go this way or that way. **Which way** shall we go?
  ... *In welche Richtung gehen wir?*
  (*Es gibt nur zwei Richtungen.*)
- There are four umbrellas here. **Which** is yours?
  ... *Welcher (der vier Regenschirme) gehört Ihnen?*

? oder ? oder ? oder ? WHICH?

What verwendet man, wenn die möglichen Antworten nicht von vornherein eingegrenzt werden:
- **What's** the capital of Argentina? *Was/Welches ist die Hauptstadt von Argentinien?*
- **What sort** of music do you like? (*of all kinds of music*) *Was für / Welche Musik magst du?*

Vergleichen Sie:
- **What colour** are his eyes? (*nicht* Which colour)
  Which colour do you prefer, **pink or yellow**? *Welche Farbe gefällt dir besser ... ?*
- **What** is the longest river in the world? *Was ist der längste Fluss ... ?*
  Which is the longest river – **the Mississippi, the Amazon or the Nile**?
  Welcher Fluss ist der längste ... ?

D

How ... ? = *Wie ... ?*
- '**How** was the party last night?' 'It was great.' '*Wie war das Fest ... ?*' ...
- '**How** do you usually go to work?' 'By bus.' '*Wie kommen Sie normalerweise zur Arbeit?*' ...

How verwendet man oft in Verbindung mit Adjektiven und Adverbien, zum Beispiel **how tall** / **how old** / **how often** usw.

'How	**tall** are you?'	'I'm 1 metre 70.'	'Wie groß ... ?'
	big is the house?'	'Not very big.'	'Wie groß ... ?'
	old is your mother?'	'She's 45.'	'Wie alt ... ?'
	far is it from here to the airport?'	'Five kilometres.'	'Wie weit ... ?'
	often do you use your car?'	'Every day.'	'Wie oft ... ?'
	long have they been married?'	'Ten years.'	'Wie lange ... ?'
	much was the meal?'	'Thirty pounds.'	'Wie viel ... ?'

Fragen → **Units 45–47**   How long does it take? → **Unit 49**   which one(s) → **Unit 75**

Übungen

48.1 Stellen Sie Fragen mit **what** über die Äußerungen (links).

1. I've got a new TV. (make?) — What make is it?
2. I want a job. (kind?) — What kind of job do you want?
3. I bought a new sweater. (colour?) — What ....
4. I got up early this morning. (time?) — .... get up?
5. I like music. (type?) — ....
6. I want to buy a car. (kind?) — ....

48.2 Vervollständigen Sie die Fragen. Beginnen Sie mit **Which**.

1. Which way shall we go?
2. .... is yours?
3. .... do you want to see?
4. .... goes to the centre?

48.3 Setzen Sie **what**/**which**/**who** ein.

1. What is that man's name?
2. Which way shall we go? Left or right?
3. You can have tea or coffee. .... do you prefer?
4. '.............. day is it today?' 'Friday.'
5. This is a nice office. .... desk is yours?
6. .... is your favourite sport?
7. .... is more expensive, meat or fish?
8. .... is older, Liz or Steve?
9. .... kind of camera do you have?
10. A: I have three cameras. B: .... camera do you use most?
11. .... nationality are you?

48.4 Vervollständigen Sie die Fragen mit **How** + **high**/**long**/**often** usw.

1. How high is Mount Everest? — Nearly 9000 metres.
2. .... is it to the station? — It's about two kilometres from here.
3. .... is Helen? — She's 26.
4. .... do the buses run? — Every ten minutes.
5. .... is the water in the pool? — Two metres.
6. .... have you lived here? — Nearly three years.

48.5 Stellen Sie eine Frage mit **How ... ?**, um jede der folgenden Informationen zu erfragen.

1. Are you 1 metre 70? 1.75? 1.80? — How tall are you?
2. Is this box one kilogram? Two? Three?
3. Are you 20 years old? 22? 25?
4. Did you spend £20? £30? £50?
5. Do you watch TV every day? Once a week? Never?
6. Is it 1000 miles from Paris to Moscow? 1500? 2000?

48.6 Übersetzen Sie ins Englische.

1. Was ist das?
2. Welche Farbe hat Ihr Auto?
3. Wie alt sind Ihre Kinder?
4. Wie oft gehen Sie ins Theater?
5. Was für Filme magst du?
6. Wie groß ist Michael?
7. Wie weit ist es zum Zentrum?
8. Hier sind zwei Mäntel. Welcher ist Ihrer?
9. Welcher Berg ist der höchste der Welt?
10. Welches gefällt dir – das grüne oder das rote Kleid?

Unit 49

How long does it take ... ?

A How long does it take from ... to ... ?

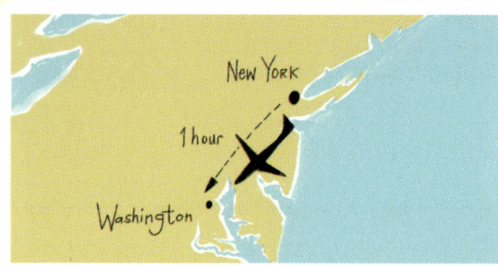

How long **does it take** by plane from New York to Washington?
Wie lange dauert es mit dem Flugzeug von New York nach Washington? / Wie lange braucht man ... ?

It takes an hour.
Es dauert eine Stunde. / Man braucht ...

It takes entspricht im Deutschen 'es dauert' / 'man braucht':
- **It takes** two hours by train from London to Manchester.
  Es dauert zwei Stunden mit dem Zug von London nach Manchester. / Man braucht ...

B How long does it take to do something?

How long	does / did / will	it take to ... ?

It	takes / took / will take		a week / a long time / three hours	to ...
	doesn't / didn't / won't	take	long	

- How long **does it take to cross** the Atlantic by ship?
  Wie lange dauert es, den Atlantik mit dem Schiff zu überqueren? / Wie lange braucht man ... ?
- A: I came by train.
  B: Did you? How long **did it take** (**to get** here)? ... *Wie lange hat es gedauert (hierher zu kommen)?*
- How long **will it take to get** from here to the hotel?
  Wie lange dauert es, von hier zum Hotel zu kommen?

- **It takes** a long time **to learn** a language. *Es dauert lange eine Sprache zu lernen.*
- **It doesn't take** long **to cook** an omelette. *Es dauert nicht lange ...*
- **It won't take** long **to fix** the computer. *Es wird nicht lange dauern ...*

C

How long	does / did / will	it take	you / Tom / them	to ... ?

It	takes / took / will take	me / Tom / them	a week / a long time / three hours	to ...

I started reading the book on Monday.
I finished it on Wednesday evening.

It **took me** three days **to read** it. *Ich habe drei Tage gebraucht, um es zu lesen.*

- How long **will it take me to learn** to drive?
  Wie lange werde ich brauchen, um Autofahren zu lernen?
- **It takes Tom** 20 minutes **to get** to work in the morning.
  Tom braucht 20 Minuten, um in der Früh zur Arbeit zu kommen.
- **It took us** an hour **to do** the shopping. *Wir haben eine Stunde gebraucht, ...*
- **Did it take you** a long time **to find** a job? *Hast du lange gebraucht, um eine Stelle zu finden?*
- **It will take me** an hour **to cook** dinner. *Ich werde eine Stunde brauchen, ...*

Übungen

Unit 49

49.1 Schreiben Sie für jedes Bild eine Frage über die Reisezeit mit **How long ... ?**

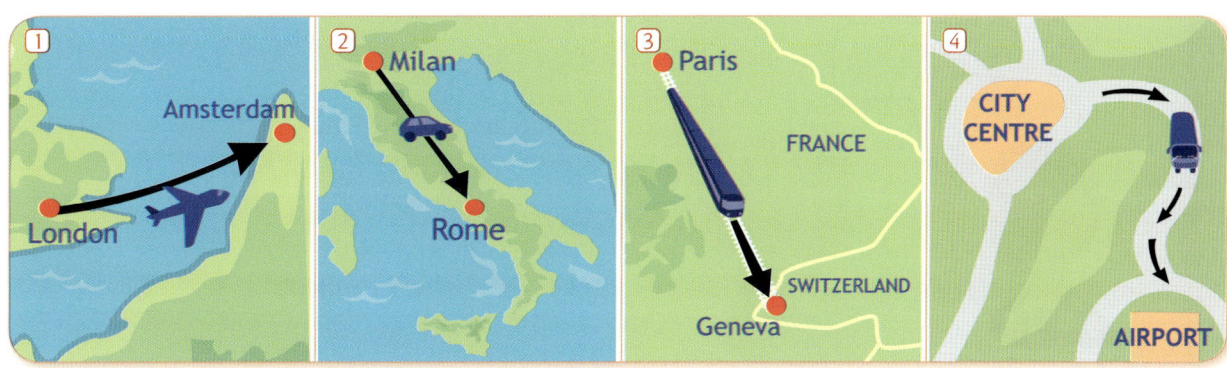

1 How long does it take by plane from London to Amsterdam?
2
3
4

49.2 Wie lange braucht man für folgende Tätigkeiten? Schreiben Sie vollständige Sätze mit **It takes ...** .

1 fly from your city/country to London
   It takes two hours to fly from Stuttgart to London.
2 fly from your city/country to New York

3 study to be a doctor in your country

4 walk from your home to the nearest shop

5 get from your home to the nearest airport

49.3 Stellen Sie Fragen über die Sätze. Verwenden Sie **How long did it take ... ?**

1 (Jane found a job.)   How long did it take her to find a job?
2 (I walked to the station.)   .... you ....
3 (Tom painted the bathroom.)
4 (I learnt to ski.)
5 (They repaired the car.)

49.4 Bilden Sie Sätze mit **It took ...** , die folgende Situationen beschreiben.

1 I read a book last week. I started reading it on Monday. I finished it three days later.
   It took me three days to read the book.
2 We walked home last night. We left at 10 o'clock and we arrived home at 10.20.

3 I learnt to drive last year. I had my first driving lesson in January. I passed my driving test six months later.

4 Mark drove to London yesterday. He left home at 7 o'clock and got to London at 10.

5 Lisa began looking for a job a long time ago. She got a job last week.

6 *Schreiben Sie eine wahre Aussage über sich selbst.*

49.5 Übersetzen Sie ins Englische.

1 'Wie lange dauert es mit dem Bus zum Zentrum?' 'Es dauert fünf Minuten.'
2 Wie lange brauchst du, um eine Seite zu lesen?
3 Wir brauchen zwei Tage, um das Haus zu putzen.
4 Lucy braucht nicht lange, um zur Arbeit zu kommen.
5 'Wie lange hat es gedauert mit dem Auto nach Paris zu fahren?' 'Es hat ungefähr zehn Stunden gedauert.'
6 Ich habe gestern zwei Stunden gebraucht, um meine Hausaufgaben zu machen.
7 Wir haben nicht lange gebraucht, um eine Wohnung zu finden.

Unit 50

Do you know where … ?
I don't know what … usw.

A

Do you know where Paula is?

Man sagt: Where **is** Paula? *Wo ist Paula?*

aber **Do you know** where Paula **is**? *Weißt du, wo Paula ist?*
(*nicht* Do you know where is Paula?)

Ähnlich sagt man:
I know
I don't know   } where **Paula is**.
Can you tell me

Subjekt Verb
↓ ↓

Wenn eine Frage wie **Where is Paula?** *Teil eines längeren Satzes ist (***Do you know where Paula is?***), ist die Wortstellung in der zweiten Satzhälfte wie im Aussagesatz (…* **where Paula is**, *nicht* where is Paula*).*

Who **are those people**?	aber	Do you know / Can you tell me	who **those people are** / how old **Nicola is** / what time **it is** / where **I can** go	?
How old **is Nicola**?				
What time **is it**?				
Where **can I** go?				
How much **is this camera**?		I know / I don't know / I don't remember	how much **this camera is** / when **you're** going away / where **they have** gone / what **Kate was** wearing	.
When **are you** going away?				
Where **have they** gone?				
What **was Kate** wearing?				

B

Fragen dieser Art im present simple *und* past simple *bildet man nicht mit* **do/does/did**, *sondern mit der Aussageform (in der zweiten Satzhälfte):*

Where **does he live**? *Wo wohnt er?*

aber **Do you know** where **he lives**? *Wissen Sie, wo er wohnt?*
(*nicht* Do you know where does he live?)

Vergleichen Sie:

How **do airplanes** fly?	aber	Do you know	how **airplanes fly**	?
What **does Jane** want?		I don't know / I don't remember / I know	what **Jane wants** / why **she went** home / where **I put** the key	.
Why **did she** go home?				
Where **did I** put the key?				

C

Fragen mit **Is … ?** / **Do … ?** / **Can … ?** *usw.*

*Bei Fragen dieser Art, die kein Fragewort (***where/who/when** *usw.) enthalten, verwendet man* **if** *oder* **whether** *(= ob).*

Vergleichen Sie:

Is Jack at home?   aber   **Do you know if Jack is** at home?
Ist Jack zu Hause?   *Weißt du, ob Jack zu Hause ist?*

Have they got a car?	aber	Do you know	if *oder* whether	**they've got** a car / **Ben can** swim / **they live** near here / **anybody saw** you	?
Can Ben swim?					
Do they live near here?		I don't know			.
Did anybody see you?					

Man kann hier entweder **if** *oder* **whether** *verwenden:*
 ○ Do you know **if** they've got a car?   *oder*
    Do you know **whether** they've got a car?
 ○ I don't know **if** anybody saw me.   *oder*
    I don't know **whether** anybody saw me.

110

Übungen

Unit 50

50.1 Beantworten Sie diese Fragen mit **I don't know where**/**when**/**why** ... usw.

1	Have your friends gone home?	(where)	I don't know where they've gone.
2	Is Kate in her office?	(where)	I don't know ....
3	Is the castle very old?	(how old)	....
4	Will Paul be here soon?	(when)	....
5	Was he angry because I was late?	(why)	....
6	Has Emily lived here a long time?	(how long)	....

50.2 Vervollständigen Sie die Sätze.

1 (How do airplanes fly?)   Do you know **how airplanes fly** ?
2 (Where does Susan work?)   I don't know ....
3 (What did Peter say?)   Do you remember .... ?
4 (Why did he go home early?)   I don't know ....
5 (What time does the meeting begin?)   Do you know .... ?
6 (How did the accident happen?)   I don't remember ....

50.3 Was ist richtig?

1 Do you know what time ~~is it~~ / it is? (Do you know what time **it is**? *ist richtig*)
2 Why <u>are you / you are</u> going away?
3 I don't know where <u>are they / they are</u> going.
4 Can you tell me where <u>is the museum / the museum is</u>?
5 Where <u>do you want / you want</u> to go for your holidays?
6 Do you know what <u>do elephants eat / elephants eat</u>?
7 I don't know how far <u>is it / it is</u> from the hotel to the station.

50.4 Bilden Sie Fragen mit **Do you know if ... ?**

1 (Have they got a car?)   Do you know if they've got a car?
2 (Are they married?)   Do you know ....
3 (Does Sue know Bill?)   ....
4 (Will Gary be here tomorrow?)   ....
5 (Did he pass his exam?)   ....

50.5 Bilden Sie Fragen mit **Do you know ... ?**

1 (What does Laura want?)   Do you know what Laura wants?
2 (Where is Paula?)   Do ....
3 (Is she working today?)   ....
4 (What time does she start work?)   ....
5 (Are the shops open tomorrow?)   ....
6 (Where do Sarah and Jack live?)   ....
7 (Did they go to Jane's party?)   ....

50.6 Verwenden Sie Ihre eigenen Ideen, um die Sätze zu vervollständigen.

1 Do you know why **the bus was late** ?
2 Do you know what time .... ?
3 Excuse me, can you tell me where .... ?
4 I don't know what ....
5 Do you know if .... ?
6 Do you know how much .... ?

50.7 Übersetzen Sie ins Englische.

1 Wissen Sie, wer das ist?
2 Können Sie mir sagen, wo der Bahnhof ist?
3 Ich weiß nicht, warum er sich ärgert.
4 Ich kann mich nicht erinnern, wo Rachel wohnt.
5 Ich weiß nicht, wie das funktioniert.
6 Wann ist Anna weggegangen?
7 Ich weiß, was wir machen können.
8 Wissen Sie, ob das Museum heute offen hat?
9 Weißt du, wann John weggegangen ist?

sich ärgern = be angry
funktionieren = work

Unit 51

She said that ... He told me that ...
(die indirekte Rede)

A Wenn man berichtet, was jemand gesagt hat, ist das Verb nach **said that** ('hat gesagt, dass') in der Vergangenheit.

Letzte Woche sind Sie auf ein Fest gegangen. Viele Ihrer Freunde waren da. Hier sind einige Dinge, die sie Ihnen gesagt haben:

Heute treffen Sie Paul. Sie erzählen ihm von dem Fest. Sie sagen Paul, was Ihre Freunde gesagt haben:

CLARE: *I'm enjoying my new job.* / *My father isn't well.*

am / is → was

- Clare said that **she was** enjoying her new job.
  Clare sagte, dass ihr die neue Arbeit gefalle.
- She said that **her father wasn't** well.
  ... dass es ihrem Vater nicht gut gehe.

SARAH / BEN: *We're going to buy a house.*

are → were

- Sarah and Ben said that **they were** going to buy a house. *... kaufen würden.*

PETER: *I have to leave early.* / *My sister has gone to Australia.*

have / has → had

- Peter said that **he had** to leave early.
  ... gehen müsse.
- He said that **his sister had** gone to Australia. *... gegangen sei.*

KATE: *I can't find a job.*

can → could

- Kate said that **she couldn't** find a job.
  ... nicht finden könne.

STEVE: *I'll phone you.*

will → would

- Steve said that **he would** phone me.
  ... anrufen würde.

RACHEL: *I don't like my job.* / *My son doesn't like school.*

do / does → did

- Rachel said that **she didn't** like her job.
  ... nicht gefalle.
- She said that **her son didn't** like school.

MIKE: *You look tired.* / *I feel fine.* YOU

look → looked
feel → felt
usw. usw.
(Gegenwart) (Vergangenheit)

- Mike said that **I looked** tired.
  ... müde aussähe.
- I said that **I felt** fine.
  ... prima fühlen würde.

B **Say** und **tell** entsprechen beide im Deutschen 'sagen'. Auf **tell** folgt jedoch immer direkt **me/you** usw.:

say (→ **said**)
- He **said** that he was tired.
  (*nicht* He said me)
  Er hat gesagt, dass er müde sei.
- What did she **say to** you?
  (*nicht* say you)
  Was hat sie dir gesagt?

Man sagt **he said to me**, **I said to Ann** usw. aber nicht 'he said me', 'I said Ann' usw.

tell (→ **told**)
- He **told me** that he was tired.
  (*nicht* He told that)
  Er hat mir gesagt, dass er müde sei.
- What did she **tell you**?
  (*nicht* tell to you)
  Was hat sie dir gesagt?

Man sagt **he told me**, **I told Ann** usw. aber nicht 'he told to me', 'I told to Ann' usw.

C Man kann auch **that** nach **say** oder **tell** weglassen:
- He said **that** he was tired. oder He said he was tired. (*ohne* that)
  Er hat gesagt, dass er müde sei. *Er hat gesagt, er sei müde.*
- Kate told me **that** she couldn't find a job. oder Kate told me she couldn't find a job.

I told you to ... → Unit 54

Übungen

51.1 Lesen Sie, was folgende Personen gesagt haben, und berichten Sie Ihre Aussagen mit **He**/**She**/**They said** (**that**) ... .

1 I've lost my watch. — He said he had lost his watch.
2 I'm very busy.
3 I can't go to the party.
4 I have to go out.
5 I'm learning Russian.
6 I don't feel very well.
7 We'll be home late.
8 I've just come back from holiday.
9 I'm going to buy a guitar.
10 We haven't got a key.

51.2 Vervollständigen Sie die Sätze, indem Sie die Aussagen der Leute in den Bildern mit der indirekten Rede wiedergeben.

1 I met Clare last week. She said ...she was enjoying her new job... .
2 Emma didn't want anything to eat. She said ....
3 I wanted to borrow Mike's ladder, but he said ....
4 Hannah was invited to the party, but she said ....
5 Susan told me she didn't want the picture. She said ....
6 Martin has just gone away on holiday. He said ....
7 I was looking for Robert. Nicola said ....
8 'Why did David stay at home?' 'He said ....'
9 'Has Mary gone out?' 'I think so. She said ....'

51.3 Vervollständigen Sie die Sätze mit **say**/**said** oder **tell**/**told**.

1 He ...said... he was tired.
2 What did she ...tell... you?
3 Anna .... she didn't like Peter.
4 Jack .... me that you were ill.
5 Please don't .... Dan what happened.
6 Did Lucy .... she would be late?
7 The woman .... she was a reporter.
8 The woman .... us she was a reporter.
9 They asked me a lot of questions, but I didn't .... them anything.
10 They asked me a lot of questions, but I didn't .... anything.

51.4 Übersetzen Sie ins Englische.

1 Matt hat gesagt, dass Emma krank sei.
2 Mary hat gesagt, dass sie später kommen würde.
3 Amy und Michael haben gesagt, dass sie heute Tennis spielen wollten.
4 Tom hat mir gesagt, dass er keinen Kaffee mag.
5 Jenny hat gesagt, sie werde heute nicht zu Hause sein.
6 Peter hat mir gesagt, dass er kein Fleisch isst.
7 Hat Kate dir gesagt, dass sie nicht kommen kann?
8 Was hat Andy dir gesagt?

Unit 52: work/working go/going do/doing

A
Der Infinitiv im Englischen wird in manchen Fällen mit **to** (**to play**) und in manchen Fällen ohne **to** (**play**) gebildet:
- Jane wants **to play** tennis. *Jane will Tennis spielen.*
- Jane can **play** tennis. *Jane kann Tennis spielen.*

B
work/go/be usw. (Infinitiv)

Nach **will/can/must** usw. verwendet man den Infinitiv ohne **to**:

will	Anna **will be** here soon.	→ Units 28–29
shall	**Shall** I **open** the window?	
might	I **might phone** you later.	→ Unit 30
may	**May** I **sit** here?	
can	I **can't meet** you tomorrow.	→ Unit 31
could	**Could** you **pass** the salt, please?	
must	It's late. I **must go** now.	→ Unit 32
should	You **shouldn't work** so hard.	→ Unit 33
would	**Would** you **like** some coffee?	→ Unit 35

Nach **do/does** und **did** (bei der Bildung von Fragen und Verneinungen) verwendet man auch den Infinitiv ohne **to**:

do/does (present simple)	**Do** you **work**?	→ Units 7–8
	They **don't work** very hard.	
	Helen **doesn't know** many people.	
	How much **does** it **cost**?	
did (past simple)	What time **did** the train **leave**?	→ Unit 13
	We **didn't sleep** well.	

C
to work / **to go** / **to be** usw. (**to** + Infinitiv)

Nach folgenden Verben verwendet man den Infinitiv mit **to**:

(I'm) **going to** …	I'm **going to play** tennis tomorrow.	→ Unit 27
	What **are** you **going to do**?	
(I) **have to** …	I **have to go** now.	→ Unit 34
	Everybody **has to eat**.	
(I) **want to** …	Do you **want to go** out?	→ Unit 53
	They don't **want to come** with us.	
(I) **would like to** …	I'**d like to talk** to you.	→ Unit 35
	Would you **like to go** out?	
(I) **used to** …	Dave **used to work** in a factory.	→ Unit 37

D
working/going/playing usw.

Beim continuous benutzt man die Form **-ing** (**working/going/playing** usw.):

am/is/are + **-ing** (present continuous)	Please be quiet. I'**m working**.	→ Units 4–5, 9, 26
	Tom **isn't working** today.	
	What time **are** you **going** out?	
was/were + **-ing** (past continuous)	It **was raining**, so we didn't go out.	→ Units 14–15
	What **were** you **doing** at 11.30 yesterday?	

Verben + **to** … und **-ing** (I want to do / I enjoy doing) → Unit 53   go und **-ing** → Unit 56

Übungen

52.1 Vervollständigen Sie die Sätze mit **… phone Paul** oder **… to phone Paul**.

1. I'll _phone Paul_ .
2. I'm going _to phone Paul_ .
3. Can you _____ Paul?
4. Shall I _____ ?
5. I'd like _____ .
6. Do you have _____ ?
7. You should _____ .
8. I want _____ .
9. I might _____ .
10. You must _____ .

52.2 Vervollständigen Sie die Sätze mit einem Verb aus dem Kästchen. Manchmal brauchen Sie den Infinitiv (**work**/**go** usw.) und manchmal **-ing** (**working**/**going** usw.).

do/doing	get/getting	~~sleep/sleeping~~	watch/watching
eat/eating	go/going	stay/staying	wear/wearing
fly/flying	listen/listening	wait/waiting	~~work/working~~

1. Please be quiet. I'm _working_ .
2. I feel tired today. I didn't _sleep_ very well last night.
3. What time do you usually _____ up in the morning?
4. 'Where are you _____ ?' 'To the office.'
5. Did you _____ TV last night?
6. Look at that plane! It's _____ very low.
7. You can turn off the radio. I'm not _____ to it.
8. They didn't _____ anything because they weren't hungry.
9. My friends were _____ for me when I arrived.
10. 'Does Susan always _____ glasses?' 'No, only for reading.'
11. 'What are you _____ tonight?' 'I'm _____ at home.'

52.3 Setzen Sie das Verb in die passende Form:

Infinitiv (**work**/**go** usw.) oder
to + Infinitiv (**to work** / **to go** usw.) oder
-ing (**working**/**going** usw.).

1. Shall I _open_ the window? (open)
2. It's late. I have _to go_ now. (go)
3. Amanda isn't _working_ this week. She's on holiday. (work)
4. I'm tired. I don't want _____ out. (go)
5. It might _____ , so take an umbrella with you. (rain)
6. What time do you have _____ tomorrow morning? (leave)
7. I'm sorry I can't _____ you. (help)
8. My brother is a student. He's _____ physics. (study)
9. Would you like _____ on a trip round the world? (go)
10. When you saw Maria, what was she _____ ? (wear)
11. When you go to London, where are you going _____ ? (stay)
12. I'm hungry. I must _____ something to eat. (have)
13. 'Where's Gary?' 'He's _____ a bath.' (have)
14. I used _____ a car, but I sold it last year. (have)
15. He spoke very quietly. I couldn't _____ him. (hear)
16. You don't look well. I don't think you should _____ to work today. (go)
17. I don't know what he said. I wasn't _____ to him. (listen)
18. I missed the bus and had _____ home. (walk)
19. I want _____ what happened. (know) You must _____ me. (tell)
20. May I _____ this book? (borrow)

52.4 Übersetzen Sie ins Englische.

1. Dave kann nicht Auto fahren.
2. Darf ich deinen Bleistift benutzen?
3. Kennen Sie meinen Bruder?
4. Ich werde morgen zu Hause sein.
5. Ich will einen neuen Laptop kaufen.
6. Könnten Sie bitte die Türe schließen?
7. Wir sind gestern nicht ausgegangen.
8. Das Wetter ist heute sehr schön. Die Sonne scheint.
9. Möchten Sie ein Stück Kuchen essen?
10. Wir fahren morgen in die Berge.
11. 'Wo sind die Kinder?' 'Sie spielen im Garten.'

Unit 53: to ... (I want to do) und -ing (I enjoy doing)

A

Nach folgenden Verben verwendet man den Infinitiv mit **to**:

want	plan	decide	try
hope	expect	offer	forget
need	promise	refuse	learn

+ **to** ... (**to do** / **to work** / **to be** usw.)

- What do you **want to do** this evening? *Was willst du heute Abend machen?*
- It's not very late. We don't **need to go** home yet. *... Wir müssen noch nicht nach Hause gehen.*
- Tina has **decided to sell** her car. *Tina hat beschlossen ihr Auto zu verkaufen.*
- You **forgot to switch** off the light when you went out. *Du hast vergessen das Licht auszuschalten ...*
- My brother is **learning to drive**. *Mein Bruder lernt (gerade) Auto zu fahren.*
- I **tried to read** my book, but I was too tired. *Ich habe versucht mein Buch zu lesen, ...*

B

Nach folgenden Verben verwendet man **-ing**:

| enjoy | stop | suggest |
| mind | finish | |

+ **-ing** (**doing** / **working** / **being** usw.)

- I **enjoy dancing**. (*nicht* enjoy to dance)
  Ich tanze gerne. (wörtlich: 'Ich genieße das Tanzen.')
- I don't **mind getting** up early.
  Es stört mich nicht früh aufzustehen.
- Has it **stopped raining**?
  Hat es aufgehört zu regnen?
- Sonia **suggested going** to the cinema.
  Sonia hat vorgeschlagen ins Kino zu gehen.

> I enjoy dancing.

C

Nach folgenden Verben ist es möglich, **-ing** oder **to** + Infinitiv zu verwenden:

| like | love | start | continue |
| prefer | hate | begin | |

+ **-ing** (**doing** usw.) oder **to** ... (**to do** usw.)

- Do you **like getting** up early? *oder* Do you **like to get** up early?
  Stehst du gerne früh auf? (wörtlich: 'Gefällt es dir, früh aufzustehen?')
- I **prefer travelling** by car. *oder* I **prefer to travel** by car.
  Ich reise lieber mit dem Auto. (wörtlich: 'Ich ziehe es vor, mit dem Auto zu reisen.')
- Anna **loves dancing**. *oder* Anna **loves to dance**.
  Ann tanzt für ihr Leben gern. (wörtlich: 'Ann liebt es zu tanzen.')
- I **hate being** late. *oder* I **hate to be** late.
  Ich komme sehr ungern zu spät. (wörtlich: 'Ich hasse es, zu spät zu kommen.')
- It **started raining**. *oder* It **started to rain**. *Es hat angefangen zu regnen.*

D

Nach folgenden Verben mit **would** verwendet man **to** + Infinitiv:

| would like | would love |
| would prefer | would hate |

+ **to** ... (**to do** / **to work** / **to be** usw.)

- Amy **would like to meet** you. (*nicht* would like meeting)
  Amy würde dich gerne kennen lernen.
- I**'d love to go** to Australia. (**I'd** = I would)
  Ich würde sehr gern nach Australien reisen.
- A: **Would** you **like to sit** down? *Möchten Sie sich setzen?*
  B: No, I**'d prefer to stand**, thank you. *Nein, ich möchte lieber stehen / ich stehe lieber, danke.*
- I like this apartment. I **wouldn't like to move**. *... Ich würde ungern umziehen.*
- I live in a small village. I**'d hate to live** in a big city. *... Ich würde sehr ungern in einer Großstadt wohnen.*

would like → Unit 35   I want you to ... → Unit 54   go und -ing → Unit 56   Präpositionen + -ing → Unit 112

Übungen

53.1 Setzen Sie das Verb in die passende Form: **to ...** oder **-ing**.

1. I enjoy _dancing_. (dance)
2. What do you want _to do_ tonight? (do)
3. Bye! I hope .... you again soon. (see)
4. I learnt .... when I was five years old. (swim)
5. Have you finished .... the kitchen? (clean)
6. Where's Anna? I need .... her something. (ask)
7. Do you enjoy .... other countries? (visit)
8. What have you decided .... ? (do)
9. Where's Ben? He promised .... here on time. (be)
10. I'm not in a hurry. I don't mind .... (wait)
11. The weather was nice, so I suggested .... for a walk by the river. (go)
12. Dan was very angry and refused .... to me. (speak)
13. I'm tired. I want .... to bed. (go)
14. I was very upset and started .... (cry)
15. I'm trying .... (work) Please stop .... (talk)

53.2 Vervollständigen Sie die Sätze mit der passenden Form (**to ...** oder **-ing**) eines der folgenden Verben:

~~go~~   go   help   lose   rain   read   see   send   wait   watch

1. 'Have you ever been to Australia?' 'No, but I'd love _to go_.'
2. Amy had a lot to do, so I offered .... her.
3. I'm surprised that you're here. I didn't expect .... you.
4. Kate has a lot of books. She enjoys ....
5. This ring was my grandmother's. I'd hate .... it.
6. Don't forget .... us a postcard when you're on holiday.
7. I'm not going out until it stops ....
8. What shall we do this afternoon? Would you like .... to the beach?
9. When I'm tired in the evenings, I like .... TV.
10. 'Shall we go now?' 'No, I'd prefer .... a few minutes.'

53.3 Vervollständigen Sie die Antworten. Achten Sie dabei auf die Form des Verbs (**to ...** oder **-ing**).

1	Do you usually get up early?	Yes, I like _to get up early_.
2	Do you ever go to museums?	Yes, I enjoy ....
3	Would you like to go to a museum now?	No, I'm hungry. I'd prefer .... to a restaurant.
4	Do you drive a lot?	No, I don't like ....
5	Have you ever been to New York?	No, but I'd love .... one day.
6	Do you often travel by train?	Yes, I enjoy ....
7	Shall we walk home or take a taxi?	I don't mind .... , but a taxi would be quicker.

53.4 Vervollständigen Sie die Sätze mit Aussagen über sich selbst. Verwenden Sie **to ...** oder **-ing**.

1. I enjoy ....
2. I don't like ....
3. If it's a nice day tomorrow, I'd like ....
4. When I'm on holiday, I like ....
5. I don't mind .... , but ....
6. I wouldn't like ....

53.5 Übersetzen Sie ins Englische.

1. Willst du mit mir kommen?
2. Paul geht sehr ungern auf Feste.
3. Wir planen nächstes Jahr nach Australien zu reisen.
4. Tania isst für ihr Leben gern Schokolade.
5. Ich habe beschlossen, Englisch zu studieren.
6. Es stört mich nicht, abends zu arbeiten.
7. Das Baby hat aufgehört zu weinen.
8. Gehen Sie gerne ins Kino?
9. Ich würde gerne ein Jahr in den USA leben.
10. Ich habe gestern versucht, dich anzurufen.
11. A: Möchten Sie mit dem Bus fahren?
    B: Nein, ich gehe lieber zu Fuß.

→ Zusätzliche Übungen 32 (Seite 268)

Unit 54
I want you to ...   I told you to ...

A   I want you to ...

The woman **wants to go**.
Die Frau will gehen.

The man **doesn't want** the woman **to go**.
He **wants** her **to stay**.
Der Mann will nicht, dass die Frau geht.
Er will, dass sie bleibt.

Man sagt:

I want	you somebody Sarah	to do something

○ I **want you to be** happy. (*nicht* I want that you are happy) *Ich will, dass du glücklich bist.*
○ They didn't **want anybody to know** their secret. *Sie wollten nicht, dass jemand ihr Geheimnis erfährt.*
○ Do you **want me to lend** you some money? *Willst du, dass ich dir etwas Geld leihe? / Soll ich dir ... ?*

Man verwendet **would like** auf gleiche Art:
○ **Would** you **like me to lend** you some money? *Möchtest du, dass ich dir etwas Geld leihe?*

B
Diese Form verwendet man auch mit anderen Verben, zum Beispiel: **ask**, **tell**, **advise**, **expect**, **persuade**, **teach**:
○ Sue **asked** a friend **to lend** her some money. *... hat einen Freund gebeten ihr Geld zu leihen.*
○ I **told** you **to be** careful. *Ich habe dir gesagt, dass du vorsichtig sein solltest.*
○ What do you **advise** me **to do**? *Was raten Sie mir zu tun?*
○ I didn't **expect** them **to be** here. *Ich habe nicht erwartet, dass sie hier sein würden.*
○ We **persuaded** Gary **to come** with us. *Wir haben Gary überredet mit uns zu kommen.*
○ I **am teaching** my brother **to swim**. *Ich bringe meinem Bruder das Schwimmen bei.*

C   I told you to ... / I told you not to ...
Bei indirekten Aufforderungen verwendet man **tell** + **somebody** + **to**:

JANE   ME

→ Jane **told** me **to wait** for her.
Jane hat mir gesagt, dass ich auf sie warten soll.

PAUL   SUE

→ Paul **told** Sue **not to wait** for him.
Paul hat Sue gesagt, dass sie nicht auf ihn warten soll.

D   make und let
Nach **make** und **let** verwendet man nicht **to**:
make somebody do ... = *jemanden veranlassen / jemanden dazu bringen etwas zu tun*:
○ He's very funny. He **makes** me **laugh**. (*nicht* makes me to laugh)
   Er bringt mich zum Lachen.
○ At school our teacher **made** us **work** very hard.
   ... wir mussten bei unserem Lehrer fleißig arbeiten. (wörtlich: '... hat uns veranlasst fleißig zu arbeiten.')

let somebody do ... = *jemandem erlauben etwas zu tun*:
○ I didn't have my phone with me, so Sue **let** me **use** hers. (*nicht* let me to use)
   Ich hatte mein Handy nicht dabei, also hat Sue mir erlaubt ihres zu benutzen.

Man verwendet auch **Let's** (= **Let us**) um vorzuschlagen mit jemandem etwas gemeinsam zu tun:
○ Come on! **Let's dance**! *Kommt! Tanzen wir!* (wörtlich: 'Lasst uns tanzen!')
○ 'Do you want to go out tonight?' 'No, I'm tired. **Let's stay** at home.' '... Bleiben wir zu Hause.'

Let's ... → Unit 36   He told me that ... → Unit 51

Übungen

Unit 54

54.1 Verwenden Sie die Sätze in Klammern um neue Sätze mit **I want you ... / I don't want you ... / Do you want me ... ?** zu schreiben.

1 (you must come with me)   I want you to come with me.
2 (listen carefully)   I want ....
3 (please don't be angry)   I don't ....
4 (shall I wait for you?)   Do you ....
5 (don't call me tonight)   ....
6 (you must meet Sarah)   ....

54.2 Vervollständigen Sie die Sätze anhand der Situationen in den Bildern.

1 Dan persuaded me to go to the cinema.
2 I wanted to get to the station. A woman told ....
3 Ben wasn't well. I advised ....
4 Laura had a lot of luggage. She asked ....
5 I was too busy to talk to Tom. I told ....
6 I wanted to make a phone call. Paul let ....
7 Sue is going to call me later. I told ....
8 Amy's mother taught ....

54.3 Vervollständigen Sie folgende Sätze mit Verben aus der Liste. In manchen Fällen ist **to** erforderlich (**to go / to wait** usw.), manchmal nicht (**go/wait** usw.).

| arrive | borrow | get | ~~go~~ | go | make | repeat | tell | think | wait |

1 Please stay here. I don't want you to go yet.
2 I didn't hear what she said, so I asked her .... it.
3 'Shall we begin?'   'No, let's .... a few minutes.'
4 Are they already here? I expected them .... much later.
5 Kevin's parents didn't want him .... married.
6 I want to stay here. You can't make me .... with you.
7 'Is that your bike?'   'No, it's John's. He let me .... it.'
8 Rachel can't come to the party. She told me .... you.
9 Would you like a drink? Would you like me .... some coffee?
10 'Kate doesn't like me.'   'What makes you .... that?'

54.4 Übersetzen Sie ins Englische.

1 Ich will, dass du etwas isst.
2 Ich möchte nicht, dass du traurig bist.
3 Willst du, dass ich mit dir gehe?
4 Möchten Sie, dass ich Ihnen helfe?
5 Sam wollte, dass ich ihn heute Abend anrufe.
6 Hannah hat mich gebeten, mit Ihnen zu sprechen.
7 Ich habe dir gesagt, du sollst die Tür schließen.
8 Was erwartest du, dass ich dir sage?
9 Sein Arzt hat ihm geraten, zu Hause zu bleiben.

Unit 55
I went to the shop to …

A

Paula wanted a newspaper, so she went to the shop.

Why did she go to the shop?
To get a newspaper.
Um eine Zeitung zu kaufen.

She went to the shop **to get** a newspaper.
Sie ist zum Laden gegangen, um eine Zeitung zu kaufen.

Man verwendet **to** *…* (**to get** / **to see** *usw.*) *um zu sagen, warum man etwas tut:*
- 'Why are you going out?'   'ced**To buy** some food.'   … 'Um Essen zu kaufen.'
- Catherine went to the station **to meet** her friend.
  … , *um ihren Freund / ihre Freundin zu treffen.*
- Sue turned on the television **to watch** the news.
  … , *um die Nachrichten zu sehen.*
- I'd like to go to Spain **to learn** Spanish.
  … , *um Spanisch zu lernen.*

money/time to (do something):
- We need some **money to buy** food.   *Wir brauchen Geld um Essen zu kaufen.*
- I don't have **time to watch** TV.   … *keine Zeit fernzusehen.*

B

to … *und* **for** …

Den Grund für eine Handlung kann man entweder mit **to** + *Verb oder* **for** + *Nomen ausdrücken:*

to + *Verb* (**to get** / **to see** *usw.*)	**for** + *Nomen* (**for a newspaper** / **for food** *usw.*)
○ I went to the shop **to get** a newspaper. (*nicht* for get)	○ I went to the shop **for a newspaper**.
○ They're going to Brazil **to see** their friends.	○ They're going to Brazil **for a holiday**.
○ We need some money **to buy** food.	○ We need some money **for food**.

C

wait for … :

wait for (somebody/something) = *auf jemanden / auf etwas warten:*
- Please **wait for** me.   *Warte(t) bitte auf mich.*
- Are you **waiting for** the bus?   *Warten Sie auf den Bus?*

wait to (do something) = *darauf warten etwas zu tun:*
- Hurry up! I'm **waiting to go**.   *Ich warte darauf wegzugehen.*
- Are you **waiting to see** the doctor?
  Warten Sie darauf den Arzt zu sehen?

wait for (somebody/something) **to** … = *darauf warten, dass jemand etwas tut / dass (bis) etwas passiert:*
- The lights are red. You have to **wait for them to change**.
  … *Sie müssen warten, bis die Ampel rot/grün wird.*
- Are you **waiting for the doctor to come**?
  Warten Sie darauf, dass der Arzt kommt?

They're **waiting for the lights to change**.

---

go to … *und* **go for** … → **Unit 56**   **something to eat** / **nothing to do** *usw.* → **Unit 79**
enough + **to/for** … → **Unit 91**   **too** + **to/for** … → **Unit 92**

Übungen

Unit 55

55.1
Schreiben Sie, wo Sie hingegangen sind und warum. Verwenden Sie Begriffe aus beiden Kästchen.

| a coffee shop   ~~the station~~ | + | buy some vegetables   get some medicine |
| the chemist   the market | | meet a friend   ~~get a train ticket~~ |

1 _I went to the station to get a train ticket._
2 I went ....
3 ....
4 ....

55.2
Vervollständigen Sie die Sätze mit den Satzhälften aus dem Kästchen.

| to get some fresh air   to read the newspaper   to wake him up |
| to open this door   to see who it was   ~~to watch the news~~ |

1 I turned on the TV _to watch the news_.
2 Alice sat down in an armchair ....
3 Do I need a key ....?
4 I went for a walk by the river ....
5 I knocked on the door of David's room ....
6 The doorbell rang, so I looked out of the window ....

55.3
Vervollständigen Sie die Sätze, indem Sie einen Grund für die Handlung mit **to ...** angeben.

1 I went to the shop _to get a newspaper_.
2 I'm very busy. I don't have time ....
3 I phoned Amy ....
4 I'm going out ....
5 I borrowed some money ....

55.4
Setzen Sie **to** oder **for** ein.

1 I went out _to_ get some bread.
2 We went to a restaurant .... have dinner.
3 Robert wants to go to university .... study economics.
4 I'm going to London .... an interview next week.
5 I'm going to London .... visit some friends of mine.
6 Do you have time .... a cup of coffee?
7 I got up late this morning. I didn't have time .... wash.
8 Everybody needs money .... live.
9 We didn't have any money .... a taxi, so we walked home.
10 The office is very small. There's space only .... a desk and chair.
11 A: Excuse me, are you waiting .... be served?
  B: No, I'm already being served, thanks.

55.5
Vervollständigen Sie die Sätze. Benutzen Sie die folgenden möglichen Satzendungen und fügen Sie **for** oder **to** ein:

| it / to arrive   you / tell me   ~~them / change~~   the film / begin |

1 We stopped at the lights and waited _for them to change_.
2 I sat down in the cinema and waited ....
3 We called an ambulance and waited ....
4 'Do you know what to do?' 'No, I'm waiting ....'

55.6
Übersetzen Sie ins Englische.

Geldautomat = cashpoint

1 Kate ist zum Geldautomaten gegangen, um Geld zu holen.
2 Ich habe keine Zeit zum Kochen.
3 Rachel und John sind in die Stadt gefahren, um einzukaufen.
4 Wir haben kein Geld, um ein Haus zu kaufen.
5 Warten Sie bitte hier, um Mr Jones zu sehen.
6 Sandra braucht Geld für ein neues Auto.
7 Warten Sie darauf, mit Mrs Anderson zu sprechen?
8 A: Warum guckst du aus dem Fenster?
  B: Um zu sehen, ob es regnet.
9 Tom wartet darauf, dass Jenny ihn anruft.

Unit 56

go to ...   go on ...   go for ...   go -ing

A
go to ... = *gehen zu/in/nach ...* (**go to work** / **go to London** / **go to a concert** *usw.*)

- What time do you usually **go to work**?   *... gehen Sie meistens zur Arbeit?*
- I'm **going to China** next week.
- Sophie didn't want to **go to the concert**.
- 'Where's Tom?'   'He's **gone to bed**.'
- I **went to the dentist** yesterday.
  Ich bin ... zum Zahnarzt gegangen.

go to →

Aber man sagt **go home** (*ohne* **to**):
- I'm **going home** now.   (*nicht* going to home)   *Ich gehe jetzt nach Hause.*

go to sleep = *einschlafen*
- I was very tired and **went to sleep** quickly.   *... und bin schnell eingeschlafen.*

B
go on ...

go on	holiday	*in Urlaub gehen*	
	a trip	*eine Reise*	
	a tour	*eine Rundfahrt*	*machen*
	a cruise	*eine Kreuzfahrt*	
	strike	*in den Streik treten*	

- We're **going on holiday** next week.
- Children often **go on school trips**.
- Workers at the airport have **gone on strike**.
  (= they are refusing to work)

C
go for ... *verwendet man für viele Freizeitaktivitäten:*

go (somewhere) for	a walk	*spazieren gehen*
	a run	*joggen gehen*
	a swim	*schwimmen gehen / baden gehen*
	a drink	*etwas trinken*
	a meal	*essen gehen*

- 'Where's Emma?'   'She's **gone for a walk**.'
- Do you **go for a run** every morning?
- The water looks nice. I'm **going for a swim**.
- I met Chris in town, so we **went for coffee**.
- Shall we **go** out **for a meal**? I know a good restaurant.

D
Man verwendet auch **go** + **-ing** *für viele Freizeitaktivitäten und Sportarten, ebenso wie für* **shopping**:

I go	shopping
he is **going**	swimming
we **went**	fishing
they have **gone**	sailing
she wants to **go**	skiing
	jogging *usw.*

I'm going skiing.

- Are you **going shopping** this afternoon?
  Gehst du heute Nachmittag einkaufen?
- It's a nice day. Let's **go swimming**.
  ... Gehen wir schwimmen.
- Richard has a small boat and he often **goes sailing**.
  ... und er geht oft segeln.
- I **went jogging** before breakfast this morning.
  Ich bin ... joggen gegangen.

122

Übungen

56.1 Schreiben Sie bei Bedarf to/on/for.

1. I'm going ...to... China next week.
2. Richard often goes ...–... sailing. (*keine Präposition*)
3. Sue went .... Mexico last year.
4. Jack goes .... jogging every morning.
5. I'm going out .... a walk. Do you want to come?
6. I'm tired because I went .... bed very late last night.
7. Mark is going .... holiday .... Italy next week.
8. The weather was warm and the river was clean, so we went .... a swim.
9. The taxi drivers went .... strike when I was in New York.
10. Let's go .... the cinema this evening.
11. It's late. I have to go .... home now.
12. Would you like to go .... a tour of the city?
13. Shall we go out .... dinner this evening?
14. My parents are going .... a cruise this summer.

56.2 Vervollständigen Sie die Sätze. Verwenden Sie go/goes/going/went + -ing.

① often — RICHARD
② last Saturday — EMILY
③ every day — DAN
④ next month — JESSICA
⑤ later — PETER
⑥ yesterday — SARAH

1. Richard has a boat. He often ...goes sailing....
2. Last Saturday Emily went ....
3. Dan .... every day.
4. Jessica is going on holiday next month. She is ....
5. Peter is going out later. He has to ....
6. Sarah .... after work yesterday.

56.3 Vervollständigen Sie die Sätze mit Wörtern aus dem Kästchen. Verwenden Sie außerdem to/on/for, wenn erforderlich.

| a swim | holiday | Portugal | shopping | sleep |
| a walk | home | riding | skiing | university |

1. The water looks nice. Let's go ...for a swim... .
2. After leaving school, Tina went .... where she studied psychology.
3. I'm going .... now. I have to buy a few things.
4. I was very tired last night. I sat down in an armchair and went ....
5. I wasn't enjoying the party, so I went .... early.
6. We live near the mountains. In winter we go .... most weekends.
7. Robert has got a horse. He goes .... a lot.
8. The weather is nice. Shall we go .... along the river?
9. A: Are you going .... soon?
   B: Yes, next month. We're going .... We've never been there before.

56.4 Übersetzen Sie ins Englische.

Karibik = Caribbean

1. Wir gehen nicht sehr oft in die Oper.
2. Wann gehst du zum Arzt? Heute oder morgen?
3. 'Wo ist Karen?' 'Sie ist nach Hause gegangen.'
4. Ich bin letzte Woche nach Paris gefahren.
5. Möchten Sie etwas trinken gehen?
6. Bist du heute Früh joggen gegangen?
7. Julie ist heute einkaufen gegangen und hat ein neues Kleid gekauft.
8. Dieses Jahr fahren wir nach Portugal in Urlaub.
9. Meine Eltern haben letztes Jahr eine Kreuzfahrt in der Karibik gemacht.

Unit 57: get

Get hat im Englischen verschiedene Bedeutungen und im Deutschen mehrere unterschiedliche Übersetzungen. Die wichtigsten Verwendungen von **get** werden hier gezeigt.

A

get an email / **get a job** usw. (**get** + Nomen) = bekommen/erhalten/kaufen/holen/finden/bringen

you **don't have** something → you **get** it → you **have** it

- I **got an email** from Sam this morning.   Ich habe heute früh eine E-mail von Sam bekommen.
- I like your sweater. Where did you **get it**?   … Wo hast du ihn gekauft?
- It's hard to **get a job** at the moment.   Es ist zur Zeit schwierig eine Arbeit zu finden.
- (am Telefon) 'Is Lisa here?' 'Yes, I'll **get her** for you.'   … 'Ja, ich hole sie …'

Man sagt auch **get a bus** / **a train** / **a taxi** (= ein(en) Bus/Zug/Taxi nehmen):
- 'Did you walk here?' 'No, I **got the bus**.'   … 'Nein, ich habe den Bus genommen.'

B

get hungry / **get cold** / **get tired** usw. (**get** + Adjektiv) = werden:

you're **not hungry** → you **get hungry** → you **are hungry**

- If you don't eat, you **get hungry**.   Wenn man nicht isst, wird man hungrig.
- Drink your coffee. It**'s getting cold**.   … er wird kalt.
- I'm sorry your mother is ill. I hope she **gets better** soon.   … Hoffentlich wird sie bald wieder gesund.
- It was raining very hard. We didn't have an umbrella, so we **got** very **wet**.
  … wir sind sehr nass geworden.

Einige Begriffe mit **get** + Adjektiv haben im Deutschen eine andere Übersetzung:

get married = heiraten
get dressed = sich anziehen
get lost = sich verlaufen/verfahren

- Nicola and Frank are **getting married** soon.
- I got up and **got dressed** quickly.
- We didn't have a map, so we **got lost**.
  Wir hatten keine Landkarte, also haben wir uns verfahren.

C

get to a place = ankommen/(hin)kommen (in / an einem Ort / an eine Stelle):
- I usually **get to work** before 8.30.   Ich komme meistens vor 8.30 Uhr zur Arbeit.
- We left London at 10 o'clock and **got to Manchester** at 12.45.
  … und sind um 12.45 Uhr … angekommen.

get here/there (ohne **to**):
- How did you **get here**? By bus? Wie sind Sie hergekommen? …

get home (ohne **to**) = nach Hause kommen:
- What time did you **get home** last night?

D

get in/out/on/off = einsteigen/aussteigen (bei Transportmitteln):

get in (a car)   **get out** (of a car)   **get on**   **get off**
(a bus / a train / a plane)

- Kate **got in** (oder **into**) **the car** and drove away. Kate ist ins Auto eingestiegen …
- A car stopped and a man **got out**. (aber A man got out **of the car**.)   … ein Mann ist ausgestiegen.
- We **got on the bus** outside the hotel and **got off** in Church Street.
  Wir sind … in den Bus eingestiegen und … ausgestiegen.

---

get to → Unit 108   in/out/on/off → Units 110, 114   get up → Unit 114   get on → Anhang 6

Übungen

Unit 57

57.1 Vervollständigen Sie die Sätze. Verwenden Sie **get**/**gets** und einen Begriff aus dem Kästchen.

| a doctor | a lot of rain | a taxi | ~~my email~~ | the job |
| a good salary | a new laptop | a ticket | some milk | your boots |

1. Did you _get my email_? I sent it a week ago.
2. Where did you _____? They're very nice.
3. Quick! This man is ill. We need to _____.
4. I don't want to walk home. Let's _____.
5. Tom has an interview tomorrow. I hope he _____.
6. When you go to the shop, can you _____?
7. 'Are you going to the concert?' 'Yes, if I can _____.'
8. Helen has a well-paid job. She _____.
9. The weather is horrible here in winter. We _____.
10. I'm going to _____. The one I have is too slow.

57.2 Vervollständigen Sie die Sätze mit **getting** + einem der folgenden Wörter:

| ~~cold~~ | dark | late | married | ready |

1. Drink your coffee. It's _getting cold_.
2. Turn on the light. It's _____.
3. 'I'm _____ next week.' 'Really? Congratulations!'
4. 'Where's Karen?' 'She's _____ to go out.'
5. It's _____. It's time to go home.

57.3 Vervollständigen Sie die Sätze mit **get**/**gets**/**got** + einem der folgenden Wörter:

| angry | better | ~~hungry~~ | lost | married | old | wet |

1. If you don't eat, you _get hungry_.
2. Don't go out in the rain. You'll _____.
3. My brother _____ last year. His wife's name is Sarah.
4. Mark is always very calm. He never _____.
5. We tried to find the hotel, but we _____.
6. Everybody wants to stay young, but we all _____.
7. Yesterday the weather wasn't so good at first, but it _____ during the day.

57.4 Bilden Sie Sätze mit **I left ...** und **got to ...** .

1. home / 7.30 → work / 8.15
   I left home at 7.30 and got to work at 8.15.
2. London / 10.15 → Bristol / 11.45
   I left London at 10.15 and _____
3. the party / 11.15 → home / midnight
   _____
4. *Schreiben Sie einen Satz über sich selbst.*
   I left _____

57.5 Vervollständigen Sie die Sätze mit **got in** / **got out of** / **got on** / **got off**.

1. Kate _got in_ the car and drove away.
2. I _____ the bus and walked to my house from the bus stop.
3. Isabel _____ the car, shut the door and went into a shop.
4. I made a stupid mistake. I _____ the wrong train.

57.6 Übersetzen Sie ins Englische. Verwenden Sie **get**.

1. Thomas hat ein Taxi zum Bahnhof genommen.
2. A: Ich gehe zum Laden.
   B: Kannst du mir Milch mitbringen?
3. Ich werde müde. Ich gehe jetzt ins Bett.
4. Ich habe gestern angerufen. Hast du meine Nachricht bekommen?
5. Wann haben Ben und Jenny geheiratet?
6. Um wie viel Uhr kommen Sie meistens in die Arbeit?
7. Komm jetzt ins Haus. Es wird kalt.
8. Sei vorsichtig, wenn du aus dem Auto steigst.
9. Lisa ist in den Zug eingestiegen, eine Minute bevor er abgefahren ist.

Nachricht = message
abfahren = leave

Unit 58

do und make

A

Do (= machen/tun) verwendet man allgemein für Handlungen:
- What are you **doing** this evening? (nicht What are you making?) *Was machst/tust du heute Abend?*
- 'Shall I open the window?' 'No, it's OK. I'll **do** it.' *'... Ich mach'/tu' es.'*
- Rachel's job is very boring. She **does** the same thing every day. *... Sie macht/tut jeden Tag das Gleiche.*
- I **did** a lot of things yesterday. *Ich habe gestern viel gemacht/getan.*

What do you do? = *Was machen Sie beruflich?*:
- 'What do you **do**?' 'I work in a bank'.

B

Make verwendet man, wenn es sich darum handelt etwas herzustellen oder zu erzeugen, und wird manchmal mit *'machen'*, manchmal mit anderen Verben übersetzt, zum Beispiel:

She's **making** coffee.
Sie kocht Kaffee.

He has **made** a cake.
Er hat einen Kuchen gebacken.

They **make** umbrellas.
Sie stellen Regenschirme her.

It was **made** in China.
Es wurde in China hergestellt.

Vergleichen Sie **do** *und* **make**:
- I **did** a lot yesterday. I **cleaned** my room, I **wrote** some letters and I **made** a cake.
  Ich habe gestern viel getan/gemacht. Ich habe mein Zimmer sauber gemacht, ich habe Briefe geschrieben und ich habe einen Kuchen gebacken.
- A: What do you **do** in your free time? Sport? Reading? Hobbies? *Was machst/tust du ... ?*
  B: I **make** clothes. I **make** dresses and jackets. I also **make** toys for my children.
  Ich nähe Kleider ... Ich bastele auch Spielzeug ...

C

In folgenden Redewendungen verwendet man immer **do**:

do		
	an exam / a test	eine Prüfung machen
	a course	einen Kurs machen
	homework	Hausaufgaben machen
	housework	den Haushalt machen
	somebody a favour	jemandem einen Gefallen tun
	an exercise	eine Übung machen

- I'm **doing my driving test** next week.
- John has just **done a training course**.
- Our children have to **do** a lot of **homework**.
- I hate **doing housework**, especially cleaning.
- Sue, could you **do me a favour**?
- I go for a run and **do exercises** every morning.

Außerdem sagt man **do the shopping** (*Einkäufe/Besorgungen machen*) / **do the cooking** (*kochen*) / **do the washing** (*die Wäsche waschen*) / **do the washing-up** (*das Geschirr spülen*) usw. :
- I **did the washing**, but I didn't **do the shopping**.

D

In folgenden Redewendungen verwendet man immer **make**:

make		
	a mistake	einen Fehler machen
	an appointment	einen Termin vereinbaren
	a phone call	telefonieren / ein Telefongespräch führen
	a list	eine Liste machen
	a noise	ein Geräusch machen
	a bed	ein Bett machen

- I'm sorry, I **made a mistake**.
- I need to **make an appointment** to see the doctor.
- Excuse me, I have to **make a phone call**.
- Have you **made a shopping list**?
- It's late. Don't **make a noise**.
- Sometimes I forget to **make my bed** in the morning.

Man sagt **make a film** (= *einen Film drehen*) aber **take a photo** / **take a picture** (= *ein Foto machen*):
- When was **this film made**? *Wann wurde dieser Film gedreht?*

aber
- When was **this photo taken**? *... dieses Foto gemacht?*

do/does/did (Verneinungen und Fragen) → Units 44–45   make somebody do something → Unit 54

Übungen

58.1 Vervollständigen Sie die Sätze mit make/making/made oder do/doing/did/done.

1. 'Shall I open the window?'   'No, it's OK. I'll ...do... it.'
2. What did you .... at the weekend? Did you go away?
3. Do you know how to .... bread?
4. Paper is .... from wood.
5. Richard didn't help me. He sat in an armchair and .... nothing.
6. 'What do you ....?'   'I'm a doctor.'
7. I asked you to clean the bathroom. Have you .... it?
8. 'What do they .... in that factory?'   'Shoes.'
9. I'm .... some coffee. Would you like some?
10. Why are you angry with me? I didn't .... anything wrong.
11. 'What are you .... tomorrow afternoon?'   'I'm working.'

58.2 Was machen diese Personen?

1. He's making a cake.
2. They ....
3. He ....
4. ....
5. ....
6. ....
7. ....
8. ....
9. ....
10. ....

58.3 Vervollständigen Sie die Sätze mit der passenden Form von make oder do.

1. I hate ...doing... housework, especially cleaning.
2. Why do you always .... the same mistake?
3. 'Can you .... me a favour?'   'It depends what it is.'
4. 'Have you .... your homework?'   'Not yet.'
5. I need to see the dentist, but I haven't .... an appointment.
6. I'm .... a course in photography at the moment. It's very good.
7. The last time I .... an exam was ten years ago.
8. How many phone calls did you .... yesterday?
9. When you've finished Exercise 1, you can .... Exercise 2.
10. There's something wrong with the car. The engine is .... a strange noise.
11. It was a bad mistake. It was the worst mistake I've ever ....
12. Let's .... a list of all the things we have to .... today.

58.4 Übersetzen Sie ins Englische.

Firma = company

1. Die Firma stellt Computer her.
2. Was machen Sie gewöhnlich nach dem Abendessen?
3. Am Wochenende mache ich meistens die Besorgungen und den Haushalt.
4. 'Was machst du?'   'Ich backe Brot.'
5. Letztes Wochenende haben wir nicht viel gemacht.
6. Hast du dein Bett gemacht?
7. Könnten Sie ein Foto von uns machen?
8. Meine Tochter hat gestern ihre Prüfung gemacht.
9. Dieser Film wurde in Italien gedreht.
10. Könnte ich bitte einen Termin mit Dr Saunders vereinbaren?

Unit 59: have

A
have und **have got**

I have (something) *oder* **I've got** (something) = *Ich habe (etwas)*:
- **I have** a new car. *oder* **I've got** a new car. *Ich habe ein neues Auto.*
- Sue **has** long hair. *oder* Sue **has got** long hair. *Sue hat lange Haare.*
- **Do** they **have** any children? *oder* **Have** they **got** any children? *Haben sie Kinder?*
- Tom **doesn't have** a job. *oder* Tom **hasn't got** a job. *Tom hat keine Arbeit.*
- How much time **do** you **have**? *oder* How much time **have** you **got**? *Wie viel Zeit haben Sie?*
- **I have** a headache. *oder* **I've got** a headache. *Ich habe Kopfschmerzen.*
- **Do** you **have** a cold? *oder* **Have** you **got** a cold? *Sind Sie erkältet? / Haben Sie eine Erkältung?*

Die Vergangenheit ist **I had** *(ohne* **got***) /* **I didn't have** */* **Did you have**? *usw.*:
- When I first met Sue, she **had** short hair. *… hatte sie kurze Haare.*
- He **didn't have** any money because he **didn't have** a job.
  Er hatte kein Geld, weil er keine Arbeit hatte.
- **Did** you **have** enough time to do everything you wanted?
  Hattest du genügend Zeit um alles zu tun, was du vorhattest?

B
have breakfast / **have a shower** *usw.*

Bei folgenden Redewendungen bedeutet **have** *(ohne* **got***) 'essen' oder 'trinken':*

have	breakfast / lunch / dinner
	a meal / a sandwich / a pizza *usw.*
	a cup of coffee / a glass of milk *usw.*
	something to eat/drink

- 'Where's Lisa?' 'She**'s having** lunch.'
  … 'Sie ist beim Mittagessen.'
- I **don't** usually **have** breakfast.
  Ich frühstücke normalerweise nicht.
- I **had** three cups of coffee this morning.
  Heute früh habe ich drei Tassen Kaffee getrunken.
- '**Have** a biscuit!' 'Oh, thank you.' *'Nehmen Sie …'*

Have *(ohne* **got***) hat unterschiedliche Übersetzungen in folgenden Redewendungen:*

have	a bath / a shower
	a rest / a holiday / a party
	a nice time / fun *usw.*
	a walk / a swim / a game (of tennis *usw.*)
	a dream / an accident
	a baby
	a look (at something)

- I **had** a shower this morning.
  Ich habe mich … geduscht.
- We**'re having** a party next week. You must come.
  Wir machen … ein Fest. …
- **Did** you **have** a good time in Tokyo?
  Haben Sie eine schöne Zeit … verbracht?
- Sandra **has** just **had** a baby.
  Sandra hat gerade ein Baby bekommen.
- Can I **have** a look at your magazine?
  … einen Blick auf deine Zeitschrift werfen?

Außerdem:
- **Have** fun / a nice time / a good time! = *Viel Spaß!*
- **Have** a good trip/flight/holiday! = *Gute Reise! / Guten Flug! / Schönen Urlaub!*

C
Vergleichen Sie:

Have *oder* **have got**
- I **have** / I**'ve got** a new shower. It's very good.
  Ich habe eine neue Dusche.

Have *(nicht* **have got***)*
- I **have** a shower every morning. *(nicht* I**'ve got***)*
  Ich dusche mich jeden Morgen.
- A: Where's Paul?
  B: He**'s having** a shower. *Er duscht sich gerade.*

I've got a new shower.

I'm having a shower.

I have / I've got → Unit 10   I've (done) (present perfect) → Units 16–19   I have to … → Unit 34

Übungen

Unit 59

59.1 Vervollständigen Sie die Sätze mit den Wörtern in Klammern. Verwenden Sie die passende Form von **have** oder **have got**.

1. _I didn't have_ time to do the shopping yesterday. (I / not / have)
2. '_Has Lisa got_ oder _Does Lisa have_ a car?' 'No, she can't drive.' (Lisa / have?)
3. He can't open the door. _____ a key. (he / not / have)
4. _____ a cold last week. He's better now. (Gary / have)
5. What's wrong? _____ a headache? (you / have?)
6. We wanted to go by taxi, but _____ enough money. (we / not / have)
7. Laura is very busy. _____ much free time. (she / not / have)
8. _____ any problems when you were on holiday? (you / have?)

59.2 Was machen die Personen? Schreiben Sie Sätze, in denen Sie folgende Begriffe verwenden.

a bath   ~~breakfast~~   a cup of tea   dinner   a good time   a rest

1. _They're having breakfast._
2. She _____
3. He _____
4. They _____
5. _____
6. _____

59.3 Was sagt man in den folgenden Situationen? Verwenden Sie **have**.

1. Emily is going on holiday. What do you say to her before she goes?
   Have a nice holiday!
2. You meet Clare at the airport. She has just got off her plane. Ask her about the flight.
   Did you have a good flight?
3. Tom is going on a long trip. What do you say to him before he leaves?
4. It's Monday morning. You are at work. Ask Paula about her weekend.
5. Paul has just come home after playing tennis with a friend. Ask him about the game.
6. Rachel is going out this evening. What do you say to her before she goes?
7. Mark has just returned from holiday. Ask him about his holiday.

59.4 Vervollständigen Sie die Sätze mit **have**/**had** und Begriffen aus der Liste.

an accident   a glass of water   a look   a walk   ~~a party~~   something to eat

1. We _had a party_ a few weeks ago. We invited 50 people.
2. 'Shall we _____ ?' 'No, I'm not hungry.'
3. I was thirsty, so I _____ .
4. I like to get up early and _____ before breakfast.
5. Tina is a very good driver. She has never _____ .
6. There's something wrong with the engine of my car. Can you _____ at it?

59.5 Übersetzen Sie ins Englische. Verwenden Sie **have** oder **have got**.

1. Terry hat blaue Augen.
2. Ich habe keinen Fernseher.
3. Haben Sie einen Hund?
4. Ich bin gestern zum Zahnarzt gegangen, weil ich Zahnweh hatte.
5. Um wie viel Uhr hast du zu Mittag gegessen?
6. Ich nehme nicht sehr oft ein Bad. Meistens dusche ich mich.
7. 'Wo ist Kate?' 'Sie ruht sich gerade aus.'
8. Wir haben Urlaub in der Türkei gemacht.
9. Kannst du einen Blick auf diese E-mail werfen?
10. Viel Spaß beim Fest!

Zahnweh = toothache
Türkei = Turkey

Unit 60

I/me   he/him   they/them usw.

A   Menschen

Subjekt	I	we	you	he	she	they
Objekt	me	us	you	him	her	them

Subjekt			Objekt		
I	I know Tom.	Tom knows me.	me	Ich kenne Tom. / Tom kennt mich.
we	We know Tom.	Tom knows us.	us	Wir kennen Tom. / Tom kennt uns.
you	You know Tom.	Tom knows you.	you	Du kennst Tom. / Tom kennt dich.*
he	He knows Tom.	Tom knows him.	him	Er kennt Tom. / Tom kennt ihn.
she	She knows Tom.	Tom knows her.	her	Sie kennt Tom. / Tom kennt sie.
they	They know Tom.	Tom knows them.	them	Sie kennen Tom. / Tom kennt sie.

*__You__ bezeichnet immer eine Person oder mehrere Personen, die man anredet, und bedeutet sowohl 'du' als auch 'ihr'. Im Englischen unterscheidet man nicht zwischen 'du' und 'Sie'; in beiden Fällen verwendet man **you**:
- **You** know Tom.   Du kennst Tom. / Sie kennen … / Ihr kennt …
- Tom knows **you**.   Tom kennt dich/Sie/euch.

Beachten Sie, dass 'sie' (kleingeschrieben) im Englischen den Pronomen **she**, **her**, **they** oder **them** entsprechen kann:
- **She** knows Tom.   Tom knows **her**.   Sie kennt Tom.   Tom kennt sie.
- **They** know Tom.   Tom knows **them**.   Sie kennen Tom.   Tom kennt sie.

B   Gegenstände

Subjekt	it	they
Objekt	it	them

- I don't want **this book**. You can have **it**.   … dieses Buch.   Du kannst es haben.
- I don't want **these books**. You can have **them**.   … diese Bücher.   Du kannst sie haben.
- Kate never drinks **milk**. She doesn't like **it**.   Kate trinkt nie Milch.   Sie schmeckt ihr nicht.
- I never go to **parties**. I don't like **them**.   Ich gehe nie …   Ich mag sie nicht.

Im Englischen verwendet man für Gegenstände immer **it** (Singular). **He** und **she** beziehen sich nur auf Personen:
- **This hat** is nice. I like **it**.   Dieser Hut …   Er gefällt mir.

C

Nach Präpositionen (**for**/**to**/**with** usw.) verwendet man **me**/**her**/**them** usw. (Objekt):
- This letter isn't **for me**. It's **for you**.   Dieser Brief ist nicht für mich.   Er ist für Sie/dich.
- Who is that woman? Why are you looking **at her**?   … Warum siehst du sie an?
- We're going to the cinema. Do you want to come **with us**?   … Möchtest du mit uns kommen?
- Sue and Kevin are going to the cinema. Do you want to go **with them**?   … mit ihnen gehen?
- 'Where's the newspaper?'   'You're sitting **on it**.'   … 'Du sitzt darauf.'

give it/them to … :
- I want that book. Please give **it to me**.   … Bitte gib es mir.   (wörtlich: 'gib es zu mir')
- Robert needs these books. Can you give **them to him**?   … Kannst du sie ihm geben?

my/his/their usw. → Unit 61   Give me that book / Give it to me → Unit 96

Übungen

60.1 Vervollständigen Sie die Sätze mit **him**/**her**/**them**.
1. I don't know those girls. Do you know ...them... ?
2. I don't know that man. Do you know .... ?
3. I don't know those people. Do you know .... ?
4. I don't know David's wife. Do you know .... ?
5. I don't know Mr Stevens. Do you know .... ?
6. I don't know Sarah's parents. Do you know .... ?
7. I don't know the woman in the black coat. Do you know .... ?

60.2 Vervollständigen Sie die Sätze mit den passenden Pronomen (Subjekt und Objekt): **I**/**me**/**you**/**she**/**her** usw.
1. **I** want to see **her**, but ...she... doesn't want to see ...me... .
2. **They** want to see **me**, but .... don't want to see ....
3. **She** wants to see **him**, but .... doesn't want to see ....
4. **We** want to see **them**, but .... don't want to see ....
5. **He** wants to see **us**, but .... don't want to see ....
6. **They** want to see **her**, but .... doesn't want to see ....
7. **I** want to see **them**, but .... don't want to see ....
8. **You** want to see **her**, but .... doesn't want to see ....

60.3 Schreiben Sie einen Kommentar oder eine Frage zu jedem Satz. Beginnen Sie mit **I like ...** , **I don't like ...** oder **Do you like ... ?**
1. I don't eat tomatoes.   ...I don't like them... .
2. George is a very nice man. I like ....
3. This jacket isn't very nice. I don't ....
4. This is my new car. Do .... ?
5. Mrs Clark is not very friendly. I ....
6. These are my new shoes. .... ?

60.4 Vervollständigen Sie die Sätze mit **I**/**me**/**he**/**him** usw.
1. Who is that woman? Why are you looking at ...her... ?
2. 'Do you know that man?'   'Yes, I work with ....'
3. Where are the tickets? I can't find ....
4. I can't find my keys. Where are .... ?
5. We're going out. You can come with ....
6. I've got a new motorbike. Do you want to see .... ?
7. Maria likes music. .... plays the piano.
8. I don't like dogs. I'm afraid of ....
9. I'm talking to you. Please listen to ....
10. Where is Anna? I want to talk to ....
11. You can have these CDs. I don't want ....
12. My brother has a new job, but .... doesn't like .... very much.

60.5 Vervollständigen Sie die Sätze so wie im Beispiel.
1. I need that book. Can you ...give it to me... ?
2. He wants the key. Can you give .... ?
3. She wants the keys. Can you .... ?
4. I need my bag. Can you .... ?
5. They want the money. Can you .... ?
6. We want the pictures. Can you .... ?

60.6 Übersetzen Sie ins Englische.
1. Dieses Buch ist für Sie.
2. John liebt Mary, aber sie liebt ihn nicht.
3. Ich kann Jim sehen, aber er kann mich nicht sehen.
4. 'Kennst du Jenny?'   'Nein, ich kenne sie nicht.'
5. Dieser Kaffee ist zu stark. Er schmeckt mir nicht.
6. Die Musik ist schön. Kannst du sie hören?
7. Ist dieses Geschenk von dir?
8. Wo sind die Kinder? Hast du sie gesehen?
9. Ich brauche die Papiere. Kannst du sie mir bitte geben?
10. Möchtest du mit uns in den Park gehen?

Unit 61 my/his/their usw.

A

| my umbrella | our umbrella | your umbrella | his umbrella | her umbrella | their umbrella |
| mein Schirm | unser Schirm | Ihr/dein Schirm | sein Schirm | ihr Schirm | ihr Schirm |

I	→	my	I	like	my	house.
we	→	our	We	like	our	house.
you	→	your	You	like	your	house.
he	→	his	He	likes	his	house.
she	→	her	She	likes	her	house.
they	→	their	They	like	their	house.

| it | → | its | Oxford (= it) is famous for its university. |

Man verwendet **my**/**your**/**his** usw. mit einem Nomen:

| **my** hands | meine Hände | **his** new **car** | sein neues Auto | **her parents** | ihre Eltern |
| **our clothes** | unsere Kleider | **your** best **friend** | dein bester Freund / deine beste Freundin | **their room** | ihr Zimmer |

B

her/**their**/**your** werden leicht verwechselt, da alle drei mit 'ihr'/'ihre' oder 'Ihr'/'Ihre' ins Deutsche übersetzt werden können:

AMY

her car
ihr Auto

her sister
ihre Schwester

MR AND MRS LEE

their son
ihr Sohn

their children
ihre Kinder

YOU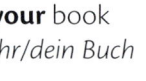

your book
Ihr/dein Buch

your keys
Ihre/eure Schlüssel

Your verwendet man, egal ob man eine ('dein'/'Ihr') oder mehrere ('euer'/'Ihre') Personen anspricht.

C

its und **it's**

Man verwendet **its** für nicht-menschliche Nomen (Tiere, Städte usw.):
- The lion opened **its** mouth and roared.   Der Löwe hat sein Maul geöffnet und gebrüllt.
- Oxford is famous for **its** university.   Oxford ist für seine Universität berühmt.

Nicht verwechseln mit **it's** (= **it is**):
- I like Oxford. **It's** a nice place.   (= It **is** a nice place)   … Es ist eine schöne Stadt.

D

My/**your**/**her** usw. werden verwendet, wenn von Kleidungsstücken und Körperteilen die Rede ist. (Im Deutschen wird oft 'der'/'die'/'das' verwendet):
- Please take off **your** coat.   Legen Sie doch bitte den Mantel ab.
- I'm going to wash **my** hands.   Ich werde mir die Hände waschen.
- He's broken **his** leg.   Er hat sich das Bein gebrochen.

mine/yours usw. → Unit 62   I/me/my/mine → Unit 63

Übungen

61.1 Vervollständigen Sie die Sätze nach dem Beispiel.
1. I'm going to wash _my hands_ .
2. She's going to wash .... hands.
3. We're going to wash ....
4. He's going to wash ....
5. They're going to wash ....
6. Are you going to wash .... ?

61.2 Vervollständigen Sie die Sätze nach dem Beispiel.
1. He _lives with his parents_ .
2. They live with .... parents.
3. We .... parents.
4. Martina lives ....
5. I .... parents.
6. John ....
7. Do you live .... ?
8. Most children ....

61.3 Vervollständigen Sie die Sätze mit **his**/**her**/**their** anhand des Familienstammbaumes.

1. I saw Sarah with _her_ husband, Philip.
2. I saw Laura and Steve with .... children.
3. I saw Steve with .... wife, Laura.
4. I saw Ben with .... brother, Will.
5. I saw Laura with .... brother, Will.
6. I saw Sarah and Philip with .... son, Will.
7. I saw Laura with .... parents.
8. I saw Beth and Robert with .... parents.

61.4 Vervollständigen Sie die Sätze mit **my**/**our**/**your**/**his**/**her**/**their**/**its**.
1. Do you like _your_ job?
2. I know Mr Watson, but I don't know .... wife.
3. Alice and Tom live in London. .... son lives in Australia.
4. We're going to have a party. We're going to invite all .... friends.
5. Anna is going out with .... friends this evening.
6. I like tennis. It's .... favourite sport.
7. 'Is that .... car?' 'No, I don't have a car.'
8. I want to contact Maria. Do you know .... number?
9. Do you think most people are happy in .... jobs?
10. I'm going to wash .... hair before I go out.
11. This is a beautiful tree. .... leaves are a beautiful colour.
12. John has a brother and a sister. .... brother is 25, and .... sister is 21.

61.5 Vervollständigen Sie die Sätze. Verwenden Sie **my**/**his**/**their** usw. zusammen mit einem der folgenden Wörter:

| coat | homework | house | husband | ~~job~~ | key | name |

1. James doesn't enjoy _his job_ . It's not very interesting.
2. I can't get in. I don't have ....
3. Sally is married. .... works in a bank.
4. Please take off .... and sit down.
5. 'What are the children doing?' 'They're doing ....'
6. 'Do you know that man?' 'Yes, but I don't know ....'
7. We live in Barton Street. .... is at the end on the left.

61.6 Übersetzen Sie ins Englische.
1. Ich wohne bei meinen Eltern.
2. Ich kenne ihren Mann.
3. Vergessen Sie nicht Ihren Hut!
4. Unsere Wohnung ist sehr schön.
5. Wasch dir die Hände!
6. Wo sind eure Kinder?
7. Toby und Sarah essen meistens in ihrer Küche.
8. Er putzt sich immer nach dem Abendessen die Zähne.
9. Canterbury ist für seine Kathedrale berühmt.
10. Wie alt ist euer Sohn?

Unit 62

Whose is this? It's mine/yours/hers usw.

A

mine	ours	yours	his	hers	theirs
meines	unseres	deines/Ihres/eures	seines	ihres	ihres

I	→	my	→	mine
we	→	our	→	ours
you	→	your	→	yours
he	→	his	→	his
she	→	her	→	hers
they	→	their	→	theirs

It's **my** money.	It's **mine**.
It's **our** money.	It's **ours**.
It's **your** money.	It's **yours**.
It's **his** money.	It's **his**.
It's **her** money.	It's **hers**.
It's **their** money.	It's **theirs**.

B

Man verwendet **my**/**your** usw. mit Nomen (**my hands** / **your book** usw.):
- **My hands** are cold. Meine Hände sind kalt.
- Is this **your book**? Ist das Ihr Buch?
- Helen gave me **her umbrella**. Helen hat mir ihren Regenschirm gegeben.
- It's **their problem**, not **our problem**. Es ist ihr Problem, nicht unser Problem.

Man verwendet **mine**/**yours** usw. ohne Nomen:
- Is this book **mine** or **yours**? Ist dieses Buch meines oder deines?
- I didn't have an umbrella, so Sarah gave me **hers**.
  Ich hatte keinen Regenschirm, also hat Sarah mir ihren gegeben.
- It's their problem, not **ours**. Es ist ihr Problem, nicht unseres.
- We went in our car, and they went in **theirs**. Wir sind mit unserem Auto gefahren, und sie mit ihrem.

his kann mit oder ohne Nomen verwendet werden:
- 'Is this **his camera** or **hers**?' 'It's **his**.'
  'Ist das sein Fotoapparat oder ihrer?' 'Das ist seiner.'

C

a friend **of mine** / a friend **of his** / some friends **of yours** usw. = ein Freund von mir / ein Freund von ihm / Freunde von dir usw.
- I went out to meet a friend **of mine**. (nicht a friend of me)
  … um einen Freund / eine Freundin von mir zu treffen.
- Tom was in a restaurant with a friend **of his**. (nicht a friend of him)
  … mit einem seiner Freunde.
- Are those people friends **of yours**? (nicht friends of you)
  … Freunde von euch?

D

Whose … ? = Wessen … ?
- **Whose phone** is this? Wessen Handy ist das?

Man kann **whose** mit oder ohne Nomen verwenden:
- **Whose money** is this?
  Wessen Geld ist das?   } It's mine.
  Whose is this?
  Wessen ist das?
- **Whose shoes** are these?
  Wessen Schuhe sind das? } They're John's.
  Whose are these?
  Wessen sind das?

Whose phone is this?

---

my/his/their usw. → Unit 61   I/me/my/mine → Unit 63   Kate's camera / my brother's car → Unit 65

Übungen

Unit 62

62.1 Vervollständigen Sie die Sätze mit **mine**/**yours** usw.

1. It's your money. It's ...yours... .
2. It's my bag. It's ....
3. It's our car. It's ....
4. They're her shoes. They're ....
5. It's their house. It's ....
6. They're your books. They're ....
7. They're my glasses. They're ....
8. It's his coat. It's ....

62.2 Wählen Sie die korrekte Form (**my** oder **mine**, **your** oder **yours** usw.).

1. It's their/~~theirs~~ problem, not ~~our~~/ours.   (their und ours sind richtig)
2. This is a nice camera. Is it your/yours?
3. That's not my/mine umbrella. My/Mine is black.
4. Whose books are these? Your/Yours or my/mine?
5. Catherine is going out with her/hers friends this evening.
6. My/Mine room is bigger than her/hers.
7. They have two children, but I don't know their/theirs names.
8. Can we use your washing machine? Our/Ours isn't working.

62.3 Vervollständigen Sie die Sätze mit **friend**(**s**) **of mine**/**yours** usw.

1. I went to the cinema with a ...friend of mine... .
2. They went on holiday with some ...friends of theirs... .
3. She's going out with a friend ....
4. We had dinner with some ....
5. I played tennis with a ....
6. Tom is going to meet a ....
7. Do you know those people? Are they .... ?

62.4 Was sagen die Personen auf in den Bildern? Schreiben Sie die Dialoge in die Sprechblasen.

62.5 Übersetzen Sie ins Englische.

1. Das ist unser Haus.
2. Wo ist Ihr Auto?
3. Das ist sein Schreibtisch und ihrer ist neben dem Fenster.
4. Könnten Sie mir bitte das Handy geben? Es ist meines.
5. Ein Freund von mir hat ein Pferd.
6. 'Wessen sind das?'   'Das sind unsere.'
7. Das ist nicht meine Tasche; das ist Ihre.
8. Eine Freundin von ihr wohnt in unserer Straße.
9. 'Wessen Mantel ist das?'   'Das ist seiner.'
10. 'Ist das euer Hund?'   'Nein, das ist ihrer.'

Unit 63
I/me/my/mine

A

	I usw. (→ Unit 60)	**me** usw. (→ Unit 60)	**my** usw. (→ Unit 61)	**mine** usw. (→ Unit 62)
	I know Tom.	Tom knows **me**.	It's **my** car.	It's **mine**.
	We know Tom.	Tom knows **us**.	It's **our** car.	It's **ours**.
	You know Tom.	Tom knows **you**.	It's **your** car.	It's **yours**.
	He knows Tom.	Tom knows **him**.	It's **his** car.	It's **his**.
	She knows Tom.	Tom knows **her**.	It's **her** car.	It's **hers**.
	They know Tom.	Tom knows **them**.	It's **their** car.	It's **theirs**.

B

Studieren Sie die Beispiele:

- A: Do **you** know that man? *Kennst du diesen Mann?*
  B: Yes, **I** know **him**, but **I** can't remember **his name**.
  Ja, ich kenne ihn, aber ich kann mich nicht an seinen Namen erinnern.
- **She** was very pleased because **we** invited **her** to stay with **us** at **our house**.
  Sie hat sich sehr gefreut, weil wir sie zu uns nach Hause eingeladen haben.
- A: Where are the children? Have **you** seen them? ... *Hast du sie gesehen?*
  B: Yes, **they** are playing with **their friends** in the park. ... *spielen mit ihren Freunden ...*
- That's **my pen**. Can **you** give it to **me**, please? *Das ist mein Stift. Kannst du ihn mir bitte geben?*
- A: Is this **your umbrella**? *Ist das Ihr Regenschirm?*
  B: No, it's **yours**. *Nein, das ist Ihrer.*
- **He** didn't have an umbrella, so **she** gave **him hers**.
  Er hatte keinen Regenschirm, also hat sie ihm ihren gegeben.
- **I**'m going out with a friend of **mine** this evening. (*nicht* a friend of me)
  Ich treffe mich heute Abend mit einem Freund von mir.

myself/yourself *usw.* → Unit 64   Give me that book / Give it to me → Unit 96

Übungen

63.1 Beantworten Sie die Fragen wie im Beispiel.

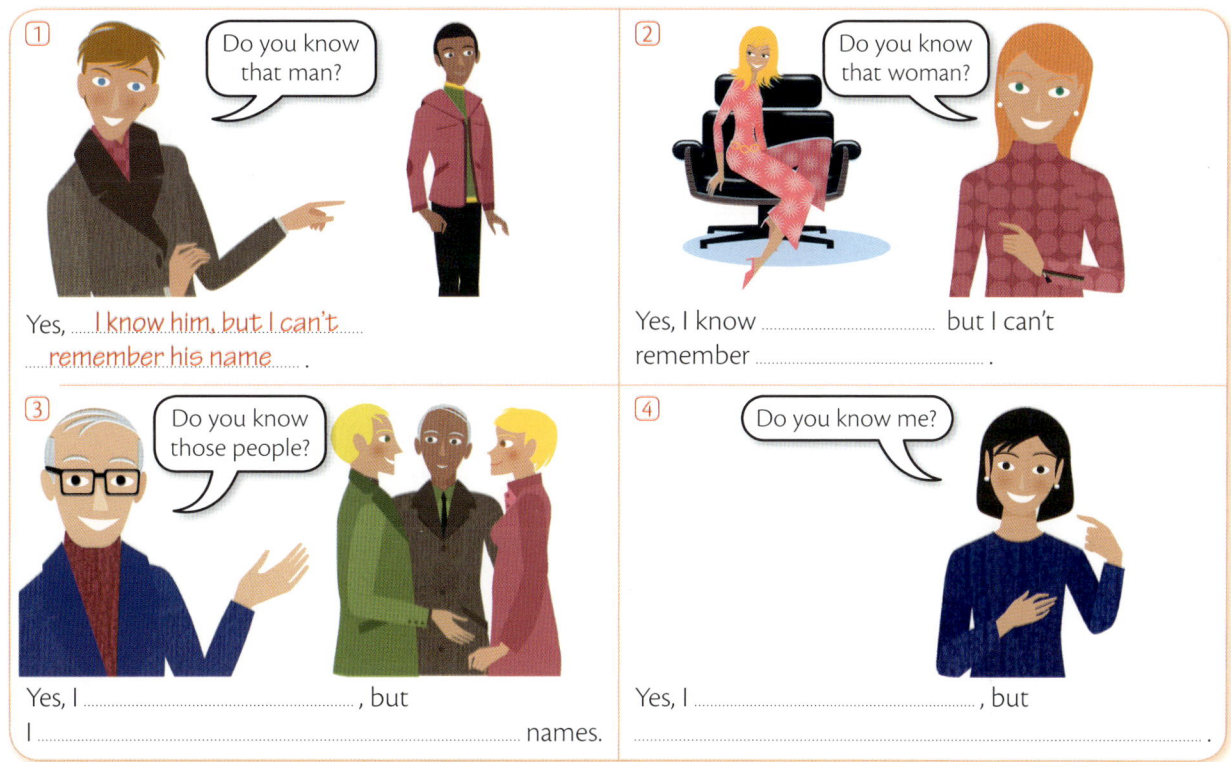

1. Do you know that man? — Yes, I know him, but I can't remember his name.
2. Do you know that woman? — Yes, I know .... but I can't remember ....
3. Do you know those people? — Yes, I ...., but I .... names.
4. Do you know me? — Yes, I ...., but ....

63.2 Vervollständigen Sie die Sätze wie im Beispiel.

1. We invited her to stay with us at our house.
2. He invited us to stay with .... at his house.
3. They invited me to stay with .... house.
4. I invited them to stay .... house.
5. She invited us to stay .... house.
6. Did you invite him .... house?

63.3 Vervollständigen Sie die Sätze wie im Beispiel.

1. I gave him my phone number, and he gave me his.
2. I gave her my phone number, and she gave me ....
3. He gave me his phone number, and I gave ....
4. We gave them .... phone number, and they gave ....
5. She gave him .... phone number, and he gave ....
6. You gave us .... phone number, and we gave ....
7. They gave you .... phone number, and you gave ....

63.4 Vervollständigen Sie die Sätze mit **him/her/yours** usw.

1. Where's Amanda? Have you seen her?
2. Where are my keys? Where did I put ....?
3. This book belongs to Ben. Can you give it to ....?
4. We don't see .... neighbours much. They're not at home very often.
5. 'I can't find my phone. Can I use ....?' 'Yes, of course.'
6. We're going to the cinema. Why don't you come with ....?
7. Did your sister pass .... exams?
8. Some people talk about .... work all the time.
9. Last night I went out for a meal with a friend of ....

63.5 Übersetzen Sie ins Englische.

Visitenkarte = business card

1. Ich liebe ihn, und er liebt mich.
2. Wir haben viele Blumen in unserem Garten.
3. 'Wo ist Anna?' 'Sie ist in ihrem Zimmer.'
4. Möchtest du mit mir kommen, oder mit ihm gehen?
5. 'Ist das euer Auto?' 'Nein, das ist ihres.'
6. Ein Freund von ihm geht morgen mit uns ins Kino.
7. Hier ist meine Visitenkarte. Könnten Sie mir Ihre geben?
8. Sie hatten keinen Schlüssel, also habe ich ihnen meinen gegeben.

Unit 64

myself/yourself/themselves usw.

A

He's looking at **himself**.

Help **yourself**!

They're enjoying **themselves**.

myself	mich/mir
himself	sich
herself	sich
yourself	dich/dir/sich
yourselves	euch/sich
ourselves	uns
themselves	sich

○ I looked at **myself** in the mirror. Ich habe mich im Spiegel angesehen.
○ He cut **himself** with a knife. Er hat sich mit einem Messer geschnitten.
○ She fell off her bike, but she didn't hurt **herself**. … aber sie hat sich nicht wehgetan.
○ Please help **yourself**. (zu einer Person) Bitte bedienen Sie sich.
○ Please help **yourselves**. (zu mehreren Personen) Bitte bedient euch.
○ We are enjoying **ourselves**. Wir amüsieren uns.
○ They had a good holiday. **They** enjoyed **themselves**.
  Sie hatten schöne Ferien. Sie haben sich amüsiert.

B

Vergleichen Sie:

me/him/them usw.

 She is looking at him .
unterschiedliche Personen
Sie sieht ihn an.

○ You never talk to **me**.
  Du sprichst nie mit mir.
○ I didn't pay for **them**.
  Ich habe nicht für sie bezahlt.
○ I'm sorry. Did I hurt **you**?
  Es tut mir leid. Habe ich dir wehgetan?

myself/himself/themselves usw.

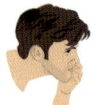 He is looking at himself .
die gleiche Person
Er sieht sich (im Spiegel) an.

○ Sometimes I talk to **myself**.
  Manchmal spreche ich mit mir selbst.
○ They paid for **themselves**.
  Sie haben selber bezahlt.
○ Be careful. Don't hurt **yourself**.
  … Tu dir nicht weh.

C

by myself / by yourself usw. = alleine:
○ I went on holiday **by myself**. Ich bin alleine in Urlaub gefahren.
○ 'Was she with friends?' 'No, she was **by herself**.' … 'Nein, sie war alleine.'

D

each other = einander / sich (gegenseitig):
○ Kate and Helen are good friends. They know **each other** well. … Sie kennen einander/sich gut.
○ Paul and I live near **each other**, but we don't see **each other** very often.
  Paul und ich wohnen nah bei einander, aber wir sehen uns nicht sehr oft.

○ James and Sue looked at **each other**.
  … haben einander/sich gegenseitig angesehen.

○ James and Sue looked at **themselves**.
  … haben sich selbst (im Spiegel) angesehen.

Folgende Verben sind im Deutschen reflexiv, jedoch nicht im Englischen:
○ I don't **feel** well today. Ich fühle mich heute nicht wohl.
○ Please **sit down**. Setzen Sie sich bitte.
○ Where shall we **meet**? Wo sollen wir uns treffen?
auch **wash** = sich waschen   **lie down** = sich hinlegen   **get ready** = sich fertig machen
  get dressed/undressed = sich anziehen/ausziehen (→ Unit 57B)

me/him/them usw. → Unit 60

Übungen

64.1 Vervollständigen Sie die Sätze mit **myself**/**yourself** usw.
1. He looked at ..himself.. in the mirror.
2. I'm not angry with you. I'm angry with ....
3. Karen had a good time in Australia. She enjoyed ....
4. My friends had a good time in Australia. They enjoyed ....
5. I picked up a very hot plate and burnt ....
6. He never thinks about other people. He only thinks about ....
7. I want to know more about you. Tell me about .... (eine Person)
8. Goodbye! Have a good trip and take care of .... ! (zwei Personen)

64.2 Schreiben Sie die Sätze mit **by myself** / **by yourself** usw. anstelle von **alone**.
1. I went on holiday alone. — I went on holiday by myself.
2. When I saw him, he was alone. — When I saw him, he ....
3. Don't go out alone. — Don't ....
4. I went to the cinema alone. — I ....
5. My sister lives alone. — My sister ....
6. Many people live alone. — Many people ....

64.3 Schreiben Sie Sätze mit **each other** über die Situationen in den Bildern:

1. They like each other.
2. They can't ....
3. They ....
4. ....
5. ....
6. ....

64.4 Vervollständigen Sie die Sätze mit **each other** oder **ourselves**/**yourselves**/**themselves** oder **us**/**you**/**them**.
1. Paul and I live near ..each other.. .
2. Who are those people? Do you know ..them.. ?
3. You can help Tom, and Tom can help you. So you and Tom can help ....
4. There's food in the kitchen. If you and Chris are hungry, you can help ....
5. We didn't go to Emily's party. She didn't invite ....
6. When we go on holiday, we always enjoy ....
7. Helen and Jane were at school together, but they never see .... now.
8. Karen and I are very good friends. We've known .... for a long time.
9. 'Did you see Sam and Laura at the party?' 'Yes, but I didn't speak to ....'
10. Many people talk to .... when they're alone.

64.5 Übersetzen Sie ins Englische.

Karneval = carnival
hinfallen = fall down
aussehen = look
lustig = funny

1. Ich habe mich beim Karneval sehr amüsiert.
2. Es tut mir leid. Ich wollte dir nicht wehtun.
3. Helen spricht oft mit sich selbst.
4. Wir möchten alleine sein.
5. Mein Vater ist hingefallen und hat sich verletzt.
6. Wir lieben einander sehr.
7. Sind die Kinder allein zu Hause?
8. Du siehst lustig aus. Guck dich im Spiegel an!
9. Ich habe mich gestern mit Laura getroffen.
10. Wie fühlen Sie sich heute?

Unit 65

-'s (Kate's camera / my brother's car usw.)

A

Kate's camera — Kates Fotoapparat
my brother's car — Das Auto meines Bruders
the manager's office — Das Büro des Leiters / der Leiterin

Normalerweise verwendet man **-'s** für Personen um Besitz oder Zugehörigkeit zu zeigen (man verwendet nicht **of**):
- I stayed at **my sister's** house. (*nicht* the house of my sister) … im Haus meiner Schwester …
- Have you met **Mr Black's** wife? (*nicht* the wife of Mr Black) … die Frau von Herrn Black?
- Are you going to **James's** party? (*nicht* the party of James) … das Fest von James?
- Paul is **a man's** name. Paula is **a woman's** name. Paul ist ein Männername (wörtlich: 'der Name eines Mannes'). Paula ist ein Frauenname (wörtlich: 'der Name einer Frau').

Man kann auch **-'s** ohne Nomen benutzen:
- Sophie's hair is longer than **Kate's**. (= Kate's hair) Sophies Haare sind länger als Kates.
- A: Whose umbrella is this?
  B: It's **my mother's**. … der meiner Mutter.
- A: Where were you last night?
  A: I was at **Paul's**. (= at Paul's house) Ich war bei Paul.

B

friend's und **friends'**

my **friend's** house (= **his** house *oder* **her** house)
das Haus meines Freundes / meiner Freundin

Man schreibt **'s** nach
friend/student/mother usw. (Singular):
  my mother**'s** car   das Auto meiner Mutter

my **friends'** house (= **their** house)
das Haus meiner Freunde

Man schreibt **'** nach
friend**s**/student**s**/parent**s** usw. (Plural):
  my parent**s'** car   das Auto meiner Eltern

C

Normalerweise verwendet man **of** … für Gegenstände, Ortsangaben usw.:
- Look at the roof **of that building**. (*nicht* that building's roof)
  … das Dach des Gebäudes.
- We didn't see the beginning **of the film**. (*nicht* the film's beginning)
  … den Anfang des Films.
- What's the name **of this village**? … der Name dieses Dorfes?
- Do you know the cause **of the problem**? … den Grund für das Problem?
- You can sit in the back **of the car**. … auf dem Rücksitz des Autos …
- Madrid is the capital **of Spain**. … die Hauptstadt von Spanien.

mine/yours usw. → Unit 62   whose … ? → Unit 62   -'s (he's / Kate's usw.) → Anhang 4.5

Übungen

65.1
Sehen Sie sich diesen Familienstammbaum an. Schreiben Sie, wie die Familienmitglieder verwandt sind.

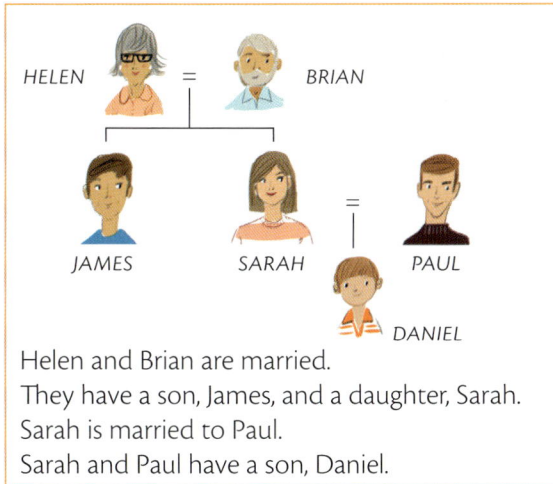

Helen and Brian are married.
They have a son, James, and a daughter, Sarah.
Sarah is married to Paul.
Sarah and Paul have a son, Daniel.

1 Brian is Helen's husband.
2 Sarah is Daniel's mother.
3 Helen is .... wife.
4 James is Sarah's ....
5 James is .... uncle.
6 Sarah is .... wife.
7 Helen is Daniel's ....
8 Sarah is James's ....
9 Paul is .... husband.
10 Paul is Daniel's ....
11 Daniel is .... nephew.

65.2
Beantworten Sie die Fragen über die Personen auf den Bildern. Verwenden Sie nur ein Wort (wie im Beispiel).

1 Whose is this? Alice's
2 Whose is this? ....
3 And this? ....
4 And these? ....
5 And this? ....
6 And these? ....

65.3
Sind diese Sätze korrekt? Korrigieren Sie die Fehler oder schreiben Sie **OK**, wenn der Satz richtig ist.

1 I stayed at the house of my sister.   my sister's house
2 What is the name of this village?   OK
3 Do you like the colour of this coat?
4 Do you have the phone number of Simon?
5 The job of my brother is very interesting.
6 Write your name at the top of the page.
7 For me, the morning is the best part of the day.
8 The favourite colour of Paula is blue.
9 When is the birthday of your mother?
10 The house of my parents isn't very big.
11 The walls of this house are very thin.
12 The car stopped at the end of the street.
13 Are you going to the party of Silvia next week?
14 The manager of the hotel is not here at the moment.

65.4
Übersetzen Sie ins Englische.

Werkstatt = garage
Stock = floor

1 Das ist Tobys Buch.
2 Das Auto meiner Frau ist in der Werkstatt.
3 'Wessen Mantel ist das?' 'Sarahs.'
4 Die Fenster des Hauses sind sehr klein.
5 Das Büro von Mrs Murray ist im zweiten Stock.
6 Ich war letztes Wochenende bei meinem Bruder.
7 Der Garten meiner Eltern ist sehr schön.
8 Hat dir der Anfang des Films gefallen?
9 Am Ende der Woche war ich sehr müde.

Unit 66

a/an ...

A

He's got **a** camera.
Er hat einen Fotoapparat.

She's waiting for **a** taxi.
Sie wartet auf ein Taxi.

It's **a** beautiful day.
Es ist ein schöner Tag.

a ... entspricht generell dem Deutschen 'ein'/'eine' ('einen, einem, einer'):
- Rachel works in **a bank**. (*nicht* in bank) ... in einer Bank.
- Can I ask **a question**? (*nicht* ask question) ... eine Frage stellen?
- There's **a woman** at the bus stop. Da ist eine Frau ...

B

Beginnt das Folgewort mit **a/e/i/o/u** (einem Vokal) verwendet man **an** (*nicht* a):
- Do you want **an a**pple or **a b**anana? ... einen Apfel oder eine Banane?
- I'm going to buy **a h**at and **an u**mbrella. ... einen Hut und einen Regenschirm ...
- There was **an i**nteresting programme on TV last night. ... eine interessante Sendung ...

Außerdem **an hour** (*das h wird nicht ausgesprochen* an ḫour)
aber vor dem Laut /ju:/ man verwendet **a**: **a university**, **a European** country

another (= **an** + **other**) bedeutet 'noch ein/eine' und wird als ein Wort geschrieben:
- Can I have **another** cup of tea? ... noch eine Tasse Tee ... ?

C

Man verwendet **a/an** ... um eine Sache oder eine Person zu definieren, oder genauer zu bezeichnen, zum Beispiel:
- Dallas is **a city in Texas**. Dallas ist eine Stadt ...
- A mouse is **an animal**. It's **a small animal**.
  ... ein Tier. ... ein kleines Tier.
- Joe is **a very nice person**. ... ein sehr netter Mensch.

I'm a dentist.

Man verwendet **a/an** ... für Berufe/Tätigkeiten
(im Deutschen wird meistens kein Artikel verwendet):
- A: What's your job? Was ist Ihr Beruf?
  B: I'm **a dentist**. (*nicht* I'm dentist) Ich bin Zahnarzt.
- A: What does Mark do? Was macht Mark beruflich?
  B: He's **an engineer**. Er ist Ingenieur.
- Would you like to be **a teacher**?
  Möchtest du gerne Lehrer werden?
- Beethoven was **a composer**. Beethoven war Komponist.
- Are you **a student**? Bist du Student/in?

D

Bei der Verneinung verwendet man auch **a/an** ... (im Deutschen wird meistens 'kein'/'keine' verwendet):
- I don't have **a job**. Ich habe keine Arbeit.
- He isn't wearing **a coat**. ... keinen Mantel.

E

a/an ... verwendet man auch bei Angaben über Häufigkeit/Geschwindigkeit usw. wie:

twice **a** week	100 kilometres **an** hour	$60,000 **a** year	£2.50 **a** kilo
zweimal pro/die Woche	100 km pro/die Stunde	... pro/im Jahr	... pro/das Kilo

- I usually run three miles **a day**. Ich laufe in der Regel drei Meilen pro Tag.

---

a car / some money (zählbar und nicht zählbar) → **Units 68–69**   the → **Unit 70**

Übungen

66.1 Setzen Sie **a** oder **an** vor das Wort.

1. *an* old book
2. .... window
3. .... horse
4. .... airport
5. .... new airport
6. .... organisation
7. .... university
8. .... hour
9. .... economic problem

66.2 Wählen Sie eine passende Definition aus dem Kästchen für jeden der Begriffe in 1–10 und vervollständigen Sie die Sätze.

~~bird~~	fruit	mountain	river	musical instrument
flower	game	planet	tool	vegetable

1. A duck is *a bird*.
2. A carrot is ....
3. Tennis is ....
4. A hammer is ....
5. Everest is ....
6. Saturn is ....
7. A banana is ....
8. The Amazon is ....
9. A rose is ....
10. A trumpet is ....

66.3 Welchen Beruf üben die Personen auf den Bildern aus? Wählen Sie Berufe aus der Liste und vervollständigen Sie die Sätze.

architect	~~dentist~~	shop assistant	photographer
electrician	nurse	taxi driver	

1. *She's a dentist.*
2. He's ....
3. She ....
4. ....
5. ....
6. ....
7. ....
8. And you? I'm ....

66.4 Bilden Sie Sätze, indem Sie Satzhälften zusammenfügen. Verwenden Sie bei Bedarf **a/an**.

~~I want to ask you~~	Rebecca works in		old house	artist
Tom never wears	Jane wants to learn	+	party	~~question~~
I can't ride	Mike lives in		bookshop	foreign language
My brother is	This evening I'm going to		hat	bike

1. *I want to ask you a question.*
2.
3.
4.
5.
6.
7.
8.

66.5 Übersetzen Sie ins Englische.

1. Cricket ist ein Sport.
2. Lisa arbeitet in einem Büro.
3. Möchtest du einen Apfel?
4. Ich habe kein Fahrrad.
5. Meine Mutter ist Ärztin.
6. Gibt es in Cardiff eine Universität?
7. Könnte ich bitte einen Orangensaft haben?
8. John hat einen interessanten Beruf. Er ist Fotograf.
9. Wir spielen dreimal pro Woche Tennis.

Unit 67: train(s) bus(es) (Singular und Plural)

A

Den Plural bildet man in der Regel mit **-s**:

Singular			Plural	
a flower	eine Blume	→	some **flowers**	Blumen
a train	ein Zug	→	two **trains**	zwei Züge
one week	eine Woche	→	a few **weeks**	ein paar Wochen
a nice place	ein schöner Platz	→	some nice **places**	schöne Plätze
this student	dieser Student	→	these **students**	diese Studenten

a flower   some **flowers**

Rechtschreibung (→ Anhang 5):

-s / -sh / -ch / -x	→	-es	bu**s** → bu**ses** di**sh** → di**shes**
			chur**ch** → chur**ches** bo**x** → bo**xes**
	Außerdem		potato → potato**es** tomato → tomato**es**
-y	→	-ies	ba**by** → ba**bies** dictiona**ry** → dictiona**ries** par**ty** → par**ties**
aber -ay / -ey / -oy	→	-ys	d**ay** → d**ays** monk**ey** → monk**eys** b**oy** → b**oys**
-f / -fe	→	-ves	shel**f** → shel**ves** kni**fe** → kni**ves** wi**fe** → wi**ves**

B

Bei folgenden Gegenständen verwendet man im Englischen immer den Plural:

scissors	**glasses**	**trousers**	**jeans**	**shorts**	**tights**	**pyjamas**
eine Schere	eine Brille	eine Hose/ Hosen	(eine) Jeans	(eine) Shorts	eine Strumpfhose/ Strumpfhosen	ein Schlafanzug

- ☐ Do you wear **glasses**? *Tragen Sie eine Brille?*
- ☐ Where **are** the **scissors**? I need **them**. *Wo ist die Schere? Ich brauche sie.*

Man kann auch sagen **a pair of scissors / a pair of trousers / a pair of tights** usw. (*ein Paar …*):
- ☐ I need **a** new **pair of jeans**. oder I need **some** new **jeans**. (*nicht* a new jeans)
  Ich brauche ein neues Paar Jeans. / Ich brauche eine neue Jeans.

C

Einige Wörter bilden den Plural nicht mit **-s**:

this **man** → these **men**	one **foot** → two **feet**	that **sheep** → those **sheep**
a **woman** → some **women**	a **tooth** → all my **teeth**	a **fish** → a lot of **fish**
a **child** → many **children**	a **mouse** → some **mice**	

Beachten Sie außerdem **a person** → **two people** / **some people** / **a lot of people** usw.:
- ☐ **She**'s a nice **person**. *Sie ist eine nette Person.*

aber
- ☐ **They** are nice **people**. (*nicht* nice persons)
  Sie sind nette Leute/Personen.

D

People (*Leute/Menschen/Personen*) ist eine Pluralform; darum sagt man **people are / people have** usw.:
- ☐ **A lot of people speak** English. (*nicht* speaks)
  Viele Leute sprechen Englisch.
- ☐ I like **the people** here. **They are** very friendly.
  Mir gefallen die Menschen hier. Sie sind sehr freundlich.

Police (*die Polizei*) ist auch Plural:
- ☐ **The police want** to talk to anybody who saw the accident. (*nicht* The police wants)

Übungen

Unit 67

67.1 Schreiben Sie den Plural folgender Wörter.

1. flower — flowers
2. boat
3. woman
4. city
5. umbrella
6. address
7. knife
8. sandwich
9. family
10. foot
11. holiday
12. potato

67.2 Vervollständigen Sie die Sätze zu jedem Bild.

1 2 3 4 LUCY 5 6

1. There are a lot of ...sheep... in the field.
2. Gary is cleaning his ....
3. There are three .... at the bus stop.
4. Lucy has two ....
5. There are a lot of .... in the river.
6. The .... are falling from the tree.

67.3 Sind diese Sätze korrekt? Korrigieren Sie die Fehler, oder schreiben Sie OK.

1. I'm going to buy some flowers. — OK
2. I need a new jeans. — I need a new pair of jeans. oder I need some new jeans.
3. It's a lovely park with a lot of beautiful tree.
4. There was a woman in the car with two mens.
5. Sheep eat grass.
6. David is married and has three childs.
7. Most of my friend are student.
8. He put on his pyjama and went to bed.
9. We went fishing, but we didn't catch many fish.
10. Do you know many persons in this town?
11. I like your trouser. Where did you get it?
12. The town centre is usually full of tourist.
13. I don't like mice. I'm scared of them.
14. This scissor isn't very sharp.

67.4 Vervollständigen Sie die Sätze. Wählen Sie die korrekte Form.

1. It's a nice place. Many people ...go... there on holiday. — **go** oder **goes**?
2. Some people .... always late. — **is** oder **are**?
3. The new city hall is not a beautiful building. Most people .... like it. — **don't** oder **doesn't**?
4. A lot of people .... TV every day. — **watch** oder **watches**?
5. Three people .... injured in the accident. — **was** oder **were**?
6. How many people .... in that house? — **live** oder **lives**?
7. .... the police know the cause of the explosion? — **Do** oder **Does**?
8. The police .... looking for the stolen car. — **is** oder **are**?
9. I need my glasses, but I can't find .... — **it** oder **them**?
10. I'm going to buy .... new jeans today. — **a** oder **some**?

67.5 Übersetzen Sie ins Englische.

1. Ich habe zwei Brüder und eine Schwester.
2. Sandra hat zwei rote Kleider.
3. Es sind heute viele Leute im Park.
4. Trägt Michael gewöhnlich eine Brille?
5. Die Schuhe passen mir nicht. Meine Füße sind zu groß.
6. Diese Tomaten schmecken sehr gut.
7. Die Polizei sucht einen Bankräuber.
8. Wir haben sechs Frauen und vier Männer in unserem Englischkurs.
9. Ich brauche eine neue Strumpfhose und einen Schlafanzug.

passen = fit
schmecken = taste
Bankräuber = bank robber

Unit 68

a bottle / some water
(zählbar / nicht zählbar 1)

A *Ein Nomen kann zählbar oder nicht zählbar sein.*

Zählbare Nomen

Zum Beispiel: (a) **car**   (a) **man**   (a) **bottle**   (a) **house**   (a) **key**   (an) **idea**   (an) **accident**

*Diese Nomen bezeichnen Dinge, die man zählen kann (**one**/**two**/**three** usw.):*

 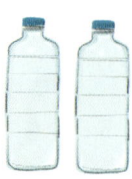  

one **bottle**   two **bottles**   three **men**   four **houses**

Zählbare Nomen haben eine Singular- und eine Pluralform:

Singular	a car	the car	my car	usw.
Plural	cars	two cars	the cars	some cars	many cars	usw.

- I've got **a car**. *Ich habe ein Auto.*
- New **cars** are very expensive. *Neue Autos sind sehr teuer.*
- There aren't **many cars** in the car park. *Es sind nicht viele Autos auf dem Parkplatz.*

*Nomen in der Einzahl (**car**/**bottle**/**key** usw.) können nicht alleine verwendet werden. Man braucht **a/an**:*
- We can't get into the house without **a key**. (*nicht* without key)
  Wir können nicht ohne Schlüssel ins Haus hinein.

B *Nicht zählbare Nomen*

Zum Beispiel: **water   air   rice   salt   plastic   money   music   tennis**

water   salt   money   music

Diese Nomen bezeichnen Dinge, die man nicht zählen kann: ~~one water~~   ~~two musics~~

Nicht zählbare Nomen haben nur eine Form:
money   the **money**   my **money**   some **money**   much **money**   usw.

- I've got **some money**. *Ich habe Geld. / Ich habe etwas Geld.*
- There isn't **much money** in the box. *Es ist nicht viel Geld …*
- **Money** isn't everything. *Geld ist nicht alles.*

*Man kann nicht zählbare Nomen auch alleine (ohne **some**, **the** usw.) verwenden:*
- You can't live without **water**. *Man kann nicht ohne Wasser leben.*

*Man kann **a/an** nicht mit nicht zählbaren Nomen verwenden:*   ✗ money   ✗ music   ✗ water

*Man kann jedoch sagen **a piece of** … / **a bottle of** … usw. + nicht zählbares Nomen:*

a bottle of water	**a carton of** milk	**a bar of** chocolate
eine Flasche Wasser	*ein Karton Milch*	*ein Schokoladenriegel*
a piece of cheese	**a bottle of** perfume	**a piece of** music
ein Stück Käse	*eine Flasche Parfüm*	*ein Musikstück*
a bowl of rice	**a cup of** coffee	**a game of** tennis
eine Schüssel Reis	*eine Tasse Kaffee*	*ein Tennisspiel*

*Man sagt **a bottle of water** (*nicht* a bottle water), **a cup of coffee** (*nicht* a cup coffee) usw.*

a/an ➔ Unit 66   zählbar / nicht zählbar 2 ➔ Unit 69

Übungen

Unit 68

68.1 Wie heißen diese Gegenstände? Manche sind zählbar und manche nicht. Schreiben Sie den Namen (aus der Liste) unter das Bild. Verwenden Sie bei Bedarf **a/an**.

bucket	envelope	money	sand	toothbrush	wallet
egg	jug	~~salt~~	~~spoon~~	toothpaste	water

1. It's _salt_.
2. It's _a spoon_.
3. It's _____.
4. It's _____.
5. It's _____.
6. It's _____.
7. It's _____.
8. It's _____.
9. It's _____.
10. It's _____.
11. It's _____.
12. It's _____.

68.2 Einige dieser Sätze sind korrekt, aber bei manchen fehlt **a/an**. Fügen Sie **a/an** ein, oder schreiben Sie **OK**.

1. I don't have watch.   _a watch_
2. Do you like cheese?   _OK_
3. I never wear hat.   _____
4. Are you looking for job?   _____
5. Kate doesn't eat meat.   _____
6. Kate eats apple every day.   _____
7. I'm going to party tonight.   _____
8. Music is wonderful thing.   _____
9. Jamaica is island.   _____
10. I don't need key.   _____
11. Everybody needs food.   _____
12. I've got good idea.   _____
13. Can you drive car?   _____
14. Do you want cup of coffee?   _____
15. I don't like coffee without milk.   _____
16. Don't go out without umbrella.   _____

68.3 Was zeigen diese Bilder? Schreiben Sie den passenden Begriff mit **a ... of ...** , indem Sie aus jedem Kästchen ein Wort wählen.

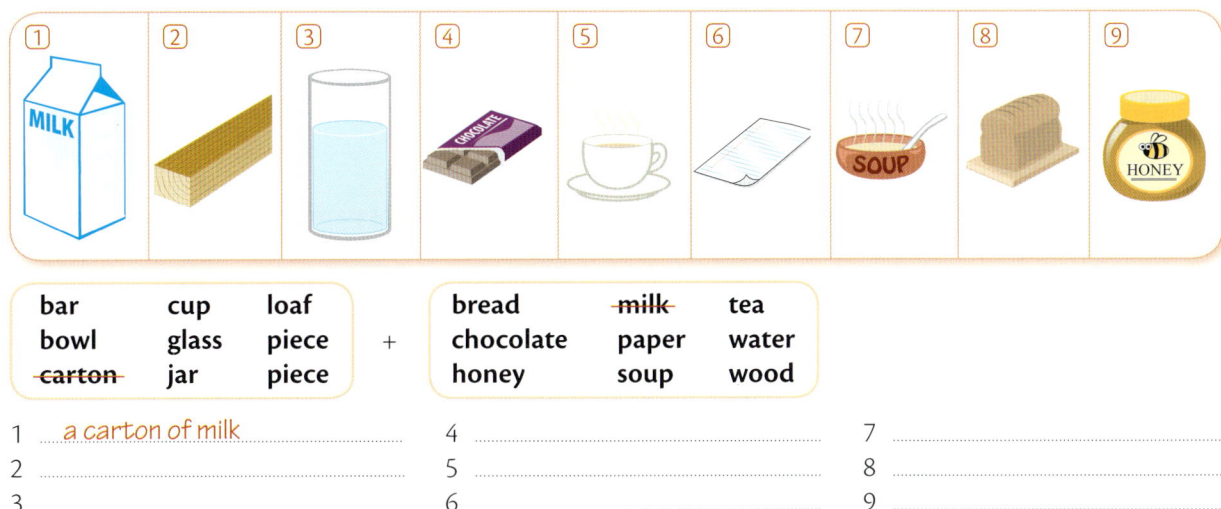

bar	cup	loaf		bread	~~milk~~	tea
bowl	glass	piece	+	chocolate	paper	water
~~carton~~	jar	piece		honey	soup	wood

1. _a carton of milk_
2. _____
3. _____
4. _____
5. _____
6. _____
7. _____
8. _____
9. _____

68.4 Übersetzen Sie ins Englische.   man = you

1. Wir brauchen Milch und vier Eier.
2. Terry geht nie ohne Schlips zur Arbeit.
3. Man braucht Luft und Wasser zum Leben.
4. Ich trinke jeden Tag einen Liter Wasser.
5. Rita hat zwei Katzen und einen Hund.
6. Möchten Sie ein Stück Kuchen?
7. Ein Glas Orangensaft und eine Schüssel Cornflakes, bitte.
8. Ich höre oft Musik, wenn ich arbeite.

147

Unit 69

a cake / some cake / some cakes
(zählbar / nicht zählbar 2)

A a/an und some

a/an (= *ein, eine usw.*) verwendet man nur mit einem zählbaren Nomen im Singular (**car/apple/shoe** *usw.*):
- I need **a** new **car**. *Ich brauche ein neues Auto.*
- Would you like **an apple**? *Möchten Sie einen Apfel?*

an apple

some (= *einige, ein paar*) verwendet man mit zählbaren Nomen im Plural (**cars/apples/shoes** *usw.*):
- I need **some** new **shoes**. *Ich brauche neue Schuhe.*
- Would you like **some apples**? *Möchten Sie ein paar Äpfel?*

some apples

some (*etwas*) verwendet man auch mit nicht zählbaren Nomen (**water/money/music** *usw.*).
Beachten Sie, dass hier im Deutschen 'etwas' auch weggelassen werden kann:
- I need **some money**. *Ich brauche (etwas) Geld.*
- Would you like **some cheese**? *Möchten Sie etwas Käse?*
  (*oder* Would you like **a piece of** cheese?) *… ein Stück Käse?*

some cheese *oder*
a piece of cheese

Vergleichen Sie **a** *und* **some**:
- Nicola bought **a hat**, **some shoes** and **some perfume**.
  Nicola hat einen Hut, Schuhe und Parfüm gekauft.
- I read **a newspaper**, made **some phone calls**, and listened to **some music**.
  Ich habe eine Zeitung gelesen, einige Telefonate gemacht und etwas Musik gehört.

B Es gibt viele Wörter, die zählbar oder nicht zählbar sein können, zum Beispiel:

a cake	**some cakes**	**some cake** *oder* **a piece of cake**
ein Kuchen	*einige Kuchen*	*Kuchen oder ein Stück Kuchen*
a chicken	**some chickens**	**some chicken** *oder* **a piece of chicken**
ein Hähnchen	*einige Hähnchen*	*Hähnchen oder ein Stück Hähnchen*

a paper / **a newspaper** (*zählbar*) = *eine Zeitung*:
- I want something to read. I'm going to buy **a paper**.

some paper (*nicht zählbar*) = *Papier*:
- I want to make a shopping list. I need **some paper** / **a piece of paper**. (*nicht* a paper)

C Beachten Sie, dass folgende Wörter meistens nicht zählbar sind:

| advice | bread | furniture | hair | information | news | weather |

- Can I talk to you? I need **some advice**. (*nicht* an advice) *Ich brauche einen Ratschlag.*
- I'm going to buy **some bread**. (*nicht* a bread) *Ich werde Brot / ein Brot kaufen.*
- They've got **some** nice **furniture** in their house. (*nicht* furnitures) *Sie haben (einige) schöne Möbel …*
- Silvia has got very long **hair**. (*nicht* hairs) *Silvia hat sehr langes Haar / lange Haare.*
- Where can I get **some information** about hotels here? (*nicht* an information)
  Wo kann ich eine Auskunft über …
- Listen! I've just had **some** good **news**. (*nicht* a good news) *… eine gute Nachricht …*
- What lovely **weather**! *Was für ein schönes Wetter!*

Man sagt **a job** (*eine Arbeit / eine Arbeitsstelle*), aber nicht a work.
- I've got a new **job**. (*nicht* a new work) *Ich habe eine neue Stelle.*

zählbar / nicht zählbar 1 ➔ Unit 68   some *und* any ➔ Unit 76

Übungen

69.1 Was sehen Sie in diesen Bildern? Verwenden Sie **a** oder **some**.

1. some perfume, a hat and some shoes
2.
3.
4.

69.2 Bieten Sie jemandem die Speisen oder Getränke in den Bildern an. Bilden Sie Sätze mit **Would you like a … ?** oder **Would you like some … ?**

1. Would you like some cheese?
2. Would you like .... ?
3. Would .... ?
4. .... ?
5. .... ?
6. .... ?

69.3 Vervollständigen Sie die Sätze mit **a/an** oder **some**.

1. I read ...a... book and listened to ...some... music.
2. I need .... money. I want to buy .... food.
3. We met .... interesting people at the party.
4. I'm going to open .... window to get .... fresh air.
5. Rachel didn't eat much for lunch – only .... apple and .... bread.
6. We live in .... big house. There's .... nice garden with .... beautiful trees.
7. I'm going to make a table. First I need .... wood.
8. Listen to me carefully. I'm going to give you .... advice.
9. I want to make a list of things to do. I need .... paper and .... pen.

69.4 Wählen Sie die korrekte Alternative.

1. I'm going to buy some new ~~shoe~~/shoes.   (shoes ist richtig)
2. Mark has brown eye/eyes.
3. Paula has short black hair/hairs.
4. The tour guide gave us some information/informations about the city.
5. We're going to buy some new chair/chairs.
6. We're going to buy some new furniture/furnitures.
7. It's hard to find a work/job at the moment.
8. We had wonderful weather / a wonderful weather when we were on holiday.

69.5 Übersetzen Sie ins Englische.

Brötchen = bread roll

1. Ich brauche Geld.
2. Das ist ein schöner Geburtstagskuchen.
3. Könntest du bitte Bananen kaufen?
4. Jenny hat mir einen guten Ratschlag gegeben.
5. Wie oft wäschst du dir die Haare?
6. Könnten Sie mir bitte eine Auskunft geben?
7. Martha sucht eine andere Arbeitsstelle.
8. Tom hat eine Zeitung, etwas Käse und einige Brötchen gekauft.

Unit 70: the ...

A

Allgemein entspricht **the** im Deutschen 'der'/'die'/'das' usw.:

- ○ **The sky** is blue and **the sun** is shining.
  Der Himmel ... und die Sonne ...
- ○ I'm going to clean **the car** tomorrow. ... das Auto ...
- ○ Excuse me, where is **the nearest bank**? ... die nächste Bank?
- ○ I'd like to live in **the country**. ... auf dem Land ... .
- ○ My brother is in **the police**. ... bei der Polizei.
- ○ What is **the name** of this street?
  Wie heißt diese Straße? (wörtlich: 'Wie ist der Name dieser Straße?')
- ○ We go to **the same school**. ... in dieselbe Schule.
- ○ What do you use **the internet** for?
  Wofür benutzt du das Internet?

B

Man verwendet **the** auch in den folgenden Fällen:

the top (oben) / **the bottom** (unten / am Fuße)
the left (links) / **the right** (rechts)
the middle (die Mitte / mitten in)

- ○ Write your name at **the top of** the page.
  ... oben auf das Blatt.
- ○ The hotel is at **the bottom of** the mountain.
  ... am Fuße des Berges.
- ○ Do you drive on **the right** or on **the left** in your country?
  Fährt man rechts oder links ... ?
- ○ The table is in **the middle of** the room.
  ... in der Mitte des Zimmers.

C

Man verwendet **the** auch in den folgenden Fällen:

(play) **the piano** / **the guitar** / **the trumpet** usw. (Musikinstrumente)
- ○ Paula is learning to play **the piano**.
  Paula lernt gerade Klavier spielen.

the radio (= Radio hören)
- ○ I listen to **the radio** a lot. (*nicht* listen to radio)
  Ich höre viel Radio.

D

Man verwendet **the** nicht bei:

television/TV
- ○ I watch **TV** a lot. Ich sehe viel fern.
- ○ What's on **television** tonight? (*nicht* on the television)
  Was gibt's heute Abend im Fernsehen?

aber   Can you turn off **the TV**? Kannst du den Fernseher ausschalten?

Mahlzeiten: **breakfast/lunch/dinner**
- ○ What did you have for **breakfast**? (*nicht* the breakfast)
- ○ **Dinner** is ready! Das Abendessen ist fertig!

Namen von Familienmitgliedern (**Mum/Dad** usw.) oder Eigennamen (**Mary/Tom** usw.):
- ○ Give **Grandma** a kiss. Gib (der) Oma einen Kuss.
- ○ I saw **Stephen** yesterday. Ich habe (den) Stephen gestern gesehen.

andere Gebräuche von **the** → Units 71–73   **the oldest** / **the most expensive** *usw.* → Unit 90

Übungen

70.1 Fügen Sie **the** ein oder schreiben Sie **OK**, wenn der Satz so korrekt ist.

1. What is name of this street? — the name
2. What's on TV tonight? — OK
3. You should call police.
4. Would you like to go to moon?
5. There's a big house at top of the hill.
6. What time is lunch?
7. How far is it to city centre?
8. Go down this street and you'll see a supermarket on left.
9. Can you play piano?
10. What's biggest city in the world?
11. I'm going out after dinner.
12. It's easy to get information from internet.
13. I don't listen to radio much.
14. My dictionary is on top shelf on right.
15. We live in country about ten miles from nearest town.

70.2 Vervollständigen Sie die Sätze. Verwenden Sie **the same** und folgende Worter:

age   colour   problem   ~~street~~   time

1. I live in North Street and you live in North Street. We live in _the same street_.
2. I arrived at 8.30 and you arrived at 8.30. We arrived at _____.
3. James is 25 and Sue is 25. James and Sue are _____.
4. My shirt is dark blue and so is my jacket. My shirt and jacket are _____.
5. I have no money and you have no money. We have _____.

70.3 Vervollständigen Sie die Sätze anhand der dazugehörigen Bilder. Verwenden Sie **the**, wenn erforderlich.

1. _The sun_ is shining.
2. She's playing _____.
3. They're having _____.
4. He's watching _____.
5. They're swimming in _____.
6. Tom's name is at _____ of the list.

70.4 Vervollständigen Sie die Sätze mit Wörtern aus der Liste. Verwenden Sie **the**, wenn erforderlich.

capital   ~~dinner~~   police   lunch   middle   name   sky   TV

1. We had _dinner_ at a restaurant last night.
2. We stayed at a very nice hotel, but I don't remember _____.
3. _____ is very clear tonight. You can see all the stars.
4. Sometimes there are some good films on _____ late at night.
5. Somebody was trying to break into the shop, so I called _____.
6. Tokyo is _____ of Japan.
7. 'What did you have for _____?' 'A salad.'
8. I woke up in _____ of the night.

70.5 Übersetzen Sie ins Englische.

1. Joe und ich wohnen in derselben Straße.
2. Wo ist die Mama?
3. Das Haus steht mitten in einem Park.
4. Kannst du Gitarre spielen?
5. Wie heißt der Mann neben Rachel?
6. Unser Haus ist links neben der Kirche.
7. Das Mittagessen steht auf dem Tisch!
8. Heute gibt es nichts Interessantes im Fernsehen.
9. Wohnen Sie in einer Stadt oder auf dem Land?

neben = next to
nichts = nothing
steht = is

Unit 71

go to work   go home   go to the cinema

A

She's **at work**.   They're going **to school**.   He's **in bed**.

*Bei folgenden Redewendungen verwendet man nicht **the** (anders als im Deutschen, wo man meistens 'der'/'die'/'das' sagt):*

(go) **to work**, (be) **at work**, start **work**, finish **work**
- Bye! I'm **going to work** now.   (*nicht* to the work)   *Ich gehe jetzt zur Arbeit.*
- I **finish work** at 5 o'clock every day.   *Ich bin jeden Tag um … mit der Arbeit fertig.*
- Why weren't you **at work** yesterday?   *Warum warst du gestern nicht bei der Arbeit?*

(go) **to school**, (be) **at school**, start **school**, leave **school** *usw.*
- What did you learn **at school** today?   (*nicht* at the school)
  Was hast du heute in der Schule gelernt?
- Some children don't like **school**.
  Manche Kinder gehen nicht gerne in die Schule. (wörtlich: '… mögen die Schule nicht.')
- John left **school** when he was 16.   *John ist mit 16 von der Schule abgegangen.*

(go) **to university/college**, (be) **at university/college**
- Helen wants to **go to university** when she **leaves school**.
  Helen will zur Universität gehen …
- What did you study **at college**?   *Was hast du an der Kolleg/Universität studiert?*

(go) **to hospital**, (be) **in hospital**
- Jack had an accident. He had to go **to hospital**.   *… Er musste ins Krankenhaus.*

(go) **to prison**, (be) **in prison**
- Why is he **in prison**? What did he do?   *Warum ist er im Gefängnis …*

(go) **to church**, (be) **in/at church**
- David usually goes **to church** on Sundays.   *David geht sonntags meistens in die Kirche.*

(go) **to bed**, (be) **in bed**
- I'm tired. I'm **going to bed**.   (*nicht* to the bed)   *… Ich gehe ins Bett.*
- 'Where's Alice?' 'She's **in bed**.'   *… 'Sie ist im Bett.'*

(go) **home**, (be) **at home** *usw.*
- I'm tired. I'm **going home**.   (*nicht* to home)   *… Ich gehe nach Hause.*
- Are you going out tonight, or are you **staying at home**?   *… oder bleibst du zu Hause?*

B

*Bei folgenden Redewendungen verwendet man jedoch **the**:*

(go to) **the cinema / the theatre / the bank / the post office / the station / the airport / the city centre**
- I never go to **the theatre**, but I go to **the cinema** a lot.
  Ich gehe nie ins Theater, aber ich gehe oft ins Kino.
- Are you going to **the city centre**?   *Fahren Sie ins Stadtzentrum?*
- I have to go to **the bank** today.   *Ich muss heute zur Bank.*

(go to) **the doctor, the dentist** (= *zum Arzt/Zahnarzt gehen*):
- You're not well. Why don't you go to **the doctor**?
- I have to go to **the dentist** tomorrow.

---

the → Units 70, 72–73   in/at → Units 106–107   to/in/at → Unit 108   (at) home → Unit 108

Übungen

71.1
Wo befinden sich die Personen auf den Bildern? Vervollständigen Sie die Sätze und verwenden Sie bei Bedarf **the**.

1 He's in ..bed................. .
2 They're at ....
3 She's in ....
4 She's at ....
5 They're at ....
6 He's in ....

71.2
Vervollständigen Sie die Sätze mit Wörtern aus der Liste, und verwenden Sie bei Bedarf **the**.

> ~~bank~~   bed   ~~church~~   home   post office   school   station

1 I need to change some money. I have to go to ...the bank....... .
2 David usually goes to ...church... on Sundays.
3 In Britain, children go to .... from the age of five.
4 There were a lot of people at .... waiting for the train.
5 We went to their house, but they weren't at ....
6 I'm going to .... now. Goodnight!
7 I'm going to .... to get some stamps.

71.3
Vervollständigen Sie die Sätze und verwenden Sie bei Bedarf **the**.

1 If you want to catch a plane, you ...go to the airport................. .
2 If you want to see a film, you go to ....
3 If you are tired and you want to sleep, you ....
4 If you rob a bank and the police catch you, you ....
5 If you have a problem with your teeth, you ....
6 If you want to study after you leave school, you ....
7 If you are badly injured in an accident, you ....

71.4
Korrigieren Sie die Sätze, in denen **the** fehlt. Schreiben Sie **OK**, wenn der Satz keinen Fehler enthält.

1 We went to cinema last night. — to the cinema
2 I finish work at 5 o'clock every day. — OK
3 Lisa wasn't feeling well yesterday, so she went to doctor.
4 I wasn't feeling well this morning, so I stayed in bed.
5 Why is Angela always late for work?
6 'Where are your children?' 'They're at school.'
7 We have no money in bank.
8 When I was younger, I went to church every Sunday.
9 What time do you usually get home from work?
10 Do you live far from city centre?
11 'Where shall we meet?' 'At station.'
12 James is ill. He's in hospital.
13 Kate takes her children to school every day.
14 Would you like to go to university?
15 Would you like to go to theatre this evening?

71.5
Übersetzen Sie ins Englische.

1 Jessica fängt um 8.30 mit der Arbeit an.
2 Ich gehe meistens um Mitternacht ins Bett.
3 (am Telefon) 'Wo bist du?' 'Am Bahnhof.'
4 Wo sind Sie zur Schule gegangen?
5 Meine Eltern sind heute nicht zu Hause.
6 Möchtest du mit uns ins Kino gehen?
7 Ihr Bruder war fünf Jahre im Gefängnis.
8 Wir gehen zur Bank und dann zur Post.
9 Tom war fünf Jahre an der Universität.

Unit 72

I like **music**   I hate **exams**

A

Bei allgemeinen Aussagen verwendet man nicht **the** (wie im Deutschen):
- I like **music**, especially **classical music**. (nicht the music ... the classical music)
  Ich mag Musik, besonders klassische Musik.
- **Life** is not possible without **water**. (nicht The life ... the water)
  Es gibt kein Leben ohne Wasser.
- I hate **exams**. (nicht the exams) *Ich hasse Prüfungen.*
- My favourite sports are **football** and **skiing**. (nicht the football ... the skiing)
  Meine liebsten Sportarten sind Fußball und Skifahren.
- Tom's brother is studying **English** and **history**. *... studiert Englisch und Geschichte*
- Is there a shop near here that sells **newspapers**? *... , der Zeitungen verkauft?*

Die Verneinung bei allgemeinen Aussagen ist auch ohne **the** (im Deutschen verwendet man 'kein' /'keine' usw.):
- We don't eat **meat**. *Wir essen kein Fleisch.*
- I don't like **crowds**. *Ich mag keine Menschenmengen.*

Bei abstrakten Begriffen verwendet man nicht **the** (anders als im Deutschen):
- That's **life**. (nicht the life) *So ist das Leben.*
- People say **love** is blind. (nicht the love) *... die Liebe blind ist.*
- Is **marriage** still important in our society? *Ist die Ehe immer noch wichtig in unserer Gesellschaft?*

Bei der **-ing** Form verwendet man nicht **the**:
- **Living** in a big city is exciting, but very expensive. (nicht The living)
  Das Leben in einer Großstadt ist aufregend, aber ...

B

flowers oder **the flowers**?

Vergleichen Sie:

- **Flowers** are beautiful.
  Blumen sind schön.
  (Blumen allgemein)

- We don't eat **fish** very often.
  Wir essen nicht sehr oft Fisch.

- **Life** is wonderful.
  Das Leben ist schön/wunderbar.
  (das Leben allgemein)

- **Wind** is a source of energy.
  Der Wind ist eine Energiequelle.
  (der Wind allgemein)

- I love this garden.
  The flowers are beautiful.
  Die Blumen sind schön.
  (die Blumen in diesem Garten)

- We had a great meal last night.
  The fish was excellent.
  ... Der Fisch war ausgezeichnet.

- I'm reading a book about
  the life of Van Gogh.
  ... das Leben von Van Gogh.

- **The wind** is very strong today.
  Der Wind ist heute sehr stark.

andere Gebräuche von **the** → Units 70–71, 73

Übungen

Unit 72

72.1 Was halten Sie davon?

| big cities | computer games | exams | jazz | parties |
| chocolate | dogs | housework | museums | tennis |

Wählen Sie sieben der Themen aus dem Kästchen und schreiben Sie jeweils einen Satz, in dem Sie ihre Einstellung dazu ausdrücken. Beginnen Sie mit:

I like ...   I don't like ...   I love ... oder **I hate ...**

1 _I hate exams._ oder _I like exams._ (usw.)
2 ......
3 ......
4 ......
5 ......
6 ......
7 ......
8 ......

72.2 Wissen Sie etwas über folgende Sachen? Schreiben Sie Sätze mit:

| I'm (very) interested in ... | I know a lot about ... | I don't know much about ... |
| I'm not interested in ... | I know a little about ... | I don't know anything about ... |

1 (history)   _I'm very interested in history._
2 (politics)   I ......
3 (sport)   ......
4 (art)   ......
5 (astronomy)   ......
6 (economics)   ......

72.3 Entscheiden Sie, welcher Satz richtig ist.

1 My favourite sport is <u>football</u> / <s>the football</s>. (*football* ist richtig)
2 I like this hotel. <s>Rooms</s> / <u>The rooms</u> are very nice. (*The rooms* ist richtig)
3 Everybody needs <u>friends / the friends</u>.
4 Jane doesn't go to <u>parties / the parties</u> very often.
5 I went shopping this morning. <u>Shops / The shops</u> were very busy.
6 'Where's <u>milk / the milk</u>?' 'It's in the fridge.'
7 I don't like <u>milk / the milk</u>. I never drink it.
8 'Do you do any sports?' 'Yes, I play <u>basketball / the basketball</u>.'
9 An architect is a person who designs <u>buildings / the buildings</u>.
10 We went for a swim in the river. <u>Water / The water</u> was very cold.
11 I don't like swimming in <u>cold water / the cold water</u>.
12 Excuse me, can you pass <u>salt / the salt</u>, please?
13 I like this town. I like <u>people / the people</u> here.
14 <u>Vegetables / The vegetables</u> are good for you.
15 <u>Houses / The houses</u> in this street are all the same.
16 I can't sing this song. I don't know <u>words / the words</u>.
17 I enjoy taking <u>pictures / the pictures</u>. It's my hobby.
18 Do you want to see <u>pictures / the pictures</u> that I took when I was on holiday?
19 <u>English / The English</u> is used a lot in <u>international business / the international business</u>.
20 <u>Money / The money</u> doesn't always bring <u>happiness / the happiness</u>.

72.4 Übersetzen Sie ins Englische.

1 Mein Sohn mag Geschichte und Englisch.
2 Das Leben ist nicht einfach.
3 Harry trinkt keinen Kaffee.
4 Jenny interessiert sich für moderne Kunst.
5 Die Menschen in dieser Stadt sind sehr nett.
6 Das Wetter ist heute nicht sehr gut.
7 Maria mag kein kaltes Wetter.
8 In diesem Museum können Sie viel über die Wissenschaft lernen.

sich interessieren für = be interested in
Wissenschaft = science

Unit 73

the ... (geographische Bezeichnungen)

A   Länder, Städte, Kontinente, usw.

Im allgemeinen verwendet man nicht **the** mit Namen von Ländern, Städten, Kontinenten usw.:
- **Cairo** is the capital of **Egypt**. Kairo ist die Hauptstadt von Ägypten.
- **Corsica** is an island in the Mediterranean. Korsika ... im Mittelmeer.
- **Peru** is in **South America**.

Beachten Sie folgende Unterschiede zwischen dem Englischen und dem Deutschen bei Ländernamen:
- I was in **Turkey** last summer. ... in der Türkei ...
- **Switzerland** has three official languages. Die Schweiz ...

Man verwendet jedoch **the** bei Ländernamen mit 'republic'/'states'/'kingdom':
the Czech **Republic**   **the** United **Kingdom** (**the** UK)
the United **States** of America (**the** USA)

B   the -s (Plural)

Mit Namen von Ländern, Inseln und Bergen, die im Plural stehen, verwendet man **the**:
the Netherlands   **the** Canary Islands   **the** Philippines   **the** Alps

C   Meere, Flüsse, Berge und Seen

Mit Namen von Meeren und Flüssen verwendet man **the**:
| **the** Atlantic (Ocean) | **the** Mediterranean (Sea) | **the** Amazon | **the** Suez Canal |
| der Atlantische Ozean | das Mittelmeer | der Amazonas | der Sueskanal |

Meistens verwendet man jedoch **the** nicht mit Namen von Bergen und Seen:
| **Everest** | **Vesuvius** | **Lake Garda** | **Lake Constance** |
| (der) Everest | der Vesuv | der Gardasee | der Bodensee |

D   Ortsbezeichnungen in Städten (Straßen, Gebäude, usw.)

Meistens verwendet man **the** nicht mit Namen von Straßen und Plätzen:
- Where is **Highfield Road**, please?
- **Times Square** is in New York.

Vergleichen Sie:
Trafalgar Square   aber   der Marienplatz
Oxford Street   aber   die Friedrichstraße

Man verwendet **the** nicht mit Namen von Flugplätzen, Bahnhöfen, Universitäten und anderen wichtigen Gebäuden, zum Beispiel:
Kennedy Airport   **Westminster Abbey**   **London Zoo**
Victoria Station   **Edinburgh Castle**   **Cambridge University**

Vergleichen Sie:
Harvard University   aber   die Marburger Universität
Windsor Castle   aber   das Heidelberger Schloss
Canterbury Cathedral   aber   der Kölner Dom

Aber meistens verwendet man **the** mit Namen von Hotels, Museen, Theatern und Kinos:
the Regent Hotel   **the** National Theatre
the Science Museum   **the** Odeon (cinema)

E   the ... of ...

Mit Namen von Ländern, Gebäuden, Einrichtungen, die **of** enthalten, verwendet man **the**:
the Museum **of** Modern Art   **the** University **of** California
the Great Wall **of** China   **the** Tower **of** London

Man sagt **the north** / **the south** / **the east** / **the west** / **the middle** (of ...):
- I've been to **the north of Italy**, but not to **the south**.
  Ich bin schon einmal im Norden Italiens gewesen, aber nicht im Süden.

andere Gebräuche von **the** ➔ Units 70–72

Übungen

73.1 Hier sind einige Geographie-Fragen. Wählen Sie die richtige Antwort aus dem Kästchen. In manchen Fällen müssen Sie **The** vor den Begriff setzen.

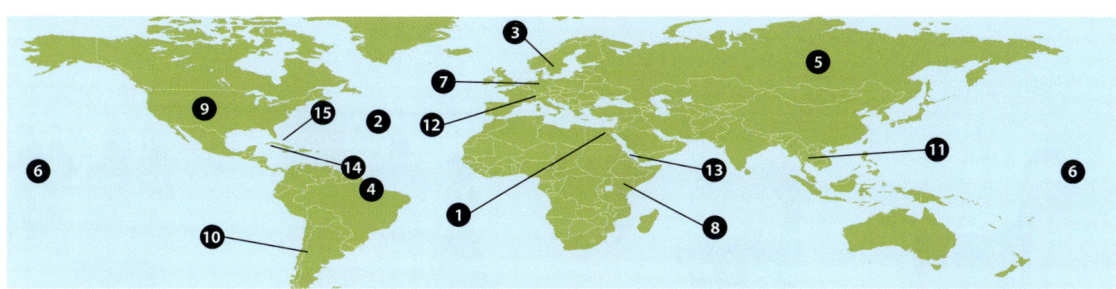

1	*Cairo*	is the capital of Egypt.	Alps
2	*The Atlantic*	is between Africa and America.	Amazon
3	....	is a country in northern Europe.	Andes
4	....	is a river in South America.	Asia
5	....	is the largest continent in the world.	~~Atlantic~~
6	....	is the largest ocean.	Bahamas
7	....	is a river in Europe.	Bangkok
8	....	is a country in East Africa.	~~Cairo~~
9	....	is between Canada and Mexico.	Jamaica
10	....	are mountains in South America.	Kenya
11	....	is the capital of Thailand.	Pacific
12	....	are mountains in central Europe.	Red Sea
13	....	is between Saudi Arabia and Africa.	Rhine
14	....	is an island in the Caribbean.	Sweden
15	....	are a group of islands near Florida.	United States

73.2 Fügen Sie **the** in den Satz ein, wenn erforderlich. Wenn der Satz so richtig ist, schreiben Sie **OK**.

1. Kevin lives in Newton Street. — *OK*
2. We went to see a play at National Theatre. — *at the National Theatre*
3. Have you ever been to China?
4. Have you ever been to Philippines?
5. Have you ever been to south of France?
6. Can you tell me where Regal Cinema is?
7. Can you tell me where Merrion Street is?
8. Can you tell me where Museum of Art is?
9. Europe is bigger than Australia.
10. Belgium is smaller than Netherlands.
11. Which river is longer – Mississippi or Nile?
12. Did you go to National Gallery when you were in London?
13. We stayed at Park Hotel in Hudson Road.
14. How far is it from Trafalgar Square to Victoria Station (*in London*)?
15. Rocky Mountains are in North America.
16. Texas is famous for oil and cowboys.
17. I hope to go to United States next year.
18. Mary comes from west of Ireland.
19. Alan is a student at Manchester University.
20. Panama Canal joins Atlantic Ocean and Pacific Ocean.

73.3 Übersetzen Sie ins Englische.

1. Der Genfer See ist in der Schweiz.
2. Michael und Amy verbringen ihren Urlaub immer in der Türkei.
3. Die Heidelberger Universität ist sehr alt.
4. Everest ist höher als der Kilimandscharo.
5. Wir fahren morgen mit dem Zug zum Frankfurter Flughafen.
6. Der Nil ist im Norden Afrikas.
7. A: In welchem Hotel wohnen Sie?
   B: Im Hilton.
8. Wir wollen nächsten Sommer ans Mittelmeer fahren – vielleicht nach Griechenland.
9. A: Ist Idaho im Osten der USA?
   B: Nein, im Westen.

Genf = Geneva
verbringen = spend
wohnen = stay

→ Zusätzliche Übungen 33–34 (Seiten 269–70)

Unit 74 this/that/these/those

A

this (singular)	**these** (plural)	**that** (singular)	**those** (plural)
Do you like **this** picture?	**These** flowers are for you.	Do you like **that** picture?	Who are **those** people?

this / these

this picture = dieses Bild (hier)
these flowers = diese Blumen (hier)

that / those

that picture = das/dieses Bild (dort)
those people = die/diese Leute (dort)

B

Man kann **this/that/these/those** mit einem Nomen (**this picture** / **those girls** usw.) oder ohne Nomen verwenden:

- **This hotel** is expensive, but it's very nice.   *Dieses Hotel …*
- 'Who's **that girl**?' 'I don't know.'   *'Wer ist dieses Mädchen?' …*
- Do you like **these shoes**? I bought them last week.   *Gefallen dir diese Schuhe? …*
- **Those apples** look nice. Can I have one?   *Diese Äpfel sehen gut aus. …*

} mit Nomen

- **This** is a nice hotel, but it's very expensive.   *Dies ist ein schönes Hotel …*
- 'Excuse me, is **this** your bag?' 'Oh yes, thank you.'   *'… ist das Ihre Tasche?' …*
- Who's **that**?   *Wer ist das?*
- Which shoes do you prefer – **these** or **those**?
  … diese hier oder diese da (oder die anderen)?

} ohne Nomen

C

that (= das) kann sich auf etwas beziehen, was vorher passiert ist:

- 'I'm sorry I forgot to phone you.' '**That**'s all right.'   *'Das macht nichts.'*
- **That** was a really nice meal. Thank you very much.   *Das war ein ausgezeichnetes Essen. …*

that kann sich auch auf etwas beziehen, was gerade erwähnt wurde:

- 'You're a teacher, aren't you?' 'Yes, **that**'s right.'   *'… (das) stimmt / (das ist) richtig.'*
- 'Martin has a new job.' 'Really? I didn't know **that**.'   *'… Das wusste ich nicht.'*
- 'I'm going on holiday next week.' 'Oh, **that**'s nice.'   *'Wie schön.'*
- 'Jenny can't come for dinner.' 'Oh, **that**'s a shame.'   *'Schade.'*

D

like this / like that = so:

- Which way should I hold it? **Like this**?   *Wie soll ich es halten? So?*
- Why are you looking at me **like that**?   *Warum guckst du mich so an?*

E

Am Telefon sagt man **this is** … und **is that** … ?:

- Hello. **This is** David. **Is that** Sarah?
  … Hier ist/spricht David. Ist das Sarah?

Man verwendet auch **this is** …, um jemanden vorzustellen:

- A: Ben, **this is** Chris.
  Ben, hier ist Chris.
  B: Hello, Chris – nice to meet you.
  Guten Tag, Chris – freut mich.
  C: Hi. *Guten Tag.*

DAVID — Hi Sarah, this is David.

Ben, this is Chris.

AMANDA   BEN   CHRIS

---

this one / that one ➔ Unit 75

Übungen

Unit 74

74.1 Vervollständigen Sie die Sprechblasen mit this/that/these/those und einem der folgenden Wörter:

birds   house   plates   postcards   seat   ~~shoes~~

1. Do you like these shoes?
2. Who lives in ....?
3. How much are ....?
4. Look at ....
5. Excuse me, is .... free?
6. .... are dirty.

74.2 Schreiben Sie passende Fragen in die Sprechblasen. Verwenden Sie **Is this/that your ... ?** oder **Are these/those your ... ?**

1. Is this your bag?

74.3 Vervollständigen Sie die Sätze mit **this is** oder **that's** oder **that**.

1. A: I'm sorry I'm late.
   B: That's all right.
2. A: I can't come to the party tomorrow.
   B: Oh, ... a shame. Why not?
3. *am Telefon*
   SUE: Hello, Jane. .... Sue.
   JANE: Oh, hello Sue. How are you?
4. A: You're lazy.
   B: .... not true!
5. A: Jill plays the piano very well.
   B: Does she? I didn't know ....
6. *Mark lernt Pauls Schwester, Helen, zu kennen.*
   PAUL: Mark, ... my sister, Helen.
   MARK: Hi, Helen.
7. A: I'm sorry I was angry yesterday.
   B: .... OK. Forget it!
8. A: You're a friend of Tom's, aren't you?
   B: Yes, ... right.

74.4 Übersetzen Sie ins Englische. Verwenden Sie **this/that/these/those**.

lecker = delicious

1. Der Mann (dort) ist der Manager.
2. Ist das (hier) Ihr Regenschirm?
3. Was machen die Leute (dort)?
4. Dieses Kleid (hier) ist schön, aber es ist teuer.
5. (*am Telefon*) Hier spricht Anna. Ist das Michael?
6. 'Ich war letzte Woche in Paris.' 'Wie schön!'
7. Gefallen dir diese Blumen (hier)?
8. Megan, das ist mein Freund Peter.
9. Diese Suppe schmeckt lecker.
10. Guck mal die Wolken an. Die sind schön.
11. Wie sollen wir den Tisch stellen? So?
12. Das war ein sehr schöner Abend. Vielen Dank!

Unit 75: one/ones

A

one = eine/einer/eines usw.

"These chocolates are good. Would you like **one**?"

Would you like **one**? *Möchtest du eine?*
= Would you like **a chocolate**? *... eine Praline?*

*Man verwendet **one** anstelle von **a/an** ... + Nomen (a chocolate / an apple usw.) um das Wort nicht wiederholen zu müssen.*

- I need **a pen**. Do you have **one**? *Ich brauche einen Stift. Haben Sie einen?*
- A: Is there **a bank** near here? *Gibt es eine Bank hier in der Nähe?*
  B: Yes, there's **one** at the end of this street. *Ja, da ist eine am Ende der Straße.*

B

one und **ones**

*Ein Nomen im Singular kann man mit **one** und ein Nomen im Plural mit **ones** ersetzen. Beachten Sie, dass in den folgenden Beispielen **one/ones** nicht 'eine'/'einer'/'eines' entspricht:*

one (Singular)

"Which **one** do you want?" "This **one**."

Which **one**? = Which **hat**?

one = hat/car/girl usw.

this one / that one
= diese/dieser/dieses usw.
- Which **car** is yours? **This one** or **that one**? *Welches Auto ist Ihres? Dieses hier oder dieses da?*

the one ... = der/die/das usw.
- A: Which **hotel** did you stay at? *In welchem Hotel ... ?*
  B: **The one** opposite the station. *In dem gegenüber vom Bahnhof.*

the ... one
- I don't like the black **coat**, but I like the **brown one**. *Ich mag den schwarzen Mantel nicht, aber mir gefällt der Braune.*

a/an ... one
- This **cup** is dirty. Can I have **a clean one**? (nicht one clean) *... Kann ich eine Saubere haben?*

another one = noch eine/einer/eines usw.
- That **biscuit** was nice. I'm going to have **another one**. *... Ich esse noch eins.*

ones (Plural)

"Which **ones** do you want?" "The white **ones**."

Which **ones**? = Which **flowers**?

ones = flowers/cars/girls usw.

these/those oder **these ones / those ones**
= diese/diesen
- Which **flowers** do you want? **These** or **those**? oder **These ones** or **those ones**? *Welche Blumen möchten Sie? Diese (hier) oder diese dort?*

the ones ... = die/denen
- A: Which **books** are yours? *Welche Bücher ... ?*
  B: **The ones** on the table. *Die auf dem Tisch.*

the ... ones
- Don't buy those **apples**. Buy **the other ones**. *... die anderen.*

some ... ones
- These **cups** are dirty. Can we have **some clean ones**? (nicht some clean) *... Können wir Saubere haben?*
- My **shoes** are very old. I'm going to buy **some new ones**. *... Ich werde neue kaufen.*

which ... ? → Unit 48   another → Unit 66   this/that usw. → Unit 74

Übungen

Unit 75

75.1 Schreiben Sie die Antworten von B auf die Fragen von A anhand der Informationen in dem Kästchen. Verwenden Sie **one** anstatt **a/an** ... .

| B doesn't need a car | B has just had a cup of coffee | there's a chemist in Mill Road |
| B is going to get a bike | ~~B doesn't have a pen~~ | B doesn't have an umbrella |

1 A: Can you lend me a pen? B: I'm sorry, _I don't have one_ .
2 A: Would you like to have a car? B: No, I don't ....
3 A: Do you have a bike? B: No, but ....
4 A: Can you lend me an umbrella? B: I'm sorry, but ....
5 A: Would you like a cup of coffee? B: No, thank you. ....
6 A: Is there a chemist near here? B: Yes, ...

75.2 Vervollständigen Sie die Sätze mit **a/an ... one** und den Wörtern aus der Liste.

| better   big   ~~clean~~   different   new   old |

1 This cup is dirty. Can I have _a clean one_ ?
2 I'm going to sell my car and buy ....
3 That's not a very good photo, but this is ....
4 I want today's newspaper. This is ....
5 This box is too small. I need ....
6 Why do we always go to the same restaurant? Let's go to ....

75.3 Vervollständigen Sie die Dialoge anhand der Informationen. Verwenden Sie **one/ones**.

1 A stayed at a hotel. It was opposite the station. A: We stayed at a hotel. B: _Which one_ ? A: _The one opposite the station._	6 A is looking at a picture. It's on the wall. A: That's an interesting picture. B: .... ? A: ....
2 A sees some shoes in a shop window. They're green. A: I like those shoes. B: Which .... ? A: The	7 A sees a girl in a group of people. She's tall with long hair. A: Do you know that girl? B: .... ? A: ....
3 A is looking at a house. It has a red door. A: That's a nice house. B: .... ? A: .... with	8 A is looking at some flowers in the garden. They're yellow. A: Those flowers are beautiful. B: .... ? A: ....
4 A is looking at some CDs. They're on the top shelf. A: Are those your CDs? B: .... ? A:	9 A is looking at a man in a restaurant. He has a moustache and glasses. A: Who's that man? B: .... ? A: ....
5 A is looking at a jacket in a shop. It's black. A: Do you like that jacket? B: .... ? A:	10 A took some photos at the party last week. A: Did I show you my photos? B: .... ? A: ....

75.4 Übersetzen Sie ins Englische.

Brot = sandwich
Handschuh = glove

1 'Haben Sie einen Laptop?' 'Nein, aber ich möchte einen kaufen.'
2 Ich habe Brote gemacht. Möchtest du eins?
3 Welches Stück möchten Sie? Dieses (hier) oder das?
4 'In welchem Haus wohnt Ben?' 'In dem mit dem schönen Garten.'
5 Welche Ohrringe gefallen dir? Diese (hier) oder diese (dort)?
6 'Möchten Sie diese Äpfel?' 'Nein, die anderen.'
7 Welches Kleid soll ich anziehen? Das Rote oder das Schwarze?
8 Wir haben ein Kind, und wir möchten noch eins.
9 Meine Hände sind kalt in diesen Handschuhen. Ich brauche wärmere.

Unit 76

some und any

A

some und any bezeichnen eine unbestimmte Menge:

some

I have **some** money.

Man verwendet **some** in bejahten Aussagen:
- I'm going to buy **some** clothes.
  Ich gehe Kleider kaufen. / Ich werde …
- There's **some** milk in the fridge.
  Es ist etwas Milch im Kühlschrank.
- We made **some** mistakes.
  Wir haben einige Fehler gemacht.

Some entspricht im Deutschen oft 'etwas/einige'.

any

I **don't** have **any** money.

Man verwendet **any** bei verneinten Aussagen:
- I'm **not** going to buy **any** clothes.
  Ich werde keine Kleider kaufen.
- There **isn't any** milk in the fridge.
  Es ist keine Milch …
- We **didn't** make **any** mistakes.
  Wir haben keine Fehler …

Im Deutschen verwendet man hier 'kein'/'keine'.

B

any und **some** in Fragen

In den meisten Fragen verwendet man **any**:
- Is there **any** milk in the fridge? *Ist etwas Milch im Kühlschrank?*
- Does he have **any** friends? *Hat er (irgendwelche) Freunde?*
- Do you need **any** help? *Brauchst du Hilfe?*

Do you have **any** money?

Meistens verwendet man **some** (nicht **any**), wenn man etwas anbietet
(**Would you like** … **?**):
- A: Would you like **some** coffee? *Möchten Sie etwas Kaffee?*
  B: Yes, please.

oder wenn man um etwas bittet (**Can I have** … **?** usw.):
- A: Can I have **some** soup, please? *… etwas Suppe haben?*
  B: Yes. Help yourself. *Ja, nimm dir.*
- A: Can you lend me **some** money? *… mir etwas Geld leihen?*
  B: Sure. How much do you need?

Would you like **some** coffee?

C

some und **any** ohne Nomen

In diesem Fall entspricht **some** im Deutschen 'welche(n)'/'welches':
- I didn't take any pictures, but Jessica took **some**. *… aber Jessica hat welche gemacht.*
- I've just made some coffee. Would you like **some**? *… Möchten Sie welchen?*

not … **any** entspricht hier 'keine(n)'/'keines':
- You can have some coffee, but I don't want **any**. *Du kannst Kaffee trinken, aber ich möchte keinen.*
- 'Where's your luggage?' 'I don't have **any**.' *… 'Ich habe keines.'*

D

Vergleichen Sie:

- She said **something**. *… etwas gesagt.*
- I saw **somebody** (oder **someone**).
  … jemanden gesehen.
- Would you like **something** to eat?
  … etwas essen?
- **Somebody's** at the door.
  Jemand ist an der Tür.

- She **didn't** say **anything**. *… nichts gesagt.*
- I **didn't** see **anybody** (oder **anyone**).
  … niemanden gesehen.
- Are you doing **anything** tonight?
  Machst du etwas …?
- Where's Sue? Has **anybody** seen her?
  … Hat jemand sie gesehen?

---

a und some → Unit 69   somebody/anything usw. → Unit 79

Übungen

Unit 76

76.1 Schreiben Sie **some** oder **any**.

1. I bought ....*some*.... cheese, but I didn't buy ....*any*.... bread.
2. In the middle of the room there was a table and .... chairs.
3. There aren't .... shops in this part of town.
4. Gary and Alice don't have .... children.
5. Do you have .... brothers or sisters?
6. There are .... beautiful flowers in the garden.
7. Do you know .... good hotels in London?
8. 'Would you like .... tea?' 'Yes, please.'
9. When we were on holiday, we visited .... interesting places.
10. Don't buy .... rice. We don't need ....
11. I went out to buy .... bananas, but they didn't have .... in the shop.
12. I'm thirsty. Can I have .... water, please?

76.2 Vervollständigen Sie die Sätze mit **some** oder **any** und einem der folgenden Wörter:

air	cheese	help	milk	questions
batteries	friends	languages	pictures	~~shampoo~~

1. I want to wash my hair. Is there ....*any shampoo*.... ?
2. The police want to talk to you. They want to ask you ....
3. I had my camera, but I didn't take ....
4. Do you speak .... foreign .... ?
5. Yesterday evening I went to a restaurant with .... of mine.
6. Can I have .... in my coffee, please?
7. The radio isn't working. There aren't .... in it.
8. It's hot in this office. I'm going out for .... fresh ....
9. A: Would you like .... ?
    B: No, thank you. I've had enough to eat.
10. I can do this job alone. I don't need ....

76.3 Vervollständigen Sie die Sätze mit den Wörtern in Klammern und **some** oder **any**.

1. Kate didn't take any pictures, but ....*I took some*.... . (I/take)
2. 'Where's your luggage?' '....*I don't have any*....' (I/not/have)
3. 'Do you need any money?' 'No, thank you. ....' (I/have)
4. 'Can you lend me some money?' 'I'm sorry, but ....' (I/not/have)
5. The tomatoes in the shop didn't look very good, so .... (I/not/buy)
6. There were some nice oranges in the shop, so .... (I/buy)
7. 'How much coffee did you drink yesterday?' '...............' (I/not/drink)

76.4 Vervollständigen Sie die Sätze mit **something/somebody/anything/anybody**.

1. A woman stopped me and said ....*something*...., but I didn't understand.
2. 'What's wrong?' 'There's .... in my eye.'
3. Do you know .... about politics?
4. I went to the shop, but I didn't buy ....
5. .... has broken the window. I don't know who.
6. There isn't .... in the bag. It's empty.
7. I'm looking for my keys. Has .... seen them?
8. Would you like .... to drink?
9. I didn't eat .... because I wasn't hungry.
10. This is a secret. Please don't tell ....

76.5 Übersetzen Sie ins Englische. Verwenden Sie **some/any/somebody/anybody** usw.

1. Es ist etwas Brot auf dem Tisch.
2. Wir haben kein Essen im Haus.
3. Möchten Sie etwas Kuchen?
4. Wir haben einige Freunde in der Stadt getroffen.
5. Hat irgendjemand angerufen?
6. Wir haben keine Milch. Könnt ihr uns welche geben?
7. A: Hast du gestern Bananen gekauft?
    B: Nein, aber ich habe Äpfel gekauft.
8. Es gibt keine Geschäfte in dieser Straße, aber in der nächsten Straße gibt es welche.
9. Martha hat etwas im Garten gesehen, aber ich habe nichts gesehen.

Unit 77: not + any   no   none

A

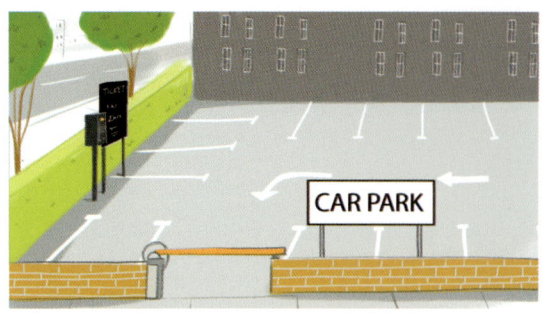

The car park is empty.   Der Parkplatz ist leer.

There are**n't any** cars   in the car park. } Es sind keine Autos …
There are **no** cars

How many cars are there in the car park?
None.   Keine.

not (-n't) + any
- There are**n't any** cars in the car park.   Es sind keine Autos …
- Tracey and Jack do**n't** have **any** children.   … haben keine Kinder.
- You can have some coffee, but I do**n't** want **any**.   … aber ich möchte keinen.

no + Nomen (**no cars** / **no garden** usw.)

no … = **not any** … oder **not a**
- There are **no cars** in the car park. (= there are**n't any** cars)
- We have **no coffee**. (= we do**n't** have **any** coffee)
- It's a nice house, but there's **no garden**. (= there is**n't a** garden)

Man verwendet **no** … (anstelle von **not** + **any**) besonders nach **have** und **there is/are**.

Beachten Sie:
verneintes Verb + **any** = bejahtes Verb + **no**
- They **don't** have **any** children.   oder   They **have no** children.   (nicht They don't have no children.)
  Sie haben keine Kinder.
- There **isn't any** sugar in your coffee.   oder   There**'s no** sugar in your coffee.
  Es ist kein Zucker in deinem Kaffee.

B

no und **none**

no + Nomen (**no money** / **no children** usw.)
- We have **no money**.   Wir haben kein Geld.
- Everything was OK.   There were **no problems**.
  … Es gab keine Probleme.

none steht alleine (ohne Nomen):
- 'How much money do you have?'   '**None**.' (= no money)
  'Wie viel Geld hast du?'   'Keins.'
- 'Were there any problems?'   'No, **none**.' (= no problems)
  'Gab es Probleme?'   'Nein, keine.'

C

none und **no-one**

none   = keinen/keine/keines (nichts)
no-one = niemand

None beantwortet die Frage **How much**? / **How many**? (Wie viel? / Wie viele Dinge oder Menschen?):
- A: **How much** money do you have?
  B: **None**. (= no money)
- A: **How many** people did you meet?
  B: **None**. (= no people)

No-one beantwortet die Frage **Who**? (Wer?/Wen?/Wem?):
- A: **Who** did you meet?   Wen hast du getroffen/kennen gelernt?
  B: **No-one**.   oder   **Nobody**.   Niemanden.

164   die Verneinung → Unit 44   some und any → Unit 76   anybody/nobody/nothing usw. → Units 78–79

Übungen

Unit 77

77.1 Formulieren Sie die Sätze um, indem Sie **no** verwenden.

1. We don't have any money. — We have no money.
2. There aren't any shops near here. — There are ....
3. Carla doesn't have any free time. — ....
4. There isn't a light in this room. — ....

Formulieren Sie die Sätze um, indem Sie any verwenden.

5. We have no money. — We don't have any money.
6. There's no milk in the fridge. — ....
7. There are no buses today. — ....
8. Tom has no brothers or sisters. — ....

77.2 Vervollständigen Sie die Sätze mit **no** oder **any**.

1. There's ...no... sugar in your coffee.
2. My brother is married, but he doesn't have .... children.
3. Sue doesn't speak .... foreign languages.
4. I'm afraid there's .... coffee. Would you like some tea?
5. 'Look at those birds!' 'Birds? Where? I can't see .... birds.'
6. 'Do you know where Jessica is?' 'No, I have .... idea.'

Vervollständigen Sie die Sätze mit no, any oder none.

7. There aren't .... pictures on the wall.
8. The weather was cold, but there was .... wind.
9. I wanted to buy some oranges, but they didn't have .... in the shop.
10. Everything was correct. There were .... mistakes.
11. 'How much luggage do you have?' '............ .'
12. 'How much luggage do you have?' 'I don't have ....'

77.3 Vervollständigen Sie die Sätze mit **any** oder **no** und einem der folgenden Wörter.

| difference | friends | furniture | heating | idea |
| money | ~~problems~~ | questions | queue | |

1. Everything was OK. There were ...no problems... .
2. Jack and Emily would like to go on holiday, but they have ....
3. I'm not going to answer ....
4. He's always alone. He has ....
5. There is .... between these two machines. They're exactly the same.
6. There wasn't .... in the room. It was completely empty.
7. 'Do you know how the accident happened?' 'No, I have ....'
8. The house is cold because there isn't ....
9. We didn't have to wait to get our train tickets. There was ....

77.4 Schreiben Sie kurze Antworten (ein oder zwei Wörter) zu diesen Fragen. Verwenden Sie bei Bedarf **none**.

1. How many letters did you write yesterday? — Two. oder A lot. oder None.
2. How many sisters do you have? — ....
3. How much coffee did you drink yesterday? — ....
4. How many photos have you taken today? — ....
5. How many legs does a snake have? — ....

77.5 Übersetzen Sie ins Englische.

sagen = tell

1. Es sind keine Kinder im Park.
2. Wir haben kein Brot.
3. 'Wie viele Leute sind da?' 'Keine.'
4. 'Wer hat dir das gesagt?' 'Niemand.'
5. Ich brauche neue Kleider, aber ich habe kein Geld.
6. A: Wie viele Kinder haben sie?
   B: Keine.
7. Tom macht nicht viel in seiner Freizeit. Er hat keine Hobbys.
8. A: Gab es irgendwelche Fehler in meiner E-Mail?
   B: Nein, keine.

Unit 78: not + anybody/anyone/anything — nobody/no-one/nothing

A

not + anybody/anyone
nobody/no-one } *niemand*
(für Menschen)

not + anything
nothing } *nichts*
(für Gegenstände/Sachen)

- There **isn't** { **anybody** / **anyone** } in the room.
  Es ist niemand im Zimmer.
- There **is** { **nobody** / **no-one** } in the room.
  Es ist niemand …
- A: **Who** is in the room?
  Wer ist im Zimmer?
  B: **Nobody**. / **No-one**. *Niemand.*

- There **isn't anything** in the bag.
  Es ist nichts in der Tasche.
- There **is nothing** in the bag.
  Es ist nichts …
- A: **What**'s in the bag?
  Was ist in der Tasche?
  B: **Nothing**. *Nichts.*

-**body** und -**one** haben die gleiche Bedeutung: any**body** = any**one**   no**body** = no-**one**

B

not + anybody/anyone
- I do**n't** know **anybody** (*oder* **anyone**) here.
  Ich kenne niemanden hier.

nobody = **not** + **anybody**
no-one = **not** + **anyone**
- I'm lonely. I have **nobody** to talk to.
  (= I do**n't** have **anybody**)
  Ich fühle mich einsam. Ich habe niemanden, mit dem ich reden kann.
- The house is empty. There is **no-one** in it.
  (= There is**n't anyone** in it.)
  Das Haus ist leer. Es ist niemand darin.

not + anything
- I ca**n't** remember **anything**.
  Ich kann mich an nichts erinnern.

nothing = **not** + **anything**
- She said **nothing**.
  (= She did**n't** say **anything**.)
  Sie hat nichts gesagt.
- There's **nothing** to eat.
  (= There is**n't anything** to eat.)
  Es gibt nichts zu essen.

C

Man kann **nobody/no-one/nothing** entweder am Anfang eines Satzes oder alleine verwenden:

- The house is empty. **Nobody** lives there. … *Dort wohnt niemand.*
- 'Who did you speak to?' '**No-one**.'
  'Mit wem haben Sie gesprochen?' 'Mit niemandem.'

- **Nothing** happened.
  Nichts ist passiert.
- 'What did you say?' '**Nothing**.'
  'Was hast du gesagt?' 'Nichts.'

D

Beachten Sie: verneintes Verb + **anybody/anyone/anything**
bejahtes Verb + **nobody/no-one/nothing**

- He does**n't** know **anything**. (*nicht* He doesn't know nothing)
- Do**n't** tell **anybody**. (*nicht* Don't tell nobody)
- There **is nothing** to do in this town. (*nicht* There isn't nothing)

some *und* any → Unit 76   any *und* no → Unit 77   somebody/anything/nowhere *usw.* → Unit 79

Übungen

Unit 78

78.1 Formulieren Sie die Sätze um mit **nobody/no-one** oder **nothing**.

1. There isn't anything in the bag. — There's nothing in the bag.
2. There isn't anybody in the office. — There's _____
3. I don't have anything to do. — I _____
4. There isn't anything on TV. — _____
5. There wasn't anyone at home. — _____
6. We didn't find anything. — _____

78.2 Formulieren Sie die Sätze um mit **anybody/anyone** oder **anything**.

1. There's nothing in the bag. — There isn't anything in the bag.
2. There was nobody on the bus. — There wasn't _____
3. I have nothing to read. — _____
4. I have no-one to help me. — _____
5. She heard nothing. — _____
6. We have nothing for dinner. — _____

78.3 Beantworten Sie die Fragen mit **nobody/no-one** oder **nothing**.

1a What did you say? Nothing.
2a Who saw you? Nobody.
3a What do you want? _____
4a Who did you meet? _____
5a Who knows the answer? _____
6a What did you buy? _____
7a What happened? _____
8a Who was late? _____

Beantworten Sie nun die selben Fragen mit vollständigen Sätzen.
Verwenden Sie **nobody/no-one/nothing** oder **anybody/anyone/anything**.

1b I didn't say anything.
2b Nobody saw me.
3b I don't _____
4b I _____
5b _____ the answer.
6b _____
7b _____
8b _____

78.4 Vervollständigen Sie die Sätze. Verwenden Sie **nobody/no-one/nothing** oder **anybody/anyone/anything**.

1. That house is empty. Nobody lives there.
2. Jack has a bad memory. He can't remember anything.
3. Be quiet! Don't say _____ .
4. I didn't know about the meeting. _____ told me.
5. 'What did you have to eat?' '_____ . I wasn't hungry.'
6. I didn't eat _____ . I wasn't hungry.
7. Helen was sitting alone. She wasn't with _____ .
8. I'm afraid I can't help you. There's _____ I can do.
9. I don't know _____ about car engines.
10. The museum is free. It doesn't cost _____ to go in.
11. I heard a knock on the door, but when I opened it, there was _____ there.
12. The hotel receptionist spoke very fast. I didn't understand _____ .
13. 'What are you doing tonight?' '_____ . Why?'
14. Sophie has gone away. _____ knows where she is. She didn't tell _____ where she was going.

78.5 Übersetzen Sie ins Englische.

faul = lazy

1. 'Was ist in diesem Schrank?' 'Nichts.'
2. Niemand hat mich gestern angerufen.
3. Es tut uns leid, wir können nichts tun.
4. Ich habe es alleine gemacht. Niemand hat mir geholfen.
5. 'Wer ist morgen hier?' 'Niemand.'
6. 'Warum antwortest du nicht?' 'Ich habe nichts zu sagen.'
7. Ich war gestern bei deinem Haus, aber es war niemand zu Hause.
8. Gestern war John sehr faul. Er hat nichts gemacht.
9. Sarah hat nie Besuch. Sie sieht niemanden.

Unit 79
somebody/anything/nowhere usw.

A

Somebody (oder **Someone**) has broken the window.

somebody/someone = jemand

There is **something** in her mouth.

something = etwas

Tom lives **somewhere** near London.

somewhere = irgendwo

B

Menschen (**-body** oder **-one**)

| somebody oder someone |
| anybody oder anyone |
| nobody oder no-one |

- There is **somebody** (oder **someone**) at the door.   Es ist jemand …
- Is there **anybody** (oder **anyone**) at the door?   Ist (irgend) jemand … ?
- There isn't **anybody** (oder **anyone**) at the door.   Es ist niemand …
- There is **nobody** (oder **no-one**) at the door.   Es ist niemand …

-body und **-one** haben die gleiche Bedeutung: **somebody** = **someone**, **nobody** = **no-one** usw.

Gegenstände/Sachen (**-thing**)

| something |
| anything |
| nothing |

- Lucy said **something**, but I didn't understand what she said.   Lucy hat etwas …
- Are you doing **anything** at the weekend?   Machst du (irgend) etwas … ?
- I was angry, but I did**n't** say **anything**.   … , aber ich habe nichts gesagt.
- 'What did you say?'   '**Nothing**.'   … 'Nichts.'

Ort und Stelle (**-where**)

| somewhere |
| anywhere |
| nowhere |

- Ruth's parents live **somewhere** in the south of England.   … leben irgendwo …
- Did you go **anywhere** last weekend?   Bist du irgendwo hingegangen … ?
- I'm staying here. I'm **not** going **anywhere**.   … Ich gehe nirgends hin.
- 'Where are you going?'   '**Nowhere**.'   … 'Nirgends.'

C

something/anybody usw. + **big/cheap/interesting** usw.
- Did you meet **anybody interesting** at the party?
  Hast du jemanden Interessanten auf dem Fest getroffen?
- Let's go out to eat. Let's go **somewhere nice**.   … Lasst uns irgendwohin gehen, wo es nett ist.
- 'What's that letter?'   'It's **nothing important**.'   … 'Es ist nichts Wichtiges.'

D

somebody else / **anything else** usw. = jemand anderer / etwas anderes usw. (oder sonst jemand/etwas usw.):
- 'Did you meet David?'   'No, **somebody else**.'   … 'Nein, jemand anderen.'
- He watches TV all the time. He doesn't do **anything else**.
  Er sieht immer fern. Er macht sonst nichts.
- We stayed at an expensive hotel. There was **nowhere else** to stay.   … Sonst gab es nirgendwo zu bleiben.

E

something/anybody usw. + **to** …
- I'm hungry. I want **something to eat**.   … Ich will etwas zu essen / etwas essen.
- I didn't bring **anything to read**.   Ich habe nichts zu lesen / zum Lesen mitgebracht.
- Tony doesn't have **anybody to talk** to.   Tony hat niemanden, mit dem er reden kann.
- There is **nowhere to go** in this town.   Man kann nirgendwo in dieser Stadt hingehen.

---

some und any → Unit 76   any und no → Unit 77   anybody/nothing usw. → Unit 78
everything/-body/-where → Unit 80

Übungen

Unit 79

79.1 Vervollständigen Sie die Sätze mit **somebody** (oder **someone**) / **something** / **somewhere**.

1 Lucy said ___something___ . — What did she say?
2 I've lost _____ . — What have you lost?
3 Sue and Tom went _____ . — Where did they go?
4 I'm going to phone _____ . — Who are you going to phone?

79.2 Beantworten Sie die Fragen mit **nobody** (oder **no-one**) / **nothing** / **nowhere**.

1a What did you say? — ___Nothing.___
2a Where are you going? — _____
3a What do you want? — _____
4a Who are you looking for? — _____

Beantworten Sie nun die Fragen. Verwenden Sie **not** + **anybody**/**anything**/**anywhere**.

1b ___I didn't say anything.___   3b _____
2b I'm not _____   4b _____

79.3 Vervollständigen Sie die Sätze mit **somebody**/**anything**/**nowhere** usw.

1 It's dark. I can't see ___anything___ .
2 Tom lives ___somewhere___ near London.
3 Do you know _____ about computers?
4 'Listen!' 'What? I can't hear _____ .'
5 'What are you doing here?' 'I'm waiting for _____ .'
6 We need to talk. There's _____ I want to tell you.
7 'Did _____ see the accident?' 'No, _____ .'
8 We weren't hungry, so we didn't eat _____ .
9 'What's going to happen?' 'I don't know. _____ knows.'
10 'Do you know _____ in Paris?' 'Yes, a few people.'
11 'What's in that cupboard?' '_____ . It's empty.'
12 I'm looking for my glasses. I can't find them _____ .
13 I don't like cold weather. I want to live _____ warm.
14 Is there _____ interesting on TV tonight?
15 Have you ever met _____ famous?

79.4 Vervollständigen Sie die Sätze mit Wörtern aus den Kästchen.

something	anything	nothing
something	anywhere	~~nowhere~~
somewhere		nowhere

| do | eat | park | sit |
| drink | ~~go~~ | read | stay |

1 We don't go out very much because there's ___nowhere to go___ .
2 There isn't any food in the house. We don't have _____ .
3 I'm bored. I've got _____ .
4 'Why are you standing?' 'Because there isn't _____ .'
5 'Would you like _____ ?' 'Yes, please – a glass of water.'
6 If you're going to the city centre, take the bus. Don't drive because there's _____ .
7 I want _____ . I'm going to buy a magazine.
8 I need _____ in London. Can you recommend a hotel?

79.5 Übersetzen Sie ins Englische.

Flohmarkt = flea market

1 Jemand hat meine Schokolade gegessen.
2 Ist irgendjemand da?
3 'Guck mal!' 'Was? Ich kann nichts sehen.'
4 Mein Stift ist hier irgendwo, aber ich kann ihn nicht finden.
5 Kann ich noch etwas für Sie tun?
6 Es gibt hier nichts zum Lesen.
7 'Ist Toby im Café?' 'Nein, er ist woanders.'
8 A: Hast du gestern etwas auf dem Flohmarkt gekauft?
   B: Nein, ich habe nichts Billiges gefunden.
9 Dieses Wochenende möchte ich etwas anderes machen.
10 Jessica hat das Fest nicht gefallen. Sie hat niemanden Interessanten getroffen.

Unit 80: every und all

A every

Every house in the street is the same.

every house in the street =
all the houses in the street
jedes Haus in der Straße = alle Häuser in der Straße

every = *jeder/jede/jedes*

every + Singular (**every house** / **every country** usw. **is**/ **has** usw.):
- **Every country** has interesting places to visit. *Jedes Land ...*
- **Every summer** we have a holiday by the sea. *Jeden Sommer ...*
- She looks different **every time** I see her. *Jedesmal, wenn ich sie sehe, sieht sie anders aus.*

Vergleichen Sie **every** *und* **all**:

- **Every student** in the class passed the exam.
  Jeder Schüler in der Klasse hat ... bestanden.
- **Every country has** a national flag.
  (*nicht* have) *Jedes Land hat ...*

- **All the students** in the class passed the exam.
  Alle Schüler in der Klasse haben ...
- **All countries have** a national flag.
  Alle Länder haben ...

B every day und all day

every day = *jeden Tag*:

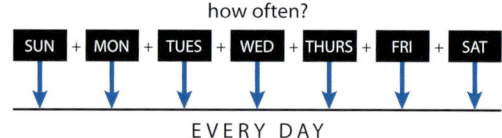

all day = *den ganzen Tag*:

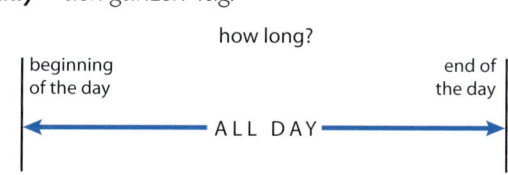

- It rained **every day** last week.
  Es hat letze Woche jeden Tag geregnet.
- Ben watches TV for about two hours **every evening**. *... jeden Abend ...*

- It rained **all day** yesterday.
  Es hat gestern den ganzen Tag geregnet.
- On Monday, I watched TV **all evening**.
  ... den ganzen Abend ...

Man sagt auch **every morning/night/summer** *usw.*

Man sagt auch **all morning/night/summer** *usw.*

C everybody (oder everyone) / everything / everywhere

everybody *oder* **everyone**
(*jeder/jedermann/alle*)
everything
(*alles*)
everywhere
(*überall*)

- **Everybody** (*oder* **Everyone**) needs friends.
  Jeder/Jedermann braucht Freunde. / Alle Menschen brauchen ...
- Do you have **everything** you need?
  Hast du alles, was du brauchst?
- I lost my watch. I've looked **everywhere** for it.
  ... Ich habe überall danach gesucht.

Nach **everybody/everyone/everything** *steht das Verb im Singular*:
- **Everybody has** problems. (*nicht* Everybody have)
  Jeder/Jedermann hat Probleme. / Alle haben Probleme.

D everybody/everything und all

Meistens wird **all** *mit einem Nomen verwendet* (**all the children** / **all the money** *usw.*).
Anders als im Deutschen wird **all** *in der Regel nicht ohne Nomen verwendet. Man sagt*:

- **All the students** passed the exam. (**all** + *Nomen*) *Alle Studenten ...*

aber **Everybody** passed the exam. (*nicht* All passed) *Alle ...*

- I'm going to tell you **all the news**. *... alle Neuigkeiten ...*

aber I'm going to tell you **everything**. (*nicht* tell you all) *Ich werde dir alles erzählen.*

all ➔ Unit 81

Übungen

80.1
Vervollständigen Sie die Sätze mit **every** und einem der folgenden Wörter:

> day   room   ~~student~~   time   word

1. _Every student_ in the class passed the exam.
2. My job is very boring. _____ is the same.
3. Kate is a very good tennis player. When we play, she wins _____ .
4. _____ in the hotel has free wi-fi and a minibar.
5. 'Did you understand what she said?' 'Most of it, but not _____ .'

80.2
Vervollständigen Sie die Sätze mit **every day** oder **all day**.

1. Yesterday it rained _all day_ .
2. I buy a newspaper _____ , but sometimes I don't read it.
3. I'm not going out tomorrow. I'll be at home _____ .
4. I usually drink about four cups of coffee _____ .
5. Paula was ill yesterday, so she stayed in bed _____ .
6. I'm tired now because I've been working hard _____ .
7. Last year we went to the seaside for a week, and it rained _____ .

80.3
Fügen Sie **every** oder **all** ein.

1. Bill watches TV for about two hours _every_ evening.
2. Julia gets up at 6.30 _____ morning.
3. The weather was nice yesterday, so we sat outside _____ afternoon.
4. I'm going away on Monday. I'll be away _____ week.
5. 'How often do you go skiing?' '_____ year. Usually in March.'
6. A: Were you at home at 10 o'clock yesterday?
   B: Yes, I was at home _____ morning. I went out after lunch.
7. My sister loves new cars. She buys one _____ year.
8. I saw Sam at the party, but he didn't speak to me _____ evening.
9. We go away on holiday for two or three weeks _____ summer.

80.4
Vervollständigen Sie die Sätze mit **everybody**/**everything**/**everywhere**.

1. _Everybody_ needs friends.
2. Chris knows _____ about computers.
3. I like the people here. _____ is very friendly.
4. This is a nice hotel. It's comfortable and _____ is very clean.
5. Kevin never uses his car. He goes _____ by motorcycle.
6. Let's get something to eat. _____ is hungry.
7. Sue's house is full of books. There are books _____ .
8. You are right. _____ you say is true.

80.5
Setzen Sie in jeden Satz ein Verb (nur ein Wort) ein.

1. Everybody _has_ problems.
2. Are you ready yet? Everybody _____ waiting for you.
3. The house is empty. Everyone _____ gone out.
4. Gary is very popular. Everybody _____ him.
5. This town is completely different now. Everything _____ changed.
6. I got home very late last night. I came in quietly because everyone _____ asleep.
7. Everybody _____ mistakes!
8. A: _____ everything clear? _____ everybody know what to do?
   B: Yes, we all understand.

80.6
Übersetzen Sie ins Englische.

> Sportverein = sports club

1. Jeder Garten in dieser Straße ist schön.
2. Es hat den ganzen Sommer geregnet.
3. Jeder braucht Liebe.
4. Gehen Sie jeden Tag einkaufen?
5. Dan geht jede Woche zum Sportverein.
6. Wir haben die ganze Nacht nicht geschlafen.
7. 'Ist alles in Ordnung?' 'Ja, alles ist wunderbar.'
8. Jedesmal wenn ich ausgehe, komme ich spät nach Hause.
9. Ich habe gestern den ganzen Tag nichts gemacht.
10. Es ist niemand hier. Alle sind nach Hause gegangen.
11. Becky hat überall in den USA gelebt.

Unit 81: all   most   some   any   no/none

A
Vergleichen Sie:

children/money/books usw. (allgemein):
- **Children** like playing.
  Kinder spielen gerne. (Kinder allgemein)
- **Money** isn't everything.
  Geld ist nicht alles. (Geld allgemein)
- I enjoy reading **books**.
  Ich lese gerne Bücher.
- Everybody needs **friends**.
  Jeder braucht Freunde.

the children / **the** money / **these** books usw. (bestimmte Kinder, bestimmte Bücher usw.):
- Where are **the children**? Wo sind die Kinder? (hier the children = unsere Kinder)
- I want to buy a car, but I don't have **the money**. ... ich habe das Geld (dafür) nicht.
- Have you read **these books**?
  ... diese Bücher gelesen?
- I often go out with **my friends**.
  ... mit meinen Freunden.

B
most / most of ... , some / some of ... usw.

 all    most    some    any    no / none / not + any

most/some usw. + Nomen für allgemeine Aussagen

all / most / some / any / no	~~of~~	cities / children / books / money

most of/some of usw. + **the/this/my** ... usw.

all / most / some / any / none	(of) / of	the ... / this/that ... / these/those ... / my/your ... usw.

- **Most children** like playing.
  Die meisten Kinder spielen gerne. (Kinder allgemein)
- I don't want **any money**.
  Ich will kein Geld.
- **Some books** are better than others.
  Manche Bücher sind besser als andere.
- He has **no friends**. Er hat keine Freunde.
- **All cities** have the same problems.
  Alle Städte haben ... (Städte allgemein)

Beachten Sie: **most** = die meisten
- **Most people** drive too fast.
  (nicht Most of people)
  Die meisten Leute fahren zu schnell.

- **Most of the children at this school** are under 11 years old.
  Die meisten dieser Kinder ...
- I don't want **any of this money**.
  Von diesem Geld will ich nichts.
- **Some of these books** are very old.
  Einige dieser Bücher ...
- **None of my friends** live near me. Keiner meiner Freunde wohnt bei mir in der Nähe.

Man sagt **all the** ... / **all my** ... usw. (meistens ohne **of**):
- **All (of) the students in our class** passed the exam. Alle Schüler ...
- Amy has lived in London **all (of) her life**.
  ... ihr ganzes Leben ...

C
all of it / most of them / none of us usw.

all / most / some / any / none	of	it / them / us / you

- You can have **some of this cake**, but not **all of it**.
  ... ein Stück von diesem Kuchen haben, aber nicht alles (davon).
- A: Do you know those people?
  B: **Most of them**, but not **all of them**. Die meisten (von ihnen), aber nicht alle.
- I have a lot of books, but I haven't read **any of them**. ... ich habe keine davon gelesen.
- 'How many of these books have you read?' '**None of them**.' 'Keine davon.'

Beachten Sie, dass **of it** und **of them** (für Gegenstände) in diesem Zusammenhang im Deutschen 'davon' entsprechen:
   none of it / none of them = keins/keine(r) davon
   most of it / most of them = das meiste davon
   some of it = ein Teil davon   **some of them** = einige (davon)

the ... (children / the children usw.) ➔ Unit 72   some und any ➔ Unit 76   no/none/any ➔ Unit 77
all und every ➔ Unit 80

Übungen

81.1 Vervollständigen Sie die Sätze. Verwenden Sie die Wörter in Klammern (**some**/**most** usw.). In manchen Fällen müssen Sie **of** (**some of** / **most of** usw.) hinzufügen.

1. ..Most.. children like playing. (**most**)
2. ..Some of.. this money is yours. (**some**)
3. .... people never stop talking. (**some**)
4. .... the shops in the city centre close at 6.30. (**most**)
5. .... people have mobile phones these days. (**most**)
6. I don't like .... the pictures in the living room. (**any**)
7. He's lost .... his money. (**all**)
8. .... my friends are married. (**none**)
9. Do you know .... the people in this picture? (**any**)
10. .... birds can fly. (**most**)
11. I enjoyed .... the film, but I didn't like the ending. (**most**)
12. .... sports are very dangerous. (**some**)
13. We can't find anywhere to stay. .... the hotels are full. (**all**)
14. You must have .... this cheese. It's delicious. (**some**)
15. The weather was bad when we were on holiday. It rained .... the time. (**most**)

81.2 Beantworten Sie die Fragen zu den Bildern. Verwenden Sie **all**/**most**/**some**/**none** + **of them** / **of it**.

1. How many of the people are women? — Most of them.
2. How many of the boxes are on the table? — ....
3. How many of the men are wearing hats? — ....
4. How many of the windows are open? — ....
5. How many of the people are standing? — ....
6. How much of the money is Ben's? — ....

81.3 Sind diese Sätze korrekt? Korrigieren Sie die Sätze, die Fehler enthalten. Wenn der Satz so korrekt ist, schreiben Sie **OK**.

1. <u>Most of children</u> like playing. — Most children
2. All the students failed the exam. — OK
3. Some of people work too hard. — ....
4. Some of questions in the exam were very easy. — ....
5. I haven't seen any of those people before. — ....
6. All of insects have six legs. — ....
7. Have you read all these books? — ....
8. Most of students in our class are very nice. — ....
9. Most of my friends are going to the party. — ....
10. I'm very tired this morning – I was awake most of night. — ....

81.4 Übersetzen Sie ins Englische.

1. Alle Kinder brauchen Liebe.
2. Keines dieser Häuser ist groß.
3. Die meisten Leute essen zu viel.
4. Einige meiner Freunde haben Kinder.
5. Das kleine Mädchen will nichts von ihrem Essen.
6. Manche Tiere sind gefährlich.
7. Die meisten meiner Kollegen sind nett, aber einige von ihnen sind unfreundlich.
8. Ich kenne keinen dieser Menschen.
9. In meiner Familie haben alle (von uns) blaue Augen, aber keiner hat blonde Haare.
10. A: Hat dir der Film gefallen?
    B: Ein Teil davon, aber nicht alles.
11. Alle diese Kleider sind teuer, aber keines davon ist schön.

Unit 82: both   either   neither

A

both/either/neither verwendet man, um über zwei Sachen oder Menschen zu reden:

  oder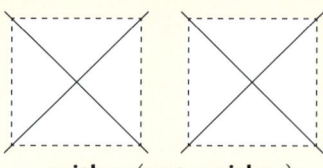

both
beide(s)

either
entweder … oder …
(eins/eine(r) von beiden)

neither (not + either)
keins/keine(r) von beiden

- Rebecca has two children. **Both** are married. … *Beide sind verheiratet.*
- Would you like tea or coffee? You can have **either**. … *beides …*
- A: Do you want to go to the cinema or the theatre?
  B: **Neither**. I want to stay at home. *Keins von beiden. Ich will zu Hause bleiben.*

Vergleichen Sie **either** *und* **neither**:

- 'Would you like **tea** or **coffee**?'
  - '**Either**. I don't mind.' *'Entweder oder. Es ist mir egal.'*
  - 'I **don't** want **either**.' (nicht I don't want neither) *'Ich möchte keins von beiden.'*
  - '**Neither**.' *'Keins von beiden.'*

B

both/either/neither + *Nomen*

both + Plural	both	windows/books/children usw.
either / neither + Singular	either / neither	window/book/child usw.

- Last year I went to Paris and Rome. I liked **both cities** very much.
  … *Beide Städte haben mir sehr gut gefallen.*
- First I worked in an office, and later in a shop. **Neither job** was very interesting.
  … *Keine der beiden Stellen …*
- There are two ways from here to the station. You can go **either way**.
  … *Sie können so oder so gehen. (Es ist egal, welchen Weg Sie nehmen.)*

C

both of … / either of … / neither of …

both	(of)	the …
either / neither	of	these/those … my/your/Paul's … usw.

I like both of those pictures.

- **Neither of my brothers** has children.
  Keiner meiner (zwei) Brüder hat Kinder.
- I **haven't** read **either of these books**.
  Ich habe keines dieser beiden Bücher gelesen.

Man kann sagen **both of the/those/my** … *oder* **both the/those/my** … (*mit oder ohne* **of**):

- I like **both of** those pictures. *oder*
  I like **both** those pictures.
- **Both of** Paul's sisters are married. *oder*
  Both Paul's sisters are married.

aber
- **Neither of** Paul's sisters is married. (*nicht* Neither Paul's sisters)

D

both of them / neither of us usw. = *beide von ihnen / keiner von beiden usw.*

both / either / neither	of	them / us / you

- Paul has two sisters. **Both of them** are married. … *Beide sind verheiratet.*
  (*Man kann auch sagen* Both are married, *wie oben.*)
- Sue and I didn't eat anything. **Neither of us** was hungry. … *Keiner von uns (beiden) hatte Hunger.*
- Who are those two people? I **don't** know **either of them**. … *Ich kenne keinen von beiden.*

I can't either / neither can I → Unit 43

Übungen

82.1
Vervollständigen Sie die Sätze mit **both**/**either**/**neither**, und verwenden Sie bei Bedarf **of**.

1. Last year I went to Paris and Rome. I liked ......**both**...... cities very much.
2. There were two pictures on the wall. I didn't like ......**either of**...... them.
3. It was a good football match. .... teams played well.
4. It wasn't a good football match. .... team played well.
5. 'Is your friend English or American?' '.................. . She's Australian.'
6. We went away for two days, but the weather wasn't good. It rained .... days.
7. A: I bought two newspapers. Which one do you want?
   B: .... It doesn't matter which one.
8. I invited Sam and Chris to the party, but .... them came.
9. 'Do you go to work by car or by bus?' '.................. . I always walk.'
10. 'Which jacket do you prefer, this one or that one?' 'I don't like .... them.'
11. 'Do you work or are you a student?' '.................. . I work and I'm a student too.'
12. My friend and I went to the cinema, but .... us liked the film. It was really bad.
13. Helen has two sisters and a brother. .... sisters are married.
14. Helen has two sisters and a brother. I've met her brother, but I haven't met .... her sisters.

82.2
Beschreiben Sie die Situationen in den Bildern mit **Both ...** oder **Neither ...** .

1. ......**Both cups are**...................................... empty.
2. .... are open.
3. .... wearing a hat.
4. .... beards.
5. .... to the airport.
6. .... correct.

82.3
Ein Mann und eine Frau haben die gleichen Antworten auf folgende Fragen gegeben. Schreiben Sie die Ergebnisse der Befragung mit **Both**/**Neither of them ...** .

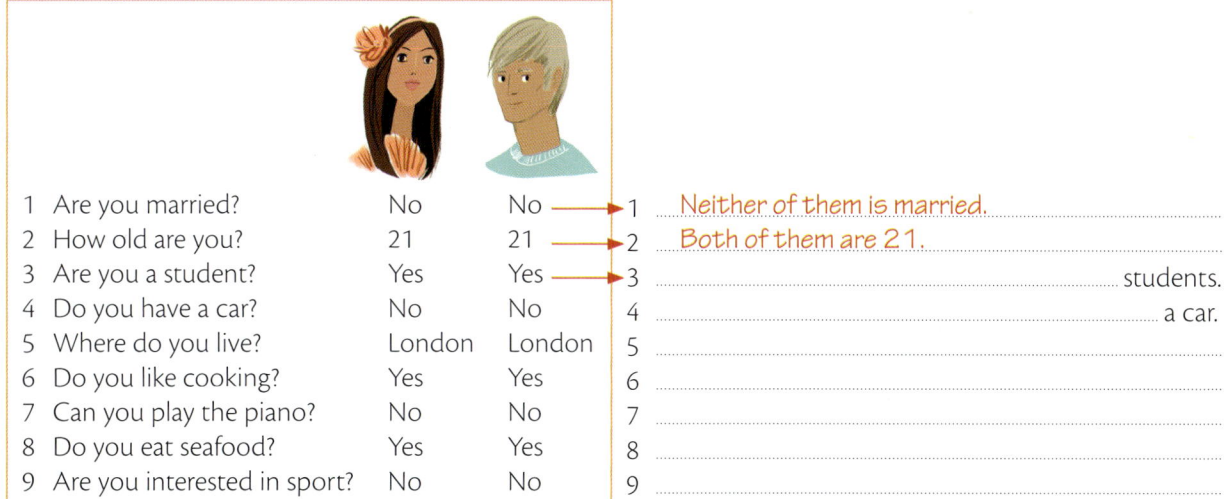

1	Are you married?	No	No	1	Neither of them is married.
2	How old are you?	21	21	2	Both of them are 21.
3	Are you a student?	Yes	Yes	3	.... students.
4	Do you have a car?	No	No	4	.... a car.
5	Where do you live?	London	London	5	
6	Do you like cooking?	Yes	Yes	6	
7	Can you play the piano?	No	No	7	
8	Do you eat seafood?	Yes	Yes	8	
9	Are you interested in sport?	No	No	9	

82.4
Übersetzen Sie ins Englische.

1. Wir haben zwei Autos, aber beide sind alt.
2. Beide meiner Brüder wohnen in London.
3. 'Möchten Sie Apfelsaft oder Orangensaft?' 'Keins von beiden, danke. Ich habe keinen Durst.'
4. Ich mag London und Paris, aber beide Städte sind sehr teuer.
5. Ich habe beide Filme gesehen, aber keiner von beiden war gut.
6. 'Sollen wir heute Abend ins Kino gehen oder zum Konzert?' 'Entweder oder. Es ist mir egal.'
7. Tom und Suzanne haben ein Mädchen und einen Jungen. Keines der Kinder geht in die Schule.
8. Wir sind heute beide müde. Keiner von uns beiden hat gut geschlafen.
9. 'Kennst du Jim und Tina Brown?' 'Ja, beide sind sehr nett.'
10. 'Wo sind Ann und Sally?' 'Ich weiß nicht. Ich habe keine von beiden gesehen.'

Unit 83   a lot   much   many

A

| **a lot of money** | **not much money** | **a lot of books** | **not many books** |
| viel Geld | nicht viel Geld | viele Bücher | nicht viele Bücher |

much = *viel*
Man verwendet **much** mit nicht zählbaren Nomen (die in der Regel nur im Singular verwendet werden) (**much food** / **much money** usw.):
- Did you buy **much food**?
- We don't have **much luggage**.
- A: Do you have any **money**?
  B: I have some, but **not much**.

How much … ? = *Wie viel … ?*
- **How much money** do you want?

many = *viele*
Man verwendet **many** mit einem Nomen im Plural (**many books** / **many people** usw.):
- Did you buy **many books**?
- We don't know **many people**.
- A: Did you take any **photos**?
  B: I took some, but **not many**.

How many … ? = *Wie viele … ?*
- **How many photos** did you take?

a lot of kann man mit allen Nomen verwenden:
a lot of = *viel*
- We bought **a lot of food**.
- Paula doesn't have **a lot of** free **time**.

Man sagt:
- There **is** a lot of **food/money/water** usw.
  Es gibt viel …

a lot of = *viele*
- We bought **a lot of books**.
- Did they ask **a lot of questions**?

- There **are** a lot of **trees/shops/people** usw.
  Es gibt viele …
- A lot of **people speak** English.
  (*nicht* speaks)

B

Man verwendet **much** in Fragen und Verneinungen:
- Do you drink **much coffee**?
- I don't drink **much coffee**.

Aber man verwendet **much** selten in bejahten Sätzen:
- I drink **a lot of coffee**. (*nicht* I drink much coffee)
- 'Do you drink much coffee?' 'Yes, **a lot**.' (*nicht* Yes, much)

Man verwendet **many** und **a lot** in allen Satzarten:
- We have **many** friends / **a lot of** friends.
- We don't have **many** friends / **a lot of** friends.
- Do you have **many** friends / **a lot of** friends?

C

Man kann **much** und **a lot** auch alleine (ohne Nomen) verwenden:
- Amy spoke to me, but she didn't say **much**.   … aber sie hat nicht viel gesagt.
- 'Do you watch TV **much**?' 'No, **not much**.' 'Sehen Sie viel fern?' 'Nein, nicht viel.'
- We like films, so we go to the cinema **a lot**. (*nicht* go to the cinema much)
  … also gehen wir viel ins Kino.
- I don't like him very **much**. Ich mag ihn nicht besonders.

Vergleichen Sie **a lot** und **a lot of** … :
- He eats **a lot**. (*nicht* a lot of)   Er isst viel.
- He eats **a lot of rice**. (**a lot of** + *Nomen*)   Er isst viel Reis.

zählbar / nicht zählbar ➔ Units 68–69

Übungen

Unit 83

83.1 Setzen Sie **much** oder **many** ein.

1. Did you buy _much_ food?
2. There aren't .... hotels in this town.
3. We don't have .... petrol. We need to stop and get some.
4. Were there .... people on the train?
5. Did .... students fail the exam?
6. Paula doesn't have .... money.
7. I wasn't hungry, so I didn't eat ....
8. I don't know where Gary lives these days. I haven't seen him for .... years.

Setzen Sie **How much** oder **How many** ein.

9. .... people are coming to the party?
10. .... milk do you want in your coffee?
11. .... bread did you buy?
12. .... players are there in a football team?

83.2 Vervollständigen Sie die Sätze mit **much** oder **many** und einem der folgenden Wörter:

| ~~books~~   countries   luggage   people   time   times |

1. I don't read very much. I don't have _many books_ .
2. Hurry up! We don't have ....
3. Do you travel a lot? Have you been to .... ?
4. Tina hasn't lived here very long, so she doesn't know ....
5. 'Do you have .... ?' 'No, only this bag.'
6. I know Tokyo well. I've been there ....

83.3 Vervollständigen Sie die Sätze mit **a lot of** und einem der folgenden Wörter:

| accidents   ~~books~~   fun   interesting things   traffic |

1. I like reading. I have _a lot of books_ .
2. We enjoyed our visit to the museum. We saw ....
3. This road is very dangerous. There are ....
4. We enjoyed our holiday. We had ....
5. It took me a long time to drive here. There was ....

83.4 In einigen dieser Sätze klingt **much** nicht natürlich. Ändern Sie die Sätze oder schreiben Sie **OK**.

1. Do you drink <u>much coffee</u>? _OK_
2. I drink <u>much tea</u>. _a lot of tea_
3. It was a cold winter. We had <u>much snow</u>. ....
4. There wasn't <u>much snow</u> last winter. ....
5. It costs <u>much money</u> to travel around the world. ....
6. We had a cheap holiday. It didn't cost <u>much</u>. ....
7. Do you know <u>much</u> about computers? ....
8. 'Do you have any luggage?' 'Yes, <u>much</u>.' ....

83.5 Schreiben Sie Sätze über diese Leute. Verwenden Sie **much** und **a lot**.

1. James loves films. (go to the cinema) _He goes to the cinema a lot._
2. Nicola thinks TV is boring. (watch TV) _She doesn't watch TV much._
3. Tina is a good tennis player. (play tennis) She ....
4. Mark doesn't like driving. (use his car) He ....
5. Paul spends most of the time at home. (go out) ....
6. Sue has been all over the world. (travel) ....

83.6 Übersetzen Sie ins Englische.

1. Ich esse viel Obst.
2. Wir haben nicht viel Brot.
3. Hast du auf dem Fest viele Leute kennen gelernt?
4. Meine Nachbarn haben viele Blumen in ihrem Garten.
5. Gehen Sie oft ins Theater?
6. Wie viele Bücher hast du letztes Jahr gelesen?
7. Becky geht meistens früh ins Bett. Sie schläft viel.
8. A: Wie viel Zeit haben wir?
   B: Nicht viel.

Unit 84: (a) little   (a) few

A

(a) **little** verwendet man mit nicht zählbaren Nomen (die in der Regel nur im Singular verwendet werden):

(a) **little** water
(a) **little** time
(a) **little** money
(a) **little** soup

a little water
etwas Wasser

(a) **few** verwendet man mit einem Nomen im Plural:

(a) **few** books
(a) **few** questions
(a) **few** people
(a) **few** days

a few books
einige Bücher

B

a little = etwas / ein wenig

- She didn't eat anything, but she drank **a little water**.
  … , aber sie hat etwas Wasser getrunken.
- I speak **a little Spanish**.
  Ich spreche etwas Spanisch.
- A: Can you speak Spanish?
  B: **A little**. *Ein wenig.*

a few = einige

- Excuse me, I have to make **a few phone calls**. … einige Telefonate …
- We're going away for **a few days**.
  … für einige Tage … .
- I speak **a few words** of Spanish.
  Ich spreche einige Worte Spanisch.
- A: Are there any shops near here?
  B: Yes, **a few**. *Ja, einige.*

C

~~a~~ **little** (ohne **a**) = wenig

- There was **little food** in the fridge.
  It was nearly empty.
  Es war wenig zu essen im Kühlschrank. …

very little = sehr wenig
- Dan is very thin because he eats **very little**.
  … weil er sehr wenig isst.

~~a~~ **few** (ohne **a**) = wenige

- There were **few people** in the theatre.
  It was nearly empty.
  Es waren wenige Leute im Theater. …

very few = sehr wenige
- Your English is very good. You make **very few mistakes**.
  … Sie machen sehr wenige Fehler.

D

Vergleichen Sie **little** und **a little**:

- They have **a little** money, so they're not poor. *Sie haben etwas Geld, …*
- They have **little** money. They are very poor.
  Sie haben wenig Geld. …

Vergleichen Sie **few** und **a few**:

- I have **a few** friends, so I'm not lonely.
  Ich habe einige Freunde, …
- I'm sad and I'm lonely. I have **few** friends.
  … *Ich habe wenige Freunde.*

I have a little money.   I have little money.   I have a few friends.   I have few friends.

zählbar / nicht zählbar → Units 68–69

Übungen

Unit 84

84.1 Beantworten Sie die Fragen mit **a little** oder **a few**.

1 'Do you have any money?'   'Yes, _a little_.'
2 'Do you have any envelopes?'   'Yes, _____.'
3 'Do you want sugar in your coffee?'   'Yes, _____, please.'
4 'Did you take any photos when you were on holiday?'   'Yes, _____.'
5 'Does your friend speak English?'   'Yes, _____.'
6 'Are there any good restaurants in this town?'   'Yes, _____.'

84.2 Vervollständigen Sie die Sätze mit **a little** oder **a few** und einem der folgenden Wörter:

> chairs   days   fresh air   friends   milk   Russian   times   ~~years~~

1 Mark speaks Italian well. He lived in Italy for _a few years_.
2 Can I have _____ in my coffee, please?
3 'When did Amy go away?'   '_____ ago.'
4 'Do you speak any foreign languages?'   'I can speak _____.'
5 'Are you going out alone?'   'No, I'm going with _____.'
6 'Have you ever been to Mexico?'   'Yes, _____.'
7 There wasn't much furniture in the room – just a table and _____.
8 I'm going out for a walk. I need _____.

84.3 Vervollständigen Sie die Sätze mit **very little** oder **very few** und einem der folgenden Wörter:

> coffee   hotels   ~~mistakes~~   people   rain   time   work

1 Your English is very good. You make _very few mistakes_.
2 I drink _____. I prefer tea.
3 The weather here is very dry in summer. There is _____.
4 It's difficult to find a place to stay in this town. There are _____.
5 Hurry up. We have _____.
6 The town is very quiet at night. _____ go out.
7 Some people in the office are very lazy. They do _____.

84.4 Vervollständigen Sie die Sätze mit **little** / **a little** oder **few** / **a few**.

1 There was _little_ food in the fridge. It was nearly empty.
2 'When did Sarah go out?'   '_____ minutes ago.'
3 I can't decide now. I need _____ time to think about it.
4 There was _____ traffic, so we arrived earlier than we expected.
5 The bus service isn't very good at night – there are _____ buses after 9 o'clock.
6 'Would you like some soup?'   'Yes, _____, please.'
7 I'd like to practise my English more, but I have _____ opportunity.

84.5 Richtig oder falsch? Korrigieren Sie die Sätze, wenn erforderlich, oder schreiben Sie **OK**, wenn der Satz so richtig ist.

1 We're going away for few days next week.   _for a few days_
2 Everybody needs little luck.
3 I can't talk to you now – I have few things to do.
4 I eat very little meat – I don't like it very much.
5 Excuse me, can I ask you few questions?
6 There were little people on the bus – it was nearly empty.
7 Mark is a very private person. Few people know him well.

84.6 Übersetzen Sie ins Englische.

1 Wir haben einige Pflanzen in unserer Wohnung.
2 'Was möchten Sie trinken?'   'Etwas Orangensaft, bitte.'
3 'Haben wir Butter im Kühlschrank?'   'Ja, ein wenig.'
4 'Gibt es in diesem Ort ein Kino?'   'Ja, es gibt einige.'
5 Wenige Leute haben genug Freizeit.
6 Es ist kalt hier im Winter, aber es schneit sehr wenig.
7 Tom hat einige Freunde, aber wenige gute Freunde.
8 Ich habe heute sehr wenig Zeit, aber morgen habe ich etwas mehr Zeit.

Unit 85: old/nice/interesting usw. (Adjektive)

A

nice day / **blue eyes** usw. (Adjektiv + Nomen)

Adjektiv + Nomen

It's a	**nice**	**day** today.	... ein schöner Tag ...
Laura has	**brown**	**eyes**.	... braune Augen.
There's a very	**old**	**bridge** in this village.	... eine sehr alte Brücke ...
Do you like	**Italian**	**food**?	... italienisches Essen?
I don't speak any	**foreign**	**languages**.	... keine Fremdsprachen.
There are some	**beautiful yellow**	**flowers** in the garden.	... schöne gelbe Blumen ...

Beachten Sie, dass im Englischen Adjektive nicht veränderbar sind, zum Beispiel:

beautiful = schöner, schöne, schönes

a beautiful house **beautiful houses**
ein schönes Haus schöne Häuser

B

be (**am**/**is**/**are**/**was** usw.) + Adjektiv (**nice**/**interesting** usw.)

- The weather **is nice** today.
  Das Wetter ist heute schön.
- These flowers **are** very **beautiful**.
  Diese Blumen sind sehr schön.
- The film **wasn't** very **good**. It **was boring**.
  Der Film war nicht sehr interessant. Er war langweilig.
- Please **be quiet**. I'm reading.
  Bitte sei still. ...

Beachten Sie, dass **be** + Adjektiv manchmal anderen Konstruktionen im Deutschen entspricht (→ Unit 3):

- I**'m hungry**/**thirsty**. Ich habe Hunger/Durst. (Ich bin hungrig/durstig.)
- He**'s scared** of dogs. Er hat Angst vor Hunden.
- **Are** you **cold**/**warm**? Ist dir kalt/warm?

C

Man verwendet **look**/**feel**/**smell**/**taste**/**sound** + Adjektiv, um Wahrnehmungen durch die verschiedenen Sinne zu beschreiben:

You look tired.
I feel tired.

You sound happy.

It smells good.
It tastes good.

- 'You **look tired**'. 'Yes, I **feel tired**'.
  'Du siehst müde aus.' 'Ja, ich fühle mich müde.'
- Joe told me about his new job. It **sounds** very **interesting**.
  ... Sie klingt sehr interessant.
- I'm not going to eat this fish. It doesn't **smell good**.
  ... Er riecht nicht gut.
- This **tastes delicious**. Das schmeckt lecker.

Beachten Sie die gleiche Satzstruktur in folgenden Beispielen:

| He | is
feels
looks | tired. | They | are
look
sound | happy. | It | is
smells
tastes | good. |

---

get + Adjektiv (get hungry/tired usw.) → Unit 57   something/anybody + Adjektiv → Unit 79

Übungen

85.1
Vervollständigen Sie die Sätze mit je einem Adjektiv (**black**/**foreign** usw.) und einem Nomen (**air**/**job** usw.) aus dem Kästchen.

air	clouds	~~foreign~~	holiday	job	~~languages~~	sharp
black	dangerous	fresh	hot	knife	long	water

1 Do you speak any foreign languages ?
2 Look at those _____ . It's going to rain.
3 Sue works very hard, and she's very tired. She needs a _____ .
4 I would like to have a shower, but there's no _____ .
5 Can you open the window? We need some _____ .
6 I need a _____ to cut these onions.
7 Fire-fighting is a _____ .

85.2
Vervollständigen Sie die Sprechblasen in den Bildern. Verwenden Sie ein Verb und ein Adjektiv.

feel(s)	look(s)	~~sound(s)~~		~~happy~~	ill	nice
look(s)	smell(s)	taste(s)	+	horrible	new	surprised

1 You sound happy .
2 It _____ .
3 I _____ .
4 You _____ .
5 They _____ .
6 It _____ .

85.3
B widerspricht A in den Sätzen unten. Vervollständigen Sie die Erwiderungen von B mit den Wörtern in Klammern.

	A		B	
1	You look tired.	Do I? I don't feel tired .	(feel)
2	This is a new coat.	Is it? It doesn't _____ .	(look)
3	I'm American.	Are you? You _____ .	(sound)
4	You look cold.	Do I? I _____ .	(feel)
5	These bags are heavy.	Are they? They _____ .	(look)
6	That soup looks good.	Maybe, but it _____ .	(taste)

85.4
Übersetzen Sie ins Englische.

miserabel = terrible, awful

1 Terry hat blaue Augen und blonde Haare.
2 Das Wetter war gestern nicht sehr schön.
3 Amy und Max wohnen in einem großen modernen Haus.
4 'Du siehst gut aus.' 'Danke.'
5 Es gibt in diesem Park schöne alte Bäume.
6 Haben Sie Durst? Möchten Sie etwas trinken?
7 Joe kennt viele interessante Leute.
8 Was kochst du? Es riecht wunderbar!
9 Mir ist kalt. Könntest du bitte das Fenster schließen?
10 (am Telefon) 'Ich fühle mich miserabel.' 'Du klingst nicht gut.'

Unit 86: quickly/badly/suddenly usw. (Adverbien)

A

He ate his dinner very **quickly**.
Er hat ... sehr schnell gegessen.

Suddenly the shelf fell down.
Plötzlich ist das Regal heruntergefallen.

Quickly und **suddenly** sind Adverbien. Adverbien bildet man, indem man **-ly** an das Adjektiv (**quick/sudden** usw.) anhängt. Beachten Sie, dass im Deutschen Adjektive und Adverbien die gleiche Form haben.

Adjektiv	quick	bad	sudden	careful	heavy	
Adverb	quickly	badly	suddenly	carefully	heavily	
	schnell	*schlecht*	*plötzlich*	*vorsichtig*	*schwer/stark*	*usw.*

Rechtschreibung (→ Anhang 5): eas**y** → eas**ily**   heav**y** → heav**ily**

B

Adverbien besagen wie etwas passiert, oder wie jemand etwas macht:

- The train **stopped suddenly**.
  Der Zug hat plötzlich angehalten.
- I **opened** the door **slowly**.
  Ich habe ... langsam aufgemacht.
- Please **listen carefully**.   Bitte hör gut/genau zu.
- I **understand** you **perfectly**.   Ich verstehe dich genau.

It's **raining heavily**.

Vergleichen Sie:

Adjektiv	Adverb
Sue is very **quiet**. *Sue ist sehr leise/still.*	Sue **speaks** very **quietly**. (*nicht* speaks very quiet) *... spricht sehr leise.*
Be careful! *Sei vorsichtig!*	**Open it carefully**! *Mach es vorsichtig auf!*
It was **a bad game**. *Es war ein schlechtes Spiel.*	Our team **played badly**. (*nicht* played bad) *... schlecht gespielt.*
I **felt nervous**. *Ich fühlte mich nervös.*	I **waited nervously**. *Ich habe nervös gewartet.*

C

hard, **fast**, **late** und **early** sind Adjektive und Adverbien:

Sue's job **is** very **hard**. *... ist sehr schwer.*	Sue **works** very **hard**. (*nicht* hardly) *... arbeitet sehr fleißig/hart.*
Ben is **a fast runner**. *... ein schneller Läufer.*	Ben can **run fast**. *... kann schnell laufen.*
The bus **was late/early**. *Der Bus kam zu spät/früh.*	I **went** to bed **late/early**. *Ich bin spät/früh ins Bett gegangen.*

D

Dem Adjektiv **good** entspricht das Adverb **well**:

Your English **is** very **good**. *Ihr Englisch ist sehr gut.*	You **speak** English very **well**. (*nicht* very good) *Sie sprechen sehr gut Englisch.*
It was **a good game**. *... ein gutes Spiel.*	Our team **played well**. *... hat gut gespielt.*

well kann auch ein Adjektiv sein:

- 'How are you?'   'I**'m** very **well**, thank you. And you?'   ... 'Mir geht es sehr gut ...'

Adjektive → Unit 85

Übungen

86.1
Vervollständigen Sie die Sätze mit einem der folgenden Adverbien passend zu den Situationen in den Bildern.

> angrily   badly   dangerously   fast   ~~heavily~~   quietly

1 It's raining _heavily_ .
2 He sings very _____ .
3 They came in _____ .
4 She shouted at me _____ .
5 She can run very _____ .
6 He was driving _____ .

86.2
Verwenden Sie ein Verb und ein Adverb, um die Sätze zu vervollständigen.

> come   know   sleep   win   ~~carefully~~   clearly   hard   well
> explain   ~~listen~~   think   work   carefully   easily   quickly   well

1 I'm going to tell you something very important, so please _listen carefully_ .
2 They _____ . At the end of the day they're always tired.
3 I'm tired this morning. I didn't _____ last night.
4 You play tennis much better than me. When we play, you always _____ .
5 _____ before you answer the question.
6 I've met Alice a few times, but I don't _____ her very _____ .
7 Our teacher doesn't _____ things very _____ . We never understand him.
8 Helen! I need your help. _____ !

86.3
Was ist richtig?

1 Don't eat so ~~quick~~/quickly. It's not good for you. (quickly ist richtig)
2 Why are you angry/angrily? I haven't done anything.
3 Can you speak slow/slowly, please?
4 Come on, Dave! Why are you always so slow/slowly?
5 Sam is a very careful/carefully driver.
6 Amy is studying hard/hardly for her examinations.
7 'Where's Anna?' 'She was here, but she left sudden/suddenly.'
8 Please be quiet/quietly. I'm studying.
9 Some companies pay their workers very bad/badly.
10 Those oranges look nice/nicely. Can I have one?
11 I don't remember much about the accident. Everything happened quick/quickly.

86.4
Setzen Sie **good** oder **well** in die Sätze ein.

1 Your English is very _good_ . You speak it very _well_ .
2 Jackie did very _____ in her exams.
3 The party was very _____ . I enjoyed it very much.
4 Mark has a difficult job, but he does it _____ .
5 How are your parents? Are they _____ ?
6 Did you have a _____ holiday? Was the weather _____ ?

86.5
Übersetzen Sie ins Englische.

überqueren = cross

1 Ich bin morgens sehr langsam.
2 Warum gehst du so langsam? Bist du müde?
3 Plötzlich hat sie James gesehen.
4 Sei vorsichtig, wenn du die Straße überquerst.
5 A: Kannst du Spanisch sprechen?
   B: Ja, aber nicht sehr gut.
6 A: Wie geht es euren Kindern?
   B: Es geht ihnen sehr gut, danke.
7 Tom arbeitet schnell, aber schlecht.
8 Wir haben heute sehr fleißig gearbeitet.
9 A: Wie gut spricht Jenny Japanisch?
   B: Sie spricht es perfekt!

Unit 87

old/older   expensive / more expensive

A

| old | older | heavy | heavier | expensive | more expensive |
| alt | älter | schwer | schwerer | teuer | teurer |

Older / heavier / more expensive sind Komparativformen.
Den Komparativ bildet man mit **-er** (**older**) oder **more** ... (**more expensive**).

B

Der Komparativ mit **-er** (**older/heavier** usw.)

Kurze Adjektive (1 Silbe) bilden den Komparativ mit **-er**:
  old → **older**   slow → **slower**   cheap → **cheaper**
  nice → **nicer**   late → **later**   big → **bigger**

Rechtschreibung (→ Anhang 5):   bi**g** → bi**gg**er   ho**t** → ho**tt**er   thi**n** → thi**nn**er

Bei Adjektiven (meistens 2 Silben), die auf **-y** enden, **-y** → **-ier**:
  easy → **easier**   heavy → **heavier**   early → **earlier**

- Rome is **old**, but Athens is **older**. (nicht more old)   ... alt ... älter.
- Is it **cheaper** to go by car or by train? Ist es billiger ... ?
- Helen wants a **bigger** car. ... ein größeres Auto.
- This coat is OK, but I think the other one is **nicer**. ... der andere ist schöner.
- Don't take the bus. It's **easier** to take a taxi. (nicht more easy)
  ... Es ist einfacher mit einem Taxi zu fahren.

far → **further**:
- A: How far is it to the station? A mile? Wie weit ... ?
  B: No, it's **further**. About two miles. Nein, es ist weiter. ...

C

Der Komparativ mit **more** ...

Längere Adjektive (zwei oder mehr Silben) bilden den Komparativ mit **more** ... :
  careful → **more careful**   polite → **more polite**
  expensive → **more expensive**   interesting → **more interesting**

- You must be **more careful**. (nicht carefuller)
  Du musst vorsichtiger sein.
- I don't like my job. I want to do something **more interesting**.
  ... Ich will etwas Interessanteres tun.
- Is it **more expensive** to go by car or by train? Ist es teurer ... ?

D

Unregelmäßige Komparativformen

| good/well | → | better | bad | → | worse |
| gut | | besser | schlecht | | schlechter/schlimmer |

- The weather wasn't very **good** yesterday, but it's **better** today.
- A: Do you feel **better** today?
  B: No, I feel **worse**. Nein, ich fühle mich schlechter.
- Which is **worse** – a headache or a toothache?
  Welches ist schlimmer ... ?

older than ... / more expensive than ... → Unit 88   the oldest / the most expensive → Unit 90

Übungen

87.1 Schreiben Sie den Komparativ für jedes Bild (**older** / **more interesting** usw.).

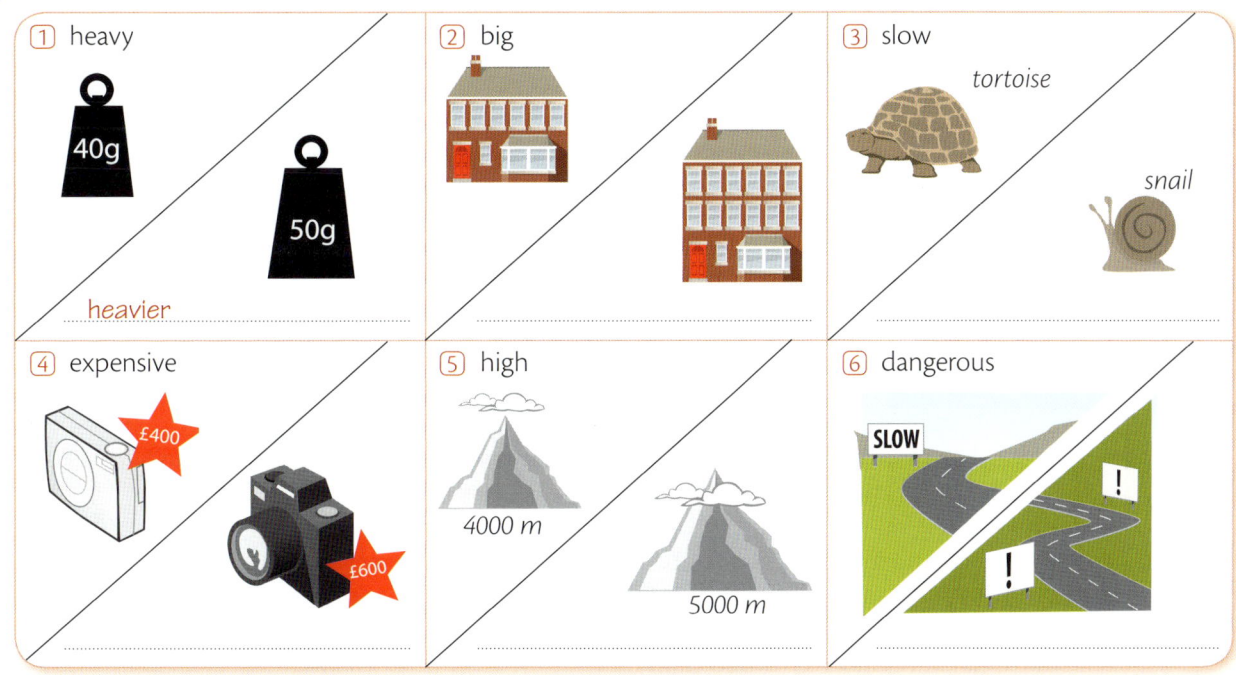

① heavy — heavier
② big
③ slow (tortoise, snail)
④ expensive (£400, £600)
⑤ high (4000 m, 5000 m)
⑥ dangerous

87.2 Schreiben Sie den Komparativ.

1 old — older
2 strong
3 happy
4 modern
5 important
6 good
7 large
8 serious
9 pretty
10 crowded

87.3 Schreiben Sie das Gegenteil.

1 younger — older
2 colder
3 cheaper
4 better
5 nearer
6 easier

87.4 Vervollständigen Sie die Sätze mit dem Komparativ.

1 Helen's car isn't very big. She wants a ...bigger... one.
2 My job isn't very interesting. I want to do something ...more interesting... .
3 You're not very tall. Your brother is ....
4 David doesn't work very hard. I work ....
5 My chair isn't very comfortable. Yours is ....
6 Your idea isn't very good. My idea is ....
7 These flowers aren't very nice. The blue ones are ....
8 My bag isn't very heavy. Your bag is ....
9 I'm not very interested in art. I'm .... in history.
10 It isn't very warm today. It was .... yesterday.
11 These tomatoes don't taste very good. The other ones tasted ....
12 Britain isn't very big. France is ....
13 London isn't very beautiful. Paris is ....
14 This knife isn't very sharp. Do you have a .... one?
15 People today aren't very polite. In the past they were ....
16 The weather isn't too bad today. Often it is much ....

87.5 Übersetzen Sie ins Englische.

sollen = should

1 Der Zug ist schnell, aber das Flugzeug ist schneller.
2 A: Welches Kleid gefällt dir?
   B: Dieses hier ist schöner.
3 Ich kann den großen Koffer nehmen. Er ist schwerer.
4 Was ist weiter? Paris oder Rom?
5 Paris ist teuer, aber London ist teurer.
6 Du hast nicht 'danke' gesagt. Du solltest höflicher sein.
7 Der Film ist gut, aber das Buch ist besser.
8 David ist im Bett. Sein Kopfschmerzen ist schlimmer.

Unit 88: older than ... more expensive than ...

A

She's **taller than** him.
Sie ist größer als er.

The Europa Hotel is **more expensive than** the Grand.
Das Europa Hotel ist teurer als das Grand Hotel.

Hotel Prices (per room per night)
Europa Hotel £150
Grand Hotel £130
Royal Hotel £120
Hotel £115

Man verwendet **than** (= als) nach einem Komparativ (**older than** ... / **more expensive than** ... usw.):
- Athens is **older than** Rome. (nicht older as)
  Athen ist älter als Rom.
- Are oranges **more expensive than** bananas? Sind Orangen teurer als Bananen?
- It's **easier** to take a taxi **than** to take the bus. Es ist leichter mit dem Taxi zu fahren, als ...
- 'How are you today?' 'Not bad. **Better than** yesterday.' ... '... Besser als gestern.'
- The restaurant is **more crowded than** usual. ... ist voller als gewöhnlich.

B

Man sagt: than **me** / than **him** / than **her** / than **us** / than **them**.
Man kann entweder sagen:
- I can run faster **than him**. oder I can run faster **than he can**.
- You are a better singer **than me**. oder You are a better singer **than I am**.
- I got up earlier **than her**. oder I got up earlier **than she did**.

C

more/less than ... = mehr/weniger als
- A: How much did your shoes cost? £60?
  B: No, **more than** that. (= **more than** £60) Nein, mehr.
- The film was very short – **less than** an hour.
  ... – weniger als eine Stunde.
- They have **more money than** they need.
  Sie haben mehr Geld als sie brauchen.
- You go out **more than** me.
  Du gehst mehr/öfter aus als ich.

60 — MORE THAN 50
50
40 — LESS THAN 50

D

a bit older (= etwas älter) / **much older** (= viel älter) usw.

Box A is **a bit bigger** than Box B.
... etwas größer als ...

Box C is **much bigger** than Box D.
... viel größer als ...

a bit / much	bigger / older / better / more difficult / more expensive	than ...

- Canada is **much bigger** than France.
  ... viel größer als ...
- Sue is **a bit older** than Joe – she's 25 and he's 24.
  ... etwas älter als ...
- The hotel was **much more expensive** than I expected.
  ... viel teurer als ...
- You go out **much more** than me.
  ... viel mehr als ...

old → older, expensive → more expensive ➜ Unit 87   not as ... as ➜ Unit 89

Übungen

88.1
Schreiben Sie Sätze, in denen Sie Kate und Ben vergleichen. Verwenden Sie **than**.

Kate
1. I'm 26.
2. I'm not a very good swimmer.
3. I'm 1 metre 68 tall.
4. I start work at 8 o'clock.
5. I don't work very hard.
6. I don't have much money.
7. I'm a very good driver.
8. I'm not very patient.
9. I'm not a very good dancer.
10. I'm very intelligent.
11. I speak French very well.
12. I don't go to the cinema very much.

Ben
1. I'm 24.
2. I'm a very good swimmer.
3. I'm 1 metre 63 tall.
4. I start work at 8.30.
5. I work very hard.
6. I have a lot of money.
7. I'm not a very good driver.
8. I'm very patient.
9. I'm a good dancer.
10. I'm not very intelligent.
11. I don't speak French very well.
12. I go to the cinema a lot.

1. Kate _is older than Ben_.
2. Ben _is a better swimmer than Kate_.
3. Kate is _____.
4. Kate starts _____ Ben.
5. Ben _____.
6. Ben has _____.
7. Kate is a _____.
8. Ben _____.
9. Ben _____.
10. Kate _____.
11. Kate _____.
12. Ben _____.

88.2
Vervollständigen Sie die Sätze. Verwenden Sie **than**.

1. He isn't very tall. You're _taller than him_ oder _taller than he is_.
2. She isn't very old. You're _____.
3. I don't work very hard. You work _____.
4. He doesn't watch TV very much. You _____.
5. I'm not a very good cook. You _____.
6. We don't know many people. You _____.
7. They don't have much money. You _____.
8. I can't run very fast. You can _____.
9. She hasn't been here very long. You _____.
10. They didn't get up very early. You _____.
11. He wasn't very surprised. You _____.

88.3
Vervollständigen Sie die Sätze mit **a bit** oder **much** und einem Komparativ (**older**/**better** usw.).

1. Emma is 25. Joe is 24½.
   Emma _is a bit older than Joe_.
2. Jack's mother is 52. His father is 69.
   Jack's mother _____.
3. My camera cost £120. Yours cost £112.
   My camera _____.
4. Yesterday I felt terrible. Today I feel OK.
   I feel _____.
5. Today the temperature is 12 degrees. Yesterday it was 10 degrees.
   It's _____.
6. Sarah is an excellent tennis player. I'm not a very good player.
   Sarah _____.

88.4
Übersetzen Sie ins Englische.

beim Arzt = at the doctor's

1. Du bist jünger als ich.
2. Ist Französisch schwieriger zu lernen als Englisch?
3. Du kannst schneller lesen als ich.
4. Unser neues Haus ist viel größer als unsere alte Wohnung.
5. A: Wie viele Leute waren auf der Party?
   B: Mehr als 30.
6. Tom hat viel mehr Zeit als Dave.
7. A: Wie lange hast du beim Arzt gewartet? Eine halbe Stunde?
   B: Nein, weniger als 20 Minuten.
8. Das blaue Kleid ist etwas teurer als das Schwarze, aber es ist viel schöner.

Unit 89: not as ... as

A

not as ... as = *nicht so ... wie*

She's old, but she's **not as old as** he is.
Sie ist alt, aber sie ist nicht so alt wie er.

Box A is**n't as big as** Box B.
... ist nicht so groß wie ...

- Rome **is not as old as** Athens.
  Rom ist nicht so alt wie Athen.
- The Grand Hotel **isn't as expensive as** the Europa.
  Das Grand Hotel ist nicht so teuer wie das Europa.
- I **don't** play tennis **as often as** you.
  Ich spiele nicht so oft Tennis wie du.
- The weather is better than it was yesterday. It **isn't as cold**.
  ... Es ist nicht so kalt.

B

not as much as ... / **not as many as** ... = *nicht so viel/viele wie* ...
- I don't have **as much money as** you. *Ich habe nicht so viel Geld wie du.*
- I don't know **as many people as** you. *Ich kenne nicht so viele Leute wie du.*
- I don't go out **as much as** you. *Ich gehe nicht so viel aus wie du.*

C

Vergleichen Sie **not as ... as** *und* **than**:
- Rome is **not as old as** Athens. *Rom ist nicht so alt wie Athen.*
- Athens is **older than** Rome. *Athen ist älter als Rom.*

- Tennis **isn't as popular as** football. *Tennis ist nicht so beliebt wie Fußball.*
- Football is **more popular than** tennis. *Fußball ist mehr beliebt als ...*

- I **don't** go out **as much as** you.
- You go out **more than** me.

D

Man sagt: as **me** / as **him** / as **her** *usw.*
Man kann entweder sagen:
- She's not as old **as him**. *oder* She's not as old **as he is**.
- You don't work as hard **as me**. *oder* You don't work as hard **as I do**.

E

The same as ... = *genauso wie ... , der/die/das Selbe (oder Gleiche) wie ...* :
- The weather today is **the same as** yesterday.
  Das Wetter ist heute genauso wie gestern.
- My hair is **the same colour as** yours.
  Meine Haare haben die gleiche Farbe wie deine.
- I arrived at **the same time as** Tom.
  Ich bin um dieselbe Zeit wie Tom angekommen.

much/many → Unit 83   older than ... / more expensive than ... → Unit 88

Übungen

Unit 89

89.1 Schreiben Sie Sätze, in denen Sie A, B und C in jedem Bild vergleichen.

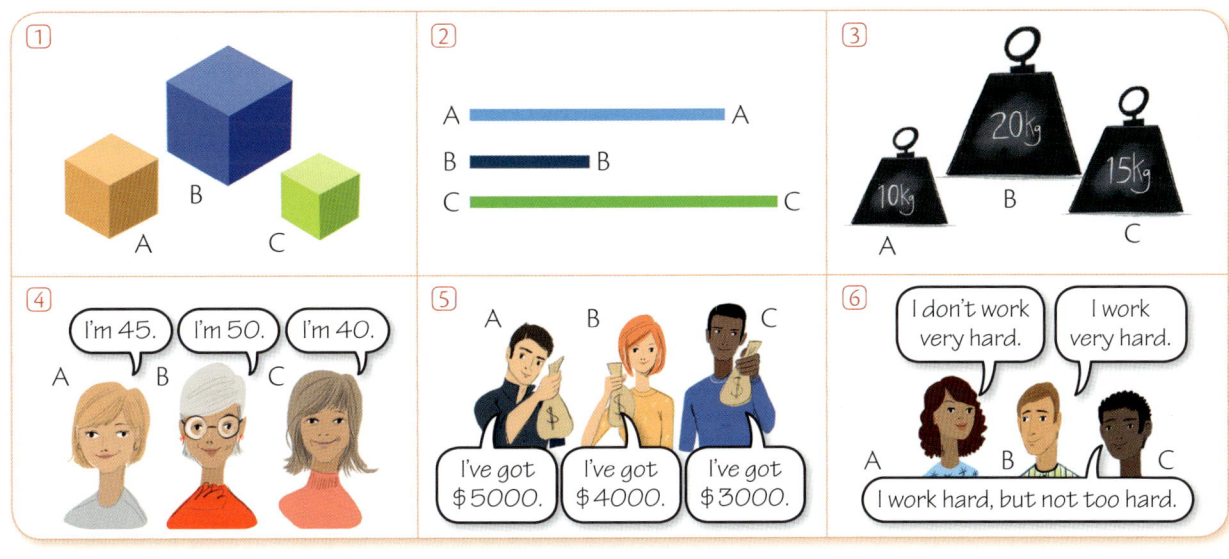

1 A is _bigger than C, but not as big as B_ .
2 A is .... B, but not .... C.
3 C is .... A, but ....
4 A is .... , but ....
5 B has got ....
6 C works ....

89.2 Schreiben Sie Sätze mit **as … as …** .

1 Athens is older than Rome. Rome _isn't as old as Athens_ .
2 My room is bigger than yours. Your room isn't ....
3 You got up earlier than me. I didn't ....
4 We played better than them. They ....
5 I've been here longer than you. You ....
6 She's more nervous than him. He ....

89.3 Vervollständigen Sie die Sätze mit **as** oder **than**.

1 Athens is older _than_ Rome.
2 I don't watch TV as much .... you.
3 You eat more .... me.
4 I'm more tired today .... I was yesterday.
5 Joe isn't as intelligent .... he thinks.
6 Belgium is smaller .... Switzerland.
7 Brazil isn't as big .... Canada.
8 I can't wait longer .... an hour.

89.4 Vergleichen Sie die Aussagen von Julia, Andy und Laura, und vervollständigen Sie die Sätze mit **the same age** / **the same street** usw.

Julia   Andy   Laura

1 (age)   _Andy is the same age as Laura_ .
2 (street) Julia lives ....
3 (time)   Julia got up ....
4 (colour) Andy's ....

89.5 Übersetzen Sie ins Englische.

1 Deutschland ist nicht so groß wie Frankreich.
2 Frankreich ist größer als Deutschland.
3 Ich habe den gleichen Hut wie Sie.
4 Ben ist größer als Joe, aber nicht so groß wie Mark.
5 A: Wie fühlst du dich heute?
   B: Genauso wie gestern – nicht sehr gut.
6 Ich wohne in der selben Straße wie mein Kollege.
7 Ich habe nicht so viele Bücher wie du.
8 München ist nicht so teuer wie London, aber es ist teurer als Frankfurt.
9 Jenny schläft nicht so viel wie Tom. Sie steht nicht so spät auf wie er.

groß (für Personen) = tall
Kollege = colleague

Unit 90: the oldest   the most expensive

A

HOTEL PRICES IN KINTON
(Per room per night)

Europa Hotel	£150	Grosvenor	£110
Grand Hotel	£130	Bennets	£100
Royal	£120	Carlton	£98
Astoria	£115	Star	£85
Palace	£115	Station	£75

Box A is **bigger than** Box B.

Box A is **bigger than** all the other boxes.
… ist größer als …

Box A is **the biggest** box.
… ist der größte Kasten.

The Europa Hotel is **more expensive than** the Grand.

The Europa Hotel is **more expensive than** all the other hotels in the city.
… ist teurer als …

The Europa Hotel is **the most expensive** hotel in the city.
… ist das teuerste Hotel …

Bigger und **more expensive** usw. sind Komparativformen (→ Unit 87).
Biggest und **most expensive** usw. sind Superlativformen.

B

Den Superlativ bildet man mit **-est** (**oldest**) oder **most** … (**most expensive**).

*Kurze Adjektive (1 Silbe: **old**/**cheap**/**nice** usw.) → **the -est**:*
old → **the oldest**   cheap → **the cheapest**   nice → **the nicest**

Rechtschreibung (→ Anhang 5):   bi**g** → the bi**gg**est   ho**t** → the ho**tt**est

Unregelmäßige Superlative: good → **the best**   bad → **the worst**

*Bei Adjektiven (meistens 2 Silben), die auf **-y** enden (**easy**/**heavy** usw.) → **the -iest**:*
easy → **the easiest**   heavy → **the heaviest**   pretty → **the prettiest**

*Längere Adjektive (**careful**/**expensive**/**interesting** usw.) → **the most** … :*
careful → **the most careful**   interesting → **the most interesting**

C

Man sagt **the** oldest … / **the** most expensive … usw. :
- The church is very old. It's **the oldest** building in the town. … das älteste Gebäude der Stadt.
- What is **the longest** river in the world? … der längste Fluss der Welt?
- Money is important, but it isn't **the most important** thing in life.
  … , aber es ist nicht die wichtigste Sache im Leben.
- Excuse me, where is **the nearest** bank? … wo ist die nächste Bank?

Man kann den Superlativ auch ohne Nomen verwenden:
- Luke is a good player, but he isn't **the best** in the team. … , aber er ist nicht der Beste der Mannschaft.

Man sagt:
- the oldest building **in** the town (nicht *of* the town) das älteste Gebäude der Stadt
- the longest river **in** the world (nicht *of* the world) der längste Fluss der Welt

D

Der Superlativ + **I've ever** … / **you've ever** … usw. :
- The film was very bad. I think it's **the worst** film **I've ever seen**.
  … Ich glaube es ist der schlechteste Film, den ich je gesehen habe.
- What is **the most unusual** thing **you've ever done**?
  Was ist das Ungewöhnlichste, das du je gemacht hast?

---

present perfect + ever → Unit 18   older / more expensive → Units 87–88

Übungen

90.1 Schreiben Sie Sätze mit dem Komparativ (**older** usw.) und dem Superlativ (**the oldest** usw.).

1. big/small
   - (A/D) A is bigger than D.
   - (A) A is the biggest.
   - (B) B is the smallest.

2. long/short
   - (C/A) C is .... A.
   - (D) D is ....
   - (B) B ....

3. young/old
   - (D/C) D ....
   - (B) ....
   - (C) ....

4. expensive/cheap
   - (D/A) ....
   - (C) ....
   - (A) ....

5. good/bad
   - (A/C) ....
   - (A) ....
   - (D) ....

90.2 Vervollständigen Sie die Sätze mit dem Superlativ (**the oldest** usw.).

1. This building is very old. It's ...**the oldest building**... in the town.
2. It was a very happy day. It was .... of my life.
3. It's a very good film. It's .... I've ever seen.
4. She's a very popular singer. She's .... in the country.
5. It was a very bad mistake. It was .... I've ever made.
6. It's a very pretty village. It's .... I've ever seen.
7. It was a very cold day. It was .... of the year.
8. He's a very boring person. He's .... I've ever met.

90.3 Verwenden Sie die Wörter in den Kästchen, um Sätze mit einem Superlativ (**the longest** usw.) zu bilden.

~~Sydney~~	Alaska	high	country	river	Africa	South America
Everest	the Nile	large	~~city~~	state	~~Australia~~	the world
Brazil	Jupiter	long	mountain	planet	the USA	the solar system

1. Sydney is the largest city in Australia.
2. Everest ....
3. ....
4. ....
5. ....
6. ....

90.4 Übersetzen Sie ins Englische.

1. Mandy ist das größte Mädchen in ihrer Klasse.
2. Ist München die teuerste Stadt in Deutschland?
3. Was war der beste Tag deines Lebens?
4. A: Wie war eure Reise nach Australien?
   B: Es war der interessanteste Urlaub, den wir gemacht haben.
5. Das waren die leichtesten Übungen, die wir je gemacht haben.
6. Mark ist ein schlechter Schüler, aber Sam ist schlechter. Sam ist der schlechteste der Klasse.
7. Dieser hier ist der größte Koffer, aber er ist je nicht der schwerste.

Unit 91: enough

A

I've only got five pounds – not enough for a taxi.

She isn't going to take a taxi.
She doesn't have **enough money**.
Sie hat nicht genug Geld.

He can't reach the shelf.
He isn't **tall enough**.
Er ist nicht groß genug.

B

enough + *Nomen* (**enough money** / **enough people** usw.)

- 'Is there **enough milk** in your coffee?' 'Yes, thank you.'
  'Hast du genug Milch in deinem Kaffee?' ...
- We wanted to play football, but we didn't have **enough players**.
  ... wir hatten nicht genügend Spieler.
- Why don't you buy a car? You've got **enough money**. *... Du hast genug Geld.*

enough *ohne Nomen*

- I've got some money, but not **enough** to buy a car.
  ... aber nicht genug, um ein Auto zu kaufen.
- 'Would you like some more to eat?' 'No, thanks. I've had **enough**.'
  ... 'Ich habe genug gegessen.'
- You're always at home. You don't go out **enough**.
  ... Du gehst nicht oft genug aus.

C

Adjektiv + **enough** (**good enough** / **tall enough** usw.)

- 'Shall we sit outside?' 'No, it isn't **warm enough**.' *'... es ist nicht warm genug.'*
- Can you hear the radio? Is it **loud enough** for you? *... Ist es laut genug für dich?*
- Don't buy that coat. It's nice, but it isn't **long enough**. *... Er ist schön, aber er ist nicht lang genug.*

enough + *Nomen*	aber	*Adjektiv* + **enough**
enough money	tall	**enough**
enough time	good	**enough**
enough people	old	**enough**

D

Man sagt:

enough for somebody/something	This pullover isn't **big enough for me**. *... ist nicht groß genug für mich.*
	I don't have **enough money for a new car**. *Ich habe nicht genug Geld für ein neues Auto.*
enough to do something	I don't have **enough money to buy** a new car. *... nicht genug Geld um ein neues Auto zu kaufen.*
	Is your English **good enough to have** a conversation? *Ist Ihr Englisch gut genug um ein Gespräch zu führen?*
enough for somebody/something **to do** something	There aren't **enough chairs for everybody to sit** down. *Es gibt nicht genug Stühle für alle zum Sitzen.*
	He didn't speak loudly **enough for me to hear** him. *Er hat nicht laut genug gesprochen, dass ich ihn hören konnte.*

to ... und for ... → Unit 55   too → Unit 92

Übungen

Unit 91

91.1
Vervollständigen Sie die Sätze. Verwenden Sie **enough** und eines der folgenden Wörter:

chairs   ~~money~~   paint   wind

1 She doesn't have *enough money* .
2 There aren't ....
3 She doesn't have ....
4 There isn't ....

91.2
Vervollständigen Sie die Sätze. Verwenden Sie eines der folgenden Adjektive + **enough**:

big   long   strong   ~~tall~~

1 He *isn't tall enough* .
2 The car ....
3 His legs aren't ....
4 He ....

91.3
Vervollständigen Sie die Sätze mit **enough** und einem der folgenden Wörter:

big   eat   ~~loud~~   ~~milk~~   old   practise   space   time   tired

1 'Is there *enough milk* in your coffee?' 'Yes, thank you.'
2 Can you hear the radio? Is it *loud enough* for you?
3 He can leave school if he wants – he's ....
4 When I visited New York last year, I didn't have .... to see all the things I wanted to see.
5 This house isn't .... for a large family.
6 Tina is very thin. She doesn't ....
7 My office is very small. There isn't ....
8 It's late, but I don't want to go to bed now. I'm not ....
9 Lisa isn't a very good tennis player because she doesn't ....

91.4
Vervollständigen Sie die Sätze mit **enough** und den Wörtern in Klammern.

1 We don't have *enough money to buy* a new car. (money/buy)
2 This knife isn't .... tomatoes. (sharp/cut)
3 The water wasn't .... swimming. (warm/go)
4 Do we have .... sandwiches? (bread/make)
5 We played well, but not .... the game. (well/win)
6 I don't have .... newspapers. (time/read)

91.5
Übersetzen Sie ins Englische.

1 Hast du genug gegessen?
2 Joe geht nicht viel aus. Er hat nicht genug Zeit.
3 A: Geht Ihr Sohn zur Schule?
   B: Nein, er ist noch nicht alt genug.
4 Wir haben nicht genug Essen fürs Wochenende.
5 Ist das Zimmer warm genug für dich?
6 Jenny und Michael haben nicht genug Geld, um ein Haus zu kaufen.
7 Unsere Wohnung ist nicht groß genug für ein Fest.
8 Wir haben nicht genug Zeit zum Essen, bevor wir ausgehen.
9 Unsere Wohnung ist nicht groß genug, dass die Kinder darin spielen können.

Unit 92: too

A

His shoes are **too big** for him.
… zu groß …

There is **too much** sugar in it.
… zu viel …

B

too + Adjektiv / Adverb (**too big** / **too hard** usw.)
- Can you turn the music down? It's **too loud**.
  Kannst du die Musik leiser stellen? Sie ist zu laut.
- I can't work. I'm **too tired**. … *Ich bin zu müde.*
- We're going to be late. You're walking **too slowly**.
  … *Du gehst zu langsam.*

It's too loud.

C

too much = *zu viel*
- I don't like the weather here. There is **too much rain**. … *Es regnet zu viel.*
- Emily studies all the time. I think she studies **too much**. … *sie lernt zu viel.*

too many = *zu viele*
- Let's go to another restaurant. There are **too many people** here. … *Es sind zu viele Leute hier.*
- Traffic is a problem in this town. There are **too many cars**. … *Es gibt zu viele Autos.*

D

Vergleichen Sie **too** und **not enough** ('nicht genug'):

too big   *zu groß*

- The hat is **too big** for him.
- The music is **too loud**. Can you turn it down, please?
- There's **too much sugar** in my coffee.
  (= more sugar than I want)
- I don't feel very well. I ate **too much**. … *Ich habe zu viel gegessen.*

not big enough   *nicht groß genug*

- The hat is**n't big enough** for him. (= it's **too small**)
- The music is**n't loud enough**. Can you turn it up, please?
- There's **not enough sugar** in my coffee.
  (= I need more sugar)
- You're very thin. You do**n't** eat **enough**. … *Du isst nicht genug.*

Beachten Sie, dass man im Englischen in der Regel **not enough** ('nicht genug') anstatt **too little** ('zu wenig') sagt:
- We do**n't** have **enough** money. (*nicht* We have too little money.) *Wir haben zu wenig Geld.*

E

Folgende Konstruktionen mit **too** sind möglich:

too … for somebody/something	• These shoes are **too big for me**. … *zu groß für mich.* • It's a small house – **too small for a large family**. … *zu klein für eine große Familie.*
too … to do something	• I'm **too tired to go** out. (*nicht* for go out) *Ich bin zu müde um auszugehen.* • It's **too cold to sit** outside. *Es ist zu kalt um draußen zu sitzen.*
too … for somebody **to do** something	• She speaks **too fast for me to understand**. *Sie spricht so schnell, dass ich sie nicht verstehen kann.*

to … und for … → Unit 55   much/many → Unit 83   enough → Unit 91

Übungen

Unit 92

92.1 Vervollständigen Sie die Sätze mit **too** + einem der folgenden Wörter passend zu den Situationen auf den Bildern.

> big   crowded   fast   heavy   ~~loud~~   low

1 The music is ....*too loud*..................... .
2 The box is ....
3 The net is ....
4 She's driving ....
5 His jacket is ....
6 The museum is ....

92.2 Vervollständigen Sie die Sätze mit **too / too much / too many** oder **enough**.

1 You're always at home. You don't go out ....*enough*.... .
2 I don't like the weather here. There's ....*too much*.... rain.
3 I can't wait for them. I don't have .... time.
4 There was nowhere to sit on the beach. There were .... people.
5 You're always tired. I think you work .... hard.
6 'Did you have .... to eat?' 'Yes, thank you.'
7 You drink .... coffee. It's not good for you.
8 You don't eat vegetables. You should eat more.
9 I don't like the weather here. It's .... cold.
10 Our team didn't play well. We made .... mistakes.
11 'Would you like some milk in your tea?' 'Yes, but not ....'

92.3 Geben Sie einen Grund für jede Aussage an. Verwenden Sie **too** oder **enough** zusammen mit den Wörtern in Klammern.

1 I couldn't work. I ....*was too tired*.................... . (tired)
2 Can you turn the radio up, please? It ....*isn't loud enough*.... . (loud)
3 I don't want to walk home. It's .... (far)
4 Don't buy anything in that shop. It .... (expensive)
5 You can't put all your things in this bag. It .... (big)
6 I couldn't do the exercise. It .... (difficult)
7 Your work needs to be better. It .... (good)
8 I can't talk to you now. I .... (busy)
9 I thought the film was boring. It .... (long)

92.4 Vervollständigen Sie die Sätze. Verwenden Sie **too** (+ Adjektiv) + **to ...** .

1 (I'm not going out / cold)   It's ....*too cold to go out*.................... .
2 (I'm not going to bed / early)   It's ....
3 (they're not getting married / young)   They're ....
4 (nobody goes out at night / dangerous) It's ....
5 (don't phone Sue now / late)   It's ....
6 (I didn't say anything / surprised)   I was ....

92.5 Übersetzen Sie ins Englische.

umziehen = move
Kriminalität = crime
leiser stellen = turn down

1 Das ist ein gutes Restaurant, aber es ist zu teuer.
2 Das Wetter hier gefällt mir nicht. Es regnet zu viel.
3 Unsere Klasse ist zu groß. Wir haben zu viele Schüler.
4 Wir wollen umziehen. Unsere Wohnung ist nicht groß genug für uns.
5 Diese Stadt ist gefährlich. Es gibt hier zu viel Kriminalität.
6 Ich kann jetzt nicht mit ihm reden. Ich habe nicht genug Zeit.
7 Es ist zu heiß, um Tennis zu spielen.
8 Es ist langweilig hier. Es gibt nicht genug zu tun.
9 Kannst du die Musik leiser stellen? Sie ist zu laut, dass ich dabei arbeiten könnte.

Unit 93: He speaks English very well. (Satzbau 1)

A Stellung des Verbs und des Objekts

Sue **bought** **some new shoes** yesterday.
Subjekt   Verb   Objekt

In der Regel folgt das Objekt direkt auf das Verb:
- Sue **bought some new shoes** yesterday.
  (*nicht* Sue bought yesterday some new shoes)

SUE (Subjekt)   SOME NEW SHOES (Objekt)

Verb + Objekt

He **speaks**	**English** very well.	(*nicht* He speaks very well English)
I **like**	**Italian food** very much.	(*nicht* I like very much Italian food.)
We **invited**	**a lot of people** to the party.	(*nicht* We invited to the party a lot of people.)
Why do you always **make**	**the same mistake**?	(*nicht* Why do you make always … ?)

Beachten Sie, dass die Wortstellung im Englischen oft anders ist als im Deutschen:
- I **listen to the radio** every day.   *Ich höre jeden Tag Radio.*
- Did you **watch TV** all evening?   *Hast du den ganzen Abend ferngesehen?*

B Stellung von Orts- und Zeitangaben

We went **to a party** **last night**. *Wir sind gestern Abend auf ein Fest gegangen.*
          wohin?   wann?

	Ortsangabe (wohin?)	+	Zeitangabe (wann? wie lange? wie oft?)	
Lisa walks	**to work**		**every day**.	*Lisa geht jeden Tag zu Fuß zur Arbeit.*
Will you be	**at home**		**this evening**?	*Wirst du heute Abend zu Hause sein?*
I usually go	**to bed**		**early**.	*Ich gehe meistens früh ins Bett.*
We arrived	**at the airport**		**at 7 o'clock**.	*Wir sind um 7 Uhr am Flughafen angekommen.*
Joe's father has been	**in hospital**		**since June**.	*Joes Vater ist seit Juni im Krankenhaus.*

Beachten Sie, dass im Englischen – anders als im Deutschen – die Zeitangabe meistens am Ende des Satzes steht:
- I went to the bank **yesterday**.   *Ich bin gestern zur Bank gegangen.*

C Wortstellung bei zwei Verben

Im Deutschen steht in einem Satz mit zwei Verben (Hilfsverb + Vollverb, zum Beispiel 'hat … verloren') das Vollverb am Ende des Satzes. Im Englischen jedoch bleiben die zwei Verben (bei Aussagesätzen) in der Regel zusammen:
- Ann **has lost** her key.   (*nicht* has her key lost)
  Ann hat ihren Schlüssel verloren.

Robert	**wants**	**to buy** a new computer.	*Robert will einen neuen Computer kaufen.*
Joe and Sue	**have**	**travelled** to many countries.	*… sind (schon) in viele Länder gereist.*
Jenny	**will**	**be** in Tokyo tomorrow.	*Jenny wird morgen in Tokio sein.*

Satzbau bei Fragen → Units 45–47   *always/usually/often usw.* → Unit 94

Übungen

93.1 Richtig oder falsch? Korrigieren Sie die Sätze, die Fehler enthalten oder schreiben Sie **OK**, wenn der Satz so richtig ist.

1. Did you watch all evening TV? — *Did you watch TV all evening?*
2. Sue bought some new shoes yesterday. — *OK*
3. I like very much this picture.
4. Tom started last week his new job.
5. I want to speak English fluently.
6. Jessica bought for her friend a present.
7. I drink every day three cups of coffee.
8. Don't eat your dinner too quickly!
9. I borrowed from my brother fifty pounds.

93.2 Setzen Sie die Wörter in die richtige Reihenfolge.

1. (the door / opened / I / slowly) — *I opened the door slowly.*
2. (a new phone / I / last week / got) I
3. (finished / Paul / quickly / his work)
4. (Emily / speak / very well / doesn't / French)
5. (a lot of shopping / did / I / yesterday)
6. (London / know / do you / well?)
7. (we / enjoyed / very much / the party)
8. (the problem / carefully / I / explained)
9. (we / at the airport / some friends / met)
10. (did you / in England / buy / that jacket?)
11. (every day / do / the same thing / we)
12. (football / like / very much / don't / I)

93.3 Setzen Sie die Wörter in die richtige Reihenfolge.

1. (to work / every day / walks / Lisa) — *Lisa walks to work every day.*
2. (at the hotel / I / early / arrived) I
3. (goes / every year / to Italy / Julia) Julia
4. (we / since 1998 / have / here / lived) We
5. (in London / Sue / born / in 1990 / was) Sue
6. (didn't / yesterday / Paul / to work / go) Paul
7. (to a wedding / last weekend / went / Helen) Helen
8. (I / in bed / this morning / my breakfast / had) I
9. (in September / Amy / to university / is going) Amy
10. (I / a beautiful bird / this morning / in the garden / saw) I
11. (many times / been / my parents / have / to the United States) My
12. (my umbrella / I / last night / left / in the restaurant) I
13. (to the cinema / tomorrow evening / are you going?) Are
14. (the children / I / took / this morning / to school) I

93.4 Übersetzen Sie ins Englische.

Handtasche = handbag

1. Ich esse jeden Tag einen Apfel.
2. Wir haben gestern einen interessanten Film gesehen.
3. Kate kann sehr gut Klavier spielen.
4. Wir wollen nächstes Wochenende in die Berge fahren.
5. Jenny und Tom fahren jeden Sommer nach Irland.
6. Wir haben gestern Abend in einem guten Restaurant gegessen.
7. Anna ist jeden Tag um 8 Uhr bei der Arbeit.
8. Ich habe gestern meine Handtasche im Bus gelassen.
9. Mary ist 90 Jahre alt. Sie hat in ihrem Leben (schon) viel gesehen.

Unit 94: always/usually/often usw. (Satzbau 2)

A

Diese Wörter (**always**/**never** usw.) stehen oft zusammen mit dem Verb in der Mitte des Satzes:

always	immer	**ever**	jemals/schon mal … ?	**just**	gerade
usually	meistens	**never**	nie	**already**	schon
often	oft	**rarely**	selten	**still**	immer noch
sometimes	manchmal	**seldom**	selten	**also**	auch
				all	alle
				both	beide

○ My brother **never speaks** to me. *Mein Bruder redet nie mit mir.*
○ She**'s always** late. *Sie kommt immer zu spät.*
○ Do you **often go** to restaurants? *Gehen Sie oft … ?*
○ I **sometimes eat** too much. (*oder* **Sometimes** I eat too much.)
Ich esse manchmal … (Manchmal esse ich …)
○ A: Don't forget to phone Laura.
  B: I**'ve already phoned** her. *Ich habe sie schon angerufen.*
○ I have three sisters. They**'re all** married. *… Sie sind alle verheiratet.*

B

Always/**never** usw. stehen vor dem Verb:

	Verb
always	go
often	play
never	have
usw.	usw.

○ I **always drink** coffee in the morning. (*nicht* I drink always coffee)
○ Helen **often goes** to London. (*nicht* Helen goes often)
○ You **sometimes look** unhappy. *Du siehst manchmal traurig aus.*
○ They **usually have** dinner at 7 o'clock.
○ We **rarely watch** TV. *oder* We **seldom watch** TV.
○ Richard is a good footballer. He **also plays** tennis and volleyball.
○ I have three sisters. They **all live** in London.

Vergleichen Sie die Wortstellung im Englischen und im Deutschen:
○ My brother **never speaks** to me. *… redet nie …*

Aber **always**/**never** usw. kommen nach **am**/**is**/**are**/**was**/**were**:

am	always
is	often
are	never
was	usw.
were	

○ I **am always** tired. (*nicht* I always am tired)
Ich bin immer müde.
○ They **are never** at home during the day. *Sie sind … nie zu Hause.*
○ It **is usually** very cold here in winter.
○ When I was a child, I **was often** late for school. *… kam ich oft zu spät …*
○ A: Where's Laura?
  B: She**'s still** in bed. *Sie ist immer noch im Bett.*
○ I have two brothers. They**'re both** doctors. *… Sie sind beide Ärzte.*

C

Bei zwei Verben stehen **always**/**never** usw. zwischen den zwei Verben (Hilfsverb + Vollverb):

Hilfsverb		Vollverb
will		go
can	always	find
do	often	remember
usw.	never	usw.
have	usw.	gone
has		been
		usw.

○ I **will always remember** you.
Ich werde mich immer an dich erinnern.
○ It **doesn't often rain** here.
○ Do you **usually go** to work by car? *Fährst du meistens … ?*
○ I **can never find** my keys.
○ **Have** you **ever been** to Egypt? *Waren Sie schon mal in Ägypten?*
○ A: Where's Laura?
  B: She**'s just gone** out. (She's = She has)
○ My friends **have all gone** to the cinema.

Vergleichen Sie die Wortstellung im Englischen und im Deutschen (→ Unit 93):
○ I've **already** seen **the film**. *Ich habe den Film schon gesehen.*
○ I'll **never** forget **that**. *Ich werde das nie vergessen.*

---

always/**never** + present simple → Unit 6   **just**/**already** + present perfect → Unit 17   **all** → Units 80–81
both → Unit 82   **hardly** → Unit 86   **still** → Unit 95

Übungen

94.1 Verwenden Sie Pauls Antworten, um Sätze mit **often**/**never** usw. zu schreiben.

1	Do you ever play tennis?	Yes, often.	Paul often plays tennis.
2	Do you get up early?	Yes, always.	He ....
3	Are you ever late for work?	No, never.	He ....
4	Do you ever get angry?	Sometimes.	....
5	Do you ever go swimming?	Rarely.	....
6	Are you at home in the evenings?	Yes, usually.	....

94.2 Schreiben Sie die Sätze noch einmal und fügen Sie das Wort in Klammern ein.

1 My brother speaks to me. (never) *My brother never speaks to me.*
2 Susan is polite. (always) Susan ....
3 I finish work at 5 o'clock. (usually) I ....
4 Sarah has started a new job. (just) Sarah ....
5 I go to bed before midnight. (rarely) ....
6 The bus isn't late. (usually) ....
7 I don't eat fish. (often) ....
8 I will forget what you said. (never) ....
9 Have you lost your passport? (ever) ....
10 Do you work in the same place? (still) ....
11 They stay in the same hotel. (always) ....
12 Jane doesn't work on Saturdays. (usually) ....
13 Is Tina here? (already) ....
14 What do you have for breakfast? (usually) ....
15 I can remember his name. (never) ....

94.3 Ergänzen Sie die Antworten mit den Angaben in Klammern. Verwenden Sie **also**.

1 Do you play football? (tennis)   *Yes, and I also play tennis.*
2 Do you speak Italian? (French)   Yes, and I ....
3 Are you tired? (hungry)   Yes, and ....
4 Have you been to England? (Ireland)   Yes, ...
5 Did you buy any clothes? (some books)   ....

94.4 Was haben diese Personen gemeinsam? Schreiben Sie Sätze mit **both** und **all**.

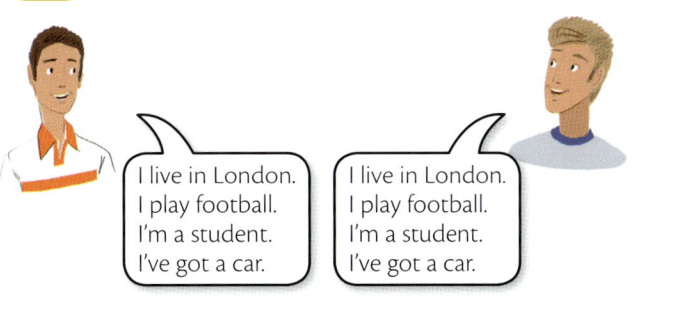 

1 *They both live in London.*
  They .... football.
  .... students.
  .... cars.

2 They .... married.
  They .... England.

94.5 Übersetzen Sie ins Englische.

denken an = think of

1 Wir sehen abends manchmal fern.
2 Megan steht oft um 7 Uhr auf.
3 Ich bin am Freitagabend immer müde.
4 Wir gehen selten ins Theater.
5 Um wie viel Uhr gehst du meistens ins Bett?
6 Ich habe dieses Buch schon gelesen.
7 Tina ist noch nie in Italien gewesen.
8 Ich habe Paul gerade gesehen.
9 Ich werde oft an diesen Tag denken.
10 Ich habe zwei Brüder und eine Schwester. Sie sind alle in Amerika.
11 Es ist nicht sehr spät. Wir können immer noch ausgehen, wenn du willst.

Unit 95

still yet already

A still

An hour ago it was raining. *Es regnete vor einer Stunde.*

It is **still** raining now. *Es regnet jetzt immer noch.*

still = *immer noch*
- I had a lot to eat, but I'm **still** hungry. *Ich habe viel gegessen, aber ich habe immer noch Hunger.*
- 'Did you sell your car?' 'No, I've **still** got it.' … *'Nein, ich habe es immer noch.'*
- 'Do you **still** live in Barcelona?' 'No, I live in Madrid now.' *'Leben Sie immer noch in Barcelona?'* …

B yet

Twenty minutes ago they were waiting for Ben.

They are **still** waiting for Ben. Ben **hasn't come yet**. *Sie warten immer noch auf Ben. Ben ist noch nicht gekommen.*

Man verwendet **yet** bei der Verneinung (He **hasn't** come yet.) und bei Fragen (**Has he** come yet?). Meistens steht **yet** am Ende des Satzes.

not yet = *noch nicht*
- A: Where's Emma?
  B: She **isn't** here **yet**. *Sie ist noch nicht hier.*
- A: What are you doing this evening?
  B: I **don't** know **yet**. *Ich weiß noch nicht.*

yet? = *schon?*
- A: Are you ready to go **yet**? *Bist du schon fertig zum Gehen?*
  B: **Not yet**. In a minute. *Noch nicht …*
- A: Have you finished with the newspaper **yet**? *Bist du schon mit der Zeitung fertig?*
  B: No, I'm still reading it. *Nein, ich lese sie immer noch.*

Vergleichen Sie **yet** und **still**:
- She hasn't gone **yet**. = She's **still** here. (nicht *She is yet here*)
- I haven't finished eating **yet**. = I'm **still** eating.

C already = *schon (früher als erwartet)*
- 'What time is Joe coming?' 'He's **already** here.' … *'Er ist schon hier.'*
- A: I'm going to tell you what happened.
  B: That's not necessary. I **already** know. *Das ist nicht nötig. Ich weiß es schon.*
- Sarah isn't coming to the cinema with us. She has **already** seen the film.
  … *Sie hat den Film schon gesehen.*

Bemerken Sie, dass **already** in bejahten Aussagesätzen und **yet** in Fragen beide mit 'schon' ins Deutsche übersetzt werden.

already/yet + present perfect → Unit 17   Stellung von **still/already** → Unit 94

Übungen

95.1
Sie sehen Tina nach zwei Jahren wieder. Damals hat sie Ihnen Folgendes (siehe Bild) über sich erzählt. Fragen Sie Tina, ob das alles immer noch stimmt. Verwenden Sie **still**.

Tina – two years ago
1. I play the piano.
2. I live in Clare Street.
3. I'm a student.
4. I've got a motorbike.
5. I go to the cinema a lot.
6. I want to be a teacher.

1. _Do you still play the piano?_
2. Do you ....
3. Are ....
4. ....
5. ....
6. ....

95.2
Schreiben Sie drei Sätze für jede Situation wie im Beispiel. Was haben die Leute vorher gemacht? Was machen Sie jetzt?

1. (vorher) _They were waiting for the bus._
   (still) _They are still waiting._
   (yet) _The bus hasn't come yet._

2. I'm looking for a job.
   (vorher) He was ....
   (still) He ....
   (yet) .... yet.

3. (vorher) She .... asleep.
   (still) ....
   (yet) ....

4. (vorher) They ....
   (still) ....
   (yet) ....

95.3
Stellen Sie für jede Situation eine Frage mit **yet**.

1. You and Sue are going out together. You are waiting for her to get ready. Perhaps she is ready now.
   Sie fragen Sue: _Are you ready yet?_
2. You are waiting for Helen to arrive. She wasn't here ten minutes ago. Perhaps she is here now.
   Sie fragen jemanden: .... Helen ....
3. Anna did an exam and is waiting for the results. Perhaps she has her results now.
   Sie fragen Anna: .... you ....
4. A few days ago you spoke to Tom. He wasn't sure where to go on holiday. Perhaps he has decided now.
   Sie fragen ihn: ....

95.4
Vervollständigen Sie die Antworten auf die Fragen. Verwenden Sie **already**.

1. What time is Joe coming? — _He's already_ here.
2. Do they want to see the film? — No, _they've already seen_ it.
3. I have to see Julia before she goes. — It's too late. She ....
4. Do you need a pen? — No, thanks. I .... one.
5. Shall I pay the bill? — No, it's OK. I ....
6. Shall I tell Paul about the meeting? — No, he .... I told him.

95.5
Übersetzen Sie ins Englische.

1. Gehst du immer noch tanzen?
2. Es ist spät, aber ich bin noch nicht müde.
3. Ich habe schon ein Glas Wasser getrunken, aber ich bin immer noch durstig.
4. 'Hast du deine Hausaufgaben schon gemacht?' 'Nein, noch nicht.'
5. 'Sind eure Gäste noch da?' 'Nein, sie sind schon abgereist.'
6. 'Möchten Sie etwas Kaffee?' 'Nein danke, ich habe schon eine Tasse getrunken.'
7. Ich habe ihm schon drei SMS geschickt, aber er hat mich noch nicht zurückgerufen.
8. 'Habt ihr euren Urlaub schon gebucht?' 'Nein, noch nicht.'

SMS = text
buchen = book

Unit 96

Give me that book!   Give it to me!

A

| give (geben/schenken) | lend (leihen) | pass (reichen) |
| send (schicken/senden) | show (zeigen) | |

SARAH

Nach diesen Verben sind zwei Satzmuster möglich:

give something to somebody
○ I gave **the keys to Sarah**.   *Ich habe die Schlüssel Sarah gegeben.*

give somebody something
○ I gave **Sarah the keys**.   *Ich habe Sarah die Schlüssel gegeben.*

B   give something to somebody

		something (etwas)	to somebody (jemandem)	
That's my book.	**Give**	it	**to** me.	… *Gib es mir.*
These are Sue's keys. Can you	**give**	them	**to** her?	… *Kannst du sie ihr geben?*
Can you	**give**	these flowers	**to** your mother?	*Kannst du deiner Mutter diese Blumen geben?*
I	**lent**	my car	**to** a friend of mine.	*Ich habe einem Freund mein Auto geliehen.*
Did you	**send**	the money	**to** Kate?	*Hast du Kate das Geld geschickt?*
We've seen these photos. You	**showed**	them	**to** us.	… *Ihr habt sie uns gezeigt.*

C   give somebody something

		somebody (jemandem)	something (etwas)	
	Give	me	that book. It's mine.	*Gib mir das Buch.* …
Tom	**gave**	his mother	some flowers.	*Tom hat seiner Mutter Blumen geschenkt.*
I	**lent**	Joe	some money.	*Ich habe Joe etwas Geld geliehen.*
How much money did you	**lend**	him?		… *hast du ihm geliehen?*
I	**sent**	you	an email. Did you get it?	*Ich habe dir eine E-Mail geschickt.* …
Nicola	**showed**	us	her holiday photos.	… *uns ihre Urlaubsfotos gezeigt.*
Can you	**pass**	me	the salt, please?	*Können Sie mir bitte das Salz reichen?*

Dieses Satzmuster ist auch mit **buy** (= *kaufen*) *und* **get** (= *besorgen/holen/bringen*) *möglich:*
○ I **bought my mother** some flowers.   (= I bought some flowers **for** my mother.)
   Ich habe meiner Mutter Blumen gekauft.
○ I'm going to the shop. Can I **get you** anything?   (= get anything **for** you)
   … *Kann ich dir etwas mitbringen?*

D

Man kann sagen:
○ I **gave** the keys **to Sarah**.
und   I **gave Sarah** the keys. (*aber nicht* I gave to Sarah the keys)

○ That's my book. Can you **give** it **to me**?
und   Can you **give me** that book? (*aber nicht* Can you give to me that book?)

Das erste Satzmuster (**give** *something* **to** *somebody*) *wird vorgezogen, wenn das Objekt* **it** *oder* **them** *ist:*
○ I gave **it to her**. (*nicht* I gave her it)
○ Here are the keys. Give **them to your father**. (*nicht* Give your father them)

it/him/them usw. ➜ Unit 60

Übungen

96.1
Mark hatte einige Sachen, die er nicht mehr haben wollte. Er hat sie verschiedenen Leuten gegeben.

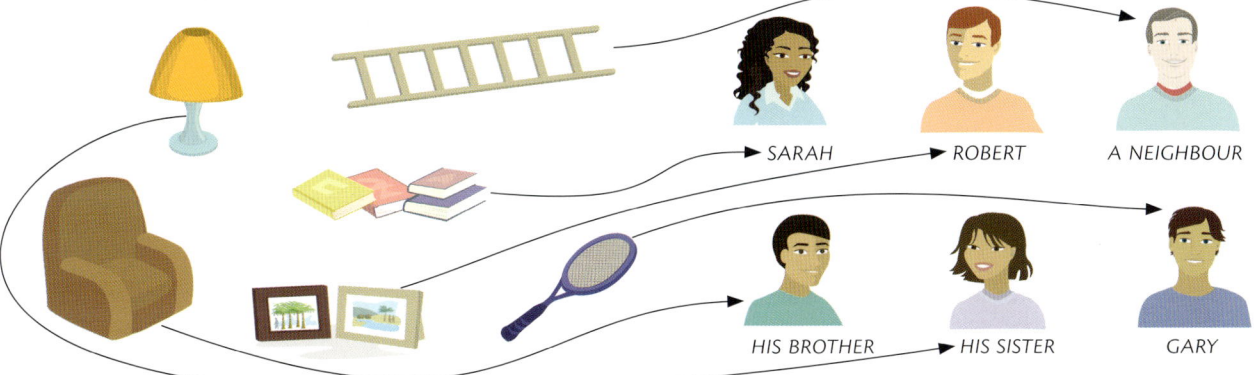

SARAH ROBERT A NEIGHBOUR
HIS BROTHER HIS SISTER GARY

Beantworten Sie die Fragen: beginnen Sie mit **He gave …** .

1 What did Mark do with the armchair?   *He gave it to his brother.*
2 What did he do with the tennis racket?   He gave ....
3 What happened to the books?   He ....
4 What about the lamp?   ....
5 What did he do with the pictures?   ....
6 And the ladder?   ....

96.2
Sie haben Ihren Freunden die Sachen geschenkt, die Sie in den Bildern sehen. Schreiben Sie, was Sie jeder Person geschenkt haben.

1 PAUL 2 JOANNA 3 RICHARD 4 EMMA 5 RACHEL 6 KEVIN

1 *I gave Paul a book.*   4 ....
2 I gave ....   5 ....
3 I ....   6 ....

96.3
Formulieren Sie Bitten mit den Wörtern in Klammern. Beginnen Sie mit **Can you give me … ?** / **Can you pass me … ?** usw.

1 (you want the salt)   (pass)   *Can you pass me the salt?*
2 (you need an umbrella)   (lend)   Can you ....
3 (you want my address)   (give)   Can .... your ....
4 (you need twenty pounds)   (lend)   ....
5 (you want more information)   (send)   ....
6 (you want to see the letter)   (show)   ....

96.4
Welcher Satz ist richtig?

1 ~~I gave to Sarah the keys~~. / I gave Sarah the keys. (I gave Sarah the keys *ist richtig*)
2 I'll lend to you some money if you want. / I'll lend you some money if you want.
3 Did you send the bill me? / Did you send the bill to me?
4 I want to buy for you a present. / I want to buy you a present.
5 Can you pass to me the sugar, please? / Can you pass me the sugar, please?
6 This is Lisa's bag. Can you give it to her? / Can you give her it?
7 I showed to the policeman my identity card. / I showed the policeman my identity card.

96.5
Übersetzen Sie ins Englische.

Paket = package

1 Kannst du bitte Jenny diese Tasche geben?
2 Zeig mir dein neues Fahrrad.
3 Können Sie mir bitte Ihren Stift leihen?
4 A: Habt ihr ein Geschenk für Beth und Chris?
   B: Ja, wir haben ihnen eine Hauspflanze gekauft.
5 Brauchst du dieses Buch, oder kannst du es mir leihen?
6 Das sind Toms Handschuhe. Kannst du sie ihm bitte geben?
7 A: Ben und Kate haben ein neues Auto.
   B: Ja, ich weiß. Sie haben es uns gezeigt.
8 Ich habe meinen Freunden in Australien ein Paket zu Weihnachten geschickt.

Unit 97: and but or so because

A

and = und   **but** = aber   **or** = oder   **so** = also   **because** = weil

Wörter wie diese (Konjunktionen) verwendet man, um zwei Sätze zu einem längeren Satz zu verbinden:

Satz A The car stopped. ─── The driver got out. Satz B

The car stopped **and** the driver got out.

B and/but/or

Satz A		Satz B
We stayed at home	**and**	(we)* watched television.
My sister is married	**and**	(she)* lives in London.
He doesn't like her,	**and**	she doesn't like him.
I bought a sandwich,	**but**	I didn't eat it.
It's a nice house,	**but**	it doesn't have a garden.
Do you want to go out,	**or**	are you too tired?

* Es ist nicht notwendig we und she zu wiederholen.

Wenn ein Satz mehrere Handlungen auflistet, werden diese mit Komma voneinander getrennt. Zwischen den zwei letzten Handlungen steht **and**:

- I got home, had something to eat, sat down in an armchair **and** fell asleep.
- Karen is at work, Sue has gone shopping **and** Chris is playing football.

C so

Satz A		Satz B
It was very hot,	**so**	I opened the window.
Joe does a lot of sport,	**so**	he's very fit.
They don't like travelling,	**so**	they haven't been to many places.

Beachten Sie, dass sich im Englischen die Wortstellung nach **so** sich nicht ändert:

- I love the sun, **so** I go to Spain for my holidays. (nicht so go I)
  Ich liebe die Sonne, also mache ich in Spanien Urlaub.

D because

Satz A		Satz B
I opened the window	**because**	it was very hot.
Joe can't come to the party	**because**	he's going away.
Lisa is hungry	**because**	she didn't have breakfast.

Because kann auch am Anfang des Satzes stehen:

- **Because it was very hot**, I opened the window.
  Weil es sehr heiß war, ...

E

Man kann längere Sätze mit mehreren Konjunktionen bilden:

- It was late **and** I was tired, **so** I went to bed.
  Es war spät und ich war müde, also bin ich ins Bett gegangen.
- I always enjoy visiting London, **but** I wouldn't like to live there **because** it's too big.
  Ich fahre immer gerne nach London, aber ich würde nicht gerne dort leben, weil es zu groß ist.

when/while/before usw. → Unit 98

Übungen

Unit 97

97.1 Verbinden Sie Sätze aus den zwei Kästchen mit **and**/**but**/**or**.

~~I stayed at home.~~	I didn't have your number.
~~I bought a sandwich.~~	Shall I wait here?
I went to the window.	~~I didn't eat it.~~
I wanted to phone you.	I went by bus this morning.
I jumped into the river.	~~I watched TV.~~
I usually drive to work.	I swam to the other side.
Do you want me to come with you?	I looked out.

1 I stayed at home and watched TV.
2 I bought a sandwich, but I didn't eat it.
3 I
4
5
6
7

97.2 Vervollständigen Sie die Sätze zu jedem Bild. Verwenden Sie **and**/**but**/**so**/**because**.

1 It was very hot, so he opened the window.
2 They couldn't play tennis
3 They went to the museum,
4 Ben wasn't hungry,
5 Helen was late
6 Sue said

97.3 Schreiben Sie, was Sie gestern gemacht haben. Verwenden Sie **and**/**but** usw.

1 (and)   In the evening I stayed at home and studied.
2 (because)   I went to bed very early because I was tired.
3 (but)
4 (and)
5 (so)
6 (because)

97.4 Übersetzen Sie ins Englische.

1 Ich bin müde, aber ich will nicht ins Bett gehen.
2 Wir könnten heute Abend ins Kino gehen, oder wir könnten zu Hause bleiben.
3 Michael hat sich gestern nicht sehr wohl gefühlt, also ist er ins Bett gegangen.
4 Das Wetter war kalt und es regnete, also sind wir zu Hause geblieben.
5 Jeden Morgen steht Sarah um 7 Uhr auf, trinkt eine Tasse Kaffee und fährt ins Büro.
6 Ich kann nicht mit euch gehen, weil ich zu viel zu tun habe.

aufstehen = get up
zu viel = too much

Unit 98

When ...

A

When I went out, it was raining.
Als ich hinausgegangen bin, regnete es.

Dieser Satz hat zwei Teile:
    Teil A   Teil B

| when I went out | + | it was raining |

Man kann sagen:
- **When I went out**, it was raining.   *oder*
  It was raining when I went out.

*Wenn Teil A (**When** …) vor Teil B kommt, setzt man ein Komma (,) zwischen die Satzteile:*
- **When** you're tired, don't drive.
  Don't drive **when** you're tired.
  Fahr nicht Auto, wenn du müde bist.
- Helen was 25 **when** she got married.
  When Helen got married, she was 25.
  Als Helen geheiratet hat, …

*Beachten Sie, dass **when** manchmal mit 'wenn' und manchmal mit 'als' ins Deutsche übersetzt wird:*
- **When** I went out, it was raining.   *Als ich hinausgegangen bin, regnete es.*
- **When** the sun shines, my office is very bright.   *Wenn die Sonne scheint, ist mein Büro sehr hell.*

*Sätze mit **before/while/after** (= bevor/während/nachdem) verhalten sich ähnlich wie Sätze mit **when**:*
- Always look both ways **before** you cross the road.
  Before you cross the road, always look both ways.
  Bevor du die Straße überquerst, guck immer in beide Richtungen.
- **While** I was waiting for the bus, it began to rain.
  It began to rain **while** I was waiting for the bus.
  Es fing an zu regnen, während ich auf den Bus wartete.
- He never played football again **after** he broke his leg.
  After he broke his leg, he never played football again.
  Nachdem er sich das Bein gebrochen hatte, hat er nie wieder Fußball gespielt.

B

When I am … / When I go … usw.

*Man verwendet (wie im Deutschen) die Gegenwartsform (**I am / I go** usw.) für Zukunftshandlungen, die nach **when** stehen:*
- **When** I **get** home this evening, I'm going to have a shower.
  Wenn ich heute Abend nach Hause komme, werde ich mich duschen.
- I can't talk to you now. I'll talk to you later **when** I **have** more time.
  … Ich spreche später mit dir, wenn ich mehr Zeit habe.

*Das Gleiche gilt nach **before/while/after/until**:*
- Please close the window **before** you **go** out.   (*nicht* before you will go)
  … bevor du weggehst.
- Rachel is going to stay in our flat **while** we **are** away.   (*nicht* while we will be)
  Rachel wird in unser Wohnung bleiben, während wir weg sind.

Beachten Sie, dass man in der anderen Satzhälfte (die nicht mit when, before, until usw. beginnt) nicht die Gegenwartsform verwendet, um sich auf die Zukunft zu beziehen:
- I**'ll talk** to you later when I have more time.   (*nicht* I talk)
  Ich spreche dich später, wenn ich mehr Zeit habe.
- We**'ll stay** here until you come back.   (*nicht* I stay)
  Wir bleiben hier, bis du zurückkommst.

---

will → Units 28–29   *if* und *when* → Unit 99   until → Unit 104   before/while/after → Unit 105

Übungen

98.1 Bilden Sie Sätze mit Satzteilen aus beiden Kästchen. Beginnen Sie jeden Satz mit **when** … .

When +
~~I went out~~	I turned off the TV
I'm tired	I always go to the same place
I knocked on the door	there were no rooms
I go on holiday	~~it was raining~~
the programme ended	there was no answer
I got to the hotel	I like to watch TV

1. *When I went out, it was raining.*
2.
3.
4.
5.
6.

98.2 Vervollständigen Sie die Sätze mit Satzteilen aus dem Kästchen.

somebody broke into the house   before they came here   when they heard the news
~~before they crossed the road~~   while they were away   they didn't believe me
they went to live in New Zealand

1. They looked both ways *before they crossed the road*.
2. They were very surprised _____.
3. After they got married, _____.
4. Their house was damaged in a storm _____.
5. Where did they live _____?
6. While we were asleep, _____.
7. When I told them what happened, _____.

98.3 Wählen Sie die korrekte Form.

1. ~~I stay~~ / I'll stay here until you come / ~~you'll come~~ back. (I'll stay und you come sind korrekt)
2. I'm going to bed when I finish / I'll finish my work.
3. We must do something before it's / it will be too late.
4. Helen is going away soon. I'm / I'll be very sad when she leaves / she'll leave.
5. Don't go out yet. Wait until the rain stops / will stop.
6. We come / We'll come and visit you when we're / we'll be in England again.
7. When I come to see you tomorrow, I bring / I'll bring our holiday photos.
8. I'm going to Paris next week. I hope to see some friends of mine while I'm / I'll be there.
9. Let's go out for a walk before it gets / it will get dark.
10. I'm not ready yet. I tell / I'll tell you when I'm / I'll be ready.

98.4 Verwenden Sie Ihre eigenen Ideen, um die Sätze zu vervollständigen.

1. Can you close the window before *you go out* ?
2. What are you going to do when _____?
3. When I have enough money, _____.
4. I'll wait for you while _____.
5. When I start my new job, _____.
6. Will you be here when _____?

98.5 Übersetzen Sie ins Englische.

1. Ich trinke Kaffee, wenn ich müde bin.
2. Das Wetter war schön, als ich in England war.
3. Bevor sie nach Deutschland gekommen ist, hat Sophie in Frankreich gelebt.
4. Ich rufe dich an, wenn ich nach Hause komme.
5. Als ich in der Stadt war, habe ich John gesehen.
6. Ich warte, bis du mich anrufst.
7. Nachdem die Kinder ins Bett gegangen sind, haben wir ferngesehen.
8. Während wir in Urlaub sind, wird unser Nachbar unsere Katze füttern.

in der Stadt = in town
füttern = feed

Unit 99

If we go ...   If you see ...   usw.

A
If = *wenn (falls)*

If *kann (wie 'wenn') am Anfang oder in der Mitte des Satzes stehen:*

If *am Anfang des Satzes*

If we go by bus,	it will be cheaper.	*Wenn wir mit dem Bus fahren, ist es billiger.*
If you don't hurry,	you'll miss the train.	*Wenn du dich nicht beeilst, wirst du den Zug verpassen.*
If you're hungry,	have something to eat.	*Wenn Sie Hunger haben, essen Sie etwas.*
If the phone rings,	can you answer it, please?	*Wenn das Telefon klingelt, können Sie bitte drangehen?*

if *in der Mitte des Satzes*

It will be cheaper	**if** we go by bus.	*Es ist billiger, wenn ...*
You'll miss the train	**if** you don't hurry.	*Du wirst den Zug verpassen, wenn ...*
I'm going to the concert	**if** I can get a ticket.	*Ich gehe ins Konzert, wenn ich eine Karte bekommen kann.*
Is it OK	**if** I use your phone?	*Geht es, wenn ich Ihr Telefon benutze?*

Beim Sprechen verwendet man den Nebensatz mit **if** *auch alleine:*
○ 'Are you going to the concert?'   'Yes, **if I can get a ticket**.'

B
Nach **if** *verwendet man die Gegenwartsform für Zukunftshandlungen (wie im Deutschen nach 'wenn').*
○ **If** you **see** Ann tomorrow, can you ask her to call me?   (*nicht* if you will see)
  Wenn du Ann morgen siehst ...

Beachten Sie, dass man in der anderen Satzhälfte (die nicht mit if *beginnt) nicht die Gegenwartsform verwendet, um sich auf die Zukunft zu beziehen:*
○ If I don't feel well tomorrow, I**'ll stay** at home.   (*nicht* I stay at home)
  ... bleibe ich zu Hause.

C
if und **when** *können beide mit 'wenn' übersetzt werden.*

If I go out = *wenn/falls ich weggehe (es ist möglich, dass ich weggehe, aber ich bin nicht sicher):*
○ A: Are you going out later? *Gehst du später weg?*
  B: Maybe. **If I go out**, I'll close the windows. *Vielleicht. Wenn/Falls ich weggehe ...*

When I go out = *ich bin sicher, dass ich weggehe:*
○ A: Are you going out later?
  B: Yes, I am. **When I go out**, I'll close the windows. *Ja. Wenn ich weggehe ...*

Vergleichen Sie **when** *und* **if**:
○ **When** I get home this evening, I'm going to have a shower.
  Wenn ich heute Abend nach Hause komme ...
○ **If** I'm late this evening, don't wait for me.   (*nicht* When I'm late)
  Wenn/Falls ich spät komme ...
○ We're going to play tennis **if** it doesn't rain.   (*nicht* when it doesn't rain)
  ... wenn/falls es nicht regnet.

Übungen

Unit 99

99.1 Bilden Sie Sätze mit Satzteilen aus beiden Kästchen. Beginnen Sie mit If.

If +
- ~~you don't hurry~~
- you pass the exam
- you fail the exam
- you don't want this magazine
- you want those pictures
- you're busy now
- you're hungry
- you need money

\+
- we can have lunch now
- you can have them
- I can lend you some
- you'll get a certificate
- ~~you'll be late~~
- I'll throw it away
- we can talk later
- you can do it again

1. _If you don't hurry, you'll be late._
2. If you pass ....
3. If ....
4. ....
5. ....
6. ....
7. ....
8. ....

99.2 Welche Form ist richtig?

1. If <u>I'm</u> / ~~I'll be~~ late this evening, don't wait for me. (<u>I'm</u> ist richtig)
2. Will you call me if <u>I give</u> / <u>I'll give</u> you my phone number?
3. If there <u>is</u> / <u>will be</u> a fire, the alarm will ring.
4. If I don't see you tomorrow morning, <u>I call</u> / <u>I'll call</u> you in the evening.
5. <u>I'm</u> / <u>I'll be</u> surprised if Michael and Jane <u>get</u> / <u>will get</u> married.
6. <u>Do you go</u> / <u>Will you go</u> to the party if <u>they invite</u> / <u>they'll invite</u> you?

99.3 Verwenden Sie Ihre eigenen Ideen um die Sätze zu vervollständigen.

1. I'm going to the concert if _I can get a ticket._
2. If you don't hurry, _you'll miss the train._
3. I don't want to disturb you if ....
4. If you go to bed early tonight, ...
5. Turn the TV off if ....
6. Tina won't pass her exams if ....
7. If I have time tomorrow, ...
8. We can go to the beach tomorrow if ....
9. I'll be surprised if ....

99.4 Setzen Sie if oder when ein.

1. _If_ I'm late this evening, don't wait for me.
2. I'm going to do some shopping now. .... I come back, we can have lunch.
3. I'm thinking of going to see Tom. .... I go, will you come with me?
4. .... you don't want to go out tonight, we can stay at home.
5. Is it OK .... I close the window?
6. John is still at school. .... he leaves school, he wants to go to college.
7. Shall we have a picnic tomorrow .... the weather is good?
8. We're going to Madrid next week. We don't have anywhere to stay – we hope to find a hotel .... we get there. I don't know what we'll do .... we don't find a room.

99.5 Übersetzen Sie ins Englische.

1. Wenn ich morgen Zeit habe, gehe ich einkaufen.
2. Ich rufe dich an, wenn ich nach Hause komme.
3. Geh ins Bett, wenn du müde bist.
4. Wenn Sie möchten, kann ich Ihnen die Information schicken.
5. Ich rede nicht mit dir, wenn du schreist.
6. Tims Eltern kaufen ihm ein neues Fahrrad, wenn er die Prüfung besteht.
7. Wollen wir morgen schwimmen gehen, wenn das Wetter gut ist?
8. Wenn Paula mit der Uni fertig ist, will sie in London arbeiten.

schreien = shout
Wollen wir? = Shall we?
fertig sein mit = finish

Unit 100: If I had ...   If we went ...   usw.

A

Dan likes fast cars, but he doesn't have one.
He doesn't have enough money.

If he **had** the money, he **would buy** a fast car.
Wenn er das Geld hätte, würde er ein schnelles Auto kaufen.

Meistens benutzt man **had** *für die Vergangenheit, aber hier bezieht sich* **had** *auf einen Zustand in der Gegenwart:* **If** he **had** the money = *Wenn er (jetzt) genug Geld hätte (aber er hat es nicht).*

*Dieser Gebrauch des past simple (***If I had** / **If I knew** / **If I lived** *usw.) entspricht im Deutschen dem Konjunktiv II (wenn ich hätte/wüsste/lebte usw.).*

If	I / you / it / they	**had** / **knew** / **lived** (usw.) ... , **didn't have** / **didn't know** (usw.) ... , **were** ... , **could** ... ,	I / you / it / they	**would** ... **wouldn't** ... **could** ... **couldn't** ...

I'd / **she'd** / **they'd** usw. = I **would** / she **would** / they **would** usw. Hier entspricht **would** dem Deutschen 'würde':

- I don't know the answer. **If** I **knew** the answer, I**'d tell** you. *Wenn ich ... wüsste, würde ich sie dir sagen.*
- It's raining, so we're not going out. We**'d get** wet **if** we **went** out. *Wir würden nass werden, wenn ...*
- Jane lives in a city. She likes cities. She **wouldn't be** happy **if** she **lived** in the country.
  ... Sie wäre nicht glücklich, wenn sie auf dem Land lebte.
- **If** you **didn't have** a job, what **would** you **do**? *Wenn Sie keine Arbeit hätten, was würden Sie tun?*

Im Deutschen verwendet man manchmal in beiden Satzhälften 'würde', im Englischen jedoch nicht:

- I **would get** better grades if I **studied** more. (nicht if I would study)
  Ich würde bessere Noten bekommen, wenn ich mehr lernen würde.

could = *könnte*
- I'm sorry I can't help you. I**'d help** you **if** I **could**. (aber ich kann leider nicht helfen)
- **If** we **had** a car, we **could travel** more. *Wenn wir ein Auto hätten, könnten wir mehr reisen.*

B

If (I) **was**/**were** ...

Man sagt: **if** I/he/she/it **was**   *oder*
             if I/he/she/it **were**

- I'm not hungry. **If I were** hungry, I'd have something to eat. (*oder* **If I was** hungry, ...)
  Wenn ich Hunger hätte, würde ich ...
- It would be nice **if the weather was** better.
  (*oder* ... **if the weather were** better)
  Es wäre schön, wenn das Wetter besser wäre.

Beachten Sie, dass 'wäre' entweder mit **would be** *oder mit* **was**/**were** *ins Englische übersetzt werden kann.*

If I were/**was you** = *an deiner/Ihrer Stelle:*
- It's not a very nice place. I wouldn't go there **if I were you**. (*oder* ... **if I was you**)
  ... An deiner Stelle würde ich nicht dorthin gehen.

C

Vergleichen Sie:

if I have / **if it is** usw.
- I must go and see Helen.
  If I **have** time, I **will go** today.
  Wenn ich Zeit habe, gehe ich heute.
- I like that jacket.
  I**'ll buy** it **if** it **isn't** too expensive.
  Ich kaufe sie, wenn sie nicht zu teuer ist.
- I**'ll help** you **if** I **can**.
  Ich helfe Ihnen, wenn ich kann.

if I had / **if it was** usw.
- I must go and see Helen.
  If I **had** time, I **would go** today.
  Wenn ich Zeit hätte, würde ich heute gehen.
- I like this jacket, but it's very expensive.
  I**'d buy** it **if** it **wasn't** so expensive.
  Ich würde sie kaufen, wenn sie nicht so teuer wäre.
- I**'d help** you **if** I **could**, but I can't.
  Ich würde Ihnen helfen, wenn ich könnte ...

if we go / if I have / if I can usw. ➔ Unit 99

Übungen

Unit 100

100.1 Vervollständigen Sie die Sätze.
1 I don't know the answer. If I ..*knew*.. the answer, I'd tell you.
2 I have a car. I couldn't travel very much if I ..*didn't have*.. a car.
3 I don't want to go out. If I .... to go out, I'd go.
4 We don't have a key. If we .... a key, we could get into the house.
5 I'm not hungry. I would have something to eat if I .... hungry.
6 Sue enjoys her work. She wouldn't do it if she .... it.
7 He can't speak any foreign languages. If he .... speak a foreign language, perhaps he would get a better job.
8 You don't try hard enough. If you .... harder, you would have more success.
9 I have a lot to do today. If I .... so much to do, we could go out.

100.2 Setzen Sie das Verb in Klammern in die passende Form.
1 If ..*he had*.. the money, he would buy a fast car. (he/have)
2 Jane likes living in a city. ..*She wouldn't be*.. happy if she lived in the country. (she/not/be)
3 If I wanted to learn Italian, ... to Italy. (I/go)
4 I haven't told Helen what happened. She'd be angry if .... (she/know)
5 If .... a map, I could show you where I live. (we/have)
6 What would you do if .... a lot of money? (you/win)
7 It's not a very good hotel. .... there if I were you. (I/not/stay)
8 If .... nearer London, we would go there more often. (we/live)
9 It's a shame you have to go now. .... nice if you had more time. (it/be)
10 I'm not going to take the job. I'd take it if .... better. (the salary/be)
11 I don't know anything about cars. If the car broke down, ... what to do. (I/not/know)
12 If you could change one thing in the world, what .... ? (you/change)

100.3 Vervollständigen Sie die Sätze mit den Angaben aus dem Kästchen. Setzen Sie das Verb in die passende Form.

we (have) a bigger house	~~it (be) a bit cheaper~~
we (buy) a bigger house	the air (be) cleaner
we (have) some pictures on the wall	I (watch) it
every day (be) the same	I (be) bored

1 I'd buy that jacket if ..*it was a bit cheaper*.. .
2 If there was a good film on TV tonight, ...
3 This room would be nicer if ....
4 If there wasn't so much traffic, ...
5 Life would be boring if ....
6 If I had nothing to do, ...
7 We could invite all our friends to stay if ....
8 If we had more money, ...

100.4 Verwenden Sie Ihre eigenen Ideen um die Sätze zu vervollständigen.
1 I'd be happier if ..*I could get a better job*..
2 If I could go anywhere in the world, ...
3 I wouldn't be very happy if ....
4 I'd buy .... if ....
5 If I saw an accident in the street, ...
6 The world would be a better place if ....

100.5 Übersetzen Sie ins Englische.
leihen = lend
sparen = save

1 Wenn ich Zeit hätte, würde ich mehr lesen.
2 Ich würde dir Geld leihen, wenn ich genug hätte.
3 An Ihrer Stelle würde ich das nicht machen.
4 Du würdest Geld sparen, wenn du zu Hause essen würdest.
5 Was würde Tom sagen, wenn er das wüsste?
6 Wenn das Wetter schön wäre, könnten wir Tennis spielen.
7 Jenny würde mit uns kommen, wenn sie nicht krank wäre.
8 Was würden Sie tun, wenn Sie mehr Freizeit hätten?

Unit 101: a person **who** ... a thing **that/which** ...
(Relativsätze 1)

A

who ... / **that** ... / **which** ... = *der* ... / *die* ... / *das* ...

"I can speak six languages."

I met a woman. **She** can speak six languages.
—— 2 Sätze ——

she → who

—— 1 Satz ——
I met **a woman who** can speak six languages.
... *eine Frau, die sechs Sprachen sprechen kann.*

JACK

Jack was wearing a hat. **It** was too big for him.
—— 2 Sätze ——

it → **that** *oder* **which**

—— 1 Satz ——
Jack was wearing **a hat that** was too big for him.
oder
Jack was wearing **a hat which** was too big for him.
... *einen Hut, der zu groß für ihn war.*

B

who *verwendet man für Menschen (nicht für Gegenstände):*

A thief is **a person**	**who** steals things.		... *ein Mensch, der Sachen stiehlt.*
Do you know **anybody**	**who** can play the piano?		... *jemanden, der ... spielen kann?*
The man	**who** phoned	didn't give his name.	*Der Mann, der angerufen hat, hat ...*
The people	**who** work in the office	are very friendly.	*Die Leute, die im Büro arbeiten, ...*

C

that *verwendet man für Gegenstände oder Menschen:*

An airplane is **a machine**	**that** flies.		... *eine Maschine, die fliegt.*
Emma lives in **a house**	**that** is 400 years old.		... *in einem Haus, das 400 Jahre alt ist.*
The people	**that** work in the office	are very friendly.	*Die Leute, die im Büro arbeiten, ...*

D

which *verwendet man für Gegenstände (nicht für Menschen):*

An airplane is **a machine**	**which** flies. (*nicht* a machine who ...)
Emma lives in **a house**	**which** is 400 years old. (*nicht* a house who ...)

Beachten Sie, dass man im Deutschen 'der'/'die'/'das' für Menschen und Gegenstände verwenden kann:
- I need **a desk which** fits into my room.
  Ich brauche einen Schreibtisch, der in mein Zimmer passt.
- I know **some people who** live in that building. ... *Leute, die ...*

Im Englischen verwendet man **which** *jedoch nicht für Menschen:*
- Do you remember **the woman who** was playing the piano at the party?
  (*nicht* the woman which ...)
  Erinnerst du dich an die Frau, die auf dem Fest Klavier gespielt hat?

---

who *und* **which** *bei Fragen* → **Units 46, 48**   the people we met (*Relativsätze 2*) → **Unit 102**

Übungen

Unit 101

101.1
Wie würden Sie die Personen im linken Kästchen beschreiben? Verwenden Sie die Angaben aus dem rechten Kästchen und schreiben Sie **A ... is a person who ...** . (Schlagen Sie unbekannte Vokabeln in einem Wörterbuch nach.)

a thief	a dentist		doesn't tell the truth	is ill in hospital
a butcher	a fool		takes care of your teeth	steals things
a musician	a genius		is very intelligent	does stupid things
a patient	a liar		plays a musical instrument	sells meat

1 A thief is a person who steals things.
2 A butcher is a person ....
3 A musician ....
4 ....
5 ....
6 ....
7 ....
8 ....

101.2
Machen Sie aus den zwei Sätzen einen Satz.

1 (A man phoned. He didn't give his name.)
   The man who phoned didn't give his name.

2 (A woman opened the door. She was wearing a yellow dress.)
   The woman .... a yellow dress.

3 (Some students took the exam. Most of them passed.)
   Most of the students ....

4 (A policeman stopped our car. He wasn't very friendly.)
   The ....

101.3
Setzen Sie **who** oder **which** ein.

1 I met a woman ..who.. can speak six languages.
2 What's the name of the man .... has just started work in your office?
3 What's the name of the river .... flows through the town?
4 Where is the picture .... was hanging on the wall?
5 Do you know anybody .... wants to buy a car?
6 You always ask questions .... are difficult to answer.
7 I have a friend .... is very good at repairing cars.
8 I think everybody .... went to the party enjoyed it very much.
9 Why does he always wear clothes .... are too small for him?

101.4
Richtig oder falsch? Korrigieren Sie die Fehler oder schreiben Sie **OK**.

1 A thief is a person which steals things. — a person who steals
2 An airplane is a machine that flies. — OK
3 A coffee maker is a machine who makes coffee.
4 What's happened to the money that was on the table?
5 I don't like people which never stop talking.
6 I know somebody that can help you.
7 I know somebody who works in that shop.
8 Correct the sentences who are wrong.
9 My neighbour bought a car who cost £40,000.

101.5
Übersetzen Sie ins Englische.

Firma = company

1 Ich habe eine Freundin, die in Paris lebt.
2 Wir haben einen Garten, der sehr groß ist.
3 Ich kenne jemanden, der in dieser Straße wohnt.
4 Rachel arbeitet in einer Firma, die Software verkauft.
5 Wo ist das Buch, das auf dem Tisch lag?
6 Hast du den Schlüssel gesehen, der in der Tür war?
7 Der Mann, der hier war, hatte blonde Haare.
8 Die Frau, die uns geholfen hat, war sehr nett.

Unit 102: the people **we met** · the hotel **you stayed at** (Relativsätze 2)

A

The man is carrying a bag.
It's very heavy. } 2 Sätze

------- 1 Satz -------
The bag (that) he is carrying is very heavy.
Der Sack, den er trägt, ist sehr schwer.

Kate won some money.
What is she going to do with it? } 2 Sätze

------- 1 Satz -------
What is Kate going to do with **the money (that) she won**?
Was wird Kate mit dem Geld, das sie gewonnen hat, tun?

KATE

Man kann sagen:
- The bag **that** he is carrying … *oder* The bag he is carrying … (*mit oder ohne* **that**)
- … the money **that** Kate won? *oder* … the money Kate won?

Wenn **that/who/which** Objekt des Nebensatzes ist, kann es weggelassen werden:

Subjekt	Verb	Objekt	
The man	was carrying	a bag	→ **the bag** (that) **the man was carrying**
Kate	won	some money	→ **the money** (that) **Kate won**
You	wanted	some books	→ **the books** (that) **you wanted**
We	met	some people	→ **the people** (who) **we met**

- Did you find **the books you wanted**? (*oder* … the books **that** you wanted?)
  Haben Sie die Bücher, die Sie haben wollten, gefunden?
- **The people we met** were very friendly. (*oder* The people **who** we met …)
  Die Leute, die wir kennen gelernt haben, …
- **Everything I said** was true. (*oder* Everything **that** I said …)
  Alles, was ich gesagt habe, ist wahr.

B

*Manchmal steht eine Präposition (***to/in/at*** usw.) nach dem Verb:*

Eve **is talking to** a man.	→	Do you know **the man Eve is talking to**?
		Kennst du den Mann, mit dem Eve redet?
We **stayed at** a hotel.	→	**The hotel we stayed at** was near the station.
		Das Hotel, in dem wir gewohnt haben, war …
I **told** you **about** some books.	→	These are **the books I told you about**.
		Das sind die Bücher, von denen ich dir erzählt habe.

Man benutzt auch **where** (= wo), *wenn von einem Aufenthaltsort die Rede ist:*
- **The hotel where** we stayed was near the station. (= The hotel we stayed at …)
  Das Hotel, in dem wir gewohnt haben, war …

C

Man muss **who/that/which** *verwenden, wenn es Subjekt des Nebensatzes ist (→ Unit 101):*
- I met a woman **who can speak** six languages. (**who** *ist Subjekt des Nebensatzes*)
- Jack was wearing a hat **that was** too big for him. (**that** *ist Subjekt des Nebensatzes*)

a person who … , a thing that/which … (Relativsätze 1) → Unit 101

Übungen

Unit 102

102.1 Machen Sie aus den zwei Sätzen einen Satz.
1. (Helen took some pictures. Have you seen them?)
   Have you seen the pictures Helen took?
2. (You gave me a pen. I've lost it.)
   I've lost the _____
3. (Sue is wearing a jacket. I like it.)
   I like the _____
4. (I gave you some flowers. Where are they?)
   Where are the _____ ?
5. (He told us a story. I didn't believe it.)
   I _____
6. (You bought some oranges. How much were they?)
   How _____ ?

102.2 Machen Sie aus den zwei Sätzen einen Satz.
1. (I was carrying a bag. It was very heavy.)
   The bag I was carrying was very heavy.
2. (You cooked a meal. It was excellent.)
   The _____
3. (I'm wearing shoes. They aren't very comfortable.)
   The shoes _____
4. (We invited some people to dinner. They didn't come.)
   The _____

102.3 Stellen Sie ihrem Freund Fragen, die zu den angegebenen Situationen passen.
1. Your friend stayed at a hotel. You ask:
   What's the name of the hotel you stayed at ?
2. Your friend was talking to some people. You ask:
   Who are the people _____ ?
3. Your friend was looking for some keys. You ask:
   Did you find the _____ ?
4. Your friend is going to a party. You ask:
   Where is the _____ ?
5. Your friend was talking about a film. You ask:
   What's the name of _____ ?
6. Your friend is listening to some music. You ask:
   What's that _____ ?
7. Your friend applied for a job. You ask:
   Did you get _____ ?

102.4 Stellen Sie Fragen, die zu den angegebenen Situationen passen. Verwenden Sie **where**.
1. John stayed at a hotel. You ask him:
   Did you like the hotel where you stayed ?
2. Sue had dinner in a restaurant. You ask her:
   What's the name of the restaurant _____ ?
3. Sarah lives in a village. You ask her:
   How big is the _____ ?
4. Richard works in a factory. You ask him:
   Where exactly is _____ ?

102.5 Übersetzen Sie ins Englische.

leihen = lend

1. Der Vogel, den ich gesehen habe, war blau.
2. Die Frau, die mir geholfen hat, war sehr nett.
3. Wie war der Film, den ihr gestern Abend gesehen habt?
4. Die Frau, mit der ich sprechen wollte, war nicht da.
5. Der Mann, den ich gesehen habe, trug ein rotes Hemd.
6. Das Fest, auf das wir gestern gegangen sind, war fantastisch.
7. Wo ist das Buch, das ich dir geliehen habe?
8. Das Restaurant, wo wir gegessen haben, war sehr gut.

215

Unit 103: at 8 o'clock   on Monday   in April

A

at *verwendet man mit der Uhrzeit:*

at	8 o'clock 10.30 midnight *usw.*

- I start work **at 8 o'clock**. ... *um 8 Uhr.*
- The shops close **at 5.30**. ... *um 5.30.*

on *sagt man vor Tagen und Daten:*

on	Sunday(s) / Monday(s) *usw.* 25 April / 6 June *usw.* New Year's Day *usw.*

- Bye! I'll see you **on Friday**. ... *Bis Freitag.*
- What do you usually do **on Sundays**?
  ... *gewöhnlicherweise sonntags?*
- The concert is **on 22 November**.
  ... *am 22. November.*

in *sagt man in Verbindung mit dem Monat, dem Jahr, der Jahreszeit:*

in	April/June *usw.* 2013/1988 *usw.* summer/spring *usw.*

- I'm going on holiday **in October**.
  ... *im Oktober ...*
- Emma was born **in 1995**.
  Emma wurde (im Jahr) 1995 geboren.
- The park is beautiful **in spring**. ... *im Frühling.*

B

Man sagt:

at the weekend = *am Wochenende*
at night = *in der Nacht/nachts*
at Christmas = *Weihnachten*
at the end of ... = *(am) Ende*
at the moment = *gerade / momentan /* *im Augenblick*

- Are you going away **at the weekend**?
- I can't sleep **at night**. *Ich kann nachts nicht schlafen.*
- Where will you be **at Christmas**? (*aber* **on** Christmas **Day**)
- I'm going on holiday **at the end of** October.
- Are you busy **at the moment**?
  Hast du im Augenblick zu tun?

C

in the morning = *am Morgen / morgens* *(am Vormittag / vormittags)*
in the afternoon = *am Nachmittag / nachmittags*
in the evening = *am Abend / abends*

- I always feel good **in the morning**.
- Do you often go out **in the evening**?

aber
on Monday morning / **on Tuesday afternoon** / **on Friday evening** / **on Saturday night** *usw.* :
- I'm meeting Jackie **on Monday morning**. ... *am Montagvormittag.*
- Are you doing anything **on Saturday night**? ... *am Samstagabend?*
- I couldn't sleep **on Tuesday night**. ... *in der Nacht von Dienstag ...*

D

at/on/in *verwendet man nicht vor:*

this ... = *diese(n) / heute* ...
last ... = *letzte(n)* ...
next ... = *nächste(n)* ...
every ... = *jede(n)* ...

- Are you going out **this evening**?
- We go on holiday **every summer**. **Last summer** we went to Canada.
- I'm leaving **next Monday**.
  (*nicht* on next Monday)

E

in five minutes / in a few days / in six weeks / in two years *usw.*

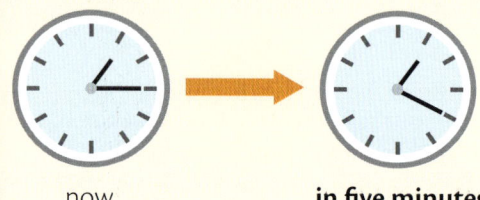

now → in five minutes

- Hurry! The train leaves **in five minutes**.
  Mach schnell! Der Zug fährt in fünf Minuten ab.
- Bye! I'll see you **in a few days**.
  ... *Wir sehen uns in ein paar Tagen.*

---

in/at/on (räumliche Präpositionen) → Units 106–107

Übungen

Unit 103

103.1 Setzen Sie at/on/in vor die Zeitangaben.

1. on 6 June
2. in the evening
3. ___ half past two
4. ___ Wednesday
5. ___ 2007
6. ___ September
7. ___ 24 September
8. ___ Thursday
9. ___ 11.45
10. ___ Christmas Day
11. ___ Christmas
12. ___ the morning
13. ___ Friday morning
14. ___ Saturday night
15. ___ night
16. ___ the end of the day
17. ___ the weekend
18. ___ winter

103.2 Vervollständigen Sie die Sätze mit at/on/in.

1. Bye! See you on Friday.
2. Where were you ___ 28 February?
3. I got up ___ 8 o'clock this morning.
4. I like getting up early ___ the morning.
5. My sister got married ___ May.
6. Jessica and I first met ___ 2006.
7. Did you go out ___ Tuesday?
8. Did you go out ___ Tuesday evening?
9. Do you often go out ___ the evening?
10. Let's meet ___ 7.30 tomorrow evening.
11. I often go away ___ the weekend.
12. I'm starting my new job ___ 3 July.
13. We often go to the beach ___ summer.
14. George isn't here ___ the moment.
15. Jane's birthday is ___ December.
16. Do you work ___ Saturdays?
17. The company started ___ 1999.
18. I like to look at the stars ___ night.
19. I'll send you the money ___ the end of the month.

103.3 Vervollständigen Sie die Sätze anhand von Lisas Terminkalender für die nächste Woche.

1. Lisa is going to the cinema on Wednesday evening.
2. She has to phone Chris ___.
3. She isn't doing anything special ___.
4. She's got a driving lesson ___.
5. She's going to a party ___.
6. She's meeting Sam ___.

103.4 Lesen Sie die Informationen und schreiben Sie Sätze mit in … .

1. It's 8.25 now. The train leaves at 8.30. — The train leaves in five minutes.
2. It's Monday today. I'll call you on Thursday. — I'll ___ days.
3. Today is 14 June. My exam is on 28 June. — My ___.
4. It's 3 o'clock now. Tom will be here at 3.30. — Tom ___.

103.5 Vervollständigen Sie die Sätze mit at/on/in, wenn erforderlich. In manchen Fällen ist der Satz so vollständig, und Sie brauchen nichts einzusetzen.

1. I'm going on Friday.
2. I'm going – next Friday. (nichts)
3. I always feel tired ___ the evening.
4. Will you be at home ___ this evening?
5. We went to France ___ last summer.
6. Laura was born ___ 1997.
7. What are you doing ___ the weekend?
8. I phone Robert ___ every Sunday.
9. Shall we play tennis ___ next Sunday?
10. I can't go to the party ___ Sunday.
11. I'm going out. I'll be back ___ an hour.
12. I don't often go out ___ night.

103.6 Übersetzen Sie ins Englische.

Termin = appointment

1. Ich gehe um 8 Uhr zur Arbeit.
2. Michael ist 2007 nach Berlin gekommen.
3. A: Was macht ihr Ostern?
   B: Wir fahren nach Italien.
4. Samstagvormittag stehe ich immer spät auf.
5. Das Projekt wird Ende Mai fertig sein.
6. Wo waren Sie letzten Donnerstag?
7. Sind Sie abends meistens zu Hause?
8. Nächsten Sommer wollen wir nach Kanada.
9. Ich muss in ein paar Minuten gehen.
10. Ich habe am Mittwoch um 11.30 einen Termin.
11. Auf Wiedersehen! Wir sehen uns am Wochenende.

Unit 104: from ... to   until   since   for

A

from ... to ... = *von ... bis ...*

- We lived in Japan **from** 2003 **to** 2010.
- I work **from** Monday **to** Friday.

Man kann auch sagen **from ... until ...** (= *von ... bis*):

- We lived in Japan **from** 2003 **until** 2010.

from Monday to Friday
Monday — Friday

B

until ... = *bis*

| until | Friday
December
3 o'clock
I come back |

- They're going away tomorrow. They'll be away **until Friday**.
- I went to bed early, but I wasn't tired. I read a book **until 3 o'clock**.
- Wait here **until I come back**.

until Friday — Friday

Mann kann auch **till** (= **until**) *sagen*:

- Wait here **till** I come back.

Vergleichen Sie:

- '**How long** will you be away?'   '**Until** Monday.'   'Bis Montag.'
- '**When** are you coming back?'   '**On** Monday.'   'Am Montag.'

C

since + *ein Zeitpunkt in der Vergangenheit* (= *seit/seitdem*)

Since *verwendet man in Verbindung mit dem* present perfect (**have been** / **have done** *usw.*).
Beachten Sie, dass man im Deutschen hier die Gegenwartsform verwendet:

| since | Monday
1998
2.30
I arrived |

- Joe is in hospital. He has been in hospital **since Monday**.
  ... *Er ist seit Montag im Krankenhaus.*
- Sue and Dave have been married **since 1998**.
  ... *sind seit 1998 verheiratet.*
- It has been raining **since I arrived**.
  Es regnet seitdem ich angekommen bin.

since Monday
Monday — now

Vergleichen Sie:

- We lived in Japan **from** 2003 **to** 2010.
  We lived in Japan **until** 2010.
  Wir haben bis 2010 in Japan gelebt.
- Now we live in Canada. We came to Canada **in** 2010.
  Jetzt leben wir in Kanada. Wir sind 2010 nach Kanada gekommen.
  We have lived in Canada **since** 2010.   *Wir leben seit 2010 in Kanada.*

Mit einem Zeitraum (**three days** / **ten years** *usw.*) *verwendet man* **for** (*nicht* **since**):

- Joe has been in hospital **for three days**. (*nicht* since three days)
  ... *ist seit drei Tagen im Krankenhaus.*

D

for ... + *ein Zeitraum*

Beachten Sie, dass **for** *je nach Zeitform auf unterschiedliche Weise ins Deutsche übersetzt wird:*

| for | three days
ten years
five minutes
a long time |

- Gary stayed with us **for three days**.
  Gary ist drei Tage lang bei uns geblieben.
- I'm going away **for a few weeks**.
  Ich fahre für ein paar Wochen weg.
- I'm going away **for the weekend**.
  Ich fahre fürs/übers Wochenende weg.

for three days
Sunday — Monday — Tuesday

Mit dem present perfect *entspricht* **for** *im Deutschen 'seit':*

- They've been married **for ten years**.
  Sie sind seit zehn Jahren verheiratet.

---

present perfect + **for/since** ➔ Units 19–20   present perfect (**I have lived**) *und* past simple (**I lived**) ➔ Unit 21

Übungen

104.1 Lesen Sie die Informationen über diese Personen und vervollständigen Sie die Sätze mit den Wörtern in Klammern. Verwenden Sie **from ... to** / **until** / **since**.

ALEX  KAREN  CLARE  ADAM

ALEX: I live in England now. I lived in Canada before. I came to England in 2009.

KAREN: I live in Switzerland now. I lived in France before. I came to Switzerland in 2011.

CLARE: I work in a hotel now. I worked in a restaurant before. I started work in the hotel in 2012.

ADAM: I'm a journalist now. I was a teacher before. I started work as a journalist in 2008.

1. (Alex / Canada / 2001 → 2009)   Alex lived _in Canada from 2001 to 2009_.
2. (Alex / Canada / → 2009)   Alex lived in Canada .... 2009.
3. (Alex / England / 2009 →)   Alex has lived in England ....
4. (Karen / France / → 2011)   Karen lived in ....
5. (Karen / Switzerland / 2011 →)   Karen has lived in ....
6. (Clare / a restaurant / 2010 → 2012)   Clare worked .... 2010 ....
7. (Clare / a hotel / 2012 →)   Clare has worked ....
8. (Adam / a teacher / 2002 → 2008)   Adam was a ....
9. (Adam / a journalist / 2008 →)   Adam has been ....

Schreiben Sie nun Sätze mit **for**.

10. (Alex / Canada)   _Alex lived in Canada for eight years_ .
11. (Alex / England)   Alex has lived in England ....
12. (Karen / Switzerland)   Karen has ....
13. (Clare / a restaurant)   Clare worked ....
14. (Clare / a hotel)   Clare ....
15. (Adam / a teacher)   Adam ....
16. (Adam / a journalist)   Adam ....

104.2 Vervollständigen Sie die Sätze mit **until**/**since**/**for**.

1. Sue and Dave have been married _since_ 1998.
2. I was tired this morning. I stayed in bed .... 10 o'clock.
3. We waited for Sue .... half an hour, but she didn't come.
4. 'Have you just arrived?' 'No, I've been here .... half past seven.'
5. 'How long did you stay at the party last night?' '.. midnight.'
6. Dan and I are good friends. We have known each other .... ten years.
7. I'm tired. I'm going to lie down .... a few minutes.
8. Don't open the door of the train .... the train stops.
9. This is my house. I've lived here .... I was seven years old.
10. Jack has gone away. He'll be away .... Wednesday.
11. Next week I'm going to Paris .... three days.
12. I usually finish work at 5.30, but sometimes I work .... six.
13. 'How long have you known Anna?' '.. we were at school together.'
14. Where have you been? I've been waiting for you .... twenty minutes.

104.3 Übersetzen Sie ins Englische.

Chef = boss
ans Meer = to the seaside

1. Wir waren von Juli bis September in den USA.
2. Unser Chef wird bis Mittwoch in London sein.
3. A: Wie lange werden Sie in England sein?
   B: Bis Juni.
4. Wir wollen fürs Wochenende ans Meer fahren.
5. Jenny ist seit drei Tagen krank.
6. Jenny war drei Tage lang krank.
7. Ich lebe seit 2005 in München.
8. Thomas lebt in dieser Wohnung seitdem er nach Hamburg gekommen ist.

Unit 105: before after during while

A before, during und after

before the film
vor dem Film

during the film
während des Films

after the film
nach dem Film

- Everybody feels nervous **before exams**.   *Jeder ist vor Prüfungen nervös.*
- I fell asleep **during the film**.   *Ich bin während des Films eingeschlafen.*
- We were tired **after our visit** to the museum.   *Wir waren nach unserem Museumsbesuch müde.*

B before, while und after

before we played
bevor wir gespielt haben

while we were playing
während wir spielten / beim Spielen

after we played
nachdem wir gespielt hatten

- Don't forget to close the window **before you go out**.   … *bevor du weggehst.*
- I often fall asleep **while I'm reading**.   *Ich schlafe oft beim Lesen ein. / … während ich lese.*
- They went home **after they did the shopping**.   … *nachdem sie die Besorgungen gemacht hatten.*

C during, while und for

Man verwendet **during** (= während) mit einem Nomen (during **the film**).
Man verwendet **while** (= während) mit einem Verb (while **I'm reading**).
- We didn't speak **during the meal**.   *Wir haben während des Essens nicht geredet.*
aber   We didn't speak **while we were eating**.   *Wir haben beim Essen nicht geredet.*

Mit einem Zeitraum (**three days** / **two hours** / **a year** usw.) verwendet man **for** (nicht during):
- We played tennis **for two hours**.   (nicht during two hours)   *Wir haben zwei Stunden lang Tennis gespielt.*
- I lived in London **for a year**.   (nicht during a year)   *Ich habe ein Jahr lang in London gelebt.*

D

Nach **before** und **after** sind zwei Konstruktionen möglich:
- I always have breakfast { **before I go** to work. / **before going** to work. }   *Ich frühstücke immer bevor ich zur Arbeit gehe.*
- { **After they did** / **After doing** } the shopping, they went home.   *Nachdem sie die Besorgungen gemacht hatten, …*

Man sagt **before going** (nicht before to go), **after doing** (nicht after to go) usw.:
- **Before eating** the apple, I washed it carefully.
  Bevor ich den Apfel aß, …
- I started work **after reading** the newspaper.
  … *nachdem ich die Zeitung gelesen hatte.*

---

past continuous (**I was -ing**) ➔ Units 14–15   before/after/while/when ➔ Unit 98   for ➔ Unit 104
Präpositionen + **-ing** ➔ Unit 112

Übungen

105.1 Vervollständigen Sie die Sätze mit den passenden Wortkombinationen aus beiden Kästchen.

after	during	+	lunch	the end	they went to Australia
before	while		the concert	~~the exam~~	you're waiting
			the course	the night	

1 Everybody was nervous *before the exam*.
2 I usually work four hours in the morning, and another three hours ....
3 The film was really boring. We left ....
4 Anna went to evening classes to learn German. She learnt a lot ....
5 My aunt and uncle lived in London ....
6 A: Somebody broke a window .... Did you hear anything?
   B: No, I was asleep all the time.
7 Would you like to sit down .... ?
8 A: Are you going home .... ?
   B: Yes, I have to get up early tomorrow.

105.2 Schreiben Sie **during**/**while**/**for**.

1 We didn't speak *while* we were eating.
2 We didn't speak *during* the meal.
3 Gary called .... you were out.
4 Amy went to Italy and stayed in Rome .... five days.
5 I didn't check my email .... I was away.
6 The students looked very bored .... the lesson.
7 I fell out of bed .... I was asleep.
8 Last night I watched TV .... three hours.
9 I don't usually watch TV .... the day.
10 Do you ever watch TV .... you are having dinner?

105.3 Vervollständigen Sie die Sätze mit einem Verb in **-ing** (**doing**, **having** usw.).

1 After *doing* the shopping, they went home.
2 I felt sick after .... too much chocolate.
3 I'm going to ask you a question. Think carefully before .... it.
4 I felt awful when I got up this morning. I felt better after .... a shower.
5 After .... my work, I left the office and went home.
6 Before .... to a foreign country, it's good to try and learn a little of the language.

105.4 Bilden Sie Sätze mit **before** + **-ing** und **after** + **-ing**.

1 They did the shopping. Then they went home.
   After *doing the shopping, they went home.*
2 John left school. Then he worked in a bookshop for two years.
   John worked ....
3 I read for a few minutes. Then I went to sleep.
   Before ....
4 We walked for three hours. We were very tired.
   After ....
5 Let's have a cup of coffee. Then we'll go out.
   Let's ....

105.5 Übersetzen Sie ins Englische.

1 Tina steht nie vor 8 Uhr auf.   immer = all the time
2 Was möchtest du nach dem Film machen?
3 Ich höre beim Kochen oft Radio.
4 Ich möchte dieses Buch fertig lesen, bevor ich ins Bett gehe.
5 Tom war zwei Wochen lang im Krankenhaus.
6 Nach dem Aufstehen, trinke ich ein Glas Wasser.
7 Zwei Leute haben während des Konzerts immer geredet.
8 Nachdem wir das Haus sauber gemacht hatten, haben wir das Auto gewaschen.

Unit 106 in at on (räumliche Präpositionen 1)

A in

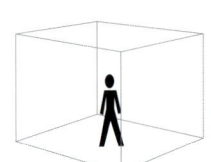
in a room
in a box
in a car
in the water

in a garden
in a town
in the city centre
in Brazil

in entspricht im Deutschen meistens 'in':
- 'Where's David?' '**In the kitchen. / In the garden. / In London.**' ... 'In der Küche. / Im Garten. / In London.'
- Rachel works **in a shop / in a bank / in a factory**. ... in einem Laden / in einer Bank / in einer Fabrik.
- I went for a swim **in the river / in the pool / in the sea**. ... im Fluss / in Schwimmbad / im Meer.
- Milan is **in the north of Italy**. Mailand ist im Norden von Italien.

Man sagt **in bed / in hospital / in prison**:
- 'Where's Kate?' 'She's **in bed**.' ... 'Sie ist im Bett.'
- David's father is ill. He's **in hospital**. ... Er ist im Krankenhaus.

B at

at the bus stop
an der Bushaltestelle

at the door
an der Tür

at the traffic lights
an der Ampel

at her desk
an ihrem Schreibtisch

at entspricht im Deutschen oft 'an':
- There's somebody **at the bus stop / at the door**.
- Do you want me to meet you **at the station / at the airport**? ... am Bahnhof / am Flughafen?
- My house is **at the end of the street**. ... am Ende der Straße.

Man sagt auch **at** university / **at** college (= an der Universität / an der Fachhochschule):
- Helen is studying law **at university**.

C on

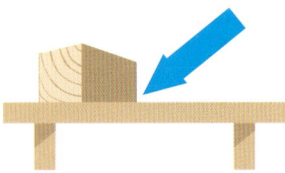
on a shelf = *auf einem Regalbrett*
on a plate = *auf einem Teller*
on the floor = *auf dem Fußboden*
on the balcony = *auf dem Balkon*

on entspricht im Deutschen oft 'auf':
- Don't sit **on the grass**. It's wet. Setz dich nicht auf den Rasen. ...
- There is a stamp **on the envelope**. ... auf dem Briefumschlag.

aber
- There are some books **on the shelf**. ... Bücher im Regal.

Außerdem sagt man:
on a horse / on a bicycle / on a motorbike
- Who is that man **on the motorbike**? ... auf dem Motorrad?

on the way to ... = *unterwegs / auf dem Weg nach/zu* ...
- I met Anna **on the way to work**. ... Anna auf dem Weg zur Arbeit ...

— stamp
— envelope

---

at/on/in (zeitliche Präpositionen) → **Unit 103** in/at/on (räumliche Präpositionen 2) → **Unit 107**
to/in/at (räumliche Präpositionen 3) → **Unit 108** on the left/right → **Unit 109**

Übungen

106.1 Beantworten Sie die Fragen. Verwenden Sie **in**/**at**/**on** zusammen mit dem Wort in jedem Bild.

1 Where is he? In the kitchen.
2 Where are the shoes? ....
3 Where is the pen? ....
4 Where are they? ....
5 Where is the bus? ....
6 Where are the horses? ....
7 Where are they standing? ....
8 Where is she swimming? ....
9 Where is he standing? ....
10 Where is he? ....
11 Where is he sitting? ....
12 Where is she sitting? ....

106.2 Vervollständigen Sie die Sätze mit **in**/**at**/**on**.

1 Don't sit ...on... the grass. It's wet.
2 What do you have .... your bag?
3 Look! There's a man .... the roof. What's he doing?
4 There are a lot of fish .... this river.
5 Charlie is .... hospital. He's going to have an operation.
6 A: Is the hospital near here?
   B: Yes, turn left .... the traffic lights.
7 It's difficult to park .... the centre of town. It's better to take the bus.
8 My sister lives .... Brussels.
9 Write your address .... the envelope.
10 I think I heard the doorbell. There's somebody .... the door.
11 Munich is a large city .... the south of Germany.
12 There are a few shops .... the end of the street.
13 It's difficult to carry a lot of things .... a bike.
14 George is late. I'm going to meet him .... the station.
15 I'm sorry I'm late. My car broke down .... the way here.

106.3 Übersetzen Sie ins Englische.

1 A: Wo ist mein blauer Pullover?
   B: Im Kleiderschrank.
2 Amy sitzt manchmal auf dem Fußboden.
3 Emily arbeitet in einer Bank im Zentrum der Stadt.
4 Im Sommer sitzen wir oft auf unserem Balkon.
5 Wann landet deine Maschine? Ich kann dich am Flughafen abholen.
6 Wo ist David? Er ist nicht an seinem Schreibtisch.
7 Wir waren im Mai in Spanien und haben im Meer gebadet.
8 Wir haben lange an der Ampel gewartet.
9 Das Zimmer ist am Ende des Ganges.
10 Ich habe auf dem Weg nach Hause einen Unfall gesehen.

Kleiderschrank = wardrobe
jemanden abholen = pick somebody up
Gang = corridor
Unfall = accident

Unit 107: in at on (räumliche Präpositionen 2)

A

in entspricht im Deutschen nicht immer 'in':

in the sky = *am Himmel*	
in the country = *auf dem Land*	
in the world = *der Welt*	
in a photo(graph) / **in** a picture = *auf einem Foto / einem Bild*	
in the middle (of …) = *mitten in*	

- I like to look at the stars **in the sky** at night.
- I live **in a town**, but I want to live **in the country**.
- What's the largest city **in the world**? *Welche ist die größte Stadt der Welt?*
- You look sad **in this picture**. *Du siehst auf diesem Foto traurig aus.*
- There's a big tree **in the middle of** the garden.

B

at

at home = *zu Hause*
at work / **at** school = *auf der Arbeit / in der Schule*
at a party = *auf einem Fest*

- Will you be **at home** this evening?
- 'Where's Kate?' 'She's **at work**.'
- We had a good time **at the party**.

at entspricht im Deutschen oft 'bei':

at Lisa's (house) / **at** my sister's (house) *usw.* *bei Lisa (zu Hause) / bei meiner Schwester usw.*
at the doctor's / **at** the hairdresser's *usw.* *(zu Hause) / beim Arzt / beim Friseur usw.*
at a concert / **at** a football match *usw.* *bei einem Konzert / bei einem Fußballspiel usw.*

- A: Where were you yesterday? B: **At my sister's**.
- I saw Tom **at the doctor's**.
- There were a lot of people **at the football match**.

at the top / at the bottom (of …) = *oben / unten (am Fuße):*
- Write your name **at the top of the page**. *… oben auf das Blatt.*
- The letter is **at the bottom of the pile**. *… ganz unten im Stapel.*

C

on entspricht im Deutschen nicht immer 'auf':

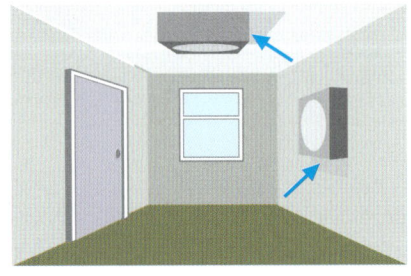
on the ceiling   **on** a wall

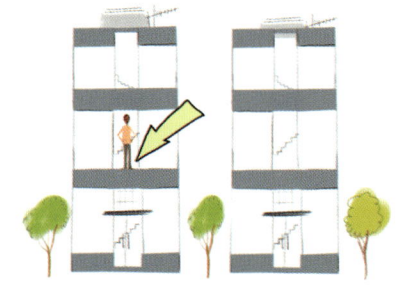
on the first floor

on a bus

- There are some pictures **on the wall**. *… an der Wand.*
- Is that a spider **on the ceiling**? *… eine Spinne an der Decke?*
- There's a mirror **on the door**. *… ein Spiegel an der Tür.*
- The office is **on the first floor**. *… im ersten Stock.*

Man sagt:
on a bus / **on** a train /
on a plane / **on** a ship
aber
in a car / **in** a taxi

- Did you come **on the bus**? *Sind Sie mit dem Bus gekommen?*
- I slept **on the plane**. *Ich habe im Flugzeug geschlafen.*
- Did you come **in your car**? *Sind Sie mit Ihrem Auto gekommen?*

---

the top / the bottom *usw.* → Unit 70   in/at/on (räumliche Präpositionen 1) → Unit 106   to/in/at → Unit 108
on the left/right → Unit 109

Übungen

107.1 Beantworten Sie die Fragen unten anhand der Situationen in den Bildern. Verwenden Sie **in/at/on** zusammen mit dem Wort in jedem Kästchen.

① (the wall) ② (a ship) ③ (the sky) ④ (a party)
⑤ (the ceiling) ⑥ (the doctor's) ⑦ (the second floor) ⑧ (work)
⑨ (a plane) ⑩ (a taxi) ⑪ (a wedding) ⑫ (the top of the hill)

1 Where is the clock?   *On the wall.*
2 Where are they? ....
3 Where are the stars? ....
4 Where are they? ....
5 Where is the spider? ....
6 Where is Steve? ....
7 Where is the restaurant? ....
8 Where is she? ....
9 Where are they? ....
10 Where are they? ....
11 Where are they? ....
12 Where is the house? ....

107.2 Vervollständigen Sie die Sätze mit **in/at/on**.

1 There weren't many people ....*at*.... the party.
2 I walked to work but I came home .... the bus.
3 Will you be .... home tomorrow afternoon?
4 Were there many people .... the concert last night?
5 There was a big table .... the middle of the room.
6 Sandy and Dave have a house .... the country.
7 Our house is number 45 – the number is .... the door.
8 I looked at the list of names. My name was .... the bottom of the list.
9 What is the longest river .... the world?
10 Where are your children? Are they .... school?
11 'Are you hungry after your journey?' 'No, I had something to eat .... the train.'
12 I've got a map .... my car.
13 'Is Tom here?' 'No, he's .... his friend's house.'
14 Who is that man .... this photo? Do you know him?
15 There's a mirror .... the wall .... the top of the stairs.

107.3 Übersetzen Sie ins Englische.

1 Thomas ist heute nicht bei der Arbeit. Er ist beim Arzt.
2 Warum steht dieser Stuhl mitten im Zimmer?
3 Everest ist der höchste Berg der Welt.
4 Das ist ein schönes Bild an der Wand.
5 Jenny war heute beim Friseur.
6 Wir wohnen im dritten Stock.
7 Ich schlafe oft im Zug.
8 Bist du das auf diesem Bild?
9 A: Bist du gestern Abend ausgegangen?
   B: Nein, ich bin zu Hause geblieben.
10 Können Sie bitte unten auf diesem Blatt unterschreiben?

sich treffen = meet
unterschreiben = sign your name

Unit 108: to   in   at (räumliche Präpositionen 3)

A

to (= nach/zu/in/auf) verwendet man, um die Bewegung auf ein Ziel hin zu beschreiben:

go/come/return/walk (usw.) **to** …

- We're **going to London** on Sunday.
  … nach London …
- I want to **go to Italy** next year.
  … nach Italien …
- We **walked** from my house **to the centre of town**.
  … von meinem Haus bis zur Innenstadt …
- What time do you **go to bed**? … ins Bett?

- The bus is **going to the airport**.
  … zum Flughafen.
- Karen didn't **go to work** yesterday.
  … zur Arbeit …
- I **went to a party** last night.
  … auf ein Fest …
- You must **come to our house**.
  … zu uns nach Hause …

in/at verwendet man, um zu beschreiben, wo sich etwas/jemand befindet (→ Units 106–107):

be/stay/do something (usw.) **in** …

- Piccadilly Circus **is in London**.
  … in London.
- My brother **lives in Italy**.
  … in Italien.
- The main shops **are in the centre of town**.
  … im Zentrum …
- I like **reading in bed**. … im Bett.

be/stay/do something (usw.) **at** …
(= bei/an/in/auf)

- The bus **is at the airport**.
  … am Flughafen.
- Sarah **wasn't at work** yesterday.
  … bei der Arbeit.
- I **met a lot of people at the party**.
  … auf dem Fest …
- Helen **stayed at her brother's house**.
  Helen hat bei ihrem Bruder übernachtet.

B

home

go/come/walk (usw.) **home** (ohne **to**) = nach Hause:
- I'm tired. I'm **going home**. (nicht to home)
- Did you **walk home**? (nicht to home)

be/stay/do something (usw.) **at home** = zu Hause:
- I'm **staying at home** tonight.
- Dan doesn't work in an office.
  He **works at home**.

C

arrive und **get** = ankommen

arrive in + ein Land oder eine Stadt (**arrive in Italy** / **arrive in Paris** usw.):
- They **arrived in this country** last week.   Sie sind … hier in diesem Land angekommen.

arrive at + andere Ziele (**arrive at the station** / **arrive at work** usw.):
- What time did you **arrive at the hotel**? … im Hotel angekommen?

get to + alle Ziele:
- What time did you **get to the hotel**?   … im Hotel angekommen?
- What time did you **get to Paris**? … in Paris angekommen?

get home / **arrive home** (keine Präposition):
- I was tired when I **got home**.   oder   I was tired when I **arrived home**.
  … als ich zu Hause angekommen war.

been to → Unit 18   get (to …) → Unit 57   in/at → Units 106–107

Übungen

Unit 108

108.1 Vervollständigen Sie die Sätze mit **to** oder **in**.
1. I like reading _in_ bed.
2. We're going _____ Italy next month.
3. Sue is on holiday _____ Italy at the moment.
4. I have to go _____ the hospital tomorrow.
5. I was tired, so I stayed _____ bed late.
6. What time do you usually go _____ bed?
7. Does this bus go _____ the centre?
8. Would you like to live _____ another country?

108.2 Vervollständigen Sie die Sätze mit **to** oder **at**, wenn erforderlich.
1. Paula didn't go _to_ work yesterday.
2. I'm tired. I'm going _−_ home. *(ohne Präposition)*
3. Tina is not very well. She has gone _____ the doctor.
4. Would you like to come _____ a party on Saturday?
5. 'Is Lisa _____ home?' 'No, she's gone _____ work.'
6. There were 20,000 people _____ the football match.
7. Why did you go _____ home early last night?
8. A boy jumped into the river and swam _____ the other side.
9. There were a lot of people waiting _____ the bus stop.
10. We had a good meal _____ a restaurant, and then we went back _____ the hotel.

108.3 Vervollständigen Sie die Sätze mit **to**, **at** oder **in**, wenn erforderlich.
1. I'm not going out this afternoon. I'm staying _at_ home.
2. We're going _____ a concert tomorrow evening.
3. I went _____ New York last year.
4. How long did you stay _____ New York?
5. Next year we hope to go _____ Canada to visit some friends.
6. Do you want to go _____ the cinema this evening?
7. Did you park your car _____ the station?
8. After the accident three people were taken _____ hospital.
9. How often do you go _____ the dentist?
10. 'Is Sarah here?' 'No, she's _____ Helen's.'
11. My house is _____ the end of the street on the left.
12. I went _____ Maria's house, but she wasn't _____ home.
13. There were no taxis, so we had to walk _____ home.
14. 'Who did you meet _____ the party?' 'I didn't go _____ the party.'

108.4 Vervollständigen Sie die Sätze mit **to**, **at** oder **in**, wenn erforderlich.
1. What time do you usually get _____ work?
2. What time do you usually get _____ home?
3. What time did you arrive _____ the party?
4. When did you arrive _____ London?
5. What time does the train get _____ Paris?
6. We arrived _____ home very late.

108.5 Vervollständigen Sie die Sätze mit Angaben über sich selbst. Verwenden Sie **to/in/at**.
1. At 3 o'clock this morning I was _in bed_ .
2. Yesterday I went _____ .
3. At 11 o'clock yesterday morning I was _____ .
4. One day I'd like to go _____ .
5. I don't like going _____ .
6. At 9 o'clock yesterday evening I was _____ .

108.6 Übersetzen Sie ins Englische.
1. Unser Büro ist im Stadtzentrum.
2. Becky arbeitet am Flughafen.
3. Fährt dieser Zug nach Hamburg?
4. Bist du heute Abend zu Hause?
5. Wann kommt der Zug in Wien an?
6. Ich bin heute früh um 9.30 in die Arbeit gekommen.
7. Nächsten Sommer wollen wir nach Thailand reisen.
8. Tom ist um 8 Uhr im Restaurant angekommen, aber Rachel war nicht da.
9. Um wie viel Uhr bist du gestern Abend nach Hause gekommen?

Unit 109: under, behind, opposite usw.

A next to / beside / between / in front of / behind

A is **next to** B.   oder   A is **beside** B.   ... neben B.
B is **between** A and C.   ... zwischen A und C.
D is **in front of** B.   ... vor B.
E is **behind** B.   ... hinter B.

außerdem:
A is **on the left**.   ... auf der linken Seite.
C is **on the right**.   ... auf der rechten Seite.
B is **in the middle** (of the group).   ... in der Mitte (der Gruppe).

B opposite (= gegenüber) und in front of (= vor)

A is sitting **in front of** B.   A sitzt vor B.
A is sitting **opposite** C.   A sitzt gegenüber von C.
C is sitting **opposite** A.   C sitzt gegenüber von A.

C by = an / neben

by the window

- Our house is **by the sea**.   Unser Haus ist am Meer.
- Who is that man standing **by the window**?
  ... der Mann am Fenster?
- If you feel cold, why don't you sit **by the fire**?   ... ans Feuer.

Beachten Sie: **by** entspricht in der Regel nicht 'bei' (→ Unit 107).
Sehen Sie Unit 111 für weitere Bedeutungen von **by**.

D under = unter

under the table

under a tree

- The cat is **under the table**.
- The girl is standing **under a tree**.
- I'm wearing a jacket **under my coat**.
  Ich trage eine Jacke unter meinem Mantel.

E above (= über / oberhalb von) und below (= unter / unterhalb von)

A is **above the line**.
A ist über/oberhalb der Linie.

B is **below the line**.
B ist unter/unterhalb der Linie.

The pictures are **above the shelves**.
Die Bilder sind über den Regalen.

The shelves are **below the pictures**.
Die Regale sind unter den Bildern / unterhalb der Bilder.

Vergleichen Sie **below** und **under**:

below besagt lediglich, dass ein Objekt sich auf einer tieferen Ebene als ein anderes befindet:
- The shelves are **below the pictures**.   ... unter/unterhalb ...

under verwendet man, wenn ein (kleineres) Objekt sich unter einem anderen (größeren) befindet und davon verdeckt wird:
- The cat is **under the table**.   ... unter ...

in/at/on → Units 106–107   to → Unit 108   up/over/through usw. → Unit 110   by → Unit 111

Übungen

109.1 Wo stehen oder sitzen die Personen in diesem Bild? Vervollständigen Sie die Sätze.

ALAN BECKY CARL
DANIELA EMMA FRANK

1 Carl is standing ……behind…… Frank.
2 Frank is sitting …………………… Emma.
3 Emma is sitting …………………… Becky.
4 Emma is sitting …………………… Daniela and Frank.
5 Daniela is sitting …………………… Emma.
6 Frank is sitting …………………… Carl.
7 Alan is standing …………………… Daniela.
8 Alan is standing …………………… left.
9 Becky is standing …………………… middle.

109.2 Vervollständigen Sie die Sätze unten mit einer passenden Präposition für jedes Bild.

FIONA PAUL

1 The cat is ……under…… the table.
2 There is a big tree …………………… the house.
3 The plane is flying …………………… the clouds.
4 She is standing …………………… the piano.
5 The cinema is …………………… the right.
6 She's standing …………………… the fridge.
7 The switch is …………………… the window.
8 The cupboard is …………………… the sink.
9 There are some shoes …………………… the bed.
10 The plant is …………………… the piano.
11 Paul is sitting …………………… Fiona.
12 In Britain people drive …………………… the left.

109.3 Beschreiben Sie die Lage der Gebäude und Einrichtungen auf dem Bild.

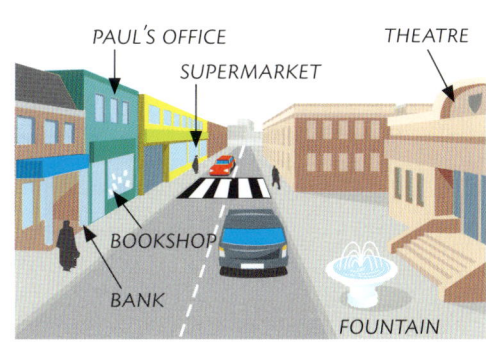

PAUL'S OFFICE SUPERMARKET THEATRE
BOOKSHOP BANK FOUNTAIN

1 (next to) The bank is next to the bookshop.
2 (in front of) The …………………………………………… in front of ……………………
3 (opposite) ……………………………………………………………………………
4 (next to) ……………………………………………………………………………
5 (above) ……………………………………………………………………………
6 (between) ……………………………………………………………………………

109.4 Übersetzen Sie ins Englische.

1 Die Post ist neben dem Bahnhof.
2 Unser Haus ist gegenüber von einem Café.
3 Das Restaurant ist auf der linken Seite.
4 Emma sitzt neben Ben.
5 Was ist hinter der Tür?
6 Vor dem Haus steht ein alter Baum.
7 Der Tisch ist zwischen der Tür und dem Fenster.
8 'Wo ist mein Stift?' 'Unter deiner Zeitung.'
9 Dein Koffer ist neben der Tür.
10 Über uns wohnt eine Familie mit zwei Kindern.
11 A: Wo ist das Kino?
   B: Es ist unter dem Café.

Unit 110: up, over, through usw.

Folgende Präpositionen beschreiben bestimmte Bewegungen, wie sie in den Diagrammen veranschaulicht werden.

to — nach/zu
- Jane is going **to** France next week. *… nach …*
- We walked **from** the hotel **to** the station. *… von … zu …*
- A lot of English words come **from** Latin.
  … kommen aus dem Lateinischen.

from — von/aus

into (in) — in
- We jumped **into** the water.
- A man came **out of** the house and got **into** a car.
  … ist aus dem Haus gekommen und in ein Auto eingestiegen.
- Why are you looking **out of** the window?
- I took the old batteries **out of** the radio.
  Ich habe die alten Batterien aus dem Radio herausgenommen.

Man sagt meistens **put** *something* **in** *… (anstatt into):*
- I **put** new batteries **in** the radio. *… ins Radio eingesetzt.*

out of — aus

on — auf (an/in)
- Don't put your feet **on** the table.
- Please take your feet **off** the table. *… vom Tisch.*
- I'm going to hang some pictures **on** the wall.
  … an die Wand hängen.
- Be careful! Don't fall **off** your bike.
  Fall nicht von deinem Fahrrad (runter).
- We got **on** the bus in Princes Street. *… in den Bus eingestiegen.*

off — (runter/weg) von

up — hinauf
- We walked **up** the hill to the house.
- Be careful! Don't fall **down** the stairs.

down — hinunter

over — über
- The plane flew **over** the mountains.
- I jumped **over** the wall into the garden.
- Some people say it is unlucky to walk **under** a ladder.
  … unter einer Leiter durchzugehen.

under — unter

through — durch
- A bird flew into the room **through** a window.
- The old road goes **through** the village.
- The new road goes **round** the village.
  … um das Dorf herum.
- The bus stop is just **round** the corner. *… um die Ecke.*
- I walked **round** the town and took some photos.
  Ich bin in der Stadt herumgegangen und …

Man kann auch **around** *sagen:*
- We walked **around** (= round) the town.

round — um … herum

round the town — in der Stadt herum

along — entlang
- I was walking **along** the road with my dog.
  … die Straße entlang …
- Let's go for a walk **along** the river.
- The dog swam **across** the river. *… über den Fluss.*

across — über

past — vorbei
- They walked **past** me without speaking.
  Sie sind an mir vorbeigegangen, ohne etwas zu sagen.
- A: Excuse me, how do I get to the hospital?
  B: Go along this road, **past** the cinema, under the bridge and the hospital is on the left.
  … am Kino vorbei …

get in/on usw. → Unit 57   in/on → Units 106–107   to → Unit 108   fall off / run away usw. → Unit 114

Übungen

110.1 Jemand fragt Sie nach dem Weg. Schreiben Sie passende Anweisungen unter jedes Bild mit **Go ...** .

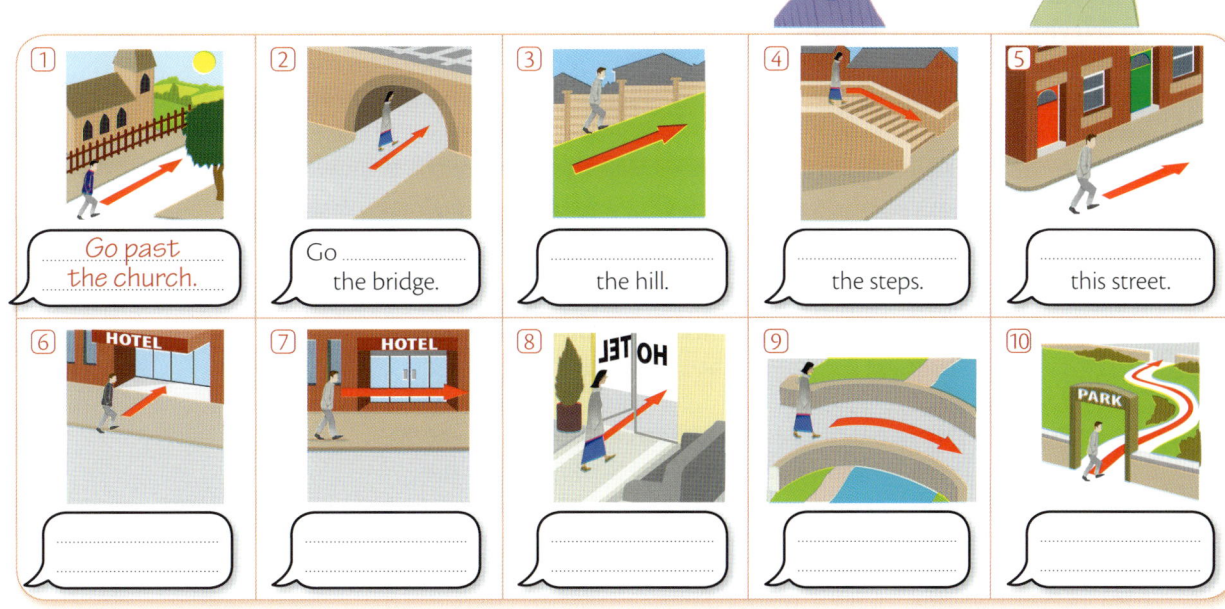

1. Go past the church.
2. Go .... the bridge.
3. .... the hill.
4. .... the steps.
5. .... this street.
6.
7.
8.
9.
10.

110.2 Vervollständigen Sie die Sätze unten mit einer Präposition passend zu den Handlungen in den Bildern.

1. The dog swam ___across___ the river.
2. A book fell .... the shelf.
3. A plane flew .... the village.
4. A woman got .... the car.
5. A girl ran .... the road.
6. Suddenly a car came .... the corner.
7. They drove .... the village.
8. They got .... the train.
9. The moon travels .... the earth.
10. They got .... the house .... a window.

110.3 Vervollständigen Sie die Sätze mit **over/from/into** usw.

1. I looked .... the window and watched the people in the street.
2. My house is very near here. It's just .... the corner.
3. 'Where's my phone?' 'You put it .... your bag.'
4. How far is it .... here .... the airport?
5. We walked .... the museum for an hour and saw a lot of interesting things.
6. You can put your coat .... the back of the chair.
7. In tennis, you have to hit the ball .... the net.
8. Silvia took a key .... her bag and opened the door.

110.4 Übersetzen Sie ins Englische.

Flur = corridor

1. Kannst du bitte die Blumen auf den Tisch stellen?
2. Wir sind durch den Tunnel gefahren.
3. Wie weit ist es vom Bahnhof zur Innenstadt?
4. Nimm deine Sachen bitte vom Tisch.
5. Gehen Sie die Treppe hinauf und den Flur entlang.
6. Julia ist aus dem Hotel gekommen und in ein Taxi eingestiegen.
7. Ich bin müde, weil ich den ganzen Tag in der Stadt herumgelaufen bin.
8. Gehen Sie an der Kirche vorbei und über die Straße.

Unit 111: on at by with about

A on

In folgenden Redewendungen wird **on** unterschiedlich ins Deutsche übersetzt oder umschrieben.

on holiday = *im Urlaub* **on television / on TV** = *im Fernsehen* **on the radio** = *im Radio* **on the phone** = *am Telefon* **on fire** = *in Flammen / brennen* **on time** = *rechtzeitig/pünktlich*	○ Jane isn't at work this week. She's **on holiday**. ○ We watched the news **on TV**. ○ We listened to the news **on the radio**. ○ I spoke to Rachel **on the phone** last night. ○ The house is **on fire**! Call the fire brigade. *Das Haus brennt! …* ○ 'Was the train late?' 'No, it was **on time**.'

B at

In folgenden Redewendungen wird **at** unterschiedlich ins Deutsche übersetzt.

at (the age of) 21 / at 50 kilometres an hour / at 100 degrees usw. :
- ○ Lisa got married **at 21**. (oder… **at the age of 21**.)
   Lisa hat mit 21 geheiratet. (oder … im Alter von 21.)
- ○ A car uses more petrol **at 120 kilometres an hour** than **at 90**.
   Ein Auto verbraucht mehr Benzin mit 120 Stunden-Kilometer …
- ○ Water boils **at 100 degrees Celsius**. *Wasser kocht bei 100 Grad Celsius.*

C by

In den folgenden Redewendungen wird **by** unterschiedlich ins Deutsche übersetzt.

by car / by bus / by plane / by bike usw. :
- ○ Do you like travelling **by train**? … *mit dem Zug?*
- ○ Jane usually goes to work **by bike**. … *mit dem Fahrrad.*

aber **on foot** (= *zu Fuß*):
- ○ You can't get there **by car**. You have to go **on foot**.
   (= you have to walk)

a book **by** … / a painting **by** … / a piece of music **by** … usw. :
- ○ Have you read any books **by Charles Dickens**?
   Hast du Bücher von Charles Dickens gelesen?
- ○ **Who** is that painting **by**? Picasso?
   Von wem ist das Gemälde? …

by verwendet man nach dem Passiv (→ Unit 22):
- ○ I was bitten **by a dog**. *Ich bin von einem Hund gebissen worden.*

by bus — *on foot* — *the title* — *by* — *the writer*

D with/without = *mit/ohne*:
- ○ Do you like your coffee **with** or **without milk**?
   … *mit oder ohne Milch?*
- ○ I cut the paper **with a pair of scissors**. … *mit einer Schere.*
- ○ Wait for me. Please don't go **without me**.
- ○ Do you know that man **with the beard**?
- ○ I'd like to have a house **with a big garden**.

Manchmal entspricht **with** jedoch im Deutschen 'bei':
- ○ Did you stay at a hotel or **with friends**?
   Hast du in einem Hotel oder bei Freunden übernachtet?

a man **with** a beard — a woman **with** glasses

E about = *über/von*

talk/speak/think/hear/know about … :
- ○ Some people **talk about their work** all the time. *Manche Leute reden immer über ihre Arbeit.*
- ○ I don't **know** much **about cars**. *Ich verstehe nicht viel von Autos.*

a book / a question / a programme / information (usw.) **about** … :
- ○ There was **a programme about** volcanoes on TV last night. Did you see it?
   Gestern Abend gab es eine Sendung im Fernsehen über Vulkane. …

by → Units 22, 64, 109   at/on → Units 103, 106–107   Präpositionen + -ing → Unit 112

Übungen

Unit 111

111.1 Vervollständigen Sie die Sätze mit **on** und einem der folgenden Wörter:

> holiday   the phone   ~~the radio~~   TV   time

1. We heard the news ...... on the radio ....
2. Please don't be late. Try to be here ....
3. I won't be here next week. I'm going ....
4. 'Did you see Linda?' 'No, but I talked to her ....'
5. 'What's .... this evening?' 'Nothing that I want to watch.'

111.2 Vervollständigen Sie die Sätze mit einer Präposition (**at**/**by**/**with** usw.) passend zu den Bildern.

1. I cut the paper ..with.. a pair of scissors.
2. She usually goes to work .... car.
3. Who is the woman .... short hair?
4. They are talking .... the weather.
5. The car is .... fire.
6. She's listening to some music .... Mozart.
7. The plane is flying .... 600 miles an hour.
8. They're .... holiday.
9. Do you know the man .... sunglasses?
10. He's reading a book .... grammar .... Vera P. Bull.

111.3 Vervollständigen Sie die Sätze mit **at**/**by**/**with** usw.

1. In tennis, you hit the ball .... a racket.
2. It's cold today. Don't go out .... a coat.
3. *Hamlet*, *Othello* and *Macbeth* are plays .... William Shakespeare.
4. Do you know anything .... computers?
5. My grandmother died .... the age of 98.
6. How long does it take from New York to Los Angeles .... plane?
7. I didn't go to the football match, but I watched it .... TV.
8. My house is the one .... the red door on the right.
9. These trains are very fast. They can travel .... very high speeds.
10. I don't use my car very often. I prefer to go .... bike.
11. Can you give me some information .... hotels in this town?
12. I was arrested .... two policemen and taken to the police station.
13. The buses here are very good. They're nearly always .... time.
14. What would you like to drink .... your meal?
15. We travelled from Paris to Moscow .... train.
16. The museum has some paintings .... Rembrandt.

111.4 Übersetzen Sie ins Englische.

kennen lernen = meet

1. Ich fahre meistens mit dem Bus zur Arbeit.
2. Ich war letzte Woche in Urlaub.
3. *Pride and Prejudice* ist ein Buch von Jane Austen.
4. Sue kommt meistens pünktlich zur Arbeit.
5. Mark hat mit 25 seine Frau kennen gelernt.
6. Wer ist der Mann mit dem Hut?
7. Heute Abend ist ein guter Film im Fernsehen.
8. Hast du von Monicas Problem gewusst?
9. Tom hat in London bei Freunden übernachtet.
10. 'Wie bist du hergekommen?' 'Mit dem Auto.'

Unit 112: good at ... , interested in ... usw.
of/at/for usw. (Präpositionen) + -ing

A interested in ... / good at ... usw. (Adjektiv + Präposition)

angry with somebody	Why are you **angry with** me? What have I done? *Warum bist du mir böse? ...*
angry about something	Are you **angry about** last night? *Ärgerst du dich wegen ... ?*
different from ... *oder* **different to** ...	Lisa is very **different from** (*oder* **to**) her sister. *... anders als ...*
fed up with ...	I'm **fed up with** my job. I want to do something different. *Ich habe meine Arbeit satt ...*
full of ...	The room was **full of people**. *... voller Leute.*
good at ...	Are you **good at** maths? *Bist du gut in Mathe?*
interested in ...	I'm not **interested in** sport. *Ich interessiere mich nicht für Sport.*
married to ...	Sue is **married to** a dentist. *... mit einem Zahnarzt verheiratet.*
nice/kind of somebody to ...	It was **kind of** you to help us. Thank you very much. *Es war nett von Ihnen uns zu helfen. ...*
be **nice/kind to** somebody	David is very friendly. He's always very **nice to** me. *... Er ist immer sehr nett zu mir.*
scared of ... / **afraid of** ...	Are you **scared of** dogs? *oder* Are you **afraid of** dogs? *... Angst vor ...*
sorry about a situation	I'm afraid I can't help you. I'm **sorry about** that. *... Das tut mir leid.*
sorry for/about doing something	I'm **sorry for/about** not phoning you yesterday. (*oder* I'm sorry I didn't phone you) *Es tut mir leid, dass ich dich ...*
be/feel **sorry for** somebody	I feel **sorry for** them. They are in a very difficult situation. *Sie tun mir leid ...*

B Präposition + -ing

Nach einer Präposition (**at/with/for** usw.) endet das Verb in **-ing**:

- I'm not very good **at telling** stories. *Ich kann nicht sehr gut Geschichten erzählen.*
- Are you fed up **with doing** the same thing every day? *Hast du es satt jeden Tag das Gleiche zu tun?*
- I'm sorry **for** not **phoning** you yesterday. *Es tut mir leid, dass ich dich gestern nicht angerufen habe.*
- Thank you **for helping** me. *Danke, dass du mir geholfen hast.*
- Mark is thinking **of buying** a new car. *Mark überlegt sich ein neues Auto zu kaufen.*
- Tom left **without saying** goodbye. *... ohne sich zu verabschieden.*
- **After doing** the shopping, they went home. *Nachdem sie die Besorgungen gemacht hatten, ...*

before/after -ing → Unit 105   think about/of → Unit 113

Übungen

112.1 Vervollständigen Sie die Sätze zu jedem Bild mit of/in/with usw.

1. He's afraid _of_ dogs.
2. She's interested .... science.
3. She's married .... a footballer.
4. She's very good .... languages.
5. He's fed up .... the weather.
6. A: Can I help you?
   B: Thanks, that's very kind .... you.

112.2 Vervollständigen Sie die Sätze mit of/in/with usw.

1. I'm not interested _in_ sport.
2. I'm not very good .... sport.
3. I like Sarah. She's always very kind .... me.
4. I'm sorry .... your broken window. It was an accident.
5. He's very brave. He isn't scared .... anything.
6. It was very nice .... Jane to let us stay in her apartment.
7. Life today is very different .... life 50 years ago.
8. Are you interested .... politics?
9. I feel sorry .... her, but I can't help her.
10. Chris was angry .... what happened.
11. These boxes are very heavy. They are full .... books.
12. I'm sorry .... getting angry .... you yesterday.

112.3 Vervollständigen Sie die Sätze mit den Wörtern in Klammern und der dazugehörigen Präposition.

1. I'm not very _good at telling_ stories. (good/tell)
2. I wanted to go to the cinema, but Paula wasn't .... (interested/go)
3. Sue isn't very .... up in the morning. (good/get)
4. Let's go! I'm .... (fed up / wait)
5. I'm .... you up in the middle of the night. (sorry/wake)
6. Sorry I'm late! .... (thank you / wait)

112.4 Bilden Sie Sätze mit den Wörtern in Klammern. Verwenden Sie without -ing.

1. (Tom left / he didn't say goodbye) _Tom left without saying goodbye._
2. (Sue walked past me / she didn't speak)
   Sue walked ....
3. (Don't do anything / ask me first)
   Don't ....
4. (I went out / I didn't lock the door)
   I ....

112.5 Schreiben Sie Sätze über sich selbst. Verwenden Sie die Wörter in Klammern.

1. (interested) _I'm interested in sport._
2. (scared) I'm ....
3. (not very good) I'm not ....
4. (not interested) ....
5. (fed up) ....

112.6 Übersetzen Sie ins Englische.

Biologie = biology
sollen = shall

1. Ich interessiere mich für Theater.
2. Die deutschen Häuser sind anders als die englischen Häuser.
3. David ist mit einer Lehrerin verheiratet.
4. Johns Schreibtisch ist voller Papiere.
5. Unsere Tochter ist sehr gut in Biologie.
6. Kate ist böse auf Tony.
7. Ich habe es satt, so viel zu arbeiten.
8. A: Soll ich Ihnen die Türe aufmachen?
   B: Danke, das ist sehr nett von Ihnen.
9. Es tut mir leid, dass ich gestern nicht mit dir geredet habe.

Unit 113: listen to ... , look at ... usw. (Verb + Präposition)

A

Folgende Verben verwendet man mit einer Präposition. Beachten Sie, dass im Deutschen nicht immer eine Präposition gebraucht wird.

ask (somebody) **for** ... *jemanden um etwas bitten*	○ Don't **ask** me **for** money. I don't have any.
belong to ... *gehören*	○ This house doesn't **belong to** me.
happen to ... *passieren*	○ I can't find my phone. What's **happened to** it?
listen to ... *hören/zuhören/anhören*	○ **Listen to** this music. It's great.
talk to somebody (**about** ...) **speak to** somebody (**about** ...) *mit jemandem über ... reden*	○ Did you **talk to** Paul **about** the problem? ○ (am Telefon) Can I **speak to** Chris, please?
thank somebody **for** ... *sich (bei jemandem) bedanken für*	○ I **thanked** Helen **for** her help.
think about / **of** ... *an jemanden / etwas denken, überlegen*	○ He never **thinks about** (*oder* **of**) other people. ○ Mark is **thinking of** (*oder* **about**) buying a car.
wait for ... *warten auf*	○ **Wait for** me. I'm nearly ready.

Beachten Sie, man sagt **call**/**phone**/**text**/**email** somebody (ohne Präposition):
○ I have to **phone my parents** today.
   ... meine Eltern anrufen.
○ Shall I **text you** or **email you**?
   Soll ich dich anrufen oder dir eine SMS schicken?

B

look at / **look for** / **look after**

look at ...
= *ansehen /
auf etwas
sehen*
	○ He's **looking at** his watch. *Er sieht auf seine Uhr.*
	○ **Look at** these flowers! They're beautiful.
	   Guck dir diese Blumen an! ...
	○ Why are you **looking at** me like that?
	   Warum siehst du mich so an?

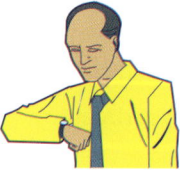

look for ...
= *suchen*
	○ She's lost her key. She's **looking for** it.
	   Sie hat ihren Schlüssel verloren. Sie sucht ihn.
	○ I'm **looking for** Sarah. Have you seen her?
	   Ich suche Sarah. Hast du sie gesehen?

look after ...
= *aufpassen auf*
	○ When Emily is at work, a friend of hers
	   looks after her children.
	   ... passt ein(e) Freund(in) auf ihre Kinder auf.
	○ Don't lose this book. **Look after** it.
	   ... Pass (gut) darauf auf.

C

depend = *darauf ankommen / davon abhängen*

It depends on ... :
○ A: Do you like eating in restaurants?
   B: Sometimes. It **depends on** the restaurant.
      ... *Das kommt aufs Restaurant an.*

Man kann **it depends what**/**where**/**how** (*usw.*) mit oder ohne **on** verwenden:
○ A: Do you want to come out with us?
   B: It **depends where** you're going. *oder* It **depends on where** ...
      Es kommt darauf an, wo ihr hingeht.

wait → Unit 55   Präpositionen + -ing → Unit 112

Übungen

113.1 Vervollständigen Sie die Sätze zu jedem Bild mit einer passenden Präposition (**to/for/at** usw.).

1 She's looking ...at... her watch.
2 He's listening .... the radio.
3 They're waiting .... a taxi.
4 Paul is talking .... Jane.
5 They're looking .... a picture.
6 Sue is looking .... Tom.

113.2 Vervollständigen Sie die Sätze mit **to/for/about** usw. In manchen Fällen ist keine Präposition notwendig.

1 Thank you very much ...for... your help.
2 This isn't my umbrella. It belongs .... a friend of mine.
3 I saw Steve, but I didn't speak .... him.
4 Don't forget to phone .... your mother tonight.
5 Thank you .... the present. It was lovely.
6 What happened .... Ella last night? Why didn't she come to the party?
7 We're thinking .... going to Australia next year.
8 We asked the waiter .... coffee, but he brought us tea.
9 'Do you like reading books?' 'It depends .... the book.'
10 John was talking, but nobody was listening .... what he was saying.
11 We waited .... Karen until 2 o'clock, but she didn't come.
12 I texted .... Lisa to tell her I would be late.
13 He's alone all day. He never talks .... anybody.
14 'How much does it cost to stay at this hotel?' 'It depends .... the type of room.'
15 Catherine is thinking .... changing her job.

113.3 Vervollständigen Sie die Sätze mit **at/for/after**.

1 I looked .... the letter, but I didn't read it carefully.
2 When you are ill, you need somebody to look .... you.
3 Excuse me, I'm looking .... Hill Street. Is it near here?
4 Bye! Have a great holiday and look .... yourself.
5 I want to take a picture of you. Please look .... the camera and smile.
6 Ben is looking .... a job. He wants to work in a hotel.

113.4 Beantworten Sie die Fragen mit **It depends ...** .

1 Do you want to go out with us?   It depends where you're going.
2 Do you like eating in restaurants? It depends on the restaurant.
3 Do you enjoy watching TV?   It depends ....
4 Can you do something for me?   It ....
5 Are you going away this weekend?
6 Can you lend me some money?

113.5 Übersetzen Sie ins Englische.

weinen = cry

1 Ich höre oft Musik.
2 Guck mal den schönen Garten an!
3 Gehört Ihnen dieser Regenschirm?
4 Ich habe gestern mit Thomas geredet.
5 Vielen Dank für die Schokolade.
6 Was suchst du?
7 Warum weinst du? Was ist passiert?
8 A: Mögen Sie Musik?
   B: Es kommt auf die Musik an.
9 Wir haben auf den Bus gewartet, aber er ist nicht gekommen.
10 Kannst du bitte einen Moment auf meinen Koffer aufpassen?

Unit 114

go in, fall off, run away usw. (phrasal verbs 1)

Phrasal verbs *bestehen aus zwei Teilen:* **go/look/be** *usw.* + **in/out/up/down** *usw. Sie entsprechen oft ähnlichen, teilbaren Verben im Deutschen (zum Beispiel* **go out** = *hinausgehen).*

in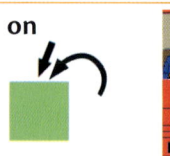
GO IN

- I waited outside the shop. I didn't **go in**.
  Ich bin nicht hineingegangen.
- Sarah opened the door of the car and **got in**.
  (= **into** the car) *... und ist eingestiegen.*

out
LOOK OUT

- I went to the window and **looked out**.
  ... und habe hinausgeschaut.
- The car stopped and a woman **got out**.
  (= **out of** the car) *... eine Frau ist ausgestiegen.*

on
GET ON

- The bus came, and I **got on**.
  ... und ich bin eingestiegen.

off
FALL OFF

- Be careful! Don't **fall off**.
  ... Fall nicht runter.

Man verwendet **on/off** *für Busse, Züge und Flugzeuge, aber* **in/out** *für Autos (→ Unit 57).*

up
STAND UP

- He **stood up** and left the room.
  Er ist aufgestanden ...
  (**stand up** = *vom Sitzen aufstehen*)
- I usually **get up** early. *Ich stehe ... früh auf.*
  (**get up** = *aus dem Bett aufstehen*)
- We **looked up** at the stars in the sky.

down
FALL DOWN

- The picture **fell down**.
  Das Bild ist hinuntergefallen.
- Would you like to **sit down**?
  Möchten Sie sich (hin)setzen?
- **Lie down** on the floor.
  Leg dich auf den Boden (hin).

away *oder* **off**
RUN AWAY

- The thief **ran away**. (*oder* ... **ran off**)
  Der Dieb ist weggelaufen/davongelaufen.
- Emma got into the car and **drove away**.
  (*oder* ... **drove off**) *... und ist weggefahren.*

be/go away = *weg sein / weggehen / wegfahren*
- Tom has **gone away** for a few days.
  Tom ist ... weggefahren.

back  GO
COME BACK

- Go away and don't **come back**!
  Geh fort und komm nicht zurück!
- We went out for dinner and then **went back**
  to our hotel. *... und sind dann ... zurückgekehrt.*

be back = *wieder da sein*
- Tom is away. He'll **be back** on Monday.
  ... Er wird am Montag wieder da sein.

over
CLIMB OVER   TURN OVER

- The wall wasn't very high, so we **climbed over**. *... , also sind wir drübergeklettert.*
- **Turn over** and look at the next page.
  Blätter um und schau die nächste Seite an.

round (*oder* **around**)
LOOK ROUND

- Somebody shouted my name, so I **looked round** (*oder* **around**).
  ... , also habe ich mich umgedreht.
- We went for a long walk. After an hour we **turned round** (*oder* **around**) and went back. *... sind wir umgekehrt ...*

238 | **get** → Unit 57 | **put on / take off** *usw.* (phrasal verbs 2) → Unit 115 | *weitere* phrasal verbs → Anhang 6

Übungen

Unit 114

114.1 Vervollständigen Sie die Sätze. Verwenden Sie die Verben aus der Liste + **in**/**out**/**up** usw.

got   got   ~~looked~~   looked   rode   sat   turned   went

1 I went to the window and _looked out_ .   5 I said hello, and he ....
2 The door was open, so we ....   6 The bus stopped, and she ....
3 He heard a plane, so he ....   7 There was a free seat, so she ....
4 She got on her bike and ....   8 A car stopped, and two men ....

114.2 Vervollständigen Sie die Sätze mit **out**/**away**/**back** usw.

1 'What happened to the picture on the wall?'   'It fell _down_ .'
2 Wait a minute. Don't go .... I want to ask you something.
3 Lisa heard a noise behind her, so she looked .... to see what it was.
4 I'm going .... now to do some shopping. I'll be .... at 5 o'clock.
5 I'm feeling very tired. I'm going to lie .... on the sofa.
6 When you have read this page, turn .... and read the other side.
7 Mark is from Canada. He lives in London now, but he wants to go .... to Canada.
8 We don't have a key to the house, so we can't get ....
9 I was very tired this morning. I couldn't get ....
10 A: When are you going .... ?
    B: On the 5th. And I'm coming .... on the 24th.

114.3 Lernen Sie zuerst die Verben in Anhang 6 auf Seite 250, bevor Sie diese Übung machen. Vervollständigen Sie die Sätze mit einem Verb aus dem Kästchen + **on**/**off**/**up** usw. Wenn erforderlich, setzen Sie das Verb in die richtige Form (zum Beispiel Vergangenheit).

| break | fall | give | hold | speak | ~~wake~~ | |
| carry | get | go | slow | take | | + on/off/up/down/over |

1 I went to sleep at 10 o'clock and _woke up_ at 8 o'clock the next morning.
2 'It's time to go.'   '................................. a minute. I'm not ready yet.'
3 The train .... and finally stopped.
4 I like flying, but I'm always nervous when the plane ....
5 How are your children? How are they .... at school?
6 It's difficult to hear you. Can you .... a little?
7 This car isn't very good. It has .... many times.
8 When babies try to walk, they sometimes ....
9 The hotel isn't far from here. If you .... along this road, you'll see it on the left.
10 I tried to find a job, but I .... It was impossible.
11 The fire alarm .... and everyone had to leave the building.

114.4 Übersetzen Sie ins Englische.

1 Guten Tag. Kommen Sie herein.
2 Um wie viel Uhr stehst du meistens auf?
3 Julia ist hereingekommen und hat sich hingesetzt.
4 Kannst du bitte die Gardinen öffnen? Ich will hinausgucken.
5 Komm heute Nacht nicht zu spät zurück.
6 Hier ist mein Auto. Steig ein!
7 A: Wo ist Monika?
    B: Sie ist für eine Woche weggefahren.
8 Er ist davongelaufen und hat sich nicht umgedreht.
9 Das Flugzeug hatte Verspätung. Wir sind eingestiegen, aber es ist nicht gestartet.

Gardinen = curtains
Verspätung haben = be delayed

Unit 115: put on your shoes / put your shoes on (phrasal verbs 2)

A

Manche phrasal verbs können ein Objekt haben, zum Beispiel:

Verb	Objekt		Verb	Objekt
put on	your coat		**take off**	your shoes

PUT ON

TAKE OFF

Man kann sagen:
    put on your coat
oder **put** your coat **on**
zieh deinen Mantel an

Man kann sagen:
    take off your shoes
oder **take** your shoes **off**
zieh deine Schuhe aus

aber **it/them** (Pronomen) kommen immer vor **on/off** usw.:
    put **it on** (nicht put on it)
    take **them off** (nicht take off them)

- It was cold, so I **put on** my coat.
  oder … I **put** my coat **on**.
- Here's your coat. **Put it on**.
  … Zieh ihn an.
- I'm going to **take off** my shoes.
  oder … **take** my shoes **off**.
- Your shoes are dirty. **Take them off**.
  … Zieh sie aus.

B

Weitere phrasal verbs + Objekt:

turn on / **turn off** (lights, machines, taps usw.):
(Lichter, Maschinen usw. anmachen, einschalten usw., ausmachen, ausschalten usw.)

- It was dark, so I **turned on** the light.
  oder … I **turned** the light **on**.
  … also habe ich das Licht angemacht.
- I don't want to watch this programme.
  You can **turn it off**. *Du kannst es ausschalten.*

TURN OFF

ON   OFF

SWITCH

Man kann auch sagen **switch on** / **switch off** (lights, machines usw.):
- I **switched on** the light and **switched off** the television.

pick up *(aufheben)* / **put down** *(hinlegen)*:

- Those are my keys on the floor.
  Can you **pick them up** for me?
  Kannst du sie für mich aufheben?
- I stopped reading and **put** my book **down**. oder
  … **put down** my book. … *und habe mein Buch hingelegt.*

PICK UP

PUT DOWN

bring back = *zurückbringen (hierher zurück)*
- You can take my umbrella, but please
  bring it back. … *aber bring ihn bitte zurück.*

take back = *zurückbringen (dorthin zurück)*
- I **took** my new sweater **back** to the shop. It was too
  small for me. … *zum Laden zurückgebracht …*

give back = *zurückgeben*
- I've got Rachel's keys. I have to **give them back** to her.
  … *Ich muss sie ihr zurückgeben.*

put back = *zurücktun*
- I read the letter and then **put it back** in the envelope.
  Ich habe den Brief gelesen und ihn dann zurück in den Umschlag getan.

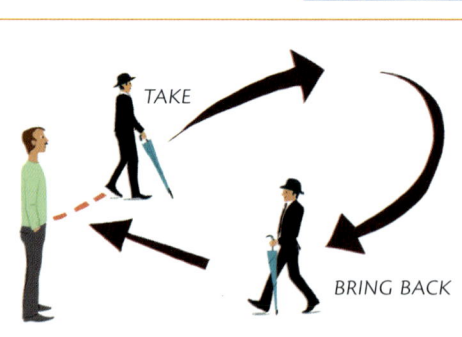
TAKE

BRING BACK

---

go in / **fall off** usw. (phrasal verbs 1) → Unit 114   weitere phrasal verbs → Anhang 6–7

240

Übungen

115.1 Was haben die Personen auf den Bildern gemacht? Schreiben Sie für jedes Bild einen Satz.

1 He _turned on the light_.
2 She ....
3 He ....
4 She ....
5 He ....
6 She ....

115.2 Es gibt drei verschiedene Möglichkeiten, die folgenden Sätze zu schreiben. Vervollständigen Sie die Tabelle.

1	I turned on the radio.	I turned the radio on.	I turned it on.
2	He put on his jacket.	He	He ....
3	She	She took her glasses off.	....
4	I picked up the phone.	....	....
5	They gave back the key.	....	....
6	....	We turned the lights off.	....

115.3 Vervollständigen Sie die Sätze mit den folgenden Verben + **it** oder **them**.

> bring back   pick up   switch off   take back   ~~turn on~~

1 I wanted to watch something on TV, so I _turned it on_.
2 My new lamp doesn't work. I'm going to .... to the shop.
3 There were some gloves on the floor, so I .... and put them on the table.
4 The heating was on but it was too warm, so I ....
5 Thank you for lending me these books. I won't forget to ....

115.4 Lernen Sie zuerst die Verben in Anhang 7, bevor Sie diese Übung machen. Vervollständigen Sie die Sätze mit Verben aus dem Kästchen. In manchen Fällen brauchen Sie außerdem **it**/**them**/**me**.

> fill in   ~~knock down~~   look up   show round   ~~turn down~~
> give up   knock over   put out   throw away   try on

1 They _knocked_ a lot of houses _down_ when they built the new road.
2 That music is very loud. Can you _turn it down_?
3 I .... a glass and broke it.
4 'What does this word mean?' 'Why don't you ....?'
5 I want to keep these magazines. Please don't ....
6 I .... a pair of shoes in the shop, but I didn't buy them.
7 I visited a school last week. One of the teachers ....
8 'Do you play the piano?' 'No, I started to learn, but I .... after a month.'
9 Somebody gave me a form and told me to ....
10 Smoking isn't allowed here. Please .... your cigarette.

115.5 Übersetzen Sie ins Englische.

1 Zieh deine Jacke aus. Es ist warm hier.
2 Mach bitte das Licht aus, wenn du ins Bett gehst.
3 'Hier ist Ihr Stift.' 'Könnten Sie ihn bitte zurück auf meinen Schreibtisch legen?'
4 Es ist Zeit für die Nachrichten. Kannst du bitte den Fernseher einschalten?
5 Warum sind deine Kleider auf dem Boden? Kannst du sie bitte aufheben?
6 'Kann ich dieses Buch mitnehmen?' 'Ja, aber bring es bitte zurück.'
7 Hast du die Waschmaschine ausgeschaltet?

Anhang 1
Aktiv und Passiv

1.1 *Gegenwart und Vergangenheit*

	Aktiv	Passiv
present simple	○ We **make** butter from milk. ○ Somebody **cleans** these rooms every day. ○ People never **invite** me to parties. ○ How **do** they **make** butter?	○ Butter **is made** from milk. ○ These rooms **are cleaned** every day. ○ I **am** never **invited** to parties. ○ How **is** butter **made**?
past simple	○ Somebody **stole** my car last week. ○ Somebody **stole** my keys yesterday. ○ They **didn't invite** me to the party. ○ When **did** they **build** these houses?	○ My car **was stolen** last week. ○ My keys **were stolen** yesterday. ○ I **wasn't invited** to the party. ○ When **were** these houses **built**?
present continuous	○ They **are building** a new airport at the moment. (= it isn't finished) ○ They **are building** some new houses near the river.	○ A new airport **is being built** at the moment. ○ Some new houses **are being built** near the river.
past continuous	○ When I was here a few years ago, they **were building** a new airport. (= it wasn't finished at that time)	○ When I was here a few years ago, a new airport **was being built**.
present perfect	○ Look! They **have painted** the door. ○ These shirts are clean. Somebody **has washed** them. ○ Somebody **has stolen** my car.	○ Look! The door **has been painted**. ○ These shirts are clean. They **have been washed**. ○ My car **has been stolen**.
past perfect	○ Tina said that somebody **had stolen** her car.	○ Tina said that her car **had been stolen**.

1.2 **will** / **can** / **must** / **have to** *usw*.

Aktiv	Passiv
○ Somebody **will clean** the office tomorrow. ○ Somebody **must clean** the office. ○ I think they**'ll invite** you to the party. ○ They **can't repair** my watch. ○ You **should wash** this sweater by hand. ○ They **are going to build** a new airport. ○ Somebody **has to wash** these clothes. ○ They **had to take** the injured man to hospital.	○ The office **will be cleaned** tomorrow. ○ The office **must be cleaned**. ○ I think you**'ll be invited** to the party. ○ My watch **can't be repaired**. ○ This sweater **should be washed** by hand. ○ A new airport **is going to be built**. ○ These clothes **have to be washed**. ○ The injured man **had to be taken** to hospital.

Anhang 2
Liste der unregelmäßigen Verben (→ Unit 25)

Infinitiv		past simple	past participle
be	(sein)	was/were	been
beat	(schlagen)	beat	beaten
become	(werden)	became	become
begin	(anfangen)	began	begun
bite	(beißen)	bit	bitten
blow	(blasen)	blew	blown
break	(brechen)	broke	broken
bring	(bringen)	brought	brought
build	(bauen)	built	built
buy	(kaufen)	bought	bought
catch	(fangen)	caught	caught
choose	(wählen)	chose	chosen
come	(kommen)	came	come
cost	(kosten)	cost	cost
cut	(schneiden)	cut	cut
do	(tun/machen)	did	done
draw	(zeichnen)	drew	drawn
drink	(trinken)	drank	drunk
drive	(fahren)	drove	driven
eat	(essen)	ate	eaten
fall	(fallen)	fell	fallen
feel	(fühlen)	felt	felt
fight	(kämpfen)	fought	fought
find	(finden)	found	found
fly	(fliegen)	flew	flown
forget	(vergessen)	forgot	forgotten
get		got	got
give	(geben)	gave	given
go	(gehen)	went	gone
grow	(wachsen)	grew	grown
hang	(hängen)	hung	hung
have	(haben)	had	had
hear	(hören)	heard	heard
hide	(verstecken)	hid	hidden
hit	(schlagen)	hit	hit
hold	(halten)	held	held
hurt	(verletzen/wehtun)	hurt	hurt
keep	(behalten)	kept	kept
know	(wissen/kennen)	knew	known
leave	(fortgehen)	left	left
lend	(leihen)	lent	lent

Infinitiv		past simple	past participle
let	(erlauben)	let	let
lie	(liegen)	lay	lain
light	(anzünden)	lit	lit
lose	(verlieren)	lost	lost
make	(machen)	made	made
mean	(bedeuten)	meant	meant
meet	(treffen)	met	met
pay	(bezahlen)	paid	paid
put	(legen/stellen)	put	put
read (/riːd/)*	(lesen)	read (/red/)*	read (/red/)*
ride	(reiten/mitfahren)	rode	ridden
ring	(läuten/anrufen)	rang	rung
rise	(steigen)	rose	risen
run	(rennen/laufen)	ran	run
say	(sagen)	said	said
see	(sehen)	saw	seen
sell	(verkaufen)	sold	sold
send	(schicken/senden)	sent	sent
shine	(scheinen)	shone	shone
shoot	(schießen)	shot	shot
show	(zeigen)	showed	shown
shut	(schließen)	shut	shut
sing	(singen)	sang	sung
sit	(sitzen)	sat	sat
sleep	(schlafen)	slept	slept
speak	(sprechen)	spoke	spoken
spend	(ausgeben)	spent	spent
stand	(stehen)	stood	stood
steal	(stehlen)	stole	stolen
swim	(schwimmen)	swam	swum
take	(nehmen)	took	taken
teach	(lehren)	taught	taught
tear	(reißen)	tore	torn
tell	(sagen/erzählen)	told	told
think	(denken)	thought	thought
throw	(werfen)	threw	thrown
understand	(verstehen)	understood	understood
wake (up)	(aufwachen)	woke	woken
wear	(tragen)	wore	worn
win	(gewinnen)	won	won
write	(schreiben)	wrote	written

* Aussprache

Folgende Verben können regelmäßig (**-ed**) oder unregelmäßig sein (**-t**):

Infinitiv	past simple / past participle
burn (brennen)	**burned** oder **burnt**
dream (träumen)	**dreamed** oder **dreamt**

Infinitiv	past simple / past participle
learn (lernen)	**learned** oder **learnt**
smell (riechen)	**smelled** oder **smelt**

Anhang 3
Unregelmäßige Verben nach Gruppen

past simple *und* past participle *sind gleich*:

1
cost	→	cost
cut	→	cut
hit	→	hit
hurt	→	hurt

let	→	let
put	→	put
shut	→	shut

2
lend	→	lent
send	→	sent
spend	→	spent
build	→	built

lost	→	lost
shoot	→	shot
get	→	got
light	→	lit
sit	→	sat

burn	→	burnt
learn	→	learnt
smell	→	smelt

| keep | → | kept |
| sleep | → | slept |

feel	→	felt
leave	→	left
meet	→	met
dream	→	dreamt /dremt/*
mean	→	meant /ment/*

3
bring	→	brought /brɔ:t/*
buy	→	bought /bɔ:t/*
fight	→	fought /fɔ:t/*
think	→	thought /θɔ:t/*
catch	→	caught /kɔ:t/*
teach	→	taught /tɔ:t/*

4
| sell | → | sold |
| tell | → | told |

find	→	found
have	→	had
hear	→	heard
hold	→	held
read	→	read /red/*
say	→	said /sed/*

| pay | → | paid |
| make | → | made |

| stand | → | stood |
| understand | → | understood |

* Aussprache

past simple *und* past participle *sind verschieden*:

1
break	→	broke	broken
choose	→	chose	chosen
speak	→	spoke	spoken
steal	→	stole	stolen
wake	→	woke	woken

2
drive	→	drove	driven
ride	→	rode	ridden
rise	→	rose	risen
write	→	wrote	written

beat	→	beat	beaten
bite	→	bit	bitten
hide	→	hid	hidden

3
eat	→	ate	eaten
fall	→	fell	fallen
forget	→	forgot	forgotten
give	→	gave	given
see	→	saw	seen
take	→	took	taken

4
blow	→	blew	blown
grow	→	grew	grown
know	→	knew	known
throw	→	threw	thrown
fly	→	flew	flown
draw	→	drew	drawn
show	→	showed	shown

5
begin	→	began	begun
drink	→	drank	drunk
swim	→	swam	swum

ring	→	rang	rung
sing	→	sang	sung
run	→	ran	run

6
| come | → | came | come |
| become | → | became | become |

245

Anhang 4
Kurzformen (he's / I'd / don't usw.)

4.1 *Beim Sprechen wird* **I am** *meistens als ein Wort ausgesprochen. Beim Schreiben wird dies durch die Kurzform* **I'm** *wiedergegeben:*

I am	→	I'm
it is	→	it's
they have	→	they've
		usw.

- **I'm** feeling tired this morning.
- 'Do you like this jacket?' 'Yes, **it's** nice.'
- 'Where are your friends?' '**They've** gone home.'

Beim Schreiben setzt man einen Apostroph (') anstelle der nichtausgesprochenen Buchstaben:

I a̶m → I**'m**   he i̶s̶ → he**'s**   you h̶a̶ve → you**'ve**   she w̶i̶ll → she**'ll**

4.2 *Mit* **I/he/she** *usw. werden folgende Kurzformen verwendet:*

am	→	'm	I'm						
is	→	's		he's	she's	it's			
are	→	're					we're	you're	they're
have	→	've	I've				we've	you've	they've
has	→	's		he's	she's	it's			
had	→	'd	I'd	he'd	she'd		we'd	you'd	they'd
will	→	'll	I'll	he'll	she'll		we'll	you'll	they'll
would	→	'd	I'd	he'd	she'd		we'd	you'd	they'd

- I**'ve** got some new shoes.
- We**'ll** probably go out this evening.
- It**'s** 10 o'clock. You**'re** late again.

's *kann die Kurzform für* **is** *oder* **has** *sein:*
- She**'s** going out this evening. (she**'s** going = she **is** going)
- She**'s** gone out. (she**'s** gone = she **has** gone)

'd *kann die Kurzform für* **would** *oder* **had** *sein:*
- A: What would you like to eat?
  B: I**'d** like a salad, please. (I**'d** like = I **would** like)
- I told the police that I**'d** lost my passport. (I**'d** lost = I **had** lost)

Man verwendet Kurzformen **'m/'s/'d** *usw. nicht am Ende eines Satzes (→ Unit 41):*
- A: Are you tired?
  B: Yes, I **am**. (*nicht* Yes, I'm.)

4.3 *Kurzformen werden vor allem mit* **I/you/he/she** *usw. gebraucht, aber man verwendet sie auch bei anderen Wörtern, zum Beispiel:*

- **Who's** your favourite singer? (= who **is**)
- **What's** the time? (= what **is**)
- **There's** a big tree in the garden. (= there **is**)
- **My sister's** working in London. (= my sister **is** working)
- **Paul's** gone out. (= Paul **has** gone out)
- **What colour's** your car? (= What colour **is** your car?)

4.4 Verneinte Kurzformen (→ Unit 44):

isn't	(= is not)	**don't**	(= do not)	**can't**	(= cannot)
aren't	(= are not)	**doesn't**	(= does not)	**couldn't**	(= could not)
wasn't	(= was not)	**didn't**	(= did not)	**won't**	(= will not)
weren't	(= were not)			**wouldn't**	(= would not)
hasn't	(= has not)			**shouldn't**	(= should not)
haven't	(= have not)			**mustn't**	(= must not)
hadn't	(= had not)				

- We went to her house, but she **wasn't** at home.
- 'Where's David?' 'I **don't** know. I **haven't** seen him.'
- You work all the time. You **shouldn't** work so hard.
- I **won't** be here tomorrow. (= I will not)

4.5 **'s** (Apostrophe + **s**) kann unterschiedliche Bedeutungen haben:

(1) **'s** = **is** oder **has** (→ Teil 4.2 dieses Anhangs)

- It**'s** raining. (= It **is** raining) Es regnet.
- It**'s** stopped raining. (= It **has** stopped) Es hat aufgehört zu regnen.

(2) let's = let **us** (→ Units 36, 54)
- It's a lovely day. **Let's** go out. (= Let **us** go out.)

(3) Kate**'s** camera (Kate's = Kates/von Kate) / my brother**'s** car (das Auto meines Bruders) / the manager**'s** office (das Büro des Leiters / der Leiterin) usw. (→ Unit 65)

Vergleichen Sie:
- **Kate's** camera was very expensive. (**Kate's** camera = Kates Fotoapparat)
- **Kate's** a very good photographer. (**Kate's** = Kate **is**)
- **Kate's** got a new camera. (**Kate's** got = Kate **has** got)

Anhang 5
Rechtschreibung

5.1 *Die Endungen* **-s** *und* **-es** (bird**s**/watch**es** *usw.*)

Nomen + **s** (*Plural*) (→ Unit 67)
  bird → bird**s**   mistake → mistake**s**   hotel → hotel**s**

Verb + **s** (he/she/it **-s**) (→ Unit 6)
  think → think**s**   live → live**s**   remember → remember**s**

aber

Man schreibt **-es** *nach* **-s** / **-sh** / **-ch** / **-x**:
  bu**s** → bus**es**   pas**s** → pass**es**   addres**s** → address**es**
  di**sh** → dish**es**   wa**sh** → wash**es**   fini**sh** → finish**es**
  wat**ch** → watch**es**   tea**ch** → teach**es**   sandwi**ch** → sandwich**es**
  bo**x** → box**es**

Außerdem bei
  potato → potato**es**   tomato → tomato**es**
  do → do**es**   go → go**es**

Wörter die auf **-f** / **-fe** *enden, bilden den Plural in der Regel mit* **-ves**:
  shel**f** → shel**ves**   kni**fe** → kni**ves**   *aber* roo**f** → roo**fs**

5.2 *Wörter die auf* **-y** *enden* (bab**y** → bab**ies** / stud**y** → stud**ied** *usw.*)

-y → **-ies**
  stud**y** → stud**ies**   (*nicht* studys)   famil**y** → famil**ies**   (*nicht* familys)
  stor**y** → stor**ies**   cit**y** → cit**ies**   bab**y** → bab**ies**
  tr**y** → tr**ies**   marr**y** → marr**ies**   fl**y** → fl**ies**

-y → **-ied** (→ Unit 12)
  stud**y** → stud**ied**   (*nicht* studyed)
  tr**y** → tr**ied**   marr**y** → marr**ied**   cop**y** → cop**ied**

-y → **-ier/-iest** (→ Units 87, 90)
  eas**y** → eas**ier**/eas**iest**   (*nicht* easyer/easyest)
  happ**y** → happ**ier**/happ**iest**   luck**y** → luck**ier**/luck**iest**
  heav**y** → heav**ier**/heav**iest**   funn**y** → funn**ier**/funn**iest**

-y → **-ily** (→ Unit 86)
  eas**y** → eas**ily**   (*nicht* easyly)
  happ**y** → happ**ily**   heav**y** → heav**ily**   luck**y** → luck**ily**

y wird nicht durch **i** *ersetzt bei Wörtern mit Endungen* **-ay/-ey/-oy/-uy**:
  holid**ay** → holid**ays**   (*nicht* holidaies)
  enj**oy** → enj**oys**/enj**oyed**   st**ay** → st**ays**/st**ayed**   b**uy** → b**uys**   k**ey** → k**eys**

aber
  say → **said**   **pay** → **paid**   (*unregelmäßige Verben*)

5.3 -ing

Verben die auf -e (make/write/drive usw.) enden -ing:
  mak**e** → mak**ing**   writ**e** → writ**ing**   com**e** → com**ing**   danc**e** → danc**ing**

Verben die auf -ie enden -ying:
  l**ie** → l**ying**   d**ie** → d**ying**   t**ie** → t**ying**

5.4

*Verdoppelung des letzten Buchstabens (sto**p** → sto**pp**ed, bi**g** → bi**gg**er usw.)*

Diese Buchstaben sind Vokale: a e i o u
Diese Buchstaben sind Konsonanten: b c d f g k l m n p r s t w y

Manche Wörter enden mit einem Vokal + einem Konsonant, zum Beispiel st**op**, b**ig**, g**et**.
Bevor man **-ing**/**-ed**/**-er**/**-est** anhängt, wird der letzte Buchstabe (**p/g/t** usw.) dieser Wörter verdoppelt (**pp/gg/tt** usw.).

Zum Beispiel:

	V+K			
stop	ST **O P**	p → **pp**	sto**pp**ing	sto**pp**ed
run	R **U N**	n → **nn**	ru**nn**ing	
get	G **E T**	t → **tt**	ge**tt**ing	
swim	SW **I M**	m → **mm**	swi**mm**ing	
big	B **I G**	g → **gg**	bi**gg**er	bi**gg**est
hot	H **O T**	t → **tt**	ho**tt**er	ho**tt**est
thin	TH **I N**	n → **nn**	thi**nn**er	thi**nn**est

V = Vokal
K = Konsonant

Der letzte Buchstabe (Konsonant) wird nicht verdoppelt:
(1) wenn das Wort mit zwei Konsonanten endet (K + K):

	K+K		
help	HE **L P**	hel**p**ing	hel**p**ed
work	WO **R K**	wor**k**ing	wor**k**ed
fast	FA **S T**	fas**t**er	fas**t**est

(2) wenn das Wort mit zwei Vokalen + einem Konsonanten endet (V + V + K):

	V+V+K		
need	N **E E D**	nee**d**ing	nee**d**ed
wait	W **A I T**	wai**t**ing	wai**t**ed
cheap	CH **E A P**	chea**p**er	chea**p**est

(3) bei längeren Wörtern (zweisilbig oder mehr), wenn die letzte Silbe nicht betont wird:

	Betonung	
happen	**HAP**-pen	→ happe**n**ing/happe**n**ed (*nicht* happenned)
visit	**VIS**-it	→ visi**t**ing/visi**t**ed
remember	re-**MEM**-ber	→ remembe**r**ing/remembe**r**ed

aber

| prefer | pre-**FER** | *(letzte Silbe betont)* | → prefe**rr**ing/prefe**rr**ed |
| begin | be-**GIN** | *(letzte Silbe betont)* | → begi**nn**ing |

(4) wenn das Wort auf **-y** oder **-w** endet (am Ende eines Wortes sind **y** und **w** keine Konsonanten):
  enjo**y** → enjo**y**ing/enjo**y**ed   sno**w** → sno**w**ing/sno**w**ed   fe**w** → fe**w**er/fe**w**est

Anhang 6
Phrasal verbs (**take off** / **give up** *usw.*)

In dieser Liste finden Sie einige der wichtigsten phrasal verbs (→ Unit 114):

on

carry on = *weitermachen/weitergehen*
- Don't stop working. **Carry on**. *… mach (ruhig) weiter.*
- A: Excuse me, where is the station?
  B: **Carry on** along this road and turn right at the lights. *Gehen Sie weiter … entlang …*

außerdem: **go on** / **walk on** / **drive on** (= *weitergehen/weiterlaufen/weiterfahren*)
- Don't stop here. **Drive on**. *… Fahren Sie weiter.*

come on = *schnell machen / sich beeilen*
- **Come on**! Everybody is waiting for you. *Mach schnell! Alle warten auf dich.*

get on = *zurecht kommen (mit der Arbeit, in der Schule, bei einer Prüfung usw.)*
- How are you **getting on** in your new job? *Wie kommst du mit deiner neuen Arbeit zurecht?*

hold on = *warten*
- Can you **hold on** a minute? *Können Sie einen Moment warten?*

(Hold on a minute.)

off

take off = *starten (bei einem Flugzeug)*
- The plane **took off** 20 minutes late, but arrived on time. *Die Maschine ist mit 20 Minuten Verspätung gestartet, aber …*

TAKE OFF

go off = *explodieren (eine Bombe), klingeln (ein Wecker), ausgelöst werden (eine Alarmanlage)*
- A bomb **went off** and caused a lot of damage. *Eine Bombe ist explodiert …*
- A car alarm **goes off** if somebody tries to break into the car. *Die Alarmanlage eines Autos wird ausgelöst, wenn …*

GO OFF

up

give up = *aufgeben*
- I know it's difficult, but don't **give up**. *… , aber gib nicht auf.*

grow up = *aufwachsen / groß werden*
- What does your son want to do when he **grows up**? *… wenn er groß ist?*

GROW UP

hurry up = *sich beeilen*
- **Hurry up**! We don't have much time. *Beeil dich! …*

speak up = *lauter sprechen*
- I can't hear you. Can you **speak up**, please? *… Können Sie lauter sprechen?*

wake up = *aufwachen*
- I often **wake up** in the middle of the night.

WAKE UP

wash up = *(das Geschirr) abwaschen/spülen*
- Do you want me to **wash up**? (*oder* … to do the washing-up?) *Soll ich das Geschirr spülen?*

WASH UP

down

slow down = *langsamer fahren/gehen (verlangsamen)*
- You're driving too fast. **Slow down**! *… Fahr langsamer!*

break down = *eine Panne haben / kaputt gehen*
- Sue was very late because her car **broke down**. *… weil sie eine Panne hatte.*

BREAK DOWN

over

fall over = *hinfallen/umfallen*
- I **fell over** because my shoes were too big for me. *Ich bin hingefallen, weil …*

FALL OVER

Anhang 7 Phrasal verbs + *Objekt*
(**put out** a fire / **give up** your job *usw.*)

In dieser Liste finden Sie einige der wichtigsten phrasal verbs + Objekt (→ Unit 115):

in/out   **fill in** / **fill out** a form = *ein Formular ausfüllen*
- Can you **fill in this form**, please? *oder*
  Can you **fill out this form**, please?

out   **put out** a fire, a cigarette *usw.* = *löschen*
- The fire brigade arrived and **put the fire out**.

       cross out a mistake, a word *usw.* = *durchstreichen*
- If you make a mistake, **cross it out**.

PUT OUT

CROSS OUT

on   **try on** clothes = *Kleidung anprobieren*
- *(in einem Kleidergeschäft)* This is a nice jacket. Shall I **try it on**? … *Soll ich sie anprobieren?*

up   **give up** something = *(etwas) aufgeben / mit etwas aufhören*
- Sue **gave up her job** when her baby was born. *Sue hat mit der Arbeit aufgehört, als …*
- 'Are you still learning Italian?' 'No, I **gave it up**.' … '*Nein, ich habe damit aufgehört.*'

       look up a word in a dictionary *usw.* = *ein Wort im Wörterbuch nachschlagen*
- I didn't know the meaning of the word, so I **looked it up** in a dictionary.

       turn up the TV, radio, music, heating *usw.* = *lauter stellen*
- Can you **turn the radio up**? I can't hear it.

       wake up somebody = *jemanden wecken*
- I have to get up early tomorrow. Can you **wake me up** at 6.30?
  Kannst du mich um 6.30 Uhr wecken?

down   **knock down** a building = *abreißen*
- They are going to **knock down** the school and build a new one.

KNOCK DOWN

       turn down the TV, radio, music *usw.* = *leiser stellen*
- The music is too loud. Can you **turn it down**?

over   **knock over** a cup, a glass, a person *usw.* = *umwerfen*
- Be careful. Don't **knock your cup over**.
  auch: **knocked over** by a car = *von einem Auto angefahren/umgefahren werden*
- There was an accident at the end of the road.
  A man was **knocked over** by a car.
  (*oder* A man was **knocked down** by a car.)

KNOCK OVER

KNOCK OVER *oder* KNOCK DOWN

away   **throw away** rubbish = *Abfall wegwerfen*
- These apples are bad. Shall I **throw them away**?
- Don't **throw away that picture**. I want it.

THROW AWAY

       put something **away** = *wegtun/wegräumen*
- After they finished playing, the children **put their toys away**.
  … , haben die Kinder ihre Spielsachen weggeräumt.

back   **pay** somebody **back** = *jemandem (Geld) zurückzahlen*
- Thank you for lending me the money. I'll **pay you back** next week.

round/around   **show** somebody **round/around** the town, the house *usw.* = *jemandem die Stadt, das Haus usw. zeigen*
- The manager **showed us round** the factory. *Der Leiter hat uns die Fabrik gezeigt.*

Zusätzliche Übungen

Liste der Übungen

1–2	**am/is/are**	Units 1–3
3	present continuous	Units 4–5
4	present simple	Units 6–8
5–7	present simple, **am/is/are** und **have** (**got**)	Units 1–3, 6–8, 10
8–9	present continuous und present simple	Units 4–9
10–13	**was/were** und past simple	Units 11–13
14	past simple und past continuous	Units 12–15
15	Gegenwart und Vergangenheit	Units 4–15
16–18	present perfect	Units 16–20
19–22	present perfect und past simple	Units 19–21
23	Gegenwart, Vergangenheit und present perfect	Units 4–21
24–27	Passiv	Units 22–23
28	Zukunft	Units 26–29
29	Vergangenheit, Gegenwart und Zukunft	Units 4–21, 26–29
30–31	Vergangenheit, Gegenwart und Zukunft	Units 4–23, 26–29, 53, 55, 98, 105
32	**-ing** und **to** …	Units 52–56,105,112
33–34	**a** und **the**	Units 66, 70–73
35	Präpositionen	Units 103–108,111

am/is/are   Units 1–3

1 Schreiben Sie Sätze, welche die Situationen in den Bildern beschreiben. Verwenden Sie Wörter aus beiden Kästchen + **is/isn't/are/aren't**.

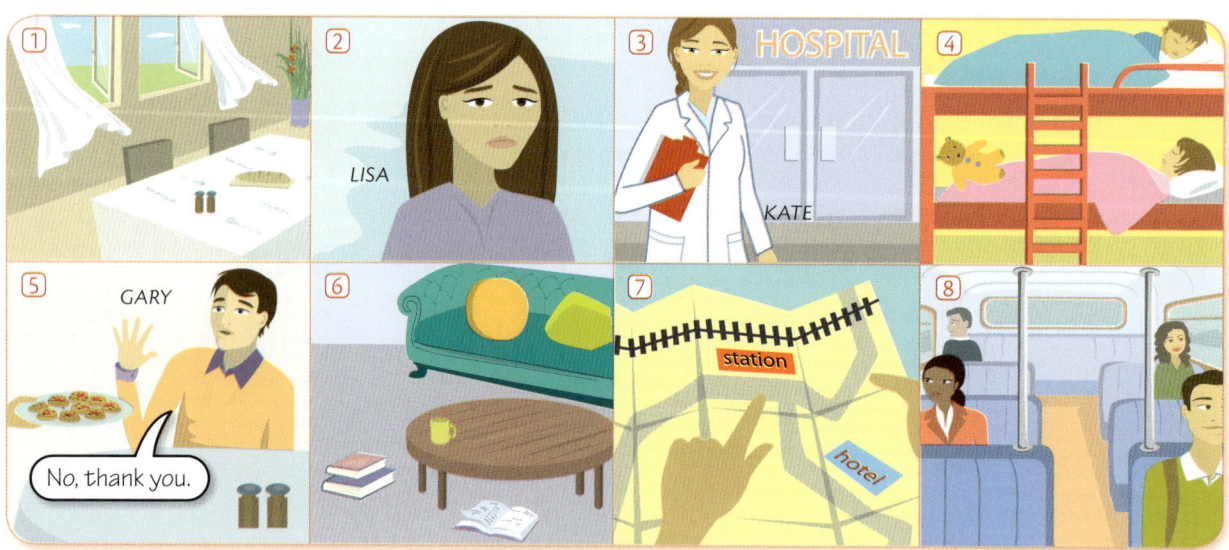

~~The windows~~	on the table
~~Lisa~~	hungry
Kate	asleep
The children	~~open~~
Gary	full
The books	near the station
The hotel	a doctor
The bus	~~happy~~

1 The windows are open.
2 Lisa isn't happy.
3 Kate
4
5
6
7
8

Zusätzliche Übungen

2 Vervollständigen Sie die Sätze.
1. 'Are you hungry?' 'No, but *I'm* thirsty.'
2. '*How are* your parents?' 'They're fine.'
3. 'Is Anna at home?' 'No, ... at work.'
4. '.............. my keys?' 'On your desk.'
5. Where is Paul from? .... American or British?
6. .... very hot today. The temperature is 38 degrees.
7. 'Are you a teacher?' 'No, ... a student.'
8. '.............. your umbrella?' 'Green.'
9. Where's your car? .... in the car park?
10. '.............. tired?' 'No, I'm fine.'
11. 'These shoes are nice. How ....?' 'Sixty pounds.'

---

present continuous (I'm working / are you working? usw.) — Units 4–5

3 Bilden Sie Aussagen oder Fragen mit den Wörtern in Klammern.
1. A: Where are your parents?
   B: *They're watching TV.* (they / watch / TV)
2. A: Paula is going out.
   B: *Where's she going?* (where / she / go?)
3. A: Where's David?
   B: .... (he / have / a shower)
4. A: .... ? (the children / play?)
   B: No, they're asleep.
5. A: .... ? (it / rain?)
   B: No, not at the moment.
6. A: Where are Sue and Steve?
   B: .... (they / come / now)
7. A: .... ? (why / you / stand / here?)
   B: .... (I / wait / for somebody)

---

present simple (I work / she doesn't work / do you work? usw.) — Units 6–8

4 Vervollständigen Sie die Sätze mit den Wörtern in Klammern. Verwenden Sie das **present simple**.
1. *Sue always gets* to work early. (Sue / always / get)
2. *We don't watch* TV very often. (we / not / watch)
3. How often *do you wash* your hair? (you / wash)
4. I want to go to the cinema, but .... to go. (Sam / not / want)
5. .... to go out tonight? (you / want)
6. .... near here? (Helen / live)
7. .... a lot of people. (Sarah / know)
8. I enjoy travelling, but .... very much. (I / not / travel)
9. What time .... in the morning? (you / usually / get up)
10. My parents are usually at home in the evening. .... very often. (they / not / go out)
11. .... work at five o'clock. (Tom / always / finish)
12. A: What .... ? (Jessica / do)
    B: .... in a hotel. (she / work)

Zusätzliche Übungen

present simple, am/is/are und have (got) — Units 1–3, 6–8, 10

5 Clare wurden folgende Fragen gestellt. Schreiben Sie Aussagen über Clare anhand ihrer Antworten.

1	Are you married?	No.	1	She isn't married.
2	Do you live in London?	Yes.	2	She lives in London.
3	Are you a student?	Yes.	3	
4	Have you got a car?	No.	4	
5	Do you go out a lot?	Yes.	5	
6	Have you got a lot of friends?	Yes.	6	
7	Do you like London?	No.	7	
8	Do you like dancing?	Yes.	8	
9	Are you interested in sport?	No.	9	

6 Vervollständigen Sie die Fragen.

1.
- What's your name ? — Ben.
- .... married? — Yes, I am.
- Where .... ? — In Barton Road.
- .... any children? — Yes, a daughter.
- How .... ? — She's three.

2.
- .... ? — I'm 29.
- .... ? — I work in a supermarket.
- .... your job? — No, I hate it.
- .... a car? — Yes, I have.
- .... to work by car? — No, I usually go by bus.

3.
- Who is this man ? — That's my brother.
- .... ? — Michael.
- .... ? — He's a travel agent.
- .... in London? — No, in Manchester.

7 Bilden Sie Sätze mit diesen Wörtern.

1. Sarah often / tennis — Sarah often plays tennis.
2. my parents / a new car — My parents have got a new car.
3. my shoes / dirty — My shoes are dirty.
4. Sonia / 32 years old — Sonia ....
5. I / two sisters
6. we often / TV in the evening
7. Amy never / a hat
8. a bicycle / two wheels
9. these flowers / beautiful
10. Emma / German very well

Zusätzliche Übungen

present continuous (I'm working) und present simple (I work) Units 4–9

8 Vervollständigen Sie die Sprechblasen.

1. Please be quiet. I'm working (I/work).
2. Do you often go (you/often/go) to the cinema?
3. What .... (you/cook)?
4. Jack .... (play) the piano very well.
5. .... (I/go) now. Goodbye!
6. .... (it/rain). Can I take this umbrella?
7. .... (I/not/watch) TV very much.
8. Excuse me, ... (we/look) for the museum.
9. What's this word? How .... (you/pronounce) it?

9 Was ist richtig?

1. '<s>Are you speaking</s> / Do you speak English?' 'Yes, a little.' (Do you speak ist richtig)
2. Sometimes we're going / we go away at weekends.
3. It's a nice day today. The sun is shining / shines.
4. (Sie treffen Kate auf der Straße.) Hello, Kate. Where are you going / do you go?
5. How often are you going / do you go on holiday?
6. Emily is a writer. She's writing / She writes books for children.
7. I'm never reading / I never read newspapers.
8. 'Where are Mark and Laura?' 'They're watching / They watch TV in the living room.'
9. Helen is in her office. She's talking / She talks to somebody.
10. What time are you usually having / do you usually have dinner?
11. Joe isn't at home at the moment. He's visiting / He visits some friends.
12. 'Would you like some tea?' 'No, thank you. I'm not drinking / I don't drink tea.'

Zusätzliche Übungen

was/were und past simple (I worked / did you work? usw.) — Units 11–13

10 Vervollständigen Sie die Sätze mit nur einem Wort.

1. I got up early and ...had... a shower.
2. Tom was tired last night, so he .... to bed early.
3. I .... this key on the floor. Is it yours?
4. Kate got married when she .... 23.
5. Helen is learning to drive. She .... her first lesson yesterday.
6. 'I've got a new job.' 'Yes, I know. David .... me.'
7. 'Where did you buy that book?' 'It was a present. Amy .... it to me.'
8. We .... hungry, so we had something to eat.
9. 'Did you enjoy the film?' 'Yes, I .... it was very good.'
10. 'Did Andy come to your party?' 'No, we .... him, but he didn't come.'

11 Joe wurden folgende Fragen über seine Kindheit gestellt. Schreiben Sie, anhand seiner Antworten, Aussagen über Joe, als er ein Kind war.

When you were a child …
- Were you tall? — No. 1 He wasn't tall.
- Did you like school? — Yes. 2 He liked school.
- Were you good at sport? — Yes. 3 He ....
- Did you play football? — Yes. 4 ....
- Did you work hard at school? — No. 5 ....
- Did you have a lot of friends? — Yes. 6 ....
- Did you have a bike? — No. 7 ....
- Were you a quiet child? — No. 8 ....

12 Vervollständigen Sie die Fragen.

1. Did you have a nice holiday? — Yes, it was great, thanks.
2. Where did you go? — To Amsterdam.
3. .... there? — Five days.
4. .... Amsterdam? — Yes, very much.
5. ....? — I have friends in Amsterdam, so I stayed with them.
6. .... good? — Yes, it was warm and sunny.
7. .... back? — Yesterday.

13 Setzen Sie das Verb in die passende Form (bejahte Form, Verneinung oder Frage).

1. It was a good party. I enjoyed it. (I / enjoy)
2. 'Did you do the shopping?' (you / do) 'No, I didn't have time.' (I / have)
3. 'Did you phone Adam?' 'No, I'm afraid ....' (I / forget)
4. I like your new watch. Where .... it? (you / get)
5. I saw Lucy at the party, but .... to her. (I / speak)
6. A: .... a nice weekend? (you / have)
   B: Yes, I went to stay with some friends of mine.
7. Paul wasn't well yesterday, so .... to work. (he / go)
8. 'Is Mary here?' 'Yes, ... five minutes ago.' (she / arrive)
9. Where .... before he moved here? (Robert / live)
10. The restaurant wasn't expensive. .... very much. (the meal / cost)

Zusätzliche Übungen

past simple (I worked) *und* past continuous (I was working) — Units 12–15

14 Vervollständigen Sie die Sätze anhand der Situationen in den Bildern. Verwenden Sie **past simple** oder **past continuous**.

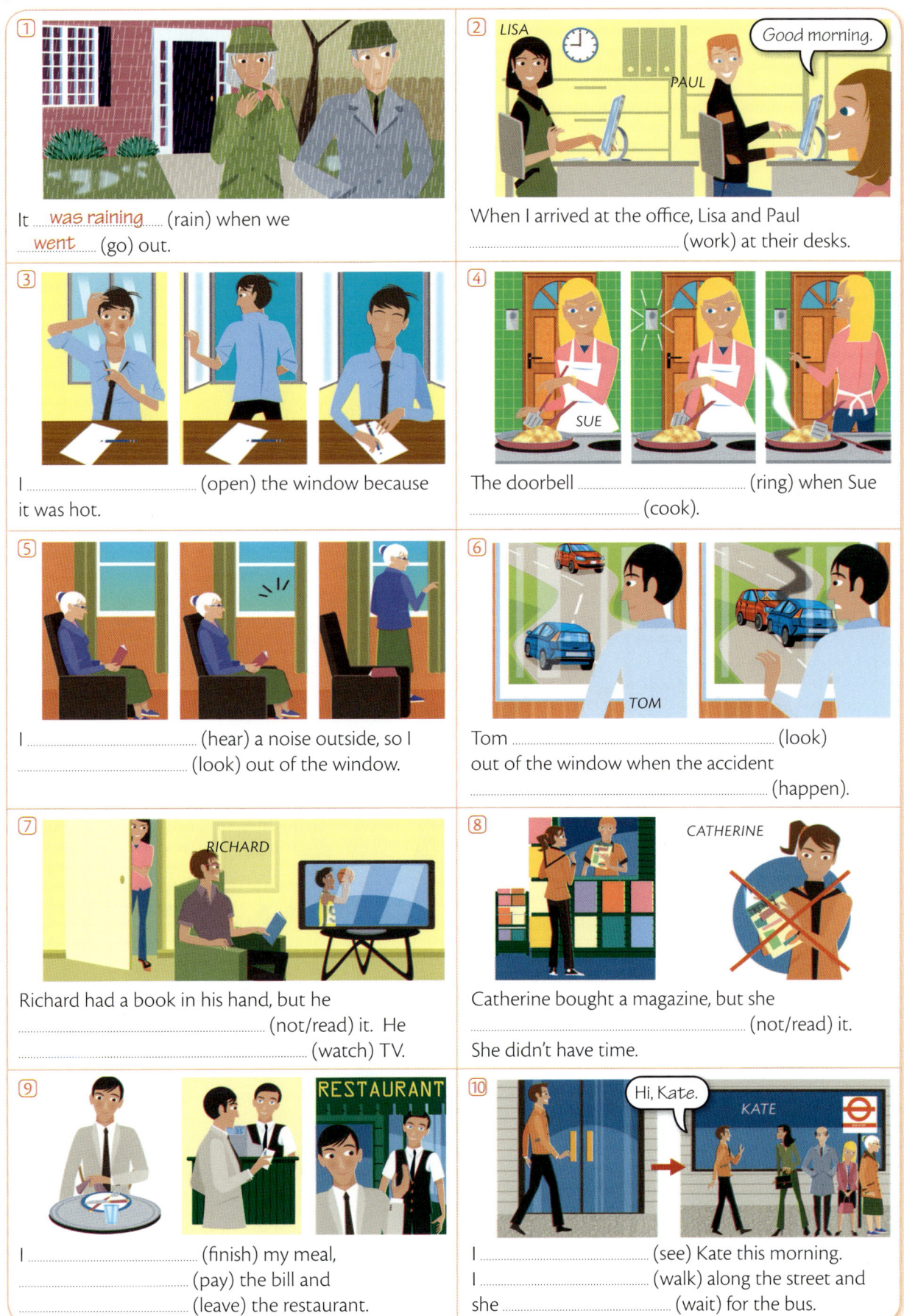

1. It **was raining** (rain) when we **went** (go) out.

2. When I arrived at the office, Lisa and Paul .... (work) at their desks.

3. I .... (open) the window because it was hot.

4. The doorbell .... (ring) when Sue .... (cook).

5. I .... (hear) a noise outside, so I .... (look) out of the window.

6. Tom .... (look) out of the window when the accident .... (happen).

7. Richard had a book in his hand, but he .... (not/read) it. He .... (watch) TV.

8. Catherine bought a magazine, but she .... (not/read) it. She didn't have time.

9. I .... (finish) my meal, ... (pay) the bill and .... (leave) the restaurant.

10. I .... (see) Kate this morning. I .... (walk) along the street and she .... (wait) for the bus.

Zusätzliche Übungen

Gegenwart und Vergangenheit   Units 4–15

15 Vervollständigen Sie die Sätze. Verwenden Sie die passende Zeitform für jeden Satz:

present simple (**I work**/**drive** usw.)   present continuous (**I am working**/**driving** usw.)
past simple (**I worked**/**drove** usw.)   past continuous (**I was working**/**driving** usw.)

1. You can turn off the television. I ___'m not watching___ (not/watch) it.
2. Last night Jenny ___fell___ (fall) asleep while she ___was reading___ (read).
3. Listen! Somebody .... (play) the piano.
4. 'Have you got my key?'   'No, I .... (give) it back to you.'
5. David is very lazy. He .... (not/like) hard work.
6. Where .... (your parents / go) for their holidays last year?
7. I .... (see) Laura yesterday. She .... (drive) her new car.
8. A: .... (you/watch) TV very much?
   B: No, I haven't got a TV.
9. A: What .... (you/do) at 6 o'clock last Sunday morning?
   B: I was in bed asleep.
10. Andy isn't at home very much. He .... (go) away a lot.
11. I .... (try) to find a job at the moment. It's not easy.
12. I'm tired this morning. I .... (not/sleep) very well last night.

present perfect (I have done / she has been usw.)   Units 16–20

16 Vervollständigen Sie die Sprechblasen anhand der Situationen in den Bildern. Verwenden Sie das **present perfect**.

258

Zusätzliche Übungen

17 Vervollständigen Sie die Sätze mit einem, zwei oder drei Wörtern.
1. Mark and Sarah are married. They _have been_ married for five years.
2. David has been watching TV _since_ 5 o'clock.
3. Joe is at work. He _____ at work since 8.30.
4. 'Have you just arrived in London?' 'No, I've been here _____ five days.'
5. I've known Helen _____ we were at school together.
6. 'My brother lives in Los Angeles.' 'Really? How long _____ there?'
7. George has had the same job _____ 20 years.
8. Some friends of ours are staying with us at the moment. They _____ here since Monday.

18 Vervollständigen Sie die Sätze mit Aussagen über sich selbst.
1. I've never _ridden a horse._
2. I've _been to London_ many times.
3. I've just _____
4. I've _____ (once / twice / a few times / many times)
5. I haven't _____ yet.
6. I've never _____
7. I've _____ since _____
8. I've _____ for _____

---

present perfect (I have done usw.) und past simple (I did usw.) — Units 19–21

19 **Present perfect** oder **past simple**? Vervollständigen Sie die Sätze mit der passenden Zeitform (bejaht oder verneint).
1. A: Do you like London?
   B: I don't know. I _haven't been_ there.
2. A: Have you seen Kate?
   B: Yes, I _saw_ her five minutes ago.
3. A: That's a nice sweater. Is it new?
   B: Yes, I _____ it last week.
4. A: Are you tired this morning?
   B: Yes, I _____ to bed late last night.
5. A: Do you want this newspaper, or can I have it?
   B: You can have it. I _____ it.
6. A: Are you enjoying your new job?
   B: I _____ yet. My first day is next Monday.
7. A: The weather isn't very nice today, is it?
   B: No, but it _____ nice yesterday.
8. A: Was Helen at the party on Saturday?
   B: I don't think so. I _____ her there.
9. A: Is your son still at school?
   B: No, he _____ school two years ago.
10. A: Is Silvia married?
    B: Yes, she _____ married for five years.
11. A: Have you heard of George Washington?
    B: Of course. He _____ the first President of the United States.
12. A: How long does it take to make a pizza?
    B: I don't know. I _____ a pizza.

Zusätzliche Übungen

20 Bilden Sie Sätze mit den Wörtern in Klammern. Verwenden Sie **present perfect** oder **past simple**.

1 A: Have you been to Thailand?
  B: Yes, _I went there last year._ (I / go / there / last year)
2 A: Do you like London?
  B: I don't know. _I've never been there._ (I / never / there)
3 A: What time is Paul going out?
  B: .... (he / already / go)
4 A: Has Catherine gone home?
  B: Yes, ... (she / leave / at 4 o'clock)
5 A: New York is my favourite city.
  B: Is it? ....? (how many times / you / there?)
6 A: What are you doing this weekend?
  B: I don't know. .... (I / not / decide / yet)
7 A: I can't find my address book. Have you seen it?
  B: .... (it / on the table / last night)
8 A: Do you know the Japanese restaurant in Leeson Street?
  B: Yes, ... (I / eat / there a few times)
9 A: Paula and Sue are here.
  B: Are they? ....? (what time / they / arrive?)

21 **Present perfect** oder **past simple**? Vervollständigen Sie die Sätze mit der passenden Zeitform.

1 A: _Have you been_ to France?
  B: Yes, many times.
  A: When .... the last time?
  B: Two years ago.

2 A: Is this your car?
  B: Yes, it is.
  A: How long .... it?
  B: It's new. I .... it yesterday.

3 A: Where do you live?
  B: In Harold Street.
  A: How long .... there?
  B: Five years. Before that .... in Mill Road.
  A: How long .... in Mill Road?
  B: About three years.

4 A: What do you do?
  B: I work in a shop.
  A: How long .... there?
  B: Nearly two years.
  A: What .... before that?
  B: I .... a taxi driver.

Zusätzliche Übungen

22 Schreiben Sie Sätze über sich selbst. Verwenden Sie die folgenden Wörter.
1 (yesterday morning) I was late for work yesterday morning.
2 (last night)
3 (yesterday afternoon)
4 (… days ago)
5 (last week)
6 (last year)

Gegenwart, Vergangenheit und present perfect   Units 4–21

23 Was ist richtig: A, B, C oder D?
1 ' Is Sue working?   (C) ' 'No, she's on holiday.'
   A Does Sue work?   B Is working Sue?   C Is Sue working?   D Does work Sue?

2 'Where ....?' 'In a village near London.'
   A lives your uncle   B does your uncle live   C your uncle lives   D does live your uncle

3 I speak Italian, but .... French.
   A I speak not   B I'm not speaking   C I doesn't speak   D I don't speak

4 'Where's Tom?' '............................ a shower at the moment.'
   A He's having   B He have   C He has   D He has had

5 Why .... angry with me yesterday?
   A were you   B was you   C you were   D have you been

6 My favourite film is *Cleo's Dream*. .... it four times.
   A I'm seeing   B I see   C I was seeing   D I've seen

7 I .... out last night. I was too tired.
   A don't go   B didn't went   C didn't go   D haven't gone

8 Tina is from Chicago. She .... there all her life.
   A is living   B has lived   C lives   D lived

9 My friend .... for me when I arrived.
   A waited   B has waited   C was waiting   D has been waiting

10 'How long .... English?' 'Six months.'
   A do you learn   B are you learning   C you are learning   D have you been learning

11 Paul is Canadian, but he lives in France. He has been there ....
   A for three years   B since three years   C three years ago   D during three years

12 'What time ....?' 'About an hour ago.'
   A has Lisa phoned   B Lisa has phoned   C did Lisa phone   D is Lisa phoning

13 What .... when you saw her?
   A did Sue wear   B was Sue wearing   C has Sue worn   D was wearing Sue

14 'Can you drive?' 'No, ... a car, but I want to learn.'
   A I never drive   B I'm never driving   C I've never driven   D I was never driving

15 I saw Helen at the station when I was going to work this morning, but she .... me.
   A didn't see   B don't see   C hasn't seen   D didn't saw

Passiv

Units 22–23, Anhang 1

24 Vervollständigen Sie die Texte zu den Bildern. Verwenden Sie die Verben in Klammern in der Passivform.

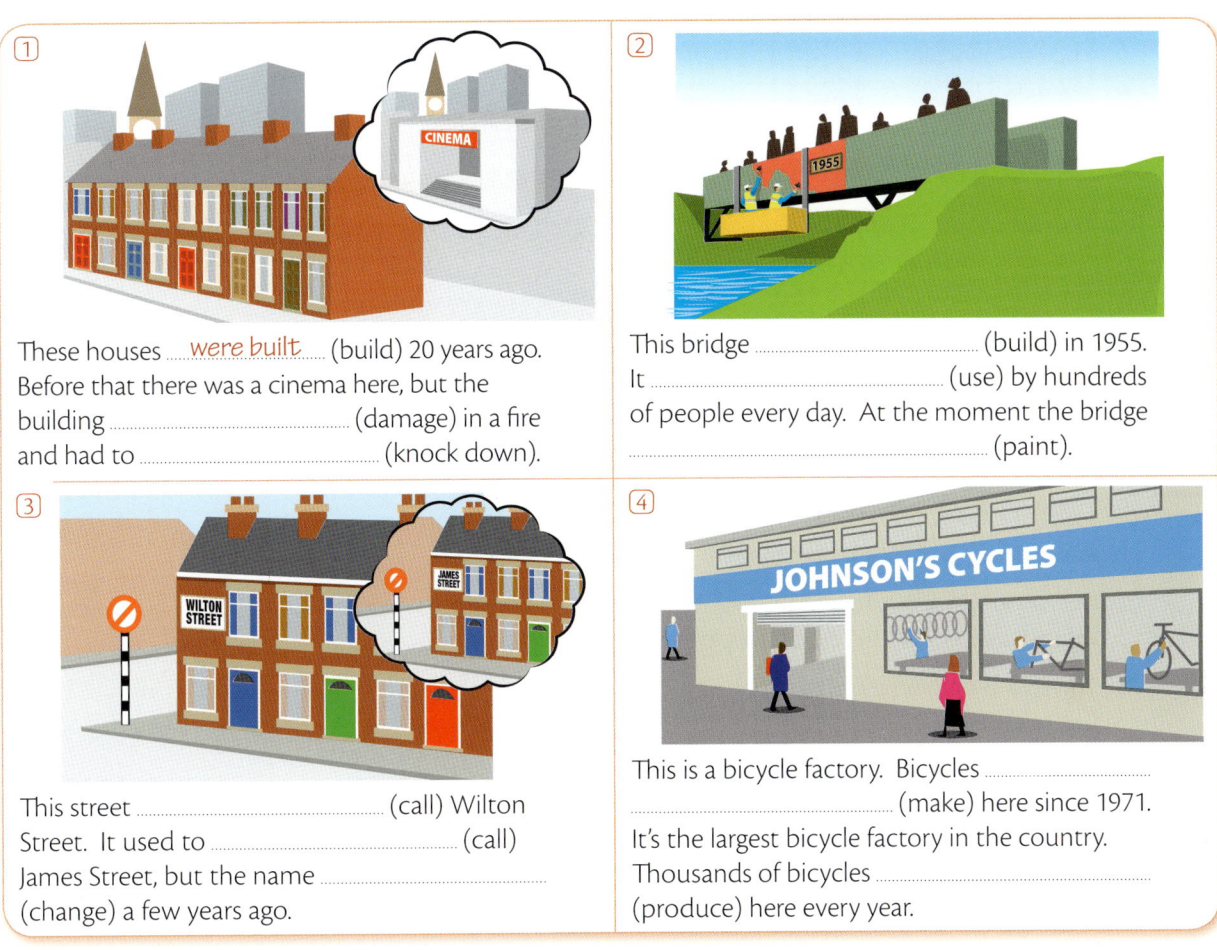

1. These houses ....were built.... (build) 20 years ago. Before that there was a cinema here, but the building .... (damage) in a fire and had to .... (knock down).

2. This bridge .... (build) in 1955. It .... (use) by hundreds of people every day. At the moment the bridge .... (paint).

3. This street .... (call) Wilton Street. It used to .... (call) James Street, but the name .... (change) a few years ago.

4. This is a bicycle factory. Bicycles .... (make) here since 1971. It's the largest bicycle factory in the country. Thousands of bicycles .... (produce) here every year.

25 Vervollständigen Sie die Sätze mit dem Passiv der Wörter in Klammern.

1. We ....were invited.... (invite) to the party, but we didn't go.
2. The museum is very popular. Every year it .... (visit) by thousands of people.
3. Many buildings .... (damage) in the storm last week.
4. A new road is going to .... (build) next year.
5. 'Where's your jacket?' 'It .... (clean). It will be ready tomorrow.'
6. She's famous now, but in a few years her name will .... (forget).
7. 'Shall I do the washing-up?' 'No, it .... (already/do).'
8. Milk should .... (keep) in a fridge.
9. .... (you/ever/bite) by a snake?
10. My bag .... (steal) from my car yesterday afternoon.

26 Wie kann man folgende Aussagen im Passiv ausdrücken? Bilden Sie neue Sätze.

1. Somebody has stolen my keys. — My keys have been stolen.
2. Somebody stole my car last week. — My car ....
3. Somebody has eaten all the bananas. — All the ....
4. Somebody will repair the machine. — The ....
5. Somebody is watching us. — We ....
6. Somebody has to do the housework. — The ....

Zusätzliche Übungen

27 Aktiv oder Passiv? Vervollständigen Sie die Sätze.
1. They __are building__ (build) a new airport at the moment.
2. I can't find my bag. I think it __has been stolen__ (steal).
3. I can't find my bag. Somebody _____ (take) it!
4. 'How did you fall?' 'Somebody _____ (push) me.'
5. 'How did you fall?' 'I _____ (push).'
6. My watch is broken. It _____ (repair) at the moment.
7. Who _____ (invent) the camera?
8. When _____ (the camera/invent)?
9. These shirts are clean now. They _____ (wash).
10. These shirts are clean now. I _____ (wash) them.
11. The letter was for me, so why _____ (they/send) it to you?
12. The information will _____ (send) to you as soon as possible.

Zukunft
Units 26–29

28 Welche ist die beste Alternative: A, B oder C?
1. __We're having (B)__ a party next Sunday. I hope you can come.
   A We have   **B** We're having   **C** We'll have

2. Do you know about Karen? _____ her job. She told me last week.
   A She leaves   **B** She's going to leave   **C** She'll leave

3. There's a programme on TV that I want to watch. _____ in five minutes.
   A It starts   **B** It's starting   **C** It will start

4. The weather is nice now, but I think _____ later.
   A it rains   **B** it's raining   **C** it will rain

5. 'What _____ next weekend?' 'Nothing. I've got no plans.'
   A do you do   **B** are you doing   **C** will you do

6. 'When you see Tina, can you ask her to phone me?' 'OK, _____ her.'
   A I ask   **B** I'm going to ask   **C** I'll ask

7. 'What would you like to drink, tea or coffee?' '_____ tea, please.'
   A I have   **B** I'm going to have   **C** I'll have

8. Don't take that magazine away. _____ it.
   A I read   **B** I'm going to read   **C** I'll read

9. Rachel is ill, so _____ to the party tomorrow night.
   A she doesn't come   **B** she isn't coming   **C** she won't come

10. I want to meet Sarah at the station. What time _____ ?
    A does her train arrive   **B** is her train going to arrive   **C** is her train arriving

11. 'Will you be at home tomorrow evening?' 'No. _____ .'
    A I go out   **B** I'm going out   **C** I'll go out

12. '_____ you tomorrow?' 'Yes, OK.'
    A Do I phone   **B** Am I going to phone   **C** Shall I phone

Vergangenheit, Gegenwart und Zukunft

Units 4–21, 26–29

29 Vervollständigen Sie die Dialoge mit den Wörtern in Klammern. Verwenden Sie die passende Zeitform.

1. A: *Did you go* (you/go) out last night?
   B: No, ... (I/stay) at home.
   A: What .... (you/do)?
   B: .... (I/watch) TV.
   A: .... (you/go) out tomorrow night?
   B: Yes, ... (I/go) to the cinema.
   A: Which film .... (you/see)?
   B: .... (I/not/know). .... (I/not/decide) yet.

2. A: Are you on holiday here?
   B: Yes, we are.
   A: How long .... (you/be) here?
   B: .... (we/arrive) yesterday.
   A: And how long .... (you/stay)?
   B: Until the end of next week.
   A: And .... (you/like) it here?
   B: Yes, ... (we/have) a wonderful time.

3. A: .... (I/go) out with Chris and Steve this evening. .... (you/want) to come with us?
   B: Yes, where .... (you/go)?
   A: To the Italian restaurant in North Street. .... (you/ever/eat) there?
   B: Yes, ... (I/be) there two or three times. In fact I .... (go) there last night, but I'd love to go again!

4. A: .... (I/lose) my glasses again. .... (you/see) them?
   B: .... (you/wear) them when .... (I/come) in.
   A: Well, ... (I/not/wear) them now, so where are they?
   B: .... (you/look) in the kitchen?
   A: No, ... (I/go) and look now.

Zusätzliche Übungen

Vergangenheit, Gegenwart und Zukunft   Units 4–23, 26–29, 53, 55, 98, 105

30 Rachel redet über ihre beste Freundin, Carolyn. Setzen Sie die Verben in die jeweils passende Zeitform.

Carolyn is my best friend. I remember very well the first time (1) .... (we/meet). It was our first day at secondary school, and (2) .... (we/sit) next to each other for the first lesson. (3) .... (we/not/know) any other students in our class, and so (4) .... (we/become) friends. We found that (5) .... (we/like) the same things, especially music and sport, and so (6) .... (we/spend) a lot of time together.

(7) .... (we/leave) school five years ago, but (8) .... (we/meet) as often as we can. For the last six months Carolyn (9) .... (be) in Mexico – at the moment (10) .... (she/work) in a school as a teaching assistant. (11) .... (she/come) back to England next month, and when (12) .... (she/come) back, (13) .... (we/have) lots of things to talk about. (14) .... (it/be) really nice to see her again.

31 Nick und sein Freund Jon machen eine Weltreise. Lesen Sie die E-mails zwischen Nick und seinen Eltern, und setzen Sie die Verben in die jeweils passende Zeitform.

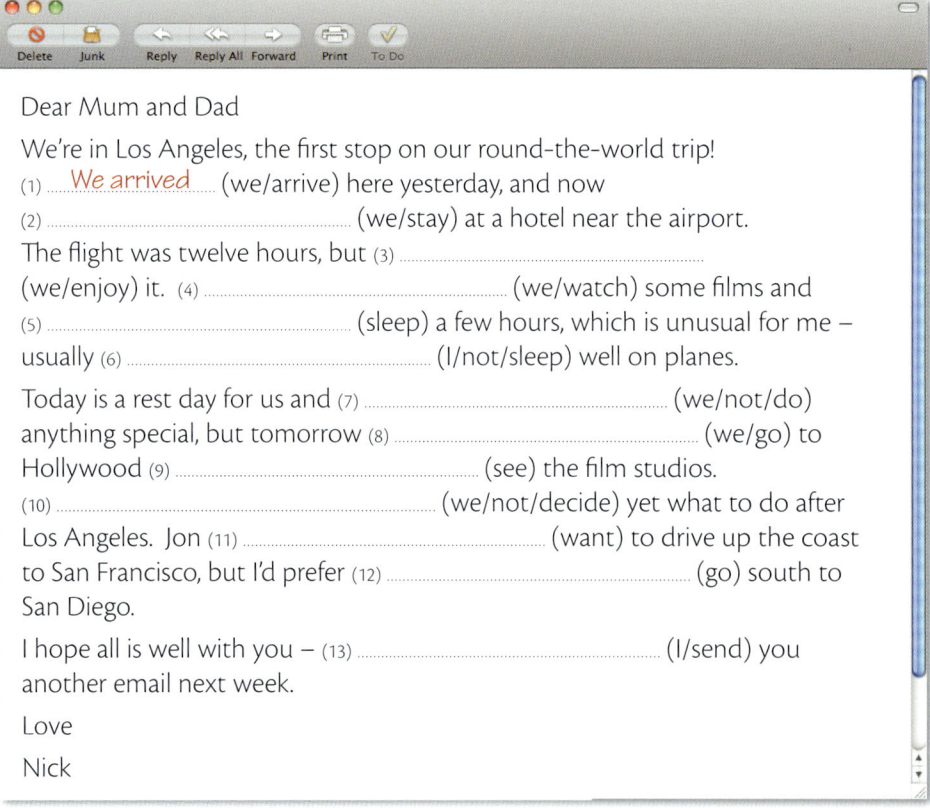

Dear Mum and Dad

We're in Los Angeles, the first stop on our round-the-world trip!
(1) *We arrived* (we/arrive) here yesterday, and now
(2) .... (we/stay) at a hotel near the airport.
The flight was twelve hours, but (3) ....
(we/enjoy) it. (4) .... (we/watch) some films and
(5) .... (sleep) a few hours, which is unusual for me –
usually (6) .... (I/not/sleep) well on planes.
Today is a rest day for us and (7) .... (we/not/do)
anything special, but tomorrow (8) .... (we/go) to
Hollywood (9) .... (see) the film studios.
(10) .... (we/not/decide) yet what to do after
Los Angeles. Jon (11) .... (want) to drive up the coast
to San Francisco, but I'd prefer (12) .... (go) south to
San Diego.
I hope all is well with you – (13) .... (I/send) you
another email next week.
Love
Nick

Nick

266

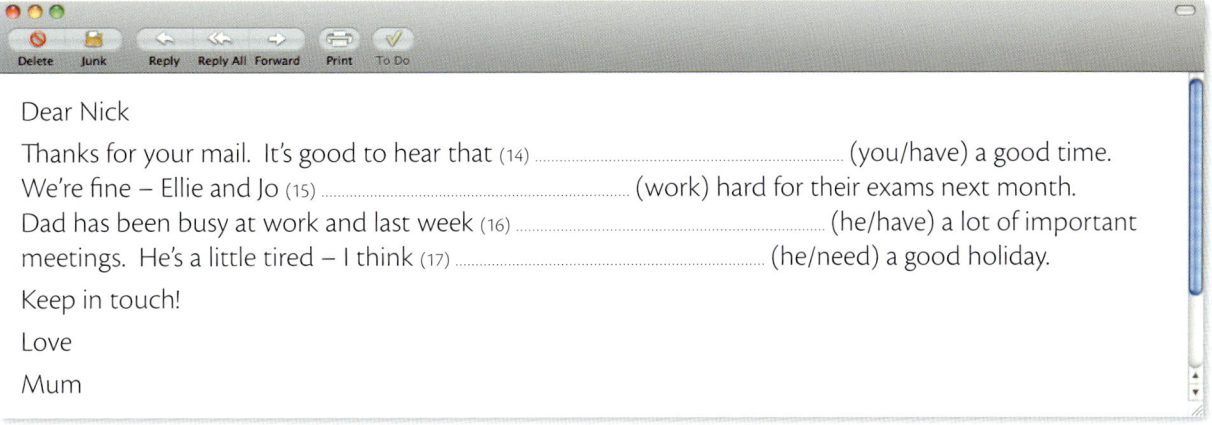

Dear Nick

Thanks for your mail. It's good to hear that (14) .... (you/have) a good time. We're fine – Ellie and Jo (15) .... (work) hard for their exams next month. Dad has been busy at work and last week (16) .... (he/have) a lot of important meetings. He's a little tired – I think (17) .... (he/need) a good holiday.

Keep in touch!

Love

Mum

Einen Monat später …

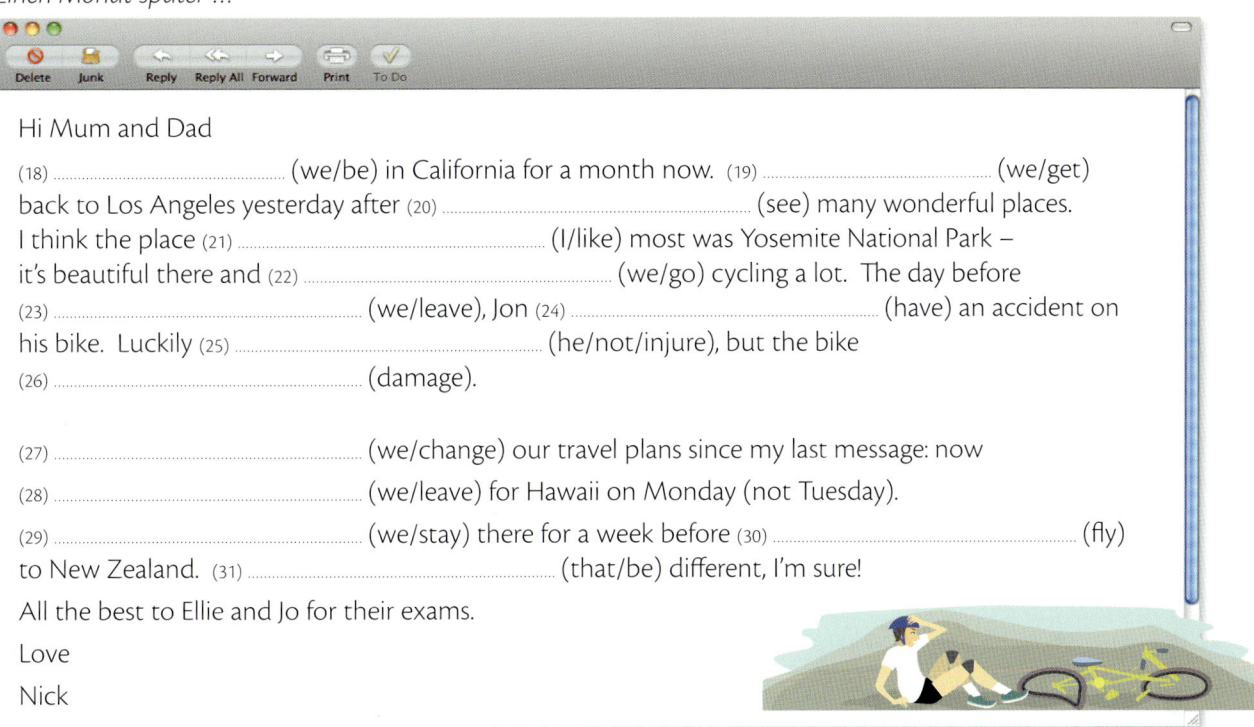

Hi Mum and Dad

(18) .... (we/be) in California for a month now. (19) .... (we/get) back to Los Angeles yesterday after (20) .... (see) many wonderful places. I think the place (21) .... (I/like) most was Yosemite National Park – it's beautiful there and (22) .... (we/go) cycling a lot. The day before (23) .... (we/leave), Jon (24) .... (have) an accident on his bike. Luckily (25) .... (he/not/injure), but the bike (26) .... (damage).

(27) .... (we/change) our travel plans since my last message: now (28) .... (we/leave) for Hawaii on Monday (not Tuesday). (29) .... (we/stay) there for a week before (30) .... (fly) to New Zealand. (31) .... (that/be) different, I'm sure!

All the best to Ellie and Jo for their exams.

Love

Nick

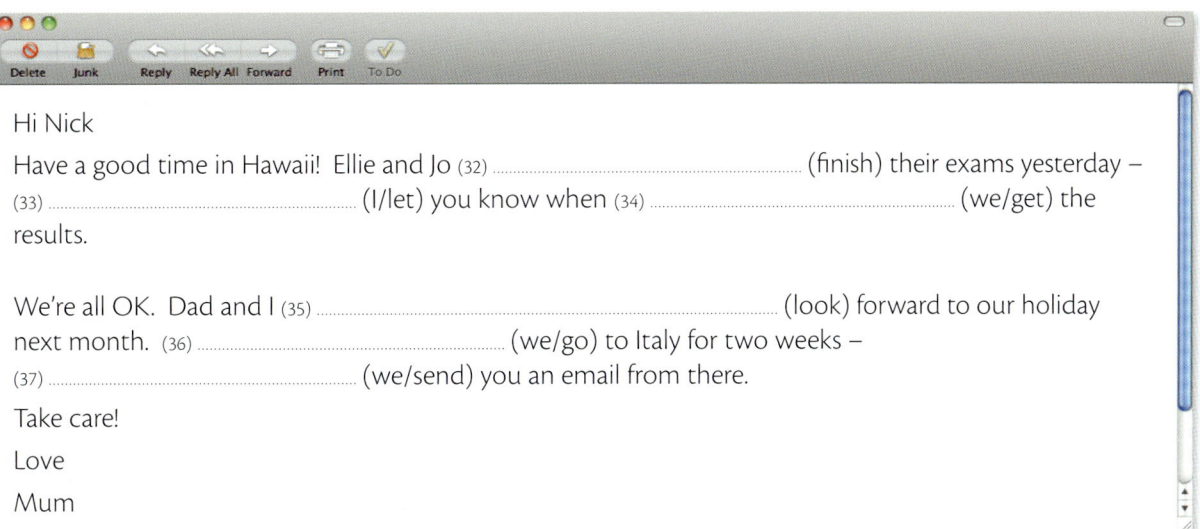

Hi Nick

Have a good time in Hawaii! Ellie and Jo (32) .... (finish) their exams yesterday – (33) .... (I/let) you know when (34) .... (we/get) the results.

We're all OK. Dad and I (35) .... (look) forward to our holiday next month. (36) .... (we/go) to Italy for two weeks – (37) .... (we/send) you an email from there.

Take care!

Love

Mum

Zusätzliche Übungen

-ing und Infinitiv
Units 52–56, 105, 112

32 Was ist richtig: A, B oder C?

1 Don't forget ...to switch (B)... off the light before you go out.
   A switch   **B** to switch   **C** switching

2 It's late. I must .... now.
   A go   **B** to go   **C** going

3 I'm sorry, but I don't have time .... to you now.
   A for talking   **B** to talk   **C** talking

4 Gary is always in the kitchen. He enjoys ....
   A cook   **B** to cook   **C** cooking

5 We've decided .... away for a few days.
   A go   **B** to go   **C** going

6 You're making too much noise. Can you please stop .... ?
   A shout   **B** to shout   **C** shouting

7 Would you like .... and eat with us on Sunday?
   A come   **B** to come   **C** coming

8 That bag is too heavy for you. Let me .... you.
   A help   **B** to help   **C** helping

9 There's a swimming pool near my house. I go .... every day.
   A to swim   **B** to swimming   **C** swimming

10 I need to go shopping .... some food.
   A to buy   **B** for buy   **C** for buying

11 I'd love .... a car like yours.
   A have   **B** to have   **C** having

12 Could you .... me with this bag, please?
   A help   **B** to help   **C** helping

13 I don't mind .... here, but I'd prefer to sit by the window.
   A sit   **B** to sit   **C** sitting

14 Do you want .... you?
   A that I help   **B** me to help   **C** me helping

15 You should think carefully before .... an important decision.
   A make   **B** to make   **C** making

16 I wasn't feeling very well, but the medicine made me .... better.
   A feel   **B** to feel   **C** feeling

17 Shall I phone the restaurant .... a table?
   A for reserve   **B** for reserving   **C** to reserve

18 Tom looked at me without .... anything.
   A say   **B** saying   **C** to say

Zusätzliche Übungen

a und the — Units 66, 70–73

33 Ergänzen Sie die Sprechblasen anhand der Situationen in den Bildern.

Zusätzliche Übungen

34 Setzen Sie bei Bedarf **a/an** oder **the** ein. Wenn **a/an/the** nicht erforderlich sind, lassen Sie die Lücke frei **–**.

1. Who is ...*the*... best player in your team?
2. I don't watch ...*–*... TV very often.
3. 'Is there ...*a*... bank near here?' 'Yes, at ...*the*... end of this street.'
4. I can't ride .... horse.
5. .... sky is very clear tonight.
6. Do you live here, or are you .... tourist?
7. What did you have for .... lunch?
8. Who was .... first President of .... United States?
9. I'm not feeling very good. I've got .... headache.
10. I'm sorry, but I've forgotten your name. I can never remember .... names.
11. What time is .... next train to London?
12. Kate doesn't often send .... emails. She prefers to call people.
13. 'Where's Sue?' 'She's in .... garden.'
14. Excuse me, I'm looking for .... Majestic Hotel. Is it near here?
15. Gary was ill .... last week, so he didn't go to .... work.
16. Everest is .... highest mountain in .... world.
17. I usually listen to .... radio while I'm having .... breakfast.
18. I like .... sport. My favourite sport is .... basketball.
19. Emily is .... doctor. Her husband is .... art teacher.
20. My apartment is on .... second floor. Turn left at .... top of .... stairs, and it's on .... right.
21. After .... dinner, we watched .... TV.
22. Last year we had .... wonderful holiday in .... south of .... France.

Präpositionen
Units 103–108, 111

35 Setzen Sie eine Präposition ein (**in**/**for**/**by** usw.).

1. Helen is studying law ...*at*... university.
2. What is the longest river .... Europe?
3. Is there anything .... TV this evening?
4. We arrived .... the hotel after midnight.
5. 'Where's Mark?' 'He's .... holiday.'
6. Tom hasn't got up yet. He's still .... bed.
7. Lisa is away. She's been away .... Monday.
8. The next meeting is .... 15 April.
9. I usually go to work .... car.
10. There's too much sugar .... my coffee.
11. Joe lived in London .... six months. He didn't like it very much.
12. Were there a lot of people .... the party?
13. What are you doing .... the moment? Are you working?
14. I don't know any of the people .... this photo.
15. The train was very slow. It stopped .... every station.
16. I like this room. I like the pictures .... the walls.
17. 'Did you buy that picture?' 'No, it was given to me .... a friend of mine.'
18. I'm going away .... a few days. I'll be back .... Thursday.
19. Silvia has gone .... Italy. She's .... Milan at the moment.
20. Emma left school .... sixteen and got a job .... a shop.

Lernhilfe

Wenn Sie unsicher sind, welche Units relevant für Sie sind, verwenden Sie diese Lernhilfe.

Entscheiden Sie, welche Alternative (A, B, C usw.) richtig ist. MANCHMAL IST MEHR ALS EINE ALTERNATIVE MÖGLICH.

Wenn Sie nicht wissen bzw. unsicher sind, welche Alternativen richtig sind, sehen Sie sich die rechts aufgelistete(n) Unit(s) an. Sie finden den korrekten Satz in der jeweiligen Unit.

Den Schlüssel zu dieser Lernhilfe finden Sie auf Seite 314.

WENN SIE UNSICHER SIND, WAS RICHTIG IST	STUDIEREN SIE DIE FOLGENDEN UNITS

Gegenwart

1.1 My name is Lisa. .... a student.   **1**
    A I be   **B** I am   **C** I'm   **D** I is

1.2 '....................?' 'No, she's out.'   **2**
    A Is at home your mother   **B** Does your mother at home
    C Is your mother at home   **D** Are your mother at home

1.3 Jenny .... in music.   **3**
    A isn't very interested   **B** not very interested
    C doesn't very interested   **D** doesn't very interest

1.4 The children **3**
    A have thirst   **B** have thirsty   **C** is thirsty   **D** are thirsty

1.5 .... scared of dogs?   **3**
    A Are you   **B** Have you   **C** Do you   **D** You are

1.6 Look, there's Sarah. .... a brown coat.   **4, 24**
    A She wearing   **B** She has wearing   **C** She is wearing   **D** She's wearing

1.7 You can turn off the television. .... it.   **4, 24**
    A I'm not watch   **B** I'm not watching   **C** I not watching   **D** I don't watching

1.8 '.................... today?' 'No, he's at home.'   **5, 24**
    A Is working Ben   **B** Is work Ben   **C** Is Ben work   **D** Is Ben working

1.9 Look, there's Emily! **5, 24**
    A Where she is going?   **B** Where she go?   **C** Where's she going?   **D** Where she going?

1.10 The earth .... round the sun.   **6, 24**
    A going   **B** go   **C** goes   **D** does go   **E** is go

1.11 We .... away at weekends.   **6, 24,**
    A often go   **B** go often   **C** often going   **D** are often go

1.12 We .... TV very often.   **7, 24**
    A not watch   **B** doesn't watch   **C** don't watch   **D** don't watching   **E** watch not

1.13 '.................... the guitar?' 'Yes, but I'm not very good.'   **8, 24**
    A Do you play   **B** Are you play   **C** Does you play   **D** Do you playing   **E** Play you

1.14 I don't understand this sentence. What ....?   **8, 24**
    A mean this word   **B** means this word   **C** does mean this word
    D does this word mean   **E** this word means

1.15 Please be quiet. **9, 24**
    A I working.   **B** I work.   **C** I'm working.   **D** I'm work.

1.16 Tom .... a shower every morning.   **9, 59**
    A has   **B** having   **C** is having   **D** have

271

Lernhilfe

WENN SIE UNSICHER SIND, WAS RICHTIG IST — **STUDIEREN SIE DIE FOLGENDEN UNITS**

1.17 What .... at weekends?
 A do you usually   B are you usually doing   C are you usually do
 D do you usually do   E you do usually — 9, 24

1.18 Sarah isn't feeling well. .... a headache.
 A She have   B She have got   C She has   D She's got — 10, 59

1.19 They .... any children.
 A don't have   B doesn't have   C no have   D haven't got   E hasn't got — 10, 59

Vergangenheit

2.1 The weather .... last week.
 A is good   B was good   C were good   D good   E had good — 11

2.2 Why .... late this morning?
 A you was   B did you   C was you   D you were   E were you — 11

2.3 Terry .... in a bank from 2005 to 2011.
 A work   B working   C works   D worked   E was work — 12

2.4 Caroline .... to the cinema three times last week.
 A go   B went   C goes   D got   E was — 12

2.5 I .... TV yesterday.
 A didn't watch   B didn't watched   C wasn't watched   D don't watch
 E didn't watching — 13, 24

2.6 'How ....?' 'I don't know. I didn't see it.'
 A happened the accident   B did happen the accident   C does the accident happen
 D did the accident happen   E the accident happened — 13

2.7 What .... at 11.30 yesterday?
 A were you doing   B was you doing   C you were doing
 D were you do   E you was doing — 14

2.8 Jack was reading a book when his phone ....
 A ringing   B ring   C rang   D was ringing   E was ring — 15

2.9 .... television when I phoned you?
 A Watched you   B Did you watch   C Were you watching   D Watching you — 15

Present perfect

3.1 'Where's Rebecca?' '.......... to bed.'
 A She is gone   B She has gone   C She goes   D She have gone   E She's gone — 16

3.2 'Are Laura and Paul here?' 'No, they ....'
 A don't arrive yet   B have already arrived   C haven't already arrived
 D haven't arrived yet — 17

3.3 My sister .... by plane.
 A has never travel   B has never travelled   C is never travelled
 D has never been travelled   E have never travelled — 18, 24

3.4 .... that woman before, but I can't remember where.
 A I see   B I seen   C I've saw   D I've seen   E I've seeing — 18, 24

3.5 'How long .... married?' 'Since 2007.'
 A you are   B you have been   C has you been   D are you   E have you been — 19

3.6 'Do you know Lisa?' 'Yes, ... her for a long time.'
 A I knew   B I've known   C I know   D I am knowing — 19

272

Lernhilfe

| WENN SIE UNSICHER SIND, WAS RICHTIG IST | STUDIEREN SIE DIE FOLGENDEN UNITS |

3.7 Richard has been in Canada 20, 104
     A for six months   **B** since six months   **C** six months ago   **D** in six months

3.8 'When did Tom go out?' '............ .'   20
     A For ten minutes.   **B** Since ten minutes   **C** Ten minutes ago.   **D** In ten minutes.

3.9 We .... a holiday last year.   21
     A don't have   **B** haven't had   **C** hasn't had   **D** didn't have   **E** didn't had

3.10 Where .... on Sunday afternoon? I couldn't find you.   21
     A you were   **B** you have been   **C** was you   **D** have you been   **E** were you

Passiv

4.1 This house .... 100 years ago.   22, 24
     A is built   **B** is building   **C** was building   **D** was built   **E** built

4.2 We .... to the party last week.   22, 24
     A didn't invite   **B** didn't invited   **C** weren't invited   **D** wasn't invited
     E haven't been invited

4.3 'Where .... born?' 'In Cairo.'   22
     A you are   **B** you were   **C** was you   **D** are you   **E** were you

4.4 My car is at the garage. It   23
     A is being repaired   **B** is repairing   **C** have been repaired   **D** repaired   **E** repairs

4.5 I can't find my keys. I think   23
     A they've been stolen   **B** they are stolen   **C** they've stolen   **D** they're being stolen

Verbformen

5.1 It .... , so we didn't need an umbrella.   24
     A wasn't rained   **B** wasn't rain   **C** didn't raining   **D** wasn't raining

5.2 Somebody .... this window.   25
     A has broke   **B** has broken   **C** has breaked   **D** has break

Zukunft

6.1 Andrew .... tennis tomorrow.   26
     A is playing   **B** play   **C** plays   **D** is play

6.2 .... out tonight?   26
     A Are you going   **B** Are you go   **C** Do you go   **D** Go you   **E** Do you going

6.3 'What time is the concert tonight?' 'It .... at 7.30.'   26
     A is start   **B** is starting   **C** starts   **D** start   **E** starting

6.4 What .... to the wedding next week?   27
     A are you wearing   **B** are you going to wear   **C** do you wear   **D** you are going to wear

6.5 I think Kelly .... the exam.   28
     A passes   **B** will pass   **C** will be pass   **D** will passing

6.6 .... to the cinema on Saturday. Do you want to come with us?   28
     A We go   **B** We'll go   **C** We're going   **D** We will going

6.7 '............ you tomorrow, OK?' 'OK, bye.'   29
     A I phone   **B** I phoning   **C** I'm phoning   **D** I'll phone

6.8 .... tomorrow, so I can't meet you.   29
     A I work   **B** I'll work   **C** I'm working   **D** I'll working

6.9 It's a nice day. .... for a walk?   29
     A Do we go   **B** Shall we go   **C** Are we go   **D** We go   **E** Go we

Lernhilfe

WENN SIE UNSICHER SIND, WAS RICHTIG IST	STUDIEREN SIE DIE FOLGENDEN UNITS

Modale Hilfsverben, Imperativ usw.

7.1 .... to the cinema this evening, but I'm not sure. — 30
   A I'll go   B I'm going   C I may go   D I might go

7.2 '............... here?' 'Yes, of course.' — 30, 31
   A Can I sit   B Do I sit   C May I sit   D Can I to sit

7.3 I'm having a party next week, but Paul and Rachel .... — 31
   A can't come   B can't to come   C can't coming   D couldn't come

7.4 Before Maria came to Britain, she .... understand much English. — 31
   A can   B can't   C not   D couldn't   E doesn't

7.5 We .... walk home last night. There were no buses. — 32, 34
   A have to   B had to   C must   D must to   E must have

7.6 I .... go yet. I can stay a little longer. — 32
   A must   B mustn't   C must not   D don't need   E don't need to

7.7 It's a good film. You .... go and see it. — 33
   A should to   B ought to   C ought   D should   E need

7.8 What time .... go to the dentist tomorrow? — 34
   A you must   B you have to   C have you to   D do you have to

7.9 We .... wait long for the bus – it came in a few minutes. — 34
   A don't have to   B hadn't to   C didn't have to   D didn't had to   E mustn't

7.10 '............... some coffee?' 'No, thank you.' — 35
   A Are you liking   B You like   C Would you like   D Do you like

7.11 Please .... Stay here with me. — 36
   A don't go   B you no go   C go not   D you don't go

7.12 Dave .... in a factory. Now he works in a supermarket. — 37
   A working   B works   C worked   D use to work   E used to work

There und it

8.1 Excuse me, ... a hotel near here? — 38
   A has there   B is there   C there is   D is it

8.2 .... a lot of accidents on this road. It's very dangerous. — 38
   A Have   B It has   C There have   D They are   E There are

8.3 I was hungry when I got home, but .... anything to eat. — 39
   A there wasn't   B there weren't   C it wasn't   D there hasn't been

8.4 .... three kilometres from our house to the city centre. — 40
   A It's   B It has   C There is   D There are

8.5 .... very often? — 40
   A Snows it   B Does it snow   C Is it snow   D It snows

Hilfsverben

9.1 I haven't got a car, but my sister .... — 41
   A have   B is   C has   D hasn't   E has got

9.2 I don't like hot weather, but Sue .... — 41
   A does   B doesn't   C do   D does like   E likes

9.3 'Nicola got married last week.' '............... Really?' — 42
   A Is she?   B Got she?   C Did she?   D Has she?

274

Lernhilfe

| WENN SIE UNSICHER SIND, WAS RICHTIG IST | STUDIEREN SIE DIE FOLGENDEN UNITS |

9.4   You haven't met my mother, ... ?   **42**
      A haven't you   **B** have you   **C** did you   **D** you have   **E** you haven't

9.5   Ben doesn't watch TV. He doesn't read newspapers **43**
      A too   **B** either   **C** neither   **D** never

9.6   'I'd like to go to Australia.' '...................'   **43**
      A So do I.   **B** So am I.   **C** So would I.   **D** Neither do I.   **E** So I would.

9.7   Sue .... much at weekends.   **44**
      A don't   **B** doesn't   **C** don't do   **D** doesn't do

Fragen

10.1   'When .... ?' 'I'm not sure.'   **45**
      A will they here be   **B** they will be here   **C** they here will be   **D** will they be here

10.2   'I broke my finger last week.' 'How .... that?'   **45**
      A did you   **B** you did   **C** you did do   **D** did you do

10.3   Why .... me last night? I was waiting for you to phone.   **45**
      A didn't you phone   **B** you not phone   **C** you don't phone   **D** you didn't phone

10.4   'Who .... in this house?' 'I don't know.'   **46**
      A lives   **B** does live   **C** does lives   **D** living

10.5   What .... when you told him the story?   **46**
      A said Paul   **B** did Paul say   **C** Paul said   **D** did Paul said

10.6   'Tom's father is in hospital.' '...................'   **47**
      A In which hospital he is?   **B** In which hospital he is in?
      C Which hospital he is in?   **D** Which hospital is he in?

10.7   Did you have a good holiday? **47**
      A How was the weather like?   **B** What was the weather like?
      C What the weather was like?   **D** Was the weather like?

10.8   .... taller – Joe or Gary?   **48**
      A Who is   **B** What is   **C** Which is   **D** Who has

10.9   There are four umbrellas here. .... is yours?   **48, 75**
      A What   **B** Who   **C** Which   **D** How   **E** Which one

10.10   How long .... to cross the Atlantic by ship?   **49**
      A is it   **B** does it need   **C** does it take   **D** does it want

10.11   I don't remember what .... at the party.   **50**
      A Kate was wearing   **B** was wearing Kate   **C** was Kate wearing

10.12   'Do you know .... ?' 'Yes, I think so.'   **50**
      A if Jack is at home   **B** is Jack at home   **C** whether Jack is at home
      D that Jack is at home

Die indirekte Rede

11.1   I saw Steve a week ago. He said that .... me, but he didn't.   **51**
      A he phone   **B** he phones   **C** he'll phone   **D** he's going to phone
      E he would phone

11.2   'Why did Tim go to bed so early?' 'He ....'   **51**
      A said he was tired   **B** said that he was tired   **C** said me he was tired
      D told me he was tired   **E** told that he was tired

Lernhilfe

WENN SIE UNSICHER SIND, WAS RICHTIG IST — **STUDIEREN SIE DIE FOLGENDEN UNITS**

-ing und to ...

12.1 You shouldn't .... so hard. — 52
 A working B work C to work D worked

12.2 It's late. I .... now. — 52
 A must to go B have go C have to going D have to go

12.3 Tina has decided .... her car. — 53
 A sell B to sell C selling D to selling

12.4 I don't mind .... early. — 53
 A get up B to get up C getting up D to getting up

12.5 Do you like .... early? — 53
 A get up B to get up C getting up D to getting up

12.6 Do you want .... you some money? — 54
 A me lend B me lending C me to lend D that I lend

12.7 He's very funny. He makes .... — 54
 A me laugh B me laughing C me to laugh D that I laugh

12.8 Paula went to the shop .... a newspaper. — 55
 A for get B for to get C for getting D to get E get

Go, get, do, make und have

13.1 It's a nice day. Let's go .... — 56
 A for a swim B on a swim C to swimming D swimming

13.2 I'm sorry your mother is ill. I hope she .... better soon. — 57
 A has B makes C gets D goes

13.3 Kate .... the car and drove away. — 57
 A went into B went in C got in D got into

13.4 'Shall I open the window?' 'No, it's OK. I'll .... it.' — 58
 A do B make C get D open

13.5 I'm sorry, I .... a mistake. — 58
 A did B made C got D had

13.6 '.................. a good time in Tokyo?' 'Yes, it was great.' — 59
 A Have you B Had you C Do you have D Did you have

Pronomen und Possessivbegleiter

14.1 I don't want this book. You can have .... — 60, 63
 A it B them C her D him

14.2 Sue and Kevin are going to the cinema. Do you want to go with .... ? — 60, 63
 A her B they C them D him

14.3 I know Amy, but I don't know .... husband. — 61, 63
 A their B his C she D her

14.4 Oxford is famous for .... university. — 61
 A his B its C it's D their

14.5 I didn't have an umbrella, so Sarah gave me .... — 62, 63
 A her B hers C her umbrella D she's

14.6 I went out to meet a friend of .... — 62, 63
 A mine B my C me D I E myself

276

Lernhilfe

	WENN SIE UNSICHER SIND, WAS RICHTIG IST	STUDIEREN SIE DIE FOLGENDEN UNITS
14.7	We had a good holiday. We enjoyed .... **A** us **B** our **C** ours **D** ourself **E** ourselves	64
14.8	Kate and Helen are good friends. They know .... well. **A** each other **B** them **C** themselves **D** theirselves	64
14.9	Have you met .... ? **A** the wife of Mr Black **B** Mr Black wife **C** the wife Mr Black **D** Mr Black's wife **E** the Mr Black's wife	65
14.10	Have you seen .... ? **A** the car of my parents **B** my parent's car **C** my parents' car **D** my parents car	65

A *und* the

15.1	I'm going to buy .... **A** hat and umbrella **B** a hat and a umbrella **C** a hat and an umbrella **D** an hat and an umbrella	66, 68
15.2	'What's your job?' '............' **A** I dentist. **B** I'm a dentist. **C** I'm dentist. **D** I do dentist.	66
15.3	I'm going shopping. I need .... **A** some new jeans **B** a new jeans **C** a new pair of jeans **D** a new pair jeans	67
15.4	I like the people here. .... very friendly. **A** She is **B** They are **C** They is **D** It is **E** He is	67
15.5	We can't get into the house without .... **A** some key **B** a key **C** key	68
15.6	Where can I get .... about hotels here? **A** some information **B** some informations **C** an information	69
15.7	The table is .... **A** in middle of the room **B** in middle of room **C** in the middle of the room **D** middle in room	70
15.8	Paula is learning to .... **A** play the piano **B** play piano **C** play a piano	70
15.9	What did you have for .... ? **A** the breakfast **B** breakfast **C** a breakfast	70
15.10	I finish .... at 5 o'clock every day. **A** the work **B** work **C** a work	71
15.11	I'm tired. I'm going .... **A** in bed **B** in the bed **C** to a bed **D** to the bed **E** to bed	71
15.12	We don't eat .... **A** the meat **B** some meat **C** a meat **D** meat	72
15.13	I was in .... last summer. **A** the Turkey **B** Turkey	73
15.14	My friends are staying at .... **A** the Regent Hotel **B** Regent Hotel	73

Bestimmungswörter und Pronomen

16.1	'I'm going on holiday next week.' 'Oh, ... nice.' **A** it's **B** this is **C** that's	74

277

Lernhilfe

WENN SIE UNSICHER SIND, WAS RICHTIG IST — **STUDIEREN SIE DIE FOLGENDEN UNITS**

			Units
16.2	'Is there a bank near here?' 'Yes, there's .... at the end of this street.' **A** some **B** it **C** one **D** a one		75
16.3	This cup is dirty. Can I have .... ? **A** clean one **B** a clean one **C** clean **D** a clean		75
16.4	I'm going shopping. I'm going to buy .... clothes. **A** any **B** some		76
16.5	'Where's your luggage?' 'I don't have ....' **A** one **B** some **C** any		76
16.6	Tracey and Jack .... **A** have no children **B** don't have no children **C** don't have any children **D** have any children		76, 77
16.7	'How much money do you have?' '............ ' **A** No. **B** No-one. **C** Any. **D** None.		77
16.8	There is .... in the room. It's empty. **A** anybody **B** nobody **C** anyone **D** no-one		78, 79
16.9	'What did you say?' '............ ' **A** Nothing. **B** Nobody. **C** Anything. **D** Not anything.		78, 79
16.10	I'm hungry. I want .... **A** something for eat **B** something to eat **C** something for eating		79
16.11	Ben watches TV for about two hours .... **A** all evening **B** all evenings **C** all the evenings **D** every evenings **E** every evening		80
16.12	.... friends. **A** Everybody need **B** Everybody needs **C** Everyone need **D** Everyone needs		80
16.13	.... children like playing. **A** Most **B** The most **C** Most of **D** The most of		81
16.14	I like .... those pictures. **A** both **B** both of **C** either **D** either of		82
16.15	I haven't read .... these books. **A** neither **B** neither of **C** either **D** either of		82
16.16	Do you have .... friends? **A** a lot of **B** much **C** many **D** much of **E** many of		83
16.17	We like films, so we go to the cinema .... **A** a lot of **B** much **C** many **D** a lot		83
16.18	There were .... people in the theatre. It was nearly empty. **A** a little **B** few **C** little **D** a few of		84
16.19	They have .... money, so they're not poor. **A** a little **B** a few **C** few **D** little **E** little of		84

Adjektive und Adverbien

17.1	I don't speak any .... **A** foreign languages **B** languages foreign **C** languages foreigns		85
17.2	He ate his dinner very .... **A** quick **B** quicker **C** quickly		86
17.3	You speak English very .... **A** good **B** fluent **C** well **D** slow		86

Lernhilfe

WENN SIE UNSICHER SIND, WAS RICHTIG IST — **STUDIEREN SIE DIE FOLGENDEN UNITS**

17.4	Helen wants .... **A** a more big car **B** a car more big **C** a car bigger **D** a bigger car	87
17.5	'Do you feel better today?' 'No, I feel ....' **A** good **B** worse **C** more bad **D** more worse	87
17.6	Athens is older .... Rome. **A** as **B** than **C** that **D** of	88
17.7	I can run faster .... **A** than him **B** that he can **C** than he can **D** as he can **E** as he	88
17.8	Tennis isn't .... football. **A** popular as **B** popular than **C** as popular than **D** so popular that **E** as popular as	89
17.9	The weather today is the same .... yesterday. **A** as **B** that **C** than **D** like	89
17.10	The Europa Hotel is .... in the city. **A** the more expensive hotel **B** the most expensive hotel **C** the hotel most expensive **D** the hotel the more expensive **E** the hotel more expensive	90
17.11	The film was very bad. I think it's the .... film I've ever seen. **A** worse **B** baddest **C** most bad **D** worst **E** more worse	90
17.12	Why don't you buy a car? You've got .... **A** enough money **B** money enough **C** enough of money	91
17.13	Is your English .... a conversation? **A** enough good to have **B** good enough for have **C** enough good for **D** good enough to have	91
17.14	I'm .... out. **A** too tired for go **B** too much tired for going **C** too tired to go **D** too much tired to go	92

Satzbau

18.1	Sue .... They're very nice. **A** bought yesterday some new shoes **B** bought some new shoes yesterday **C** yesterday bought some new shoes	93
18.2	.... coffee in the morning. **A** I drink always **B** Always I drink **C** I always drink	94
18.3	.... during the day. **A** They are at home never **B** They are never at home **C** They never are at home **D** Never they are at home	94
18.4	'Where's Emma?' 'She ....' **A** isn't here yet **B** isn't here already **C** isn't here still	95
18.5	I locked the door and I gave .... **A** Sarah the keys **B** to Sarah the keys **C** the keys Sarah **D** the keys to Sarah	96

Konjunktionen und Relativsätze

19.1	I can't talk to you now. I'll talk to you later when .... more time. **A** I'll have **B** I had **C** I have **D** I'm going to have	98
19.2	.... late this evening, don't wait for me. **A** If I'm **B** If I'll be **C** When I'm **D** When I'll be	99

Lernhilfe

	WENN SIE UNSICHER SIND, WAS RICHTIG IST	STUDIEREN SIE DIE FOLGENDEN UNITS
19.3	I don't know the answer. If I _____ the answer, I'd tell you. **A** know **B** would know **C** have known **D** knew	100
19.4	I like this jacket. _____ it if it wasn't so expensive. **A** I buy **B** I'll buy **C** I bought **D** I'd bought **E** I'd buy	100
19.5	Emma lives in a house _____ is 400 years old. **A** who **B** that **C** which **D** it **E** what	101
19.6	The people _____ work in the office are very friendly. **A** who **B** that **C** they **D** which **E** what	101
19.7	Did you find the books _____ ? **A** who you wanted **B** that you wanted **C** what you wanted **D** you wanted **E** you wanted it	102
19.8	I met _____ can speak six languages. **A** a woman who **B** a woman which **C** a woman **D** a woman she	102

Präpositionen

20.1	Bye! I'll see you _____ . **A** until Friday **B** at Friday **C** in Friday **D** on Friday	103
20.2	Hurry! The train leaves _____ five minutes. **A** at **B** on **C** from **D** after **E** in	103
20.3	'How long will you be away?' '_____ Monday.' **A** On **B** To **C** Until **D** Till **E** Since	104
20.4	We played tennis yesterday. We played _____ two hours. **A** in **B** for **C** since **D** during	105
20.5	I always have breakfast before _____ to work. **A** I go **B** go **C** to go **D** going	105
20.6	I met Anna _____ the way to work. **A** in **B** on **C** during **D** at	106
20.7	Write your name _____ the top of the page. **A** at **B** on **C** in **D** to	107
20.8	There are some pictures _____ the wall. **A** at **B** on **C** in **D** to	107
20.9	The office is _____ the first floor. **A** at **B** on **C** in **D** to	107
20.10	I met a lot of people _____ the party. **A** on **B** to **C** in **D** at	108
20.11	I want to go _____ Italy next year. **A** at **B** on **C** in **D** to	108
20.12	What time did you arrive _____ the hotel? **A** at **B** on **C** in **D** to	108
20.13	'Where is David in this picture?' 'He's _____ Ben.' **A** at front of **B** in the front of **C** in front of **D** in front from	109
20.14	I jumped _____ the wall into the garden. **A** on **B** through **C** across **D** over **E** above	110
20.15	Jane isn't at work this week. She's _____ holiday. **A** on **B** in **C** for **D** to **E** at	111

WENN SIE UNSICHER SIND, WAS RICHTIG IST STUDIEREN SIE DIE FOLGENDEN UNITS — **STUDY UNIT**

20.16 Do you like travelling .... ? — 111
 A with train **B** with the train **C** in train **D** on train **E** by train

20.17 I'm not very good .... telling stories. — 112
 A on **B** with **C** at **D** in **E** for

2018 Tom left without .... goodbye. — 112
 A say **B** saying **C** to say **D** that he said

20.19 I have to phone .... today. — 113
 A with my parents **B** to my parents **C** at my parents **D** my parents

20.20 'Do you like eating in restaurants?' 'It depends .... the restaurant.' — 113
 A in **B** at **C** of **D** on **E** over

Phrasal verbs

21.1 The car stopped and a woman got .... — 114
 A off **B** down **C** out **D** out of

21.2 It was cold, so I .... — 115
 A put on my coat **B** put my coat on **C** put the coat on me **D** put me the coat on

21.3 I've got Rachel's keys. I have to .... to her. — 115
 A give back **B** give them back **C** give back them **D** give it back

Schlüssel zu den Übungen

UNIT 1

1.1
2 they're
3 it isn't / it's not
4 that's
5 I'm not
6 you aren't / you're not

1.2
2 'm/am
3 is
4 are
5 's/is
6 are
7 is … are
8 'm/am … is

1.3
2 I'm / I am
3 He's / He is
4 they're / they are
5 It's / It is
6 You're / You are
7 She's / She is
8 Here's / Here is

1.4
Beispiel-Antworten:
1 My name is Robert.
2 I'm from Australia.
3 I'm 25.
4 I'm a gardener.
5 My favourite colours are black and white.
6 I am interested in plants.

1.5
2 He's / He is strong.
3 They're / They are tired.
4 He's / He is sad.
5 She's / She is tall.
6 They're / They are angry.

1.6
2 It's / It is windy today. *oder* It isn't / It's not windy today.
3 My hands are cold. *oder* My hands aren't / are not cold.
4 Brazil is a very big country.
5 Diamonds aren't / are not cheap.
6 Toronto isn't / is not in the US.
8 I'm / I am fit. *oder* I'm not / I am not fit.
9 I'm / I am a good swimmer. *oder* I'm not / I am not a good swimmer.

1.7
1 Claire is French. She's / She is from Paris.
2 Mike is very strong.
3 Your friends are nice.
4 I'm very busy today.
5 We aren't / We're not / We are not married.
6 The children are tired today.
7 I'm/I am a teacher.
8 Tom isn't / is not at home.
9 The street is very noisy.
10 The weather isn't / is not nice today, but it isn't / it's not cold.

UNIT 2

2.1
2 F
3 H
4 C
5 I
6 B
7 A
8 E
9 D

2.2
3 Is your job interesting?
4 Are these seats free?
5 Are you a student?
6 Is the station near here?
7 Are your children at school?
8 Why are you sad?

2.3
2 Where's / Where is
3 How old are
4 What's / What is
5 Who's / Who is
6 What colour are

2.4
2 Are you American?
3 How old are you?
4 Are you a teacher?
5 Are you married?
6 Is your wife a lawyer?
7 Where's / Where is she from?
8 What's / What is her name?
9 How old is she?

2.5
2 Yes, I am. *oder* No, I'm not.
3 Yes, it is. *oder* No, it isn't. / No, it's not.
4 Yes, they are. *oder* No, they aren't. / No, they're not.
5 Yes, it is. *oder* No, it isn't. / No, it's not.
6 Yes, I am. *oder* No, I'm not.

2.6
1 Are you German?
2 Where are we?
3 Is your coat new?
4 Who's / Who is that?
5 Are the children at home?
6 Are you tired?
7 Are your parents at work?
8 What's / What is that?
9 How old are your cats?
10 'Is your mother a teacher?' 'No, she's a doctor.'

UNIT 3

3.1
2 She's / She is thirsty.
3 They're / They are asleep.
4 He's / He is scared.
5 The shop's / The shop is closed.
6 They're / They are hungry.
7 She's / She is in a hurry.
8 They're / They are cold.

3.2
3 they're / they are
4 are you
5 He's / He is
6 are they
7 I'm / I am *oder* we're / we are
8 Is she
9 Are you
10 It's / It is
11 is he

3.3
Beispiel-Antworten:
2 I'm / I am hungry. *oder* I'm not / I am not hungry.
3 I'm / I am in a hurry. *oder* I'm not / I am not in a hurry.
4 I'm / I am scared of dogs. *oder* I'm not / I am not scared of dogs.
5 I'm / I am cold. *oder* I'm not / I am not cold.
6 I'm / I am interested in films. *oder* I'm not / I am not interested in films.
7 I'm / I am thirsty. *oder* I'm not / I am not thirsty.

3.4
1 I'm / I am hot.
2 You're / You are right.
3 Are you hungry?
4 I'm not / I am not afraid of spiders.
5 I'm not / I am not interested in cars.
6 Is the shop open?
7 Where are Paula and Michael from?
8 How's / How is your sister?
9 Am I late?
10 How much are the apples?

UNIT 4

4.1
2 's/is waiting
3 're/are playing
4 He's / He is lying
5 They're / They are having
6 She's / She is sitting

4.2
2 's/is cooking
3 're/are standing
4 's/is swimming
5 're/are staying
6 's/is having
7 're/are building
8 'm/am going

4.3
3 She's / She is sitting on the floor.
4 She isn't / She's not reading a book.
5 She isn't / She's not playing the piano.
6 She's / She is laughing.
7 She's / She is wearing a hat.
8 She isn't / She's not drinking coffee.

4.4
3 I'm sitting on a chair. *oder* I'm not sitting on a chair.
4 I'm eating. *oder* I'm not eating.

Schlüssel zu den Übungen

5 It's raining. *oder* It isn't raining. / It's not raining.
6 I'm learning English.
7 I'm listening to music. *oder* I'm not listening to music.
8 The sun is shining. *oder* The sun isn't shining.
9 I'm wearing shoes *oder* I'm not wearing shoes.
10 I'm not reading a newspaper.

4.5

1 I haven't got / don't have any time now. I'm / I am writing an email.
2 Look at Matt. He's / He is dancing with Steph.
3 I'm / I am having lunch. Are you hungry?
4 She isn't / She's not working; she's / she is watching TV.
5 'Where are Tom and Sue?' 'They're / They are playing tennis.'
6 The sun is shining and we're / we are lying on the beach.
7 The children aren't / are not playing; they're / they are sleeping/ asleep.
8 Jamie is wearing a new tie today.
9 Amy can't/cannot come to the phone/telephone. She's / She is having a bath.

UNIT 5

5.1

2 Are you going now?
3 Is it raining?
4 Are you enjoying the film?
5 Is that clock working?
6 Are you waiting for a bus?

5.2

2 Where is she going?
3 What are you eating?
4 Why are you crying?
5 What are they looking at?
6 Why is he laughing?

5.3

3 Are you listening to me?
4 Where are your friends going?
5 Are your parents watching TV?
6 What is Jessica cooking?
7 Why are you looking at me?
8 Is the bus coming?

5.4

2 Yes, I am. *oder* No, I'm not.
3 Yes, I am. *oder* No, I'm not.
4 Yes, it is. *oder* No, it isn't. / No, it's not.
5 Yes, I am. *oder* No, I'm not.
6 Yes, I am. *oder* No, I'm not.

5.5

1 Is John wearing a tie today?
2 'Is it snowing?' 'No, it's / it is raining.'
3 'What are you doing?' 'I'm / I am thinking.'
4 There's Emily. Where's / Where is she going?

5 Why are they laughing? It/That isn't funny. *oder* It's/That's not funny.
6 Where's / Where is James? Is he working today?
7 A: What are you reading?
   B: A very interesting book.
8 A: Are the children watching TV?
   B: No, they're / they are playing in the garden.

UNIT 6

6.1

2 thinks   5 has
3 flies   6 finishes
4 dances

6.2

2 live   5 They go
3 She eats   6 He sleeps
4 He plays

6.3

2 open   7 costs
3 closes   8 cost
4 teaches   9 boils
5 meet   10 like ... likes
6 washes

6.4

2 I never go to the cinema.
3 Martina always works hard.
4 Children usually like chocolate.
5 Jackie always enjoys parties.
6 I often forget people's names.
7 Sam never watches TV.
8 We usually have dinner at 7.30.
9 Kate always wears nice clothes.

6.5

Beispiel-Antworten:
2 I sometimes read in bed.
3 I often get up before 7 o'clock.
4 I never go to work by bus.
5 I usually drink two cups of coffee in the morning.

6.6

1 I like chocolate.
2 We live in Frankfurt.
3 The bank closes at 3.30.
4 The sun rises early in (the) summer.
5 Sam always watches TV in the evening.
6 Rachel and Mark often go to the cinema.
7 He never does his homework.
8 I usually go by train, but I sometimes go by car. *oder* ... but sometimes I go by car.

UNIT 7

7.1

2 Anna doesn't play the piano very well.
3 They don't know my phone number.
4 We don't work very hard.
5 He doesn't have a bath every day.
6 You don't do the same thing every day.

7.2

1 Kate doesn't like classical music. I like (*oder* I don't like) classical music.
2 Ben and Sophie don't like boxing. Kate likes boxing. I like (*oder* I don't like) boxing.
3 Ben and Sophie like horror movies. Kate doesn't like horror movies. I like (*oder* I don't like) horror movies.

7.3

Beispiel-Antworten:
2 I never go to the theatre.
3 I don't ride a bike very often.
4 I never eat in restaurants.
5 I often travel by train.

7.4

2 doesn't use   5 don't know
3 don't go   6 doesn't cost
4 doesn't wear   7 don't see

7.5

3 don't know   6 don't believe
4 doesn't talk   7 like
5 drinks   8 doesn't eat

7.6

1 I don't / do not know your brother.
2 Ben doesn't / does not get up early on Sundays. *oder* On Sundays Ben doesn't / does not get up early.
3 I don't / do not like that dress very much.
4 We don't / do not go out very often.
5 Jenny likes apples, but she doesn't / does not like bananas.
6 Steve and Amy don't / do not do very much at the weekend.
7 Lisa doesn't / does not play tennis, but she plays squash.

UNIT 8

8.1

2 Do you play tennis?
3 Does Lucy live near here?
4 Do Tom's friends play tennis? / Do they play tennis?
5 Does your brother speak English? / Does he speak English?
6 Do you do yoga every morning?
7 Does Paul go away a lot? / Does he go away a lot? *oder* Does Paul go away much? / Does he go away much?
8 Do you want to be famous?
9 Does Anna work hard? / Does she work hard?

8.2

3 How often do you watch TV?
4 What do you want for dinner?
5 Do you like football?
6 Does your brother like football?
7 What do you do in your free time?
8 Where does your sister work?
9 Do you always have breakfast?
10 What does this word mean?
11 Does it snow here in winter?
12 What time do you usually go to bed?

283

Schlüssel zu den Übungen

13 How much does it cost to phone New York?
14 What do you usually have for breakfast?

8.3
2 Do you enjoy / Do you like
3 do you start
4 Do you work
5 do you go
6 does he do
7 does he teach
8 Does he enjoy / Does he like

8.4
2 Yes, I do. oder No, I don't.
3 Yes, I do. oder No, I don't.
4 Yes, it does. oder No, it doesn't
5 Yes, I do. oder No, I don't.

8.5
1 Do you like my dress?
2 Does he work very much/hard?
3 Do you like fish?
4 Where does Tom live?
5 Does she play the guitar?
6 How often do you go out in the evening/evenings?
7 Do they often go to London?
8 What does your mother do?
9 What do you usually do after work?
10 How much does it cost to rent a car?

UNIT 9

9.1
2 No, she isn't.
  Yes, she does.
  She's playing the piano.
3 Yes, he does.
  Yes, he is.
  He's cleaning a window.
4 No, they aren't.
  Yes, they do.
  They teach.

9.2
2 don't   6 do
3 are   7 does
4 does   8 doesn't
5 's/is … don't

9.3
4 is singing
5 She wants
6 do you use
7 you're sitting
8 I don't understand
9 I'm going … Are you coming
10 does your father finish
11 I'm not listening
12 He's / He is cooking
13 doesn't usually drive … usually walks
14 doesn't like … She prefers

9.4
1 A: What are you doing?
  B: I'm doing my homework.
2 My little son sleeps a lot, but now he's crying.
3 Do you understand what I mean?
4 The children don't want to go to bed.

5 That's / That is impossible. I don't believe it/that.
6 Do you often go to the cinema?
7 A: Are you working?
  B: No, I'm playing a game.
8 'Where are the children?' 'They're / They are playing in the garden.'
9 Jane studies a lot / very hard, but at the moment / now she's playing / is playing with the cat.

UNIT 10

10.1
3 He's got a new job.
4 Have you got an umbrella?
5 We've got a lot of work to do.
6 I haven't got your phone number.
7 Has your father got a car?
8 How much money have we got?

10.2
2 I don't have many clothes.
3 Does Tom have a brother?
4 How many children do they have?
5 Do you have any questions?
6 Sam doesn't have a job.

10.3
2 He's got a bike. oder He has a bike.
3 He hasn't got a dog. oder
  He doesn't have a dog.
4 He's got a mobile phone. oder
  He has a mobile phone.
5 He hasn't got a watch. oder
  He doesn't have a watch.
6 He's got two brothers and a sister. oder He has two brothers and a sister.
  (Beispiel-Antwort)
7 I've got a dog. / I have a dog. oder
  I haven't got a dog. / I don't have a dog.
8 I've got a bike. / I have a bike. oder
  I haven't got a bike. / I don't have a bike.
9 I've got a brother and a sister. oder
  I have a brother and a sister.

10.4
3 has   6 don't have
4 don't have   7 doesn't have
5 have

10.5
2 's got / has got a lot of friends
3 hasn't got a key
4 haven't got much time
5 has got six legs
6 haven't got a job

10.6
1 Tom has / has got a new laptop.
2 We don't have / haven't got a television/TV.
3 How much time do we have / have we got?
4 Does Emily have a bicycle/bike?
  oder Has Emily got a bicycle/bike?
5 A: Do you have / Have you got (any) children?
  B: Yes, we have a girl and a boy. oder
  Yes, we've got a girl and a boy.

6 Kate has / has got three brothers, but she doesn't have / hasn't got (any) sisters.
7 It's / It is a big house, but it has / it's got a small kitchen.

UNIT 11

11.1
2 Jack and Kate were at/in the cinema.
3 Sue was at the station.
4 Mr and Mrs Hall were in/at a restaurant.
5 Ben was on the beach / on a beach / at the seaside.
6 (Beispiel-Antwort) I was at work.

11.2
2 is … was   6 're/are
3 'm/am   7 Was
4 was   8 was
5 were   9 are … were

11.3
2 wasn't … was
3 was … were
4 '**Were** Kate and Ben at the party?'
  'Kate **was** there, but Ben **wasn't**.'
  oder 'Kate **wasn't** there, but Ben **was**.'
5 were
6 weren't … were

11.4
2 Was your exam difficult?
3 Where were Sue and Chris last week?
4 How much was your new camera?
5 Why were you angry yesterday?
6 Was the weather nice last week?

11.5
1 Last night / Yesterday evening I was at a party and today I'm / I am very tired!
2 Ben was in hospital last week, but now he's / he is at work again.
3 Was Jenny at school yesterday?
4 'Where were you last weekend?'
  'We were in the mountains.'
5 Why were you tired this morning?
6 'Where are my brown shoes?'
  'I don't know. Yesterday they were under the table.'
7 When Beth was small/little, she was scared of the dark.

UNIT 12

12.1
2 opened
3 started … finished
4 wanted
5 happened
6 rained
7 enjoyed … stayed
8 died

Schlüssel zu den Übungen

12.2
2 saw
3 played
4 paid
5 visited
6 bought
7 went
8 thought
9 copied
10 knew
11 put
12 spoke

12.3
2 got
3 had
4 left
5 drove
6 got
7 parked
8 walked
9 checked
10 had
11 waited
12 departed
13 arrived
14 took

12.4
2 lost her keys
3 met her friends
4 bought a newspaper
5 went to the cinema
6 ate an orange
7 had a shower
8 came (to see us)

12.5
Beispiel-Antworten:
2 I got up late yesterday.
3 I met some friends at lunchtime.
4 I went to the supermarket.
5 I phoned a lot of people.
6 I lost my keys.

12.6
1 Lisa danced with Tom at the party.
2 When I was a child, I had a dog.
3 My sister worked in France from 2010 to 2012.
4 I usually go away at the weekend, but last weekend I stayed at home.
5 Yesterday Kate and I went to town and I bought a dress.
6 My parents came home late last night.

UNIT 13

13.1
2 didn't work
3 didn't go
4 didn't have
5 didn't do

13.2
2 Did you enjoy the party?
3 Did you have a good holiday?
4 Did you finish work early?
5 Did you sleep well last night?

13.3
2 I got up before 7 o'clock. *oder* I didn't get up before 7 o'clock.
3 I had a shower. *oder* I didn't have a shower.
4 I bought a magazine. *oder* I didn't buy a magazine.
5 I ate meat. *oder* I didn't eat meat.
6 I went to bed before 10.30. *oder* I didn't go to bed before 10.30.

13.4
2 did you arrive
3 Did you win
4 did you go
5 did it cost
6 Did you go to bed late
7 Did you have a nice time
8 did it happen / did that happen

13.5
2 bought
3 Did it rain
4 didn't stay
5 opened
6 didn't have
7 did you do
8 didn't know

13.6
1 Did you see David last week?
2 Lisa didn't phone/call me yesterday.
3 How did you break your arm?
4 We ate in a restaurant yesterday, but we didn't like/enjoy the food.
5 What did the children do yesterday?
6 I didn't have breakfast this morning.
7 A: Did you go to the party last night?
   B: No, we stayed at home.
8 I didn't do very much in/during my holidays.

UNIT 14

14.1
2 Jack and Kate were at the cinema. They were watching a film.
3 Tom was in his car. He was driving.
4 Tracey was at the station. She was waiting for a train.
5 Mr and Mrs Hall were in the park. They were walking.
6 (*Beispiel-Antwort*) I was in a café. I was having a drink with some friends.

14.2
2 she was playing tennis
3 she was reading a/the paper/newspaper
4 she was cooking (lunch)
5 she was having breakfast
6 she was cleaning the kitchen

14.3
2 What were you doing
3 Was it raining
4 Why was Sue driving
5 Was Tom wearing

14.4
2 He was carrying a bag.
3 He wasn't going to the dentist.
4 He was eating an ice cream.
5 He wasn't carrying an umbrella.
6 He wasn't going home.
7 He was wearing a hat.
8 He wasn't riding a bicycle.

14.5
1 At 7.30 I was having a shower.
2 It wasn't snowing this morning.
3 Jenny was wearing a warm coat, but she wasn't wearing a hat.
4 We were playing cards last night at 10 o'clock.
5 The weather was strange this morning. It was raining, but the sun was shining too.
6 Joe is wearing a tie today, but he wasn't wearing one yesterday. *oder* … but yesterday he wasn't …
7 Why was the baby crying at 2 o'clock in the morning?

UNIT 15

15.1
1 happened … was painting … fell
2 arrived … got … were waiting
3 was walking … met … was going … was carrying … stopped

15.2
2 was studying
3 Did Paul call … called … was having
4 didn't go
5 were you driving … stopped … wasn't driving
6 Did your team win … didn't play
7 did you break … were playing … kicked … hit
8 Did you see … was wearing
9 were you doing
10 lost … did you get … climbed

15.3
1 When did your airplane/plane arrive?
2 I was having a shower when my phone/telephone rang.
3 What was Joe doing when you saw him?
4 'How did you break your leg?' 'I fell (over) when/while I was skiing.'
5 I saw Tom and Anna in town / in the city yesterday. They were shopping.
6 Did you see Jenny at the party on Saturday night? She was wearing a very nice/beautiful dress.
7 'What were the children doing when you got home?' 'They were playing.'
8 We were going to bed when we heard a strange noise.

UNIT 16

16.1
2 She has / She's closed the door.
3 They have / They've gone to bed.
4 It has / It's stopped raining.
5 He has / He's had a shower.
6 The picture has fallen down.

16.2
2 've bought / have bought
3 's gone / has gone
4 Have you seen
5 has broken
6 've told / have told
7 has taken
8 haven't seen
9 has she gone
10 've forgotten / have forgotten
11 's invited / has invited
12 Have you decided
13 haven't told
14 've finished / have finished

285

Schlüssel zu den Übungen

16.3
1. Laura has bought a new phone.
2. I've / I have lost my handbag!
3. Have you cleaned/brushed your teeth?
4. You haven't drunk your milk.
5. 'Where is / Where's Rachel?' 'She's / She has gone to work.'
6. I'm sorry. I've / I have broken the glass.
7. Has the train arrived?
8. The car is dirty. We haven't washed it.
9. A: Where are the children?
   B: They've / They have gone to bed.

UNIT 17

17.1
2. He's / He has just got up.
3. They've / They have just bought a car.
4. The race has just started.

17.2
2. they've / they have already seen it.
3. I've / I have already phoned him.
4. He's / He has already gone (away).
5. I've / I have already read it.
6. She's / She has already started (it).

17.3
2. The bus has just gone.
3. The train hasn't left yet.
4. He hasn't opened it yet.
5. They've / They have just finished their dinner.
6. It's / It has just stopped raining.

17.4
2. Have you met your new neighbours yet?
3. Have you paid your electricity bill yet?
4. Has Tom/he sold his car yet?

17.5
1. A: Would you like a cup of coffee?
   B: No thank you / No thanks. I've / I have just had/drunk a coffee.
2. A: Don't forget to close the window.
   B: I've / I have already done it.
3. The plane hasn't / has not arrived yet.
4. It's / It is a beautiful day. Have you been outside yet?
5. Have you cleaned your room yet?
6. 'Where's the bus?'   'It's / It has already left.'

UNIT 18

18.1
3. Have you ever been to Australia?
4. Have you ever lost your passport?
5. Have you ever flown in a helicopter?
6. Have you ever won a race?
7. Have you ever been to New York?
8. Have you ever driven a bus?
9. Have you ever broken your leg?

18.2
Helen:
2. She's / She has been to Australia once.
3. She's / She has never won a race.
4. She's / She has flown in a helicopter a few times.

Sie (Beispiel-Antworten):
5. I've / I have never been to New York.
6. I've / I have played tennis many times.
7. I've / I have never driven a lorry.
8. I've / I have been late for work a few times.

18.3
2. I've never met / I have never met
3. he's read / he has read
4. Have you ever written
5. I haven't been to China … my brother has been
6. They've visited / They have visited

18.4
2–6
She's / She has done a lot of interesting things.
She's / She has travelled all over the world. oder She's / She has been all over the world.
She's / She has been married three times.
She's / She has written ten books.
She's / She has met a lot of interesting people.

18.5
1. I've seen that/this film three times.
2. 'Have you ever been to Ireland?' 'Yes, many times.'
3. A: Have you ever eaten Mexican food?
   B: No, never.
4. My brother has never been to the USA.
5. We've / We have never visited him.
6. 'How many times / How often has he seen her?'   'Only once.'
7. Has he ever been married?
8. Sarah and Michael have been to Las Vegas three times.

UNIT 19

19.1
3. have been
4. has been
5. have lived / have been living
6. has worked / has been working
7. has had
8. have been learning

19.2
2. How long have they been there? oder … been in Brazil?
3. How long have you known her? oder … known Amy?
4. How long has she been learning Italian?
5. How long has he lived in Canada? / How long has he been living …?
6. How long have you been a teacher?
7. How long has it been raining?

19.3
2. She has lived in Wales all her life.
3. They have been on holiday since Sunday.
4. The sun has been shining all day.
5. She has been waiting for ten minutes.
6. He has had a beard since he was 20.

19.4
2. I know
3. I've known
4. have you been waiting
5. works
6. She has been reading
7. have you lived
8. I've had
9. is … He has been

19.5
1. A: Anna is in England now.
   B: How long has she been there?
2. A: My brother lives in Hamburg.
   B: How long has he lived there? oder How long has he been living there?
3. A: How long have you known John?
   B: I've / I have known him for 10 years.
4. Jenny has had a new car since May.
5. A: Where's / Where is Helen?
   B: I don't know. We've / We have been waiting for her for 20 minutes.
6. How long have you been learning English?
7. It's / It has been raining for a week.

UNIT 20

20.1
3. for
4. since
5. since
6. for
7. for
8. for … since

20.2
Beispiel-Antworten:
2. A year ago.
3. A few weeks ago.
4. Two hours ago.
5. Six months ago.

20.3
3. for 20 years
4. 20 years ago
5. an hour ago
6. a few days ago
7. for six months
8. for a long time

20.4
2. Jack has been here since Tuesday.
3. It's been raining for an hour.
4. I've known Sue since 2008.
5. Claire and Matt have been married for six months.
6. Laura has been studying medicine (at university) for three years.
7. David has played / David has been playing the piano since he was seven years old.

Schlüssel zu den Übungen

20.5
Beispiel-Antworten:
1 I've lived in … all my life.
2 I've been in the same job for ten years.
3 I've been learning English for six months.
4 I've known Chris for a long time.
5 I've had a headache since I got up this morning.

20.6
1 I've / I have been at home since 5 o'clock.
2 John has been in Australia for two weeks.
3 We came to Germany three years ago.
4 James and Ali left five minutes ago.
5 Hannah has been ill/sick since Thursday.
6 A: How long have you lived / been living in Boston?
   B: Since 2010.
7 I have known Ben for three months.
8 A: When did the train arrive?
   B: An/One hour ago.

UNIT 21

21.1
2 I started (it)   4 she went (away)
3 they arrived   5 I wore it

21.2
3 I finished
4 OK
5 did you finish
6 OK
7 (Steve's grandmother) died
8 Where were you / Where did you go

21.3
3 played
4 did you go
5 Have you ever met
6 wasn't
7 's/has visited
8 switched
9 lived
10 haven't been

21.4
1 Did you have
  was
2 Have you seen went
  haven't seen
3 has worked / has been working
  was worked
  didn't enjoy
4 've/have seen
  've/have never spoken
  Have you ever spoken
  met

21.5
1 Jane arrived last night / yesterday evening.
2 'Where's / Where is John?' 'He's / He has gone to the supermarket.'
3 We have been living / have lived in New York for six months.
4 I studied in London from 2010 to 2012.
5 Has your son ever been to the USA?
6 What did you do last weekend?
7 A: When did you have breakfast?
   B: Three hours ago.
8 Have you ever eaten/had lobster?
9 We've / We have (just) cleaned the house.
10 A: That's / That is a nice/beautiful dress.
    B: I bought it yesterday.

UNIT 22

22.1
3 Glass is made from sand.
4 The windows are cleaned every two weeks.
5 This room isn't used very much.
6 Are we allowed to park here?
7 How is this word pronounced?
9 The house was painted last month.
10 My phone was stolen a few days ago.
11 Three people were injured in the accident.
12 When was this bridge built?
13 I wasn't woken up by the noise.
14 How were these windows broken?
15 Were you invited to Jon's party last week?

22.2
2 Football **is played** in most …
3 Why **was the letter sent** to … ?
4 … where films **are made**.
5 Where **were** you born?
6 How many languages **are spoken** … ?
7 … but nothing **was** stolen.
8 When **was** the bicycle **invented**?

22.3
3 is made
4 were damaged
5 was given
6 are shown
7 were invited
8 was made
9 was stolen … was found

22.4
2 Sarah was born in Manchester.
3 Her parents were born in Ireland.
4 I was born in …
5 My mother was born in …

22.5
1 The streets are cleaned every day.
2 The house was damaged in the storm yesterday. *oder* … damaged yesterday in the storm.
3 When was this church built?
4 Two computers were stolen from the office yesterday. *oder* … stolen yesterday from the office.
5 When were your parents born?
6 What/Which languages are spoken in South America?
7 Two men were arrested yesterday by the police. *oder* … arrested by the police yesterday.

UNIT 23

23.1
2 A bridge is being built.
3 The windows are being cleaned.
4 The grass is being cut.

23.2
3 The window **has been** broken.
4 The roof **is being** repaired.
5 The car **has been** damaged.
6 The houses **are being** knocked down.
7 The trees **have been** cut down.
8 They **have been** invited to a party.

23.3
3 has been repaired
4 was repaired
5 are made
6 were they built
7 Is the photocopier being used? (*oder* Is anybody using the photocopier?)
8 are they called
9 were stolen
10 was damaged … hasn't been repaired

23.4
1 'Where's / Where is your bike?' 'It's / It is being repaired.'
2 Dinner is served every evening at 7 o'clock. *oder* … at 7 o'clock every evening.
3 I can't/cannot find my money. I think it's / it has been stolen.
4 A picture was stolen from the museum yesterday. *oder* Yesterday a picture was stolen …
5 Look at the houses! They've / They have been damaged in the storm. *oder* They were damaged …
6 Last week the office wasn't / was not cleaned. *oder* The office wasn't cleaned last week.
7 David is being examined by the doctor.

UNIT 24

24.1
3 are   7 do
4 Does   8 Is
5 Do   9 does
6 Is   10 Are

24.2
2 don't   6 doesn't
3 'm/am not   7 'm/am not
4 isn't   8 aren't / 're not
5 don't

24.3
2 Did   7 were
3 were   8 Has
4 was   9 did
5 Has   10 have
6 did

24.4
2 was   6 've/have
3 Have   7 is
4 are   8 was
5 were   9 has

287

Schlüssel zu den Übungen

24.5
3 eaten
4 enjoying
5 damaged
6 use
7 gone
8 understand
9 listening
10 pronounced
11 open

24.6
1 Look! It's / It is snowing.
2 We didn't / did not go out yesterday afternoon because it was raining.
3 Yoghurt is made from milk.
4 My office wasn't / was not cleaned yesterday.
5 'What are the children doing?' 'They're / They are playing.'
6 I don't / do not go to the theatre very often.
7 Do you like Japanese food?
8 What did you do last weekend?
9 Amy and Steven have bought a new house.
10 Jenny didn't / did not go to work yesterday.
11 Ben has finished his homework and now he's / he is watching TV.
12 Our house was built in 1950.

UNIT 25

25.1
3 got
4 brought
5 paid
6 enjoyed
7 bought
8 sat
9 left
10 happened
11 heard
12 put
13 caught
14 watched
15 understood

25.2
2 began — begun
3 ate — eaten
4 drank — drunk
5 drove — driven
6 spoke — spoken
7 wrote — written
8 came — come
9 knew — known
10 took — taken
11 went — gone
12 gave — given
13 threw — thrown
14 forgot — forgotten
15 ran — run

25.3
3 slept
4 saw
5 rained
6 lost ... seen
7 stolen
8 went
9 finished
10 built
11 learnt/learned
12 ridden
13 known
14 fell ... hurt
15 ran ... run

25.4
2 told
3 won
4 met
5 woken up
6 swam
7 thought
8 spoken
9 cost
10 driven
11 sold
12 flew

25.5
1 I studied English at university.
2 I've / I have made/baked a cake. Would you like a piece?
3 Emma went to the theatre yesterday.
4 'Where's / Where is Joe?' 'He's / He has gone out.'
5 The stairs are cleaned every Thursday.
6 *Romeo and Juliet* was written by William Shakespeare.
7 Lisa is tired. She's / She has driven 500 kilometres today.
8 Where is our car? It's / It has been stolen!
9 I ate and drank a lot at the party. *oder* At the party I ate …

UNIT 26

26.1
2 Richard is going to the cinema.
3 Rachel is meeting Dave.
4 Karen is having lunch with Will.
5 Tom and Sue are going to a party.

26.2
2 Are you working next week?
3 What are you doing tomorrow evening?
4 What time are your friends coming?
5 When is Lisa going on holiday?

26.3
Beispiel-Antworten:
3 I'm going away at the weekend.
4 I'm playing basketball tomorrow.
5 I'm meeting a friend this evening.
6 I'm going to the cinema on Thursday evening.

26.4
3 She's getting
4 are going … are they going
5 finishes
6 I'm not going
7 I'm going … We're meeting
8 are you getting … leaves
9 Are you coming … does the film begin
10 are you doing … I'm working

26.5
1 I'm / I am going to the mountains at the weekend.
2 Tom isn't going to work tomorrow.
3 Are you going to the party tonight?
4 Sarah and Michael are going to Ireland next summer.
5 What time are you coming home tonight?
6 The football match starts at 4 o'clock today.
7 'What are you doing on Friday evening?' 'We're / We are going to the cinema.'
8 What time does your plane arrive tomorrow?

UNIT 27

27.1
2 I'm going to have a bath.
3 I'm going to buy a car.
4 We're going to play football.

27.2
3 'm/am going to walk
4 's/is going to stay
5 'm/am going to eat
6 're/are going to give
7 's/is going to lie down
8 Are you going to watch
9 is Rachel going to do

27.3
2 The shelf is going to fall (down).
3 The car is going to turn (right).
4 He's / He is going to kick the ball.

27.4
Beispiel-Antworten:
1 I'm going to phone Maria this evening.
2 I'm going to get up early tomorrow.
3 I'm going to buy some shoes tomorrow.

27.5
1 I'm tired. I'm / I am going to stay at home tonight.
2 Paul is going to buy a new smartphone.
3 What are the children going to do in the school holidays?
4 Helen and Ben are going to get married.
5 Is your mother going to visit us on Sunday?
6 When is Sarah going to have a holiday?
7 It's / It is cold. I think it's / it is going to snow.
8 Hurry up! We're / We are going to be late.

UNIT 28

28.1
2 she'll be
3 she was
4 she'll be
5 she's
6 she was
7 she'll be

28.2
Beispiel-Antworten:
2 I'll be at home.
3 I'll probably be in bed.
4 I'll be at work.
5 I don't know where I'll be.

28.3
2 'll/will
3 won't
4 won't
5 'll/will
6 'll/will
7 won't

28.4
3 I think we'll win the game.
4 I don't think I'll be here tomorrow.
5 I think Sue will like her present.
6 I don't think they'll get married.
7 I don't think you'll enjoy the film.

Schlüssel zu den Übungen

28.5
2 are you doing
3 They're going
4 will lend
5 I'm going
6 will phone
7 He's working
8 Will you
9 are coming

28.6
1 The American president will be in Ireland tomorrow.
2 You can call/ring/phone me tomorrow. I'll/I will be in the office all day.
3 We'll / We will / We shall be home in an hour.
4 I think Tom will marry Kelly
5 I won't / I will not be at work tomorrow.
6 Do you think it will rain tomorrow?
7 It won't / It will not be very difficult.
8 I don't / I do not think Jenny will come to the party.

UNIT 29

29.1
2 I'll eat   5 I'll stay
3 I'll sit   6 I'll show
4 I'll do

29.2
2 I think I'll have
3 I don't think I'll play
4 I think I'll buy
5 I don't think I'll buy

29.3
2 I'll do
3 I watch
4 I'll go
5 is going to buy
6 I'll give
7 Are you doing … I'm going
8 I'm working

29.4
2 Shall I turn off the TV?
3 Shall I make some sandwiches?
4 Shall I turn on the light?

29.5
2 where shall we go?
3 what shall we buy?
4 who shall we invite?

29.6
1 'It's cold.' 'I'll / I will close the window.'
2 It's very hot today. I think I'll / I will go swimming.
3 A: My homework is very difficult/ hard.
   B: I'll / I will help you.'
4 Where shall we meet tomorrow?
5 I don't feel well. I don't think I'll / I will go out tonight / this evening.
6 The weather is nice/beautiful. Shall we go/drive to the mountains?
7 A: Shall I open the door?
   B: No, I'll do it.

UNIT 30

30.1
2 I might see you tomorrow.
3 Sarah might forget to phone.
4 It might snow today.
5 I might be late tonight.
6 Mark might not be here next week.
7 I might not have time to go out.

30.2
2 I might go away.
3 I might see her on Monday.
4 I might have fish.
5 I might get/take a taxi. *oder* … go by taxi.
6 I might buy/get a new car.

30.3
3 He might get up early.
4 He isn't / He's not working tomorrow.
5 He might be at home tomorrow morning.
6 He might watch TV.
7 He's going out in the afternoon.
8 He might go shopping.

30.4
Beispiel-Antworten:
1 I might buy some new clothes.
2 I might go out with some friends.
3 I might have an egg for breakfast.

30.5
1 I might go to the theatre tonight / this evening.
2 It might snow tomorrow.
3 'Are the boys playing football tomorrow?' 'They might.'
4 Tina might visit us tomorrow.
5 James isn't / is not feeling well. He might not go out tonight / this evening.
6 'What are you doing / going to do this afternoon?' 'We might work in the garden.'
7 I might not be at home this afternoon, but I'll / I will be there this evening / in the evening.
8 May/Can I come in?

UNIT 31

31.1
2 Can you ski?
3 Can you play chess?
4 Can you run ten kilometres?
5 Can you drive (a car)?
6 Can you ride (a horse)?
7 I can/can't swim.
8 I can/can't ski.
9 I can/can't play chess.
10 I can/can't run ten kilometres.
11 I can/can't drive (a car).
12 I can/can't ride (a horse).

31.2
2 can see   4 can't find
3 can't hear   5 can speak

31.3
2 couldn't eat
3 can't decide
4 couldn't find
5 can't go
6 couldn't go

31.4
2 Can/Could you pass the salt (please)?
3 Can/Could I have these postcards (please)?
4 Can/Could you turn off the radio (please)?
5 Can/Could I borrow your newspaper (please)?
6 Can/Could I use your pen (please)?

31.5
1 Alice can speak four languages.
2 James can't/cannot play tennis.
3 Can you come at 3 o'clock?
4 Michael and Anna can dance the tango.
5 I can't/cannot find my key.
6 Can/Could you help me, please?
7 When Laura was young, she could run ten kilometres.
8 Could/Can I use your telephone/ phone?
9 We couldn't go out at the weekend. We didn't / did not have time.

UNIT 32

32.1
2 must meet   5 must go
3 must wash   6 must win
4 must learn   7 must be

32.2
2 I must   5 I had to
3 I had to   6 I had to
4 I must   7 I must

32.3
2 don't need to rush
3 mustn't lose
4 don't need to wait
5 mustn't forget
6 don't need to phone

32.4
2 C   4 B
3 A   5 D

32.5
3 don't need to   7 must
4 had to   8 had to
5 must   9 don't need to
6 mustn't   10 mustn't

32.6
1 I must clean the house this weekend.
2 Simon had to get up early today.
3 You mustn't do that!
4 You must be careful.
5 You don't need to come if you're tired.
6 We mustn't forget to buy (some) milk.
7 I can do it alone. You don't need to help me.
8 Our plane was delayed. We had to wait (for) four hours at the airport.

289

Schlüssel zu den Übungen

UNIT 33

33.1
2 You should go
3 You should eat
4 you should visit
5 you should wear
6 You should take

33.2
2 He shouldn't eat so much.
3 She shouldn't work so hard.
4 He shouldn't drive so fast.

33.3
3 I think you should sell it.
4 I think she should have a holiday.
5 I don't think they should get married.
6 I don't think you should go to work.
7 I think he should go to the doctor.
8 I don't think we should stay there.

33.4
Beispiel-Antworten:
2 I think everybody should have enough food.
3 I think people should drive more carefully.
4 I don't think the police should carry guns.
5 I think I should take more exercise.

33.5
1 You should go swimming more often.
2 Children should read more books.
3 You shouldn't / should not always come/be so late. *oder* You shouldn't / should not come/be so late all the time.
4 Do you think I should wear this dress?
5 Tom shouldn't / should not go out so much/often. He's / He is always tired. *oder* He's / He is tired all the time.
6 I think we should buy Jenny a book for her birthday.
7 Do you think I should go to the police?
8 I don't think we should stay so long.
9 I don't think you should eat so much meat. You should eat more salad.

UNIT 34

34.1
2 have to do
3 has to read
4 have to speak
5 has to travel
6 have to hit

34.2
2 have to go
3 had to buy
4 have to change
5 had to answer

34.3
2 did he have to wait
3 does she have to go
4 did you have to pay
5 do you have to do

34.4
2 doesn't have to wait.
3 didn't have to get up early.
4 doesn't have to work (so) hard.
5 don't have to leave now.

34.5
3 have to pay
4 had to borrow
5 must stop *oder* have to stop (*beides ist möglich*)
6 has to meet
7 must tell *oder* have to tell (*beides ist möglich*)

34.6
Beispiel-Antworten:
2 I have to go to work every day.
3 I had to go to the dentist yesterday.
4 I have to go shopping tomorrow.

34.7
1 I have to be in the office at 8 o'clock every morning.
2 Ben has to study for his exam tonight / this evening.
3 I have to / must clean the windows. They're / They are dirty.
4 For this course, you don't have to do/take a test / an exam.
5 We had to take a taxi home because there were no buses.
6 Do you have to work tomorrow?
7 Does Rachel have to wear glasses when she reads?
8 The children didn't / did not have to go to bed early yesterday.
9 It's / It is very important. You have to / must listen!

UNIT 35

35.1
2 Would you like an apple?
3 Would you like some coffee? / … a cup of coffee?
4 Would you like some cheese? / … a piece of cheese?
5 Would you like a sandwich?
6 Would you like some cake? / … a piece of cake?

35.2
2 Would you like to play tennis tomorrow?
3 Would you like to come to a concert next week?
4 Would you like to borrow my umbrella?

35.3
2 Do you like
3 Would you like
4 would you like
5 Would you like
6 I like
7 would you like
8 Would you like
9 Do you like
10 I'd like
11 I'd like
12 do you like

35.4
1 'Would you like a glass of juice?' 'Yes, please.'
2 I'd like a cup of coffee and a piece of cake, please.
3 Would you like an apple or an orange?
4 A: Would you like to go skiing with us?
  B: Yes, I'd love to.
5 Do you like going to the mountains?
6 I'd like three apples and four bananas (please).
7 A: Do you like going to the theatre?
  B: Yes, but I don't go very often.
8 I like tea, but now I'd like a glass of water (please).

UNIT 36

36.1
3 Don't buy
4 Smile
5 Don't sit
6 Have
7 Don't forget
8 Sleep
9 Be … Don't drop

36.2
2 let's take a taxi
3 let's watch TV
4 let's go to a restaurant
5 let's wait a little

36.3
3 No, let's not go out.
4 No, don't close the window.
5 No, don't phone me (tonight).
6 No, let's not wait for Andy.
7 No, don't turn on the light.
8 No, let's not go by bus.

36.4
1 The door is locked. Please open it!
2 The baby is sleeping. Please be quiet.
3 It's a secret. Don't tell our friends!
4 Let's go to town.
5 Goodbye/Bye. Have a good trip!
6 I'm tired. Let's not play tennis today.
7 A: Have another piece of cake.
  B: No thanks.
8 A: What shall we do on Saturday evening?
  B: Let's go to the cinema.

UNIT 37

37.1
2 He used to play football.
3 She used to be a taxi driver.
4 They used to live in the country.
5 He used to wear glasses.
6 This building used to be a hotel.

37.2
2–6
She used to play volleyball.
She used to go out most evenings. / She used to go out a lot.
She used to play the guitar.
She used to read a lot. / She used to like reading.
She used to go away two or three times a year. / She used to travel a lot.

37.3
3 used to have
4 used to be
5 go/travel
6 used to eat
7 watches
8 used to live
9 get
10 did you use to play

37.4
1 When I was a child / As a child I used to play football.
2 Kate used to work in a bank.
3 John and Linda used to live in Paris.
4 I didn't use to like vegetables when I was a child / as a child.
5 Tom didn't use to wear glasses.
6 We used to go to the cinema a lot / often.
7 We usually go out on Saturday evening.
8 Did you use to have long hair?

UNIT 38

38.1
3 There's / There is a hospital.
4 There isn't a swimming pool.
5 There are two cinemas.
6 There isn't a university.
7 There aren't any big hotels.

38.2
Beispiel-Antworten:
3 There is a university in …
4 There are a lot of big shops.
5 There isn't an airport.
6 There aren't many factories.

38.3
2 There's / There is
3 is there
4 There are
5 are there
6 There isn't
7 Is there
8 Are there
9 There's / There is … There aren't

38.4
2–6
There are eight planets in the solar system.
There are fifteen players in a rugby team.
There are twenty-six letters in the English alphabet.
There are thirty days in September.
There are fifty states in the USA.

38.5
2 It's
3 There's
4 There's … Is it
5 Is there … there's
6 It's
7 Is there

38.6
1 There's / There is an old church in the village.
2 There isn't an airport in our town.
3 There are a lot of / many flowers in our garden.
4 'That's / That is / This is our house.' 'It's very nice/beautiful.'
5 Is there a good restaurant near here?
6 There's / There is a cat on the sofa/couch.
7 It's / It is Sunday. There are a lot of / many people in the park today.
8 There's / There is a bag on the table. Is it yours?
9 There's / There is an old tree in front of the house. It's / It is very big.

UNIT 39

39.1
2 There was a carpet
3 There were three pictures
4 There was a small table
5 There were some flowers
6 There were some books
7 There was an armchair
8 There was a sofa

39.2
3 There was   7 Were there
4 Was there   8 There wasn't
5 there weren't   9 There was
6 There wasn't   10 there weren't

39.3
2 There are
3 There was
4 There's / There is
5 There's been / There has been *oder* There was
6 there was
7 there will be
8 there were … there are
9 There have been
10 there will be *oder* there are

39.4
1 There was a big concert here last week. *oder* Last week there was …
2 The weather was nice/beautiful yesterday. There were a lot of / many children in the park.
3 There will be a lot of snow this winter.
4 Were there a lot of people / many people at the party last night?
5 There weren't / were not any houses here 50 years ago. *oder* 50 years ago there weren't / were not any houses here.
6 Do you think there will be a lot of traffic in town / in the city this afternoon?
7 A: Why is the plane delayed?
   B: There's been / There has been a technical problem. *oder* There was …
8 There won't / will not be a football match tomorrow. *oder* Tomorrow there …

UNIT 40

40.1
2 It's cold.
3 It's windy.
4 It's sunny/fine. *oder* It's a nice day.
5 It's snowing.
6 It's cloudy.

40.2
2 It's / It is
3 Is it
4 is it … it's / it is
5 It's / It is
6 Is it
7 is it
8 It's / It is
9 It's / It is

40.3
2 How far is it from the hotel to the beach?
3 How far is it from New York to Washington?
4 How far is it from your house to the airport?

40.4
3 It   6 it
4 It … It   7 It … there
5 There   8 It

40.5
2 It's nice to see you again.
3 It's impossible to work here.
4 It's easy to make friends.
5 It's interesting to visit different places.
6 It's dangerous to go out alone

40.6
1 It's / It is very hot today.
2 It's / It is 7.30. It's / It is time to go to school.
3 It doesn't / does not snow here very often.
4 It's / It is five kilometres to the city centre.
5 There was a little / some fog at the airport this morning. *oder* … this morning at the airport.
6 How far is it from London to Paris?
7 It's / It is easy to learn English.
8 It's / It is expensive to eat in a restaurant every day.

UNIT 41

41.1
2 is   5 will
3 can   6 was
4 has

Schlüssel zu den Übungen

41.2
2 'm not
3 weren't
4 haven't
5 isn't
6 hasn't

41.3
3 doesn't
4 do
5 did
6 does
7 don't
8 didn't

41.4
Beispiel-Antworten:
2 I like sport, but my sister doesn't.
3 I don't eat meat, but Jessica does.
4 I'm American, but my husband isn't.
5 I haven't been to Japan, but Jessica has.

41.5
2 wasn't
3 are
4 has
5 can't
6 did
7 has
8 do
9 hasn't
10 will
11 might

41.6
2 Yes, I have. *oder* No, I haven't.
3 Yes, I do. *oder* No, I don't.
4 Yes, it is. *oder* No, it isn't.
5 Yes, I am. *oder* No, I'm not.
6 Yes, I do. *oder* No, I don't.
7 Yes, I will. *oder* No, I won't.
8 Yes, I have. *oder* No, I haven't.
9 Yes, I did. *oder* No, I didn't.
10 Yes, I was. *oder* No, I wasn't.

41.7
1 I'm not tall, but my sister is.
2 Sam can dance, but Sarah can't.
3 The weather wasn't nice yesterday, but today it is.
4 My brother has (got) children, but I haven't.
5 'Were you at the party yesterday?' 'I wasn't, but Emma was.'
6 I play tennis, but my husband doesn't.
7 We don't like dogs, but our children do.
8 'Did you watch the football match yesterday?' 'I did, but Jenny didn't.'
9 'Will you be at home tomorrow?' 'I won't, but Thomas will.'

UNIT 42

42.1
2 Do you?
3 Didn't you?
4 Doesn't she?
5 Do I?
6 Did she?

42.2
3 Have you?
4 Can't she?
5 Were you?
6 Didn't you?
7 Is there?
8 Aren't you?
9 Did you?
10 Does she?
11 Won't you?
12 Isn't it?

42.3
2 aren't they
3 wasn't she
4 haven't you
5 don't you
6 doesn't he
7 won't you

42.4
2 are you
3 isn't she
4 can't you
5 do you
6 didn't she
7 was it
8 doesn't she
9 will you

42.5
1 'It's / It is late.' 'Is it? What time is it? / What's the time?'
2 A: I'm / I am tired.
   B: Are you? Do you want to go home?
3 Tim isn't married, is he?
4 A: I haven't got / I don't have a TV.
   B: Haven't you? / Don't you? Why not?
5 You can drive, can't you?
6 A: Ben wasn't at work yesterday.
   B: Wasn't he? Was he ill?
7 A: Tom plays football.
   B: Does he? How often does he play?
8 You're / You are from London, aren't you? *oder* You come from London, don't you?
9 A: I saw Mia yesterday.
   B: Did you? Where?
10 You weren't at home yesterday, were you?
11 Kate didn't phone/call/ring you yesterday, did she?
12 You've / You have met my wife, haven't you?

UNIT 43

43.1
2 either
3 too
4 too
5 either
6 either
7 too

43.2
2 So am I.
3 So have I.
4 So do I.
5 So will I.
6 So was I.
7 Neither can I.
8 Neither did I.
9 Neither have I.
10 Neither am I.
11 Neither do I.

43.3
1 So am I.
2 So can I. *oder* I can't.
3 Neither am I. *oder* I am.
4 So do I. *oder* I don't.
5 Neither do I. *oder* I do.
6 So did I. *oder* I didn't.
7 Neither have I. *oder* I have.
8 Neither do I. *oder* I do.
9 So am I. *oder* I'm not.
10 Neither have I. *oder* I have.
11 Neither did I. *oder* I did.
12 So do I. *oder* I don't.

43.4
1 A: I'm from Germany / I come from Germany.
   B: I'm from Germany / I come from Germany too.
2 'I'm / I am tired.' 'So am I.'
3 Rebecca is a teacher. Jenny is a teacher too.
4 'I can't play tennis.' 'Neither can I.'
5 John goes to bed early. He gets up early too.
6 'We've got / We have got / We have a dog.' 'So have we.'
7 Tony isn't married. Anna isn't married either.
8 A: We went/drove to the mountains last weekend.
   B: So did we.
9 Ben doesn't go out very often. Neither does Nicola.

UNIT 44

44.1
2 They aren't / They're not married.
3 I haven't had dinner.
4 It isn't cold today.
5 We won't be late.
6 You shouldn't go.

44.2
2 I don't like cheese.
3 They didn't understand.
4 He doesn't live here.
5 Don't go away!
6 I didn't do the shopping.

44.3
2 They haven't arrived.
3 I didn't go to the bank.
4 He doesn't speak German.
5 We weren't angry.
6 He won't be pleased.
7 Don't call me tonight.
8 It didn't rain yesterday.
9 I couldn't hear them.
10 I don't believe you.

44.4
2 'm not / am not
3 can't
4 doesn't
5 isn't / 's not
6 don't … haven't
7 Don't
8 didn't
9 haven't
10 won't
11 didn't
12 weren't
13 hasn't
14 shouldn't / mustn't

44.5
3 He wasn't born in London.
4 He doesn't like London.
5 He'd like to live in the country.
6 He can drive.
7 He doesn't have a car. *oder* He hasn't got a car.
8 He doesn't read newspapers.
9 He isn't interested in politics.

… Schlüssel zu den Übungen

10 He watches TV most evenings.
11 He didn't watch TV last night.
12 He went out last night.

44.6
1 I'm / I am not sad.
2 David wasn't / was not at home yesterday.
3 We can't/cannot come tomorrow.
4 I don't / do not know your sister.
5 We didn't / did not go out last night / yesterday evening.
6 Don't go to bed too late!
7 It won't / will not rain tomorrow.
8 Don't be late. We haven't got / don't have much time.
9 I couldn't / could not find my key this morning.
10 You shouldn't talk about it.
11 Don't do that! It / That isn't / is not nice.

UNIT 45

45.1
3 Were you late this morning?
4 Has Kate got a key? *oder* Does Kate have a key?
5 Will you be here tomorrow?
6 Is Paul going out this evening?
7 Do you like your job?
8 Does Nicola live near here?
9 Did you enjoy the film?
10 Did you have a good holiday?

45.2
2 Do you use it a lot?
3 Did you use it yesterday?
4 Do you enjoy driving?
5 Are you a good driver?
6 Have you ever had an accident?

45.3
3 What are the children doing?
4 How is cheese made?
5 Is your sister coming to the party?
6 Why don't you tell the truth?
7 Have your guests arrived yet?
8 What time does your train leave?
9 Why didn't Emily go to work?
10 Was your car damaged in the accident?

45.4
3 What are you reading?
4 What time did she go (to bed)?
5 When are they going (on holiday)?
6 Where did you see him?
7 Why can't you come (to the party)?
8 Where has she gone?
9 How much (money) do you need?
10 Why doesn't she like you?
11 How often does it rain?
12 When did you do it? / … do the shopping?

45.5
1 Are the children tired?
2 Can Jenny speak French?
3 Was the film interesting?
4 Will you be at home tonight / this evening?
5 Do you like Chinese food?
6 Have you seen David today?
7 Where does your mother work?
8 Did Rachel call you yesterday?
9 What did you do last weekend?
10 Why don't you like Emma?

UNIT 46

46.1
2 What fell off the shelf?
3 Who wants to see me?
4 Who took your umbrella? / Who took it?
5 What made you ill?
6 Who is / Who's coming?

46.2
3 Who did you phone?
4 What happened last night?
5 Who knows the answer?
6 Who did the washing-up?
7 What did Jane do? / What did she do?
8 What woke you up?
9 Who saw the accident?
10 Who did you see?
11 Who has got it? / Who's got it? *oder* Who has got your pen? / Who's got your pen?
12 What does this word mean? *oder* What does it mean?

46.3
2 Who phoned you?
   What did she want?
3 Who did you ask?
   What did he say?
4 Who got married?
   Who told you?
5 Who did you meet?
   What did she tell you?
6 Who won?
   What did you do (after the game)?
7 Who gave you a/the book?
   What did Catherine give you?

46.4
1 Who has (got) my English book?
2 Who can answer the question?
3 Where are the children?
4 That smells good. What are you cooking?
5 Who are these people?
6 What's / What has fallen down? *oder* What fell down?
7 Who won the game on Saturday?
8 Where did you see Thomas this morning?
9 What did you have/eat for dinner/supper yesterday?
10 I can hear music. Who's / Who is playing the piano?

UNIT 47

47.1
2 What are you looking for?
3 Who did you go to the cinema with?
4 What/Who was the film about?
5 Who did you give the money to?
6 Who was the book written by?

47.2
2 What are they looking at?
3 Which restaurant is he going to?
4 What are they talking about?
5 What is she listening to?
6 Which bus are they waiting for?

47.3
2 Which hotel did you stay at?
3 Which (football) team does he play for?
4 Which school did you go to?

47.4
2 What is the food like?
3 What are the people like?
4 What is the weather like?

47.5
2 What was the film like?
3 What were the lessons like?
4 What was the hotel like?

47.6
1 'Where is Jim from?' *oder* 'Where does Jim come from?' 'From Australia.'
2 What are you thinking about?
3 What are the beaches in Thailand like? *oder* What are the beaches like in Thailand?
4 Which house does Becky live in?
5 What are you waiting for?
6 What was the food in Spain like? *oder* What was the food like in Spain?
7 A: Kate went to a party yesterday. *oder* Kate was at a party …
   B: Who did she go with?
8 'How is / How's your father?' 'He's / He is better, thank you.'
9 What's Joe like? Is he friendly/nice?

UNIT 48

48.1
3 What colour is it?
4 What time did you get up?
5 What type of music do you like?
6 What kind of car do you want (to buy)?

48.2
2 Which coat
3 Which film/movie
4 Which bus

48.3
3 Which		8	Who
4 What		9	What
5 Which		10	Which
6 What		11	What
7 Which			

48.4
2 How far   5 How deep
3 How old   6 How long
4 How often

Schlüssel zu den Übungen

48.5
2 How heavy is this box?
3 How old are you?
4 How much did you spend?
5 How often do you watch TV?
6 How far is it from Paris to Moscow?

48.6
1 What's/What is that?
2 What colour is your car?
3 How old are your children?
4 How often do you go to the theatre?
5 What kind/type/sort of films do you like?
6 How tall is Michael?
7 How far is it to the centre?
8 There are two coats here. Which is yours? *oder* Here are two coats …
9 What's / What is the highest mountain in the world?
10 Which do you like – the green or the red dress?

UNIT 49

49.1
2 How long does it take by car from Milan to Rome?
3 How long does it take by train from Paris to Geneva?
4 How long does it take by bus from the city centre to the airport?

49.2
Beispiel-Antworten:
2 It takes … hours to fly from … to New York.
3 It takes … years to study to be a doctor in … .
4 It takes … to walk from my home to the nearest shop.
5 It takes … to get from my home to the nearest airport.

49.3
2 How long did it take you to walk to the station?
3 How long did it take him to paint the bathroom?
4 How long did it take you to learn to ski?
5 How long did it take them to repair the car?

49.4
2 It took us 20 minutes to walk home. / … to get home.
3 It took me six months to learn to drive.
4 It took Mark/him three hours to drive to London. / … to get to London.
5 It took Lisa a long time to find a job. / … to get a job.
6 It took me … to …

49.5
1 'How long does it take by bus to the centre?' 'It takes five minutes.'
2 How long does it take you to read a page?
3 It takes us two days to clean the house.
4 It doesn't take Lucy long / a long time to get to work.
5 'How long did it take to get to Paris by car?' 'It took about ten hours.'
6 It took me two hours yesterday to do my homework. *oder* It took me two hours to do my homework yesterday.
7 It didn't take us long / a long time to find a flat / an apartment.

UNIT 50

50.1
2 I don't know where she is.
3 I don't know how old it is.
4 I don't know when he'll be here.
5 I don't know why he was angry.
6 I don't know how long she has lived here.

50.2
2 where Susan works
3 what Peter said
4 why he went home early
5 what time the meeting begins
6 how the accident happened

50.3
2 are you
3 they are
4 the museum is
5 do you want
6 elephants eat
7 it is

50.4
2 Do you know if/whether they are married?
3 Do you know if/whether Sue knows Bill?
4 Do you know if/whether Gary will be here tomorrow?
5 Do you know if/whether he passed his exam?

50.5
2 Do you know where Paula is?
3 Do you know if/whether she is working today? / … she's working today?
4 Do you know what time she starts work?
5 Do you know if/whether the shops are open tomorrow?
6 Do you know where Sarah and Jack live?
7 Do you know if/whether they went to Jane's party?

50.6
Beispiel-Antworten:
2 Do you know what time the bus leaves?
3 Excuse me, can you tell me where the station is?
4 I don't know what I'm going to do this evening.
5 Do you know if there's a restaurant near here?
6 Do you know how much it costs to rent a car?

50.7
1 Do you know who that is?
2 Can you tell me where the station is?
3 I don't know why he's / he is angry.
4 I don't remember where Rachel lives.
5 I don't know how that works.
6 When did Anna leave?
7 I know what we can do.
8 Do you know if/whether the museum is open today?
9 Do you know when John left?

UNIT 51

51.1
2 She said (that) she was very busy.
3 She said (that) she couldn't go to the party.
4 He said (that) he had to go out.
5 He said (that) he was learning Russian.
6 She said (that) she didn't feel very well.
7 They said (that) they would be home late. / … they'd be …
8 She said (that) she had just come back from holiday. / … she'd just come back …
9 She said (that) she was going to buy a guitar.
10 They said (that) they hadn't got a key. / They said (that) they didn't have a key.

51.2
2 She said (that) she wasn't hungry.
3 he said (that) he needed it.
4 she said (that) she didn't want to go.
5 She said (that) I could have it.
6 He said (that) he would send me a postcard. / … he'd send …
7 Nicola said (that) he had gone home. / … he'd gone home.
8 He said (that) he wanted to watch TV.
9 She said (that) she was going to the cinema.

51.3
3 said   7 said
4 told   8 told
5 tell   9 tell
6 say   10 say

51.4
1 Matt said (that) Emma was ill/sick.
2 Mary said (that) she would come later.
3 Amy and Michael said (that) they wanted to play tennis today.
4 Tom told me (that) he didn't like coffee.
5 Jenny said (that) she wouldn't be at home today.
6 Peter told me (that) he didn't eat meat.
7 Did Kate tell you (that) she couldn't come?
8 What did Andy say to you / tell you?

Schlüssel zu den Übungen

UNIT 52

52.1
3 phone
4 phone Paul
5 to phone Paul
6 to phone Paul
7 phone Paul
8 to phone Paul
9 phone Paul
10 phone Paul

52.2
3 get
4 going
5 watch
6 flying
7 listening
8 eat
9 waiting
10 wear
11 doing … staying

52.3
4 to go
5 rain
6 to leave
7 help
8 studying
9 to go
10 wearing
11 to stay
12 have
13 having
14 to have
15 hear
16 go
17 listening
18 to walk
19 to know … tell
20 borrow

52.4
1 Dave can't drive (a car).
2 May/Can I use your pencil?
3 Do you know my brother?
4 I'll / I will be at home tomorrow.
5 I want to buy a new laptop.
6 Could you close the door, please?
7 We didn't go out yesterday.
8 The weather is very nice today. The sun is shining.
9 Would you like to eat/have a piece of cake?
10 We're / We are going to go/drive to the mountains tomorrow. *oder* Tomorrow we're / we are going/driving to the mountains.
11 'Where are the children?' 'They're / They are playing in the garden.'

UNIT 53

53.1
3 to see
4 to swim
5 cleaning
6 to ask
7 visiting
8 to do
9 to be
10 waiting
11 going
12 to speak
13 to go
14 crying / to cry
15 to work … talking

53.2
2 to help
3 to see
4 reading
5 to lose
6 to send
7 raining
8 to go
9 watching / to watch
10 to wait

53.3
2 going to museums
3 to go
4 driving / to drive
5 to go (there)
6 travelling by train
7 walking

53.4
Beispiel-Antworten:
1 I enjoy cooking.
2 I don't like studying.
3 If it's a nice day tomorrow, I'd like to have a picnic by the lake.
4 When I'm on holiday, I like to do very little.
5 I don't mind travelling alone, but I prefer to travel with somebody.
6 I wouldn't like to live in a big city.

53.5
1 Do you want to come with me?
2 Paul hates going / to go to parties.
3 We plan to travel/go to Australia next year.
4 Tania loves eating / to eat chocolate.
5 I've / I have decided to study English.
6 I don't mind working evenings / in the evening.
7 The baby has stopped crying.
8 Do you like going / to go to the cinema? *oder* Do you enjoy going … ?
9 I'd like / I would like to live in the USA for a year.
10 I tried to ring/call/phone you yesterday.
11 A: Would you like to take the bus / go by bus?
   B: No, I'd / I would prefer to walk / to go on foot.

UNIT 54

54.1
2 I want you to listen carefully.
3 I don't want you to be angry.
4 Do you want me to wait for you?
5 I don't want you to call me tonight.
6 I want you to meet Sarah.

54.2
2 A woman told me to turn left after the bridge.
3 I advised him to go to the doctor.
4 She asked me to help her. / … asked me if I could help her.
5 I told him to come back in ten minutes.
6 Paul let me use his phone.
7 I told her not to phone before 8 o'clock. / … not to call (me) before 8 o'clock.
8 Amy's mother taught her to play the piano.

54.3
2 to repeat
3 wait
4 to arrive
5 to get
6 go
7 borrow
8 to tell
9 to make (*oder* to get)
10 think

54.4
1 I want you to eat something.
2 I don't want you to be sad.
3 Do you want me to go with you?
4 Would you like me to help you?
5 Sam wanted me to call/ring/phone him tonight / this evening.
6 Hannah asked me to talk/speak to you.
7 I told you to close the door.
8 What do you expect me to say?
9 His doctor advised him to stay at home.

UNIT 55

55.1
2–4
I went to the coffee shop to meet a friend.
I went to the chemist to get some medicine.
I went to the market to buy some vegetables.

55.2
2 to read the newspaper
3 to open this door
4 to get some fresh air
5 to wake him up
6 to see who it was

55.3
Beispiel-Antworten:
2 to talk to you now
3 to tell her about the party
4 to do some shopping
5 to buy a motorbike

55.4
2 to
3 to
4 for
5 to
6 for
7 to
8 to
9 for
10 for
11 to

55.5
2 for the film to begin
3 for it to arrive
4 for you to tell me

55.6
1 Kate went to the cashpoint to get (some) money.
2 I haven't got / don't have time to cook.
3 Rachel and John went to town to go shopping.
4 We haven't got / don't have money to buy a house.
5 Please wait here to see Mr Jones.
6 Sandra needs money for a new car.

Schlüssel zu den Übungen

7 Are you waiting to speak/talk to Mrs Anderson?
8 A: Why are you looking out of the window?
   B: To see if it's / it is raining.
9 Tom is waiting for Jenny to call/ring/phone him.

UNIT 56

56.1
3 to
4 – (keine Präposition)
5 for
6 to
7 on … to
8 for
9 on
10 to
11 – (keine Präposition)
12 on
13 for
14 on

56.2
2 went fishing
3 goes swimming
4 going skiing
5 go shopping
6 went jogging

56.3
2 to university
3 shopping
4 to sleep
5 home
6 skiing
7 riding
8 for a walk
9 on holiday … to Portugal

56.4
1 We don't go to the opera very often.
2 When are you going to the doctor? Today or tomorrow?
3 'Where's / Where is Karen?' 'She's / She has gone home.'
4 I went to Paris last week.
5 Would you like to go for a drink?
6 Did you go jogging this morning?
7 Julie went shopping today and bought a new dress.
8 This year we're going to Portugal on holiday.
9 My parents went on a cruise in the Caribbean last year.

UNIT 57

57.1
2 get your boots
3 get a doctor
4 get a taxi
5 gets the job
6 get some milk
7 get a ticket
8 gets a good salary
9 get a lot of rain
10 get a new laptop

57.2
2 getting dark
3 getting married
4 getting ready
5 getting late

57.3
2 get wet
3 got married
4 gets angry
5 got lost
6 get old
7 got better

57.4
2 got to Bristol at 11.45.
3 I left the party at 11.15 and got home at midnight.
4 (Beispiel-Antwort) I left home at 8.30 and got to the airport at 10 o'clock.

57.5
2 got off
3 got out of
4 got on

57.6
1 Thomas got a taxi to the station.
2 A: I'm going to the shop.
   B: Can you get me some milk?
3 I'm getting tired. I'm going to bed now.
4 I called/phoned/rang yesterday. Did you get my message?
5 When did Ben and Jenny get married?
6 What time do you usually get to work?
7 Come into the house now. It's getting cold.
8 Be careful when you get out of the car.
9 Lisa got on the train a/one minute before it left.

UNIT 58

58.1
2 do
3 make
4 made
5 did
6 do
7 done
8 make
9 making
10 do
11 doing

58.2
2 They're / They are doing (their) homework.
3 He's / He is doing the shopping. oder He is shopping.
4 She's / She is making a jacket.
5 They're / They are doing an exam. (oder … taking an exam.)
6 He's / He is making the/his bed.
7 She's / She is doing the washing-up. oder She is washing up. / She is doing the dishes. / She is washing the dishes.
8 He's / He is making a (shopping) list.
9 They're / They are making a film.
10 He's / He is taking a picture/photo/photograph.

58.3
2 make
3 do
4 done
5 made
6 doing
7 did
8 make
9 do
10 making
11 made
12 make … do

58.4
1 The company makes computers.
2 What do you usually do after dinner/ supper?
3 At the weekend, I usually do the shopping and the housework. oder I usually do … at the weekend.
4 'What are you doing?' 'I'm / I am making/baking bread.'
5 We didn't do much last weekend.
6 Have you made your bed? oder Did you make your bed?
7 Could you take a picture/ photograph/photo of us?
8 My daughter did/took her exam/ test yesterday.
9 This film was made in Italy.
10 Could I make an appointment with Dr Saunders, please?

UNIT 59

59.1
3 He doesn't have / He hasn't got
4 Gary had
5 Do you have / Have you got
6 we didn't have
7 She doesn't have / She hasn't got
8 Did you have

59.2
2 She's / She is having a cup of tea.
3 He's / He is having a rest.
4 They're / They are having a good time.
5 They're / They are having dinner.
6 He's / He is having a bath.

59.3
3 Have a nice/good trip!
4 Did you have a nice/good weekend?
5 Did you have a nice/good game (of tennis)?
6 Have a nice/good time! oder Have a nice/good evening! oder Have fun!
7 Did you have a nice/good holiday?

59.4
2 have something to eat
3 had a glass of water
4 have a walk
5 had an accident
6 have a look

59.5
1 Terry has (got) blue eyes.
2 I don't have / I haven't got a television/TV.
3 Do you have / Have you got a dog?
4 I went to the dentist yesterday because I had (a) toothache.
5 What time did you have lunch?
6 I don't often have a bath. Usually I have a shower. oder I usually have a shower.
7 'Where's / Where is Kate?' 'She's / She is having a rest.'
8 We had a holiday in Turkey.
9 Can you have a look at this email?
10 Have a good/nice time at the party! oder Have fun at the party!

Schlüssel zu den Übungen

UNIT 60

60.1
2 him
3 them
4 her
5 him
6 them
7 her

60.2
2 I ... them
3 he ... her
4 they ... us
5 we ... him
6 she ... them
7 they ... me
8 she ... you

60.3
2 I like him.
3 I don't like it.
4 Do you like it?
5 I don't like her.
6 Do you like them?

60.4
2 him
3 them
4 they
5 us
6 it
7 She
8 them
9 me
10 her
11 them
12 he ... it

60.5
2 Can you give it to him?
3 Can you give them to her?
4 Can you give it to me?
5 Can you give it to them?
6 Can you give them to us?

60.6
1 This book is for you.
2 John loves Mary, but she doesn't love him.
3 I can see Jim, but he can't see me.
4 'Do you know Jenny?' 'No, I don't know her.'
5 This coffee is too strong. I don't like it.
6 The music is nice. Can you hear it?
7 Is this present from you?
8 Where are the children? Have you seen them?
9 I need the/those papers. Can you give them to me, please?
10 Would you like to go to the park with us?

UNIT 61

61.1
2 her hands
3 our hands
4 his hands
5 their hands
6 your hands

61.2
2 They live with their parents.
3 We live with our parents.
4 Martina lives with her parents.
5 I live with my parents.
6 John lives with his parents.
7 Do you live with your parents?
8 Most children live with their parents.

61.3
2 their
3 his
4 his
5 her
6 their
7 her
8 their

61.4
2 his
3 Their
4 our
5 her
6 my
7 your
8 her
9 their
10 my
11 Its
12 His ... his

61.5
2 my key
3 Her husband
4 your coat
5 their homework
6 his name
7 Our house

61.6
1 I live with my parents.
2 I know her husband.
3 Don't forget your hat!
4 Our flat/apartment is very nice/beautiful.
5 Wash your hands!
6 Where are your children?
7 Toby and Sarah usually eat in their kitchen.
8 He always brushes/cleans his teeth after dinner.
9 Canterbury is famous for its cathedral.
10 How old is your son?

UNIT 62

62.1
2 mine
3 ours
4 hers
5 theirs
6 yours
7 mine
8 his

62.2
2 yours
3 my ... Mine
4 Yours ... mine
5 her
6 My ... hers
7 their
8 Ours

62.3
3 of hers
4 friends of ours
5 friend of mine
6 friend of his
7 friends of yours

62.4
2 Whose camera is this? It's hers.
3 Whose gloves are these? They're mine.
4 Whose hat is this? It's his.
5 Whose money is this? It's yours.
6 Whose bags are these? They're ours.

62.5
1 That's / That is our house.
2 Where's / Where is your car?
3 That's / That is his desk and hers is next to / by the window.
4 Could you please give me that/the phone? It's mine.
5 A friend of mine has a horse.
6 'Whose are these/those?' 'They're ours.'
7 That's / This is not my bag/handbag; it's yours.
8 A friend of hers lives in our street.
9 'Whose coat is this/that?' 'It's / That's his.'
10 'Is that/this your dog?' 'No, it's theirs/hers.'

UNIT 63

63.1
2 Yes, I know **her**, but I can't remember **her name**.
3 Yes, **I know them**, but **I can't remember their** names.
4 Yes, **I know you**, but I **can't remember your name**.

63.2
2 He invited us to stay with **him** at his house.
3 They invited me to stay with **them at their** house.
4 I invited them to stay **with me at my** house.
5 She invited us to stay **with her at her** house.
6 Did you invite him **to stay with you at your** house?

63.3
2 I gave her my phone number, and she gave me **hers**.
3 He gave me his phone number, and I gave **him mine**.
4 We gave them **our** phone number and they gave **us theirs**.
5 She gave him **her** phone number and he gave **her his**.
6 You gave us **your** phone number, and we gave **you ours**.
7 They gave you **their** phone number, and you gave **them yours**.

63.4
2 them
3 him
4 our
5 yours
6 us
7 her
8 their
9 mine

63.5
1 I love him and he loves me.
2 We have a lot of / many flowers in our garden.
3 'Where's / Where is Anna?' 'She's in her room.'
4 Would you like to come with me or go with him?
5 'Is that/this your car?' 'No, it's theirs/hers.'
6 A friend of his is going to the cinema with us tomorrow.
7 Here's / Here is my business card. Could you give me yours?
8 They didn't have a key, so I gave them mine.

UNIT 64

64.1
2 myself
3 herself
4 themselves
5 myself
6 himself
7 yourself
8 yourselves

Schlüssel zu den Übungen

64.2
2 When I saw him, he **was by himself**.
3 Don't **go out by yourself**.
4 I **went to the cinema by myself**.
5 My sister **lives by herself**.
6 Many people **live by themselves**.

64.3
2 They can't see each other.
3 They call each other a lot.
4 They don't know each other.
5 They're / They are sitting next to each other.
6 They gave each other presents / a present.

64.4
3 each other
4 yourselves
5 us
6 ourselves
7 each other
8 each other
9 them
10 themselves

64.5
1 I enjoyed myself very much at the carnival.
2 I'm sorry. I didn't want to hurt you.
3 Helen often talks to herself.
4 We'd / We would like to be alone / by ourselves.
5 My father fell down and hurt himself.
6 We love each other very much.
7 Are the children at home by themselves / alone?
8 You look funny. Look at yourself in the mirror!
9 I met Laura yesterday.
10 How do you feel today? *oder* How are you feeling today?

UNIT 65

65.1
3 Helen is **Brian's** wife.
4 James is Sarah's **brother**.
5 James is **Daniel's** uncle.
6 Sarah is **Paul's** wife.
7 Helen is Daniel's **grandmother**.
8 Sarah is James's **sister**.
9 Paul is **Sarah's** husband.
10 Paul is Daniel's **father**.
11 Daniel is **James's** nephew.

65.2
2 Andy's
3 Dave's
4 Jane's
5 Rachel's
6 Alice's

65.3
3 OK
4 Simon's phone number
5 My brother's job
6 OK
7 OK
8 Paula's favourite colour
9 your mother's birthday
10 My parents' house
11 OK
12 OK
13 Silvia's party
14 OK

65.4
1 That's / This is Toby's book.
2 My wife's car is at the garage.
3 'Whose coat is that/this?' 'Sarah's.'
4 The windows of the house are very small.
5 Mrs Murray's office is on the second floor.
6 I was at my brother's last weekend.
7 My parents' garden is very beautiful/ nice.
8 Did you like the beginning of the film/movie?
9 At the end of the week I was very tired.

UNIT 66

66.1
2 a
3 a
4 an
5 a
6 an
7 a
8 an
9 an

66.2
2 a vegetable
3 a game
4 a tool
5 a mountain
6 a planet
7 a fruit
8 a river
9 a flower
10 a musical instrument

66.3
2 He's a shop assistant.
3 She's an architect.
4 She's a taxi driver.
5 He's an electrician.
6 She's a photographer.
7 She's a nurse.
8 I'm a/an …

66.4
2–8
Tom never wears **a** hat.
I can't ride **a** bike.
My brother is **an** artist.
Rebecca works in **a** bookshop.
Jane wants to learn **a** foreign language.
Mike lives in **an** old house.
This evening I'm going to **a** party.

66.5
1 Cricket is a sport.
2 Lisa works in an office.
3 Would you like an apple?
4 I don't have / haven't got a bike.
5 My mother is a doctor.
6 Is there a university in Cardiff?
7 Can/Could I have an orange juice, please?
8 John has an interesting job. He's a photographer.
9 We play tennis three times a week.

UNIT 67

67.1
2 boats
3 women
4 cities
5 umbrellas
6 addresses
7 knives
8 sandwiches
9 families
10 feet
11 holidays
12 potatoes

67.2
2 teeth
3 people
4 children
5 fish
6 leaves

67.3
3 … with a lot of beautiful **trees**.
4 … with two **men**.
5 OK
6 … three **children**.
7 Most of my **friends** are **students**.
8 He put on his **pyjamas** …
9 OK
10 Do you know many **people** …
11 I like your **trousers**. Where did you get **them**?
12 … full of **tourists**.
13 OK
14 **These scissors aren't** …

67.4
2 are
3 don't
4 watch
5 were
6 live
7 Do
8 are
9 them
10 some

67.5
1 I have (got) two brothers and a sister.
2 Sandra has (got) two red dresses.
3 There are a lot of / many people in the park today.
4 Does Michael usually wear glasses?
5 The/These shoes don't fit me. My feet are too big.
6 These tomatoes taste very good.
7 The police are looking for a bank robber.
8 We have six women and four men on our English course. *oder* There are six women and …
9 I need some new tights / a new pair of tights and some pyjamas / a pair of pyjamas.

UNIT 68

68.1
3 a jug
4 water
5 toothpaste
6 a toothbrush
7 an egg
8 money
9 a wallet
10 sand
11 a bucket
12 an envelope

68.2
3 … **a** hat.
4 … **a** job?
5 OK
6 … **an** apple …
7 … **a** party …
8 … **a** wonderful thing.
9 … **an** island.
10 … **a** key.

Schlüssel zu den Übungen

11 OK
12 ... **a** good idea.
13 ... **a** car?
14 ... **a** cup of coffee?
15 OK
16 ... **an** umbrella.

68.3
2 a piece of wood
3 a glass of water
4 a bar of chocolate
5 a cup of tea
6 a piece of paper
7 a bowl of soup
8 a loaf of bread
9 a jar of honey

68.4
1 We need (some) milk and four eggs.
2 Terry never goes to work without a tie.
3 You need air and water to live.
4 I drink a litre of water every day.
5 Rita has (got) two cats and a dog.
6 Would you like a piece of cake?
7 A glass of orange juice and a bowl of cornflakes, please.
8 I often listen to music when I work / when I'm working.

UNIT 69

69.1
2 a newspaper (*oder* a paper), some flowers (*oder* a bunch of flowers) and a pen
3 some bananas, some eggs and some bread (*oder* a loaf of bread)
4 some toothpaste, some soap (*oder* a bar of soap) and a comb

69.2
2 Would you like some coffee? (*oder* ... a cup of coffee?)
3 Would you like a biscuit?
4 Would you like some bread? (*oder* ... a piece of bread? / a slice of bread?)
5 Would you like a chocolate?
6 Would you like some cake? (*oder* ... a piece of cake?)

69.3
2 some ... some
3 some
4 a ... some
5 an ... some
6 a ... a ... some
7 some
8 some
9 some ... a

69.4
2 eyes
3 hair
4 information
5 chairs
6 furniture
7 job
8 wonderful weather

69.5
1 I need some money.
2 That's / This is a nice/beautiful birthday cake.
3 Could you buy some bananas, please?
4 Jenny gave me some good advice.
5 How often do you wash your hair?
6 Could you give me some information, please?
7 Martha is looking for a different job / another job.
8 Tom bought a paper / a newspaper, some cheese and some bread rolls.

UNIT 70

70.1
3 ... **the** police.
4 ... **the** moon?
5 ... **the** top of the hill.
6 OK
7 ... **the** city centre?
8 ... **the** left.
9 ... **the** piano.
10 ... **the** biggest city in the world?
11 OK
12 ... to get information from **the** internet.
13 ... **the** radio much.
14 ... on **the** top shelf on **the** right.
15 ... in **the** country about ten miles from **the** nearest town.

70.2
2 the same time
3 the same age
4 the same colour
5 the same problem

70.3
2 **the** guitar   5 **the** sea
3 breakfast   6 **the** bottom
4 television/TV

70.4
2 **the** name   6 **the** capital
3 **The** sky   7 lunch
4 TV   8 **the** middle
5 **the** police

70.5
1 Joe and I live in the same street.
2 Where's / Where is Mum/Mummy?
3 The house is in the middle of a park.
4 Can you play the guitar?
5 What's / What is the name of the man next to Rachel?
6 Our house is on the left next to the church.
7 Lunch is on the table!
8 Today there is / there's nothing interesting on TV.
9 Do you live in a town/city or in the country?

UNIT 71

71.1
2 **the** cinema   5 home
3 hospital   6 prison
4 **the** airport

71.2
3 school   6 bed
4 **the** station   7 **the** post office
5 home

71.3
2 **the** cinema
3 go to bed
4 go to prison
5 go to **the** dentist
6 go to university/college
7 go to hospital / are taken to hospital (American speakers say 'go to the hospital', 'are taken to the hospital.')

71.4
3 **the** doctor   10 **the** city centre
4 OK   11 **the** station
5 OK   12 OK
6 OK   13 OK
7 **the** bank   14 OK
8 OK   15 **the** theatre
9 OK

71.5
1 Jessica starts/begins work at 8.30.
2 I usually go to bed at midnight.
3 'Where are you?' 'At the station.'
4 Where did you go to school?
5 My parents aren't / are not at home today.
6 Would you like to go to the cinema with us?
7 Her brother was in prison for five years.
8 We're / We are going to the bank and then to the post office.
9 Tom was at university for five years.

UNIT 72

72.1
Beispiel-Antworten:
2 I don't like dogs.
3 I hate museums.
4 I love big cities.
5 I don't like tennis.
6 I love chocolate.
7 I don't like computer games.
8 I hate parties.

72.2
Beispiel-Antworten:
2 I'm not interested in politics.
3 I'm interested in sport.
4 I don't know much about art.
5 I don't know anything about astronomy.
6 I know a little about economics.

Schlüssel zu den Übungen

72.3
3 friends
4 parties
5 **The** shops
6 **the** milk
7 milk
8 basketball
9 buildings
10 **The** water
11 cold water
12 **the** salt
13 **the** people
14 Vegetables
15 **The** houses
16 **the** words
17 pictures
18 the pictures
19 English … international business
20 Money … happiness

72.4
1 My son likes history and English.
2 Life isn't / is not easy.
3 Harry doesn't / does not drink coffee.
4 Jenny is interested in modern art.
5 The people in this town/city are very friendly/nice.
6 The weather isn't / is not very good today.
7 Maria doesn't / does not like cold weather.
8 In this museum you can learn a lot about science.

UNIT 73

73.1
3 Sweden
4 **The** Amazon
5 Asia
6 **The** Pacific
7 **The** Rhine
8 Kenya
9 **The** United States
10 **The** Andes
11 Bangkok
12 **The** Alps
13 **The** Red Sea
14 Jamaica
15 **The** Bahamas

73.2
3 OK
4 **the** Philippines
5 **the** south of France
6 **the** Regal Cinema
7 OK
8 **the** Museum of Art
9 OK
10 Belgium is smaller than **the** Netherlands.
11 **the** Mississippi … **the** Nile
12 **the** National Gallery
13 **the** Park Hotel in Hudson Road
14 OK
15 **The** Rocky Mountains are in North America.
16 OK
17 **the** United States
18 **the** west of Ireland

19 OK
20 **The** Panama Canal joins **the** Atlantic Ocean and **the** Pacific Ocean.

73.3
1 Lake Geneva is in Switzerland.
2 Michael and Amy always spend their holidays in Turkey.
3 Heidelberg University is very old.
4 (Mount) Everest is higher than (Mount) Kilimanjaro.
5 We're / We are going by train to Frankfurt Airport tomorrow. *oder* We're / We are taking the train …
6 The (River) Nile is in the north of Africa.
7 A: Which hotel are you staying at?
   B: At the Hilton.
8 We want to go to the Mediterranean next summer – maybe to Greece.
9 A: Is Idaho in the east of the USA?
   B: No, in the west.

UNIT 74

74.1
2 that house
3 these postcards
4 those birds
5 this seat
6 These plates

74.2
2 Is that your umbrella?
3 Is this your book?
4 Are those your books?
5 Is that your bicycle/bike?
6 Are these your keys?
7 Are those your keys?
8 Is this your watch?
9 Are those your glasses?
10 Are these your gloves?

74.3
2 that's
3 This is
4 That's
5 that
6 this is
7 That's
8 that's

74.4
1 That man is the manager.
2 Is this your umbrella?
3 What are those people doing?
4 This dress is nice/pretty/beautiful, but it's expensive.
5 This is Anna. Is that Michael?
6 'I was in Paris last week.' '(Oh) that's nice!'
7 Do you like these flowers?
8 Megan, this is my friend Peter.
9 This soup tastes delicious.
10 Look at those clouds. They're beautiful.
11 Which way should we put the table? Like that/this?
12 That was a very nice evening. Thank you very much!

UNIT 75

75.1
2 I don't need one
3 I'm going to get one
4 I don't have one / I haven't got one
5 I've just had one
6 there's one in Mill Road

75.2
2 a new one
3 a better one
4 an old one
5 a big one
6 a different one

75.3
2 Which ones?
   The green ones.
3 Which one?
   The one with a/the red door.
4 Which ones?
   The ones on the top shelf.
5 Which one?
   The black one.
6 Which one?
   The one on the wall.
7 Which one?
   The tall one with long hair.
8 Which ones?
   The yellow ones.
9 Which one?
   The one with a/the moustache and glasses.
10 Which ones?
   The ones I took at the party last week.

75.4
1 'Do you have / Have you got a laptop?' 'No, but I would like to buy one.'
2 I've / I have made (some) sandwiches. *oder* I made (some) sandwiches. Would you like one?
3 Which piece would you like?
   This one or that one?
4 'Which house does Ben live in?'
   'In the one with the nice/beautiful garden.'
5 Which earrings do you like?
   These (ones) or those (ones)?
6 'Would you like these apples?'
   'No, the other ones.'
7 Which dress should I wear?
   The red one or the black one?
8 We have / We've got a/one child and we would / we'd like another one.
9 My hands are cold in these gloves. I need some warmer ones.

UNIT 76

76.1
2 some
3 any
4 any
5 any
6 some
7 any
8 some
9 some
10 any … any
11 some … any
12 some

Schlüssel zu den Übungen

76.2
2 some questions
3 any pictures
4 any foreign languages
5 some friends
6 some milk
7 any batteries
8 some fresh air
9 some cheese
10 any help

76.3
3 I have some / I've got some
4 I don't have any / I haven't got any / I haven't any
5 I didn't buy any
6 I bought some
7 I didn't drink any

76.4
2 something
3 anything
4 anything
5 Somebody/Someone
6 anything
7 anybody/anyone
8 something
9 anything
10 anybody/anyone

76.5
1 There's / There is some bread on the table.
2 We don't have / We haven't got any food in the house.
3 Would you like some cake?
4 We met some friends in town.
5 Did anybody/anyone call/phone? *oder* Has anybody/anyone called/phoned?
6 We don't have / We haven't got any milk. Could you give us some?
7 A: Did you buy any bananas yesterday?
   B: No, but I bought some apples.
8 There aren't any shops in this street, but there are some in the next street. *oder* … in the next street there are some.
9 Martha saw something in the garden, but I didn't see anything.

UNIT 77

77.1
2 There are no shops near here.
3 Carla has no free time. / Carla has got no free time.
4 There is no light in this room.
6 There isn't any milk in the fridge.
7 There aren't any buses today.
8 Tom doesn't have any brothers or sisters. / Tom hasn't got any brothers or sisters.

77.2
2 any
3 any
4 no
5 any
6 no
7 any
8 no
9 any
10 no
11 None
12 any

77.3
2 no money
3 any questions
4 no friends
5 no difference
6 any furniture
7 no idea
8 any heating
9 no queue

77.4
Beispiel-Antworten:
2 Three.
3 Two cups.
4 None.
5 None.

77.5
1 There aren't any / There are no children in the park.
2 We don't have / haven't got any bread. *oder* We have (got) / We've got no bread.
3 'How many people are there?' 'None.'
4 'Who told you that?' 'No-one/Nobody.'
5 I need (some) new clothes, but I have (got) / I've got no money. *oder* … but I don't have / haven't got any money.
6 A: How many children do they have / have they got?
   B: None.
7 Tom doesn't do much in his free time. He has / He's got no hobbies. *oder* He doesn't have / hasn't got any hobbies.
8 A: Were there any mistakes in my email?
   B: No, none.

UNIT 78

78.1
2 There's nobody in the office.
3 I have nothing to do. / I've got nothing to do.
4 There's nothing on TV.
5 There was no-one at home.
6 We found nothing.

78.2
2 There wasn't anybody on the bus.
3 I don't have anything to read. / I haven't got anything to read.
4 I don't have anyone to help me. / I haven't got anyone to help me.
5 She didn't hear anything.
6 We don't have anything for dinner. / We haven't got anything for dinner.

78.3
3a Nothing.
4a Nobody./No-one.
5a Nobody./No-one.
6a Nothing.
7a Nothing.
8a Nobody./No-one.
3b I don't want anything.
4b I didn't meet anybody/anyone.
5b Nobody/No-one knows the answer.
6b I didn't buy anything.
7b Nothing happened.
8b Nobody/No-one was late.

78.4
3 anything
4 Nobody/No-one
5 Nothing
6 anything
7 anybody/anyone
8 nothing
9 anything
10 anything
11 nobody/no-one
12 anything
13 Nothing
14 Nobody/No-one … anybody/anyone

78.5
1 'What's / What is in that cupboard?' 'Nothing.'
2 Nobody phoned/rang/called me yesterday.
3 We're / We are sorry we can't/cannot do anything. *oder* … we can do nothing.
4 I did it by myself. Nobody/No-one helped me.
5 'Who's / Who is here tomorrow?' *oder* 'Who will be …' 'No-one / Nobody.'
6 'Why don't you answer?' 'I don't have / haven't got anything to say.' *oder* 'I have (got) / I've got nothing to say.'
7 I was at your house yesterday, but there was nobody/no-one at home. *oder* … there wasn't anybody/anyone at home.
8 John was very lazy yesterday. He didn't do anything. *oder* He did nothing.
9 Sarah never has visitors. She doesn't see anybody. *oder* She sees nobody.

UNIT 79

79.1
2 something
3 somewhere
4 somebody/someone

79.2
2a Nowhere.
3a Nothing.
4a Nobody./No-one.
2b I'm not going anywhere.
3b I don't want anything.
4b I'm not looking for anybody/anyone.

79.3
3 anything
4 anything
5 somebody/someone
6 something
7 anybody/anyone … nobody/no-one
8 anything
9 Nobody/No-one
10 anybody/anyone
11 Nothing
12 anywhere
13 somewhere
14 anything
15 anybody/anyone

301

Schlüssel zu den Übungen

79.4
2 anything to eat
3 nothing to do
4 anywhere to sit
5 something to drink
6 nowhere to park
7 something to read
8 somewhere to stay

79.5
1 Somebody/Someone has eaten my chocolate. *oder* … ate my chocolate.
2 Is anybody/anyone there?
3 'Look!' 'What? I can't see anything.' *oder* 'I can see nothing.'
4 My pen is here somewhere, but I can't find it.
5 Can I do anything else for you?
6 There isn't anything to read here. *oder* There's nothing to read here.
7 'Is Toby at the cafe?' 'No, he's somewhere else.'
8 A: Did you buy anything at the flea market yesterday?
B: No, I didn't find anything cheap. *oder* I found nothing cheap.
9 This weekend I want to do something else/different.
10 Jessica didn't like/enjoy the party. She didn't meet anybody/anyone interesting. *oder* She met nobody interesting.

UNIT 80

80.1
2 Every day
3 every time
4 Every room
5 every word

80.2
2 every day
3 all day
4 every day
5 all day
6 all day
7 every day

80.3
2 every
3 all
4 all
5 Every
6 all
7 every
8 all
9 every

80.4
2 everything
3 Everybody/Everyone
4 everything
5 everywhere
6 Everybody/Everyone
7 everywhere
8 Everything

80.5
2 is
3 has
4 likes
5 has
6 was
7 makes
8 Is … Does

80.6
1 Every garden in this street is nice/beautiful. *oder* All the gardens in this street are …
2 It rained all summer.
3 Everybody/Everyone needs love.
4 Do you go shopping every day?
5 Dan goes to the sports club every week.
6 We haven't slept / didn't sleep all night.
7 'Is everything OK / all right?' 'Yes, everything is wonderful/great/fine.'
8 Every time I go out, I come home late.
9 I did nothing / I didn't do anything all day yesterday.
10 There's / There is nobody/no-one here. Everybody/Everyone has gone home.
11 Becky has lived everywhere in the USA.

UNIT 81

81.1
3 Some
4 Most of
5 Most
6 any of
7 all *oder* all of
8 None of
9 any of
10 Most
11 most of
12 Some
13 All *oder* All of
14 some of
15 most of

81.2
2 All of them.
3 Some of them.
4 None of them.
5 Most of them.
6 None of it.

81.3
3 Some people …
4 Some of **the** questions … *oder* Some questions …
5 OK
6 All insects …
7 OK (*oder* … all **of** these books)
8 Most of **the** students … *oder* Most students …
9 OK
10 … most of **the** night

81.4
1 All children need love.
2 None of these houses are big.
3 Most people eat too much.
4 Some of my friends have children.
5 The little girl doesn't want any of her food.
6 Some animals are dangerous.
7 Most of my colleagues are nice/friendly, but some of them are unfriendly.
8 I don't know any of these people. *oder* I know none of these people.
9 In my family, all of us have blue eyes, but none of us have blond hair.
10 A: Did you like the film/movie?
B: Some of it / Part of it, but not all of it.
11 All (of) these dresses/clothes are expensive, but none of them are nice/beautiful.

UNIT 82

82.1
3 Both
4 Neither
5 Neither
6 both
7 Either
8 neither of
9 Neither
10 either of
11 Both
12 neither of
13 Both
14 either of

82.2
2 Both windows are open.
3 Neither man is wearing a hat. *oder* Neither of them is wearing …
4 Both men have (got) beards. *oder* Both of them have …
5 Both buses go to the airport. *oder* … are going to the airport.
6 Neither answer is correct.

82.3
3 Both of them are students.
4 Neither of them has (got) a car.
5 Both of them live in London.
6 Both of them like cooking.
7 Neither of them can play the piano.
8 Both of them eat seafood.
9 Neither of them is interested in sport.

82.4
1 We have / We've got two cars, but both (of them) are old.
2 Both (of) my brothers live in London.
3 'Would you like apple juice or orange juice?' 'Neither, thank you / thanks. I'm not thirsty.'
4 I like London and Paris, but both cities are very expensive.
5 I saw both films/movies, but neither of them was good.
6 'Shall we go to the cinema or to the concert tonight / this evening?' 'Either. I don't mind.'
7 Tom and Suzanne have (got) a girl and a boy. Neither of the children goes to school.
8 Both of us are tired today. *oder* We're both tired today. Neither of us slept well.
9 'Do you know Jim and Tina Brown?' 'Yes, both of them are very nice.'
10 'Where are Ann and Sally?' 'I don't know. I haven't seen either of them.'

UNIT 83

83.1
2 many
3 much
4 many
5 many
6 much
7 much
8 many
9 How many
10 How much
11 How much
12 How many

83.2
2 much time
3 many countries
4 many people
5 much luggage
6 many times

Schlüssel zu den Übungen

83.3
2 a lot of interesting things
3 a lot of accidents
4 a lot of fun
5 a lot of traffic

83.4
3 a lot of snow   6 OK
4 OK   7 OK
5 a lot of money   8 a lot

83.5
3 She plays tennis a lot.
4 He doesn't use his car much.
  (oder ... a lot.)
5 He doesn't go out much.
  (oder ... a lot.)
6 She travels a lot.

83.6
1 I eat a lot of fruit.
2 We don't have much bread / a lot of bread. oder We haven't got ...
3 Did you meet many people / a lot of people at the party?
4 My neighbours have a lot of flowers / many flowers in the garden.
5 Do you go to the theatre much / a lot? oder Do you often go to the theatre?
6 How many books did you read last year?
7 Becky usually goes to bed early. She sleeps a lot.
8 A: How much time do we have / have we got?
  B: Not much / a lot.

UNIT 84

84.1
2 a few   5 a little
3 a little   6 a few
4 a few

84.2
2 a little milk
3 A few days
4 a little Russian
5 a few friends
6 a few times
7 a few chairs
8 a little fresh air

84.3
2 very little coffee
3 very little rain
4 very few hotels
5 very little time
6 Very few people
7 very little work

84.4
2 A few   5 few
3 a little   6 a little
4 little   7 little

84.5
2 ... **a** little luck
3 ... **a** few things
4 OK
5 ... **a** few questions
6 ... **few** people
7 OK

84.6
1 We have a few plants in our flat/apartment.
2 'What would you like to drink?' 'A little orange juice, please.'
3 'Do we have / Have we got any butter in the fridge?' 'Yes, a little.'
4 'Is there a cinema in this town?' 'Yes, there are a few.'
5 Few people have enough free time.
6 It's cold here in (the) winter, but it snows very little.
7 Tom has (got) a few friends, but few good friends.
8 I have very little time today, but tomorrow I have a little more time.
  oder ... I'll / I will have ...

UNIT 85

85.1
2 black clouds
3 long holiday
4 hot water
5 fresh air
6 sharp knife
7 dangerous job

85.2
2 It looks new.
3 I feel ill.
4 You look surprised.
5 They smell nice.
6 It tastes horrible.

85.3
2 It doesn't look new.
3 You don't sound American.
4 I don't feel cold.
5 They don't look heavy.
6 Maybe, but it doesn't taste good.

85.4
1 Terry has (got) blue eyes and blond hair.
2 The weather wasn't very nice/good yesterday.
3 Amy and Max live in a big/large modern house.
4 'You look good.' 'Thank you.'
5 There are (some) beautiful old trees in this park.
6 Are you thirsty? Would you like something to drink?
7 Joe knows many interesting people. oder ... a lot of interesting people.
8 What are you cooking? It smells wonderful/great!
9 I'm cold. Could you close the window, please?
10 'I feel terrible/awful.' 'You don't sound good.'

UNIT 86

86.1
2 badly   5 fast
3 quietly   6 dangerously
4 angrily

86.2
2 work hard
3 sleep well
4 win easily
5 Think carefully
6 know her very well
7 explain things very clearly/well
8 Come quickly

86.3
2 angry   7 suddenly
3 slowly   8 quiet
4 slow   9 badly
5 careful   10 nice (siehe Unit 85C)
6 hard   11 quickly

86.4
2 well
3 good
4 well
5 well
6 good ... good

86.5
1 I'm / I am very slow in the morning.
2 Why are you walking so slowly? Are you tired?
3 Suddenly she saw James.
4 Be careful when you cross the street/road.
5 A: Can you speak Spanish?
  B: Yes, but not very well.
6 A: How are your children?
  B: They're / They are very well, thank you / thanks.
7 Tom works fast/quickly, but badly.
8 We worked / We've worked very hard today.
9 A: How well does Jenny speak Japanese?
  B: She speaks it perfectly!

UNIT 87

87.1
2 bigger
3 slower
4 more expensive
5 higher
6 more dangerous

87.2
2 stronger
3 happier
4 more modern
5 more important
6 better
7 larger
8 more serious
9 prettier
10 more crowded

87.3
2 hotter/warmer
3 more expensive
4 worse
5 further
6 more difficult oder harder

303

Schlüssel zu den Übungen

87.4
3 taller
4 harder
5 more comfortable
6 better
7 nicer
8 heavier
9 more interested
10 warmer
11 better
12 bigger
13 more beautiful
14 sharper
15 more polite
16 worse

87.5
1 The train is fast, but the plane is faster.
2 A: Which dress do you like?
   B: This one is nicer / prettier / more beautiful.
3 I can take the big suitcase. It's heavier.
4 Which is further? Paris or Rome?
5 Paris is expensive, but London is more expensive.
6 You didn't say 'thank you'. You should be more polite.
7 The film/movie is good, but the book is better.
8 David is in bed. His headache is worse.

UNIT 88

88.1
3 Kate is taller than Ben.
4 Kate starts work earlier than Ben.
5 Ben works harder than Kate.
6 Ben has more money than Kate. / Ben has got more money than Kate.
7 Kate is a better driver than Ben.
8 Ben is more patient than Kate.
9 Ben is a better dancer than Kate. / Ben dances better than Kate.
10 Kate is more intelligent than Ben.
11 Kate speaks French better than Ben. / Kate speaks better French than Ben. / Kate's French is better than Ben's.
12 Ben goes to the cinema more than Kate. / … more often than Kate.

88.2
2 You're older than her. / … than she is.
3 You work harder than me. / … than I do.
4 You watch TV more than him. / … than he does.
5 You're a better cook than me. / … than I am. *oder* You cook better than me. / … than I do.
6 You know more people than us. / … than we do.
7 You've got more money than them. / … than they have.
8 You can run faster than me. / … than I can.
9 You've been here longer than her. / … than she has.
10 You got up earlier than them. / … than they did.
11 You were more surprised than him. / … than he was.

88.3
2 Jack's mother is much younger than his father.
3 My camera cost a bit more than yours. / … than your camera. *oder* My camera was a bit more expensive than …
4 I feel much better today than yesterday. / … than I did yesterday. / … than I felt yesterday.
5 It's a bit warmer today than yesterday. / … than it was yesterday.
6 Sarah is a much better tennis player than me. / … than I am. *oder* Sarah is much better at tennis than me. / … than I am. *oder* Sarah plays tennis much better than me. / … than I do.

88.4
1 You're / You are younger than me / than I am.
2 Is French more difficult to learn than English?
3 You can read faster / more quickly than me / than I can.
4 Our new house is much bigger than our old flat/apartment.
5 A: How many people were at the party?
   B: More than 30.
6 Tom has much more time than Dave.
7 A: How long did you wait at the doctor's? Half an hour?
   B: No, less than 20 minutes.
8 The blue dress is a bit / a little more expensive than the black one, but it's / it is much nicer / prettier / more beautiful.

UNIT 89

89.1
2 A is longer than B, but not as long as C.
3 C is heavier than A, but not as heavy as B.
4 A is older than C, but not as old as B.
5 B has (got) more money than C, but not as much as A. *oder* … but less (money) than A.
6 C works harder than A, but not as hard as B.

89.2
2 Your room isn't as big as mine. / … as my room.
3 I didn't get up as early as you. / … as you did.
4 They didn't play as well as us. / … as we did.
5 You haven't been here as long as me. / … as I have.
6 He isn't as nervous as her. / … as she is.

89.3
2 as   6 than
3 than   7 as
4 than   8 than
5 as

89.4
2 Julia lives in the same street as Laura.
3 Julia got up at the same time as Andy.
4 Andy's car is the same colour as Laura's.

89.5
1 Germany is not as big as France.
2 France is bigger than Germany.
3 I have / I've got the same hat as you.
4 Ben is taller than Joe, but not as tall as Mark.
5 A: How do you feel / are you feeling today?
   B: The same as yesterday – not very well/good.
6 I live in the same street as my colleague.
7 I don't have / haven't got as many books as you.
8 Munich isn't / is not as expensive as London, but it's / it is more expensive than Frankfurt.
9 Jenny doesn't sleep as much as Tom. She doesn't / does not get up as late as him / as he does.

UNIT 90

90.1
2 C is longer than A.
   D is the longest.
   B is the shortest.
3 D is younger than C.
   B is the youngest.
   C is the oldest.
4 D is more expensive than A.
   C is the most expensive.
   A is the cheapest.
5 A is better than C.
   A is the best.
   D is the worst.

90.2
2 the happiest day
3 the best film
4 the most popular singer
5 the worst mistake
6 the prettiest village
7 the coldest day
8 the most boring person

90.3
2 Everest is the highest mountain in the world.
3–6
Brazil is the largest country in South America.
Alaska is the largest state in the USA.
The Nile is the longest river in Africa. / … in the world.
Jupiter is the largest planet in the solar system.

Schlüssel zu den Übungen

90.4
1 Mandy is the tallest girl in her class.
2 Is Munich the most expensive city in Germany?
3 What was the best day of your life?
4 A: How was your trip to Australia?
   B: It was the most interesting holiday we've / we have ever had.
5 Those were the easiest exercises we've ever done. *oder* … we have ever done.
6 Mark is a bad pupil/student, but Sam is worse. Sam is the worst in the class.
7 This is the biggest suitcase, but it isn't / it's not the heaviest.

UNIT 91

91.1
2 enough chairs
3 enough paint
4 enough wind

91.2
2 The car isn't big enough.
3 His legs aren't long enough.
4 He isn't strong enough.

91.3
3 old enough
4 enough time
5 big enough
6 eat enough
7 enough space
8 tired enough
9 practise enough

91.4
2 sharp enough to cut
3 warm enough to go
4 enough bread to make
5 well enough to win
6 enough time to read

91.5
1 Have you eaten enough?
2 Joe doesn't go out much. He doesn't have / hasn't got enough time.
3 A: Does your son go to school?
   B: No, he isn't old enough yet.
4 We don't have / haven't got enough food for the weekend.
5 Is the room warm enough for you?
6 Jenny and Michael don't have / haven't got enough money to buy a house.
7 Our flat/apartment isn't big enough for a party.
8 We don't have / haven't got enough time to eat before we go (out). *oder* There isn't enough time for us to eat before we go (out).
9 Our flat/apartment isn't big enough for the children to play in.

UNIT 92

92.1
2 too heavy
3 too low
4 too fast
5 too big
6 too crowded

92.2
3 enough
4 too many
5 too
6 enough
7 too much
8 enough
9 too
10 too many
11 too much

92.3
3 It's too far.
4 It's too expensive.
5 It isn't / It's not big enough.
6 It was too difficult.
7 It isn't good enough.
8 I'm too busy.
9 It was too long.

92.4
2 too early to go to bed
3 too young to get married
4 too dangerous to go out at night
5 too late to phone Sue (now)
6 too surprised to say anything

92.5
1 That's a good restaurant, but it's / it is too expensive.
2 I don't like the weather here. It rains too much.
3 Our class is too big. We have (got) / We've got too many pupils/students.
4 We want to move. Our flat/apartment isn't big enough for us.
5 This city is dangerous. There's / There is too much crime here.
6 I can't speak to him now. I don't have / haven't got enough time.
7 It's / It is too hot to play tennis.
8 It's / It is boring here. There isn't enough to do.
9 Can you turn the music down? It's / It is too loud for me to work.

UNIT 93

93.1
3 I like this picture very much.
4 Tom started his new job last week.
5 OK
6 Jessica bought a present for her friend. *oder* Jessica bought her friend a present.
7 I drink three cups of coffee every day.
8 OK
9 I borrowed fifty pounds from my brother.

93.2
2 I got a new phone last week.
3 Paul finished his work quickly.
4 Emily doesn't speak French very well.
5 I did a lot of shopping yesterday.
6 Do you know London well?
7 We enjoyed the party very much.
8 I explained the problem carefully.
9 We met some friends at the airport.
10 Did you buy that jacket in England?
11 We do the same thing every day.
12 I don't like football very much.

93.3
2 I arrived at the hotel early.
3 Julia goes to Italy every year.
4 We have lived here since 1998.
5 Sue was born in London in 1990.
6 Paul didn't go to work yesterday.
7 Helen went to a wedding last weekend.
8 I had my breakfast in bed this morning.
9 Amy is going to university in September.
10 I saw a beautiful bird in the garden this morning.
11 My parents have been to the United States many times.
12 I left my umbrella in the restaurant last night.
13 Are you going to the cinema tomorrow evening?
14 I took the children to school this morning.

93.4
1 I eat an apple every day.
2 We saw an interesting film/movie yesterday.
3 Kate can play the piano very well.
4 We want to go/drive to the mountains next weekend.
5 Jenny and Michael go to Ireland every summer.
6 We ate in a good restaurant yesterday evening / last night.
7 Anna is at work at 8 o'clock every day.
8 I left my handbag on the bus yesterday.
9 Mary is 90 years old. She's / She has seen a lot (of things) in her life.

UNIT 94

94.1
2 He always gets up early.
3 He's / He is never late for work.
4 He sometimes gets angry.
5 He rarely goes swimming.
6 He's / He is usually at home in the evenings.

94.2
2 Susan is always polite.
3 I usually finish work at 5 o'clock.
4 Sarah has just started a new job.
5 I rarely go to bed before midnight.
6 The bus isn't usually late.
7 I don't often eat fish.
8 I will never forget what you said.
9 Have you ever lost your passport?
10 Do you still work in the same place?
11 They always stay in the same hotel.

305

Schlüssel zu den Übungen

12 Jane doesn't usually work on Saturdays.
13 Is Tina already here?
14 What do you usually have for breakfast?
15 I can never remember his name.

94.3
2 Yes, and I also speak French.
3 Yes, and I'm also hungry.
4 Yes, and I've also been to Ireland.
5 Yes, and I also bought some books.

94.4
1 They both play football.
  They're / They are both students.
  They've both got cars. / They both have cars.
2 They're / They are all married.
  They were all born in England.
  They all live in New York.

94.5
1 We sometimes watch TV in the evening.
2 Megan often gets up at 7 o'clock.
3 I'm / I am always tired on Friday evening/evenings. *oder* On Friday evening/evenings I'm / I am always tired.
4 We rarely/seldom go to the theatre.
5 What time do you usually go to bed?
6 I've / I have already read this book.
7 Tina has never been to Italy.
8 I've / I have just seen Paul.
9 I'll / I will often think of this day.
10 I have (got) / I've got two brothers and one sister. They're / They are all in America.
11 It's not very late. We can still go out if you want.

UNIT 95

95.1
2 Do you still live in Clare Street?
3 Are you still a student?
4 Have you still got a motorbike? / Do you still have a motorbike?
5 Do you still go to the cinema a lot?
6 Do you still want to be a teacher?

95.2
2 He was looking for a job.
  He's / He is still looking (for a job).
  He hasn't found a job yet.
3 She was asleep. She's / She is still asleep.
  She hasn't woken up yet. / She isn't awake yet. / She hasn't got up yet. *oder* She isn't up yet.
4 They were having dinner. / They were eating.
  They're / They are still having dinner. / … still eating.
  They haven't finished (dinner) yet. / They haven't finished eating yet.

95.3
2 Is Helen here yet? *oder* Has Helen arrived/come yet?
3 Have you had your (exam) results yet? / Have you got your … / Have you received your …
4 Have you decided where to go yet? / Do you know where you're going yet?

95.4
3 She's / She has already gone/left.
4 I already have one. / I've already got one.
5 I've / I have already paid (it).
6 No, he already knows.

95.5
1 Do you still go dancing?
2 It's / It is late, but I'm not tired yet.
3 I've / I have already drunk a/one glass of water, but I'm / I am still thirsty.
4 'Have you done your homework yet?' 'No, not yet.'
5 'Are your guests still here?' 'No, they've / they have already left/gone.'
6 'Would you like some coffee?' 'No thank you / thanks. I've / I have already had/drunk a cup.'
7 I've / I have already sent him three texts, but he hasn't called me back yet.
8 'Have you booked your holiday yet?' 'No, not yet.'

UNIT 96

96.1
2 He gave it to Gary.
3 He gave them to Sarah.
4 He gave it to his sister.
5 He gave them to Robert.
6 He gave it to a neighbour.

96.2
2 I gave Joanna a plant.
3 I gave Richard a tie.
4 I gave Emma some chocolates / a box of chocolates.
5 I gave Rachel some flowers / a bunch of flowers.
6 I gave Kevin a wallet.

96.3
2 Can you lend me an umbrella?
3 Can you give me your address?
4 Can you lend me twenty pounds?
5 Can you send me more information?
6 Can you show me the letter?

96.4
2 lend you some money
3 send the bill to me
4 buy you a present
5 pass me the sugar
6 give it to her
7 showed the policeman my identity card

96.5
1 Can you give Jenny this bag, please? *oder* Can you give this bag to Jenny, please?
2 Show me your new bicycle.
3 Can you lend me your pen, please?
4 A: Do you have / Have you got a present for Beth and Chris?
  B: Yes, we bought them a house plant.
5 Do you need this book, or can you lend it to me?
6 These are Tom's gloves. Can you give them to him, please?
7 A: Ben and Kate have (got) a new car.
  B: Yes, I know. They showed it to us.
8 I sent my friends in Australia a package for Christmas.

UNIT 97

97.1
3 I went to the window and (I) looked out.
4 I wanted to phone you, but I didn't have your number.
5 I jumped into the river and (I) swam to the other side.
6 I usually drive to work, but I went by bus this morning.
7 Do you want me to come with you, or shall I wait here?

97.2
Beispiel-Antworten:
2 because it was raining / because the weather was bad
3 but it was closed
4 so he didn't eat anything / so he didn't want anything to eat
5 because there was a lot of traffic / because the traffic was bad
6 Sue said goodbye, got into her car and drove off/away

97.3
Beispiel-Antworten:
3 I went to the cinema, **but** the film wasn't very good.
4 I went to a café **and** met some friends of mine.
5 There was a film on television, **so** I watched it.
6 I got up in the middle of the night **because** I couldn't sleep.

97.4
1 I'm / I am tired, but I don't want to go to bed.
2 We could go to the cinema tonight / this evening, or we could stay at home.
3 Michael didn't feel very well yesterday, so he went to bed.
4 The weather was cold and it was raining, so we stayed at home.
5 Every morning Sarah gets up at 7 o'clock, drinks a cup of coffee and drives to the office.
6 I can't go with you because I have / I've got too much to do.

UNIT 98

98.1
2 When I'm tired, I like to watch TV.
3 When I knocked on the door, there was no answer.

Schlüssel zu den Übungen

4 When I go on holiday, I always go to the same place.
5 When the programme ended, I turned off the TV.
6 When I got to the hotel, there were no rooms.

98.2
2 when they heard the news
3 they went to live in New Zealand
4 while they were away
5 before they came here
6 somebody broke into the house
7 they didn't believe me

98.3
2 I finish
3 it's
4 I'll be … she leaves
5 stops
6 We'll come … we're
7 I'll bring
8 I'm
9 it gets
10 I'll tell … I'm

98.4
Beispiel-Antworten:
2 you finish your work
3 I'm going to buy a motorbike
4 you get ready
5 I won't have much free time
6 I come back

98.5
1 I drink coffee when I'm / I am tired.
2 The weather was nice/fine when I was in England.
3 Before she came to Germany, Sophie lived in France.
4 I'll call/phone/ring you when I get/come home. *oder* I'm going to call …
5 When I was in town, I saw John.
6 I'll wait until you call/phone/ring me. *oder* I'm going to wait …
7 After the children went to bed, we watched television/TV.
8 While we're / we are on holiday, our neighbour will / is going to feed our cat.

UNIT 99

99.1
2 If you pass the exam, you'll get a certificate.
3 If you fail the exam, you can do it again.
4 If you don't want this magazine, I'll throw it away.
5 If you want those pictures, you can have them.
6 If you're busy now, we can talk later.
7 If you're hungry, we can have lunch now.
8 If you need money, I can lend you some.

99.2
2 I give
3 is
4 I'll call

5 I'll be … get
6 Will you go … they invite

99.3
Beispiel-Antworten:
3 … you're busy
4 … you'll feel better in the morning
5 … you're not watching it
6 … she doesn't study
7 … I'll go and see Chris
8 … the weather is good
9 … it rains today

99.4
2 When   6 When
3 If   7 if
4 If   8 when … if
5 if

99.5
1 If I have time tomorrow, I'll go / I'm going to go shopping.
2 I'll call you when I get home. *oder* I'm going to call you …
3 Go to bed if you're / you are tired.
4 If you like/wish, I can send you the information.
5 I won't talk to you if you shout. *oder* I'm not going to talk to you …
6 Tim's parents will buy him a new bicycle if he passes the exam. *oder* … are going to buy …
7 Shall we go swimming tomorrow if the weather is nice/fine?
8 When Paula finishes university, she wants to work in London.

UNIT 100

100.1
3 wanted
4 had
5 were/was
6 didn't enjoy
7 could
8 tried
9 didn't have

100.2
3 I'd go / I would go
4 she knew
5 we had
6 you won
7 I wouldn't stay
8 we lived
9 It would be
10 the salary was/were
11 I wouldn't know
12 would you change

100.3
2 I'd watch it / I would watch it
3 we had some pictures on the wall
4 the air would be cleaner
5 every day was/were the same
6 I'd be bored / I would be bored
7 we had a bigger house / we bought a bigger house
8 we would/could buy a bigger house *oder* we would/could have a bigger house

100.4
Beispiel-Antworten:
2 I'd go to Antarctica
3 I didn't have any friends
4 I'd buy a house if I had enough money.
5 I'd try and help
6 there were no guns

100.5
1 If I had time, I would read more.
2 I would lend you (some) money, if I had enough.
3 If I were/was you, I wouldn't do that.
4 You would save money if you ate at home.
5 What would Tom say if he knew (that)?
6 If the weather were/was nice/fine, we could play tennis.
7 Jenny would come with us if she wasn't ill/sick. *oder* … if she weren't ill/sick.
8 What would you do if you had more free time?

UNIT 101

101.1
2 A butcher is a person who sells meat.
3 A musician is a person who plays a musical instrument.
4 A patient is a person who is ill in hospital.
5 A dentist is a person who takes care of your teeth.
6 A fool is a person who does stupid things.
7 A genius is a person who is very intelligent.
8 A liar is a person who doesn't tell the truth.

101.2
2 The woman who opened the door was wearing a yellow dress.
3 Most of the students who took the exam passed (it).
4 The policeman who stopped our car wasn't very friendly.

101.3
2 who   6 which
3 which   7 who
4 which   8 who
5 who   9 which

that ist auch korrekt in allen Sätzen.

101.4
3 … a machine **that**/**which** makes coffee
4 OK (**which** ist auch korrekt)
5 … people **who**/**that** never stop talking
6 OK (**who** ist auch korrekt)
7 OK (**that** ist auch korrekt)
8 … the sentences **that**/**which** are wrong
9 … a car **that**/**which** cost £40,000

307

Schlüssel zu den Übungen

101.5
1 I have (got) a friend/girlfriend who lives in Paris. *oder* … that lives in Paris.
2 We have (got) a garden that/which is very big.
3 I know somebody who/that lives in that/this street.
4 Rachel works in a company that/which sells software.
5 Where's / Where is the book that/which was on the table?
6 Have you seen / Did you see the key that/which was in the door?
7 The man who/that was here had blond hair.
8 The woman who/that helped us was very nice.

UNIT 102

102.1
2 I've lost the pen you gave me.
3 I like the jacket Sue is wearing.
4 Where are the flowers I gave you?
5 I didn't believe the story he told us.
6 How much were the oranges you bought?

102.2
2 The meal you cooked was excellent.
3 The shoes I'm wearing aren't very comfortable.
4 The people we invited to dinner didn't come.

102.3
2 Who are the people you were talking to?
3 Did you find the keys you were looking for?
4 Where is the party you're going to?
5 What's the name of the film you were talking about?
6 What's that music you're listening to?
7 Did you get the job you applied for?

102.4
2 What's the name of the restaurant where you had dinner?
3 How big is the village where you live?
4 Where exactly is the factory where you work?

102.5
1 The bird I saw was blue. *oder* The bird that/which I saw …
2 The woman who/that helped me was very nice/friendly.
3 How was the film/movie you saw last night / yesterday evening? *oder* … the film that/which you saw … ?
4 The woman I wanted to speak to wasn't there. *oder* The woman who/that …
5 The man I saw was wearing a red shirt. *oder* The man who/that I saw …
6 The party we went to yesterday was fantastic. *oder* The party that/which we went to …

7 Where's / Where is the book I lent you? *oder* … the book that/which I lent you?
8 The restaurant where we ate was very good. *oder* The restaurant (that/which) we ate at/in …

UNIT 103

103.1
3	at	11	at
4	on	12	in
5	in	13	on
6	in	14	on
7	on	15	at
8	on	16	at
9	at	17	at*
10	on	18	in

* Im Amerikanischen sagt man '**on** the weekend'.

103.2
2	on	11	at*
3	at	12	on
4	in	13	in
5	in	14	at
6	in	15	in
7	on	16	on
8	on	17	in
9	in	18	at
10	at	19	at

* Im Amerikanischen sagt man '**on** the weekend'.

103.3
2 on Friday
3 on Monday
4 at 4 o'clock on Thursday / on Thursday at 4 o'clock
5 on Saturday evening
6 at 2.30 on Tuesday (afternoon) / on Tuesday (afternoon) at 2.30

103.4
2 I'll call you in three days.
3 My exam is in two weeks.
4 Tom will be here in half an hour. / … in 30 minutes.

103.5
3 in
4 – (*Satz ist vollständig*)
5 – (*Satz ist vollständig*)
6 in
7 at*
8 – (*Satz ist vollständig*)
9 – (*Satz ist vollständig*)
10 on
11 in
12 at

* Im Amerikanischen sagt man '**on** the weekend'.

103.6
1 I go to work at 8 o'clock.
2 Michael came to Berlin in 2007.
3 A: What are you doing at Easter?
  B: We're / We are going to Italy.
4 I always get up late on Saturday morning/mornings. *oder* On Saturday morning/mornings I always …

5 The project will be finished at the end of May.
6 Where were you last Thursday?
7 Are you usually at home in the evening/evenings?
8 We want to go to Canada next summer.
9 I have to leave/go in a few minutes. *oder* I must leave/go …
10 I have (got) / I've got an appointment on Wednesday at 11.30.
11 Goodbye! I'll see you at/on the weekend. *oder* See you …

UNIT 104

104.1
2 Alex lived in Canada **until** 2009.
3 Alex has lived in England **since** 2009.
4 Karen lived in France **until** 2011.
5 Karen has lived in Switzerland **since** 2011.
6 Clare worked in a restaurant **from** 2010 **to** 2012.
7 Clare has worked in a hotel **since** 2012.
8 Adam was a teacher **from** 2002 **to** 2008.
9 Adam has been a journalist **since** 2008.
11 Alex has lived in England for … years.
12 Karen has lived in Switzerland for … years.
13 Clare worked in a restaurant for three years.
14 Clare has worked in a hotel for … years.
15 Adam was a teacher for six years.
16 Adam has been a journalist for … years.

104.2
2	until	9	since
3	for	10	until
4	since	11	for
5	Until	12	until
6	for	13	Since
7	for	14	for
8	until		

104.3
1 We were in the USA from July until/till September.
2 Our boss will be in London until/till Wednesday.
3 A: How long will you be in England?
  B: Until June.
4 We want to go to the seaside for the weekend.
5 Jenny has been ill/sick for three days.
6 Jenny was ill/sick for three days.
7 I've lived / I have lived in Munich since 2005.
8 Thomas has lived in this flat/apartment since he came to Hamburg.

Schlüssel zu den Übungen

UNIT 105

105.1
2 after lunch
3 before the end
4 during the course
5 before they went to Australia
6 during the night
7 while you are waiting
8 after the concert

105.2
3 while
4 for
5 while
6 during
7 while
8 for
9 during
10 while

105.3
2 eating
3 answering
4 having/taking
5 finishing/doing
6 going/travelling

105.4
2 John worked in a bookshop for two years after leaving school.
3 Before going to sleep, I read for a few minutes.
4 After walking for three hours, we were very tired.
5 Let's have a cup of coffee before going out.

105.5
1 Tina never gets up before 8 o'clock.
2 What would you like to do after the film/movie?
3 I often listen to the radio while I cook. *oder* … while I'm / I am cooking.
4 I want to finish reading this book before I go to bed. *oder* … before going to bed.
5 Tom was in hospital for two weeks.
6 After getting up, I drink a glass of water. *oder* After I get up, I …
7 Two people talked all the time during the concert.
8 After cleaning the house, we washed the car. *oder* After we (had) cleaned the house, we washed the car.

UNIT 106

106.1
2 **In** the box.
3 **On** the box.
4 **At** the airport.
5 **At** the bus stop.
6 **In** the field.
7 **On** the balcony.
8 **In** the pool.
9 **At** the window.
10 **In** bed.
11 **On** the table.
12 **At** the table.

106.2
2 in
3 on
4 in
5 in
6 at
7 in
8 in
9 on
10 at
11 in
12 at
13 on
14 at
15 on

106.3
1 A: Where's / Where is my blue pullover?
  B: In the wardrobe.
2 Amy sometimes sits on the floor.
3 Emily works in a bank in the city centre / in the centre of the city.
4 In (the) summer we often sit on our balcony.
5 When does your plane land? I can pick you up at the airport.
6 Where's / Where is David? He isn't at his desk.
7 We were in Spain in May and (we) swam in the sea.
8 We waited (for) a long time at the traffic lights. *oder* We waited at the traffic lights (for) a long time.
9 The room is at the end of the corridor.
10 I saw an accident on the way home.

UNIT 107

107.1
2 **On** a ship
3 **In** the sky
4 **At** a party
5 **On** the ceiling
6 **At** the doctor's
7 **On** the second floor
8 **At** work
9 **On** a plane
10 **In** a taxi
11 **At** a wedding
12 **At** the top of a hill

107.2
2 on
3 at
4 at
5 in
6 in
7 on
8 at
9 in
10 at
11 on
12 in
13 at
14 in
15 on … at

107.3
1 Thomas isn't at work today. He's / He is at the doctor's.
2 Why is that chair in the middle of the room?
3 Everest is the highest mountain in the world.
4 That's a nice/beautiful picture on the wall.
5 Jenny was at the hairdresser's today.
6 We live on the third floor.
7 I often sleep on the train / on trains.
8 Is that you in this picture?
9 A: Did you go out last night / yesterday evening?
  B: No, I stayed at home.
10 Could you please sign your name at the bottom of this page?

UNIT 108

108.1
2 to
3 in
4 to
5 in
6 to
7 to
8 in

108.2
3 to
4 to
5 **at** home … **to** work
6 at
7 – (keine Präposition)
8 to
9 at
10 **at** a restaurant … **to** the hotel

108.3
2 to
3 to
4 in
5 to
6 to
7 at
8 to
9 to
10 at
11 at
12 **to** Maria's house … **at** home
13 – (keine Präposition)
14 meet **at** the party … go **to** the party

108.4
1 to
2 – (keine Präposition)
3 at
4 in
5 to
6 – (keine Präposition)

108.5
Beispiel-Antworten:
2 to work
3 at work
4 to Canada
5 to parties
6 at a friend's house

108.6
1 Our office is in the city centre.
2 Becky works at the airport.
3 Does this train go to Hamburg?
4 Are you at home this evening / tonight? *oder* Will you be at home … ?
5 When does the train arrive in Vienna? *oder* … get to Vienna?
6 I got to work at 9.30 this morning. *oder* I arrived at work …
7 Next summer we want to go/travel to Thailand.
8 Tom got to the restaurant at 8 o'clock, but Rachel wasn't / was not there. *oder* Tom arrived at the restaurant …
9 What time did you get/arrive / come home last night / yesterday evening?

Schlüssel zu den Übungen

UNIT 109

109.1
2 next to / beside / by
3 in front of
4 between
5 next to / beside / by
6 in front of
7 behind
8 on the left
9 in the middle

109.2
2 behind
3 above
4 in front of
5 on
6 by / next to / beside
7 below/under
8 above
9 under
10 by / next to / beside
11 opposite
12 on

109.3
2 The fountain is in front of the theatre.
3 The bank/bookshop is opposite the theatre. *oder* Paul's office is opposite the theatre. *oder* The theatre is opposite …
4 The bank/bookshop/supermarket is next to …
5 Paul's office is above the bookshop.
6 The bookshop is between the bank and the supermarket.

109.4
1 The post office is next to / by / beside the station.
2 Our house is opposite a café.
3 The restaurant is on the left.
4 Emma is sitting next to/by/beside Ben.
5 What's / What is behind the door?
6 There's / There is an old tree in front of the house. *oder* In front of the house there's / there is an old tree.
7 The table is between the door and the window.
8 'Where's / Where is my pen?' 'Under the newspaper.'
9 Your suitcase is by the door.
10 There's / There is a family with two children above us. *oder* Above us there's …
11 A: Where's / Where is the cinema? B: It's / It is below the café.

UNIT 110

110.1
2 Go under the bridge.
3 Go up the hill.
4 Go down the steps.
5 Go along this street.
6 Go into the hotel.
7 Go past the hotel.
8 Go out of the hotel.
9 Go over the bridge.
10 Go through the park.

110.2
2 off
3 over
4 out of
5 across
6 round/around
7 through
8 on
9 round/around
10 **into** the house **through** a window

110.3
1 out of
2 round/around
3 in
4 from here to the airport
5 round/around
6 on/over
7 over
8 out of / from

110.4
1 Can/Could you put the flowers on the table, please? *oder* Can/Could you please … ?
2 We drove/went through the tunnel.
3 How far is it from the station to the city centre?
4 Take your things off the table, please. *oder* Please take …
5 Go up the stairs and along the corridor.
6 Julia came out of the hotel and got into a taxi.
7 I'm / I am tired because I walked round/around (the) town all day.
8 Go past the church and across the street.

UNIT 111

111.1
2 on time
3 on holiday
4 on the phone
5 on TV

111.2
2 by
3 with
4 about
5 on
6 by
7 at
8 on
9 with
10 **about** grammar **by** Vera P. Bull

111.3
1 with
2 without
3 by
4 about
5 at
6 by
7 on
8 with
9 at
10 by
11 about
12 by
13 on
14 with
15 by
16 by

111.4
1 I usually go to work by bus.
2 I was on holiday last week.
3 *Pride and Prejudice* is a book by Jane Austen.
4 Sue usually gets/comes to work on time. *oder* Sue usually arrives at work …
5 Mark met his wife at (the age of) 25.
6 Who is the/that man with the hat?
7 This evening / Tonight there's/there is a good film on television/TV.
8 Did you know about Monica's problem?
9 Tom stayed with friends in London.
10 'How did you get/come here?' 'By car.'

UNIT 112

112.1
2 in
3 to
4 at
5 with
6 of

112.2
2 at
3 to
4 about
5 of
6 of
7 from/to (*Man kann auch sagen* different than …)
8 in
9 for
10 about
11 of
12 **for/about** getting angry **with** you

112.3
2 interested in going
3 good at getting
4 fed up with waiting
5 sorry for/about waking
6 Thank you for waiting

112.4
2 Sue walked past me without speaking.
3 Don't do anything without asking me first.
4 I went out without locking the door.

112.5
Beispiel-Antworten:
2 I'm scared of the dark.
3 I'm not very good at drawing.
4 I'm not interested in cars.
5 I'm fed up with living here.

112.6
1 I'm / I am interested in (the) theatre.
2 German houses are different from English houses.
3 David is married to a teacher.
4 John's desk is full of papers.
5 Our daughter is very good at biology.
6 Kate is angry with Tony.
7 I'm / I am fed up with working so much / so hard.

Schlüssel zu den Übungen

8 A: Shall I open the door for you?
B: Thank you, that's / that is very kind of you.
9 I'm / I am sorry for not talking to you yesterday. *oder* I'm / I am sorry I didn't talk to you yesterday.

UNIT 113

113.1
2 to
3 for
4 to
5 at
6 for

113.2
2 to
3 to
4 – (keine Präposition)
5 for
6 to
7 of/about
8 for
9 on
10 to
11 for
12 – (keine Präposition)
13 to
14 on
15 of/about

113.3
1 at
2 after
3 for
4 after
5 at
6 for

113.4
Beispiel-Antworten:
3 It depends on the programme.
4 It depends (on) what it is.
5 It depends on the weather.
6 It depends (on) how much you want.

113.5
1 I often listen to music.
2 Look at that beautiful/nice garden!
3 Does this umbrella belong to you?
4 I spoke/talked to Thomas yesterday.
5 Thank you very much for the chocolate.
6 What are you looking for?
7 Why are you crying? What happened?
8 A: Do you like music?
B: It depends on the music.
9 We waited for the bus, but it didn't come/arrive.
10 Could you / Can you look after my suitcase for a moment please?

UNIT 114

114.1
2 went in
3 looked up
4 rode off/away
5 turned round/around
6 got off
7 sat down
8 got out

114.2
2 away
3 round/around
4 going **out** ... be **back**
5 down
6 over
7 back
8 in
9 up
10 going **away** ... coming **back**

114.3
2 Hold on
3 slowed down
4 takes off
5 getting on
6 speak up
7 broken down
8 fall over / fall down
9 went off
10 carry on
11 gave up

114.4
1 Hello / Good morning. Come in.
2 What time do you usually get up?
3 Julia came in and sat down.
4 Can you open the curtains, please? I want to look out.
5 Don't come back too late tonight.
6 Here's / Here is my car. Get in.
7 A: Where's / Where is Monika?
B: She went away for a week. *oder* She's / She has gone away ...
8 He ran away and didn't look/turn round. *oder* ... and didn't look/turn around.
9 The plane/airplane was delayed. We got on, but it didn't take off.

UNIT 115

115.1
2 She took off her hat. *oder* She took her hat off.
3 He put down his bag. *oder* He put his bag down.
4 She picked up the magazine. *oder* She picked the magazine up.
5 He put on his sunglasses. *oder* He put his sunglasses on.
6 She turned off the tap. *oder* She turned the tap off.

115.2
2 He put his jacket on.
He put it on.
3 She took off her glasses.
She took them off.
4 I picked the phone up.
I picked it up.
5 They gave the key back.
They gave it back.
6 We turned off the lights.
We turned them off.

115.3
2 take it back
3 picked them up
4 switched it off
5 bring them back

115.4
3 knocked over
4 look it up
5 throw them away
6 tried on
7 showed me round
8 gave it up *oder* gave up (*ohne* it)
9 fill it in
10 put your cigarette out

115.5
1 Take off your jacket. *oder* Take your jacket off. It's / It is warm (in) here.
2 Please turn/switch off the light when you go to bed. *oder* Please turn/switch the light off when ...
3 'Here is your pen.' 'Could you put it back on my desk, please?'
4 It's time for the news. Can you turn/switch on the television, please? *oder* Can you turn/switch the television on, please?
5 Why are your clothes on the floor? Can you pick them up, please?
6 'Can I take this book?' 'Yes, but please bring it back.'
7 Did you turn/switch off the washing machine? *oder* Have you turned/switched off ... ? *oder* Did you turn/switch the washing machine off? *oder* Have you turned/switched ... off?

Schlüssel zu den zusätzlichen Übungen

1
3   Kate is a doctor.
4   The children are asleep.
5   Gary isn't hungry.
6   The books aren't on the table.
7   The hotel is near the station.
8   The bus isn't full.

2
3   she's / she is
4   Where are
5   Is he
6   It's / It is
7   I'm / I am *oder* No, I'm not. I'm a student.
8   What colour is
9   Is it
10 Are you
11 How much are they?

3
3   He's / He is having a shower.
4   Are the children playing?
5   Is it raining?
6   They're / They are coming now.
7   Why are you standing here? I'm / I am waiting for somebody.

4
4   Sam doesn't want
5   Do you want
6   Does Helen live
7   Sarah knows
8   I don't travel
9   do you usually get up
10 They don't go out
11 Tom always finishes
12 does Jessica do … She works

5
3   She's / She is a student.
4   She hasn't got a car. *oder* She doesn't have a car.
5   She goes out a lot.
6   She's got / She has got a lot of friends. *oder* She has a lot of friends.
7   She doesn't like London.
8   She likes dancing.
9   She isn't / She's not interested in sport.

6
1   Are you married? Where do you live? Have you got any children? *oder* Do you have any children? How old is she?
2   How old are you? What do you do? / Where do you work? / What's your job? Do you like/enjoy your job? Have you got a car? *oder* Do you have a car? Do you (usually) go to work by car?
3   What's his name? / What's he called? What does he do? / What's his job? Does he live/work in London?

7
4   Sonia is 32 years old.
5   I've got / I have two sisters *oder* I have two sisters.
6   We often watch TV in the evening.
7   Amy never wears a hat.
8   A bicycle has got two wheels. / … has two wheels.
9   These flowers are beautiful.
10 Emma speaks German very well.

8
3   are you cooking
4   plays
5   I'm going
6   It's raining
7   I don't watch
8   we're looking
9   do you pronounce

9
2   we go
3   is shining
4   are you going
5   do you go
6   She writes
7   I never read
8   They're watching
9   She's talking
10 do you usually have
11 He's visiting
12 I don't drink

10
2   went   7   gave
3   found   8   were
4   was   9   thought
5   had   10   invited/asked
6   told

11
3   He was good at sport.
4   He played football.
5   He didn't work hard at school.
6   He had a lot of friends.
7   He didn't have a bike.
8   He wasn't a quiet child.

12
3   How long were you there? / How long did you stay there?
4   Did you like/enjoy Amsterdam?
5   Where did you stay?
6   Was the weather good?
7   When did you get/come back?

13
3   I forgot
4   did you get
5   I didn't speak
6   Did you have
7   he didn't go
8   she arrived
9   did Robert live
10 The meal didn't cost

14
2   were working
3   opened
4   rang … was cooking
5   heard … looked
6   was looking … happened
7   wasn't reading … was watching
8   didn't read
9   finished … paid … left
10 saw … was walking … was waiting

15
3   is playing
4   gave
5   doesn't like
6   did your parents go
7   saw … was driving
8   Do you watch
9   were you doing
10 goes
11 'm/am trying
12 didn't sleep

16
3   it's / it has just finished/ended
4   I've / I have found them! *oder* I've got them!
5   I haven't read it.
6   Have you seen her?
7   I've / I have had enough.
8   Have you (ever) been to Sweden?
9   We've / We have (just) been to the cinema.
10 They've / They have gone to a party.
11 He's / He has (just) woken up.
12 How long have you lived here? *oder* … have you been living here?
13 Yes, we've / we have known each other for a long time.
14 It's / It has been raining all day. *oder* It has rained all day. *oder* It has been horrible/bad all day.

17
3   's/has been
4   for
5   since
6   has he lived / has he been / has he been living
7   for
8   've been / have been

18
Beispiel-Antworten:
3   I've just started this exercise.
4   I've met Sarah a few times.
5   I haven't had lunch yet.
6   I've never been to Australia.
7   I've lived here since I was born.
8   I've lived here for three years.

19
3   bought/got
4   went
5   've/have read *oder* read *oder* 've/have finished with
6   haven't started (it) *oder* haven't begun (it)
7   was
8   didn't see
9   left
10 's/has been
11 was
12 've/have never made

20
3   He's / He has already gone.
4   she left at 4 o'clock.
5   How many times have you been there?
6   I haven't decided yet.

Schlüssel zu den zusätzlichen Übungen

7 It was on the table last night.
8 I've eaten there a few times.
9 What time did they arrive?

21
1 When was the last time? *oder*
 When did you go the last time?
2 How long have you had it?
 I bought/got it yesterday.
3 How long have you lived there /
 have you been there / have you
 been living there?
 Before that we lived in Mill Road.
 How long did you live in Mill Road?
4 How long have you worked there /
 have you been working there?
 What did you do before that?
 I was a taxi driver. *oder* I worked
 as a taxi driver.

22
Beispiel-Antworten:
2 I didn't go out last night.
3 I was at work yesterday afternoon.
4 I went to a party a few days ago.
5 It was my birthday last week.
6 I went to America last year.

23
2 B	7 C	12 C
3 D	8 B	13 B
4 A	9 C	14 C
5 A	10 D	15 A
6 D	11 A	

24
1 was damaged … be knocked down
2 was built … is used … is being
 painted
3 is called … be called … was changed
4 have been made … are produced

25
2 is visited
3 were damaged
4 be built
5 is being cleaned
6 be forgotten
7 has already been done
8 be kept
9 Have you ever been bitten
10 was stolen

26
2 My car was stolen last week.
3 All the bananas have been eaten.
4 The machine will be repaired.
5 We're / We are being watched.
6 The housework has to be done.

27
3 has taken
4 pushed
5 was pushed
6 is being repaired
7 invented
8 was the camera invented
9 have been washed *oder* were
 washed
10 I've / I have washed them. *oder*
 I washed them.
11 did they send *oder* have they sent
12 be sent

28
2 B	8 B
3 A	9 C
4 C	10 C
5 B	11 B
6 C	12 C
7 C	

29
1 I stayed
 did you do
 I watched
 Are you going
 I'm going are you going to see
 I don't know … I haven't decided
2 have you been
 We arrived
 are you staying / are you going to stay
 do you like
 we're having
3 I'm going … Do you want are you
 going
 Have you ever eaten
 I've been … I went
4 I've lost … Have you seen
 You were wearing … I came
 I'm not wearing
 Have you looked / Did you look
 I'll go

30
1 we met
2 we sat / we were sitting
3 We didn't know
4 we became
5 we liked
6 we spent
7 We left
8 we meet
9 has been
10 she's working
11 She's coming
12 she comes
13 we'll have / we're going to have
14 It will be

31
2 we're staying
3 we enjoyed
4 We watched
5 slept
6 I don't sleep
7 we're not doing / we're not going
 to do *oder* we aren't doing /
 we aren't going to do
8 we're going
9 to see
10 We haven't decided
11 wants
12 to go
13 I'll send
14 you're having
15 are working / have been working
16 he had
17 he needs
18 We've been
19 We got
20 seeing
21 I liked
22 we went
23 we left
24 had

25 he wasn't injured
26 was damaged
27 We've changed / We changed
28 we're leaving
29 We're staying / We're going to stay /
 We'll stay
30 flying
31 That will be / That's going to be
32 finished
33 I'll let
34 we get
35 are looking
36 We're going
37 we'll send

32
2 A	11 B
3 B	12 A
4 C	13 C
5 B	14 B
6 C	15 C
7 B	16 A
8 A	17 C
9 C	18 B
10 A	

33
2 a car
3 the fridge
4 a teacher
5 school
6 the cinema
7 a taxi
8 the piano
9 cars
10 the same

34
4 **a** horse
5 **The** sky
6 **a** tourist
7 for lunch (−)
8 **the** first President of the United States
9 **a** headache
10 remember names (−)
11 **the** next train
12 sends emails (−)
13 **the** garden
14 **the** Majestic Hotel
15 ill last week (−) … to work (−)
16 **the** highest mountain in the world
17 to **the** radio … having breakfast (−)
18 like sport (−) … is basketball (−)
19 **a** doctor … **an** art teacher
20 **the** second floor … **the** top of **the**
 stairs … on **the** right
21 After dinner (−) … watched
 television (−)
22 **a** wonderful holiday in **the** south
 of France (−)

35
2 in	12 at
3 on	13 at
4 at	14 in
5 on	15 at
6 in	16 on
7 since	17 by
8 on	18 for … on
9 by	19 to … in
10 in	20 at … in
11 for	

Schlüssel zur Lernhilfe

Gegenwart
1.1	B, C	1.11	A
1.2	C	1.12	C
1.3	A	1.13	A
1.4	D	1.14	D
1.5	A	1.15	C
1.6	C, D	1.16	A
1.7	B	1.17	D
1.8	D	1.18	C, D
1.9	C	1.19	A, D
1.10	C		

Vergangenheit
2.1	B	2.6	D
2.2	E	2.7	A
2.3	D	2.8	C
2.4	B	2.9	C
2.5	A		

Present perfect
3.1	B, E	3.6	B
3.2	D	3.7	A
3.3	B	3.8	C
3.4	D	3.9	D
3.5	E	3.10	E

Passiv
4.1	D
4.2	C
4.3	E
4.4	A
4.5	A

Verbformen
5.1	D
5.2	B

Zukunft
6.1	A	6.6	C
6.2	A	6.7	D
6.3	C	6.8	C
6.4	A, B	6.9	B
6.5	B		

Modale Hilfsverben, Imperativ usw.
7.1	C, D	7.7	B, D
7.2	A, C	7.8	D
7.3	A	7.9	C
7.4	D	7.10	C
7.5	B	7.11	A
7.6	E	7.12	E

There und it
8.1	B	8.4	A
8.2	E	8.5	B
8.3	A		

Hilfsverben
9.1	C	9.5	B
9.2	A	9.6	C
9.3	C	9.7	D
9.4	B		

Fragen
10.1	D	10.7	B
10.2	D	10.8	A
10.3	A	10.9	C, E
10.4	A	10.10	C
10.5	B	10.11	A
10.6	D	10.12	A, C

Die indirekte Rede
11.1	E
11.2	A, B, D

-ing und to ...
12.1	B	12.5	B, C
12.2	D	12.6	C
12.3	B	12.7	A
12.4	C	12.8	D

Go, get, do, make und have
13.1	A, D	13.4	A, D
13.2	C	13.5	B
13.3	C, D	13.6	D

Pronomen und Possessivbegleiter
14.1	A	14.6	A
14.2	C	14.7	E
14.3	D	14.8	A
14.4	B	14.9	D
14.5	B, C	14.10	C

A und the
15.1	C	15.8	A
15.2	B	15.9	B
15.3	A, C	15.10	B
15.4	B	15.12	D
15.5	B	15.13	B
15.6	A	15.14	A
15.7	C		

Bestimmungswörter und Pronomen
16.1	C	16.11	E
16.2	C	16.12	B, D
16.3	B	16.13	A
16.4	B	16.14	A, B
16.5	C	16.15	D
16.6	A, C	16.16	A, C
16.7	D	16.17	D
16.8	B, D	16.18	B
16.9	A	16.19	A
16.10	B		

Adjektive und Adverbien
17.1	A	17.8	E
17.2	C	17.9	A
17.3	C	17.10	B
17.4	D	17.11	D
17.5	B	17.12	A
17.6	B	17.13	D
17.7	A, C	17.14	C

Satzbau
18.1	B	18.4	A
18.2	C	18.5	A, D
18.3	B		

Konjunktionen und Relativsätze
19.1	C	19.5	B, C
19.2	A	19.6	A, B
19.3	D	19.7	B, D
19.4	E	19.8	A

Präpositionen
20.1	D	20.11	D
20.2	E	20.12	A
20.3	C, D	20.13	C
20.4	B	20.14	D
20.5	A, D	20.15	A
20.6	B	20.16	E
20.7	A	20.17	C
20.8	B	20.18	B
20.9	B	20.19	D
20.10	D	20.20	D

Phrasal verbs
1.1	C
1.2	A, B
1.3	B

Index

Die Nummern beziehen sich auf Units (nicht auf Seitennummern).

a/an 66
   a *und* some 68–69
about 111E
above 109E
across 110
Adjektive 85
   Adjektiv + Präposition (good at *usw.*) 112A
   Adjektive und Adverbien (quick/quickly) 86
   be + *Adjektiv* (I'm hungry / I'm scared *usw.*) 3, 85
   get + *Adjektiv* (get tired *usw.*) 57B
   Komparativ (older / more expensive) 87–89
   something/anybody *usw.* + *Adjektiv* 79C
   Superlativ (the oldest / the most expensive) 90
Adverbien 86
   Wortstellung (always / usually / often *usw.*) 94
advise (advise somebody to …) 54B
afraid (**of**) 112A
after 98, 105
ago 20B
Aktiv und Passiv Anhang 1
all
   all *und* every *usw.* 80
   all (of) 81
   Wortstellung 94
along 110
already 95C
   already + present perfect 17B
   Wortstellung 94
also (*Wortstellung*) 94
always
   always + present simple 6C
   Wortstellung 94
am / is / are 1–3
   am / is / are (present continuous) 4–5, 24A, 26, 52D
   there is / there are 38
an *siehe* **a**
and 97
angry (**with**/**about** …) 112A
another 66B
any
   any *und* some 76
   not + any 77
   any *und* no 77
   any (of) 81
anybody/anyone/anything 76D, 78–79
anywhere 79
Apostroph (I'm, it's *usw.*) Anhang 4
Apostroph + **'s** (my brother's car) 65
are *siehe* **am**/**is**/**are**
around 110, 114–115, Anhang 7
arrive 108C
Artikel (a/an/the) 66–73

   a/an 66, 68–69
   the 70–73
as (not as … as) 89
ask
   ask somebody to … 54B
   ask somebody for … 113A
at
   at 8 o'clock / at night *usw.* 103
   at the bus stop / at work *usw.* 106–107
   at *und* to 108
   at the age of … 111B
away
   run away / throw away *usw.* (phrasal verbs) 114–115, Anhang 7

back
   come back / give back *usw.* (phrasal verbs) 114–115, Anhang 7
be (*Infinitiv von* am/is/are)
   am/is/are 1–3
   am/is/are + -ing (present continuous) 4–5, 24A, 26, 52D
   be + *Adjektiv* (I'm hungry / I'm scared *usw.*) 3, 85B
   have/has been (present perfect) 16–19
   Passiv 22–23, Anhang 1
   was/were 11
   was/were + -ing (past continuous) 14, 24A, 52D
   will be 28
because 97
been
   have/has been (present perfect) 16–19
   there has/have been 39B
before 98, 105
begin (begin to … *oder* begin -ing) 53C
behind 109A
belong (**to**) 113A
below 109E
beside 109A
best 90B
better 87D
between 109A
bit (a bit older / a bit bigger *usw.*) 88D
born 22C
both 82
   Wortstellung 94
but 97
by 111C
   by (= beside) 109C
   by myself / by yourself *usw.* 64C
   by *nach dem Passiv* (I was bitten by a dog) 22D

can / can't 31
continue (continue to … *oder* continue -ing) 53C
could / couldn't 31C–D

depend (**on** …) 113C
did
   didn't *bei der Verneinung* 13, 24D, 41C, 44B, 52B
   did *bei Fragen* 13, 24D, 41C, 45B, 52B

different (**from**) 112A
direkte Rede und indirekte Rede 51
do 58
   do/does *bei Fragen* 8, 24D, 41C, 45B, 52B
   don't/doesn't *bei der Verneinung* 7, 24D, 41C, 44B, 52B
   don't go / don't fall *usw.* (*Imperativ*) 36C
down 110
   sit down / put down *usw.* (phrasal verbs) 114–115, Anhang 6–7
during 105

each other 64D
either
   either *und* too 43A
   either (of) 82
end (at the end of) 103B, 106B
enjoy
   enjoy -ing 53B
   enjoy myself/yourself *usw.* 64A
enough 91
   enough *und* too 92D
ever
   Have you ever … ? 18
   Superlativ + ever 90D
   Wortstellung 94
every 80
everybody/everyone/everything/everywhere 80C
expect 53A, 54B

far
   how far is it? 40A, 48D
   far → further 87B
fast 86C
fed up (**with**) 112A
few / a few 84
finish (finish -ing) 53B
for
   for ten minutes / for three years *usw.* 20, 104D
   for *und* during 105C
   for *und* to 55B
   go for a walk *usw.* 56C
Fragen 45–48
   am/is/are … ? 2
   did … ? (past simple) 13, 45B
   do/does … ? (present simple) 8, 45B
   Do you know where … ? (*indirekte Fragen*) 50
   have you? / are you? *usw.* (*Interesse zeigen*) 42A
   How long does it take? 49
   Präpositionen am Satzende (who is she talking to?) 47
   question tags (… do you? / … isn't it? *usw.*) 42B
   What / Which / How … ? 48
   Who saw you? / Who did you see? 46
   Why don't … ? / Why isn't … ? *usw.* 45C
from 104A, 110
front (in front of …) 109A–B

315

Index

full (of) 112A
further 87B

geographische Bezeichnungen mit und ohne the 73
Gerundium siehe -ing
get 57
  get on / get up *usw.* (phrasal verbs) 114, Anhang 6
  get to (a place) 57C, 108C
give
  give something to somebody / give somebody something 96
  give up / give back *usw.* (phrasal verbs) 115, Anhang 6–7
go 56
  go -ing (go swimming *usw.*) 56D
  go home / go to work / go to the cinema 71
  go in / go back *usw.* (phrasal verbs) 114
going to (I'm going to do something) 27
good
  good *und* well 86D
  good at 112A
got
  Vergangenheit von get 12C, 57
  have/has got 10, 59A
had
  had to 34B
  he said he had (done something) 51, Anhang 1.1
  Vergangenheit von have 12C
happen (to) 113A
hard 86C
has *siehe* **have**
hate 53C–D
have 10, 59
  have breakfast / have a shower *usw.* 4B, 59B
  have done / have been *usw.* (present perfect) 16–19, 24C
  have to 34
  there has/have been 39B
  have/has got 10, 59A
her 60–61, 63
hers 62–63
herself 64
Hilfsverben 24, 41–43
him 60, 63
himself 64
his 61–63
holiday (on holiday) 56B, 111A
home 56A, 71A, 108B
  get home 57C, 108C
how 48
  how big? / how old? / how far? *usw.* 48D
  How long does it take? 49
  How long have you … ? (present perfect) 19
  how much? / how many? 83A

I/you/he/she *usw.* (*Personalpronomen*) 60, 63

if 99–100
  Do you know if … ? 50C
  if I had / if we went 100
  if we go / if you see *usw.* 99
  if *und* when 99C
Imperativ (do this / don't do that *usw.* 36
in
  go in / fill in *usw.* (phrasal verbs) 114–115, Anhang 7
  in April / in summer *usw.* 103
  in a room / in the city *usw.* 106–107
  in five minutes / in three years *usw.* 103E
  in *und* to 108
  put something in 110
indirekte Fragen (Do you know what … ? *usw.*) 50
indirekte Rede He said that … / He told me that … 51
  He told me to … 54C
Infinitiv (do/see/play *usw.*)
  Adjektiv + Infinitiv (it's easy to …) 40B
  can / will / should *usw.* + Infinitiv 52B
  Infinitiv (to do / to see *usw.*) *und* to + Infinitiv (to do / to see *usw.*) 52–54
  Infinitiv *und* for 55B
  Infinitiv *und* -ing (do/doing *usw.*) 52–53
  I went to the shop to buy … (Infinitiv + Handlungsgrund) 55
  something to eat / nowhere to go *usw.* 79E
  Verben + to + Infinitiv (I want to go *usw.*) 52C, 53–54
-ing (doing/playing/going *usw.*)
  am/is/are + -ing (present continuous) 4–5, 24A, 26, 52D
  Gerundium als Subjekt (living in a big city …) 72A
  go -ing (go swimming *usw.*) 56D
  -ing *und* Infinitiv (do/doing *usw.*) 52–53
  Präpositionen + -ing 105D, 112B
  Verben + -ing (enjoy -ing *usw.*) 53B–C
  was/were + -ing (past continuous) 14, 24A, 52D
interested (in) 3B, 112A
into 110
is *siehe* **am/is/are**
it 40, 60B
  it is *und* there is 38B, 40A
  it's *und* its 61C
its 61

just
  just + present perfect 17A
  Wortstellung 94

kind (kind to somebody / kind of somebody) 112A
know (Do you know where … ?) 50
Komparativ (older / more expensive *usw.*) 87–89
Konditional (if …) 99, 100
  if I did … 100
  if I do … 99

Konjunktionen 97–100
  and/but/or/so/because 97
  if 99–100
  when/before/while/after until 98
Kurzformen (I'm/it's/you've *usw.*) Anhang 4

late (I'm late *usw.*) 3B, 11B
learn (learn to …) 53A
left (on the left) 70B, 109A
lend (lend something to somebody) 96
less 88C
let 54D
like
  (What's it like?) 47B
  like this / like that 74D
like (*Verb*)
  do you like? *und* would you like? 35C
  like to … *oder* like -ing 53C
  would like 35, 53D, 54A
listen (to) 113A
little / a little 84
look
  look + Adjektiv (look tired *usw.*) 85C
  look at/for/after 113B
lot (a lot of …) 83
love 53C–D

make 58
  make somebody do something 54D
  make *und* do 58
many
  many *und* much 83
  not as many (as) 89B
  too many 92C
married
  get married 57B
  married to 112A
may 30D
me/you/him *usw.* (*Personalpronomen*) 60, 63
middle (in the middle of) 70B, 107A, 109A
might 30
mind (I don't mind -ing) 53B
mine/yours/hers *usw.* (*Possessivpronomen*) 62–63
modale Hilfsverben (will/can/might *usw.*) 28–35, 52B
more 87C, 88
most
  most (of) 81
  the most expensive / the most difficult *usw.* 90
much
  much bigger / much more expensive 88D
  much *und* many 83
  not as much (as) 89B
  too much 92C
must 32
  must *und* have to 34D
mustn't 32C
my/your/his *usw.* (*Possessivbegleiter*) 61, 63
myself/yourself *usw.* (*Reflexivpronomen*) 64

Index

need
  don't need to   32D
  need to …   53A

neither
  Neither am I / Neither do I *usw.*   43B
  neither (of)   82

never
  never + present perfect   18
  never + present simple   6C
  Wortstellung   94

next to   109A

nice (nice to somebody / nice of somebody)   112A

nicht zählbare Nomen (salt/water/music *usw.*)   68–69

no (no money / no friends *usw.*)   77A–B, 81B

nobody/no-one/nothing   78–79
  no-one *und* none   77C

Nomen (*zählbar und nicht zählbar*)   68–69

none   77B–C, 81B–C

nor (Nor am I / Nor do I *usw.*)   43B

nowhere   79

of
  the … of …   73E
  the roof of the building *usw.*   65C

off   110
  get off / turn off *usw.* (phrasal verbs)   114–115, Anhang 6

offer (to do something)   53A

often
  often + present simple   6C
  Wortstellung   94

on
  get on / put on *usw.* (phrasal verbs)   114–115, Anhang 6–7
  go on (holiday / a trip *usw.*)   56B
  on holiday / on television *usw.*   111A
  on Monday / on 25 April *usw.*   103A
  on the left / right   109A
  on the table / on the wall *usw.*   106–107

one/ones   75

opposite   109B

or   97B

ought to   33E

our   61, 63

ours   61–63

ourselves   64

out
  out of   110
  go out / put out *usw.* (phrasal verbs)   114–115, Anhang 6–7

over   110
  climb over / knock over (phrasal verbs)   114–115, Anhang 6–7

pair (a pair of …)   67B

Passiv   22–23, 24B, Anhang 1
  present continuous (is being done) *und* present perfect (has been done)   23
  present simple (is done) *und* past simple (was done)   22
  will/can/must *usw.* be done   Anhang 1.2

past (*Präposition*)   110

past continuous (was/were + -ing)   14–15, 24A, 52D
  Passiv des past continuous   Anhang 1.1
  past continuous (I was doing) *und* past simple (I did)   15

past participle (cleaned/done/seen *usw.*)   25A
  Passiv (the room was cleaned)   22–23, 24B, Anhang 1
  present perfect (I have cleaned)   16, 24C
  regelmäßig (cleaned) *und unregelmäßig* (seen)   25, Anhang 2–3

past perfect
  Aktiv und Passiv   Anhang 1.1
  He said he had (done something)   51

past simple (did/cleaned/saw *usw.*)   12–13
  Fragen (did … ?)   13, 45B
  if + past simple (if I had / if we went)   100
  past simple + ago   20B
  past simple (I did) *und* past continuous (I was doing)   15
  past simple (I did) *und* present perfect (I have done)   21
  past simple *Passiv* (the room was cleaned)   22, 24B, Anhang 1.1
  regelmäßige (cleaned) *und unregelmäßige Verben* (saw)   12C, Anhang 2–3
  Verneinung (didn't)   13, 44B
  was/were   11

people   67C–D

Personalpronomen (I/m/you *usw.*)   60, 63

persuade (persuade somebody to …)   54B

phrasal verbs (get up / put on *usw.*)   114–115, Anhang 6–7

Plural (cup→ cups / man → men *usw.*)   67

police (*Plural*)   67D

Possessivbegleiter (my/your/his *usw.*)   61, 63

Possessivpronomen (mine/yours/his *usw.*)   62–63

Präpositionen   103–113
  about   111E
  Adjektiv + Präposition (scared of *usw.*)   112A
  at   103, 106–108, 111B
  at/on/in (*zeitliche Präpositionen*)   103
  before/after/during/while   105
  by   109C, 111C
  for/since   20, 104
  in/at/on (*räumliche Präpositionen*)   106–108
  on   103, 106–107, 109A, 111A
  Präpositionenen + -ing (in -ing / without -ing *usw.*)   105D, 112B
  Präpositionen am Satzende (Who is she talking to?)   47
  Präpositionen in Relativsätzen (the man she is talking to)   102B
  to/in/at (*räumliche Präpositionen*)   108
  under/behind/opposite *usw.* (*Lage*)   109
  until   104A–B
  up/over/through (*Bewegung*)   110
  Verb + Präposition (listen to / wait for *usw.*)   113
  with/without   111D, 112B

present continuous (am/is/are + -ing)   4–5, 24A, 52D
  Fragen (are you -ing?)   5
  Passiv des present continuous   23A, Anhang 1.1
  present continuous *für die Zukunft* (What are you doing tomorrow?)   26
  present continuous (I am doing) *und* present simple (I do)   9
  Verneinung (I'm not -ing)   4

present perfect (I have done)   16–21, 24C
  Have you ever … ?   18
  How long have you … ?   19
  Passiv des present perfect   23B, Anhang 1.1
  present perfect + already   17B
  present perfect continuous (I have been -ing)   19B
  present perfect + for/since   19–20
  present perfect + just   17A
  present perfect (I have done) *und* past simple (I did)   21
  present perfect + yet   17C, 95B
  regelmäßige und unregelmäßige Verben   16B, 25, Anhang 2–3

present simple (I work / she works *usw.*)   6–8, 24D
  Fragen (do/does … ?)   8, 45B
  Passiv des present simple (the room is cleaned)   22, 24B, Anhang 1.1
  present simple + always/usually/never *usw.*   6C
  present simple *nach* if   99B
  present simple *nach* when/while *usw.*   98B
  present simple (I do) *und* present continuous (I am doing)   9
  present simple *für die Zukunft* (The concert starts at 7.30)   26C
  Verneinung (don't/doesn't)   7, 44B

promise (promise to …)   53A

Pronomen
  one/ones   75
  Personalpronomen (I/me/you *usw.*)   60, 63
  Possessivpronomen (mine/yours *usw.*)   62–63
  reflexive Personalpronomen (myself/yourself *usw.*)   64
  Relativpronomen (who/which/that)   101–102

put
put something in …   110
put on / put out *usw.* (phrasal verbs)   115, Anhang 7

Rechtschreibung   Anhang 5

reflexive Personalpronomen (myself/yourself *usw.*)   64

Index

regelmäßige und unregelmäßige Verben 12, 25, Anhang 2–3
Relativpronomen (who/which/that) 101–102
Relativsätze 101–102
right (on the right) 70B, 109A
round 110
  turn round / show round (phrasal verbs) 114–115, Anhang 7
's (*Apostroph* + **s**) 65, Anhang 4.5
same 70A, 89E
Satzbau
  always/usually/often *usw.* 94
  Do you know where … ? (*indirekte Fragen*) 50
  Fragen 45–47
  Fragen im past simple 13D
  Fragen im present continuous 5B
  Fragen im present simple 8B
  nach give/lend/send *usw.* 96
  Passiv 22–23
  Stellung von Orts- und Zeitangaben 93B
  Verb + Objekt 93A
  Wortstellung bei zwei Verben 93C
say/said
  he said that … (*indirekte Rede*) 51
  say *und* tell 51B
scared (**of**) 112A
shall 28D, 29C
should 33
simple past *siehe* **past simple**
simple present *siehe* **present simple**
since 20A, 104C
Singular und Plural (flower → flowers) 67
so
  I was tired, so I went to bed 97
  So am I / So do I *usw.* 43B
some
  some *und* a/an 68–69
  some *und* any 76
  some (of) 81
somebody/someone/something/somewhere 76, 79
sometimes
  sometimes + present simple 6C
  Wortstellung 94
sorry (sorry about *und* sorry for) 112A
speak (to …) 113A
start (start to … *und* start -ing) 53C
still 95
  Wortstellung 94
stop (stop -ing) 53B
suggest (suggest -ing) 53B
Superlativ (the biggest / the most expensive *usw.*) 90
tags (question tags) 42B
take (How long does it take?) 49
talk (to …) 113A
tell/told
  Can you tell me where … ? 50A
  He told me that … 51
  He told me to … 54C
  tell *und* say 51B

than 88–89
that 74
  He said that … (*indirekte Rede*) 51C
  that *und* this 74
  a thing that … (*Relativsätze*) 101
the 70–73
  the biggest / the most expensive *usw.* 90
  the cinema / the theatre / the bank *usw.* 71B
  flowers / the flowers 72B
  the *bei geographischen Bezeichnungen* 73
  the same 70A
  the sun / the sky *usw.* 70A
  the top / the bottom *usw.* 70B
their 61, 63
theirs 62, 63
them 60, 63
themselves 64
there
  there has/have been 39B
  there is/are 38
  there is *und* it is 38B
  there was/were 39A
  there will be 39C
these 74
think (think about / think of) 113A
this 74
those 74
through 110
till (= until) 104B
to
  get to … 57C, 108C
  go to … 56A, 108A
  als räumliche Präposition 108, 110
  als zeitliche Präposition 104A
to + *Infinitiv* (to go / to be *usw.*) *siehe Infinitiv*
too 92
  too *und* either 43A
turn (turn round / turn on *usw.*) (phrasal verbs) 114–115, Anhang 7
under 109D, 110
unregelmäßige Verben 12C, 25B, Anhang 2–3
until 98B, 104A–B
up 110
  get up / pick up *usw.* (phrasal verbs) 114–115, Anhang 6–7
us 60, 63
used (I used to …) 37
usually
  usually + present simple 6C
  Wortstellung 94
Verben
  Fragen 45–48
  Gegenwart 1–10, 24, 26
  indirekte Rede 51
  modale Hilfsverben (will/can/should *usw.*) 28–35, 52B
  Passiv 22–23, Anhang 1
  phrasal verbs (get up / put on *usw.*) 114–115, Anhang 6–7
  present perfect 16–21, 24

regelmäßige und unregelmäßige Verben 25, Anhang 2–3
  Verben + -ing 52–53
  Verben + *Präpositionen* (look at / speak to *usw.*) 113
  Verben + to … (*Infinitiv*) 52–54
Vergangenheit 11–15, 21, 24
Verneinung 44
Zukunft 26–29
Verneinung 44
  no *und* none 77
  not *und* any 77–78
  verneinte Fragen 45C
wait (**for**) 55C, 113A
want
  (want to …) 53A
  want somebody to … 54A
was/were 11
  if I was/were … 100B
  there was/were 39A
  was/were done (*Passiv*) 22, 24B
  was/were + -ing (past continuous) 14, 24A, 52D
well 3B, 86D
were *siehe* **was**
what
  What … like? 47B
  What … ? 48
  What … ? *und* Which … ? 48C
  What … ? *und* Who … ? 46C
when 98
  when *und* if 99C
whether 50C
which
  a thing which … (*Relativsätze*) 101
  Which … ? 48
  Which one/ones? 75B
  Which … ? *und* What … ? 48C
while 98, 105
who
  a person who … (*Relativsätze*) 101
  Who … ? 46
  Who … ? *und* Where … ? 46C
whose (Whose is this?) 62D
will 28–29
  there will be 39C
  will *und* shall 28D
  won't 28A
with/without 111D
  with/without + -ing 112B
won't (= will not) 28A
worse 87D
worst 90B
Wortstellung siehe Satzbau
would
  He would buy a car if he had the money 100
  I'd like / would you like? 35
  would like/love *usw.* 53D
yet 95
  yet + present perfect 17C
you 60, 63
your 61, 63
yours 62, 63
yourself/yourselves 64

Index

zählbare *und nicht zählbare Nomen* 68–69

Zeitformen
Aktiv und Passiv Anhang 1.1
be/have/do *Gegenwarts– und Vergangenheitsformen* 24
past continuous (I was doing) 14–15, 24A, 52D
past simple (I did) 12–13, 15, 21, 24D
present continuous (am/is/are + -ing) 4–5, 24A, 26, 52D
present perfect (I have done) 16–21, 24C
present simple (I do) 6–8, 24D, 26C

Zukunft 26–29
The concert starts at 7.30 (present simple) 26C
(I'm) going to (do something) 27
I'm working tomorrow (present continuous) 26
shall 28D, 29C
will 28–29
die Zukunft nach if 99B
die Zukunft nach when/before/while *usw.* 98B